W9-CEI-354

GREAT BOOKS
for every
BOOK LOVER

I can't decide what to read…

GREAT BOOKS
for every
BOOK LOVER

*2002 great reading suggestions for the
discriminating bibliophile*

BY THOMAS J. CRAUGHWELL

BLACK DOG & LEVENTHAL PUBLISHERS
NEW YORK

Published by
BLACK DOG & LEVENTHAL PUBLISHERS, INC.
151 West 19th Street
New York, NY 10011

Distributed by
Workman Publishing Company
708 Broadway
New York, NY 10003

Cover and Book Design by Inkstone Design, Inc.
Illustrations by Joanna Yardley

Manufactured in the United States of America

ISBN: 1-57912-045-X

h g f e d c b a

ACKNOWLEDGMENTS

My first word of thanks goes to my friend, Jim Mustich. He was too busy publishing A Common Reader (the best books-by-mail catalog on the planet) to write Workman Publishing's first Book Lover's Page-A-Day Calendar, so he recommended me for the job.

Sally Kovalchick is a joy to work with. She is one of those rare editors who has half a dozen great ideas before breakfast. I owe her more than I can ever hope to repay.

My thanks to Peter Workman, J.P. Leventhal and Jessica MacMurray, who dreamed up the Book Lover's Book and transformed my unwieldy manuscript into a very handsome book.

Finally, I am especially grateful to my Mom and Dad, my sisters Karen and Kathy, my brother-in-law John Varda, and my friends James Dutcher, Candis La Prade, Kevin and Ellen Donovan, Debbie VanderBilt, Bill Soleim, and the entire Feeney clan—Dave, Lynne, Jim, and Christine. Over the years, they have brought a host of wonderful books and authors to my attention.

AUTHOR'S NOTE

. . . .

Whether you are a seasoned bibliophile who is happiest deep in the recesses of a used bookstore or a new reader whose bookstore is the Internet, finding the right book is a constantly evolving art. So, gathered here are 2002 recommendations to fit every imaginable taste and to help readers of all kinds celebrate the joys of reading and the endless possibilities of books.

Great Books for Every Book Lover is designed to appeal to all types of readers. If you like British mysteries and that's all you want to read, well and good—you'll find plenty of titles listed here. If you're curious about contemporary poetry but don't know where to begin, this book offers some solid suggestions. If you prefer horror, or romance, or true crime, we've got you covered. From offbeat travel books to expert advice on personal finance, from holiday books for kids to the novels of Nobel Prize-winning authors, here are 2002 personal recommendations of books on every conceivable subject, to fit every imaginable taste.

So dive in.

—TJC

TABLE OF CONTENTS

ALL-STAR SPORTS BOOKS

I HAD A HAMMER
by Henry Aaron and Lonnie Wheeler (HarperCollins, 1994, paperback)

Hank Aaron is the man who shattered Babe Ruth's career home run record and got plenty of hate mail for doing so (some interesting examples of the genre are reprinted in Aaron's book). Nonetheless, Aaron remains a gentleman, tells an excellent story and reveals how he followed his own quiet path to greatness. Hands down, the best sports autobiography to appear in decades.

....

THE RUNNER'S LITERARY COMPANION:
GREAT STORIES AND POEMS ABOUT RUNNING
Edited by Garth Battista (Penguin, 1996, paperback)

If you are expecting a sweat-stained anthology about endorphin highs and being "in the zone," you're in for a surprise. Sure, there a few tough pieces about manly competition (the Alan Sillitoe and John L. Parker entries), but most of the stories come from a different angle. Joyce Carol Oates, for instance, offers a stream of consciousness tale of a woman running with her boyfriend who begins to have premonitions of disaster. From James Tabor to Sara Maitland, from Evelyn Waugh to Walt Whitman, this is an imaginative collection of runner-related stories and poems.

....

FRIDAY NIGHT LIGHTS:
A TOWN, A TEAM, A DREAM
by H.G. Bissinger (HarperPerennial, 1991, paperback)

Friday night high-school football games are common in towns all across America, but the games have a special intensity in Odessa, Texas. Pulitzer Prize-winning journalist H.G. Bissinger spent a season in Odessa and found that 20,000 fans look to the Panthers of Permian High School to carry the town's self-image on their young shoulders. Bissinger interviews coaches and parents, teachers and students, politicians and ministers about the role football plays in Odessa. And he follows the Panthers on their quest for another state championship.

BALL FOUR
by Jim Bouton (Macmillan General Reference, 1990, paperback)

Back in 1970, Bouton's book outraged the baseball establishment. Sports writers said he was a Benedict Arnold. Commissioner Bowie Kuhn pressured Bouton to sign a retraction. And to this day, Bouton is not invited back to Old-Timers' Day. You see, Bouton revealed that baseball players got drunk, used drugs, slept with groupies, were nasty to the fans and Lord knows what else. He also exposed the deep-seated hatred between players and owners—a prophetic revelation in light of the 1994 baseball strike. Bouton's book would shock no one now, but it was big news when it was first published. And, it swept away forever the myth that baseball is a innocent game played by wholesome all-American boys.

OCTOBER 1964
by David Halberstam (Fawcett, 1995, paperback)

October 1964 was, of course, the year when the St. Louis Cardinals won the World Series against the New York Yankees. For the Bronx Bombers, it was the end of an era. Mickey Mantle, Roger Maris and Whitey Ford were losing their magic. Tough young players like Bob Gibson, Lou Brock and Curt Flood were on the rise. And Yogi Berra was fired and replaced by Johnny Keane, who had just led the Cardinals to victory. Halberstam brings it all back in one of the most vivid baseball narratives ever written.

* * *

IVY LEAGUE AUTUMNS:
AN ILLUSTRATED HISTORY OF COLLEGE FOOTBALL'S GRAND OLD RIVALRIES
by Richard Goldstein (St. Martin's Press, 1996, hardcover)

Hobart Amory Hare Baker, son of an old Philadelphia Main Line family, was "Princeton's version of Frank Merriwell." Yet he knew instinctively that after a touchdown, gentlemen do not dance in the end zone. Goldstein, a sportswriter who covers Ivy League football for *The New York Times*, has written a fun history of the game as it was played among the upper crust. He features plenty of history and folklore about the players, including the parts Teddy Roosevelt, Cole Porter, F. Scott Fitzgerald and the Kennedy brothers played in Ivy League football. And rivaling the great stories are 112 vintage photographs.

* * *

COWBOYS HAVE ALWAYS BEEN MY HEROES: THE DEFINITIVE HISTORY OF AMERICA'S TEAM
by Peter Golenbock (Warner Books, 1997, paperback)

Overlook the hubris of designating the Dallas Cowboys "America's Team" and just let yourself enjoy the stories and the gossip. For example, you'll find out how the Cowboys' original owner, Clint Murchison, Jr., ran through his $1.2 billion inheritance and ran up $500 million in debt. Then there's ex-player Peter Gent whose exposé, North Dallas Forty, showed the world that coach Tom Landry was hardly God's gift to football. And you'll learn that Roger Stabach became a star quarterback by ignoring his coach. A solid work of football history that is both candid and fair.

* * *

WRIGLEYVILLE: A MAGICAL HISTORY OF THE CHICAGO CUBS
by Peter Golenbock (St. Martin's Press, 1996, hardcover)

Year after year, the Chicago Cubs break their fans' hearts. They haven't won a national championship since 1908. So why does Chicago love these guys? Maybe it's nostalgia. Maybe it's history. Maybe it's hope springing eternal in the human breast. Whatever. Golenbock goes back to 1871, the year the franchise was founded and traces the great moments in Cubs' history: like their championship season (back during the Teddy Roosevelt administration); the real story of Babe Ruth's "called shot" against Charlie Root in Game 3 of the 1932 World Series; and the great Cubs team of 1969 and their pennant race against the New York Mets. Who knew rooting for bums could be so much fun?

BOSTON: A CENTURY OF RUNNING
by Hal Higdon (Rodale, 1995, paperback)

The first Boston Marathon was run in 1897. Since then it has become the most prestigious runner's event in the United States, perhaps in the world, if the number of competitors from other nations is a fair indication. Through lots of fascinating facts and more than 200 photographs, Hal

Higdon traces the history and heroes of this great event, including John A. Kelley who ran the marathon 61 times between 1928 and 1992 and Roberta Gibb, the first woman to run in 1966.

THEY'RE OFF!
HORSE RACING AT SARATOGA
by Edward Hotaling
(Syracuse University Press, 1995, hardcover)

By the 1860s, Saratoga Springs in upstate in New York was America's premier resort. In succeeding decades, Astors, Vanderbilts, presidents, gangsters and Hollywood stars all came to Saratoga, making the most of the town's gaming house, mineral springs and horse racing during the short 42-day "season." Hotaling tells Saratoga's story with tremendous energy, capturing the excitement of the town in its glory days, when throngs came to see races featuring Man o' War, Secretariat and Longfellow—the finest Thoroughbred of the 19th century. 95 illustrations and photographs enhance the lively text.

MEMORIES OF SUMMER: WHEN BASEBALL WAS AN ART AND WRITING ABOUT IT A GAME
by Roger Kahn (Hyperion, 1997, paperback)

Baseball shaped Roger Kahn's life. He grew up in Brooklyn during the Depression, rooting for the Dodgers. By 1952, he had landed his dream job-writing for the sports section of the *New York Herald Tribune* (which featured Red Smith's column). In this wonderful book, he recalls the golden days when players and sportswriters were not in opposing camps. But he especially celebrates the writers and radio commentators who, in the years before television, brought the games to life for milions of fans who couldn't make it to the ballpark. A beauty of a memoir of a much less cynical time.

IDOLS OF THE GAME: A SPORTING HISTORY OF THE AMERICAN CENTURY
by Robert Lipsyte and Peter Levine
(Turner Publishing, 1995, hardcover)

American sports fans are fickle. In Babe Ruth's case, for instance—we're willing to forgive any faults. In other cases—Babe Didrikson comes to mind—we may have to be taught a few lessons about giving women athletes the same respect and high salaries that men enjoy. In this wide-ranging discussion, the authors discuss stars from Joe Louis, whose victories over Nazi racists took our minds off racism at home, to Muhammed Ali, who insisted, "I don't have to be what you want me to be," to Arnold Schwarzenegger, who transformed himself from body builder to action hero, to Michael Jordan a superb athlete and a superb salesman of shoes, breakfast cereal, hot dogs, underwear and himself.

....

THE FRANCHISE: A HISTORY OF SPORTS ILLUSTRATED MAGAZINE
by Michael MacCambridge (Hyperion, 1997, hardcover)

In 1954, Henry Luce had a hunch that sports would make a decent topic for a weekly magazine. In those days, baseball was the only team sport that had a national following—football, basketball, hockey, even the Olympics barely registered on the national psyche. It was managing editor André Laguerre who "made" Sports Illustrated by going out and getting some serious talent for this new magazine. MacCambridge shows how great writing, outstanding photographs and an unlimited budget changed S.I. from a stodgy reporter of stats to a publication that excites its readers (especially the swimsuit issue).

....

75 SEASONS:
THE COMPLETE STORY OF THE NATIONAL FOOTBALL LEAGUE 1920-1995
by Will McDonough et al. (Turner Publishing, 1994, hardcover)

In 1938, Byron "Whizzer" White was a first round draft pick of the NFL Pittsburgh Pirates; in his rookie year he led the league in rushing with 567 yards. Later, White became a justice of the Supreme Court. A year before Jackie Robinson signed with the Brooklyn Dodgers, four black players were signed for the NFL— Kenny Washington and Woody Strode for the St. Louis Rams and Bill Willis and Marion Motley for the Cleveland Browns. Packed with great stories like these and filled with hundreds of photos, *75 Seasons* is the essential football encyclopedia.

THE ILLUSTRATED HISTORY OF MICKEY MANTLE
by Gene Schoor (Carroll & Graf, 1996, hardcover)

One of baseball's greatest players is lionized in this lavishly illustrated biography. Photos include shots from Mickey Mantle's childhood in Joplin, Missouri; his early days in baseball; his legendary plays in Yankee Stadium—including dramatic action shots of some of his greatest moments. Plus, there are pictures of Mantle with his family, with Roger Maris, Casey Stengel, Joe DiMaggio and Yogi Berra. Schoor has also included interviews with Mantle and his lifetime stats. A great tribute to a great ball player.

GREEN BAY REPLAY: THE PACKERS' RETURN TO GLORY
by Dick Schaap (Avon, 1997, paperback)

Dick Schaap is about as loyal a fan as you'll find: He's written five books about the Green Bay Packers. This one focuses on how Green Bay got to and won Super Bowl XXXI in January 1997. Schaap compares coach Mike Holmgren, quarterback Brett Favre and defensive end Reggie White with the legendary Vince Lombardi and his quarterback Bart Starr and defensive end Willie Davis. Schaap loves these guys and he hopes Holmgren will preside over a new Green Bay dynasty. An especially nice touch: Schapp doesn't forget to praise the 100,000 citizens of Green Bay, Wisconsin, almost all of whom are die-hard Packer fans.

HAUNTS OF THE BLACK MASSEUR: THE SWIMMER AS HERO
by Charles Sprawson (Pantheon, 1993, hardcover)

Charles Sprawson has always felt the mystical power of water. In one of the most graceful and unusual books you're ever likely to encounter, he takes his readers from languid Roman baths to Byron's dramatic plunge into the sea at Shelley's' seaside funeral to Johnny Weismuller doing laps in a Chicago pool to Yukio Mishima daily regimen of swimming to condition his body before his ritual suicide. Sprawson celebrates the mystique of swimmers and swimming. Worth searching for.

COBB: A BIOGRAPHY
by Al Stump (Algonquin Books, 1996, paperback)

Ty Cobb's rivals didn't like him, but his teammates hated his guts. Back in 1961, when Al Stump was ghostwriting Cobb's autobiography, he couldn't tell us everything he learned about the man. Now, 35 years later, we get to read what Ty Cobb was really like. Stump includes Cobb's astonishing career in the big leagues— his first batting championship in 1907, 96 bases stolen in 1915, three .400 seasons in 1911, 1912, 1922. But he also includes the chilling details of Cobb's personal life. Wife beating. Alcoholism. Pathological racism. And the murder of Cobb's father—by his mother. A biography that sends shivers up your spine.

GOLF DREAMS: WRITINGS ON GOLF
by John Updike (Knopf, 1996, hardcover)

Novelist John Updike admits to an "impassioned but imperfect devotion" to the game of golf. In this collection of 30 essays, articles and excerpts from his fiction, Updike reminisces about the day he first started playing; denounces the "Gimme Game"—a universally accepted way of cheating; vilifies able-bodied players who use motorized golf carts; celebrates the pleasures of playing a late-season round of golf on an empty course; and assures his readers that all those hours they spend sprawled on a couch watching golf on TV are actually productive and valuable. A golf book that's well above par.

BASEBALL: AN ILLUSTRATED HISTORY
by Geoffrey C. Ward and Ken Burns
(Random House, 1997, paperback)

The book Ward and Burns wrote in conjunction with the PBS series is fast, exciting and captures perfectly the greatest moments and greatest characters in baseball. The stunning rise of Babe Ruth, variously known as a "national heirloom" and "that big son of a bitch." The heart-wrenching Black Sox scandal and the fall of Shoeless Joe Jackson. The incredible 1947 season when Jackie Robinson took the field for the Brooklyn Dodgers. Like Walt Whitman said, "The game of ball is glorious."

MEN AT WORK: THE CRAFT OF BASEBALL
by George F. Will (HarperPerennial, 1991, paperback)

The only thing Will likes as much as a spirited political argument is a great ball game. His love song to baseball is filled with fun anecdotes and includes Will's solution to the designated hitter controversy.

AMERICAN CLASSICS

LITTLE WOMEN
by Louisa May Alcott (1869; Dover, 1997, paperback)

Somehow this novel has been relegated to "children's fiction." It's too good for that. Read it again now that you're an adult and can appreciate the sophistication of Alcott's story of the devoted March clan.

GO TELL IT ON THE MOUNTAIN
by James Baldwin (1953; Random House, 1995, paperback)

The year is 1935 and John Grimes, now 14, is expected to join his father's storefront church, the Temple of the Fire Baptized. John has definite spiritual longings, but he is also carrying the standard adolescent baggage of raging hormones and anger with his parents. His own history and the history of his family are revealed in flashbacks, each one a perfect story in itself. A powerful tale of a new generation striving to overcome a legacy of guilt, bitterness and anger.

Baldwin's non-fiction:

THE FIRE NEXT TIME
(1963; Random House, 1995, paperback).

These two blistering essays are stinging, inflammatory indictments of racism in American history.

DEATH COMES FOR THE ARCHBISHOP
by *Willa Cather* (1927; Random House, 1971, paperback)

Cather based her mystical novel on the career of Jean Baptiste Lamy, first Archbishop of Santa Fe. Jean Latour's superiors sent him from France to minister to souls in New Mexico. Yet 40 years of hard work and devotion did nothing to allay Latour's spiritual dryness. As death approaches, the archbishop hopes his dry spell will be over. This is a pretty romantic story, but Cather's command of historical detail and love for the people and landscape of New Mexico save it from descending into sentimentality.

ABSALOM, ABSALOM
by *William Faulkner* (1936; Vintage, 1991, paperback)

In early 19th-century West Virginia, Thomas Sutpen, the child of poor whites, resolves to accumulate a fortune, marry into a fine family and build a dynasty. But nothing goes quite as Sutpen planned. He leaves his first wife, an aristocratic Haitian, when he discovers she has some black ancestors. He marries again in America, but years later his daughter falls in love with a dashing young Haitian gentleman—the son from Sutpen's first marriage. There is a terrible grandeur to this multi-generational saga.

More of Faulkner:

THE SOUND AND THE FURY
(1929; Vintage, 1991, paperback).

The degeneration of an old plantation family is contrasted with the vitality of the black family that were once their slaves.

AS I LAY DYING
by *William Faulkner* (1930; Vintage, 1991, paperback)

In the 1920s and 1930s, Fitzgerald, Hemingway and Faulkner were the stars of American literature. But the most daring of the three was Faulkner. In 1930, with *As I Lay Dying*, became into full possession of his literary powers. This macabre black comedy presents the conscious thoughts, unconscious impressions and horrific hallucinations of a family in rural Mississippi as they carry the body of their matriarch to the grave. If you've never read Faulkner, you could do no better than to begin with this haunting novel.

THE GREAT GATSBY
by F. Scott Fitzgerald (1925; Longman, 1996, paperback)

The Great Gatsby is one of those very rare novels-a literary masterpiece that has always been immensely popular. Fitzgerald's tale of Jay Gatsby and his quest for love and success has the fragile, gorgeous, shimmering quality of a dream. if you've never read *Gatsby* before, you're in for a treat. And if it has been a while since you read *Gatsby*, pick it up again and discover again what a beautiful novel this is.

TENDER IS THE NIGHT
(1934; Scribner, 1995, paperback)

Dick Diver, an American psychiatrist, falls in love with and marries one of his patients—a beautiful schizophrenic named Nicole Warren. With a group of American expatriates, they live a seemingly care-free life on the Riviera. Little by little, Fitzgerald reveals just how frail the Divers' marriage is.

THE HOUSE OF THE SEVEN GABLES
by Nathaniel Hawthorne
(1851; Everyman's Classic Library, 1995, paperback)

Hawthorne's classic tale of an ancestral curse is creepy American Gothic. The mighty Pyncheon clan has fallen on hard times. Spinster Hepzibah lives in poverty in Seven Gables with her child-like brother, Clifford, just released from 30 years in prison for a murder he did not commit. Meanwhile, their conniving cousin, Judge Pyncheon, has designs on the House and a scheme to dispose of Clifford for good. More than 100 years since it was first published, *The House of the Seven Gables* is still a masterpiece of the dark twists and turns of the human heart.

THE SCARLET LETTER
by Nathaniel Hawthorne (1850; Broadview Press, 1995, paperback)

The Scarlet Letter
by Nathaniel Hawthorne

Hawthorne didn't invent the story of a woman marked with the emblem of her sin, he drew it out of his own family's history. In the 17th century, three of his ancestors—a brother and two sisters—committed incest. The brother escaped into the forest, but his sisters were condemned to wear a badge that identified their sin. From that shameful incident, Hawthorne created one of the greatest stories in American literature-of bold Hester Prynne; of her cowardly, guilt-ridden lover, Reverend Dimmesdale; of their impish child, Pearl; and of the spider-like Roger Chillingsworth.

FOR WHOM THE BELL TOLLS
by Ernest Hemingway (1940; Scribner, 1996, paperback)

Robert Jordan, an American who has joined the Loyalists in Spain's Civil War, is holed up with a guerrilla band in a cave near Segovia. Their mission: to support a Loyalist advance by blowing up a strategic bridge nearby. With Jordan is the woman he loves, Maria, the daughter of Republicans who saw her parents shot and was herself raped by Fascists. The band succeeds in destroying the bridge, but during the retreat Jordan is seriously wounded and left behind. The novel has the spare, beautiful prose that is Hemingway's hallmark and a cast of intense, introspective characters that readers find impossible to forget.

Also by Hemingway:

THE SUN ALSO RISES
(1926; Simon & Schuster, 1995, paperback)

In what may be his greatest novel, Hemingway follows a group of friends, all part of the Lost Generation, to Pamplona for the running of the bulls. At the heart of the group are Jake Barnes, tough, brave, but impotent from a war wound and Lady Brett Ashley, who is divorcing her husband, enjoying a love affair with a gallant bullfighter, but may actually be in love with Jake.

DEATH IN THE AFTERNOON

(1932; Touchstone Books, 1996, paperback).

Hemingway interprets bullfighting as a sacred ritual in which the death of the bull is a foregone conclusion, although the matador must give the bull every opportunity to kill him. Between Hemingway's musings about life and death, you learn a lot about bullfighting.

THE OLD MAN AND THE SEA

(1952; Simon & Schuster, 1995, paperback).

An old fisherman fights a huge swordfish for three days and three nights. This story of a tough man battling nature is vintage Hemingway.

THEIR EYES WERE WATCHING GOD

by Zora Neale Hurston (1937; Perennial Library, 1990, paperback)

Zora Neale Hurston's own research in African-American folklore inspired this poignant novel of Janie Crawford, a woman who is determined not to spend her life poor and downtrodden. With her husband, Joe, she founds an all-black community in the Florida Everglades. Joe brings Janie the financial security for which she's longed, but stifles her independence. Freedom comes after Joe's death, when Janie falls violently in love with Teacake, a man who appreciates Janie and encourages her to "let her hair down." Lyrical, uplifting and often funny, Hurston's novel also bears a strong message about basic human rights.

Hurston's First Novel:

JONAH'S GOURD VINE

(1934; Perennial Library, 1990, paperback).

The troubled but ultimately loving marriage of a black preacher and his wife. Hurston based the story on her own parents.

A SINGLE MAN
by Christopher Isherwood
(1964; Farrar Straus & Giroux, 1996, paperback)

George is a middle-aged Briton teaching at a California university. He's bright, funny, intelligent-his colleagues and students think George is just great. No one knows that inside, George feels sick and hollow. The young man George loved is dead and George himself does not want to admit that his lover's death has changed him fundamentally. Readers have always found this book unnerving. It breaks your heart without ever once lapsing into cheap sentimentality.

THE AMBASSADORS
by Henry James (1903; Oxford University Press, 1985, paperback)

James reveled in the clash between European sophistication and American small-town virtues. That contest is played out again when Lambert Struthers journeys to Paris to bring a wayward young American home to his mother in Woollett, Massachusetts. Naturally, Struthers' noble mission meets unexpected results. A radiant story of self-discovery and one of James' finest novels.

WASHINGTON SQUARE
by Henry James (1881; Signet Classics, 1964, paperback)

This little gem of a psychological novel is often overlooked by readers of Henry James. Catherine Sloper is plain, shy and socially awkward, but she has a large inheritance coming. When Morris Townsend, a handsome, dashing, but penniless young man starts to court her, Catherine is delighted. But her father is certain his daughter is being duped by a scoundrel. One of the most intriguing studies of character in American literature.

THE COUNTRY OF THE POINTED FIRS
by Sarah Orne Jewett (1896; Doubleday, 1974, paperback)

The psychology of people who live in out-of-the-way places intrigued Sarah Orne Jewett. In The Country of the Pointed Firs, she sets her readers down in a sleepy Maine seaport where she interweaves the histories of the town's colorful inhabitants. Old Captain Littlepage swears he found Purgatory in the Arctic. Abby Martin is known around town as "the Queen's Twin" because she was born on the same day and in the same hour as Queen Victoria. And then there's the 40-year courtship of Esther Hight and William Blackett. Read this book for its touching stories and authentic atmosphere of Maine in the 19th century.

ON THE ROAD
by Jack Kerouac (1957; Penguin, 1991, paperback)

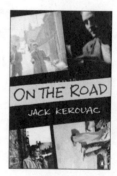

When it was originally published, Jack Kerouac's autobiographical novel was heralded by *The New York Times* as doing for the Beats what *The Sun Also Rises* had done for the Lost Generation. The story follows Sal Paradise and his friend, Dean Moriarty, on a cross-country road trip. Along the way, the boys encounter an endless parade of girls, low-lifes, local characters and new friends as they pursue their quest for something extraordinary—like a religious experience, only more fun. Kerouac's galloping prose captures the energy of youth rushing to embrace life and adventure and sex and maybe God.

Another Kerouac Classic:

DHARMA BUMS
(1958; Penguin, 1991, paperback).

Some readers say Kerouac is damn near a mystic in this road novel that mixes Zen Buddhism with the wild prose and wild parties.

CALL OF THE WILD
by Jack London
(1903; University of Oklahoma Press, 1995, hardcover)

Buck, a pampered house pet, is stolen and carried off to the Klondike to serve as a sled dog. Plunged into a hostile, unfamiliar world of brutal men and wolfish dogs, Buck learns to fight for survival before he runs away from human contact altogether and takes his natural place in the wild. This is Jack London in top form—and it's no book for children.

THE SEA-WOLF
by Jack London (1904; Penguin, 1998, paperback)

Humphrey Van Weyden, a wealthy dilettante, has been knocked on the head and dragged aboard a tramp steamer. Degraded and brutalized by Captain Wolf Larsen and his crew, Van Weyden begins to toughen up to survive. Once he's stronger, Van Weyden faces a dilemma: should he kill Larsen, or temper his new self-respect with self-restraint? A classic that wonders which force is more powerful—savagery or civilization.

WHITE FANG
by Jack London (1906; Scholastic, 1989, paperback)

White Fang is half dog and half wolf. His first owner makes him savage, the better to win professional dogfights. His second owner tames him with kindness and takes him to his home in California where White Fang proves his loyalty.

UNCLE TOM'S CABIN
by Harriet Beecher Stowe (1852; Penguin Classics, 1998, paperback)

One of the most influential novels ever written also happens to be a truly enjoyable read. Stowe used her story of a Christ-like slave to attack racial violence, denounce the hypocrisy of pro-slavery Christians in North and South and protest the outrageous Fugitive Slave Law of 1850. By the way, Eliza and her baby leaping from ice floe to ice floe on the Ohio River to escape a pack of bloodhounds is one of the most powerful scenes in 19th-century American literature.

CANE
by Jean Toomer (1923; Norton, 1988, paperback)

Langston Hughes considered this one of the great masterpieces to emerge from the Harlem Renaissance. Through a series of lyrical, even sensual, sketches, Toomer records her impressions of life among black people in rural Georgia and in the urban North.

HUCKLEBERRY FINN
by Mark Twain
(1884; Cambridge University Press, 1995, paperback)

This is not a book for children. Just look at the first line of the Duke's hapless attempt to recite Hamlet's soliloquy: "To be or not to be, that is the bare bodkin." Obviously, the jokes in Huck Finn are aimed at adults. So are the life lessons—about following your conscience and questioning the status quo and being true to your friends. Among the Great Names Of American literature, nobody is more fun to read than Mark Twain.

THE OPTIMIST'S DAUGHTER
by Eudora Welty (Vintage, 1990, paperback)

With its superb characterizations, this novel is the high-water mark of Welty's long, distinguished career. Laurel McKelva Hand, 45 years old, returns to Mississippi from Chicago to be with her dying father. She was prepared for the stress of sorting out her feelings about the dynamic, domineering old man and seeing the hometown folks again. But she wasn't ready for her father's new white-trash wife.

Also by Welty:

THE COLLECTED STORIES OF EUDORA WELTY
(Harcourt Brace, 1982, paperback).

Like Mark Twain and Flannery O'Connor, Welty has a flawless ear for dialect. Start with "The Petrified Man" and then wander at will.

NATIVE SON
by Richard Wright (1940; HarperCollins, 1993, paperback)

Bigger Thomas, a black teenager living in a Chicago slum, gets a job as a chauffeur at a rich family's house. The daughter, Mary, takes an interest in Bigger and introduces him to her Communist friends. Bigger is in unfamiliar territory here, confused by Mary's frank sexuality and the friendly-yet-patronizing attitude of the Communists. One night, when Mary gets drunk and Bigger is trying to get her back to her room, he accidentally kills her. This is a dark story and the resolution will probably please no one. But it is one of the powerful novels about American racism ever written.

AN AUTHOR YOU SHOULD KNOW

THINGS FALL APART
by Chinua Achebe (Anchor Books, 1994, paperback)

I n this story, set in an Igbo village in the last decade of the 19th century, Nigerian Chinua Achebe answers Joseph Conrad and other Western authors who have tried to write about Africa. He describes the arrival of British missionaries and British colonial adminstrators and the impact their coming has on traditional village life, particularly upon a respected village elder, Okonkwo. Best of all, Achebe uses traditional African methods to tell his story—  proverbs, folk tales and anecdotes that are the product of thousands of years of oral tradition. Make an effort to get a copy of this novel.

¡YO!
by Julia Alvarez (Plume, 1997, paperback)

T o the dismay of her family who considered her the most promising member of the clan, Yolanda Garcia—at age 33—is twice divorced, childless and stuck in an endless cycle of bush-league jobs and bush-league lovers. A large cast of narrators lead the reader through the twists and turns of Yo's life, exploring the entanglements that brought her to this sorry condition. And it is part of Alvarez's genius that while her narrators are creating a portrait of Yolanda, they are also revealing something important about themselves. A completely engaging story about a complex heroine, her large, outspoken gang of family and friends and the vagaries of fate.

The Prequel:

HOW THE GARCIA GIRLS LOST THEIR ACCENTS
by Julia Alvarez (Plume, 1992, paperback).

After a failed coup in the Latin American homeland, the Garcia family flees to the United States. Overnight the four Garcia sisters are no longer well-to-do aristocrats; now they are not-entirely-welcome Hispanic immigrants.

....

BLESS ME, ULTIMA
by Rudolfo Anaya (Warner Books, 1994, paperback)

Out West, lots of readers know and love the novels of Rudolfo Anaya. But back East this gifted Mexican-American author is barely known at all. In case you've missed Anaya, start with Bless me, Ultima, considered his finest novel. It's the story of six-year-old Antonio and Ultima the curandera, a woman with tremendous healing and mystical powers. Ultima helps Antonio move toward manhood and teaches this little boy, preparing for his First Holy Communion, to draw upon the power of Mexico's pagan past. An enchanted tale full of unexplained phenomena.

ALBURQUERQUE
by Rudolfo Anaya (University of New Mexico Press, 1992, hardcover)

No, it's not a typo. The extra "r" is emblematic of the quirkiness of this novel set in the New Mexico city of Albuquerque, where the hero, Albrán González, an ex-Golden Gloves champion, tries to find his father, has an affair with the lady mayor and fights the schemes of a local attorney to turn the town into a city of canals-a kind of Venice on the Rio Grande.

THE ROBBER BRIDE
by Margaret Atwood (Anchor Books, 1998, paperback)

Female scoundrels are rare in contemporary fiction, but Margaret Atwood makes up for it in this story of Zenia, one of the most seductively wicked and wily villains you've ever met. Atwood displays the range of Zenia's evil genius through the lives of three women, all of them former college classmates of hers and all of whom have been victims of her nasty schemes. She's betrayed their confidence, seduced their men, even lulled them into thinking she was dead. A beautiful portrait of a nasty woman.

LEVIATHAN
by Paul Auster (Penguin, 1993, paperback)

When Maria Turner finds a lost address book, she decides to adopt a new identity for herself. When Ben Sachs blows himself up in Wisconsin's North Woods, his best friend, Peter Aaron, thinks he knows why. Paul Auster writes dark, unpredictable stories about people who reinvent themselves from time to time. This may be his finest novel ever.

Also by Auster:

THE NEW YORK TRILOGY
(Penguin, 1990, paperback).

A writer of detective stories takes on a bizarre missing-person case. A college student is hired to spy on a neighbor who is spying on him. A prolific writer disappears and a boyhood friend becomes obsessed with the author's private life.

THE BIRTHDAY BOYS
by Beryl Bainbridge (Thorndike Press, 1995, paperback)

In 1912, Captain Robert Falcon Scott and four companions set out across Antarctica in a race with the Norwegian explorer

Roald Amundsen to the South Pole. Scott and his men had courage and superhuman endurance and followed the gentleman's code of the British public schools. But none of that mattered in the frozen wilderness of Antarctica. Bainbridge tells their story in five first-person narratives as each of the doomed men might have told their story. Poetic, heroic and heartbreaking.

WATSON'S APOLOGY
by *Beryl Bainbridge* (McGraw-Hill, 1988, paperback)

One day, after church services were over, the Reverend J.S. Watson went home and bludgeoned his wife to death. Basing her novel on a historical incident, Bainbridge takes a crime that shocked Victorian London and uses it as a vehicle to explore the tensions that exist between men and women. A disturbing (and sometimes wickedly funny) portrait of a marriage gone terribly wrong.

A DEAD MAN IN DEPTFORD
by *Anthony Burgess* (Carroll & Graf, 1996, paperback)

Burgess turns the life of Christopher Marlowe into an imaginative novel, scrupulously researched in its historical details. The young playwright has a couple of problems. He's gay; he's an atheist; and he's aligned himself with Sir Walter Raleigh against Sir Francis Walsingham, Elizabeth I's Machiavellian Secretary of State and head of a notoriously efficient secret police. This is an Elizabethan England of spies and state terror, not the Victorian fantasy of jolly old England under good Queen Bess. *A Dead Man in Deptford* is a great literary thriller. Don't miss it.

Another Burgess Classic:

NOTHING LIKE THE SUN
(Norton, 1996, paperback).

Burgess fills in one of the most intriguing of all the missing pieces in Shakespeare's biography—his love life.

BABEL TOWER
by A.S. Byatt (Random House, 1996, hardcover)

Frederica's marriage to a country squire ends when he becomes violent and abusive. With their young son, She runs away to London and takes a job teaching at an art school. One of the most influential figures at the school is Jude Mason, an urban guru who goes about unkempt, unwashed and largely unclothed. Jude has written a novel, *Babbletower*, about an attempt to found a utopian community in an old castle. In her most complex story since *Possession*, Byatt intertwines the tensions at the art school, the squire and Frederica's custody battle for their son and the plot of Jude's novel.

DONALD DUK
by Frank Chin (Coffee House Press, 1991, paperback)

Donald Duk is the son of a restaurateur in San Francisco's Chinatown. But what he really wants is to be the next Fred Astaire. His cultural awakening comes during Chinese New Year. Amid the celebrations, Donald learns some remarkable things— about his father, about the Chinese who built the Pacific Railroad and about the customs and civilization and he would rather ignore. A beautifully told story of growing up.

PARIS TROUT
by Pete Dexter (Penguin, 1989, paperback)

In Cotton Point, Georgia, shortly after World War II, a vicious white man named Paris Trout murders a 14-year-old black girl and can't understand why the courts and the lawyers are making such a fuss about it. A dark, terrible beauty of a novel that's as mesmerizing as a train wreck.

Also by Dexter:

BROTHERLY LOVE
(Penguin, 1992, paperback).

A story of betrayal and blood vengeance between two cousins in a Philadelphia crime family.

THE PAPERBOY
(Dell, 1996, hardcover)

In every one of his novels, Pete Dexter accomplishes what most writers can only dream of: he gets us inside the heads of his characters so we come to know them as intimately as we know ourselves. This time out, Dexter tells the story of two newspapermen investigating the case of a man sitting on death row for an especially gruesome murder. Together, the reporters write a story about the matter that wins them a Pulitzer. But is their article the truth? This is Pete Dexter at the top of his game.

THE SIN EATER
by Alice Thomas Ellis (A Common Reader Edition, 1998, paperback)

Upstairs in a large country house in Wales, an old man known as the Captain is dying. Downstairs, his family has gathered to say good-bye (although no one is exactly prostrate with grief). In fact, it seems as if at any moment the daggers will come out. Organizing the weekend death watch is Rose, the Captain's daughter-in-law, who takes pains to disconcert her troublesome relatives. To give her readers a break from this witty viper pit, Ellis introduces a wonderful subplot—the annual Village vs. Squire cricket match. And when the village wins (for the first time in living memory) a sort of Welsh orgy breaks out. A wise, wry novel of how people respond to mortality.

THE SAMURAI
by Shusaku Endo (New Directions, 1997, paperback)

From a forgotten historical event, one of Japan's most respected writers has fashioned an unusual tale. In 1613, an embassy of samurai traveled on a trade mission across the Pacific to Mexico, then on to Spain and finally to Rome to meet the Pope. By the time they return home—seven years later—Japan is a different country and they are changed men.

THE SEA AND POISON
by Shusaku Endo (New Directions, 1992, paperback)

Doctor Suguro, practicing medicine on the outskirts of Tokyo, is haunted by a terrible memory: during the war, he assisted in the vivisection of an American prisoner of war. When The Sea and Poison was first published Japanese readers were shocked that an author would address head-on the problem of individual responsibility for crimes committed during World War II. A gripping, unflinching story of Japanese war crimes—told from the Japanese perspective.

SILENCE
by Shusaku Endo (Dufour Editions, 1996, paperback)

During the persecution of Christians in 17th-century Japan, a captured Portuguese Jesuit is given a choice: renounce Christ or face a horrific death. This superb, subtle, psychological novel is based on a true story.

BIRDSONG
by Sebastian Faulks (Vintage, 1997, paperback)

This novel—a bestseller in England—cries out to be made into a Masterpiece Theater series. Twenty-year-old Stephen Wraysford takes a trip to Amiens in 1910 and falls in love with the wife of a wealthy industrialist. She runs off with him, but their life is not a romantic idyll. When World War I begins, Stephen enlists to escape his doomed affair. It's hard to resist a story that moves from passionate romance to the horrors of trench warfare. And author Sebastian Faulks adds another level of perspective to the story by flashing forward to the present day when Stephen's granddaughter find his diaries. Ideal for anyone who enjoys historical fiction.

THE HOUSE ON THE LAGOON
by Rosario Ferré (NAL-Dutton, 1996, paperback)

A husband and wife, he a macho, wealthy importer enamored of American culture and longing for Puerto Rico's statehood, she a Vassar-educated feminist and supporter of Puerto Rico's independence, clash over their own family's history. Isabel has begun a multi-generational autobiographical novel and when Quintin finds it and sees how she has interpreted family events, he gets angry and begins to write his own novel. In alternating chapters, they offer their opposing perspectives on the past, all the while writing a new chapter in their own life together. An imaginative story from one of Latin America's preeminent novelists.

·············

THE TENANTS OF TIME
by Thomas Flanagan (Dutton, 1988, paperback)

Of all the ill-advised rebellions in Irish history, the Fenian Uprising of 1867 stands out as especially quixotic. Flanagan, one of the best historical novelists on the planet, follows four friends who take part in the rebellion and whose lives seem to diverge once the uprising collapses: Hugh MacMahon takes a job as a schoolmaster; Bob Delaney becomes a Parnellite politician; Vincent Tully gets along on his good looks and his father's money; while Ned Nolan is the only one of the four who remains committed to violent struggle. Years later, all four come together again for the climatic episode.

The Prequel:

THE YEAR OF THE FRENCH
by Thomas Flanagan (Holt, 1989, paperback).

The doomed uprising of 1798 and its impact on a handful of friends in a small rural Irish village.

·············

REMEMBER THE MORNING
by Thomas Fleming (Forge, 1997, paperback)

It is 1721. Two young girls, Dutch-born Catalyntie Van Vorst and African-born Clara, have been carried off by Senecas and adopted by the tribe. Catalyntie and Clara like Indian life, especially the status Seneca women enjoy in tribal councils. Then a prisoner exchange brings the women "home." Back in white society, Catalyntie is now subject to her uncle. Clara is Catalyntie's slave. Both long to regain some degree of independence. While they work out that problem, Catalyntie and Clara become involved in a love triangle with an idealistic colonist named Malcolm Stapleton. Remember the Morning is the best kind of historical fiction-an absorbing story that gets all the period details right.

INDEPENDENCE DAY
by *Richard Ford* (Vintage, 1996, paperback)

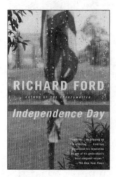

Frank Bascombe's life is still a mess. His wife has divorced him. He's not even writing sports stories any more: now he sells real estate. Over the Fourth of July weekend, Frank tries to get his life back on track. Readers and critics have been unanimous in their praise of Richard Ford's novels. They are introspective without ever becoming whiny, and they offer a vision of hope and stability even to down-and-out guys like Frank Bascombe.

The Prequel:

THE SPORTSWRITER
by *Richard Ford* (Vintage, 1995, paperback).

Frank Bascombe takes a hard look at his life. Once he was a novelist—now, he is a sportswriter, covering the lives and careers of men who are infinitely more successful than he is. A searing story of a man who wants his life to mean something again.

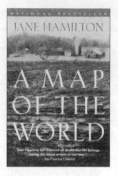

A MAP OF THE WORLD

by Jane Hamilton (Anchor Books, 1995, paperback)

One day, just for a moment, Alice Goodwin stops watching her best friend's two-year-old daughter and the child drowns in the Goodwin's' pond. The tragedy opens a Pandora's box of troubles. Alice is accused of child abuse, thrown in jail and put on trial. Yet, just as in the ancient myth of Pandora, there is still hope.

ATTICUS

by Ron Hansen
(HarperCollins, 1996, paperback)

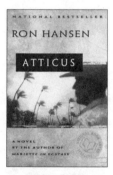

One of America's best contemporary novelists, Ron Hansen writes stories that are emotional powerhouses, addressing big themes: love and death and forgiveness. The title character of Atticus is a 67-year-old former rancher, now a rich oil man. His son Scott—his youngest boy, the child he doted on—has killed himself in Mexico, so he goes down to claim the body. There Atticus finds traces of Scott's last days that lead him to wonder if perhaps his son was murdered. And when at last he discovers the truth, it is worse than anyone could imagine. Can Atticus forgive his boy? Should he forgive him? Hansen finds a perfect resolution to this moral dilemma.

MARIETTE IN ECSTASY

by Ron Hansen (HarperCollins, 1996, paperback)

The serenity of a convent in upstate New York is shattered when a young novice finds on her hands and feet and side the wounds of Christ's crucifixion. The mother superior, the nuns, the chaplain, the physicians, everyone wants it to be a case of religious hysteria. But it appears that the stigmata is genuine. When it first appeared, this extraordinary book became a word-of-mouth sensation among booksellers and readers.

WONDERFUL YEARS, WONDERFUL YEARS
by George V. Higgins (Kensington, 1989, paperback)

Boston contractor Ken Farley's wife knows too much about the family business, so he ships her off to a nice rest home in the country. It's Bucky Arbuckle's job to make sure the missus stays there. This is a rich, wonderful novel and Higgins writes the best dialogue since Ring Lardner.

Also by Higgins:

THE PATRIOT GAME
(Knopf, 1982, hardcover)

A Justice Department agent pursues an IRA gunrunner through Boston's underworld, Irish ghettoes and the tony country clubs of the Boston Brahmins. Worth searching for.

MR. IVES' CHRISTMAS
by Oscar Hijuelos (HarperCollins, 1995, paperback)

Edward Ives was living the American dream. He had a wife he loved, two wonderful children, a successful career. And as a devout Catholic, Mr. Ives had a rich spiritual life. But then, as Christmas approaches, Mr. Ives' son Robert is gunned down in front of a church. The senselessness of Robert's death throws Mr. Ives' life in turmoil. He begins to wonder if God, his marriage and his faith in the essential goodness of people are all a delusion. Oscar Hijuelos has written a profound novel that treats love, faith, forgiveness and redemption seriously. Don't miss it.

Also by Oscar Hijuelos:

THE MAMBO KINGS PLAY SONGS OF LOVE
(HarperCollins, 1990, paperback).

A bittersweet story of two Cuban brothers—musicians playing the Latin neighborhoods of New York City in the early 1950s—who get their big break when they appear on the I Love Lucy show.

HERE ON EARTH
by Alice Hoffman (Putnam, 1997, hardcover)

Alice Hoffman has written a new version of Wuthering Heights, this time set in a remote, modern day New England village. Hollis is the dark-eyed orphan heartthrob brought into the Murray household. March is the spitfire who falls insanely in love with Hollis (and he returns the favor). Alan is March's slimy brother who persecutes Hollis. By and large, Hoffman follows the original plot faithfully, but it is her own lyrical prose which puts a pleasant spin on Bronte's dark tale of obsessive love. Many readers have observed that Wuthering Heights' story of mad love is a bit over the top. Yet in Hoffman's version Hollis and March's intense, life-long romance is perfectly credible.

PROPERTY OF
by Alice Hoffman (Berkley, 1993, paperback)

Alice Hoffman has a talent for writing gracefully about subjects that make most people uncomfortable. On the outskirts of New York City, a gang named the Orphans fights for control of the streets. The girls wear jackets emblazoned with the words "Property of the Orphans." The narrator hates these trashy girls, until she develops an erotic obsession for McKay, the Orphans' leader and becomes his property.

Also by Alice Hoffman:

ILLUMINATION NIGHT
(Fawcett Crest, 1988, paperback).

On Martha's Vineyard, a couple that has toughed out the hard times and kept their marriage intact is confronted with an unexpected crisis—the teenage girl next door is sexually obsessed with the husband.

THE UNCONSOLED
by Kazuo Ishiguro (Knopf, 1996, paperback)

There's a touch of Kafka to this tale of an internationally acclaimed pianist named Ryder who arrives in an unnamed

European city to give a concert (or so he believes). Yet everyone he meets keeps alluding to some mysterious mission he must accomplish and no one seems willing to enlighten him on the nature of this assignment. Like Stevens, the butler from Ishiguro's best-known work, *Remains of the Day*, what Ryder says to people is at odds with what he means. Once again, the interior life of Ishiguro's main character will keep readers spellbound.

Also by Ishiguro:

AN ARTIST OF THE FLOATING WORLD
(Vintage, 1989, paperback).

An artist in pre-war Japan hopes for a career as a painter, but wonders if there will be room for artists in a militaristic nation. This novel was on the short list for England's Booker Prize and launched Ishiguro's international reputation.

MIDDLE PASSAGE
by Charles Johnson (Plume, 1991, paperback)

The year is 1830. Rutherford Calhoun, a freed slave, is on the lam from a string of bad debts and an ill-starred love affair. So he signs on as a seaman aboard a slave ship bound for Africa. Yet nothing goes as the slavers or Calhoun planned. The captain is a madman and the ship's human cargo are members of a tribe of magicians. Charles Johnson writes some of the most gorgeous prose you've ever encountered about one of the strangest voyages in literature.

ORDINARY MONEY
by Louis B. Jones (Viking, 1990, hardcover)

Randy Potts, amateur suburban schemer, has printed millions of dollars in $20 bills. When he suspects that the Feds are onto him, Randy hides the crate of phony money in the garage of Wayne Paschke, an unemployed house painter and his best friend. But the Feds have tested the money and they've decided it's real. Naturally, Randy and Wayne are too smart to fall for that old ploy....

Jones has invented a new genre—the comic suspense novel. Worth searching for.

PARTICLES AND LUCK
by Louis B. Jones (Vintage, 1994, paperback)

Boy genius, Mark Perdue, 27, occupies a distinguished chair of physics at Berkeley, lives in the princely Cobblestone Hearth Village Estates and has just married an intelligent, sexy, drop-dead gorgeous woman who is entirely too good for him. So why is he spending Halloween night camped out with the owner of failing pizza franchise, waiting for representatives of a mysterious corporation who may be trying to take over their deluxe condos? Jones has a genius for catching the unpredictability, the sheer looniness of modern life.

················

ANNIE JOHN
by Jamaica Kincaid (Plume, 1986, paperback)

This especially well done coming-of-age story follows Annie John from age 10 through 17 as she grows up on the island of Antigua. Annie has insight and maturity beyond her years; even poverty and death cannot break her spirit. But what really sets this book apart is Jamaica Kincaid's genius in exposing the emotions and rebellions of adolescence. Best scenes: Annie wrestles with her feelings of both love and hatred for her mother.

More of Jamaica Kincaid:

LUCY
(Plume, 1991, Paperback).

The stakes are keeping one's innocence or learning from cruel experience in this story of an Antiguan au pair working for a wealthy family in a large U.S. city.

················

SLOWNESS
by Milan Kundera, Translated by Linda Asher
(HarperCollins, 1996, paperback)

O n a midsummer's night in a chateau near Paris, two tales of seduction, separated by more than two centuries, are remembered. In the 18th century, a young chevalier shares a memorable night with the sensuous Madame de T. His 20th-century counterpart, Vincent, comes to the now-shabby chateau for an entomological conference and meets a woman who makes her intentions clear to him almost immediately. The "slowness" of Kundera's title is his code word for arousal and his story is a lament for the leisure with which previous generations approached a night of love.

Kundera's Blockbuster:

THE UNBEARABLE LIGHTNESS OF BEING
(HarperCollins, 1988, paperback).

A man juggles life's anxieties that weigh his spirit down and its superficialities which make him feel weightless.

SOMETHING TO BE DESIRED
by Thomas McGuane (Vintage, 1994, paperback)

M cGuane is in top form in thus sharp, funny book about misguided sexual obsession. When Lucien Taylor hears that his boyhood sweetheart, Emily, shot her husband, he does what any red-blooded Romeo would do: he leaves his wife, deserts his son, declares that Emily is the misunderstood victim of a lousy marriage and rushes back to Montana to be with his long-lost love.

Also by McGuane:

KEEP THE CHANGE
(Vintage, 1994, paperback)

Joe Starling is an artist who's stopped painting, a lover who's run out on his girlfriend. But he's determined to make a success of the family ranch before it's swallowed up by a local land baron.

THE STERILE CUCKOO
by John Nichols (Norton, 1994, paperback)

Nichols published this novel when he was 24 years old and it shows (in a good way). While it was still fresh in his mind, he captured all of the joy, pain, freedom and confusion of youth. Anyone who's ever set foot on a college campus will be touched by the funny, tender, offbeat and tragic romance that grows between Jerry Payne and Pookie Adams—who, by the way, ranks as one of the most original literary heroines on record.

ABSOLUTION
by Olafur Johann Olafsson (Pantheon, 1991, hardcover)

Back home in Reykjavik, Olafsson is a best-selling author. But in the U.S., his adopted country, he is less well-known. This novel should help build Olafsson's following in America. Petersen, a nasty, wealthy old man holed up in his Park Avenue apartment, is haunted by a "little crime" he committed during the Nazi occupation of Copenhagen. Against his own inclinations, Petersen reveals his ugly secret to the reader, all the while hoping for forgiveness. Worth searching for.

THE CANNIBAL GALAXY
by Cynthia Ozick (NAL-Dutton, 1984, paperback)

Joseph Brill is headmaster of a private school in the Midwest. All his life he has been waiting for a prodigy, a genius student who would lend importance to his school and establish Brill's reputation as a first class educator. But when such a child is at last enrolled, Brill can't see it and writes the girl off as mediocre. Instead, he focuses on the girl's mother, whom he believes possesses a mind as brilliant as his own. A beautifully crafted story of pride and self-delusion.

JOSHUA THEN AND NOW
by Mordechai Richler (Bantam, 1985, paperback)

Joshua's mother was a stripper. His father was a third-rate boxer. Joshua himself was the "muscle" for a mobster. But somehow Joshua manages to rise above his past and begin a new career as a TV news commentator with a socially prominent gentile wife. Still, Joshua's past haunts him and as his father's old cronies begin to die off, Joshua finds himself returning to the family's old neighborhood, trying to recapture some sense of Jewish life in Montreal.

SOLOMON GURSKY WAS HERE
by Mordechai Richler (Random House, 1990, paperback)

A very funny Jewish Canadian family saga. Grandpa Ephraim, the founder of the dynasty, was a first rate con man. His sons, Bernard, Solomon and Morrie, made a fortune with their distillery during America's Prohibition period. The real pleasures of this novel are the scenes where the Gurskys take on English Canada's aristocratic families.

MOO
by Jane Smiley (Random House, 1995, hardcover)

Without ever slipping over the line into slapstick, Smiley mercilessly lampoons the pretensions, agendas and egomania of the faculty at a big Midwestern agricultural college, known affectionately as Moo U. The funniest send-up of academia to come along in years.

A SUMMONS TO MEMPHIS
by Peter Taylor (Ballantine, 1993, paperback)

During his life, George Carter had derailed the marriage plans of all three of his children. Now wealthy, widowed and in his eighties, Carter plans to marry a younger woman. His children—his two daughters especially—see this as their opportunity for payback. Taylor's story is deceptively simple, but after a page or two you realize that you are in the hands of a master, an author who writes with tremendous intelligence about the human heart and the old resentments that can surface even in the most devoted families.

THE JOY LUCK CLUB
by Amy Tan (Ivy Books, 1990, paperback)

Amy Tan is one of the brightest stars of contemporary fiction. Her storytelling is first-rate in this poignant tale of four Chinese "aunties" whose lives in 1940s China contrast so sharply with the lives of their assimilated daughters in contemporary California. A book that goes straight to your heart.

THE MOSQUITO COAST
by Paul Theroux (Avon, 1983, paperback)

Allie Fox, a cantankerous Yankee inventor, is fed up with modern America so he packs up his family and moves them down to Honduras where he plans to build a new society. Make no mistake, Fox may be a bit intense, but he is definitely a mechanical genius. With his clan and a willing group of Hondurans to help them, Fox builds a mini-Eden in the jungle. And it even works! But then Fox's egomania begins to undermine everything he has achieved and soon his family find they have a certifiable madman on their hands.

More of Theroux:

MY SECRET HISTORY
(Ivy Books, 1990, paperback).

Theroux's loosely autobiographical novel of a man's coming of age, from boyhood attraction to the priesthood, to adolescent sexual initiation, to young adulthood in Africa, to a husband with marriage difficulties.

CLOSE QUARTERS
by *Angela Thirkell* (Knopf, 1958)

In the 1950s, British author Angela Thirkell created a little world called Barsetshire, filled it with country manorhouses, great estates and charming villages and peopled it with some of the most engaging characters in modern fiction. This story focuses on Margot Macfadyen. She has just suffered three bereavements, but then the most promising gentleman appears on the scene. Readers new to Barsetshire are always surprised how quickly they become absorbed in Thirkell's intriguing little world. Worth searching for.

The prequel:

JUTLAND COTTAGE
by *Angela Thirkell* (Knopf, 1957).

Margot has just turned 40 and is still unmarried. So, the ladies of Barchester town exert themselves to find her a suitable husband. Of course, the results of all these good intentions are unpredictable. Worth searching for.

THE RECTOR'S WIFE
by *Joanna Trollope* (Berkley, 1996, paperback)

The great-great-great-great-great-niece of Anthony Trollope, Joanna Trollope is extremely popular in England, where The Rector's Wife is thought to be her best book. After 20 years' scrapping by on the paltry salary of her dull clergyman husband Peter, Anna Bouverie takes a job in a supermarket. As revolutions go, this one is pretty tame, but it scandalizes the parish and mortifies Peter. Censured at home, Anna finds support from three surprising sources—Patrick, a wealthy newcomer to the village; Daniel, the new archdeacon; and Jonathan, Daniel's handsome brother. As the men's affection for Anna grows, she finds that she has a lot of new choices to make.

THE CHOIR
by Joanna Trollope (Berkley, 1997, paperback)

An English cathedral requires expensive repairs, so the autocratic dean suggests jettisoning the boys' choir. This displeases the best chorister's mother, who is having an affair with the choirmaster. Meanwhile, the dean's troubled daughter is herself infatuated with the choirmaster. Before the fate of the choir is decided, a whole slew of nasty events befall the cast of characters. A light read, but very entertaining.

THE LADDER OF YEARS
by Anne Tyler (Ivy Books, 1997, paperback)

Anne Tyler's fictional characters tend to be eccentrics, but the people in this novel have both feet planted firmly on the ground. Delia Grinstead, wife to an aloof Baltimore physician and mother of three thoroughly unpleasant children, runs away to a little town in Delaware where she adopts the identity of Ms. Grinstead, a rather shy spinster lady. Tyler develops Delia's personality beautifully as she evolves from childish insecurity into a sympathetic, intelligent, tender woman. Of Tyler's many novels, this stands among the best.

THE ACCIDENTAL TOURIST
by Anne Tyler (Berkley, 1986, paperback)

Macon Leary, a buttoned-down kind of guy who hates chaos, is forced to return to his family home and endure the non-stop lunacy of his brothers and sisters. Worse yet, a love interest appears— Muriel, a fast-talking, stiletto-heeled dynamo determined to drag Macon out of his lethargy. An all-time favorite.

SEARCHING FOR CALEB
by Anne Tyler (Fawcett, 1996, paperback)

The rich, self-assured Peck clan of Baltimore is the living icon of stability. There is, however, one oddball in the family—Grandpa's brother Caleb the cello player, who ran off 60 years ago and hasn't been heard from since. To everyone's dismay, Grandpa decides it's time to find his brother before death finds them first.

DINNER AT THE HOMESICK RESTAURANT
(Ivy Books, 1992, paperback).

After a wretched childhood, Ezra opens the Homesick Restaurant to give his life direction, but his handsome, uncontrollable brother, Cody, has other plans.

MORALITY PLAY
by Barry Unsworth (Norton, 1996, paperback)

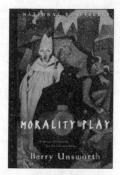

As the Black Death sweeps across England, Nicholas Barber, a priest, runs away from his post at Lincoln Cathedral and joins a band of wandering players. Hungry, tired, destitute, the players' leader strikes upon a shocking plan to make some money: they stage a play based on the murder of a young woman and perform it in the village in which she was killed. Unfortunately, like Hamlet's "Mousetrap," the play strikes a little too close to the truth and the players run afoul of the local lord. You'll enjoy Unsworth's ensemble of characters and his intense descriptions of medieval life.

More by Unsworth:

SACRED HUNGER
(Norton, 1993, paperback).

Unsworth won England's Booker Prize for this story of a slave ship in which the captive Africans and the white crew try to escape from society and build a mixed-race community.

IN THE BEAUTY OF THE LILIES
by John Updike (Fawcett, 1997, paperback)

Beginning in Paterson, New Jersey, in 1910, Updike follows a family trying to find some moral anchor for their lives. The patriarch, Reverend Clarence Wilmot, saw his faith collapse before the onslaught of Darwin and Nietzsche. His granddaughter, Esther, has become a Hollywood starlet who believes her success is a sign of ongoing divine intervention. And her son, Clark, has allied himself with a David Koresh figure (some of the novel's best scenes involve the Waco-style siege of his religious commune). This is Updike in perfect form.

An unlikely Updike novel:

THE WITCHES OF EASTWICK
(Fawcett, 1985, paperback).

Updike breaks with his usual "suburban realism" to spin a story— by turns funny and frightening—of three divorcées who are enticed by the Devil to practice witchcraft in their small Rhode Island town.

THE ENGLISHMAN'S BOY
by Guy Vanderhaeghe (Picador, 1997, paperback)

A Hollywood mogul wants to make a movie about an elderly Canadian cowboy named Shorty McAdoo. What the mogul doesn't know is 50 years back, in 1873, McAdoo took part in an Indian massacre. The story follows two parallel plot lines. One tells of McAdoo and the posse that murdered some Indian horse thieves. The other exposes ruthless doings in 1920s Hollywood. Vanderhaeghe's forceful narrative style is perfectly suited to telling stories about brutal, pitiless characters.

THE WEDDING
by Dorothy West (Anchor Books, 1996, hardcover)

After more than 45 years, Dorothy West wrote a novel. The last surviving member of that great literary flowering known as the Harlem Renaissance tells a story that sets Guess Who's Coming to Dinner on its head. In the 1950s, in a prosperous black middle-class community on Martha's Vineyard, a young woman announces that she intends to marry a white jazz musician. Her parents are appalled—as is the man from the neighborhood who loves her. The situation only gets worse as the wedding day approaches. Oprah Winfrey produced a made-for-TV-movie based on this piece in 1997, but it's no substitute for this lovely, heartbreaking book.

• • • • • • • • • • • • •

THIS BOY'S LIFE: A MEMOIR
by *Tobias Wolff* (Perennial Library/HarperCollins, 1990, paperback)

When Toby's mother remarried, she hoped she was restoring the stability her boy had lost when the family split apart. But Toby's stepfather turns out to be a tyrant more brutal than any Charles Dickens ever dreamed up. Trapped in a ratty town, saddled with a reputation as a troublemaker, Toby reinvents himself and hatches an escape plan that is so daring, so wily, so impossible, it will astonish you.

By *Tobias' Brother:*

THE DUKE OF DECEPTION
by *Geoffrey Wolff* (Vintage, 1990, paperback).

Duke Wolff, the author's father, was a con man. A liar. A cheat. A scam artist. He cheerfully swindled jewelers, sports car dealers, landlords. His resumes were masterworks of misinformation (he claimed to hold an advanced degree from the Sorbonne's non-existent Ecole d'Aeronautique). And he went to his grave denying to his own sons that he was Jewish. When you read Wolff's memoir of his life with his father, it may strike you as fiction. Duke Wolff's story is just too good to be true.

• • • • • • • • • • • • •

BEACH BOOKS

JAWS
by Peter Benchley (Fawcett, 1991, paperback)

The spell-binding story of a great white shark that terrorizes a Long Island summer resort town has kept readers out of the water for more than 20 years. If you've never read Jaws, do yourself a favor and take it with you to the beach. Benchley has packed his novel with real-life characters, genuine emotions and a thrilling chase at sea. Hands down, the ultimate beach book.

THE GLASS LAKE
by Maeve Binchy (Dell, 1996, paperback)

Kit McMahon is 12 years old when her mother disappears after a walk along Lough Glass. As the authorities find the McMahon family's boat overturned on the lake, Kit discovers a suicide note from her mother. But Helen McMahon isn't dead— she has run away to London where she builds a thriving employment agency business. One day, years later, Kit walks into the agency looking for a job.... Once again, Maeve Binchy has written a page-turner about the secrets women share.

One of Binchy's best:

THE COPPER BEECH
(Dell, 1993, paperback).

An old copper beech tree shades a schoolhouse in a tiny Irish village. For generations, students have carved their initials into the massive trunk. Binchy tells charming interlocking tales of what became of some of those children.

GONE BAMBOO
by Anthony Bourdain (Villard Books, 1997, paperback)

Henry Denard, a former assassin for the CIA, has retired to the island of St. Martin to live a life of restful hedonism with his gorgeous wife, Frances. But back in the States, Jimmy "Pazz" Calabrese, a 320-pound crossdressing mob boss, is still miffed that Denard bungled a hit the year before and left one of Jimmy Pazz's rivals alive. By introducing lots of memorable characters, a few interesting subplots, a little gunplay, a little bloodshed and really snappy dialogue, Bourdain keeps his story percolating and his readers entertained.

More by Bourdain:

BONE IN THE THROAT
(Villard Books, 1995, paperback).

Tommy Pagano, an aspiring chef, winds up working in his cousin's restaurant where the specialty of the house is minced mobsters.

THE BRIDGE BUILDER'S STORY
by Howard Fast (M.E. Sharpe, 1995, hardcover)

Berlin, 1939. Scott Waring and his wife Martha are married just eleven days when the Gestapo arrest them. Imprudently, Waring had gone to a Nazi rally carrying a pistol; now the Gestapo think he meant to assassinate Hitler. They promise they will kill Martha unless he confesses. To save his wife, Waring fabricates a confession. But the Nazis kill Martha anyway. Then the story skips ahead to 1951. Guilt over Martha's death has left Scott a psychological mess and sexually impotent. With a psychiatrist he explores his war adventures. With a waitress in Greenwich Village, a Dachau survivor, he learns to love again. Howard Fast specializes in fast-paced melodramas, and this is one of his best.

FLASHMAN AND THE ANGEL OF THE LORD

by George MacDonald Fraser (Plume, 1996, paperback)

The reluctant hero of Fraser's Flashman Papers series is British Army colonel Sir Harry Flashman. In his latest adventure, Flashman is forced to join John Brown's doomed 1859 raid on the arsenal at Harper's Ferry, Virginia. What Brown doesn't know is the U.S. government has hired Flashman as a spy to dissuade him from the attack. Meanwhile, white supremacists want Flashman to spur on Brown's mad adventure (they're sure it will unite the South and split the Union). A rollicking, sardonic adventure.

Another Flashman adventure:

FLASHMAN AND THE DRAGON

(Plume, 1987, paperback).

During China's Taiping Rebellion, Flashman is thrown into a dungeon, endures fiendish tortures, becomes the boy toy of a diminutive and insatiable princess and finally rescues his comrades from a particularly nasty death.

WISHES

by Lisa Jackson (NAL-Dutton, 1995, paperback)

Kate Summers had just lost her husband and child in a drunk driving accident when a stranger presented her with a newborn baby boy. She can have the child, but only if she asks no questions, leaves Boston immediately and always insists that he is her natural son. Jubilant, Kate takes the baby and runs. 15 years later, Deagan O'Roarke, the boy's father, shows up at Kate's door. One drunken night years earlier, Deagan and his cousin Bibi went to bed together. Fifteen-year-old Jon Summers is the product of that one-night stand. After years of secrecy, the story has gotten out. And now Bibi's immensely rich father wants his missing grandson back. Money, power, sex and the battle over a good-looking kid. What more could ask for in a beach read?

AZTEC AUTUMN
by Gary Jennings (Forge Press, 1997, paperback)

Jennings has mastered the art of the historical novel. His period details are accurate; he never lapses into stereotypes—whether he is describing Aztecs or Spanish conquistadors; and he has a vigorous prose style that keeps his story moving. The hero, Tenamaxtli, is an Aztec nobleman who is determined to find the Spaniards weakness and build an Aztec army that can exploit it. It's a classic tale of a man with a mission, enlivened by plenty of graphic battle scenes and gruesome executions, plus Tenamaxtli's considerable sexual escapades.

The Prequel:

AZTEC

by Gary Jennings (Forge, 1997, paperback).

An enormous saga (over 1000 pages!) of the life and adventures of Mixtil, an Aztec who becomes a scribe, warrior, merchant and wanderer in the years before the arrival of the Spanish conquistadors.

....

LOVERS
by Judith Krantz (Bantam, 1995, paperback)

Gigi Orsini has just started working as a copywriter at a slick Los Angeles advertising agency. The art director on her creative team is David Melville, a attractive man who shows an obvious interest in her. Gigi's future at the agency is far from certain as one of the partners, an ice queen appropriately named Victoria Frost, becomes Gigi's nemesis. Glamorous locations, jealousy, romance, intricate plot twists, plus a host of supporting characters from Krantz's two blockbuster best-sellers *Scruples* and *Scruples Two*, make this a natural for the beach.

....

GLITZ
by Elmore Leonard (Warner Books, 1987, paperback)

Vincent Mora, a Miami cop on medical leave, is recuperating in Puerto Rico when two events disrupt his vacation. A paroled rapist Mora put away has followed him to the island, bent on revenge. And a local young woman who was employed by a rich Atlantic City casino owner has turned up murdered. *Glitz* has all the action, intrigue and intelligent characterizations—plus a truly satisfying ending—that make Elmore Leonard a joy to read.

Another by Leonard:

CAT CHASER
(Avon Books, 1995, paperback).

Life gets exciting once again for George Moran, an ex-Marine running a motel in Florida, when he falls in love with the wife of a Central American general. A tightly plotted thriller with plenty of sex and violence.

PRIDE OF LIONS
by Morgan Llywelyn (Tor, 1996, paperback)

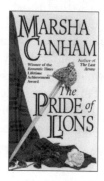

Llywelyn's fans have waited since 1979 for this sequel to his best-seller, Lion of Ireland. In the first book, Brian Boru, High King of Ireland, succeeded in driving the Vikings from Ireland, but died in the final battle. Now his sons, Donough and Teigue, contend for their father's crown and his widow schemes to regain the power she lost at her husband's death. Readers will enjoy Llywelyn's grasp of 11th-century history and his strong story of treachery in Ireland's royal family.

The first book:

LION OF IRELAND
by Morgan Llywelyn (Tor Books, 1996, paperback).

Inspired by tales of Charlemagne, Brian Boru rallies his countrymen, uniting them into a cohesive force to defeat the Viking invaders.

ANYTHING CONSIDERED
by Peter Mayle (Knopf, 1996, paperback)

In the sun-drenched Provencal village of Saint-Martin, Bennett, a down-on-his-luck Englishman, gets his hands on a secret that has eluded humankind for thousands of years: how to cultivate truffles. Bennett plans to make a fortune off his new-found expertise. Ah! but the allure of truffles extends beyond the five-star restaurants of Europe. Soon Bennett is dodging Italian gangsters, a Japanese hit man and a gorgeous former commando of the army of Israel—all of whom would kill for the truffle-growing serum. A fast plot, lots of atmosphere and plenty of laughs make this an ideal book for summer reading.

RIDE THE WIND:
THE STORY OF CYNTHIA ANN PARKER AND THE LAST DAYS OF THE COMANCHES
by Lucia St. Clair Robson (Ballantine, 1982, paperback)

In 1836, a Comanche war party attacked Parker's Fort, Texas, killed most of the inhabitants and carried off nine-year-old Cynthia Ann Parker. Cynthia spent the rest of her life with the Comanches, learning their ways and answering to the name the Comanches gave her: Naduah, Keeps Warm with Us. In time she married a warrior named Wanderer and gave birth to a son, Quanah Parker, who grew up to be the last free war chief of the Comanches. This big, sweeping novel tells Cynthia's unique story and the story of one of the greatest of the Plains tribes.

Another Robson epic:

WALK IN MY SOUL
(Ballantine, 1985, paperback).

Tiana, a Cherokee woman and young Sam Houston fall in love in the days before the Cherokee are forcibly moved west on the Trial of Tears.

NURSES
by *Marcia Rose* (Ballantine, 1996, paperback)

I f you like the television series *E.R.*, you'll love *Nurses*. Set in New York City's only nurse-run hospital, this novel is brimming with colorful characters and suspense-filled subplots. Marty Lamb is director of the hospital. Her schizophrenic husband, who tried to strangle her, has just been released from a mental health institution. Meanwhile, Marty has started an affair with the handsome Dr. Paul Giordano. A transsexual nurse, missing drugs and the mysterious appearance of gray envelopes that detail the darkest secrets of Marty and her staff help keep the plot percolating.

LAST NIGHT
by *Meryl Sawyer* (Dell, 1996, paperback)

T wenty years before this book begins, Judge Dana Hamilton killed the man who raped her and her sister. Now a blackmailer is threatening to expose her. So she hires Rob Taggett, an ex-cop and a private investigator. Taggett's first suspect is an acquaintance of Dana's—a filthy rich Hawaiian rancher called Big Daddy. When Dana and Rob go out to the ranch for a friendly visit, they finally admit their mutual attraction for each other. Sawyer keeps the story going with plenty of hidden motives among a wide cast of possible suspects. And there are lots of steamy love scenes between this very appealing couple. A solid modern romance.

HILL TOWNS
by *Anne Rivers Siddons* (HarperCollins, 1994, paperback)

B ack home in North Carolina, Hays Bennett seemed dashing and romantic, but his wife Cat begins to have second thoughts when they encounter a sexy painter in Tuscany. You'll love Siddons' bewitching descriptions of Italian landscapes and she supplies plenty of lies, manipulation and even a little danger to keep you on the edge of your beach chair.

More by Anne Rivers Siddons:

PEACHTREE ROAD
(Ballantine, 1989, paperback).

Often considered her best novel, this saga of an old Georgia family reveals the social taboos and arcane rituals of the Southern aristocracy.

THE RIVER GOD
by *Wilbur Smith* (St. Martin's Press, 1995, paperback)

Tanus, the golden boy of Pharaoh's army, has been chosen by the gods to lead a bold campaign that will reunite the two halves of divided Egypt. As his reward, Tanus chooses Lady Lostris, a legendary beauty whom the priests say the gods have reserved for themselves. Set in ancient Egypt 4000 years ago, Smith's epic story of forbidden love, military conquest and priestly intrigue is a bona fide page-turner, perfect for long, lazy days on the beach.

THE BEST ANTHOLOGIES

THE PENGUIN BOOK OF WOMEN'S HUMOR
Edited by Regina Barreca (Penguin, 1996, paperback)

You expect funny stuff from Mae West, Dorothy Parker, Molly Ivins, Cynthia Heimel, Erma Bombeck and Rita Rudner. But what about the Brontës, George Eliot, Edith Wharton and Gertrude Stein? This encyclopedic volume of women's humor includes Gwendolyn Brooks' "White Girls Are Peculiar People," Lily Tomlin "On Doctors" and Judy Holliday "On Falsies." From Flannery O'Connor's black humor to Elayne Boosler's zingers, these is a raucous collection all women—and men—can enjoy.

ROY BLOUNT'S BOOK OF SOUTHERN HUMOR
Edited by Roy Blount, Jr. (Norton, 1994, hardcover)

Face it. Yankees just aren't funny. Our best humorists have always come from below the Mason-Dixon Line. In this anthology, Blount has collected more than 150 stories, sketches, poems, essays, blues, country and rock lyrics—all of them absolutely hilarious. You'll find Twain, Faulkner, Welty, Zora Neale Hurston, Louis Armstrong, Molly Ivins, Dave Barry. Plus Blount's own contribution, "I Don't Eat Dirt Personally. " A laugh riot.

DESIRING ITALY
Edited by Susan Cahill (Fawcett, 1997, paperback)

Mary Shelley and Muriel Spark on Venice. Elizabeth Barrett Browning and Mary McCarthy on Florence. Kate Simon on Siena. Edith Wharton on Milan. Barbara Grizzuti Harrison on Sicily. Susan Cahill has collected 31 delightful observations about Italy and things Italian written by women travelers over the last 200 years. You'll find Rose Macaulay's meditation on the pleasures of ruins; Patricia Hampl on the joys of spring in Umbria; and Marcella Hazan's love song to gelati. A completely enchanting book on how Italy assaults the mind, the spirit and the senses of the traveler.

Another Great Cahill Collection:

WISE WOMEN: OVER TWO THOUSAND YEARS OF SPIRITUAL WRITING BY WOMEN
(Norton, 1997, paperback).

Ranging over 4000 years, Cahill brings together sacred writings by women from ancient Babylon and Egypt, to medieval Germany, to contemporary America.

EYEWITNESS TO HISTORY
Edited by John Carey (Avon Books, 1990, paperback).

The eruption of Vesuvius and destruction of Pompeii. Dinner with Attila the Hun. An Aztec human sacrifice. A night in the Black Hole of Calcutta. A slave auction in Virginia. Darwin in the Galapagos Islands. Gauguin in Tahiti. A stoning in Jeddah—in 1958! The first men on the moon. These are just a handful of the eyewitnesses accounts you'll find in this anthology.

THE NORTON ANTHOLOGY OF AFRICAN AMERICAN LITERATURE
general editors Henry Louis Gates and Nellie Y. McKay
(Norton, 1997, hardcover)

What a wonderful book. It features long, meaty excerpts from the writings of Phillis Wheatley, Sojourner Truth, Frederick Douglass, W.E.B. DuBois, Langston Hughes, Zora Neale Hurston, Dorothy West, Nikki Giovanni, Toni Morrison, Octavia Butler, Gloria Naylor, David Bradley, Walter Mosely, Rita Dove. But what really pushes this book over the top is the audio companion with performances by Paul Robeson, Mahalia Jackson, Louis Armstrong, Martin Luther King, Jr.'s "I Have a Dream" speech and Malcolm X's "The Ballot or the Bullet." A real celebration of more than 200 years of creative expression by African Americans.

CENTERS OF SELF
Edited by Judith A. and Martin J. Hamer
(Hill & Wang, 1994, paperback)

The subtitle of this anthology is Short Stories by Black American Women from the Nineteenth Century to the Present. Scan the table of contents and you'll find many names you recognize: Zora Neale Hurston, Dorothy West, Alice Walker, Ntozake Shange, Jamaica Kincaid. But there will be many more names that are unfamiliar as the editors reach back to 1859 to find the unique literary voices of black women. The stories wrestle with virtually every dimension of black life —"passing" as white, striving for respect, looking for love, recognition, security and a sense of self-worth. This is an impressive, moving and revealing collection of short fiction.

NEW TRAILS:
ORIGINAL STORIES OF THE WEST
Edited by John Jakes and Martin H. Greenberg
(Bantam, 1995, paperback)

Twenty-three authors, some old hands at writing westerns, some greenhorns, offer a satisfying variety of stories. Jakes himself spins a mystical tale of a trapper. Elmore Leonard offers a racially charged shoot-out. Marianne Willman takes the famous murder of Billy the Kid and looks at it from various points of view. And Loren

D. Estleman follows an old woman's clever plan to re-invigorate her husband. A great collection for devoted western fans and readers new to the genre.

....

THE UNCOLLECTED WODEHOUSE
Edited and Introduced by David A. Jansen
(International Polygonics, Ltd., 1992)

Wodehouse's official biographer scoured many long-defunct newspapers and magazines to assemble this treasury of the comic master's previously uncollected articles and short stories. It includes Wodehouse's only mystery story, accounts of British public school life, the first of his many articles for Punch, one of the few stories about Reggie Pepper (a precursor of Bertie Wooster) and his very first butler, Keggs, the prototype for the immortal Jeeves. This fascinating look at how geniuses get that way is out of print, so hunt around used books stores or your local library for a copy.

....

FIRST FICTION: AN ANTHOLOGY OF THE FIRST PUBLISHED SHORT STORIES BY FAMOUS WRITERS
Edited by Kathy Kiernan and Michael M. Moore
(Little, Brown, 1994, paperback)

Mary McCarthy based her first short story on the nasty breakup of her first marriage. Fitzgerald, flush with the $30 he got for his first story, splurged on a pair of white flannel pajamas. This collection of 41 firsts by masters of the short story include works by Raymond Carver, John Cheever, Dorothy Parker, Shirley Jackson, Isaac Bashevis Singer, Flannery O'Connor. A celebration of youth, ambition and the joys of getting into print. Worth searching for.

....

THE NEW NEGRO
Edited by Alain Locke, with an introduction by Arnold Rampersand
(1925; Atheneum, 1992, paperback)

Anyone interested in the Harlem Renaissance must own a copy of *The New Negro*, a monumental anthology of fiction and poetry, as well as essays on such topics as African American music, art, literature folklore, history and sociology. Contributors include W.E.B. DuBois, Zora Neale Hurston, Arthur Schomburg, Langston Hughes, Angelina Grimke and Countee Cullen. It is a kind of archive of that tremendous upsurge of creativity in black America that reached its zenith in the mid-1920s. This volume includes the illustrations created by Winold Reiss and Aaron Douglas for the original 1925 edition.

THE COLUMBIA BOOK OF CIVIL WAR POETRY
Edited by Richard Marius
(Columbia University Press, 1994, hardcover)

Nothing seems to strike America's "mystic chords of memory" (as Lincoln put it) more sharply than the Civil War. This masterful anthology brings together the voices of dozens of American poets who responded to the great war in remarkably unique ways. You'll find Walt Whitman's lament on Lincoln's assassination, "When Lilacs Last in the Dooryard Bloomed," Julia Ward Howe's mystically militant "Battle Hymn of the Republic" and Robert Lowell's tribute to Colonel Shaw and his black troops, "For the Union Dead." Plus, there are works by Herman Melville, Elizabeth Bishop, Langston Hughes and many more. Illustrated with more than 50 Civil War photographs and drawings, this is an especially handsome volume.

THE NEW GOTHIC: A COLLECTION OF CONTEMPORARY GOTHIC FICTION
Edited by Bradford Morrow and Patrick McGrath
(Random House, 1991, paperback)

Gothic fiction has a noble pedigree: it gave us Emily Brontë's *Wuthering Heights* and the stories of Edgar Allen Poe. This collection assembles 21 modern-day practitioners of the art. Kathy Acker brings a touch of necrophilia to "J." Sinister monks inhabit

John Hawkes' "Regulus and Maximus." And in "For Dear Life," Ruth Rendell recounts a hellish train ride for a well-born woman who has never taken the subway before. Keep this collection away from your bedside—you don't want to scare yourself before you go to sleep!

THE GOLDEN TREASURY
Edited by Francis Turner Palgrave, with new poems chosen by John Press (Penguin Classics, 1992, paperback)

The first edition of The Golden Treasury, a gold mine of British lyric poetry, was published in 1860. This new edition—the sixth—includes all the poets you would expect: Shakespeare and Thomas Wyatt, George Herbert and Robert Burns, Byron, Keats, Shelley, Wordsworth and Christina Rossetti. Now John Press, himself a poet, adds modern British and Irish poets including Philip Larkin, Seamus Heaney, Fleur Adcock and Derek Mahon. A magnificent, full-blooded anthology of verse, the one that sets the standards for all others.

THE PORTABLE DOROTHY PARKER
with a new introduction by Brendan Gill (Penguin, 1991, paperback)

A laugh-out-loud collection of Parker poems, short stories and hilarious zingers.

THE AMERICAN SHORT STORY
Edited by Thomas K. Parkes (Galahad Books, 1994, hardcover)

What an anthology. More than 1000 pages of America's best and most memorable short stories. Poe's "The Fall of the House of Usher." Melville's "Benito Cereno." Sarah Orne Jewett's "A White Heron." Willa Cather's "Paul's Case." Isaac Bashevis Singer's "Gimpel the Fool." Oates' "Where Are You Going, Where Have You Been?" Plus works by Hawthorne, Twain, Benét, Welty, Faulkner, O'Connor and Capote. A classic collection that belongs in every library.

WITNESSING AMERICA:
THE LIBRARY OF CONGRESS BOOK OF
FIRSTHAND ACCOUNTS OF LIFE IN AMERICA
1600-1900
Compiled and Edited by Noel Rae (Penguin, 1996, paperback)

Governor William Bradford's account of the Mayflower crossing the Atlantic. Benjamin Franklin on youthful passions. Louisa May Alcott's suggestions on how to make ends meet. The handsomely illustrated first person accounts of the very famous and the not-famous-at-all take readers to a Pueblo village, aboard a slave ship, inside a frontier trading post, even to a funeral in a California mining camp. *Witnessing America* is a big, lively, eclectic book that captures the diversity of the American experience.

FAILURE IS IMPOSSIBLE:
SUSAN B. ANTHONY IN HER OWN WORDS
Edited by Lynn Sherr (Times Books, 1996, paperback)

"Women," Anthony once said, "we might as well be great Newfoundland dogs out baying at the moon as to be petitioning for the passage of bills without the power to vote." Published to coincide with the 175th anniversary of Anthony's birth and the 75th anniversary of the passage of the 19th amendment, this wonderful anthology brings together selections from the great woman's speeches, letters, private papers and reminiscences and reveals Anthony's brilliance, her rapier wit and her tremendous courage in the face of the vicious attacks on her character which plagued her throughout her career as the chief advocate of women's suffrage. An excellent reference work and an inspiring resource.

LINCOLN:
SELECTED SPEECHES AND WRITINGS
with an introduction by Gore Vidal (Vintage/Library of America, 1992, paperback)

The best of Lincoln's writings are collected in this two-volume selection of his most significant and interesting work: the House Divided speech; the Lincoln-Douglas Debates; the First Inaugural Address which invoked "the better angels of our nature"; the Emancipation Proclamation; the Gettysburg Address; and the Second Inaugural Address which promised "malice towards none." In addition, there is an excellent selection of letters to Mary Todd Lincoln, McClellan, Grant and Sherman.

GUNFIGHT! THIRTEEN WESTERN STORIES
Edited with an introduction by James C. Work
(University of Nebraska Press, 1996, paperback)

Some of the best Western short stories written between 1904 and 1990 are assembled here. There's Dorothy Johnson's classic, "The Man Who Shot Liberty Valence." Luke Short's "Top Hand" features a young man with no experience as a gunslinger, but with guts and right on his side. And don't miss John M. Cunningham's hard-edged "The Tin Star"—the inspiration for the Gary Cooper-Grace Kelly movie, High Noon (by the way, the short story is significantly different from the Hollywood version).

BLOOD SISTERS: THE FRENCH
REVOLUTION IN WOMEN'S MEMORY
by Marilyn Yalom (Basic Books, 1993, hardcover)

What an incredible anthology. Here are first-hand accounts of women who were participants in one of the most dangerous eras in French history. Included are the reminiscences of peasant women who fought as soldiers; an eyewitness account of Marie

Antoinette's final days, told by the woman who served her in prison; the poignant memories of Madame Royale, the only surviving child of Louis XVI and Marie Antoinette; and the vivid recollections of Charlotte Robespierre, sister of the man who presided over the Reign of Terror. Worth searching for.

AMERICAN INDIAN STORIES
by Zitkala-sa [Gertrude Simmons Bonnin]
(1921; University of Nebraska Press, 1979, paperback)

The year Zitkala-sa was born was the high-water mark for the Lakota: in 1876, they overwhelmed General Custer and his men at the Little Bighorn. After the battle, catastrophe followed upon catastrophe for the Lakota and Zitkala-sa witnessed it all. Nonetheless, she carved out a place for herself that straddled the worlds of her own Yankton Lakota people and that of the whites. She edited the American Indian Magazine and she founded the National Council of American Indians. This anthology of Zitkala-sa's stories, essays and autobiographical sketches chronicles the dilemma of Native Americans who felt relentless pressure to abandon the traditions they loved.

THE BEST HISTORY

UNDAUNTED COURAGE:
MERIWETHER LEWIS, THOMAS JEFFERSON AND THE OPENING OF THE AMERICAN WEST
by Stephen E. Ambrose (Touchstone Books, 1997)

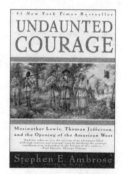

Stephen Ambrose describes this book as "a labor of love." It's also a splendid work of history that reveals once again Ambrose's extraordinary command of the facts and remarkable gifts as a storyteller. Drawing upon a lifetime of research, he explores the close friendship that existed between Jefferson and Lewis and takes his readers along on Lewis and Clark's two-year journey to the Pacific and back again. The book concludes sadly with Lewis' violent death and Thomas Jefferson's final appraisal of his young friend as a man of "courage undaunted." Buy this book. It is destined to be a classic of American history.

THE DAY LINCOLN WAS SHOT
by Jim Bishop (Scholastic, 1998, paperback)

An hour-by-hour account of Abraham Lincoln's last day of life, from 7 a.m., April 14, when he wished a White House guard good morning, until 7:22 a.m., April 15, when he died. Bishop's imaginative re-creation of the day includes the routine of the President and Mrs. Lincoln and the final maneuverings of John Wilkes Booth and his fellow conspirators.

THE SABRES OF PARADISE
by Lesley Blanch (Carroll & Graf, 1984, paperback)

In the 1950s, when this book first appeared, Blanch's history of a 19th-century war in the Caucasus must have seemed terribly obscure. But with the recent war between Russia and Chechnya The Sabres of Paradise has gotten a second life. Here is the story of Shamyl, a heroic Muslim guerrilla fighter, who led a 25-year-long resistance to Tsar Nicholas I's efforts to absorb the Caucasus region into the Russian empire. A thrilling work of history that makes contemporary events understandable.

BURY MY HEART AT WOUNDED KNEE
by Dee Brown (Owl, 1991, paperback)

In this meticulously documented account of the American West—from the natives' point of view—historian Dee Brown chronicles the savage and systematic annihilation of the American Indian in the latter half of the 19th century. Using the words of the warriors themselves, Brown describes in vivid detail the battles, betrayals and broken treaties that shaped this heartbreaking chapter of history. First published in 1970, this powerful book played a large part in bringing Native American issues into the mainstream.

A STILLNESS AT APPOMATTOX
by Bruce Catton (Peter Smith, 1992, hardcover)

A brilliant storyteller, a gifted stylist, Bruce Catton wrote the best narrative histories of the Civil War. Here he focuses on the year 1864. The Army of the Potomac has jettisoned its vision of a glorious victory and transformed itself into a ruthless war machine. The Army of Northern Virginia still dares to hope for a miracle, the men confiding all their trust in the godlike Robert E. Lee. Catton immerses his readers in the terrible details of The

Wilderness, the Bloody Angle, Cold Harbor, the Crater, sweeping you along through the last cruel months of the Civil War.

THE EASTER REBELLION: Dublin 1916
by Max Caulfield (1963; Roberts Rinehart, 1995, hardcover)

Written more than 30 years after the fact, this book has been the best and liveliest account of the fateful week that led to the birth of an independent Ireland. Max Caulfield interviewed more than 100 survivors and eyewitnesses, filling his pages with memorable anecdotes: the 57 rebels who, loaded down with all their equipment, took the streetcar to the revolution; the 25-man garrison which held Dublin Castle that day (all the other troops had gone to the races); poor Joseph Mary Plunkett, dying of tuberculosis, dragged from his sickbed to serve as an officer; and the zealous Countess Markievitz leading a platoon of women and Boy Scouts into battle. This is an outstanding story, filled with human interest.

THE SECULARIZATION OF THE EUROPEAN MIND IN THE NINETEENTH CENTURY
by Owen Chadwick (Cambridge University Press, 1990, paperback)

After 1900 years, the influence of Christianity on European society began to slip. The distinguished British historian Owen Chadwick explores the social and intellectual trends that led to this major shift in how men and women viewed their world. From the rise of technology to the expansion of the cities, from the theories of Darwin to the political philosophy of Marx, Chadwick tells a compelling story of the forces that chipped away at tradition. A classic study, from Cambridge University Press' distinguished Canto series.

A WAY THROUGH THE WILDERNESS:
THE NATCHEZ TRACE AND THE CIVILIZATION OF THE SOUTHERN FRONTIER
by William C. Davis
(1996 Louisiana State University Press, 1996, paperback)

Not long after the Revolution, settlers around Nashville began to move South, lured by stories of "land begging for occupancy." Davis offers a lively portrait of the men and women who moved into the new land—pioneers who made friends with their Choctaw neighbors, entrepreneurs who founded Southern dynasties, law-and-order types who labored to establish solid communities and scallawags who set up the ever-popular saloons, bordellos and gambling houses. A colorful page from the history of the settlement of America.

THE UNREDEEMED CAPTIVE:
A FAMILY STORY FROM EARLY AMERICA
by John Demos (Random House, 1995, paperback)

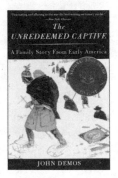

Hours before dawn, on February 29, 1704, a war party of French and Indians attacked the lightly guarded village of Deerfield in western Massachusetts, carrying off more than 100 captives. Among them were the Reverend John Williams and his five children. Two and a half years later, all the Williamses were ransomed, except the youngest daughter, Eunice. She remained in Canada, converted to Catholicism, married a Mohawk warrior and started a family. For more than 70 years, the Williams clan tried to "redeem" Eunice, but she would not come home. With the narrative power of a great novelist, John Demos tells how a single tragic incident changed an American family forever.

BOUND UPON A WHEEL OF FIRE:
WHY SO MANY GERMANY JEWS MADE THE TRAGIC DECISION TO REMAIN IN NAZI GERMANY
by John V.H. Dippel (Basic Books, 1996, hardcover)

Leo Baeck, chief rabbi of Berlin. Richard Willstätter, Nobel laureate in chemistry. Bella Fromm, society columnist. Max Warburg, banker and philanthropist. Why did prominent Jews like these stay in Nazi Germany until the last possible moment? In this compelling and heart-breaking book, John Dippel explores the reasons why so many Jews missed their opportunity to flee from Nazi Germany and he answers the implication that by failing to leave, German Jewry participated in its own destruction. *Bound Upon A Wheel of Fire* adds an important new dimension to Holocaust studies.

TERRIBLE HONESTY:
MONGREL MANHATTAN IN THE 1920s
by Ann Douglas (Farrar, Straus & Giroux, 1996, paperback)

New York City in the 1920s was witty and wicked, frivolous and flamboyant. Ann Douglas captures the glamour of the city and the people who made it the cultural capital of America: Duke Ellington, Al Jolson, Fanny Brice and George Gershwin; F. Scott Fitzgerald, Countee Cullen and Marianne Moore. And she writes brilliantly about innovations that changed the way Americans thought about themselves—including the new advertising, skyscrapers and Freud.

A STRUGGLE FOR POWER:
THE AMERICAN REVOLUTION
by Theodore Draper (Times Books, 1996, paperback)

Distinguished historian Theodore Draper has found that most American colonists were perfectly happy to be part of Great Britain's empire. But, in 1764-65, Parliament enacted a series of unpopular taxes and trade restrictions, attempted to break the power of colonial assemblies and generally did everything imaginable to infuriate the colonists and drive more and more Americans into the separatist camp. Drawing on a host of original documents, Draper conveys the discontent and mob violence in the streets and the genius of Patrick Henry, John Hancock, Thomas Jefferson and John Adams—men who put an Enlightenment spin on the revolution by appealing to the spirit of liberty, social contracts and inalienable rights.

MILLENNIUM: A HISTORY OF THE LAST THOUSAND YEARS
by Felipe Fernández-Armesto (Doubleday, 1996, paperback)

Part of the mission of this book," Fernández-Armesto says, "is to rehabilitate the overlooked... places often ignored as peripheral, peoples marginalized as inferior and individuals relegated to bit-parts." He accomplishes his goal beautifully, spinning wonderful stories: the Byzantine princess who was both repulsed and smitten by a hunky Norman Crusader; why the African kingdom of Dahomey's prosperity was so closely linked to the slave trade; and how "The Night Soil Collectors are Coming Down the Mountain" became a Top 40 hit during China's Cultural Revolution. A shamelessly entertaining and idiosyncratic history of the last thousand years.

PAUL REVERE'S RIDE AND THE BATTLE OF LEXINGTON AND CONCORD
by David Hackett Fischer
(Oxford University Press, 1995, paperback)

If you remember your Longfellow, you know that on April 18, 1775, Paul Revere made a midnight ride to spread the alarm that the British were coming. Or was it William Dawes? Finally, an eminent American historian reveals what led up to this near-mythic event, illuminates the complex character of Revere himself and tells us what really happened on that fateful night-and what followed the next morning at Lexington and Concord.

....

FAITH AND TREASON:
THE STORY OF THE GUNPOWDER PLOT
by Antonia Fraser (Doubleday, 1997, paperback)

On November 5, 1605, Guy Fawkes expected to see King James I and both houses of Parliament blown to kingdom come. Instead, he was arrested and hustled off to the Tower of London. Antonia Fraser sifts facile popular legends about the notorious Gunpowder Plot from the much more fascinating historical facts. She studies the motivations of chief conspirator Robert Catesby, "the prince of darkness at the center of the Gunpowder Plot." She reveals that the plot was just one of a host of intrigues in Jacobean England. And she explores the role of English Catholics in these conspiracies, a persecuted minority driven to the point of desperation. Fraser is one England's finest historians; and *Faith and Treason* may be her most compelling book to date.

....

ASHES OF GLORY: RICHMOND AT WAR
by Ernest B. Furgurson (Random House, 1997, paperback)

Richmond was not prepared to be the capital of the Confederacy. Politicians, lobbyists and journalists doubled the city's population overnight. It doubled again as refugees fleeing the Yankee armies poured into town. Add to this the tens of thousands of Union troops held in the city's prisons and you can understand why there were food shortages, an ever-rising crime rate and a host of other urban evils. Furgurson details it all and brings forward the stories of individual Richmond citizens like Elizabeth Van Lew, daughter of a wealthy old Virginia family who acted as a Union spy throughout the war. *Ashes of Glory* is certain to be the definitive account of Richmond's trials.

....

NO ORDINARY TIME-FRANKLIN AND ELEANOR ROOSEVELT:
THE HOMEFRONT IN WORLD WAR II
by Doris Kearns Goodwin (Simon & Schuster, 1995, paperback)

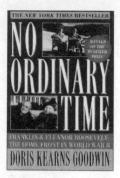

They were miserably mismatched as husband and wife, but as a political team you couldn't beat Franklin and Eleanor Roosevelt. When Hitler invaded Poland, the Roosevelts joined forces to convince America that it must enter the war. How Franklin and Eleanor wheedled, cajoled, sometimes even bludgeoned the public and Congress to prepare for war—and then to expend any effort and make any sacrifice to win it—is one of the great stories of American history. Doris Kearns Goodwin tells it with vigor, revealing fresh insights about one of history's most effective political partnerships.

THE PRIVATE LIVES OF THE ROOSEVELTS: ELEANOR AND FRANKLIN
by Joseph Lash (NAL-Dutton, 1973, paperback).

Intimate portraits of the painfully shy and emotionally starved Eleanor, the spoiled, self-satisfied mama's boy Franklin and the life they tried to build together.

THE JEWS OF SPAIN:
A HISTORY OF THE SEPHARDIC EXPERIENCE
by Jane S. Gerber (Free Press, 1994, paperback)

Under the Visigoths and the Moors, the Sephardic Jews of Spain became an intellectual, cultural and economic powerhouse. In the Christian courts of Spain they were physicians, poets, financiers, counsellors. All that ended in 1492 when Ferdinand and Isabella expelled the entire Jewish community from Spain. In this scholarly yet accessible history, Gerber describes the glories of Sephardic civilization in Spain, the tragic events of the

Expulsion, the Sephardic diaspora throughout the Old and the New World and the return of the Sephardic Jews to Spain after World War II.

. . . .

A HISTORY OF THE ARAB PEOPLE
by *Albert Hourani* (M.J.F. Books, 1997, paperback)

The West has waited a long time for this landmark history; Hourani's goal is to explain to Western readers the history and culture of the Arab world. He traces the birth of Islam and the emergence of rival and often hostile Muslim sects and offers welcome insights into such troubling issues as the rise of Islamic fundamentalism and the plight of the Palestinians. This book is essential reading for anyone who cares about what is happening in the world.

. . . .

THE FATAL SHORE:
THE EPIC OF AUSTRALIA'S FOUNDING
by *Robert Hughes* (Vintage, 1988, paperback)

In 1788, England's first fleet of transported convicts —"a Noah's Ark of small-time criminality"—landed at Botany Bay and began the European settlement of Australia. Hughes draws upon all of his genius as a narrative historian to spin a grand epic of the penal colony that evolved into a robust nation.

. . . .

MUTINY ON THE AMISTAD:
THE SAGA OF A SLAVE REVOLT AND ITS
IMPACT ON AMERICAN ABOLITION,
LAW AND DIPLOMACY
by *Howard Jones* (Oxford University Press, 1988, paperback)

In 1839, Africans aboard the Spanish ship Amistad seized control of the vessel that was carrying them into slavery and forced its captain to take them to Africa. The American Navy stopped the Amistad off Long Island and imprisoned the Africans in Connecticut. The Amistad incident became an international controversy and cause célèbre among abolitionists. The case was heard by the US Supreme Court who set the Africans free. It was the only instance in American history when Africans bound for slavery won their right to return home through due process of law.

EMPIRE'S END:
A HISTORY OF THE FAR EAST FROM HIGH COLONIALISM TO HONG KONG
by John Keay (Scribner's, 1997, hardcover)

The return of Hong Kong to Chinese rule marked the end of Britain's eastern empire and the conclusion of 500 years of European colonialism in the Far East. Yet as recently as 1930, nearly half the world's people were part of the British, Dutch, French, or American empires. How did it happen and what is the legacy of colonialism in Asia? John Keay sifts the answers from an enormous amount of material (empire builders are awfully good record keepers). Illustrated with vintage photographs and telling anecdotes. *Empire's End* is absorbing history.

DECISIVE DAY:
THE BATTLE OF BUNKER HILL
by Richard M. Ketchum

Today the Battle of Bunker Hill is a source of nationalist pride, but in 1775 Americans saw it as a humiliating defeat. For once, however, the revisionist historians are right on the money. More British officers fell in the assault on the hill than at any other battle in living memory and before they finally captured the American position at the summit, the Redcoats had lost half their forces. In time, both sides learned the lesson of Bunker Hill— that American rebels could successfully challenge the might of the British army. Worth searching for.

AMERICAN SLAVERY, 1619-1877
by Peter Kolchin (Hill & Wang, 1994, paperback)

Kolchin's concise history of the slave trade in America is full of surprises. For instance, in the 17th century, Africans were brought to America as indentured servants and were released after their period of servitude was completed. The idea of slavery as a permanent condition arose later. If you want to understand slaves, masters and the system that bound them together, read this book.

PATRIOTS: THE MEN WHO STARTED THE AMERICAN REVOLUTION
by A.J. Langguth (Touchstone Books, 1989, paperback)

Washington was a man of honor; his soldiers loved him—even if his military strategies were a bit shaky. Thomas Jefferson was a popular man in Congress; but no one liked his continual leaves of absence to visit his wife. Benedict Arnold cut a dashing figure with the ladies; but when a suitor came around to court his pretty sister, Arnold reached for his pistols. All the familiar men and women and all the legendary scenes from the Revolution come to life in this unforgettable history.

THE PROMISED LAND: THE GREAT BLACK MIGRATION AND HOW IT CHANGED AMERICA
by Nicholas Lemann (David McKay Company, 1992, paperback)

There aren't enough superlatives for this excellent history of the mass migration of blacks from the rural South to the cities of the North. Lemann explores every dimension of a dramatic moment in U.S. history and chronicles the heartbreak of black people who fled poverty and segregation in the South only to find new hardships and racism in the North.

THE SCOTCH-IRISH: A SOCIAL HISTORY
by James G. Leyburn
(University of North Carolina Press, 1989, hardcover)

The Scottish Presbyterians who settled in Northern Ireland in the 17th century prospered. But their success was minimal compared to ones who continued on to America. Their courage prompted them to be among the very first pioneers. Their independent spirit and animosity toward the English made them heroes of the American Revolution. And their belief that hard work and thrift would be rewarded became the cornerstone of the American dream. James Leyburn's book is a landmark study of a very influential group of immigrants, the people Teddy Roosevelt said were "fitted to be Americans from the very start."

THE DEATH OF A PRESIDENT: NOVEMBER 1963
by William Manchester
(Perennial Library/Harper & Row, 1988, paperback)

On February 5, 1964, Jacqueline Kennedy invited William Manchester to write an account of the assassination and funeral of her husband, President John F. Kennedy. Manchester was granted unprecedented access to the Kennedy family and to many of the President's friends and colleagues. He retraced, physically, every move the Kennedy entourage, Lee Harvey Oswald and Jack Ruby made on those fateful days. In the end, Jackie Kennedy thought Manchester had revealed too many personal details—an understandable complaint from a grieving widow. But the late author Jerzy Kosinski described the book best when he said, "It tells you what happened and it tells you how it felt while it was happening."

THE GREAT BRIDGE: THE EPIC STORY OF THE BUILDING OF THE BROOKLYN BRIDGE
by David McCullough (Simon & Schuster, 1983, paperback)

When it was completed in 1882, the Brooklyn Bridge was the tallest building in New York, the longest suspension bridge in the world and one of the top tourist attractions in the country. Honeymooners took moonlit strolls on the promenade. Tourists snapped photos of it with their newly invented Kodak cameras. And P.T. Barnum helped demonstrate its stability by parading a herd of 21 elephants across the bridge. David McCullough, one 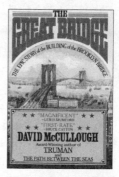 America's finest narrative historians, tells the story of the bridge, the age that produced it, the Roebling family who designed it and the impact it had on the lives and imagination of ordinary people.

. . . .

THE JOHNSTOWN FLOOD
by *David McCullough* (Touchstone Books, 1968, paperback)

On May 31, 1889, an earthen dam gave way and a mountain of water 70 feet high smashed into Johnstown, Pennsylvania. McCullough follows the chain of events that led to the terrible moment, including the criminal carelessness of Pittsburgh's wealthiest families who vacationed at the man-made lake above the town, but neglected the upkeep of the lake's dam.

. . . .

THE PATH BETWEEN THE SEAS
by *David McCullough* (Touchstone Books, 1978, paperback)

With fanfare and panache and arrogance, Ferdinand Lesseps, the Frenchman who had commandeered the digging of the Suez Canal, began to dig a canal in Panama. Soon the jungle, yellow fever and the engineering problems Lesseps had always dismissed as trivial defeated him. Then, just as the jungle began to reclaim the big trench, Teddy Roosevelt became interested in the project. A great story of how heroic determination is meaningless without a good understanding of the terrain.

ONE MORE RIVER TO CROSS:
AN AFRICAN AMERICAN PHOTOGRAPH ALBUM
by Walter Dean Myers (Harcourt Brace, 1995, hardcover)

More than 150 photographs record the black experience in America in this intriguing collection. The earliest photo is the most chilling—a building in a small town which bears a sign reading "Auction & Negro Sales." Nonetheless, this a positive, upbeat collection that tries to take in the entire spectrum of life in rural and urban communities. The running quotes are powerful: "We were set back, run out, pushed down and beat down, but we had been through too much, had seen too much, to stay down. You hear?"

A HISTORY OF VENICE
by John Julius Norwich (Vintage, 1989, paperback)

History is never dreary in Venice. It's a pageant, a spectacle, sometimes even a fireworks display. Norwich reveals it all, from the Venetian merchants who "liberated" St. Mark's body from its tomb in Egypt, to the blind Venetian Doge who personally led the attack on Constantinople, to the well-born ladies of 18th-century Venice who made Casanova feel so welcome.

BYZANTIUM: THE DECLINE AND FALL
by John Julius Norwich (Knopf, 1995, hardcover)

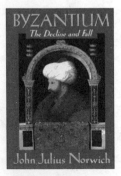

Most Westerners have only a dim idea of what was going on in Byzantium during its 1100-year-long history. John Julius Norwich has drawn the Eastern Empire out of the shadows and shown Western readers what we've been missing. *Byzantium: The Decline and Fall*, the third and final volume of his series, is an especially rich read that details the sacking of Constantinople by the Crusaders in 1204, the emperor's desperate efforts to save his empire by reuniting the Greek Orthodox Church with Rome in the 15th century and the final, heartbreaking fall of Constantinople to the Turks in 1453.

Norwich's Prequels:

BYZANTIUM: THE EARLY CENTURIES AND BYZANTIUM: THE APOGEE
(Knopf, 1989/1992, hardcover).

From riots in the Hippodrome, to depravity in the imperial palace, to iconoclasts in the churches, Norwich tells a breathtaking story of gore, glory and intrigue.

THE PRESIDENCY OF ABRAHAM LINCOLN
by Phillip Shaw Paludan
(University Press of Kansas, 1994, paperback)

Abraham Lincoln led America through the four most crucial years of its history. Here is the first book to study the Lincoln presidency, day by day. Paludan offers us a very human Lincoln, pragmatic and clever at outmaneuvering his political rivals. He demonstrates how Lincoln's great speeches were carefully timed to shape public opinion and he argues that despite what most historians say, Lincoln believed "freeing the slaves and saving the Union were linked as one goal, not two optional goals."

FRANCE AND ENGLAND IN NORTH AMERICA
by Francis Parkman (Library of America, 1983, paperback)

Parkman, a 19th-century Boston Brahmin, is still the undisputed master of American narrative history. There are no dry dates or dull factoids in this history: Parkman is telling the story of two empires struggling for control of a continent. On every page you meet men and women of remarkable heroism and incredible villainy. And no one recounts stories of fearful captures, desperate escapes and ferocious battles like Parkman.

RUSSIA UNDER THE BOLSHEVIK REGIME
by Richard Pipes (Vintage, 1995, paperback)

Unlike almost every other historian of the Russian Revolution, Pipes does not believe that Lenin, Trotsky and their comrades were disappointed utopians. Pipes says they were extremists whose desire for absolute power set the stage for Stalin's purges.

A NEW WORLD: AN EPIC OF COLONIAL AMERICA FROM THE FOUNDING OF JAMESTOWN TO THE FALL OF QUEBEC
by Arthur Quinn (Berkley, 1995, paperback)

Open this book to any page, begin at any paragraph and immediately you are carried along by the energy of Quinn's prose.

On John Smith: "a perfect specimen of lusty Elizabethan exuberance."

On the landing of the Pilgrims: "in their crowded ships [was] the first consignment of the New England conscience."

On brotherly love in Pennsylvania: "One can imagine the New Yorkers listening attentively, trying to figure out the catch."

Quinn has got a good ear for language and a great gift for storytelling. This is the history of colonial America you've been waiting for.

CITIZENS: A CHRONICLE OF THE FRENCH REVOLUTION
by Simon Schama (Knopf, 1991, hardcover)

The French Revolution started, Schama says, with an innocent desire to be a modern nation. No more feudal kings or old-fashioned religions, but a country of enlightened citizens. And if a little blood had to be spilt, well, the leaders of the Revolution could keep that under control. But as the violence spun out of control, the revolutionaries themselves found that they were turning to forms of repression that France had not seen since the Middle Ages.

THE EMBARRASSMENT OF RICHES: AN INTERPRETATION OF DUTCH CULTURE IN THE GOLDEN AGE
by Simon Schama (Random House, 1997, paperback)

With this book, Schama achieved an international reputation as a genius of narrative history. In the 17th century, the Netherlands—a flat, watery country of small farms and fishing villages—became one of the wealthiest nations in Europe. Like an enormous Rembrandt canvas, Schama's story is filled with memorable characters—shipwrecked sailors, tulip speculators, stranded whales, even professional wrestlers.

HE HAD A DREAM: MARTIN LUTHER KING, JR. AND THE CIVIL RIGHTS MOVEMENT
by Flip Schulke (Norton, 1995, paperback)

Schulke was a photojournalist during the Civil Rights movement of the 1960s. His collection of photos includes Medgar Evers' funeral in 1963 ("the first murder of a black civil rights leader the media had paid any attention to"), plus shots of beefy cops with nightsticks, mobs of wild-eyed segregationists and crowds of civil rights demonstrators, black and white, often looking frightened but determined. A tremendous visual record of what Dr. King taught America to overcome.

CHANCELLORSVILLE
by Stephen Sears (Houghton Mifflin, 1996, paperback)

Outnumbered two to one by a giant Yankee army under the command of Joseph Hooker, Robert E. Lee did the unthinkable. He split his army in two and sent Stonewall Jackson on the boldest flanking maneuver in American history. Attacked on two fronts, the Union men fled in panic. But in this triumphal

moment, Jackson was mortally wounded- accidentally, by his own men. There have been other histories of Chancellorsville, but none come close to this new account by Stephen Sears. He makes military tactics instantly understandable and he has a gift for conveying the human drama of the battle in all its power.

LANDSCAPE TURNED RED: THE BATTLE OF ANTIETAM
by Stephen Sears (Houghton Mifflin, 1983, paperback)

Stephen Sears became a household name among readers of Civil War history thanks to this first-rate account of the bloodiest day of the Civil War, when 23,000 Americans fell in the cornfields and country roads of Maryland.

THE BLACK DIASPORA
by Ronald Segal (Ginn Press, 1995, hardcover)

Beginning in the 16th century, more than 10 million Africans were carried into slavery in the western hemisphere. Today, their descendants number 100 million and are found throughout the Americas. In this ambitious book, Segal—who was born in Africa—surveys the trials and accomplishments of Africans in the New World over a period of 500 years. Especially interesting are the sections on American nations with large black populations, such as Brazil, the home to 75 million people of African descent. This is epic history, told with passion and verve.

THE RISE AND FALL OF THE THIRD REICH
by William L. Shirer (Fawcett, 1991, paperback)

Shirer's history of Nazi Germany is an absolute masterpiece of history that has been an international bestseller for over

35 years. Beginning in 1925, Shirer, a journalist, watched and reported on the Nazi movement. After the war, he spent years immersed in the documents the Allies had captured in Germany. Everything is here: inside stories about Hitler, his generals, his toadies and the horror they unleashed upon the world.

....

LONGITUDE: THE TRUE STORY OF A LONE GENIUS WHO SOLVED THE GREATEST SCIENTIFIC PROBLEM OF HIS TIME
by Dava Sobel (Penguin, 1996, paperback)

Longitude was once a theoretical problem with lots of real-world ramifications. Without longitude, sailors could not measure distance and could only guess where they were at sea. Galileo and Isaac Newton tried to find a solution to the problem, but without success. It was finally solved in 1733 by an English mechanical genius named John Harrison. He constructed a virtually friction-free clock which enabled sailors to calculate how far they had sailed by comparing what time it was at home with what time is was in their current time zone. It was a near-miraculous discovery and Sobel brings it all to life—the naval disasters before the invention, the thrill of scientific discovery and the jealousy of Harrison's university rivals.

....

THE WAR OF THE ROSES
by Desmond Stewart (Viking, 1995, hardcover)

The Losers: Jane Shore, Edward IV's mistress, forced to do penance as a harlot; she died a beggar in London. William Hastings, whose efforts to save the 12-year-old Edward V from his uncle, the future Richard III, cost him his head. The Winners: Lady Margaret Beaufort, who married Henry VII and united the houses of York and Lancaster. John Morton, Bishop of Ely, switched sides during the War and lived to be Archbishop of Canterbury.

By focusing on the pivotal players, Steward makes England's messy dynastic war comprehensible. A model of clarity and beautifully illustrated. Worth searching for.

VOICES OF TRIUMPH: PERSEVERANCE, LEADERSHIP, CREATIVE FIRE
by the Editors of Time-Life Books (Time-Life Books, 1994, hardcover)

There would be no nation known as America had no Blacks been forcibly imported to these shores," writes Henry Louis Gates, Jr., in this three-volume landmark series of African-American history and culture. You'll meet Nat Turner, Thurgood Marshall, Ella Fitzgerald and lesser-known figures such as Jean Du Sable of Haiti who founded Chicago. Meticulously researched and richly illustrated, these books trace a people's long struggle for freedom, dignity and civil rights.

A LIFE WILD AND PERILOUS: MOUNTAIN MEN AND THE PATHS TO THE PACIFIC
by Robert M. Utley (Holt, 1997, hardcover)

Mountain man Jed Smith had traveled so extensively in the American West that he had in his head a "master map" of the whole region. He was about to set it down on paper when he was killed, at age 32, by Comanches. In *A Life Wild and Perilous*, Robert Utley paints a portrait of mountain men as freedom-loving, anti-social adventurers who nonetheless charted the American wilderness and blazed the trials to Santa Fe, to Oregon and through the Rockies to California. Accompanying the exciting stories of Kit Carson and Jim Bridger are excellent maps of the West when it was still a wild, dramatic, violent place.

LINCOLN AT GETTYSBURG:
THE WORDS THAT RE-MADE AMERICA
by Garry Wills (Touchstone/Simon & Schuster, 1992, paperback)

In three minutes and 272 words, Lincoln convinced Americans that Thomas Jefferson's phrase, "all men are created equal," is the cornerstone of our society. A truly remarkable work of historical analysis.

AN EASY BURDEN:
THE CIVIL RIGHTS MOVEMENT AND THE
TRANSFORMATION OF AMERICA
by Andrew Young (HarperCollins, 1998, paperback)

To tell the story of how the civil rights movement transformed American life andrew Young begins with his own childhood in a middle class black neighborhood of New Orleans during the 1940s and 1950s. In describing his work with Martin Luther King, Jr., Ralph Abernathy and other heroes of the civil rights movement, he admits the Baptist ministers' authoritarian style made him chafe. But most surprising is Youngs' forgiving account of the whites who hated him and everything he worked for.

BIG (AND SMALL) BUSINESS

ADAMS' STREETWISE SMALL BUSINESS START-UP: YOUR COMPREHENSIVE GUIDE TO STARTING AND MANAGING A BUSINESS
by Bob Adams (Adams Media Corporation, 1996, paperback)

Bob Adams started his publishing company with $2000 while he was still a student at Harvard Business School. Today, his firm has $10 million in annual sales. In this chatty, easy-to-use handbook, Adams explains everything every entrepreneur should know, from the best sources to finance your start-up company, to the 10 most common mistakes of small business beginners (you'll want to avoid these), to how to compete with the big boys and win. Plus, you'll learn how to do the paperwork, the most important questions to ask prospective employees and much, much more. This book is like having a mentor at your side through every step of your new venture.

AGAINST THE GODS: THE REMARKABLE STORIES OF RISK
by Peter L. Bernstein
(John Wiley & Sons, 1996, hardcover)

A little biography, a little history, a little science. Bernstein brings these disciplines together to help him tell the story of scientists and philosophers who discovered the notion of risk—of methodically studying the past to predict outcomes in the future. Then, in a narrative that reads like a novel, Bernstein demonstrates the role played by risk management in every type of grand endeavor: bridges thrown across the widest rivers, lives saved by coronary bypass surgery, even the enterprise of space travel itself. Against the Gods uncovers the vital distinction between chance and skill.

THE HOUSE OF MORGAN:
AN AMERICAN BANKING DYNASTY AND THE RISE OF MODERN FINANCE
by Ron Chernow (Touchstone Books, 1991, paperback)

Depending upon your point of view, the Morgans were either old-fashioned bankers who sealed their deals with a handshake, or manipulative devils who bullied American corporations and coaxed America into war to turn a profit. "Nobody," says Chernow, "was ever neutral about the Morgans." Here is a big, full-scale saga about the swashbuckling days of American finance.

THE EXECUTIVE IN ACTION:
MANAGING FOR RESULTS
• INNOVATION AND ENTREPRENEURSHIP • THE EFFECTIVE EXECUTIVE
by Peter F. Drucker (HarperBusiness, 1996, paperback)

The Harvard Business Review once said that Peter F. Drucker's "writings are landmarks of the managerial profession." Now for the first time, three of Drucker's pathfinding classics are available in a single volume. Managing for Results teaches you what to do to make your business succeed. Innovation and Entrepreneurship teaches you how to bring originality to the work place. And The Effective Executive shows you how to be the kind of manager who gets the right things done. This omnibus edition gives you everything you need to know to be an effective manager.

More Management Advice from Peter Drucker:

MANAGING IN A TIME OF GREAT CHANGE
(Dutton, 1995, paperback).

From how to keep your family business prospering to how to tap into the markets of Japan and China, Drucker offers solid advice for thriving in a volatile business climate.

MAKING MONEY WITH YOUR COMPUTER AT HOME:
EXPANDED SECOND EDITION
by Paul and Sarah Edwards (Putnam, 1997, paperback)

Paul and Sarah Edwards are the gurus of self-employment. Now they've completely updated and expanded one of their most popular titles—*Making Money with Your Computer*. You'll discover 100 computer-based businesses that can earn income for you now; get answers to common questions about setting up and running your business; and learn dozens of ways to market your business and find clients. Whether you have a full-time or part-time business in mind, the Edwardses give you tips on how to generate income fast, how to discipline yourself so you can be your own boss, how to grow your business and much more.

FOUNDER: A PORTRAIT OF THE FIRST ROTHSCHILD AND HIS TIMES
by Amos Elon (Penguin, 1997, paperback)

When Mayer Amschel Rothschild was born in Frankfurt's cramped Judengasse ghetto in 1744, Jews were not even permitted to leave their homes after dark. Rothschild never moved out of his seedy old neighborhood, but before he died he established a banking empire and set up his five sons as financiers in the great capitals of Europe. Amos Elon, an Israeli journalist, has collected what survives of original Rothschild documents (much was destroyed during World War II—the Nazis even tried to obliterate Mayer's tombstone) to tell the life and times of one of the most successful businessmen history has ever known.

THE GREAT WAVE: PRICE REVOLUTIONS AND THE RHYTHMS OF CHANGE THROUGH HISTORY
by David Hackett Fischer
(Oxford University Press, 1996, hardcover)

How high were rents in Ming China? What did cattle cost in 10th-century Portugal? Historian David Hackett Fischer studies price changes around the globe, from the Middle Ages to the present and finds an interesting pattern. With the great waves of inflation come price collapse and times of political and social unrest, followed by periods of economic stability and cultural and intellectual rebirth. Brimming with fascinating anecdotes (did you know feudal lords charged their tenants for firewood?) this is the book which makes economic theory spring to life.

SECURITY ANALYSIS: THE ORIGINAL 1934 EDITION
by Benjamin Graham and David Dodd
(McGraw-Hill, 1996, hardcover)

Any Wall Street professional will tell you Benjamin Graham was one of the greatest investment thinkers of all time. Yet, for many years his classic text was available only in "new" editions—all of which were bowdlerized, abridged and rewritten by later editors. You could get a copy of the original Security Analysis at a rare book store, if you were willing to pay $7500 or more. But now, at long last, you can own a copy of this landmark investment handbook without spending a fortune. Here is the book that made Graham famous (and helped make Warren Buffett a multimillionaire) in its original, undiluted form.

INSIDE INTEL: ANDREW GROVE AND THE RISE OF THE WORLD'S MOST POWERFUL CHIP COMPANY
by Tim Jackson (Dutton, 1997, hardcover)

Intel has a reputation for being one of the more secretive companies in the world of high tech. Nonetheless, through more than 100 interviews, careful research into court documents and unpublished records, *Financial Times* columnist Tim Jackson has pieced together a remarkably detailed history of Intel. He reveals the aggressive marketing and tough business practices Intel uses against its competitors, how its genius for technological innovation has enabled it to dominate the market and how Intel's product modifications compel their customers to keep coming back for upgrades. An excellent job of investigative reporting.

WORLDLY GOODS:
A NEW HISTORY OF THE RENAISSANCE
by Lisa Jardine (Doubleday, 1996, hardcover)

The way Lisa Jardine tells it, the Renaissance was as much a celebration of prosperity and material goods as it was a rediscovery of classical culture. To make her point, she has collected stories about sharp deals and smooth operators in Europe—from the Christian merchants of Genoa and Venice who were negotiating new trade agreements with the sultan within days of his conquest of Constantinople, to artists like Van Eyck and Carpaccio who helped their patrons show off their new acquisitions by featuring their treasures in paintings. Here at last is a fresh, entertaining and enlightening approach to the Renaissance.

BEN & JERRY'S: THE INSIDE SCOOP
by Fred "Chico" Lager (Dove Books, 1994, paperback)

Two 1960s relics turn an ice-cream parlor in a deserted gas station into a $200 million corporation. How did they do it? Volume. And integrity. And great ingredients. Plus, a progressive social outlook. Ben & Jerry's former CEO tells how an offbeat business became an unexpected American success story.

INSANELY GREAT:
THE LIFE AND TIMES OF MACINTOSH, THE
COMPUTER THAT CHANGED EVERYTHING
by Steven Levy (Penguin, 1995, paperback)

S teve Jobs had two requirements for the computer that would become Macintosh: it had to be beautiful to look at and it had to be fun to use. Well, actually three requirements, because it also had to be, as he put it, "insanely great." This is the story of the computer that through its friendly interface, quirky personality and elegant design changed the way we deal with information and won a near-fanatical following across the globe.

STEINWAY & SONS
by Richard K. Lieberman (Yale University Press, 1995, hardcover)

S ince 1835, the Steinway clan have been makers of superb pianos as well as shrewd marketers. Both sides of the Steinway character are given their due in this chronicle of the family and their product. He recounts how Steinway's business boomed in the 19th century (they sponsored concerts of superstar performers in return for endorsements), enabling them to build a rail link from their mansions in Queens to Manhattan, a company village for their workers, even an amusement park (on the site of LaGuardia Airport). Then, he explores the factors that brought about Steinway's decline—from the advent of record players to Yamaha's mass—produced pianos.

THE BANKERS: THE NEXT GENERATION
by Martin Mayer (Dutton, 1997, hardcover)

T wenty years ago, Martin Mayer's original The Bankers spent 17 weeks on *The New York Times* best-seller list. Since then, the new information age has altered banking in ways no one could have imagined. In *The Bankers: The Next Generation*, Mayer brings the story up to date-the megamergers, the rise of nationwide banks, the genesis of electronic money. Especially interesting are his accounts of the "near-death experiences" of Citicorp and Bank of America, the collapse of Barings and why Orange County, California, went into bankruptcy. Accessible and extremely interesting, *The Bankers* uncovers the ongoing revolution within a traditionally conservative profession.

....

I SING THE BODY ELECTRONIC:
A Year with Microsoft on the Multimedia
Frontier
by Fred Moody (Penguin, 1996, paperback)

A *Seattle Weekly* reporter chronicles a year in the life of a small team of Microsoft software designers. Their assignment: to create a multimedia encyclopedia for children called *Explorapedia*. Bill Gates urges his staff to be "businesspeople every day," the young men and women Moody hangs out with tend to think of themselves as creators of a new entertainment and education medium. Best character: a 25-year-old developer who is barely articulate in English but is Shakespeare when it comes to the language of programming. A first-rate behind-the-scenes story.

....

POUR YOUR HEART INTO IT:
How Starbucks Built a Company One
Cup at a Time
by Howard Schultz and Dori Jones Yang (Hyperion, 1997, hardcover)

When Howard Schultz took a job with Starbucks in 1982 it was a small Seattle retailer with five stores. Today, Schultz is CEO of Starbucks and the company has 1,300 stores with 80,000 employees in cities and towns across North America. Starbuck's profits have grown 50% a year for the past six years. But there's more than money in the Starbucks story. The company inspires loyalty among consumers, provides long-term value to shareholders and treats its employees with respect. The last point may be the most important. "Success," Schultz writes, "is empty if you arrive at the finish line alone."

....

UNORTHODOX STRATEGIES FOR THE EVERYDAY WARRIOR: ANCIENT WISDOM FOR THE MODERN COMPETITOR

Translated, with commentary by Ralph Sawyer with the collaboration of Mei-chun Lee Sawyer (Westview Press, 1996, paperback)

I f you truly know that the enemy has a weakness that can be exploited... quickly advance your army and pound it." Some 1000 years in China, this book of 100 tactical principles was compiled as a text for young men jockeying for high-ranking government positions. Now Ralph Sawyer, a distinguished scholar and translator of Chinese military texts, has translated this compendium of tactics and added his own commentary to each principle to show they may be applied in competitive corporate environments.

DEN OF THIEVES

by James B. Stewart (Touchstone Books, 1992, paperback)

H ere is the definitive exposé of greed in the 1980s. Through his junk bond empire, Michael Milken made $550 million in a single year. Corporate boards across America lived in dread of Ivan Boesky and his $3 billion in stock-purchasing power. With investment bankers Martin Siegel and Dennis Levine, Milken and Boesky formed the biggest insider trading ring in the history of American finance—and almost brought down Wall Street. Then, a handful of detectives in off-the-rack suits dragged this quartet of high rollers into court.

WHERE ARE THE CUSTOMERS' YACHTS?
OR, A GOOD HARD LOOK AT WALL STREET

by Fred Schwed, Jr. (John Wiley & Sons, 1995, paperback)

F red Schwed spent a good part of his professional as a trader on Wall Street. Then in 1940, he published this hilarious send-up of the foibles of bankers, brokers, traders and Wall Street's hapless customers. More than 50 years later, the stories still ring true.

In fact, you'll find a touch of Mark Twain and H.L. Mencken in these comical anecdotes. This new edition comes with a foreword by Michael Lewis, author of *Liar's Poker* and is illustrated by *New Yorker* cartoonist Peter Arno. One of the funniest and most astute books ever written about American commerce.

FIRE AND ICE:
THE STORY OF CHARLES REVSON—THE MAN WHO BUILT THE REVLON EMPIRE
by Andrew Tobias

Charles Revson, one of the most ruthless entrepreneurs of our century, became a millionaire in the cutthroat world of cosmetics. But his employees and wives did not. He hired and fired top executives with lightning speed. He could never remember his first wife's name; giggled through the wedding ceremony to his second; and walked out on his third days after their 10th anniversary (he had given her $30,000 in cash in a tin can). Tobias has written a compelling story of a complicated man. Worth searching for.

MY VAST FORTUNE:
THE MONEY ADVENTURES OF A QUIXOTIC CAPITALIST
by Andrew Tobias (Random House, 1997, paperback)

Andrew Tobias, the host of *Beyond Wall Street: The Art of Investing* presents a hilarious and financially enlightening collection of stories about his own personal adventures with money. He recalls his days at Harvard where he built the *Let's Go* travel guides into a money-making publishing venture and his early years in the work force when he became Manhattan's most notorious tightwad. Plus he offers such fun tips as "never buy real estate over the phone," explains why "Ralph Nader is a big fat idiot" and reveals how your investments can do 80% better than those of your friends.

FINANCIAL SAVVY FOR THE SELF-EMPLOYED
by Grace W. Weinstein (Owl, 1996, paperback)

There's a lot more to starting your own business than setting up a computer and a fax modem in your spare bedroom. Weinstein, an expert on personal finances, has written the first book to combine solid advice on how to run your own business with practical tips on personal and business finances. You'll learn how to keep records, when you must pay your taxes and what type of insurance coverage you're going to need. Plus, Weinstein teaches the ins and outs of getting small-business loans and investing for your retirement. If you're self-employed, this book is a must.

THE BOOK IS ALWAYS BETTER THAN THE MOVIE

EMPIRE OF THE SUN
by J.G. Ballard (Pocket Books, 1987, paperback)

Jim, an 11-year-old British boy, is separated from his parents during the fall of Shanghai in 1941 and fends for himself in a series of Japanese concentration camps. A tough book, without a trace of sentimentality.

LITTLE BIG MAN
by Thomas Berger (Dell, 1985, paperback)

Jack Crabb was a white boy raised by Indians who grew up to be a plainsman, Indian scout, buffalo hunter and snake oil salesman. He crossed paths with Wyatt Earp, Wild Bill Hickock and Calamity Jane, but his biggest claim to fame was being the only surviving white man of Custer's last stand. Thomas Berger presents the novel as the memoirs of either the most neglected hero in the history of the U.S., or a liar of insane proportions. Either way, it is an exciting and amusing portrait of the Old West.

PLANET OF THE APES
by Pierre Boulle (NAL-Dutton, 1964, paperback)

This novel, in which an astronaut lands on a distant planet where evolution has taken a slightly different course, is much more frightening and exciting than the five feature films, television series and animated kids' show it inspired.

THE SHELTERING SKY
by Paul Bowles (Vintage, 1991, paperback)

After more than 40 years living in Morocco, Paul Bowles may know North Africa better than any other Westerner. The Sheltering Sky is a novel of psychological terror in which three world-weary American travelers drift through exotic cities and magnificent deserts, all the while barely noticing how this cruel, impassive land is slowly destroying them.

JURASSIC PARK
by Michael Crichton (Ballantine, 1991, paperback)

In the book, you get more chase scenes, the dinosaurs nail more victims and the intelligence of the raptors is even more chilling than you may remember from the movie. You also get a much better sense of the scientific principles involved in recovering dino-DNA. Oh, and the ending is entirely different.

THE RETURN OF MARTIN GUERRE
by Natalie Zemon Davis
(Harvard University Press, 1994, paperback)

In 16th-century France, a peasant returns to his wife, his family and his home village after many years' absence and begins his life anew. But is this the same Martin who disappeared years before, or is it a devilishly clever impostor? One of history's most fascinating episodes.

THE LOVER
by Marguerite Duras
(Perennial Library/HarperCollins, 1992, paperback)

The narrator, now in middle age, looks back to her adolescence in French Indochina when she met a wealthy Chinese man and began a torrid love affair. Her family severely complicates the situation-they have fallen on hard times and while they may deplore the affair, they hope that this connection with a rich man will raise their fortunes. A remarkable story of love, maturity and opportunism from one of the finest writers in Europe.

THE NAME OF THE ROSE
by *Umberto Eco* (Warner Books, 1988, paperback)

Perhaps the best detective novel ever written. Brother William of Baskerville is a guest at an abbey where monks are being murdered in the most grotesque fashion. Employing the logic of Aristotle, the theology of Aquinas and maybe the deductive reasoning of Sherlock Holmes, he begins to uncover the abbey's darkest secrets. But he must work fast: some old acquaintances from the Inquisition are coming and Brother William may not escape them a second time.

GORILLAS IN THE MIST
by *Dian Fossey* (Houghton Mifflin, paperback)

For years, Dian Fossey sat on the perimeter of a family of gorillas in Africa's Virunga Mountains, imitating their feeding habits and mimicking their grunts of contentment. Then one day, a male gorilla reached out, touched Fossey, and she became a member of the clan. In this enthralling book, Fossey recounts the 15 years she spent among four families of mountain gorillas on the borderlands of Rwanda, Zaire and Uganda, working to understand them and trying to protect them from poachers. It's a great read, but Fossey made certain her book would also be scientifically significant: she included census findings, described gorilla vocalizations, reprinted results of autopsy reports and included the most extensive bibliography on gorillas published up to that time. Worth searching for.

THE WORLD ACCORDING TO GARP
by John Irving (Ballantine, 1997, paperback)

An author-wrestler, a transsexual football player, a libidinous graduate student and a cult of self-mutilating feminists populate the zany world of Irving's most eccentric, most brilliant novel. Irving's gift for wordplay is hard to beat.

THE PORTRAIT OF A LADY
by Henry James (1881; Viking, 1988, paperback)

Critics say The Portrait of a Lady reflects the tension Henry James felt in his own life: how can one reconcile personal desires with society's expectations? Isabel Archer, a young American lady—intelligent, beautiful, independent and penniless—arrives in Europe with her aunt. She receives many offers of marriage from suitable men, but in the end makes the worst choice imaginable. Then, shortly after she realizes the dreadful mistake she has made, she meets a man whom she truly can love. The alternative before Isabel now is whether she should risk her place in society to follow her heart, or sacrifice her feelings and desires to her sense of duty.

SCHINDLER'S LIST
by Thomas Keneally (Touchstone Books, 1993, paperback)

Thomas Keneally first learned of Oskar Schindler when, by chance, he walked into the luggage store of Leopold Pfefferberg, one of "Schindler's Jews." A bon vivant, a war profiteer, a philanderer, a Nazi, Schindler nonetheless saved more than 1000 Jewish lives during World War II. This is an incredible story of the expansion of a human soul. Even if you've seen the movie, read this novel.

ONE FLEW OVER THE CUCKOO'S NEST
by Ken Kesey (NAL-Dutton, 1975, paperback)

Ken Kesey drew on his experiences as a ward attendant in a mental hospital for this novel about one man's tragic attempt to buck the system. Randall McMurphy feigns insanity and gets himself committed to get out of a prison work detail. However he gets more than he bargained for when he runs up against the overbearing and dictatorial keeper of the ward—Head Nurse Ratched. His amusing attempts to get her goat escalate into a grim battle for the hearts and minds of his fellow inmates.

THE SHINING
by Stephen King (Signet Books, 1978, paperback)

You could read this ghost story on a beach at high noon on the Fourth of July surrounded by thousands of people and it would still scare the bejesus out of you. Down-and-out author Jack Torrance moves his wife and five-year-old son to a vast Rocky Mountain hotel where he's landed a job as winter custodian. As the snow piles up and the roads become impassable, the hotel's legion of ghosts become bolder—they'd like Jack Torrance to join them.

THE YEAR OF LIVING DANGEROUSLY
by C.J. Koch (Penguin, 1983, paperback)

A young Australian journalist eager to make a mark in his profession travels to Sukarno's Indonesia. The Indonesian who serves as his assistant guides him through the political and social complexities of the country. The woman he falls in love with draws him into the jaded world of the expatriates. Peter Weir's film version of this political thriller captured the emotional impact of Koch's book, but not its complication.

THE LOST LANGUAGE OF THE CRANES
by David Leavitt (Bantam, 1987, paperback)

It's not going too far to say that this stands among the most poignant novels of sexual awakening ever written. At 25, Philip begins his first serious gay romance. When he comes out to his parents, Philips' father feels especially ill-at-ease. Gradually Philip's mother begins to suspect that her husband has been keeping his own homosexuality secret.

ROSEMARY'S BABY
by Ira Levin (Signet, 1997, paperback)

If you've only seen the movie and never read Levin's book, you don't know what scary is. Guy and Rosemary Woodhouse, newcomers to a spooky Manhattan high-rise, think their neighbors are a bit strange. And they get a lot stranger once Rosemary becomes pregnant. Levin is at his scary best writing about Rosemary frightened and alone in that eerie apartment building.

Also by Levin:

THE STEPFORD WIVES.

Why are all the women in this suburb so listless and why are their husbands so happy? Worth searching for.

THE BOYS FROM BRAZIL
(Random House, 1976, hardcover).

Dr. Mengele of Auschwitz has cloned 94 Adolf Hitlers. Now a Nazi hunter is trying to track down all of these budding Führers.

THE NATURAL
by Bernard Malamud (Avon, 1980, paperback)

If King Arthur and the Knights of the Round Table were a ball club, this would be their story. No book has ever captured the romance, the pure magic of baseball as beautifully as Malamud's story of Roy Hobbs and his miraculous bat, Wonderboy. You'll love the impossibly evil Judge and the hopelessly smarmy reporter Max Mercy. A real American classic.

More Malamud:

THE FIXER
(Penguin, 1994, paperback).

Malamud based this novel on actual event in czarist Russia, about 1910. A Jewish handyman living in an area closed to Jews is arrested and falsely charged with the ritual murder of a Christian boy.

AT PLAY IN THE FIELDS OF THE LORD
by *Peter Matthiessen* (Vintage, 1991, paperback)

The Aidan Quinn/Tom Berenger/Daryl Hannah film never came near the emotional intensity of this novel about the Quarriers, well-meaning American missionaries who are hopelessly out of place in the Amazon jungle and Lewis Moon, a half-Indian mercenary who tries to abandon white society and return to tribal life.

GONE WITH THE WIND
by *Margaret Mitchell* (1935; Warner Books, 1994, paperback)

Scarlett O'Hara was not beautiful, but men seldom realized it when caught by her charm." So begins Mitchell's love song to the indomitable spirit of the South. Within six months of its release, *GWTW* had sold one million copies; it soared to the top of the bestseller lists and stayed there for two years. The story is irresistible and Mitchell's psychological insights and literary gifts may surprise you.

THE INFORMER
by *Liam O'Flaherty* (1925; Harcourt Brace, 1980, paperback)

John Ford's 1935 film of The Informer starring Victor McLaglen is outstanding, but the novel has the leisure to offer more insight into the character of feckless Gypo Nolan. The story is set all in one night in the 1920s, during Ireland's civil war. Gypo, poor lummox that he is, turns in his comrade Frankie McPhillips, the commander of the local revolutionary cell, for the £20 reward money—enough, he thinks, to marry his sweetheart and emigrate with her to America. But Gypo squanders it all in pubs and fish and chips shops. And after the money is gone, the rebels come for him. A terrible beauty of a novel.

CONTACT
by Carl Sagan (Pocket Books, 1997, paperback)

Readers of science fiction consistently rank this book among the top ten "contact" novels. It's December, 1999. After years of monitoring deep space, a very determined research scientist is finally rewarded with a transmission from someone, or something, out there. A multinational team of scientists prepares to journey into the galaxy to meet this new life form, but politics, personalities and even religion soon become entangled in this tremendous adventure. The story is thrilling and readers have never ceased to praise Sagan for the rich scientific content he's brought to his story.

ROB ROY
by Sir Walter Scott (1817; New American Library, 1995, paperback)

You'll find the novel much different from the plot of the Liam Neeson/Jessica Lange movie. Here, Rob Roy is part of a valiant trio which includes a young man wrongly disinherited by his father and a beautiful high-spirited young woman. Together they work to unmask and defeat the villainous Rashleigh. A classic tale of courage and adventure.

FRANKENSTEIN
by Mary Wollestonecraft Shelley (1818; Viking, 1998, paperback)

First of all Frankenstein is the doctor, not the monster. Second, with all due respect to Boris Karloff and Kenneth Branagh, no film version of Mary Shelley's novel has ever gotten the themes or the characters straight. This is a novel that wonders how far science can go before it offends against the laws of God and nature and debates the responsibility of a creator for his creation. Packed with creepy scenes and challenging ideas, *Frankenstein* remains one of the best horror novels ever written. And did you know that Mary Wollestonecraft Shelley was only 19 when she wrote it?

101 DALMATIANS
by *Dodie Smith* (Puffin, 1989, paperback)

Dalmatian puppies are disappearing all over England and Scotland Yard is at a loss. When their own family of fifteen gets snatched, Pongo and Missis, a young, married Dalmatian couple, set out on their own to bring them home. With the help of a cross-country canine network, they brave hunger, the weather and cruel dognappers to save their pups from a shocking fate. Whether you're looking for a bedtime story for a youngster or yourself, you'll love this book. Disney based its popular animated film on this heartwarming tale of rescue.

DRACULA
by *Bram Stoker* (1897; Tor Books, 1992, paperback)

Everyone has seen at least one Dracula movie, but few people have sat down to read the 19th-century novel on which all the films are based. Stoker's story of the undead showing up in tidy, rational Victorian England is a work of genius. He maintains a constant undercurrent of tension that erupts into moments of sheer terror.

SOPHIE'S CHOICE
by *William Styron* (Random House, 1992, paperback)

Styron's most touching novel is this saga of Sophie, a Polish Catholic survivor of Auschwitz, her flamboyant Jewish lover, Nathan and their best friend, Stingo, a would-be author and Sophie's would-be lover. You'll find the story and the characters in the novel are much more complex than in the movie.

A MIDNIGHT CLEAR
by *William Wharton* (Ballantine, 1983, paperback)

This is one of the most haunting and moving novels ever published about the Second World War. It's Christmas, near the end of the war and a squad of young American soldiers on an extended reconnaissance mission encounter a squad of their young German counterparts. Both groups are cold, scared, far from home and neither wishes to kill or be killed. Together they hatch a plan for the Germans to surrender with dignity. However, the best laid plans sometimes go tragically awry.

THE BONFIRE OF THE VANITIES
by Tom Wolfe (Bantam, 1988, paperback)

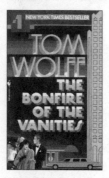

The one, the only. While picking up his mistress at the airport, hapless Sherman McCoy gets involved in a freak accident in the South Bronx. In no time, everybody wants a piece of Sherman: the alcoholic tabloid journalist who knows it's a career-making story; the jaded Bronx prosecutor who can prove that the system works if he nails a Park Avenue investment banker; the flamboyant Harlem pastor who sees another opportunity to get on TV. A vicious but funny portrayal of New York in the 1980s.

BOOKS TO SAVOR: FOOD & WINE

REAL BEER AND GOOD EATS
by Bruce Aidells and Denis Kelly (Knopf, 1992, hardcover)

The beer renaissance has arrived. You can see it in the proliferation of microbrewries producing top-quality ales, lagers and stouts. So Aidells and Kelly have produced a guide to great food that is even better when washed down with great beer. The 175 recipes included here run from Basque Chorizo, Red Pepper and Garbanzo Salad to Barbecued Shrimp New Orleans Style. There's even a tour of famous eateries where you can also find great beer, such as McSorley's Old Ale House in New York—legend says it never closed its doors during Prohibition.

FROM EARTH TO THE TABLE:
JOHN ASH'S WINE COUNTRY CUISINE
by John Ash with Sid Goldstein (Dutton, 1995, hardcover)

John Ash's philosophy—in this book and in his northern California restaurant—is to eat "seasonally and locally." Why, for instance, put cardboard-tasting tomatoes in a salad in December when you can make Warm Red Cabbage Salad with Pancetta and California Goat Cheese? Ash's recipes are innovative and tempting: Fusilli with Collards, Bacon and Garlic; Seared Ahi Tuna with Lavender-Pepper Crust; Crab Wontons with Orange-Chipotle Sauce. And of course, you'll get Ash's wine recommendations for each dish. A perfect book for cooks who like to follow the rhythm of the seasons.

························

LEAFY GREENS
by *Mark Bittman* (Macmillan, 1995, hardcover)

Arugula. Chard. Kale. Watercress. Dandelions. Leafy greens have come a long way from iceberg lettuce. And there's no end in sight to the "greening of America" as more and more of us discover that greens are among the healthiest foods we can eat. Here, then, are fresh and tasty ways to prepare all those wonderful vegetables. From Creamy Kale Soup, to Risotto with Arugula and Shrimp, to Sweet and Sour Chinese Cabbage, you'll learn more than 100 ways to take advantage of the versatility of greens.

The natural accompaniment:

THE COMPLETE BOOK OF DRESSINGS
by *Paulette Mitchell* (Macmillan, 1995, hardcover).

Basil-Sherry Vinaigrette, Herbed Anchovy Dressing, Roasted Sweet Red Pepper Dressing—there are more than 100 possibilities in this guide for "dressing for success."

························

COOKING PROVENCE:
FOUR GENERATIONS OF RECIPES AND TRADITIONS
by *Antoine Bouterin and Joan Schwartz*
(Macmillan, 1994, hardcover)

Garlic," says Antoine Bouterin, "is not only a flavor, it is the secret of happiness." The chef of New York's celebrated restaurant, Le Perigord, was born and learned to cook in the corner of France that almost worships the garlic clove: Provence. With 200 authentic mouth-watering Provençal recipes, Bouterin reveals the secrets of traditional country French cooking. Fragrant Lentil Stew. Lamb Chops Provençal sprinkled with fresh herbs. Pommes Marie-Therese Bouterin's mother's recipe for baked apples with honey and rosemary. This is the one book that brings you all the flavors of Provence.

PEDALING THROUGH BURGUNDY COOKBOOK

by Sarah Leah Chase, illustrated by Cathy Brear
(Workman, 1995, paperback)

A devoted fan of French country cuisine, a former owner of a catering business on Nantucket and an experienced leader of bicycle tours through the provinces, Sarah Leah Chase is the right person to introduce you to the wines and cuisine of Burgundy. From Frogs Legs with Pouilly Fuissé and Parsley to Spring Rabbit with Mustard and Cornichons, to Pain d'Epices (the rum-soaked Burgundian gingerbread), Chase immerses you in the pleasures of rustic cuisine. And her animated essays on travel through Burgundy will make you wish you could be in Beaune tomorrow.

On the Road Again:

PEDALING THROUGH PROVENCE COOKBOOK

by Sarah Leah Chase, illustrated by Linda Montgomery
(Workman, 1995, paperback).

Roast Rack of Lamb with Lavender Honey. Soupe au Pistou. Quayside Calamari Salad. From marvels of Mediterranean cuisine to market day inspirations, Chase offers 95 sublime Provençal recipes, plus dozens of insights into the joys of traveling through Provence á bicyclette.

THE WAY TO COOK
by Julia Child (Knopf, 1993, paperback)

The world-renowned "French Chef" shares 800 of her best recipes with you in a big, beautiful volume. Whether you are a beginner or an experienced gourmet, Julia Child makes preparing memorable meals easy. And with 600 full-color illustrations, you'll be able to see what you should be doing.

THE TRUE HISTORY OF CHOCOLATE
by Sophie D. and Michael D. Coe
(Thames & Hudson, 1996, hardcover)

The Maya celebrated it in their sacred texts. The Spanish craved it almost as much as gold. And the Grand Duke of Tuscany liked his flavored with a hint of jasmine. Now the Coes have written a very informative and entertaining illustrated history of chocolate and how it came to be the universal favorite confection. You'll learn how chocolate was first prepared in Central America 3000 years, the impact it made in Renaissance Europe, how it's grown and processed today and what distinguishes the pricey gourmet chocolate from the mass-produced stuff. *The True History of Chocolate* is a sinfully rich read.

THE MARTINI: SHAKEN NOT STIRRED
by Barnaby Conrad III (Chronicle Books, 1995, hardcover)

I must get out of these wet clothes," a drenched Robert Benchley once said, "and into a dry martini." Oh, for the days when a martini was the emblem of wit, sophistication and romance. Anecdotes from martini history (FDR plied Stalin with martinis at the 1943 Tehran Conference), martini-inspired New Yorker cartoons and movie stills from the martini's glory days in the 1930s and 1940s help Conrad trace the intoxicating history of America's high-octane cocktail.

COFFEE:
A GUIDE TO BUYING, BREWING AND ENJOYING
by Kenneth Davids (Cole Group, 1994, paperback)

Here is the book that elevates the morning cup of coffee from a familiar routine to your favorite part of the day. Davids offers the last word on the best equipment, the most delectable recipes, even the right kinds of filters. Whether you like au lait, supremo, espresso, or a regular cup of joe, with this book, you'll never make a bad cup of coffee again.

DESSERTS TO DIE FOR
by Marcel De Saulniers; recipes with Jon-Pierre Peavey; photographs by Michael Grand (Simon & Schuster, 1995, hardcover).

The title is only a pale reflection of the extravagance found between the covers. Toasted Brandy and Spice Pound Cake, Pillars of Chocolate with Cocoa Thunderheads, Rum-soaked Zombie Cake and many more indulgent treats from the author of Death by Chocolate.

VEGETARIAN TIMES COMPLETE COOKBOOK
by the Editors of Vegetarian Times and Lucy Moll (Macmillan, 1995, paperback)

Whether you're an ovo-lacto vegetarian, a lacto vegetarian, a vegan, or just somebody who would like some tasty recipes for vegetarian dishes, you won't find a better resource than this collection from the editors of *Vegetarian Times*. This book explains their philosophy and serves up 750 imaginative recipes, including Spaghetti Squash Salad, African Peanut Soup, Nutty Lentil Loaf and Spiced Pumpkin Custard Pudding. A comprehensive and innovative guide for anyone interested in vegetarian cooking.

CHINESE CUISINE
by Susanna Foo, Foreword by Amy Tan (Houghton Mifflin, 1995)

If you love Chinese cuisine, you'll discover there's a delicious difference to Susanna Foo's recipes. She takes the traditional dishes from northern China and Taiwan, where she grew up and makes some modifications. Balsamic vinegar stands in for the rice vinegars of China. Cold sesame noodles are garnished with julienned Belgian endive. And she offers lots of alternatives to stir-frying. From perfect dim sum, to Classic Hot and Sour Soup (with scallion pancakes), to Auntie Wu's Braised Red Snapper with Garlic and Ginger, you'll learn how to enliven your menu with 175 traditional and innovative Chinese recipes.

A little extra inspiration:

THE KITCHEN GOD'S WIFE
by Amy Tan (Vintage, 1993, paperback).

Three women reveal the secrets of their lives, going back to their origins in 1920 Shanghai.

* * * * * * * * * * * * *

A TASTE OF AFRICA
by Dorinda Hafner (Ten Speed Press, 1994, paperback)

A native of Ghana, Hafner has adapted 100 of Africa's most savory recipes for modern cooks. Here is Giant Crab Thermidor from the Ivory Coast, Moroccan Couscous and Shitor Din dark chili sauce from Ghana. This will be the most original cookbook in your kitchen.

* * * * * * * * * * * * *

ESSENTIALS OF ITALIAN COOKING
by Marcella Hazan (Knopf, 1992, hardcover)

Before you boil the pasta, read Marcella Hazan. Her recipes are simple, easy, delicious—and they work. For instance, all you need to make the best tomato sauce you've ever tasted is basil, garlic, olive oil, canned San Marzano tomatoes, salt, pepper and about 45 minutes for preparation and cooking. You can't go wrong.

. . . .

THE FOOD LOVER'S TIPTIONARY
by *Sharon Tyler Herbst* (Hearst, 1994, paperback)

"**A** n A to Z Guide with More Than 4500 Food and Drink Tips, Secrets, Shortcuts and Other Things Cookbooks Never Tell You." Now that's a subtitle. From how to use chopsticks to slicing onions without tears, thousands of handy tips even experienced cooks can use.

. . . .

BEAT THIS!
by *Ann Hodgman* (Houghton Mifflin, 1993, paperback)

H odgman has written the first cookbook with attitude. She doesn't just present recipes, she dares you to find any better. Try the To-Die-For Brownies ("They're so creamy and unctuous that you could spread them on top of other brownies") and Artichoke and Mushroom Salad ("a recipe you probably didn't realize you were trying the best version of"). Hodgman's cookbook is delicious and unbeatable.

. . . .

MICHAEL JACKSON'S BEER COMPANION: THE WORLD'S GREAT BEER STYLES, GASTRONOMY AND TRADITIONS
by *Michael Jackson* (Running Press, 1993, paperback)

W hat's the difference between American ales and international ales? Can you distinguish between porter and stout? Sure, you like wheat beers, but would you go near a fruit beer? And what the heck is a Lambic? Michael Jackson, one of the first guys ever to write a guide book to beer, knows his brewskys. Going country-by-country, he walks you through the world's great beer styles, recounts some local traditions that have grown up around beer and brewing, recommends the best beer to accompany virtually any kind of cuisine and visits with some innovative brewers. Features 218 full-color illsutratons, including 100 labels.

On the Road:

SECRET LIFE OF BEER:
LEGENDS, LORE & LITTLE-KNOWN FACTS
by Alan D. Eames (Storey Communications, 1995, paperback).

Eames, known as "the Indiana Jones of Beer," tramps arond the world collecting funny, surprising and interesting factoids about everybody's favorite beverage.

THE BORDER COOKBOOK:
AUTHENTIC HOME COOKING OF THE AMERICAN SOUTHWEST AND NORTHERN MEXICO
by Cheryl Alters Jamison and Bill Jamison
(Harvard Common Press, 1995, paperback)

Norteño cuisine is characterized by big tortillas, flame-broiled beef and savory cheeses. In 300 recipes, the Jamisons assemble the best dishes that blend Mexican, Native American and Anglo influences. You'll find lots of salsa recipes to choose from, the secret to perfect guacamole, plus Red Caldwell's South Texas Fajitas and Piñata Pollo stuffed with chorizo, jalapeño and goat cheese. There's even invaluable information about such unusual ingredients as nopales (cactus pads) and chiltepins (pea-sized hot chiles).

THE MAKING OF A COOK
by Madeleine Kamman (Simon & Schuster, 1994, paperback)

This is the book that is going to transform you from someone who follows recipes into a serious cook. Kamman tells you what utensils you need, explains the chemical changes the ingredients are undergoing in the pot (and how they determine if your meal is going to be a success) and then teaches you how to prepare delicious dishes, course by course—stocks and soups, vegetables, meat and fish, sauces, desserts. You'll even learn professional tricks, such as how to prepare a fine sauce if you have all afternoon or only half an hour. Essential for budding chefs.

¡CUBA COCINA! THE TANTALIZING WORLD OF CUBAN COOKING
by Joyce LaFray (Hearst, 1994, hardcover)

Cuban cooking may be just what your home menu needs. It's recipes are simple, but the flavors are complex (without being searingly hot). For instance, you can make an authentic Cuban Creole Sauce with olive oil, garlic, onion, oranges, parsley, oregano, salt and pepper. You'll find classico dishes such as Ham Croquettes and Shredded Beef in Ropa Viejo (tomato sauce) and nuevo dishes such as Grilled Snapper with Mango-Black Bean Relish. LaFray includes all the information you need, from tips on grilling fish to the right way to prepare black beans. This is the best way to bring the authentic, savory specialties of Cuba into your kitchen.

BREAD ALONE: BOLD FRESH LOAVES FROM YOUR OWN HANDS
by Daniel Leader and Judith Blahnik Morrow, 1993, hardcover)

Leader is a professional baker who is most happy when producing hearty breads in the style of old-time European village bakers. With easy-to-follow, step-by-step directions, he teaches you his secret-slow fermentation of the dough. Then, it's on to 88 flavorful Old World recipes including sourdough rye with onions, focaccia, crusty baguettes, wheat bread with walnuts.

U.S.A. COOKBOOK
by Sheila Lukins (Workman, 1997, hardcover)

Brace your palate for a star-spangled salute to great American cuisine. Sheila Lukins visited every corner of the United States-from Wiscasset, Maine, to the island of Lanai in Hawaii. And everywhere she went she collected outstanding regional recipes. This monumental book features 600 of the best American dishes: Savory Chicken Pot Pie from the heartland, Sumptuous Southwestern Brisket, Mashed Yukon Golds and The Great U.S.A. Salmon Cake. From Spiced Maple Ribs to Minty Sweet Peas to Big Time Banana Split, this is a landmark collection of American classics.

The Book Every Cook Needs:

THE SILVER PALATE COOKBOOK
by Julee Rosso & Sheila Lukins with Michael McLaughlin
(Workman, 1993, paperback).

The cookbook that launched Lukins' career collects the recipes she and Rosso made famous in their New York catering business.

....

JAMES MCNAIR COOKS SOUTHEAST ASIAN
by James McNair (Chronicle Books, 1996, hardcover)

This visually stunning full-color cookbook introduces you to 70 savory Southeast Asian recipes. Begin with a refreshing glass of Thai Limeade. Then learn to prepare Saté, the shish kebob of Indonesia and Malaysia, with a piquant marinade; Go Xao, Vietnam's zesty lemongrass chicken; Yum Goong Yahng Phet, a fiery grilled shrimp entree from Thailand, plus a host of recipes for preparing rice, noodles, curries and dipping sauces. McNair even includes a shopping guide for locating special ingredients and instructions for preparing other essential ingredients at home.

....

THE UNION SQUARE CAFE COOKBOOK
by Danny Meyer and Michael Romano
(HarperCollins, 1994, hardcover)

Night after night, New Yorkers fill the tables of Danny Meyer's legendary Union Square Cafe. Now you can prepare the signature dishes that have made this restaurant one of the best in the country. The more than 160 recipes include Marinated Tuna Fillet Mignon and Hot Garlic Potato Chips, Penne with Asparagus and Red Pepper and the to-die-for Marble Fudge Brownies. A four-star cookbook.

....

THE NEW COMPLETE JOY OF HOME BREWING
by Charlie Papazian (Avon, 1991, paperback)

Absolutely everything you need to know, from what equipment to buy to assembling ingredients to brewing different varieties of beer. You'll even learn how to control the amount of alcohol. An indispensable guide with crystal clear directions.

PARKER'S WINE BUYER'S GUIDE
by Robert M. Parker, Jr. (Fireside Paperbacks, 1995, paperback)

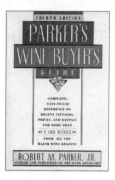

If you break out in a sweat every time you walk into a wine shop, then this book is for you. As author and publisher of *The Wine Advocate*, one of the world's most respected wine journals, Parker knows how to cut through the hype and get straight to the point: is it a good bottle of wine? More than 7,500 wines are described here and each one is graded on the 100-point system you remember from grammar school. From the rarest vintages to a simple table wine, Parker makes you feel at ease and in control.

STEAK LOVER'S COOK BOOK
by William Rice (Workman, 1997, paperback)

Carnivores, rejoice! Food journalist and steak groupie William Rice has written the definitive book on how to buy, store and prepare a perfect steak—whether it is the priciest tenderloin or the most economical skirt steak. He includes 90 recipes for steak including Pan-Broiled Porterhouse with Shallot-Lemon Butter, The True Steak au Poivre and Wine-Bathed Sirloin. Plus he features 50 more recipes for side dishes (Outrageous Onion Rings, Steak Fries, Okra with Onions) and desserts (Mississippi Mud Pie, Summer Fruit Cobbler, Rich Bread Pudding). Hands down, this is the best-ever cookbook for steak.

TASTING PLEASURE:
CONFESSIONS OF A WINE LOVER
by *Jancis Robinson* (Viking, 1997, hardcover)

In Great Britain, Jancis Robinson is a household word, renowned for her free and easy columns about wine. Now wine lovers on this side of the pond have an opportunity to learn about the pleasures of the vine from Robinson. She tours the vineyards of France, Spain, Portugal, Australia and California; explains the qualities that distinguish the finest wines; and dishes a little dirt about famous and important figures in the wine world (did you know Francis Ford Coppola has a vineyard in Napa Valley?).

THE BOOK OF JEWISH FOOD:
AN ODYSSEY FROM SAMARKAND TO NEW YORK
by *Claudia Roden* (Knopf, 1996, hardcover)

For almost 15 years, Claudia Roden traveled around the globe-from Poland and Russia to Syria, India and the Mediterranean, from the Americas to North Africa and Israel—collecting more than 800 authentic Jewish recipes, many of which have never before been published. You'll find recipes for the long-simmering Sabbath stews known as cholents and for the vegetable and noodle puddings called kugels. There are also definitive recipes for Potato Latkes, Borscht, Hallah, Carrot Tzimmes, Matzo Brei, Kreplach, Hungarian Chicken Paprikash, Rugelach and more. A cookbook that's bound to become a classic.

More Great Recipes:

SECRETS OF A JEWISH BAKER
by *George Greenstein* (Crossing Press, 1993, paperback).

An award-winning cookbook that gives you the recipes and the confidence to bake Challah, Cinnamon Raisin Bread, Millet Rye Bread, Pumpernickel Bread, Bagels and Bialys, Egg Rolls and more, using modern techniques and without spending a small fortune on special equipment.

NUEVO LATINO:
RECIPES THAT CELEBRATE THE NEW LATIN-AMERICAN CUISINE
by Douglas Rodriguez(Ten Speed Press, 1995, paperback)

Latin-American food is unfamiliar territory to most Anglos, but it could be the next "cool cuisine" if Rodriguez, co-owner of New York's Patria restaurant, has anything to say about it. This book serves up traditional Latin-American dishes such as Banana-Lentil Salad, as well as Rodriguez's own recipes: Ham Croquetas with Brie and Kale. But while Rodriguez's tremendous enthusiasm spills over on every page, he does make concessions to down-to-earth practicality, including a list of mail-order sources for hard-to-find ingredients. This is a great introduction to a vibrant cuisine.

CLASSIC HOME DESSERTS
by Richard Sax (Houghton Mifflin, 1994, hardcover)

After 10 years of searching out great home cooks and paging through old cookbooks, Bon Appétit columnist Richard Sax has produced the most comprehensive and inspiring dessert cookbook ever. Try Iowa's Favorite Custard Pie, from an authentic Iowa farm recipe. Or Mrs. Dalgairn's Scottish Seed Cake, from an 1830 Edinburgh cookbook. Sax even reveals the secret of his Russian Jewish grandmother's Legendary Honey Cake. From fruit tarts to puddings, from cookies to ice cream, this dessert cookbook is a triumph.

LICENSE TO GRILL
by Chris Schlesinger and John Willoughby
(William Morrow, 1997, hardcover)

Schlesinger and Willoughby are gurus of the grill who take you beyond the humble hamburger. Their 200+ recipes, with more emphasis on vegetables and fish than you usually find in grilling cookbooks, includes Almond-Crusted Grilled Salmon with Garlic Sauce, Grilled Lamb Skewers with Apricots, Grilled Veal Chops and Grilled Shrimp (which can be tossed with linguine). Then try

Grilled Spicy New Potato Salad, Grilled Garlicky Eggplant and Grilled Black Pepper Flatbread. Schlesinger and Willoughby also teach you basic grilling techniques.

ALMOST VEGETARIAN
by Diana Shaw (Clarkson Potter Publishers, 1994, paperback)

If you are a part-time carnivore who believes you should eat more vegetables but can't quite bring yourself to make a total commitment to vegetarianism, this book is for you. Diana Shaw has written an appetizing primer that reveals the joys of low-fat, high-fiber vegetarian cooking. Try Roast Garlic Pesto, Aromatic Leek and Potato Soup, or Winter Squash Gratin. With many recipes, Shaw even gives you the option of adding fish or chicken without feeling guilty. At last, a tantalizing collection of recipes for health-conscious chefs.

B. SMITH'S: ENTERTAINING AND COOKING FOR FRIENDS
by Barbara Smith (Workman/Artisan, 1995, hardcover)

After a glamorous career as a high-fashion model whose picture appeared on the covers of *Ebony*, *Essence* and *Mademoiselle*, Barbara Smith has opened two popular restaurants—one in New York's Theater District, another in Washington D.C.'s Union Station. This big, glossy cookbook offers Smith's signature fare—a blend of international cuisine and tasty all-American home cooking, from Mom's Fried Chicken to Flash-Roasted Salmon with Swiss Chard and Citrus Vinaigrette. For a picnic at the beach or a stylish dinner party for eight, Barbara Smith has the best menus and entertainment tips.

THE LUTÈCE COOKBOOK
by André Soltner with Seymour Britchky (Knopf, 1995, hardcover)

In New York, Lutèce is a shrine to superb cuisine. For more than 30 years, major-domo André Soltner made his patrons feel comfortable and at ease as he presented them with near-miraculous preparations. Now Soltner has collected 300 of his favorite recipes, classics of French fare as well as specialties from his native south Alsace. Among the Lutèce signature dishes you'll find here are Provençal Fish Soup, Lamb Chops in a Potato Crust, Carrot and Endive Terrine, Bavarian Cream with Grand Marnier and a heavenly Chocolate Mousse. This book, like the restaurant itself, is a classic.

VENETIAN TASTE
by Adam D. Tihany, Francesco Antonucci and Florence Fabricant (Abbeville Press, 1997, hardcover)

Everyone loves Italian cuisine, yet few home chefs know about the wonderful specialties of Venice. With seafood as its centerpiece and flavorful influences from the Greeks, Turks, Austrians, Spanish and Sephardic Jews, Venetian cuisine is perhaps the most distinctive in Italy. Start with crisp Rosemary Grissini (breadsticks). Move on to Risotto with Shrimp and Radicchio, or Tuna Ravioli with Ginger, or Polenta with Wild Mushrooms. Then finish with Venice's most delectable culinary invention, Tiramisu. A delicious collection of recipes that captures all the exuberance of the world's most delightful city.

MONDAY-TO-FRIDAY PASTA
by Michele Urvater (Workman, 1995, paperback)

What are you going to cook when you get home from work tonight? With 175 quick and tasty pasta recipes to choose from, you can count on a nutritious feast in 30 minutes or less. Urvater tells you how to stock your pantry over the weekend so the ingredients you need will be there when you need them. And she offers variations on her recipes to suit a variety of tastes and diets. For instance, you can cut the fat in Pesto Tortellini with Four

Cheeses by using low-fat cheeses and substituting chicken broth for cream. And chopped scallions will give the meal a little extra zing. These are carefully thought-out, realistic recipes for busy working people.

················

RECIPE OF MEMORY:
FIVE GENERATIONS OF MEXICAN CUISINE
by Victor M. Valle and Mary Lou Valle (New Press, 1995, hardcover)

With recipes that go back to the 1880s when the Valles lived in Guadalajara, this book offers an authentic taste of Old Mexico. From Chiles Stuffed with Shrimp to Squab on Saffron Rice to Prickly Pear Sorbet.

················

EVERYBODY EATS WELL IN BELGIUM
by Ruth Van Waerebeek (Workman, 1995, paperback)

The medieval cities and art treasures of Belgium are Europe's best-kept secrets and so is this little nation's hearty cuisine. Now Ruth Van Waerebeek, a native of Ghent who teaches Belgian cooking in New York City, expands on her family's traditional recipes to give you a solid introduction to the savory fare of Belgium. You'll learn how to make such tasty appetizers as Gratin of Belgian Endive, a flavorful Chicken Waterzooi brimming with herbs and vegetables, plus Van Waerebeek reveals the secret ingredient in traditional Belgian Waffles—yeast. Don't miss this warm, friendly introduction to the cuisine of Belgium.

················

JOHN WILLINGHAM'S WORLD OF CHAMPION BAR-B-Q
by John Willingham
(Morrow, 1996, hardcover)

For hard-core barbecuers, the secrets of great barbecuing are guarded like the family jewels. So it's astonishing that

Willingham has come out with some of his techniques. He tells you what kind of cooker you need and why to cook with wood (don't bother with charcoal and never use gas). Then its on to the recipes: Willingham's World-Champion Ribs, World-Champion Brisket, Screamin' Mean Oven-Roasted Beef Barbecue. Plus you get his secrets for the best sauces, rubs and marinades. Here at last is your key to slow-cook heaven, supplied by a master.

BRITISH CLASSICS

SENSE AND SENSIBILITY
by Jane Austen (1811; Penguin, 1996, paperback)

I n the hands of a lesser being, Sense and Sensibility would have degenerated into a dreary romance populated by one-dimensional stick figures. It is true that Elinor is fundamentally sensible and her younger sister Marianne is often swept away by her passionate sensibilities, nonetheless, Austen rounds out their personalities. As in all Austen novels, marrying off the main characters is the thing and there are plenty of false starts, meddling parents and misunderstandings to keep the story moving. And of course there's a completely satisfying ending. This is Austen's first novel and it is a very impressive, very entertaining beginning.

PRIDE AND PREJUDICE
by Jane Austen (1813; Penguin, 1996, paperback)

Austen never assembled a better cast of characters that the aloof Mr. Bennet, his vulgar wife, their three ditzy youngest daughters, the insufferably unctuous Mr. Collins and, of course, that aristocratic harridan Lady Catherine de Burgh. But dominating the action is the nonstop sparring and sniping between Elizabeth Bennet and Mr. Darcy. Funny, perceptive and very hard to put down, this is Austen at the pinnacle of her powers.

PERSUASION
by Jane Austen (1818; Penguin, 1967, paperback)

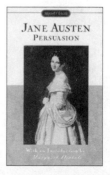

Poor Anne Elliott. At 27, she's just a step or two shy of becoming a spinster. You see, at age 19, she let herself be persuaded by Lady Russell not to marry Frederick Wentworth, a penniless naval officer. (Anne, after all, is the daughter of a baronet.) But now a kind fate has thrown

Anne one last chance for love. Published a year before she died, *Persuasion* is Austen's most mature novel, more lyrical than satirical. Give it a try.

JANE EYRE
by Charlotte Brontë (1847; Hyperion, 1995, paperback)

Intense and introspective, Jane Eyre is Charlotte Brontë's most unconventional heroine. After her wretched childhood in an orphanage, Jane takes a position as governess at the home of Edward Rochester, a violent man brooding over some dark secret. In this unusual environment, Jane becomes assertive and Rochester becomes almost tender. They fall in love. But the Rochester secret could destroy all hope of future happiness. It's a thriller. It's a romance. It's a mystery (who is that madwoman in the attic?). And it's one of the best novels to emerge from 19th-century England.

WUTHERING HEIGHTS
by Emily Brontë (1847; Oxford University Press, 1995, paperback).

Wuthering Heights
by Emily Brontë

Violent passions, restless ghosts and the wildest storms in English literature fill the pages of Wuthering Heights. Caught by a fierce tempest on the desolate Yorkshire moors, poor Mr. Lockwood is forced to seek shelter at *Wuthering Heights*, the home of his surly landlord, Mr. Heathcliff. As the storm rages outside, an elderly servant woman tells Lockwood the story of Heathcliff's mad passion for the wild and beautiful Cathy, of Cathy's betrayal of her lover and of her own nature and of Heathcliff's vengeance on everyone who ever injured him.

GREAT EXPECTATIONS
by Charles Dickens 1861, (Bantam Books, 1994, paperback)

The liveliest storyteller in 19th-century England was Charles Dickens. With wit and verve, he brought to life the entire spectrum of England's class-bound society, lambasted the cruelties of his age and held up for admiration the old-fashioned virtues—friendship, loyalty, generosity and true love. He reached the pinnacle of his career in *Great Expectations*, the story of Pip, a poor boy who finds his life dramatically changed after he brings food to a hungry escaped convict. It's a great story, packed with unforgettable characters. The pompous Mr. Pumblechook. The spectral Miss Havisham. The ominous lawyer, Mr. Jaggers. The haughty Estella. If you were forced to read it in high school, read it again now. This time you'll appreciate it.

More by Charles Dickens:

NICHOLAS NICKLEBY
(1839; Bantam, 1983, paperback).

A young man's struggle to make his way in a heartless world, full of intriguing plot twists. Some of the scenes will wring your heart.

OLIVER TWIST
by Charles Dickens (1838; Penguin, 1985, paperback)

Who can resist the story of the orphan boy who outrages the authorities of the workhouse by daring to ask for more? Although there is a healthy dollop of 19th-century sentimentality in *Oliver Twist*, you won't find any singing and dancing pickpockets and prostitutes in this novel. In fact, Dickens shocked his contemporaries by painting a harsh, dead-on portrait of life among London's criminal underclass. *Oliver Twist* has all the qualities that make Dickens great—a sharp sense of humor, a genius for delineating character in just two or three paragraphs and a story line that appeals to the reader's heart and conscience.

Another Masterwork by Dickens:

BLEAK HOUSE
(1853; Viking, 1971, paperback).

An interminable family lawsuit. A sweet, self-sacrificing heroine named Esther Summerson. An old scandal that Lady Dedlock is determined to suppress. And that's just for starters.

A TALE OF TWO CITIES
(1859; Pocket Books, 1996, paperback)

The implacable Madame Defarge knitting her way through a bloodbath. Sydney Carlton mounting the scaffold to save Lucy and her family. *A Tale of Two Cities* is the best novel about the French Revolution and arguably Dickens' greatest story.

....

JUDE THE OBSCURE
by Thomas Hardy (1895; Viking, 1978, paperback)

Thomas Hardy described story of *Jude the Obscure* as "a deadly war waged between flesh and spirit." Jude Fawley is an idealistic young man married to a barmaid. Against his better judgment, he falls in love with his unconventional (perhaps even unstable) cousin, Sue Bridehead. Readers were shocked by the resolution of this lovers' triangle. In fact, the backlash was so severe that Hardy gave up writing fiction. Even today, the twists of the plot are dismaying.

Another Hardy Shocker:

THE MAYOR OF CASTERBRIDGE
(1886; Knopf, 1993, paperback).

In a drunken stupor, Michael Henchard sells his wife Susan and infant daughter to a sailor for five guineas. The next day, when Henchard is sober, he learns too late what he has done—his family is gone. But 18 years later, when Henchard is the respectable mayor of Casterbridge, Susan and her daughter return. Once again, nothing goes as you'd expect.

TESS OF THE D'URBERVILLES
by Thomas Hardy (1891; Penguin, 1978, paperback)

Hardy's classic tale of an endlessly victimized young woman is also an unromantic view of the hard life of English country people.

....

SONS AND LOVERS
by D.H. Lawrence (1913; New American Library, 1985, paperback)

M rs. Morel deals with her unhappy marriage by transferring all her ambition and affection to her son, Paul. When he falls in love with a local girl named Miriam, Mrs. Morel becomes jealous and possessive. To please his mother, Paul gives up Miriam, in a rather shabby fashion. Next, he takes up with a married woman named Clara. As if to punish him for falling in love again, Mrs. Morel becomes deathly ill. One of the remarkable features of this novel is the way Lawrence manages to get his readers to dislike yet feel sympathy for Paul and resent yet admire Mrs. Morel.

....

1984
by George Orwell (1949; Knopf, 1992, paperback)

I n some bleak future world, a low-level government functionary named Winston Smith indulges in two unforgivable thought crimes—he has kept a secret diary and he has fallen in love with a woman name Julia. A novel that highlights Western society's failures and carries them to their ultimate, nightmarish extreme.

Also by Orwell:

ANIMAL FARM
(1945; NAL-Dutton, 1983, paperback).

Led by the pigs, the animals on Mr. Jones' farm rebel and vow to form an egalitarian society. But then the pigs are tempted to seize all power for themselves. A merciless satire of revolutions in general and of Stalin's Russia in particular.

....

BRIDESHEAD REVISITED
by Evelyn Waugh (1945; Little, Brown, 1982, paperback)

Brideshead is Waugh's most beautiful book. Charles Ryder was young and ready for romance when he met Sebastian Flyte at Oxford. Together, they share magical interludes at Oxford, in Venice and at Brideshead, the Flytes' glorious estate that comes to dominate Charles' imagination. But the idyll does not last as Sebastian begins to slide into alcoholism. A lush, sad, romantic and ultimately uplifting story about the decline of aristocracy, the end of youth and the discovery of faith.

A HANDFUL OF DUST
by Evelyn Waugh (1934; Little, Brown, 1977, paperback)

Tony Last is perfectly happy playing country squire, puttering about his beloved estate, Hetton and talking with his tenants. But his wife Brenda wants something more exciting—and she finds it in a playboy named John Beaver. From that point things pretty much go to hell. Tony refuses to give Brenda a divorce and promptly goes on a prolonged journey to Brazil. Somewhere in the Amazon he runs into trouble and is rescued by a half-crazed Englishman who expects Tony to spend the rest of his life reading Dickens aloud to him. Waugh wrote two endings for this novel— the Alternate Ending is much more cheerful.

TO THE LIGHTHOUSE
by Virginia Woolf (1927; Harcourt Brace, 1990, paperback)

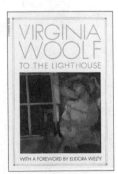

Few authors have been able to capture so succinctly the tensions and differences in perspective that complicate the life of men and women as Virginia Woolf. She wrote in a stream-of-consciousness style to convey her belief that life is a succession of meaningful moments. This enchanting story follows the Ramsey family before and after the death of Mrs. Ramsey—the heart of the clan, the heart of this novel. An excursion to a lighthouse off the

Scottish coast comes to symbolize the different perspectives of the generous Mrs. Ramsey and her cold, self-pitying husband. It is a tremendously moving work about what passes away and what remains.

More by Virginia Woolf:

ORLANDO
(1928; Penguin, 1997, paperback).

Do not grow old," Elizabeth I tells Orlando. By some miracle, Orlando manages to stay young for 400 years, although at one point he does change sexes.

MRS. DALLOWAY
(1925; Harcourt Brace, 1990, paperback).

Virginia Woolf's famous stream of consciousness technique is especially effective in this novel that follows the thoughts of a fashionable London hostess as she prepares for a dinner party she will give that evening.

CHILDREN'S CLASSICS

MADELINE
by Ludwig Bemelmans (1939; Puffin Books, 1977, paperback)

*In an old house in Paris
that was covered with vines
lived twelve little girls
in two straight lines....*

Over half a century has passed since Bemelmans first published his wonderful, rhyming children's story about a spunky little girl who has to have her appendix out. Bemelmans' humorous verse, the first draft of which was penned on the back of a menu in Pete's Tavern in New York, coupled with his illustrations of famous spots around Paris, make for a charming children's book indeed.

GOLDILOCKS AND THE THREE BEARS
by Jan Brett (PaperStar, 1996, paperback)

Jan Brett's illustrated retelling of the little fair-haired house-breaker is a feast for the eye. Her illustrations are detailed and intricate, but they don't overwhelm the story. And as an extra treat, Brett has illustrated in the frames of the main story a little tale about the mice that live in the bears' cottage. Kids are going to love this book and even adults will find themselves studying the beautiful illustrations.

ALICE'S ADVENTURES IN WONDERLAND
by Lewis Carroll,
Illustrated by Angel Dominguez
(1865; Artisan/Workman, 1996, hardcover)

More than 100 years have passed since we first fell down the rabbit hole and wound up in Wonderland. Now artist Angel Dominguez has created a deluxe new edition of Lewis Carroll's immortal story of a sensible little girl who finds herself in a very strange place indeed. The 75 new watercolor paintings capture the magic and gaiety of Alice's adventures with the Cheshire Cat, the Mad Hatter, the Mock Turtle and of course, the White Rabbit. A perfect gift for an adult who has always loved the *Alice* books, or for young readers who haven't yet made the journey to Wonderland.

JAMES AND THE GIANT PEACH
by Roald Dahl (Puffin Books, 1983, paperback)

When young James Henry Trotter accidentally spilled the bag of magic that the strange little man had given him onto the old peach tree, he thought he'd never be free of his evil Aunt Sponge and eviler Aunt Spiker. Little did he realize that his adventures were just beginning. Roald Dahl is one of the most beloved children's authors of all time. *James and the Giant Peach* was his first and one of his finest children's novels.

HARRIET THE SPY
by Louise Fitzhugh (HarperTrophy, 1990, paperback)

There are two kinds of people in the world: those who have read *Harriet the Spy* and those who haven't. If you haven't, you should because this book is an absolute milestone in children's literature. Harriet M. Welsh is an eleven-year-old New Yorker who is determined to grow up to be a famous author. To prepare herself she practices by following a daily spy route and writing down everything she sees in her secret notebook. But her life is turned upside down when her classmates find her notebook and start writing notes of their own—about her. Fitzhugh has created a brilliant portrait of childhood.

. . . .

JOHNNY TREMAIN
by *Esther Forbes* (1943; Houghton Mifflin, 1990, paperback)

This fast-paced children's classic won the Newberry Award in 1944. Johnny Tremain was a silversmith's apprentice until a bad burn cost him the use of his hand. But he's found another job in Boston—delivering newspapers for a small printer. The job brings him into contact with the Sons of Liberty and soon Johnny is involved in spying on the British and all sorts of other adventures. A gripping, very well written, historically accurate novel of the American Revolution.

. . . .

KIM
by *Rudyard Kipling* (1901; New American Library, 1991, paperback)

Kipling drew upon his own childhood in India for this tale of an orphaned yet resourceful Anglo-Indian boy growing up on the streets of Lahore. The heart of this story is "the Great Game," as imperial espionage was known in the days of the Raj. Kim gets his start running little errands for Mahbub Ali, an agent of the British Secret Service. But it's Ali's colleague, Lurgan, who gives the promising boy formal training in the arts of spying and disguise so he can go up against Russian agents in the hill country of northern India. A great adventure story that readers of all ages will enjoy.

THE JUNGLE BOOK AND THE SECOND JUNGLE BOOK
by *Rudyard Kipling*
(1894 & 1895; New American Library, 1995, paperback)

If you're only familiar with the stories of the boy Mowgli from the Disney cartoon, you're in for a surprise. There's nothing romantic about Kipling's jungle where the wild things follow a harsh code. And the strong mythic element of the stories—the jungle as a fallen Eden is a recurring motif—raises these books above their traditional designation as fables for children.

HERCULES:
THE MAN, THE MYTH, THE HERO
by Kathryn Lasky, illustrated by Mark Hess
(Hyperion, 1997, hardcover)

Kathryn Lasky has struck upon an inspired way to retell the myth of Hercules: she uses the first person so young readers can come to understand how this ancient hero felt about a career spent battling monsters and trying to avoid the wrath of his hostile stepmother, Hera. Lasky doesn't sidestep the violence of the legends, or the tragedy of Hercules' life. Still, the old adventure stories are irresistible and Mark Hess' dramatic paintings draw readers into the action.

THE QUITE REMARKABLE ADVENTURES OF THE OWL AND THE PUSSYCAT
by Eric Idle, based on the Poems, Drawings and Writings of Edward Lear (Dove, 1996, paperback)

Eric Idle, famous for his work with the genius comedy ensemble "Monty Python's Flying Circus," expands on Edward Lear's beloved children's poem. In Idle's version the rather shy owl and the winsome and resourceful pussycat sail off in the "beautiful pea green boat" to rescue the legendary Bong tree from an evil fire lord and his henchman, with wonderful comic results. Idle originally wrote this story for his daughter. Luckily he decided to share it with the rest of us.

THE CHRONICLES OF NARNIA
by C.S. Lewis
(1950-56; HarperCollins Juvenile Books, 1994, paperback)

There is no telling how many millions of readers have stepped through the magic door in the wardrobe and found themselves in the enchanted land of Narnia. In seven volumes, Lewis transports his readers to a realm where magic is real and battles are epic struggles between the powers of good and evil. Packed with grand adventures that will thrill girls and boys, the Narnia stories are one of the most absorbing fantasies ever written.

THE STORY OF DOCTOR DOLITTLE

by Hugh Lofting, illustrated by Michael Hague
(Books of Wonder/Morrow Junior Books, 1997, hardcover)

Every kid would like to be able to talk to the animals. Maybe that's why Hugh Lofting's *The Story of Doctor Dolittle* has remained a classic. The story begins when a swallow swoops into Dr. Dolittle's home with the news that monkeys are suffering from an epidemic and need help fast. So Dr. Dolittle, Jip his dog and Dab-Dab, the duck who acts as the doctor's housekeeper, hurry off to Africa. Michael Hague's fifty full-color paintings bring the story to life, especially the battle with the pirates and the scarey crossing of a chasm on a bridge made of monkeys.

PAUL REVERE'S RIDE

by Henry Wadsworth Longfellow, illustrated by Ted Rand
(Puffin/Unicorn Books, 1996, hardcover)

Listen, my children and you shall hear,
Of the midnight ride of Paul Revere.

Longfellow has pretty much disappeared from the school curriculum these days. And while probably few people miss epics like *The Song of Hiawatha* or *Evangeline*, *Paul Revere's Ride* is one Longfellow poem that deserves a come-back. It's got rhythm, rhyme and an exciting story-in other words, it's perfect for kids. Now a new edition makes the poem especially enticing, thanks to a clear design and Ted Rand's richly detailed paintings of 18th-century Massachusetts. If all editions of American classics were this attractive, getting kids to read them would be a lot easier.

CURIOUS GEORGE
by Margret and H.A. Rey (Houghton Mifflin, 1941, paperback)

Millions of boys and girls have been delighted by the adventures of Curious George, the monkey who left the jungle and went to live with the man in the large yellow hat. George is a good monkey, but he can't help getting into scrapes—like calling the fire department when there's no fire and being carried away by a bunch of balloons when he only wanted one. There are seven Curious George stories in all. Start with this one and the young readers in your life will soon be clamoring for the others.

The further adventures of Curious George:

CURIOUS GEORGE TAKES A JOB
by Margret and H.A. Rey (Houghton Mifflin, 1947, paperback).

George tries his hand at cooking, dishwashing, window washing and housepainting before discovering his true vocation as a movie star.

THE STORY OF THE TREASURE SEEKERS
by E. Nesbitt (Puffin Classics, 1994, paperback)

When their father is all but ruined by a dishonest business partner, the plucky Bastable children start roaming the streets of London looking for ways to supplement the family income. For serious scrapes, there's a friendly uncle on hand to save the children. But the real attraction of this story is watching the Bastables find inventive ways to solve their problems on their own.

WHERE THE WILD THINGS ARE

story and pictures by Maurice Sendak
(1963; HarperCollins, 1988, hardcover)

L et the wild rumpus start!" Max exclaims in Sendak's classic tale of fantastic monsters. For more than 30 years, *Wild Things* has been a favorite with children and parents. If you know a kid who doesn't have a copy, run out and buy one today.

THE SNEETCHES AND OTHER STORIES

written and Illustrated by Dr. Seuss
(Random House, 1961, hardcover)

D r. Seuss didn't just help children learn to read and rhyme. He also used his wonderful way with words and pictures to teach them the foolishness of some unfortunate human foibles. His tale of the Star Bellied Sneetches who would have "nothing to do with the plain-bellied sort" exposes the absurdity of prejudice. While the story of two stubborn Zaxes teaches the importance of cooperation and compromise. Seuss's stories are so enjoyable they mask the fact that his lessons are invaluable.

THE WONDERFUL O

by James Thurber (1957; Dove Books, 1994, paperback)

C onfusion reigns when blackhearted pirates banish the letter "O" from the language of a tiny, peaceful island. Poets become pets. People have to move from houses into huts. And a man named Otto Ott could only stutter helplessly when he introduced himself. However confusion becomes rebellion when the islanders realize that there are four "O" words they cannot and will not live without. Thurber wrote for children with the same warmth and wit he used for adults, making this fable a wonderful read indeed.

LES BRAVADES:
A GIFT FOR HIS DAUGHTER

written and illustrated by Orson Welles, afterward by Simon Callow
(Workman, 1996, paperback)

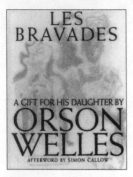

In spring of 1956, Orson Welles happened to be in St. Tropez during the festival known as Les Bravades. From his ringside seat at café tables, Welles captured the celebration in colorful sketches, drawing on whatever bit of paper he had at hand. A few months later, he collected the paintings and drawings, wrote a story to accompany them and produced a unique little book as a Christmas gift for his daughter, Rebecca. Now this exclusive Welles family heirloom is available for the first time in a fine facsimile edition which retains the different sizes of Welles' original artwork and even leaves his typos intact. A delightful work by a gifted artist, director, storyteller and devoted father.

MISTRESS MASHAM'S REPOSE
by T.H. White (1947; Ace Books, 1989, paperback)

On an overgrown island in the middle of a crumbling English estate, a lonely little girl stumbles upon some honest-to-goodness Lilliputians (straight out of Gulliver's Travels)—and sets out on the adventure of a lifetime. Best known for his brilliant retelling of the Arthurian legend, *The Once and Future King*, T.H. White had the habit of writing books that you wish would never end. This masterpiece of fantasy and wonder is one of them.

CLASSICS OF THE STAGE

WHO'S AFRAID OF VIRGINIA WOOLF
by Edward Albee (1962; NAL-Dutton, 1983, paperback)

A middle-aged couple—Martha, the brassy daughter of the president of a small new England college and George, her unsuccessful professor husband—entertain a new faculty member, Nick and his wife, Honey. As the liquor flows, George and Martha keep referring to their imaginary 21-year-old son. Nick admits he only married Honey because she said she was pregnant. And there's a whole slew of other personal revelations as well. But the best part of this play is the shameless bitchiness of the dialogue once George and Martha take the gloves off.

THE MADNESS OF GEORGE III
by Alan Bennett (Faber & Faber, 1995, paperback)

The acclaimed drama of a king ruled by a mysterious disease and a team of quack doctors who try to cure him.

THE LITTLE FOXES
by Lillian Hellman (1939; Yestermorrow, 1993, paperback)

The formerly no-account Hubbard clan has done quite well for themselves. Oscar married Birdie, a lady of the old Southern aristocracy. His brother Ben is a wealthy bachelor. And Regina has done best of all, marrying a rich financier with a bad heart. On most days, the clan has nothing but genial contempt for one another. But then a series of interesting events gives Regina the upper hand over her brothers and she plays it for all it's worth.

Never has the American stage ever seen a creature more ruthless than Regina. Best scene: Horace sends Regina for his heart medicine.

TAMBURLAINE THE GREAT

Parts I and II, by Christopher Marlowe
(1587; University of Nebraska Press, 1967, paperback)

Marlowe's two-part drama follows Tamburlaine, a shepherd whose ruthless quest for power military genius makes him the terror of Asia. London audiences thrilled to the carnage, cruelty, hubris and bombastic speeches when these plays debuted. Great poetry and a rousing good read.

THE CRUCIBLE

by Arthur Miller (1953; Penguin, 1995, paperback)

Miller pilloried Joseph McCarthy's witch hunts for Communists in the 1950s through this powerful drama set during the Salem witch hunts of 1692. When a disturbed little girl's strange malady is diagnosed as the result of witchcraft, the citizens of Salem discover an effective way of settling old scores, eliminating rivals and getting even with ex-lovers. Miller skillfully blends fact with fiction in this play and even borrowed dialogue from the actual court transcripts for the trial sequences.

More by Miller:

DEATH OF A SALESMAN

(1949; Penguin, 1976, paperback).

The Pulitzer prize-winning play that proved the downfall of a little guy could be as tragic as the undoing of Oedipus.

LONG DAY'S JOURNEY INTO NIGHT
by Eugene O'Neill (1941; Yale University Press, 1962, paperback)

It is August 1912 and Mary Tyrone has returned from a sanitarium to her family's summer home. Mary is addicted to morphine. Her husband James is an aging matinee idol. Her son Jamie is a hard-drinking cynic. Her youngest son, Edmund, has tuberculosis, although no one will admit it. As the men of the family squabble and try not to notice that Mary has not been cured of her addiction, Mary herself slips blissfully into the past, imagining that she has joined a convent, or has a glamorous career as a concert pianist, or is an innocent young belle of the ball again. For this story, O'Neill drew upon his own family history.

More of O'Neill:

THE ICEMAN COMETH
(1946; Random House, 1957, paperback).

The scene never leaves a sordid bar where the regulars wait for Hickey, a salesman who always tells the joke about his wife and the iceman. But this time, Hickey has come armed with a much nastier story.

AMADEUS
by Peter Shaffer (HarperCollins, 1981, paperback)

A romantic, lively retelling of the legendary rivalry between the boy wonder, Mozart and the staid court composer, Salieri.

PYGMALION
by George Bernard Shaw (1918; Bantam, 1992, paperback)

Henry Higgins, professor of phonetics, boasts to his friend Colonel Pickering that by teaching a Cockney flower girl to speak properly he could successfully pass her off as a duchess. Pickering takes the bet and poor Eliza Doolittle is subjected to a rigorous course of elocution lessons. As Eliza's speech improves, so does everything else about her—a fact obvious to everyone except the arrogant professor. If the story sounds familiar, its because it was the basis of the Broadway classic, *My Fair Lady*. The ending in Shaw's original, however, is not what you'd expect from a musical comedy.

Another of Shaw's Ladies:

MRS. WARREN'S PROFESSION
(1893; Amereon Ltd., 1995, paperback).

Mrs. Warren's daughter is shocked to learn her mother runs a chain of brothels in the great cities of Europe. The conflict between the two women gives this play its dramatic power, as Mrs. Warren tries to teach her daughter a hard fact—that society only pretends to disapprove of prostitution.

THE IMPORTANCE OF BEING EARNEST
by Oscar Wilde (1895; Norton, 1980, paperback)

A brilliant farce of two young women who are determined to marry men named Ernest and the strenuous, outrageously funny efforts of their beaux to change their names.

EPICS

THE RAMA QUARTET:
RENDEZVOUS WITH RAMA, RAMA II, THE GARDEN OF RAMA, RAMA REVEALED
by Arthur C. Clark with Gentry Lee (Bantam, 1995, paperback)

Clark is one of the great ones of science fiction. In this quartet, a vast cylinder enters Earth's solar system; inside it is a self-contained world filled with peril. The tension is almost unbearable as humans gradually come to understand the truth about this alien world.

....

SHOGUN
by James Clavell (Dell, 1976, paperback)

Clavell's story of shipwrecked Englishman John Blackthorne's struggle to stay alive in 17th-century Japan is based on a long-forgotten historical event. In spite of feudal intrigues, an alien language and culture and hostile Portuguese and Spanish empire builders, Blackthorne manages to carve out a place for himself in a foreign land. A grand adventure that immerses you in the world of feudal Japan.

....

THE REBEL ANGELS, WHAT'S BRED IN THE BONE, THE LYRE OF ORPHEUS
by Robertson Davies (Penguin, 1981, 1985, 1988, paperback)

Robertson Davies was one of the great champions of culture, learning and civility. In this trilogy, as in all of his novels, he explores the intricate relationship that binds together art, spirituality and psychology. In one way or another, all the characters of this trilogy are involved in the Cornish Foundation, an organization established to promote the arts. As the story unfolds, the reader is treated to discussions of gypsy lore, Jungian psychology, the secrets of art forgers, the mysteries of alchemy and astrology and observations of rural life in Canada. Dive into Davies' *Cornish Trilogy* and see if you aren't hooked by his wisdom, erudition and great sense of humor.

UNDERWORLD
by *Don DeLillo* (Scribner, 1997, hardcover)

The year is 1951. At the moment J. Edgar Hoover learns that the Soviets have just tested their first atomic bomb, Bobby Thomson hits his "shot heard 'round the world" and the New York Giants win the Penant. The tensions of the Cold War serve as the backdrop to this novel and the baseball Thomson hit is the story's elusive Holy Grail. Frank Sinatra, Jackie Gleason and Lenny Bruce have cameo appearances. There are more than a few gags about the apocalypse. This is a big novel (over 800 pages), but it's worth your time.

THE ALEXANDRIA QUARTET:
JUSTINE, BALTHASAR, MOUNTOLIVE, CLEA
by *Lawrence Durrell* (1960; Penguin, 1991, paperback)

These four novels are interlocking tales of a handful of lovers, friends and acquaintances in Alexandria, Egypt, during the early years of this century. Durrell assembles a fascinating cast—English and Irish expatriates, prostitutes and ambassadors, Jews and Coptic Christians—and draws some of the most life-like characterizations in modern fiction. But best of all is the sensuality of the stories and the powerful evocation of exotic Alexandria.

THE STUDS LONIGAN TRILOGY:
YOUNG LONIGAN, STUDS LONIGAN, THE YOUNG MANHOOD OF STUDS LONIGAN
by *James T. Farrell*
(1935; University of Illinois Press, 1993, hardcover)

Farrell did his best writing in this famous trilogy. In a working-class Irish neighborhood in Chicago during the 1920s, a street hood named Studs Lonigan has two ambitions: to become "a great guy" and to win the hand of the lovely Lucy. But, as Studs and his boys grow older, their wild behavior becomes more dangerous. A Chicago Irish boy himself, Farrell wrote this vivid, powerful story from his heart.

THE HISTORY OF TOM JONES, A FOUNDLING
by Henry Fielding (1749; Modern Library, 1994, hardcover)

Henry Fielding's brilliant account of a foundling named Tom Jones remains one of the most entertaining novels ever written. According to the family that adopts Tom, he is a charming rogue who was "born to be hanged." Young Tom's hilarious adventures get him into a host of troubles (most of them amorous). Yet he's always true in his fashion to the great love of his life, Sophia Western, the squire's daughter. Although Tom Jones is over 250 years old, it is one of those rare novels that wears its age lightly.

THE TOWER OF BEOWULF
by Parke Godwin (Avon, 1996, paperback)

In the original Anglo-Saxon, Beowulf is a thrilling read. But in modern English translations the epic tends to be heavy sledding. So Godwin has drawn upon his considerable imaginative gifts to give new life to the ancient legend. He focuses on what the poem leaves out—the characters' motivations (especially the monsters), the conflicting spiritual realms of the Danes and the Christians—and he offers his own interpretation of what makes a hero. All sagas should be this much fun to read.

YANDILLI TRILOGY
by Rodney Hall (Noonday/Farrar, Straus & Giroux, 1995, paperback)

The Yandilli Trilogy is the ultimate Outback epic. A young slave laborer narrates the settling of Australia in The Second

Bridegroom. An English missionary tells her strange story in
The Grisly Wife. And a harrowing murder mystery is featured in
Captivity Captive.

LES MISERABLES
by Victor Hugo (1862; Fawcett Books, 1989, paperback)

Long before there was the musical, there was this grand,
sweeping epic of a novel. Jean Valjean, a hardened criminal,
is at first confused—and then converted—when he encounters
strangers who treat him with kindness. But pursuing Valjean across
the years is the ruthless, vengeful Inspector Javert.

EYES OF EAGLES, DREAMS OF EAGLES, TALONS OF EAGLES
by William W. Johnstone (Pinnacle Books, 1996, paperback)

The Jamie MacCallister trilogy is a tough, terse, code-of-the-
West kind of story. In these three books, Jamie survives a
raid that massacres his family, escapes from his Shawnee captors
and meets Kate, his life-long love. Jamie and Kate head west, where
he fights at the Alamo before the family settles in Colorado. Then
the Civil War breaks out, dividing father and sons and pitting
brother against brother. Johnstone spins an action-packed saga
about the rugged men and strong women who settled the American
frontier.

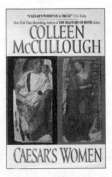

CAESAR'S WOMEN
by Colleen McCullough (Avon, 1997, paperback)

What was Julius Caesar like before he
conquered Gaul, crossed the Rubicon and
met his fate on the Ides of March? In this
wonderfully researched novel, McCullough
draws us into the private life of one of the most
influential men of the ancient world. The
women in Caesar's life play a large role in the

story—his mother, wife, daughter, lover—but the bulk of the plot is taken up with intrigue in Rome and conquest abroad during the waning days of the Roman Republic.

More by McCullough:

FORTUNE'S FAVORITES
(Avon, 1994, paperback).

A big sweeping novel that chronicles the rivalry between the dictator, Sulla and the military genius, Pompey. Plus the rise of young Julius Caesar and a historically accurate retelling of the story of Spartacus.

....

HAWAII
by James Michener (Fawcett Crest, 1986, paperback)

Of all the Michener epics, this one is the best. Michener weaves an enormously satisfying saga that includes the sub-oceanic volcanic eruption that formed the islands, the settlement of the islands by the Polynesians, the advent of zealous Calvinist missionaries from New England, the corrupting influence of Yankee sailors and the new vitality brought by Chinese and Japanese immigrants.

Also by Michener:

CENTENNIAL
(Fawcett Crest, 1987, paperback).

Indians, mountain men, Amish refugees, half-breed renegades, cattle barons, hucksters, lawmen. Some readers say this is really his best novel.

....

THE TALE OF GENJI
by Lady Murasaki (The Modern Library, 1977, hardcover)

The first book we would recognize as a novel was written in the first years of the 11th century by a lady of Japan's Imperial Court. There, Lady Murasaki found all the passions of the human heart, albeit concealed or distorted by the conventions of this elegant society. In this graceful world she set the story of the handsome Prince Genji, his wife and his primary mistress, Lady Rokujo, whose hatred for the prince's other lovers provides many interesting episodes in this novel. This is a big book, so savor it in small portions. You'll find that Lady Murasaki combines the restraint of Jane Austen with Tolstoy's profound understanding of the human heart.

THE BOUNTY TRILOGY
by Charles Nordhoff and James Norman Hall
(1932; Little, Brown, 1985, paperback)

These three novels tell the whole story of Fletcher Christian, Captain Bligh and the fate of all the men who sailed on the Bounty. *Mutiny on the Bounty* details the mutiny, the mutineer's idyllic months back on Tahiti and their trial in England. *Men Against the Sea* follows Bligh and the 19 men who remained loyal to him in their 3600-mile voyage in an open boat—still one of the most astonishing feats of human courage and navigational skill on record. *Pitcairn's Island* accompanies the escaped mutineers to their refuge on a remote South Seas island, their efforts to establish a primitive society and the bloody rivalries that nearly destroyed them all.

A DANCE TO THE MUSIC OF TIME
by Anthony Powell (University of Chicago Press, 1983, paperback).

In this novel written in four volumes, Nicholas Jenkins, an urbane and reticent upper-class Englishman, relates his most significant experiences from his days as a schoolboy in the '20s, through his days as an aspiring writer with bohemian set of friends in the '30s, through the agony of World War II and finally as an old man encountering late the counterculture of the '60s and '70s.

The novels are exquisitely written and Powell has an especially fine ear for dialogue—a serious plus as he is constantly moving through a world of brilliant conversationalists.

SWANN'S WAY
by Marcel Proust (1913; Vintage International, 1989, paperback)

By dipping a madeleine in his tea, Marcel, the narrator of *Swann's Way*, is swept back in time to his childhood. So begins the first volume of *Remembrance of Things Past*, Proust's monumental meditation on time, memory and art. This book, the first volume of the series, focuses on Swann, a Jewish bourgeois who is just beginning to make his way in Parisian society. Through Marcel's memories and Swann's experiences, Proust examines life in France at the turn of the century, when the aristocracy went into decline and the middle class began its ascendancy.

FIRE FROM HEAVEN, THE PERSIAN BOY, FUNERAL GAMES
by Mary Renault (Vintage, 1977, paperback)

This trilogy, based on the life of Alexander the Great, is one of Mary Renault's finest achievements. *Fire From Heaven* sets the young prince between his scheming mother, Olympias and his warlike father, Philip. *The Persian Boy* depicts Alexander at the pinnacle of his career, the conqueror of Persia and in love with a young male courtesan who was once the lover of the Persian Great King. Finally, *Funeral Games* records the end of Alexander's reign and the rivalries that destroyed his empire.

THE AWAKENING LAND
by Conrad Richter (Random House, 1966, hardcover)

Readers who are familiar with this epic novel of pioneer America tend to be impassioned about it. (Author David McCullough once wrote an admiring essay about Richter). The central character of *The Awakening Land* is Sayward Luckett, who comes to Ohio from Pennsylvania with her parents and her sisters in the years after the Revolution. They are rough, illiterate folk who hack out a life in a primeval wilderness. Richter's goal—and he accomplished it beautifully—was to tell the story of people who are entirely forgotten yet had an enduring impact on American history. Worth searchiong for.

LONDON
by Edward Rutherfurd (Crown, 1997, hardcover)

London is a completely satisfying epic read about every reader's favorite city. Rutherfurd assembles a core cast of several families and follows their descendants through the centuries—from 2000 years ago when the Britons prepared to repulse an invader named Julius Caesar, to the advent of Christianity, the Viking and Norman invasions, the upheavals of the Reformation, the Great Fire and the Blitz. Along the way we meet great characters such as Thomas Becket and Christopher Wren and encounter such legendary partnerships as Victoria and Albert and Fortnum and Mason. An absolutely addictive saga. Don't miss it.

Rutherfurd's First Epic:

SARUM
(Ivy Books, 1992, paperback).

A big, sweeping multi-generational chronicle of the English town we know as Salisbury.

THE RAJ QUARTET:
THE JEWEL IN THE CROWN, THE DAY OF THE SCORPION, THE TOWERS OF SILENCE, A DIVISION OF THE SPOILS
by Paul Scott (Avon, 1979, paperback)

With two terrible events—the rape of a young Englishman and the tragic end of an elderly English schoolteacher—Scott launches an epic set in India during the last years of the British Raj. His main characters include the well-bred Layton clan, the sadistic policeman Merrick and the outcast Anglo-Indian Hari Kumar—an unlikely cast whose destinies are woven together as the Empire wanes and an independent India begins to rise.

IVANHOE
by Sir Walter Scott (1819; Bantam, 1988, paperback)

I s there a novelist who wouldn't like to enjoy the enormous influence Scott had on European and American society? The impact of Scott's tales of high romance in the Middle Ages was felt in the arts, in opera, even in the Anglican Church. His tale of Ivanhoe, the fearless Saxon knight and champion of the oppressed, has always been his most popular novel because it has everything: lust, treachery, dungeons, accusations of witchcraft, trial by combat, a lovers triangle and a cast that includes Richard the Lionheart, the sniveling Prince John and Robin Hood. Just dive in.

More Scott:

THE TALISMAN
(1825; Everyman's Classic Library, 1991, paperback).

Scott based this story on an actual talisman brought back from the Crusades by Sir Simon Lockhart and kept among his descendants for centuries. This grand adventures in the Holy Land almost surpassed Ivanhoe in popularity.

WITH FIRE AND SWORD
by Henryk Sienkiewicz (Macmillan, 1993, paperback)

W hat we've got here is a Slavic *Gone with the Wind*, translated for the very first time into English. Sienkiewicz's big, splashy, action-packed novel recounts the noble deeds of Polish knights and their battles against Cossacks and Tartars. They don't write rousing novels like this anymore.

THE GREENLANDERS
by Jane Smiley (Fawcett, 1996, paperback)

S miley bases her book on an actual historical mystery. For 400 years, a Viking colony flourished in Greenland but then inexplicably disappeared. In the settlement's final days, Margaret Gunnarson forsakes her husband for an adventurous Norwegian sailor, while her quiet brother Gunnar pursues a quiet quest for wisdom that will outlive the colony. Here are all the elements of an authentic Viking saga, coupled with stunning descriptions of a wild, unknown world.

. . . .

EAST OF EDEN
by John Steinbeck (1952; Viking Press, 1984, paperback)

Steinbeck is better known for his relatively brief, tightly controlled novels. In *East of Eden*, he lets go and produces a grand saga, set in 19th-century California, of a murderous rivalry between brothers and a woman so depraved that her sins haunt her children. Steinbeck takes a family epic and lifts it into the realm of myth.

. . . .

THE ISLE OF GLASS, THE GOLDEN HORN, THE HOUNDS OF GOD
by Judith Tarr

Tarr's books are a brilliant bend of history and fantasy. This romantic trilogy, set at the time of Richard the Lionheart and the Crusades, follows the adventures of Alfred of St. Ruan, whose mystic powers permit him to move easily between the world of elves and the world of mortals. Worth searching for.

. . . .

WAR AND PEACE
by Leo Tolstoy (1866; Viking, 1982, paperback)

Look, you said you were looking for a nice fat novel, right? And this is a great story, even if it is a bit on the longish side. Tolstoy tackles the big themes here-the importance of family, the loyalty that binds friends together, the miracle of being in love. And you can't help being moved by the gallant Prince Andrei falling in battle, or the Rostov family fleeing from burning Moscow, or the bewitching Natasha growing to womanhood. Dive in.

THE SNOW QUEEN, WORLD'S END, THE SUMMER QUEEN
by Joan Vinge (Warner Books, 1989, paperback)

Vinge blends the fairy tales of Hans Christian Andersen with science fiction in this trilogy of the barbarous world of the Summer People who struggle to free themselves from their alien overlords.

EROTICA

THE FERMATA
by Nicholson Baker (Vintage, 1995, paperback)

Baker brings an adolescent fantasy to life. At age 35, Arno Stine has the power of real-life freeze-frame: he can actually stop time. So, he uses this unique magic to freeze women and then undress them. *The Fermata* leads one to believe that the obsessed, hormone-driven teenager lives on inside every man's head.

Also by Baker:

VOX
(Random House, 1993, paperback).

Jim and Abby, separated by 3000 miles but connected by the telephone, indulge in a marathon of phone sex.

THE COMPLETE KAMA SUTRA
Translated by Alain Daniélou (Park Street Press, 1995, paperback)

This is the first complete, unabridged, unexpurgated translation of the 4th-century Hindu guide to discovering "infinite delight" in more than 100 years. While it's true that some of the possibilities mentioned here require a certain agility, most of the book offers pragmatic suggestions for enhancing your partner's pleasure, as well as your own. Any book that's stayed in print for 1600 years must know what it's talking about.

VENUS BOUND:
THE EROTIC VOYAGE OF THE OLYMPIA PRESS
AND ITS WRITERS
by John de St. Jorre (Random House, 1996, hardcover)

Maurice Girodias founded the Olympia Press in Paris just after World War I. He devoted himself to publishing the books censors in Great Britain and the United States had banned. His catalog included *Lolita, The Ginger Man* and all those *Tropics* books of Henry Miller. But literary crusading is expensive, so to bankroll his revolution Girodias brought out a line of real dirty books. (Perhaps you are familiar with one of his best-sellers, a book called *Candy*). *Venus Bound* is one of those rare books that combines solid scholarship with a good sense of humor.

THE GINGER MAN
by J.P. Donleavy (1955; Atlantic Monthly Press, 1988, paperback)

In 1950s Dublin—a most unlikely capital of promiscuity— Sebastian Dangerfield has no trouble finding women willing to climb into bed with him. But his friend Kenneth cannot lose his virginity no matter how hard he tries.

BLUE EYES, BLACK HAIR
by Marguerite Duras (Pantheon, 1987, paperback)

A young man and a young woman share a rented room together. They are strangers, but the woman reminds the man of a beautiful youth he saw once and with whom he fell instantly in love. A masterpiece of sensuality, worth searching for.

SALAMMBO
by Gustave Flaubert (1862; Penguin Classics, 1977, paperback)

Readers in 19th-century France were shocked by the frank sensuality of the characters in this historical novel set during the war between Rome and Carthage. Flaubert worked especially hard to re-create the exact details of life in two ancient empires.

LADY CHATTERLEY'S LOVER
by D.H. Lawrence (1928; Bantam Books, 1987, paperback)

This is the novel that made English author D.H. Lawrence a household word. A war wound has rendered Lord Chatterley impotent, so Lady Chatterley turns to the forthright, earthy gamekeeper Mellors. For its strong language and frank descriptions of sexual situations, Lady Chatterley's Lover was banned in England until 1959 and in the United States until 1960. The 1950s expurgated version is still floating around, so be certain that you have the original.

PASSIONATE HEARTS:
THE POETRY OF SEXUAL LOVE
Edited by Wendy Maltz (New World Library, 1997, paperback)

Sex has a way of softening limbs, / oiling joints and melding hearts," writes poet Wendy Lee in this collection of sensuous love poetry. Editor Wendy Maltz, a licensed sex therapist, has no patience for the sentimental baloney that usually passes for love poetry. So she's collected, as she puts it, "poems that inspire... poems in which heart connection was at the core of the sexual experience." With works by Marge Piercy, Pablo Neruda, Galway Kinnell, e.e. cummings and Raymond Carver, among others, this anthology proves that high culture can be very sexy.

TROPIC OF CANCER
by Henry Miller (1934; Modern Library, 1983, hardcover)

Until 1961, Miller's shocking journal of a penniless American in Paris was banned in the United States. Based very closely on his own life, Miller's hero scrounges for money, devours books and makes love as vigorously and imaginatively as possible. One of the great naughty books of the 20th century.

Also by Miller:

TROPIC OF CAPRICORN
(1939; Grove Press, 1987, paperback)

A young man attempts to discover who he is through a round of sexual escapades.

SEVEN HUNDRED KISSES:
A YELLOW SILK BOOK OF EROTIC WRITING
Edited by Lily Pond (Harper San Francisco, 1997, paperback)

Yellow Silk, a magazine of literary erotica, favors writing that is as smart as it is sexy. Now Lily Pond, the founder and editor, brings together a titillating collection of erotic writing by contemporary authors. There's Carlos Fuentes' rollicking "Apollo and the Whores," a sensual flirtation excerpted from Walter Mosley's "The Little Yellow Dog" and Kathryn Steadman's "What She Wrote Him," an examination of an erotic obsession. Plus you'll find contributions from Tobias Wolff, Jane Smiley and Dorothy Allison. *Seven Hundred Kisses* is a stylish, seductive anthology.

THE LITERARY COMPANION TO SEX
Collected by Fiona Pitt-Kethley (Random House, 1994, paperback)

Remember when you were in high school and you'd fold down the pages of the "good parts" in dirty books? It seems that Fiona Pitt-Kethley did, too. Now she's collected all the best erotica from more than 2000 years of great literature. From the exotic-erotica of the Arabian Nights, to Milton's beautiful description of the First Lovers in the Garden of Eden, to Benjamin Franklin's practical "Advice on the Choice of a Mistress." Plus, excerpts from Anais Nin, D.H. Lawrence, Sappho, Henry Miller and lots more. It's naughty. It's entertaining. And since it's literature, it's good for you.

BELINDA
by Anne Rice (Jove Publications, 1988, paperback)

You may also find "Anne Rampling" given as the author for this novel—it was Anne Rice's nom de plume when she wrote erotica. Belinda, a sexually precocious 16-year-old, seeks out a distinguished illustrator of children's books and they begin an affair. Soon the artist is doing paintings of Belinda that become increasingly explicit and bizarre until they even frighten him. And then, Belinda disappears.

More by Rice/Rampling:

EXIT TO EDEN
(Ballantine, 1996, paperback).

In the Caribbean is an island devoted to sexual pleasure in all its variety. But there's trouble in paradise when the mistress of the island falls in love with one of her boy toys.

WIDE SARGASSO SEA
by Jean Rhys (Norton, 1998, paperback)

What was she like, the poor madwoman in the attic, before she married Mr. Rochester? In this imaginative prequel to *Jane Eyre*, Jean Rhys imagines Antoinette Cosway enjoyed a languid, sensuous life in the West Indies before she met the cold, proud Edward Rochester. Why did she marry? And what happened once they arrived in England? You'll find closely guarded secrets and lush sexuality on every page as Rhys unravels one of the great enigmas of English literature.

FEVER:
SENSUAL STORIES BY WOMEN WRITERS
Edited by Michele Slung (HarperCollins, 1995, paperback)

Imagine what sex would be like in the bedchamber of a Hindu bride, or in a Texas taco joint, for that matter. If there is a theme to this collection of short stories, it's that sensuous experiences can happen anywhere. Susan Musgrave's "Valentine's Day in Jail" introduces a woman reporter who regularly visits her lover, Angel, in prison. Nancy Holder's "Love in the Wax Museum" recounts what happens when a committed lesbian couple visit a nephew in California. And Susan St. Aubin's "Marian's Ears" follows the adventures of man who finds his lover's ears delicious. These are witty, sexy, intelligent stories.

THE FIRST LOVE STORIES
by *Diane Wolkstein* (HarperCollins, 1991, hardcover)

Wolkstein, a professional storyteller, narrates the world's oldest and most potent love stories. There's the Egyptian legend of Isis and Osiris, in which love is stronger than death; the Hindu tale of passion tamed in Shiva and Sati; the sensuality of the Hebrew Song of Songs; the Greco-Roman love-conquers-all myth of Psyche and Eros; and two tales of doomed love: from the Arab world, the story of Layla and Majnun and from the Celtic world, the tale of Tristan and Iseult. In her vivid retelling, Wolkstein conveys the erotic power of these ancient love stories.

EXERCISE & FITNESS

TRAILSIDE HIKING AND BACKPACKING
A Complete Guide, by Karen Berger (Norton, 1995, paperback)

What every hiker needs is good boots. What every hiker should avoid is wearing cotton. In this compendium, Karen Berger walks you through the details that can make the difference between a joyous outdoor adventure and a miserable ordeal in the wilderness. She covers food, gear, how to find your way in the woods, how to set up a tent, even how to go camping with kids. A must-have for anyone who owns boots and a backpack.

THE COMPLETE BOOK OF ABS
by Kurt Brungardt (Villard, 1998, paperback)

A best-selling, comprehensive workout guide for toning the stomach. Over 100 exercises and 300 illustrations; plus trainer's tips and advice on how to work the abs without putting stress on your back.

THE COMPLETE BOOK OF BUTT & LEGS
by Kurt, Mike and Brett Brungardt (Villard, 1995, paperback)

Your lower body doesn't get much of a workout moving from the car to the desk chair to the couch. You know it. The Brungardt boys know it. So they've put together an illustrated guide with 100 effective exercises for men and women to tone up the butt and the legs. No matter what your personal fitness level may be, there are exercises in this book you can do to improve the muscle groups of your lower body. Plus, you get essential tips about diet and mental attitude.

20-MINUTE YOGA WORKOUTS
by Alice Christensen, with the American Yoga Association
(Fawcett Books, 1995, paperback)

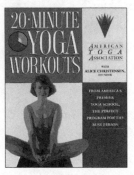

If you've got 20 minutes, you can practice yoga. This authoritative guidebook (notice that it's endorsed by the American Yoga Association) helps even the busiest people enjoy the benefits of a yoga workout. Everything you'd expect is here—breathing exercises, gentle yoga warm-up routines, classic asans and techniques for relaxation and meditation. There are even special workouts for seniors and pregnant women. This copiously illustrated, step-by-step guidebook is perfect for people who think they don't have time to practice yoga.

EXPLOSIVE POWER AND STRENGTH:
COMPLEX TRAINING FOR MAXIMUM RESULTS
by Donald A. Chu, Ph.D.(Rodale, 1996, paperback)

Explosive Power and Strength unlocks the secrets to the thing everyone who works out wants—fast, noticeable results. You'll learn to create your own customized workout program, the proper ways to train safely and how to tailor your program to your favorite sports. Find out how exercising with a medicine ball can improve your upper body strength; how single-arm rows can build powerful shoulders; which simple exercise will add inches to your vertical jump for basketball or volleyball; and how to add more strength to your running stride.

NANCY CLARK'S SPORTS NUTRITION GUIDEBOOK
by Nancy Clark, M.S., R.D.
(Human Kinetics Publishers, 1996, paperback)

It doesn't matter whether you run in the park just a couple times a week or haunt the gym everyday: you still need a winning diet to boost your energy and improve your workout routine. As the dietary consultant to the Boston Celtics, Nancy Clark can teach you low-fat eating strategies, the best pretraining and precompetition meals, secrets of effective carbo-loading, plus recipes for high-protein blender drinks. This is winning nutritional advice that will help you increase your strength and endurance.

THE ESSENTIAL GUIDE TO NATURE WALKING IN THE UNITED STATES
by Charles Cook (Henry Holt, 1997, paperback)

It would be hard to find a more enthusiastic cheerleader for walking than Charles Cook. He devotes almost a quarter of his book to describing the benefits of walking to body, mind and spirit and detailing what you will need to walk well—including what to wear and what to carry with you. Then he gets down to identifying walking sites in every state. He describes the plants and wildlife you'll encounter, lists individual walking trails by distance and level of difficulty and supplies the address and phone number of each park if you need additional information. If you are a walker, this guide will tell you some significant walking trails to consider across the country.

EAT SMART, THINK SMART:
HOW TO USE NUTRIENTS TO ACHIEVE PEAK PERFORMANCE
by Robert Haas (HarperCollins, 1995, paperback)

Yes, fish is brain food-the nutrients found in seafood improve your memory and ability to learn. Green tea will do the same thing and it will burn fat. And, the nutrients in peanuts help you stay focused on the task at hand. These are just some of the useful facts you'll encounter in this useful guide.

Also by Robert Haas:

EAT TO WIN
(NAL Dutton, 1985, paperback).

What to eat to burn fat, build muscle and improve your athletic performance.

......

BICYCLING COAST TO COAST:
A COMPLETE ROUTE GUIDE-VIRGINIA TO OREGON
by Donna Lynn Ikenberry (The Mountaineers, 1996, paperback)

Based upon the Adventure Cycling Association's "Transamerica Bicycle Route," this guide provides a 77-day tour that will take you clear across the continent. The book is wonderfully thorough with mile-by-mile directions, important observations such as when the shoulder of the road disappears, recommended sidetrips and where to find motels, campgrounds, markets and restaurants. Many detailed maps are included, as well as more than 100 photographs of what you will see along the way. Plus, you get safety tips and candid assessments of the best times of the year to ride. An excellent companion, whether you plan to do the whole stretch in one epic journey, or just follow part of the route for a day or a weekend.

......

THE ULTIMATE LEAN ROUTINE:
12-WEEK CROSS TRAINING & FAT LOSS PROGRAM
by Greg Isaacs (Summit Group, 1996, paperback)

Isaacs, the corporate fitness director for the Warner Brothers Studios, insists that his cross training and nutrition program can pay off with up to 30% loss in body fat, 50% increase in aerobic fitness and 40% increase in muscle strength—all in 12 weeks. Even if you don't achieve such amazing gains that fast, this book is a sound beginning for a fitness program.

HIGH-PERFORMANCE NUTRITION:
THE TOTAL EATING PLAN TO MAXIMIZE YOUR WORKOUT

by Susan M. Kleiner and Maggie Greenwood-Robinson
(John Wiley & Sons, 1996, hardcover)

The cornerstone to any serious workout program is good nutrition. So nutrition and fitness experts Kleiner and Greenwood-Robinson have developed a diet that will give you energy to get through intense work outs and build muscle. Their 30-day plan suggests 65% carbohydrates, 15% protein and 20% fat. Plus, they include sensible chapters on vitamin, herbal and fiber supplements and nutrition for vegetarian, pregnant and older athletes. If you're a highly motivated athlete, this is the no-nonsense nutrition book you've been looking for.

....

THE NEW YORK CITY BALLET WORKOUT:
FIFTY STRETCHES AND EXERCISES ANYONE CAN DO FOR A STRONG, GRACEFUL AND SCULPTED BODY

by Peter Martins, with photographs by Paul Kolnik and Richard Corman
(Morrow, 1997, hardcover)

Maybe you won't have a body like Baryshnikov's, but you can be stronger and enjoy more flexibility by following these 50 powerful exercises. Peter Martins, ballet master for The New York City Ballet, teaches you center exercises to develop your coordination and stability, routine movements to strength the abdomen and leg movements which can (in time) give you the legs of a dancer. More than 300 photographs of NYCB dancers demonstrate how to perform the exercises correctly. Whether you're a serious athlete or seriously out of shape, this workout program can help you attain a lean, toned body.

....

TRAILSIDE BIKING: A COMPLETE GUIDE
by Peter Oliver (Norton, 1995, paperback)

What's the point of a mountain bike if you always ride on paved roads and trails? Do you really need a rear view mirror? And how do you change a flat tire? This friendly, down-to-earth handbook is packed with reliable advice on everything from negotiating hills to emergency repairs to selecting the bike that's right for you. It's durable, waterproof vinyl covers make it ideal for the road and its compact size means you can take it along when you shop for a new bike or equipment. Peter Oliver even tells what gear not to buy. A must-have for anyone who owns a bicycle.

HARVEY PENNICK'S LITTLE RED BOOK: LESSONS AND TEACHINGS FROM A LIFETIME IN GOLF
by Harvey Pennick (Simon & Schuster,1992, paperback)

In pithy epigrams and anecdotes, Harvey Pennick, one of the game's most inspiring teachers, offers encouragement for golfers at every skill level, including practical advice on their swing, how to keep calm on the course and much more. A classic of golf literature.

FIT OVER FORTY: A REVOLUTIONARY PLAN TO ACHIEVE LIFELONG PHYSICAL AND SPIRITUAL HEALTH AND WELL-BEING
by James M. Rippe, M.D. (Morrow, 1996, hardcover)

Cardiologist James Rippe is director of the Center for Clinical and Lifestyle Research at Tufts University—and the man who established the first-ever fitness standards for people over 40. His plan for baby boomers starts with ten self-tests to evaluate your own fitness level, then moves on to a program that includes cardiovascular fitness, muscular endurance, flexibility, low body fat, good nutritional habits and stress reduction. Plus he offers case histories of out-of-shape people who turned their lives around. This is the book that could get you to the gym at last.

BACKACHE: WHAT EXERCISES WORK
by Dava Sobel and Arthur C. Klein
(St. Martin's Press, 1996, paperback)

I f you suffer from recurring backaches, these exercises can help. Like personal trainers, Sobel and Klein suggest how you can fit exercise into your daily schedule and teach you more than 30 different exercises that stretch and strengthen the muscles of your upper and lower back. Plus, you'll get tips on how to adjust your lifestyle to keep back trouble from ever returning. Here at last is a sensible, breakthrough book that offers relief from backache.

5-MINUTE MASSAGE
by Robert Thé (Sterling, 1995, paperback)

H ere are simple self-massage sequences you can perform in the office or at home to give quick relief to a stiff neck, or release tension in shoulders, back, arms, hands—anywhere. You can even apply these skills to relax a partner. Photographs illustrate each step of the techniques.

FIRST-CLASS FICTION

SOMEWHERE EAST OF LIFE
by Brian Aldiss (Carroll & Graf, 1994, hardcover)

Burnell, a nice guy who travels around the globe trying to save threatened architectural monuments, has been robbed. Somebody's stolen 10 years' worth of his memory—including the racy parts from his marriage which have been sold as soft porn. A solid, dependable type, Burnell tries to carry on with his work, but he really would like his memories back.

THE HARD TO CATCH MERCY
by William Baldwin (Fawcett, 1995, paperback)

For Willie T. Allson, the son and grandson of Confederate heroes, life in the Carolina Low Country in 1916 is not easy. His Cousin Brother hears spirit voices—some of them speaking French. His Grandpa Allson is obsessed with a rich dowry hidden from the Yankees during the Tragic War of Southern Independence—it seems no one in the family can remember where they stashed it. And now two of the family's cows have gotten themselves lost—clearly a job for the famous Hard to Catch (his first name) Mercy (his last name). One of the most outlandish Southern comedies since Flannery O'Connor.

MAPP & LUCIA
by E.F. Benson (HarperCollins, 1988, paperback)

Lucia, an Englishwoman with Italian affectations, locks horns with the imperious Miss Mapp to determine who shall preside over society in the village of Tilling. Both are women of iron will and reptilian cunning, so their feud is one of the most exquisite literary entertainments since Austen's Elizabeth Bennet duked it out with Lady Catherine De Burgh.

Also by Benson:

QUEEN LUCIA
(HarperCollins, 1988, paperback).

In her debut novel, Lucia attempts to convert stuffy British society to her bizarre personal vision of cosmopolitan culture.

MISS MAPP
(HarperCollins, 1988, paperback).

Bad enough that Mapp's neighbors fail to maintain her high standards of public and private decorum; now she must fend off the romantic advances of two retired army officers.

....

ARTHUR REX
by Thomas Berger (Dell Delacorte Press, 1970, hardcover)

The New York Times called Thomas Berger one of "our first-rate literary wise guys." In Arthur Rex, Berger has written the naughtiest version ever of the Arthurian legend. From the overpowering body odor of Uther Pendragon to Sir Gawain's heroic efforts to control his libido to the deliciously wicked team of Morgan le Fay and Mordred the Bastard, Berger puts a refreshing new spin on these familiar tales. Worth searching for.

....

THE FEUD
by Thomas Berger (Delacorte, 1983, paperback)

One Saturday morning, Dolf Beeler of Hornbeck stopped by Bud Bullard's hardware store in Millville to get a can of paint remover. Dolf was chewing an unlit stogie at the time and the store had a strict no smoking policy. The presence of the cigar is enough to cause an uproar that ends with Bud Bullard's loony cousin pulling a gun on Dolf and Dolf blubbering that he didn't want to die. Hours later, Bullard's hardware store burns to the ground. Then Beeler's car blows up in his driveway. The feud is on! And before it ends, most of the leading citizens of Hornbeck and Millville will be drawn into this wickedly funny vendetta.

PIG
by *Andrew Cowan* (Harcourt Brace, 1997, paperback)

For as long as he can remember, Danny (now 15 years old) has found refuge from his battling parents at his grandparents' cottage-and-pig-farm. When Gran dies and Grandad is hustled off to a nursing home, Danny volunteers to take care of the cottage and the family's last pig. But developers from a theme park called LeisureLand have designs on the property. Then Danny's life takes a turn for the better when he meets Surinder, a Pakistani girl. Can Danny get the girl, hold on to the cottage and save the pig?

REDEYE: A WESTERN
by *Clyde Egderton* (Algonquin Books, 1995, paperback)

In turn-of-the-century Colorado, a wacky band of frontier entrepreneurs have come together to transform the Mesa Largo cliff dwelling into the Old West's first tourist trap. Among the scoundrels, innocents and snake oil salesmen who try to cash in on this opportunity are a freelance embalmer, a Mormon bishop and his passel of "former" wives, an Indian philosopher, an unbalanced bounty hunter and his prize catch dog, Redeye. This is the strangest western you'll ever read and it springs straight out of America's tall tale tradition.

HELLO DARLING, ARE YOU WORKING?
by *Rupert Everett* (Avon, 1994, paperback)

You know Rupert Everett as the sexy star of My Best Friend's Wedding and Another Country. Now he's branched out into fiction, writing a campy, zany novel that was a blockbuster in England. His hero is Rhys Waverel, a soap-opera hunk who suddenly finds himself out of work and penniless. Deciding to market his best asset, the unflappable Rhys becomes a boy toy for a rich widow. From that point, Rhys (and the story) take off to English country homes, wild Paris nightclubs and a decadent costume ball in Tangier. Everett has revived the art of the smart English satire.

THE BOOKSHOP
by Penelope Fitzgerald
(Mariner Books/Houghton Mifflin, 1997, paperback)

It is the 1950s in Hardborough, a small English village on the Suffolk coast. Mrs. Green, a widow, has opened a bookshop in a dilapidated building where her influential neighbor, Mrs. Gamart, had planned to open a village arts center. When, in their haste to buy copies of Lolita, the villagers clog the sidewalk outside the bookshop, canny Mrs. Gamart calls the police: the throng is obstructing traffic. And because the shop assistant ringing up all those purchases of Nabokov's naughtiest book is under age, Mrs. Gamart tosses in a charge of corrupting a minor. And so we're off with a first-rate English satire. Don't pass up *The Bookshop*.

Another by Penelope Fitzgerald:

INNOCENCE
(Holt, 1986, paperback).

An 18-year-old Florentine contessa is determined to win the affection of a brilliant young doctor, who is just as determined to avoid all romantic entanglements. A hilarious Italian comedy of manners.

THE PYRATES
by George MacDonald Fraser (HarperCollins, 1995, paperback)

Imagine what would have happened if Mel Brooks had directed an Errol Flynn pirate movie and you'll get an idea of the inspired lunacy of The Pyrates. George MacDonald Fraser's characters come right out of Central Casting—a dashing, clean-cut hero; a sassy blond heroine; a roguish anti-hero; a snarling, sadistic villain; a sultry temptress; some blustering English admirals, smarmy Spanish viceroys and the obligatory ensemble of snaggle-toothed buccaneers. And to keep the story moving, Fraser throws in the occasional zany anachronism—like pirate shop stewards. All parodies should be this successful and this much fun.

ARMADILLOS & OLD LACE
by Kinky Friedman (Bantam, 1995, paperback)

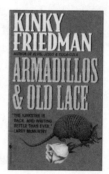

The most modest of authors, Kinky Friedman has named his wacky private detective "Kinky Friedman." This time, our hero returns to his parents' summer camp in the Texas hill country, where strange things are happening: elderly ladies are dropping dead on their 76th birthdays. Kinky could solve this mystery overnight were it not for a few distractions— the lovely camp counselor he's wooing, the disappearance of his cat and the rediscovery of his inner child. Great, goofy fun from the Kinkmeister.

More by Friedman:

GOD BLESS JOHN WAYNE
(Bantam, 1996, paperback).

Kinky's low-life friend Ratso decides to find his true parents (who, of course, aren't eager to be found). But when a string of violent episodes suddenly accompanies Ratso's search for his birth mommy, Kinky gets involved.

ELVIS, JESUS AND COCA-COLA
by Kinky Friedman (Bantam, 1994, paperback)

• *Plot #1:* Tom Baker, producer of a film on Elvis impersonators, is dead, the film is missing and Kinky Friedman (no relation to the author) suspects foul play.

• *Plot #2:* At one time, Kinky had been involved with two ladies, both named Judy-Uptown Jud and Downtown Judy. Suddenly,

Downtown Judy shows up, ready to fire up their relationship again. Just as suddenly, Uptown Judy disappears.

You'll never guess how these two story lines come together, or how Kinky solves them.

....

THE HIPPOPOTAMUS
by Stephen Fry (Soho Press, 1996, paperback)

Ted Wallace, an alcoholic and priapic poet, hears a report that his solemn little godson is performing miracles down in Norfolk. Turns out the rumor is true! The boy can cure people by the laying on of hands. But then the earnest little chap comes to believe that the purest, most natural way to pass his healing spirit on to the afflicted is to have sex with them. Women, men, even Lilac the horse. Astonishingly, the laying on of...whatever...seems to do everyone a world of good. A laugh riot from the actor who created the character of Jeeves for the "Jeeves and Wooster" PBS series.

More Laughs from Stephen Fry:

THE LIAR
(Soho Press, 1994, paperback).

Adrian Healey is certain he can fool all of the people all of the time and so he does (almost).

....

COLD COMFORT FARM
by Stella Gibbons (1933; Penguin, 1996, paperback)

Orphaned at the age of 20, Flora Poste attempts to extend her small inheritance by living with relatives and "tidying up" their lives. She chooses as her first stop the grim Stadakker clan of Cold Comfort Farm. There she meets a collection of truly-inspired wacky characters including the aging matriarch, Aunt Ada "I-saw-something-nasty-in-the-woodshed" Doom. This immensely entertaining novel has the added literary merit of being a dead-on irreverent parody of Thomas Hardy and D.H. Lawrence. (NOTE: Look for the 1964 American edition. It has great illustrations by cartoonist Charles Saxon.)

THE UNEXPECTED MRS. POLLIFAX
by Dorothy Gilman (Fawcett, 1985, paperback)

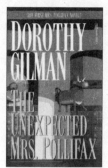

After a quiet existence of planting geraniums and volunteering at the local hospital, elderly widow Emily Pollifax decides to put some excitement in her life—by joining the CIA. As "that nice Mr. Cairstairs" down at the agency will soon learn, espionage will never be the same. Mrs. Pollifax's "routine" mission to Mexico to recover some microfilm is just the first in a delightful series of adventures.

Also by Gilman:

MRS. POLLIFAX ON SAFARI
(Fawcett, 1987, paperback).

Love finds Mrs. P. in Zambia where she is searching for a terrorist named Aristotle.

MRS. POLLIFAX AND THE CHINA SITUATION
(Fawcett, 1985, paperback).

Now indispensable to the CIA, Mrs. Pollifax toddles off to China.

THE AMAZING MRS. POLLIFAX
(Fawcett, 1985, paperback)

At time in life when most folks are winding down, Emily Pollifax is just getting warmed up. Once again the senior-citizen sleuth takes a break from gardening and volunteering in New Brunswick, New Jersey, to help out the CIA. This time out, a phone call sends her on a simple assignment to Turkey. But soon enough, her best-laid plans go awry and she teams up with an unlikely band of heroes on an adventure across the Turkish countryside.

TRAVELS WITH MY AUNT
by Graham Greene (Penguin, 1977, paperback)

Bachelor Henry Pulling's early and quiet retirement is turned upside down when he bumps into his long-lost and highly unpredictable Aunt Augusta at his mother's cremation. Shortly thereafter, Henry, Aunt Augusta and her current lover embark on a farcical adventure that takes them to Paris, Istanbul and Paraguay. Best known for thrillers and mystical melodramas, this comic masterpiece was one of Greene's first attempts at humor.

ARTISTIC DIFFERENCES
by Charlie Hauck

Producer Jimmy Hoy has the simple dream of making his new sitcom the best thing on television. All that's stopping him are some incompetent network executives, a few sleazy agents and one pain-in-the-butt prima donna whom his partner describes as "a lot like Joseph Mengele, but without the human side." Written by a veteran TV writer, this funny first novel doubles as a handbook on how to survive Hollywood. Worth searching for.

CATCH-22
by Joseph Heller (Everyman's Library, 1995, hardcover)

Undiluted genius. That's the only way to characterize this novel set during World War II. Yossarian, a B-25 bombardier flying missions out of a very unusual base in Italy, wants the doctor to ground him for insanity. But the very fact that he doesn't want to fly proves that he's sane. Will he get himself out of the sky before he's killed? This very funny story, with its wacky cast of characters, captures the absurdity and grim, grim humor of war.

NATIVE TONGUE
by Carl Hiassen (Fawcett, 1992, paperback)

Hiassen is the master of the comic thriller who puts his bizarre characters in wonderfully improbable situations. Reporter Joe Winder has sold out to the Amazing Kingdom of Thrills, a low-rent Florida theme park where the main attraction is a pair of blue-tongued mango voles. When the rare voles are stolen, the future of the Amazing Kingdom, not to mention Joe's job, is in considerable jeopardy.

DOUBLE WHAMMY
by Carl Hiassen (Warner, 1987, paperback)

Through Carl Hiassen's eyes, Florida is a strange, wondrous and wacky place indeed, populated with some of the most memorable characters you're likely to meet in a modern mystery. Double Whammy brings to life the high-stakes world of tournament large mouth bass fishing. R.J. Decker, a news photographer turned private eye is hired to investigate the death of a celebrity bass fisherman and finds himself teamed with a road-kill-eating hermit battling crooked evangelists and gun-toting rednecks in a fight for his life.

HIGH FIDELITY
by Nick Hornby (Riverhead Books, 1995, paperback)

Rob is a 35-year-old slacker. His girlfriend, Laura, has left him. His vintage record store is on the skids. And his only real occupation is making lists: The Top-Five Songs Ever, The Top-Five Cheers Episodes, The Top-Five Most Memorable Relationships. To avoid being alone, he gets himself in the most uncomfortable social situations and with nobody around the apartment anymore, Rob becomes the butt of his own jokes. Filled with allusions to pop-music and hilarious snide comments on contemporary culture, this is a funny, off-beat novel of being a single guy in the 90s.

MAXIMUM BOB
by Elmore Leonard (Delacorte, 1991, paperback)

Maximum Bob Gibbs is a Florida judge with a penchant for throwing the book at offenders. It's the kind of activity that makes a lot of enemies. So when a very big, very alive alligator turns up at Bob's house, miles from where any self-respecting alligator should be, everyone assumes that an ex-con with a grudge brought it there. However, everyone is wrong and the game, as they say, is afoot. Leonard is one of the most entertaining crime writers alive and this is one of his best.

ET TU, BABE
by Mark Leyner (Vintage Contemporaries, 1993, paperback)

Cult author Mark Leyner skewers American culture in this laugh-out-loud funny faux autobiography. In an offbeat world where the shower scene music from *Psycho* is the new U.S. National Anthem, Leyner chronicles his own rise and fall as Chief Executive Officer of the multinational corporation, "Team Leyner." If you're not already a Leyner fan, this is an excellent introduction to a comic mind.

THE TOWERS OF TREBIZOND
by Rose Macaulay (Carroll & Graf, 1995, paperback)

You've got to love a book that begins: "'Take my camel, dear,' said my Aunt Dot as she climbed down from this animal on her return from High Mass." Macaulay has been lampooning polite British society for decades and she is at her eccentric best in this wonderfully funny novel.

WITCH: THE LIFE AND TIMES OF THE WICKED WITCH OF THE WEST
by Gregory Maguire (HarperCollins, 1995, paperback)

At last the truth can be told! Oz's Wicked Witch of the West was grossly misunderstood. Raised in a single-parent household, afflicted with a strange skin condition, forced by necessity to raise her little sister and brother, Elphaba's (her given name) so-called anti-social behavior was actually her personal struggle against endemic totalitarianism in the Land of Oz. (Although the Tin Woodsman thinks her problem was hermaphroditism). Maguire is a scholar of children's literature and this wacky prequel to *The Wizard of Oz* is his first shot at fiction.

CONJUGAL BLISS
by John Treadwell Nichols (Ballantine, 1995, paperback)

Roger and Zelda, best of friends, best of lovers, get married and all hell breaks loose. According to Roger, anyway. Is Zelda really the irrational, sexually voracious wild woman Roger makes her out to be? A bawdy, sometimes outrageous comedy of contemporary sexual manners.

THE MILAGRO BEANFIELD WAR
by John Treadwell Nichols (Ballantine, 1990, paperback)

Since 1935, when the Interstate Water Compact reallocated much of Milagro's water for big-time farmers further south, the village had become somewhat of a ghost town. But then one day, Joe Mondragon, 36 and without much to show for it, impulsively and illegally decided he was going to divert some water to the little field in front of his dead parents' run-down home and grow some beans. But what seems like a simple act of irrigation sets off an all out range war and launches one of the best comic novels of the last fifty years.

THE BUBBLE REPUTATION
by Cathie Pelletier (Pocket Books, 1994, paperback)

After the sudden death of her husband, Rosemary O'Neal was content to drift into a nice, quiet widowhood in her huge Maine house. But then family and friends arrive, determined to rouse her from her depression. Her college roommate uses the house

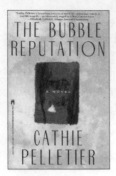

to rendezvous with her lover. Rosemary's 300-pound Uncle Bishop arrives with a new boyfriend who has a passion for ladies' shoes rivaling that of Imelda Marcos. And when a new unsettling turn of events combines with the current chaos, Rosemary comes to some moving realizations about love and family.

More by Cathie Pelletier:

THE WEIGHT OF WINTER
(Pocket Books, 1993, paperback).

Through the vivid memories of a 107-year-old woman, the inbreeding and infighting of a Maine town are revealed. A colorful, sometimes tragic, often eccentric story of small town life.

....

ANOTHER ROADSIDE ATTRACTION
by Tom Robbins (Bantam, 1995, paperback)

Captain Kendrick's Memorial Hot Dog Wildlife Preserve is not just another roadside attraction. On a good day life is strange there, but when the body of Jesus Christ (nabbed from the Vatican basement, of course) turns up, things really get out of hand. Robbins writes with a wacky prose style that will have you smiling, laughing, pondering and wishing this book would never end.

More Inspired Looniness from Tom Robbins:

SKINNY LEGS AND ALL
(Bantam, 1995, paperback).

When the apocalypse comes, it will probably start in an offbeat restaurant across the street from the United Nations. A rowdy, fun-loving book of revelations about sex, race, politics, art, religion and money. Robbins makes you laugh and makes you think.

EVEN COWGIRLS GET THE BLUES
(Bantam, 1984, paperback)

When you have giant thumbs, hitchhiking is a way of life. Sissy

Hankshaw uses her own dazzling digits to maximum advantage, hitchhiking her way into an incredible adventure. This novel became a cult classic of the 1970s and firmly established Tom Robbins, a former urban journalist, as a master of the offbeat. He has a gift not only for turning a phrase but for squeezing it until all of its natural poetry is released. His wacky way with words will alter your brainscape for the better.

MEMOIRS OF AN INVISIBLE MAN
by H.F. Saint (Simon & Schuster)

Since he became invisible, Nick Halloway has learned some interesting lessons: only wear invisible clothes; only eat clear foods; and your only chance of getting a visible woman to sleep with you is to make her think you are a ghost. Spoiling the intriguing possibilities of invisibility are the government agents who know about Nick and are determined to turn him into a superspy or a guinea pig—they haven't decided which. Worth searching for.

THE LOVE LETTER
by Cathleen Schine (Signet, 1996, paperback)

On a fine summer morning, Helen MacFarquhar opens her mailbox to find a passionate love letter that begins "Dear Goat" and is signed, "As Ever, Ram." When 20-year-old Johnny Howell, Helen's part-time help at her bookstore, reads the letter, he believes it is from Helen to him—and he is instantly smitten. But no sooner do Johnny and Helen consummate their unanticipated affair, than Helen's 11-year-old daughter returns home from camp. Then Helen's ditzy mother and haughty grandmother arrive for a prolonged visit. Schine has deft hand for comedy of manners and this book reads beautifully as Helen's tidy life gives way to merry chaos.

More by Schine:

ALICE IN BED
(Signet, 1996, paperback).

A sassy, spoiled college girl is confined to a hospital bed by an unidentifiable malady. To keep her occupied, a cast of remarkable characters parade through her sickroom, including her well-meaning mom, her mom's tacky new boyfriend and two doctors who become Alice's lovers.

THE HOUSE OF STRIFE
by Maurice Shadbolt

In 1830s London, Ferdinand Wildblood has launched a "literary" career as Henry Youngman, author of a blockbuster series of pot boilers that depict blood-soaked adventures and lascivious encounters among the Maori. But when the sailor from whom Wildblood stole the idea for his first best-seller shows up, the hack author heads out for Maori country itself. In place of romantic savagery, he finds a seedy British colony, so to liven the place up, Wildblood begins an affair with a Maori maiden and even instigates a Maori uprising against British imperialism. Worth searching for.

TROPICAL DEPRESSION
by Laurence Shames (Hyperion, 1996, paperback)

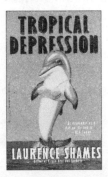

One morning Murray Zemelman "the Bra King" backs out of his garage and drives away from his trophy wife, his fancy house and his lingerie empire. He heads for Florida to see his first wife Franny, the woman he was crazy enough to leave years before. In Key West, Zemelman meets Tommy Tarpon, the last of an obscure Florida tribe and they concoct a scheme to build a casino on the swampy, alligator-infested island that is the last piece of real estate Tarpon's tribe still owns. It's a great idea, until a crooked politician and local mobster enter the picture to give the plot the necessary complications.

More Fun in the Sun:

SUNBURN
by *Laurence Shames* (Hyperion, 1996, paperback).

An aging godfather vacationing in Florida lets his half-Jewish illegitimate son talk him into writing his memoirs. Meanwhile, back in New York, the legitimate all-Italian son is not so crazy about Pop spilling his guts about the family business.

....

A CONFEDERACY OF DUNCES
by *John Kennedy Toole* (Amereon, Ltd., 1998, hardcover)

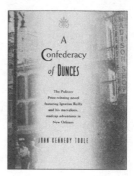

John Kennedy Toole took his own life when he was only 32 years old. Seven years later, his mother found a publisher for *A Confederacy of Dunces*, a comic masterpiece that won a Pulitzer Prize. Ignatius J. Reilly, 30 years old, is too busy planning the total reform of the 20th century to find a job. When at last his mother tosses him out into the working world, the results are hilarious.

....

SLAUGHTERHOUSE FIVE
by *Kurt Vonnegut, Jr.* (Dell, 1991, paperback)

Listen: Billy Pilgrim has come unstuck in time. The naïve hero of this powerful novel is randomly reliving episodes of his existence from cradle to grave to the far reaches of outer space, desperately trying to make sense of it all. Vonnegut based this darkly comic antiwar adventure on his own experiences as a POW in the Dresden firebombing during World War II. This is justifiably Vonnegut's best-known work and its publication in 1969 firmly established him as a literary heavyweight.

....

More by Vonnegut:

BLUEBEARD
(Dell, 1988, paperback).

You'll encounter lots of Vonnegut's famous off-beat humor in this tale the artist, Rabo Karabekian. An entertaining satire of the American art world and the philistine notion of art-as-investment.

CAT'S CRADLE
(Dell, 1992, paperback).

Vonnegut's satire of modern man and his self-destructive madness would be unbearable were it not for his brilliant bursts of humor.

THE LOVED ONE
by Evelyn Waugh (1947; Little, Brown, 1977, paperback)

After a visit to America, Waugh turned his wicked wit on Hollywood and the southern California funeral industry. The story follows Dennis Barlow, a British expatriate who used to write for a movie studio but now works at The Happier Hunting Ground—a "memorial park" for pets located in the shadow of Whispering Glades Memorial Park, a fantastically kitsch Hollywood cemetery-and-theme-park. Ruthless, sometimes damn close to vicious, *The Loved One* is one of Waugh's most hilarious satires.

More by Waugh:

SCOOP
(1938; Little Brown, 1977, paperback).

A revolution erupts a Third World backwater and the publisher of the London Beast wants his best war correspondent there to cover the carnage. He calls for Boot. Alas, he should have been more specific. Because now William Boot, the nature columnist, rather than John Boot, the seasoned battlefield journalist, is on his way to war-torn Ishmaelia. Of course, pandemonium ensues. Waugh is at his black comedy best in this hilarious send-up of the London press.

THE ROACHES HAVE NO KING

by *Daniel Evan Weiss* (High Risk Books, 1994, paperback)

When a human neat-freak takes over his kitchen of choice, the tiny roach hero of this darkly humorous novel hatches a scheme of biblical proportions to rescue his brethren from the resulting famine. It takes a writer with great skill and humor to make a roach an appealing protagonist. Weiss has both. His grasp of roach society is so extensive, one wonders if he didn't don a brown exoskeleton and go undercover like an urban Jane Goodall.

PSMITH JOURNALIST

by *P.G. Wodehouse* 1915; Buccaneer Books, 1990, hardcover)

Wodehouse's gregarious agent provocateur, Psmith (the "P" is silent) first appeared on the scene around 1909, approximately a decade before Jeeves and Wooster, the characters for which Wodehouse would become a legend, turned up. Evidently the author had already hit his stride. In this particular farce, Psmith tags along with a school chum to New York where he persuades the acting editor of *Cosy Moments* to transform his absent boss's beloved style magazine into a herald of social commentary, with unpredictably ridiculous and entertaining results.

FIRST TIME OUT

THE ROMANCE READER
by Pearl Abraham (Riverhead Books, 1995, hardcover)

Among Rachel Benjamin's Hasidic neighbors, the idea of a rabbi's daughter—anybody's daughter—wearing a bathing suit is scandalous. Reading romance novels, even Brontë romance novels, borders on sinful. Rachel lives in 1970s New York, but it might as well be 1870s Eastern Europe. And while she genuinely loves the close-knit feeling of her community, part of her chafes against the constant scrutiny of family, friends and neighbors. Abraham has written a sympathetic story of a religious young woman's flirtation with secular society.

AUDREY HEPBURN'S NECK
by Alan Brown (Pocket Books, 1996, paperback)

On his ninth birthday, Toshi Okamoto's mother takes him to the movies to see Roman Holiday. At once, he is mesmerized by the beauty of Audrey Hepburn—especially her neck. For years, he searches for a woman with the same striking physical feature with whom he can fall in love. And at last, he does. A funny, hip, offbeat first novel.

OTHER VOICES, OTHER ROOMS
by Truman Capote (1948; Vintage International, 1994, paperback)

A young boy in a slow Southern town takes his first fearful steps toward emotional maturity. Capote's first novel brought him instant recognition as a prodigious new talent.

THE LONGEST MEMORY
by Fred D'Aguiar (Pantheon, 1996, paperback)

Whitechapel is an old man and the oldest slave on a plantation in 19th-century Virginia. He remembers being a boy in Africa before he was stolen by slave traders. As he tells the story of his life on the plantation, Whitechapel reveals, gradually, the part he played in the horrible tragedy of his son, Chapel. Chapel did everything a slave ought not to do—he learned to read and write, he fell in love with the master's daughter and he ran away. *The Longest Memory* is D'Aguiar's first work of fiction. It is a devastating story.

DELIVERANCE
by James Dickey (1970; Dell, 1994, paperback)

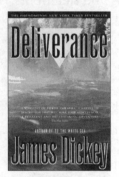

No one expected that Dickey, a National Book Award-winning poet, would write such a brilliant first novel. His story of four bored Southern businessmen who are attacked by mountain people is a spellbinding tour de force. *Deliverance* is the type of novel you wish you could read in one sitting.

Also by Dickey:

TO THE WHITE SEA
(Delta, 1994, paperback).

A brutal story of an American tail gunner shot down over Japan during World War II and trying to find sanctuary in a hostile land.

SCANDAL
by Joanna Elm (Forge, 1996, paperback)

Author Joanna Elm has worked for the supermarket tabloid, The Star and the TV tabloid show *A Current Affair*. So it's no surprise that her first mystery novel has a TV tabloid journalist as its heroine. Kitty Fitzgerald relishes her new assignment covering the murder of a talk-show host. But while Kitty is digging up dirt about the victim, someone else is revealing sordid secrets from Kitty's own past—then Kitty's son is abducted. A fun first novel that blends suspense with sensationalism.

. . . .

POSTCARDS FROM THE EDGE
by Carrie Fisher (Simon and Schuster, 1987, paperback)

Comedian Steve Martin said that Carrie Fisher's autobiographical first novel "makes Moby Dick seem like a big, fat, dumb book." Which may be an overstatement. But certainly *Postcards* has a lot more laughs in it. It's the story of Suzanne Vale, an extraordinary young actress in Los Angeles who is trying to figure out how she landed in rehab and why, despite all she has going for her, she feels like "something on the bottom of someone's shoe and not even someone interesting." Fisher's humor is unique, irreverent and hilarious.

. . . .

THIS SIDE OF PARADISE
by F. Scott Fitzgerald (1920; Modern Library, 1996, paperback)

Fitzgerald's first novel was an instant sensation. Though only 24 years old, he had captured perfectly the energy and affectations of the young people of the Jazz Age. The story follows Amory Blaine, a handsome young man drifting aimlessly through life, trying to find something he loves completely. He goes through women, literature, radical politics, booze and money only to find that, as he puts it, "I know myself... but that is all."

. . . .

WHERE ANGELS FEAR TO TREAD
by E.M. Forster (1905; Bantam, 1996, paperback)

Forster's first novel examines what happens when stuffy, conventional, upper-middle-class English people go up against the passion and warmth of Italy. Widowed Lilia Herriton travels to Italy for a little sunshine. There she meets—and marries—a young stud named Gino in the absolutely delightful town of Monteriano. Lilia's Herriton in-laws are scandalized and send out one delegation after another to bring her back.

The Best of Forster:

A PASSAGE TO INDIA
(1924; Everyman's Library, 1992, paperback).

The thinly veiled tensions between British and Indians erupts when a hysterical Englishwoman falsely accuses an Indian physician of sexual assault. This is Forster's last, most acclaimed and greatest novel.

ELLEN FOSTER
by Kaye Gibbons (Algonquin Books, 1987, paperback)

"When I was little I would think of ways to kill my daddy." Now that's on opening line that gets your attention. Ellen Foster, the narrator of this novel, is a young girl who endures her father's alcoholism, her mother's death and some unpleasantness from the people she's sent to live with. But Ellen is going to be all right. She's resilient. She thrives on the stories she finds in books (*The Canterbury Tales* is one of her sources of consolation). She's got a sharp tongue and wicked sense of humor. And she's got her friends, particularly a young black girl named Starletta. If you missed Gibbons' novel when it first came out, catch up with it now.

NATHAN'S RUN
by John Gilstrap (HarperCollins, 1996, paperback)

John Gilstrap has hit the big time with his first novel. Twelve-year-old Nathan Bailey is accused of killing a cop. With no one to turn to for help, a nationwide manhunt bearing down on him and a mysterious hit man hot on his trail, Nathan concocts a daring plan to save his skin. He hooks up with a radio talk-show host and broadcasts his side of the story over the air waves. With a sympathetic character and edge-of-your-seat action, *Nathan's Run* is a classic pageturner.

....

A PALE VIEW OF HILLS
by Kazuo Ishiguro (Putnam's Sons, 1982, paperback)

A *Pale View of Hills* is Ishiguro's first novel, published several years before his remarkable book, *Remains of the Day*, brought him great literary acclaim. It is the graceful and poignant story of Etsuko, a Japanese woman living in England, who distracts herself from thinking of her daughter's recent suicide by remembering a certain summer in Nagasaki—long enough after the bomb that some buildings have been rebuilt, but long before the people inhabiting those buildings have been able to make sense of their post-war lives.

....

COUNTRY LIVING, COUNTRY DYING
by Able Jones (Down East, 1995, paperback)

On Halloween, the manager of the town dump of Bosky Dells, Maine, finds a skeleton in the landfill with a cache of documents which suggest that the bones were once Glinda True, a village woman who disappeared back in 1967. But then Glinda shows up on the day of her funeral. So whose bones are they? Jones keeps his readers guessing as he combines recollections of the strange events of 1967 with a slew of new questions that have cropped up now that Glinda's back in town. Why did she leave? Where's she been? What does she want now, especially from her cousin Adele? An entertaining, macabre first novel.

....

LOS ALAMOS
by Joseph Kanon (Bantam Doubleday Dell, 1997, hardcover)

In the final days of WWII, Army intelligence officer Michael Connolly arrives in Santa Fe, New Mexico, to investigate the murder of a security officer on the Manhattan Project. Is it merely a grim coincidence or has security on the top secret A-bomb project been breached? The young officer soon finds himself swept up in not only a passionate love affair but a potentially deadly scheme to expose a case of high-level espionage. It's a page-turner of a debut novel.

A VISITATION OF SPIRITS
by Randall Kenan (Doubleday, 1996, paperback)

Randall Kenan set his first novel in fictional town called Tims Creek in southeastern North Carolina. The time is the mid-1980s, but Kenan reaches back to the distant past to chart the changes in the South, particularly among African Americans. The novel is filled with arresting scenes, including a hog killing and wrestles with hard topics, such as the response to homosexuality in a rural black community. Kenan brings an extraordinary sense of place and a deep understanding of human nature to his story. Readers from Kenan's part of the world say he captures the speech of rural eastern North Carolina perfectly.

THE RAVEN
by Peter Landesman (Baskerville, 1995, paperback)

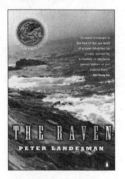

This literary novel marks an impressive debut for newcomer Peter Landesman. In 1941, a tourist cruise ship disappeared off the coast of Maine. Over the next 50 years, the web of deceit surrounding the *Raven* tragedy begins to unravel. There's the banker and his wife who withdrew from the cruise at the last minute and sent a bank secretary and her boyfriend in their place. Then there's the *Raven's* captain, a man with a history of maritime fraud. And finally, there's the lobsterman who brought up the first bodies and for reasons of his own suppressed vital evidence. Landesman is an author to watch.

THE DISHWASHER
by *Dannie Martin* (Norton, 1995, paperback)

Like Bill Malone, his dishwashing protagonist, author Dannie (Red Hog) Martin has been in prison. Paroled after 14 years in jail, Malone gets a room in a cheap motel and takes a job washing dishes at a restaurant. When his landlady's teenaged daughter is raped by a local drug dealer, Malone goes after him. And while the cops don't really care who killed the dealer, the dead man's Mafia employers do. Martin has drawn a character who is essentially decent, really wants to go straight, but sticks to the underworld's code of honor. And when he gets mad, it's incredible how much damage he can do. A very impressive first novel.

FLESH AND STONE
by *Mark Miano* (Kensington Books, 1997, hardcover)

On the coldest night on record, the body of a man is found frozen beneath the ice of New York's Central Park reservoir, his mouth gapping open in a silent scream. As TV newswriter Mark Cappo starts to investigate the murder, he learns that the victim was the owner of a posh Upper East Side art gallery and that the victim's secret lover was a woman Cappo also knew intimately. Cappo finds out more than he ever wanted to know about the art world, love, betrayal, bizarre sex acts and murder. And he finds himself torn between his obligations to his profession and his private code of honor. An impressive debut you won't want to miss.

FUGITIVE PIECES
by *Anne Michaels* (Knopf, 1997, hardcover)

Anne Michaels is a Canadian poet whose first novel, Fugitive Pieces, took the critics by storm. At the heart of the story is a seven-year-old Polish Jewish boy who sees his family murdered by the Nazis. The boy is rescued by a Greek geologist who raises him and tries to give the child hope and strength to begin a new life. But, the boy seems haunted by the ghosts of his family and he isn't sure if they want him to join them, or leave them behind and re-enter the world.

THE TRUEST PLEASURE
by Robert Morgan (Algonquin Books, 1995, paperback)

Life is hard for mountain people like Ginny Peace. Raising her children and working from dawn to dark beside her husband, Tom, on their farm takes everything out of her. The only real joy she gets is speaking in tongues at a Pentacostal church. But Tom believes Ginny and her fellow worshippers are hysterics at best, fakers at worst. His contempt for the church services and Ginny's determination to go to them drives a wedge between husband and wife. Narrated by Ginny in the twang of the North Carolina hills, this is a sublime Southern novel, in the tradition of Eudora Welty.

THE WOMEN OF BREWSTER PLACE
by Gloria Naylor (Penguin, 1982, paperback)

Gloria Naylor's first novel follows a group of women who, for a variety of reasons, have all landed at a housing project called Brewster Place. At the heart of the story is Mattie Michael, who came to Brewster Place after her son skipped bail and Mattie lost her house. Other memorable characters include Cora, who keeps having babies but doesn't know what to do with them when they grow up; Etta Mae, Mattie's childhood friend who has lousy luck with men; Lorraine and Theresa, two lesbians the other women of Brewster Place find hard to accept; and Kiswana, a college drop-out hoping to find herself away from her affluent family.

Another by Gloria Naylor:

MAMA DAY
(Vintage, 1989, paperback).

Blending African-American folklore with Shakespeare's *The Tempest*, Naylor has created an enchanting story set on an imaginary island off the coast of Georgia about a gifted healer named Mama Day.

BLOODSONG
by *Jill Neimark* (Plume Books, 1994, paperback)

"**I**'m in love with a murderer." That's how Neimark begins her sexy first novel. Lynn, a lonely New Yorker, runs a personal ad. Kim Beckett, an Adonis who lives in a seedy Times Square hotel, answers it. Immediately, they throw themselves into one of the most enthusiastic love affairs in modern American fiction. When Kim confesses his secret, Lynn starts down a dangerous road to discover who her lover really is. If Neimark's first novel is this good, imagine what her next will be like.

APPOINTMENT IN SAMARRA
by *John O'Hara* (1934; Random House, 1982, paperback)

Smart, reckless, a little risqué, John O'Hara came out of the tough-guy school of American literature. His first novel begins on Christmas Eve, 1930. Julian English, a pampered WASP and owner of the Gibbsville Cadillac Motor Car Company, has just thrown his highball into the face of Harry Reilly, a brash Irish Catholic who is on his way to becoming the new owner of the Gibbsville Cadillac Motor Car Company. O'Hara turns his jaundiced eye on the goings-on in bedrooms and speak-easies and he records flawlessly the voices of low-level mobsters, drunks, nightclub singers and crude nouveau riches.

Back in print:

BUTTERFIELD 8
by *John O'Hara* (1935; Random House, 1994, paperback).

O'Hara based his novel on a true story—the notorious case of a young woman whose body was discovered on a Long Island beach in 1931. A beautiful re-imagining of the young woman's daring but sordid life.

RAISING HOLY HELL
by *Bruce Olds* (Penguin, 1997)

John Brown is still one of the most controversial figures of the Civil War era. Was he a terrorist? A madman? God's avenging angel? To tell his story, Olds has written an unusual book, a cross between a historical novel and experimental fiction. You'll find a variety of literary devices employed here—journal entries, poetry, folktales, interior monologues, newspaper articles, eyewitness testimony. But each new device and each fresh perspective brings the reader closer to understanding the true character of this implacable enemy of slavery. An extremely impressive first novel.

IN THE PLACE OF FALLEN LEAVES
by Tim Pears (Primus Paperbacks, 1995, paperback)

For his first novel, Pears creates an enchanted summer for his 13-year-old heroine Alison Fremantle, the daughter of a Devonshire farmer. Through her grandmother's stories, Alison learns the secret histories and public tragedies of her relatives and village neighbors. But Alison is also beginning her own private adventures with Jonathan, the local viscount's son. A tender, beautiful novel about the joys of summer and the pain and pleasures of growing up.

A SHORT HISTORY OF A SMALL PLACE
by T.R. Pearson (Ballantine, 1986, paperback)

"That was the day Mrs. Pettigrew stopped being just peculiar.... Now when folks spoke of her they would say she was Not Right, which was an advancement of a sort. The town of Neely had seen a blue million peculiarities in its history, but those among its citizenry who were genuinely not right were rare and cherished." Pearson's laugh-out-loud debut novel proved him to be a sort of a weird combination of Faulkner, Twain and Uncle Remus. He transforms everyday incidents into zany, significant events that capture small town life in all its poignant and irresistible absurdity. You'll find yourself reading choice passages out loud to anyone who will listen.

Another comic classic by Pearson:

OFF FOR THE SWEET HEREAFTER
(Henry Holt, 1995, paperback)

This hilarious chronicle of the romance/crime spree of a Piedmont Bonnie and Clyde-named Benton Lynch and Jane Elizabeth Firesheets-may be even funnier than its prequel, A *Short History of a Small Place*.

● ● ● ● ● ● ● ● ● ● ● ● ● ●

RASERO

by Francisco Rebolledo, translated by Helen R. Lane
(Louisiana State University Press, 1995, paperback)

Sixteen-year-old Fausto Rasero has an uncanny paranormal gift: every time he makes love he sees some future tragedy, including horrors that he does not understand-such as the concentration camps and Hiroshima. After a lively time in Paris, during which he makes the acquaintance of Voltaire, Madame Pompadour, the boy Mozart and Robespierre, Rasero returns to Spain. There he hooks up with Goya, whose macabre paintings reflect Rasero's dark visions. A lively, racy, literary fantasy.

● ● ● ● ● ● ● ● ● ● ● ● ● ●

THE CAGE

by Audrey Schulman (Algonquin Books, 1994, hardcover)

Beryl, a wildlife photographer who has done most of her work in zoos, accepts an assignment to photograph polar bears in the Arctic. But she'll have to take her photos from inside a small steel cage plopped down in the middle of the bears' habitat. It's all supposed to be perfectly safe, yet within a few days of their arrival on the tundra, the high-tech gadgetry Beryl and her three male companions had relied upon fails. And it's going to take every reserve of strength Beryl and her friends have to get past the starving bears, survive in the murderous cold and walk miles back to town.

● ● ● ● ● ● ● ● ● ● ● ● ● ●

THE YOUNG LIONS
by *Irwin Shaw* (Bantam Doubleday Dell, 1976, paperback)

In his first novel Shaw discovered the formula for success—a gripping story, characters you believe in, lots of action. Three young men—a Nazi, an American and a Jew—meet by chance in a Bavarian forest. Beginning with this encounter, Shaw shows how their lives become intertwined during World War II. A great read from one of the best writers of popular fiction. Worth searching for.

Also by Shaw:

RICH MAN, POOR MAN.

Irwin Shaw's classic saga of the Jordache clan: Tom the prizefighter, Rudy the ambitious businessman and Gretchen the talented actress with abysmal taste in men. A story with tremendous popular appeal. Worth searching for.

A SIMPLE PLAN
by Scott Smith (St. Martin's Press, 1994, paperback)

Deep in the woods, three men discover a duffel bag stuffed with $4 million. They make a pact: hide the bag; if no one claims the money in six months, it's theirs. But some people just can't wait and the simple plan suddenly takes a downward spin into blood-chilling violence and unexpected evil. From page one Scott Smith grabs the reader by the throat and never lets go.

LIE DOWN IN DARKNESS
by *William Styron* (Vintage, 1992, paperback)

Readers of James Joyce will especially appreciate Styron's first novel—the interior monologues are thought to be among the best since *Ulysses*. Styron set his story in the South shortly after World War II, when the old biblical rhetoric is beginning to fade and skepticism and industrialization are altering the patterns of a traditional rural society. The novel revolves around the Loftis clan, a family united only by their hatreds for one another.

THE SECRET HISTORY
by Donna Tartt (Ivy Books, 1993, paperback)

Hard to believe, but this story of secret sin is Donna Tartt's first novel. A small group of exceptional college students go into a New England forest to perform a bacchanalian rite. But before the night is over, something terrible and unexpected happens. The scholars vow to keep what they've done secret forever, but their crime takes its vengeance on them one by one.

LOOK HOMEWARD, ANGEL
by Thomas Wolfe (1929; Touchstone Books, 1997, paperback)

Most novelists tell their own life story in their first novel, but few have ever succeeded in creating a work as passionate as Look Homeward, Angel. Wolfe was 29 when he published this story of Eugene Gant (his alter ego) growing up in a small Southern town where eccentricity is close to an art form. Eugene loves the place, but he can't wait to get away from it. Even today, the raw power of this coming-of-age novel strikes something deep down in a reader's soul.

Wolfe's Classic:

YOU CAN'T GO HOME AGAIN
(1940; HarperPerennial, 1989, paperback).

The attempts of a rootless young man to find something he can believe in—home, sex, literature, money, politics—take him from his Southern hometown to Nazi Germany to 1930s New York. An intense portrait of disillusionment that ends (thank God) on an upbeat note.

FOR YOUNG READERS

WEETZIE BAT
by Francesca Lia Block (HarperCollins, 1991, paperback)

Weetzie Bat has been miserable since her Hollywood parents divorced. Then a genie appears and offers her three wishes. When her wishes are granted, Weetzie expects to live "happily ever after." But Weetzie and her friends have a lot to learn about what can make us happy. This is an offbeat story about family, friendship and love. It also deals with divorce, homosexuality, AIDS, drug abuse and the Hollywood movie culture—so it may not be for everyone.

A BOY CALLED SLOW
by Joseph Bruchac, illustrated by Rocco Baviera
(Paperstar, 1998, paperback)

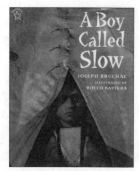

Slow, a Lakota Sioux boy, longs for the day when he will be a man as brave and wise as his father. So he devotes himself to following the ways of the warriors. When he distinguishes himself in battle against the Crow, he wins a new name, the one history calls him—Sitting Bull. Bruchac tells a gripping story of the journey to manhood and teaches youngsters about Lakota history and culture. Baviera's illustrations draw on the soft hues of the Great Plains, accented by bursts of brilliant color.

VOYAGE OF THE BASSET

by James C. Christensen with Renwick St. James and Alan Dean Foster
(Artisan/Workman, 1996, hardcover)

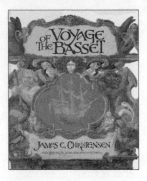

Cassandra Aisling is a nine-year-old girl who will take magic and mystery over good sense and reality any day. Naturally, a voyage aboard the H.M.S. Basset with her father, Professor Algernon Aisling, sounds very appealing, especially since the ship is manned by a crew of dwarves and gremlins. Once everyone is aboard, the Bassett is swept away to the lands of legend. The Aislings visit King Oberon and Queen Titania; they watch their step around fire-breathing dragons; they rescue the Sphinx and the Manticore; they hear the siren songs of mermaids. The entire journey is a grand adventure, illustrated with 120 incredibly opulent full-color paintings.

THE DIARY OF VICTOR FRANKENSTEIN

by Roscoe Cooper, illustrated by Timothy Basil Ering
(DK Ink, 1997, hardcover)

Readers age 10-12 will love this battered, blood-stained journal. It combines the thrill of reading someone's private diary with the chills of learning how a young medical student used human corpses to create a monster. Sketches reveal how Victor Frankenstein made his monster and even depict the creature itself. And tucked among the pages of the journal are letters from Frankenstein's family and friends, as well as other documents that show how the young genius destroyed his promising career by obsessively pursuing this doomed experiment.

MY DENALI

by Kimberley and Hannah Corral, photographs by Roy Corral
(Alaska Northwest, 1995, hardcover)

Twelve-year-old Hannah Corral leads readers on a hiking tour of one of America's most magnificent national parks. She revels in the splendor of the scenery and seeing wildlife by the hundreds. But when Hannah witnesses a grizzly taking down a moose calf, her mother tells her "Denali stays wild because of life-and-death struggles between predator and prey." Hannah's father, Roy Corral, formerly photo editor of Alaska magazine, provides the stunning photographs. An ideal introduction to Denali for children, but one that adults will appreciate, too.

THE WATSONS GO TO BIRMINGHAM-1963

by Christopher Paul Curtis (Delacorte, 1995, hardcover)

Thirteen-year-old Byron Watson has got a bad case of adolescent rebellion. So his parents decide a summer with the grandparents in Alabama might straighten their son out. It is summer, 1963 and the Watsons are black. As they leave Michigan and travel deep into the South, the family encounters the troubles that were plaguing America that summer. But the worst comes when they arrive in Birmingham—just in time for the bombing of the Sixteenth Avenue Baptist Church in which four young girls were killed. A very poignant family odyssey.

THE SLEEPING BREAD

by Stefan Czernecki and Timothy Rhodes,
illustrated by Stefan Czernecki (Hyperion, 1993, paperback)

The Fiesta of San Pedro is coming and the villagers want that scruffy beggar, Zafiro, out of town. But before he leaves, Zafiro sheds a single tear in the baker's shop. Now, strangely, the bread won't rise—until Zafiro is brought back and invited to join the celebration. Based on Guatemalan folklore.

SING A SONG OF POPCORN:
EVERY CHILD'S BOOK OF POEMS
by Beatrice Shenck De Regniers and Marcia Brown
(Scholastic, 1988, paperback)

Susie's galoshes
Make splishes and sploshes
and slooshes and sloshes
As Susie steps slowly
Along in the slush.

—from *Galoshes* by Rhoda Bacmeister

Weather and witches, camels and snails, manners and nonsense, this collection of more than 100 poems has it all. You'll find works by contemporary poets such as Eve Merriam and Charlotte Pomerantz as well as such classics by Christina Rosetti and Robert Louis Stevenson. And enlivening the pages are illustrations by nine Caldecott Medal artists, including Maurice Sendak and Jan Carr.

JOHN BROWN:
ONE MAN AGAINST SLAVERY
by Gwen Everett, illustrated by Jacob Lawrence
(Rizzoli, 1993, hardcover)

Everett tells the story of the fiery abolitionist from his daughter's point of view. "One person—one family—can make a difference," Brown tells Annie. This is an interesting way to make an important yet troubling and violent time in American history accessible to children.

LINCOLN: A
PHOTOBIOGRAPHY
by Russell Freedman
(Clarion Books, 1989, hardcover)

By far, this Newberry Medal Book is the best biography of Lincoln for young readers. Author Russell Freedman portrays

Lincoln as a living, breathing, human being—down-to-earth, witty, sensible, a doting father, a brave, determined and compassionate leader. Making the book even better are 90 period photographs and illustrations of Lincoln, his family, his friends, his opponents and his times. A wonderfully evocative book that succeeds brilliantly in making American history and biography intriguing.

DINOTOPIA

by *James Gurney* (Turner Publishing, 1992, hardcover)

I n the enchanted land of Dinotopia, humans and dinosaurs have lived together happily for centuries, undiscovered by the outside world—until a scientist and his young son are shipwrecked in this wonderful land. It's hard to say which is better, the story or the 160 spectacular full-color illustrations.

SWAMP ANGEL

by *Anne Isaacs, illustrated by Paul O. Zelinsky*
(Dutton Children's Books, 1994, paperback)

I magine what would happen if Paul Bunyan had a sister. Isaacs takes the classic American genre of the tall tale and spins a wildly entertaining yarn about Angelica Longrider, the girl who would become "the greatest woodswoman in Tennessee." At age two she builds her first log cabin. At 12, she rescues a covered wagon stuck in a swamp. When she grows up, she out-wrestles an enormous bear and tosses him into the night sky. (You can still see him up there.) Accompanied by Zelinsky's American folk art-style paintings, *Swamp Angel* is pure delight.

CINDER EDNA

by *Ellen Jackson, Illustrated by Kevin O'Malley*
(Lothrop, Lee & Shepherd, 1994, hardcover)

A s Ellen Jackson read Cinderella to her kindergarten class, she wondered how anyone could run in glass slippers—much less dance in them—and Cinder Edna was born. Cinderella's next door neighbor, Cinder Edna doesn't depend on any fairy godmother to get what she wants. Instead, Edna saves her money, puts a ball gown on layaway and takes a city bus to the royal ball where, by being herself, she meets a prince worth living happily ever after with. She's a fun and self-reliant heroine to introduce your own little princess to.

CAT, YOU BETTER COME HOME
by Garrison Keillor, Paintings by Steve Johnson and Lou Fancher (Viking, 1995, hardcover)

"She gave away gifts like she was St. Nicholas.
Her diamond bill was just ridicholas."

Puff doesn't want to be a pampered housecat anymore. She wants the high life—fame, fortune and an endless stream of foie gras. So she strikes out to become TV's queen of cat food. Puff's life in the fast lane is told in witty verses by the bard of *Lake Wobegon* and illustrated with big, lush, full-color illustrations. A story that's as much fun for adults to read as it is for kids to hear.

THE CANADA GEESE QUILT
by Natalie Kinsey-Warnock (Yearling Books, 1992, hardcover)

Ten-year-old Ariel has two major worries. First, her mother is expecting a new baby and Ariel wonders if that means her mom will love her less. More serious is Ariel's grandmother who has been sick lately. To reassure to her, Grandma suggests that in secret they make a special quilt as a gift for the baby. But before the quilt is finished, Grandma suffers a stroke. Ariel is frightened, but she hopes that seeing her struggle to piece the quilt together will inspire Grandma to get well again. What Ariel doesn't know is that Grandma has a secret gift just for Ariel.

AS LONG AS THERE ARE MOUNTAINS
by Natalie Kinsey-Warnock (Cobblehill, 1997, hardcover).

Thirteen-year-old Iris loves working on her family's farm and believes she will always live there. Then, in a single year, her grandfather dies, the barn burns down and Iris' father is crippled in an accient. It looks like the farm will have to be sold.

THE GREAT MIGRATION: AN AMERICAN STORY
written and illustrated by Jacob Lawrence
(Phillips Collection, 1993, paperback)

In 1940-41, Lawrence did a series of 60 paintings that depicted the migration of Southern blacks to the North. In this beautifully illustrated book, he adapts his paintings and makes a very complex historical event comprehensible to young readers, without shying away from topics such as segregation, poverty and race riots.

THE LEDGERBOOK OF THOMAS BLUE EAGLE
by Gay Matthaei and Jewel Grutman, illustrated by Adam Cvijanovic
(Thomasson-Grant, 1994, hardcover)

The oblong shape, blue cloth cover, the stamped border design, the rounded corners of this book give every appearance of an old-fashioned ledger. Open the book and you find ruled paper with a clear, handsome old-style script flowing beautifully across the page. And then there are the illustrations: vivid scenes of Sioux life in the 19th century, painted in glowing colors. One imagines this tale of Thomas Blue Eagle, a Sioux boy taken from his family and sent to a school for Indian children in Carlisle, Pennsylvania, was meant for children, but adults will treasure it, too.

THE PIRATE QUEEN
by Emily Arnold McCully (Putnam, 1995, hardcover)

In the 16th century, Grania O'Malley was queen of the pirates, marauding on the high seas, winning mountains of treasure one day and losing it all the next. She reached the pinnacle of her career when she appealed to a fellow monarch, Elizabeth I, for permission to spend her life freebooting. Naturally, Elizabeth granted it. McCully has a flair for storytelling and her big paintings have the technicolor grandeur Grania's legend requires.

MY DOG SKIP
by Willie Morris (Random House, 1995, hardcover)

Willie Morris was nine years old in 1943 when his dad gave him a fox terrier puppy. Willie named the puppy Skip and they developed a bond that mystified the adults around them. In fact, Willie's boyhood reads like the further adventures of Tom Sawyer, with illustrations by Norman Rockwell. In their little town on the Mississippi Delta, Willie and Skip spent their days chasing squirrels and following fire engines and their nights taking little kids into old graveyards and scaring them half to death (Skip howls on cue). All of us wish we had a childhood like Willie's. And we'd all jump at the chance to bring home a dog like Skip.

MONEY, MONEY, MONEY:
THE MEANING OF THE ART AND SYMBOLS ON UNITED STATES PAPER CURRENCY
by Nancy Winslow Parker (HarperCollins, 1995, hardcover)

Nancy Winslow Parker knows money. In this cheerful, informative little volume, she explains the strange symbols that appear on U.S. currency, traces the long line of famous people who have appeared on our bills—from Martha Washington to Union General Philip Sheridan to Pocahontas—and reveals the secret printing techniques that drive counterfeiters crazy. This may look like a book for kids, but it's packed with information adults will enjoy.

ALVIN AILEY
by Andrea Davis Pinkney, illustrated by Brian Pinkney
(Hyperion, 1993, hardcover)

He curled his shoulders from back to front and rippled his hands like an ocean wave." In this book, it's hard to say what captures the movement of the dancers best—the text or the illustrations. Here is the story of master choreographer Alvin Ailey and how he invented Revelations, his masterpiece that combines modern dance with the African-American rhythms he first heard at his Baptist church in his hometown, Rogers, Texas.

THE TWELVE DANCING PRINCESSES
by Jane Ray (Dutton, 1996, hardcover)

While everyone else in the royal palace is sound asleep, twelve sisters, all of them princesses, dance the night away. Their father the king knows something is up—every morning he awakens to find twelve pairs of worn-out dancing shoes and twelve pooped princesses—but he can't prove anything. So he comes up with a fool-proof plan: he offers a princess's hand in marriage to any man who can tell him what his daughters have been doing at night. The story takes a delightful "girls just wanna have fun" approach and the illustrations are pure magic-garlands of diamonds sparkle in the forest and the princesses' ball gowns glisten in the moonlight.

UNDER THE MOON
by Dyan Sheldon, Illustrated by Gary Blythe (Dial Books, 1995)

When Jenny finds an Indian arrowhead, she spends the afternoon trying to imagine how the first people lived on the land that is now her neighborhood. But traffic and house cats and well-tended gardens distract her. Then, Jenny camps out in her yard and in her dreams she is transported back to Indian times. An evocative story, with richly colored, realistic illustrations.

WHERE THE SIDEWALK ENDS
by Shel Silverstein (HarperCollins, 1974, paperback)

Shel Silverstein wrote the nonsensical verses and drew the comic illustrations for this volume in which readers discover what happens to Sarah Cynthia Sylvia Stout when she would not take the garbage out, or when Jimmy Jet spends too much time in front of the TV set.

GEORGE WASHINGTON'S COWS
by David Small (Farrar, Straus & Giroux, 1994, hardcover)

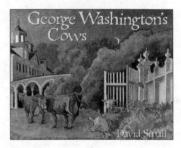

Why did George Washington go into politics? Because at Mount Vernon, the wackiest farm animals in America were driving him crazy. Take his cows, for instance:

*They had to be dressed in lavender gowns
and bedded on cushions of silk...
Begged every hour in obsequious tones,
Or they just wouldn't give any milk.*

A delightful book, illustrated with imaginative color paintings. As much fun grown-ups as for kids.

THE TRUE STORY OF THE THREE LITTLE PIGS
by Jon Scieszka, illustrated by Lane Smith (Puffin, 1997, paperback)

At long last, the much-maligned Wolf sets the record straight. First, he was only going next door to the Little Pigs' to borrow a cup of sugar. Second, it was an ill-timed sneeze that blew the First Little Pig's straw house down. Third, what kind of numb-nut builds a house out of straw, anyway? A fresh spin on a classic story for kids and adults. The illustrations are wickedly witty.

RAMA AND THE DEMON KING,
by *Jessica Souhami* (DK Ink, 1997, hardcover)

Prince Rama is everything his wicked stepmother is not—good, honest, brave, loving. So she tricks Rama's father, the King, into banishing his son to the forest for fourteen years. Rama leaves the court with his lovely wife Sita and his loyal brother Lakshman. Together they drive off the demons that dwell there and settle down to live peacefully with the animals. But the ten-headed Demon King has vowed vengeance on Prince Rama for conquering the forest demons. With a lively narrative and bold, bright illustrations, Jessica Souhami introduces Western readers to a story Indian parents have told their children for thousands of years.

SHABANU, DAUGHTER OF THE WIND
by *Suzanne Fisher Staples* (Knopf, 1989, hardcover)

Readers age 13 and over will find the story of Shabanu and her family of Pakistani nomads exciting. Shabanu's father raises camels and although Shabanu doesn't want him to sell their camels to Afghani rebels (the animals could be killed hauling weapons to battle), the insurgents offer so much money the man can't refuse. But there are other problems: Shabanu offends a clan leader when she tries to protect her older sister from a gang of men who are molesting her. The only way to resolve the issue is for Shabanu's father to agree to her betrothal to the clan leader's brother. An adolescent novel that is filled with surprises.

THE CHINESE SIAMESE CAT
by *Amy Tan, Illustrated by Gretchen Schields*
(Dove Books, 1994, paperback)

The best-selling author of *The Joy Luck Club* has written a delightful story of Sagwa, a mischievous kitten who performed a heroic deed 1000 years ago and has been famous among felines ever since. When the Foolish Magistrate decrees, "No singing until the sun goes down," Sagwa goes to work to foil the wicked man and his silly law. Children and adults will enjoy

Amy Tan's clever story and Gretchen Schields' colorful, wonderfully detailed illustrations.

IRA SLEEPS OVER
by *Bernard Waber* (Houghton Mifflin, 1972, hardcover)

Little Ira has a problem. he's been invited to sleep over next door at his friend Reggie's house. But Ira's older sister tells him Reggie will laugh if Ira shows up with his teddy bear, Tah-Tah. Waber not only explores a common childhood problem, but he does a masterful job portraying Ira's comic relationships with individual members of his family. And Waber's rhythmic prose makes this a great read-aloud book. A gem.

NEVER TAKE A PIG TO LUNCH:
AND OTHER FUN POEMS ABOUT THE FUN OF EATING
by *Nadine Bernard Westcott* (Orchard Books, 1994, hardcover)

You may know Westcott from the whimsical watercolor illustrations she does for Gourmet magazine. In this large-format book, she has brought together 60 comical poems about food, eating and table manners that are as much fun for parents as for kids. She even includes advice from such authorities as Miss Piggy: "Never eat more than you can lift."

CHARLOTTE'S WEB
by *E.B. White* (1952; HarperCollins, 1990, paperback)

When E.B. White wasn't composing scathing satire for *The New Yorker*, he was penning some of the best-loved children's books ever written. This is the story of a little girl named Fern, her pig, Wilbur, Templeton the self-centered rat and Charlotte A. Cavatica, a beautiful large grey spider—and a terrific speller—who devises a wonderfully clever plan to save Wilbur's life.

Also by E.B. White:

THE TRUMPET OF THE SWAN
(1970; HarperTrophy, 1987, paperback).

The poignant story of a young boy and his friend Louis, a trumpeter swan who can't make a sound.

STUART LITTLE
(1945; HarperCollins, 1990, paperback).

The incredible adventures of a most unusual mouse won its author the Laura Ingalls Wilder Award.

BRIAR ROSE
by Jane Yolen (Tor Books, 1993, paperback)

The old woman opened her eyes. "I was the princess in the castle in the sleeping woods. And there came a great dark mist and we all fell asleep. But the prince kissed me awake. Only me." Becca Berlin is the only one in her family who takes her grandmother seriously when she says on her deathbed, "I am Briar Rose." Becca's search to find out who her grandmother was leads to a refugee camp in Oswego, New York and a death camp in Chelmo, Poland. Yolen weaves the tale of Briar Rose and a story of the Holocaust into a seamless novel.

TAM LIN
by Jane Yolen, illustrated by Charles Mikolaycak
(Harcourt Brace, 1990, hardcover)

When brave Jennet MacKenzie lays claim to her great-grandfather's tumbledown castle, she unwittingly summons up Tam Lin, a handsome young man held prisoner by the Faery Queen. Now Jennet must fight to save Tam Lin's life and hold on to the home that is rightfully hers. An exciting story, with beautiful illustrations that capture the romance and mystery of Scotland.

SKY DOGS
by Jane Yolen, illustrated by Barry Moser
(Voyager Books, 1995, paperback)

The first time they saw horses, the Blackfeet thought they were massive dogs sent down from the sky as a gift from the Creator. A wonderful Native American story with illustrations that capture the majesty of the Great Plains.

FRESH IDEAS

THE WESTERN CANON:
THE BOOKS AND SCHOOL OF THE AGES
by Harold Bloom (Riverhead, 1995, paperback)

Yale professor and literary critic Harold Bloom is tired of the political, moral, sexual, ethnic and racial agendas that have invaded and often taken over college literature departments. To the dismay of wild-eyed activists, Bloom insists that there is such a thing as aesthetics, that we can tell one book is better than another and there most certainly are some works that will always enlarge our life and expand our imaginations. From Chaucer to Emily Dickinson, from Shakespeare to Pablo Neruda, Bloom urges us to rediscover the pleasures of great reading.

SHAMANS, SOFTWARE AND SPLEENS:
LAW AND THE CONSTRUCTION OF THE INFORMATION SOCIETY
by James Boyle (Harvard University Press, 1996, paperback)

It was Stewart Brand who popularized the phrase, "information wants to be free." So does that mean you can't copyright, trademark, or patent anything that appears on the Net and the Web? Attorney James Boyle examines such issues as the right of publicity, the right to privacy and what "intellectual property" means these days. He insists that free access to information is the heart and soul of the Net and the Web and rejects any suggestion that users should pay to use any Web site. Boyle writes in a jazzy style, which fits his cutting edge area of expertise and has a provocative point of view that will get you thinking.

THE RUIN OF KASCH
by *Roberto Calasso* (Belknap Press, 1995, paperback)

The end of the ancient world and the rise of the modern is Calasso's theme in this book. He studies the idea of sacrifice, the power of stories and the loss of idealism. At the heart of this book is Talleyrand, the man who believed in nothing and so survived every political and cultural upheaval. *The Ruin of Kasch* is filled with intriguing insights and gorgeous images that will keep you turning pages far into the night.

....

THE CULTURE OF DISBELIEF:
HOW AMERICAN LAW AND POLITICS TRIVIALIZE RELIGIOUS DEVOTION
by *Stephen L. Carter* (Basic Books, 1993, paperback)

In spite of America's long tradition of separating church and state, there has been a shift in our political culture that treats religious views and religious voices with disdain. Stephen L. Carter, an Episcopalian and a professor of law at Yale University, argues for a variety of new approaches to religion in public life. He discourages public officials from citing sacred texts to win political arguments. He insists that public schools can teach students ethics and urges protection for minority faiths. At last, a calm, rational discussion of law, politics and religion in America.

....

THE TWILIGHT OF COMMON DREAMS:
WHY AMERICA IS WRACKED BY CULTURE WARS
by *Todd Gitlin* (Metropolitan Books/Henry Holt, 1995, hardcover)

One minute Christopher Columbus was an intrepid explorer; the next he was a genocidal monster. What happened? How did our national culture disintegrate into nasty turf wars? Todd Gitlin places all the arguments about "multiculturalism" and "national unity" in a larger historical context and spares no one in his eloquent attack on the interest groups who have all but destroyed the notion of a common good as they pursue their own narrow agendas. A feisty assault on partisanship and an appeal for a return to reason, tolerance and a shared vision of America.

....

NEWS VALUES:
IDEAS FOR AN INFORMATION AGE
by Jack Fuller (University of Chicago Press, 1996, paperback)

Not long ago, Mike Wallace said that if he were covering a war and had information that U.S. troops were about to walk i nto an ambush, he would say nothing rather than break his "neutral observer" status. This claim struck many Americans as outrageous and it is one of the thorny issues Jack Fuller, the Pulitzer Prize-winning publisher of *The Chicago Tribune*, takes on in his thoughtful reassessment of contemporary journalism. His basic argument is that in spite of the arrogance of some outspoken reporters, journalism "does not exempt [the media] from the basic moral imperatives that guide all other human relationships."

....

IN DEFENSE OF ELITISM
by William A. Henry III (Doubleday, 1995, paperback)

A life-long liberal and card-carrying member of the ACLU, Henry argues that some ideas are better than others; some values more enduring; some works of art more universal; some people smarter, more productive, harder to replace. Unflinching and often funny, Henry takes on the thorniest social issues of our age-affirmative action, multicultural curriculums, radical feminism and the stupid notion (fostered by karaoke bars) that everybody is 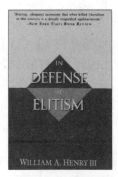 equally talented. *In Defense of Elitism* may make you uncomfortable, it may even make you angry, but it will keep you intellectually engaged from cover to cover.

....

THE DEATH OF COMMON SENSE:
HOW LAW IS SUFFOCATING AMERICA
by Philip K. Howard (Warner Books, 1996, paperback)

Your favorite rustic bed-and-breakfast establishment is probably in violation of the fire code. Sure, the "multi-story transient lodging" defined in the code is really meant for motels; nonetheless, your B&B must choose between making the prohibitively expensive renovations (which will put it out of business), or scoff at the law (and be driven out of business). As a founding partner of a New York law firm, Howard encounters inflexible, intrusive regulations all the time. In this book he lambastes modern America's infatuation with regulation and appeals for guidelines, not rigid rules; initiative, not mindless bureaucracy.

THE CULTURE OF COMPLAINT
by Robert Hughes (Warner Books, 1994, paperback)

Watching the art critic for *Time* magazine blow substandard art and substandard ideas out of the water is a beautiful thing. Diatribes should always be this much fun.

NOAH'S CHOICE:
THE FUTURE OF ENDANGERED SPECIES
by Charles C. Mann and Mark L. Plummer (Knopf, 1995, hardcover)

Noah had it easy. He took one pair of "unclean" animals, seven pairs of "clean" ones, marched them into the ark, raised the gangplank and waited for the rain to come. Today, saving wildlife is a lot more complicated. Mann and Plummer ask provocative questions about the goals of conservation. Do we preserve only creatures that are useful to humans? Or, only the ones that are beautiful to look at? Or, do we preserve them all at any cost?

QUEST FOR PERFECTION:
THE DRIVE TO BREED BETTER HUMAN
BEINGS
by Gina Maranto (Scribner, 1996, hardcover)

A prize-winning science journalist tackles the age-old dream of improving the human species. She offers an interesting historical overview of the subject, from Plato's Republic to 19th-century futuristic novels. Then, she gets down to business. For example, why were Nazi experiments in eugenics unspeakably evil, while contemporary eugenics work is considered benign? How far are we from the day when individuals—perhaps even the government—will terminate an embryo because it doesn't quite measure up in terms of appearance or intelligence? A very provocative study of the ethical, legal and religious implications of manipulating human evolution.

LIVING WITHOUT A GOAL:
FINDING THE FREEDOM TO LIVE A CREATIVE
AND INNOVATIVE LIFE
by James Ogilvy (Doubleday, 1995, hardcover)

A life enslaved to a single Goal, no matter how noble, becomes a mechanism rather than an organism, a business plan rather than a biography, a tool rather than a gift." Maybe, philosopher James Ogilvy says, if we stopped striving for the higher-paying job, the better car, the bigger house, we'd have more time for such joyous, unplanned experiences as friendship, romance and happiness. There's no denying this is a radical book, but you'll be surprised how much sense Ogilvy makes.

THE MORNING AFTER:
SEX, FEAR AND FEMINISM
by Katie Roiphe (Little, Brown, 1994, paperback)

This is the book that launched a thousand talk show segments. Roiphe argues that the definition of "date rape" promoted by some feminists is too broad—women are beginning to look like weak, passionless, perennial victims. Instead, Roiphe insists women are perfectly capable of taking responsibility for their sex lives and she suggests that there may be other reasons for the increase of accusations of date rape. A provocative and in many ways persuasive critique of the ways what is personal is made political.

GUILTY:
THE COLLAPSE OF CRIMINAL JUSTICE
by Judge Harold J. Rothwax (Random House, 1996, paperback)

In his 25 years on the bench, New York State Supreme Court Judge Harold J. Rothwax has watched criminals and defense attorneys hide behind ill-advised statutes and procedures that keep the courts from resolving the big question: Did the accused commit the crime? So Rothwax has a few radical suggestions: eliminate the Miranda warning; loosen up the current search-and-seizure laws; and abolish the insistence on unanimous jury verdicts. Sounds like harsh medicine, but after reading a few pages of the judge's book, you may find yourself agreeing with him.

CITY LIFE:
URBAN EXPECTATIONS IN A NEW WORLD
by Witold Rybczynski (Simon & Schuster, 1996, paperback)

Upon returning from Paris, a friend asked Witold Rybczynski, "Why aren't our cities like that?" It's a good question to ask a man who is professor of urbanism at the University of Pennsylvania. So Rybczynski sets out to explain the contrasting of visions of a city in America and Europe. For starters, he explains why Americans insist they don't like cities. Then he notes the types of monuments Europeans and Americans revere: Parisians pride themselves on Notre Dame, the city's cathedral; while New Yorkers boast of the Chrysler Building, a private corporation's headquarters. A book both enlightening and entertaining.

FORBIDDEN KNOWLEDGE:
FROM PROMETHEUS TO PORNOGRAPHY
by Roger Shattuck (St. Martin's Press, 1996, paperback)

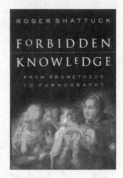

Is the quest for knowledge an absolute good? Or should some realms be off limits? Lord knows literature is filled with people—Faust, Frankenstein, Dr. Jekyll, Adam and Eve—who destroyed themselves because they presumed that humankind has a right to know everything. Roger Shattuck argues that in some cases the pursuit of knowledge has brought us nothing but trouble—the atomic bomb, for instance. Yet, Shattuck is no advocate for censorship. He would like to see more people recognize that there are repercussions even to the quest for knowledge and that sometimes the price of knowing and understanding is too high.

. . . .

QUEER IN AMERICA:
SEX, THE MEDIA AND THE CLOSETS OF POWER
by Michelangelo Signorile (Anchor Books, 1996, paperback)

Signorile is the controversial gay activist who became notorious for outing Malcolm Forbes. Here he argues forcefully that gay men and lesbians will continue to be a powerless minority so long as they are afraid to be honest about who and what they are. Signorile illustrates his points with the often frustrating, sometimes uplifting, real-life stories of actors and agents, government officials and legislators, columnists and editors who know all about being locked in the closet.

. . . .

VIRTUALLY NORMAL:
AN ARGUMENT ABOUT HOMOSEXUALITY
by Andrew Sullivan (Vintage, 1998, paperback)

Few issues spark a more intense emotional response than homosexuality. Is it immoral? Should homosexuals be allowed

to marry? Are rights for homosexuals special rights or civil rights? Any one of the these questions can set off a firestorm of argument. Now Andrew Sullivan, the brilliant, young, gay former editor of *The New Republic* tackles points of view across the spectrum, respecting their strengths, exposing their weaknesses and appealing to reason. Sullivan is nothing if not evenhanded: his conclusions are likely to irritate everyone from the Catholic hierarchy to radical gay activists.

RACE MATTERS
by Cornell West (Vintage, 1994, paperback)

West doesn't believe that what happened in Los Angeles in May 1992 was a race riot or class warfare. He describes it as a "multiracial, trans-class and largely male display of justified social outrage." As a provocative writer on race in America, West will probably get you angry, but he'll also get you thinking.

THE LEVELING WIND:
POLITICS, CULTURE & OTHER NEWS
by George F. Will (Viking, 1994, hardcover)

The Nineties provided America's most articulate conservative with plenty of column fodder. This collection includes Will's acerbic, funny, perceptive observations about the career of Bill Clinton and his merry band of bureaucrats, the Supreme Court's agonizing over the constitutionality of publicly displayed Hanukkah menorahs, the looniness of Antioch College's sexual contact code and lots more.

THE MORAL ANIMAL:
THE NEW SCIENCE OF EVOLUTIONARY
PSYCHOLOGY
by Robert Wright (Random House, 1995, paperback)

A re there genes that program us to sacrifice for our children, love our spouses, stick by our friends, cling to our principles, admire the good and deprecate the evil? The answer is a very definite "Probably." Wright argues that moral standards emerge from genetic self-interest—we do good things for others in the expectation that they will do good things for us. That's a gross oversimplification. So, to savor every intelligent, original nuance of Wright's argument, buy his book.

FRESH
TRANSLATIONS

JASON AND THE GOLDEN FLEECE
by Apollonius of Rhodes, translated by Richard Hunter
(Oxford University Press, 1993, hardcover)

F orget the sword-and-sandals movie version from the 1960s
with its chintzy special effects. This third-century B.C. epic
is the real thing. An impossible quest. A dream team of heroes
(including Hercules) who come together to win the prize. An army
of demon warriors who spring right out of the ground. And a
beautiful princess who will let nothing—NOTHING!—stand
between her and her buff Greek prince. *Jason and the Golden Fleece*
is one of the great books of the ancient world and this new
translation brings the story vividly to life for modern readers.

DON QUIJOTE
by Miguel de Cervantes, translated by Burton Raffel
(1605; Norton, 1996, paperback)

B urton Raffel is a marvel among translators: he's rendered
Beowulf into modern English from its original 8th-century
Anglo-Saxon, now he gives readers a lively English translation of
Cervantes' comic epic. *Don Quijote* is the first modern novel: the
story of the last gasp of chivalry told through the adventures
of an eccentric elderly knight, Don Quixote and his rotund
companion, Sancho Panza.

THE FIVE BOOKS OF MOSES
translated by Everett Fox (Schocken Books, 1995, hardcover)

At the beginning of God's creating
of the heavens and the earth,
when the earth was wild and waste,
darkness over the face of Ocean,
rushing-spirit of God hovering over the face of the waters-
God said: Let there be Light! And there was light.

Everett Fox, a professor of Judaica, has gone back to the Hebrew text to rediscover the literary power of the first five books of the Bible. His goal—and he has accomplished it beautifully—is to capture in English the rhythms, idioms and even the peculiarities of the Hebrew original. Fox banishes the insipid, modern, translation-by-committee versions of the Bible and restores the ancient cadences and magisterial poetry of sacred Scripture. *The Five Books of Moses* is a dazzling achievement that everyone who loves the Word and words will celebrate.

THE ARABIAN NIGHTS II:
SINDBAD AND OTHER POPULAR STORIES
translated by Husain Haddawy (Norton, 1995, hardcover)

The Seven Voyages of Sindbad. Ali Baba and the 40 Thieves. Aladdin and the Magic Lamp. You remember these stories from childhood, but you've probably never read them in their original versions. Now Husain Haddawy has created a new translation of these classic tales of adventure and enchantment that captures all the sensuality of the Arabic text.

Haddawy's prequel:

THE ARABIAN NIGHTS
(Norton, 1990, hardcover).

The complete text of the Arabic classic, in a critically acclaimed new translation for modern readers.

THE AUTUMN OF THE MIDDLE AGES

by Johan Huizinga, translated by Rodney J. Payton and Ulrich Mammitzch (University of Chicago Press, 1996, hardcover)

In 1924, Huizinga's book was translated from Dutch into English under the title *The Waning of the Middle Ages*. Since then, English-speakers have regarded it as one of the best books on life in 14th- and 15th-century France and the Low Countries. What no one knew was *Waning* was a hatchet job. The 1924 translator cut passages he didn't like, omitted Huizinga's most intriguing theories, mangled his prose and even eliminated the pictures. All of that has been remedied in this new edition-the first English translation that is absolutely faithful to the original text. If you were charmed by *The Waning of the Middle Ages*, you'll be dazzled by *The Autumn of the Middle Ages*.

THE LANDMARK THUCYDIDES, A COMPREHENSIVE GUIDE TO THE PELOPONNESIAN WAR

Edited by Robert B. Strassler (Free Press, 1996, hardcover)

As a historian Thucydides had no rivals. He was the first to see human passions (rather than the whims of the gods) as the prime force in history. And when Greek prose was still in its infancy, Thucydides set the standard future Greek writers would try to emulate. Nonetheless, modern readers have found Thucydides hard to tackle. So Robert Strassler and his team of classical scholars have created a new edition that for the first time in 2000 years makes this great work readable and enjoyable. You'll find a "Calendar of Events," an epilogue which summarizes the consequences of the war for the main players, appendices on Greek institutions, plus excellent maps. Every work of ancient history deserves an edition as good as this.

FUNNY FOLK

BRING ME THE HEAD OF WILLY THE MAILBOY!
by Scott Adams (Andrews & McMeel, 1995, paperback)

Scott Adams' Dilbert comic strip—the adventures of a luckless, cubicle-dwelling employee in the land of the clueless—is, by far, the funniest corporate satire of all time. Packed with dead-on accurate observations such as "there's a fine line between marketing and grand theft" and cautionary advice about opera "we can't let children think it's okay to dress like Vikings and go around hollering," Bring Me the Head of Willy the Mailboy is an excellent entrée into the Dilbert Zone.

DOGBERT'S TOP SECRET MANAGEMENT HANDBOOK
by Scott Adams (HarperCollins, 1996, paperback)

Dilbert's canine sidekick, Dogbert, skewers current management trends in this hilarious book of essays and cartoons designed to help new managers avoid such unforgivable mistakes as rewarding good work with good pay, communicating clearly and improving department efficiency.

THE WORLD OF CHARLES ADDAMS
(Borzoi Books/Knopf, 1991, hardcover)

Medusa at the beauty parlor. A cardinal (the Vatican kind) in a birdfeeder. A naughty Greek boy's mother scolds him, "Why can't you be more like Oedipus?" And of course, the ghoulishly hilarious Addams family. Here are 300 of Charles Addams' best cartoons, including 24 of his New Yorker covers in full color. A laugh riot.

GETTING EVEN
by *Woody Allen* (Vintage, 1978, paperback)

Death, incidentally, is one of the worst things that can happen to a Cosa Nostra member and most prefer to simply pay a fine." This is just one of the many outrageous observations from Woody Allen's first humor collection. These 17 pieces show off Allen at his best as he lampoons philosophy, organized crime, Latin American revolutionaries and other modern obsessions. Not only a volume of humor, *Getting Even* also explores great truths— "Eternal nothingness is OK if you're dressed for it."

LET'S PAVE THE STUPID RAINFORESTS & GIVE SCHOOL TEACHERS STUN GUNS: AND OTHER WAYS TO SAVE AMERICA
by *Ed Anger* (Broadway Books, 1996, paperback)

Madonna, Newt Gingrich, Bill Clinton, even Rush Limbaugh look forward to the outrageously funny columns of Ed Anger from *Weekly World News*. His over-the-top comedy is hilarious and almost guaranteed to offend somebody. On animals rights: "I'm Going Huntin' for Whale!" On Social Security: "older Americans ought to get off their butts and get back to work." On gun control: "It ain't Christmas without the gift of guns!" By the way, "Ed Anger" is a pseudonym—nobody knows who this guy really is.

DAVE BARRY'S BOOK OF BAD SONGS
by Dave Barry (Andrews and McMeel, 1997, paperback)

When *Miami Herald* columnist and professional funny guy, Dave Barry, invited his readers to vote on the worst pop songs, he was deluged with more than 10,000 responses. Having carefully tabulated the results, Barry has broken down the songs by category, including Teen Death Songs, Weenie Music and Songs That People Always Get Wrong (for years, Barry thought the opening line of the Beach Boys' "Help Me, Rhonda" was "Well, since she put me down/There's been owls pukin' in my bed"). We won't say which song is the worst ever, but Paul Anka's "(You're) Having My Baby" and Neil Diamond's "I Am, I Said" both ranked very high.

Also by Dave Barry:

DAVE BARRY IN CYBERSPACE
(Crown, 1996, paperback)

Guy-who-gets-paid-to-be-funny, Dave Barry (dbarry@techgeek. com), is just the man to help you understand the mysteries of cyberspace.

With Barry by your side, you'll learn that hardware "is the part of the computer that stops working when you spill beer on it" and a megahertz "is a really, really big hertz." Plus you get Barry's personal recommendations on special features every computer ought to have ("I strongly recommend the Auto-Defrost option"), tips on how to communicate with your computer when it crashes: ("Give me back my report or I'm going to throw your little friend the fax machine out the window!") and Barry's most astonishing revelation of all—why Bill Gates is Elvis.

DAVE BARRY'S COMPLETE GUIDE TO GUYS
(Random House, 1995, paperback)

Barry explores such guyhood essentials as scratching, the little-known link between the discovery of North America and golf and the 100% effective "Margaret Thatcher Method" of delaying orgasm. Plus, he explains to women how to talk to guys without scaring them.

DAVE BARRY'S GREATEST HITS
(Fawcett, 1989, paperback)

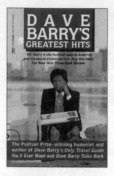

There just aren't enough words for "funny" to describe newspaper columnist Dave Barry. In this collection of essays, the master humorist introduces us to his dog (We are not sure yet whether Earnest has a working brain"), unveils his $8.95 tax plan ("There would be no deductions but you would still be permitted to cheat") and examines the search for invisible subatomic particles ("I'm starting to wonder if [physicists] don't sit around their $23 million atomic accelerators all day, drinking frozen daiquiris and shrieking, 'There goes one now!' and then laughing themselves sick").

DAVE BARRY TURNS 40
(Fawcett, 1991, paperback)

There should be books this entertaining for every milestone in life. Guy-who-gets-paid-to-be-funny Dave Barry takes a swing at the aging process with chapters on important topics such as Your Disintegrating Body ("going past age 40 is basically an affront to Nature, with exhibit A being the Gabor sisters"), Sex After 40 ("younger people seem to want to have sex with each other at every available opportunity including traffic lights, whereas older people are more likely to reserve their sexual activities for special occasions such as the installation of a new pope") and The Joys of Geezerhood ("the geezer car should be as large as possible. If a fighter jet can't land on it, you don't want to drive it").

THE BENCHLEY ROUNDUP
by Robert Benchley University of Chicago Press, 1983, paperback)

A great many people have come to me," Benchley writes, "and asked me how I manage to get so much work done while looking so dissipated. My answer is 'Don't you wish you knew?'" Back during the 1920s and 1930s, Robert Benchley was celebrated as a brilliant raconteur, a prolific reviewer and screenwriter and one of the funniest members of the legendary Algonquin Round

Table. This collection of the best of Benchley introduces a new generation to his apparently effortless wit. As James Thurber once remarked, "One of the greatest fears of the humorous writer is that he has spent three weeks writing something done faster and better by Benchley."

....

HOME LIFE QUARTET
by Alice Thomas Ellis
(A Common Reader Edition, 1997, hardcover)

Not that our everyday life is uneventful.... 'The floor fell out of the lavatory' is not altogether lacking in drama, but it doesn't have the same élan as 'At this point I shot my third husband and had to flee the country.'"

Some of our British friends regard the years when Alice Thomas Ellis wrote her weekly column in The Spectator as a kind of golden age. So it is a thrill to find all of Ellis' brilliantly witty observations about domestic life collected in four handsome volumes and available on this side of the pond. Pounce!

....

IF YOU LEAVE ME, CAN I COME TOO?
by Cynthia Heimel (Atlantic Monthly Press, 1995, paperback).

"Nature," Cynthia Heimel observes, "is not a feminist. If nature were a feminist... giving birth would be a breeze and there would be no such things as a stretch mark." In case you haven't run into Heimel before, think of her as the Dorothy Parker of the 90s—a smart, sharp-tongued woman with an outrageous opinion about everything. In this very funny collection of essays, she answer the eternal question, "How can I dump him when he hasn't called me?", explains why nice girls don't read romance novels and suggests ways for daughters to suppress their matricidal tendencies. A laugh riot from page one.

....

THE BOOK OF GUYS
Garrison Keillor (Penguin, 1994, paperback)

I magine Dionysus, 50 years old, with a wife pushing him to get help for his drinking problem. Or picture Don Giovanni as a cocktail pianist in North Dakota. Ever wonder what Zeus would be like as a Lutheran? Only the fertile imagination of Garrison Keillor could dream up these scenarios. From Al Denny, the New Age author of *Rebirthing the Me You Used to Be* , to Omoo the Wolf Boy, who grows up, gets married and has a few pups of his own, Keillor lampoons the hapless predicaments of modern guys.

Also by Garrison Keillor:

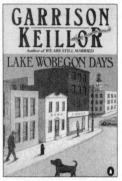

LAKE WOBEGON DAYS
(Penguin, 1995, paperback)

In the spring of 1974, Keillor accidentally left his briefcase in an Oregon train station. In it was a story that, in its loss, became the most brilliant thing he'd ever written. In an effort to replace it he penned *Lake Wobegon Days*, which (although he claims doesn't stand up to the original missing version) ranks as one of the funniest and most touching portraits of small town American life ever written. From the Sons of Knute Ice Melt contest to the history of the Living Flag, Keillor chronicles the town's history with warmth and wit that captures what is profoundly universal in American life.

WLT: A RADIO ROMANCE
(Penguin, 1992, paperback)

In 1926, the Soderbjerg brothers start up a radio station, WLT (With Lettuce and Tomato), hoping to save their floundering restaurant and become the Sandwich Kings of South Minneapolis. Inspired hilarity from one of America's best storytellers.

INTO THE TWILIGHT, ENDLESSLY GROUSING
by *Patrick F. McManus* (Simon & Schuster, 1997, paperback)

atrick F. McManus, the James Thurber of the outdoors, writes hilarious columns for *Outdoor Life* magazine. This collection features some of his best. McManus recalls the Fourth of July when, madcap child that he was, he dropped a huge but unlit firecracker down his stepfather's waders. He tells the outrageous story of how his uncle's beard got caught in the belt of the town librarian just as that prim lady was exiting the movie theater. And he offers such sharp observations as, "Eighty-seven percent of all conversations between friends are based on shared ignorance. That's the reason so many friendships last a lifetime." You'll find big laughs on every page.

GROUCHO AND ME:
THE AUTOBIOGRAPHY OF GROUCHO MARX
by (of all people) Groucho Marx
(1959; Da Capo Press, 1995, paperback)

This is the story of how the sons of the most inept tailor on Manhattan's Upper East Side became the toast of stage and screen. Groucho recalls rough nights on far-flung vaudeville stages, remembers Hollywood in its heyday and reveals the true character of Julius H. Marx, the quiet, literary man who donned the mask of Groucho to entertain the world.

THE ACCIDENTAL BUDDHIST:
MINDFULNESS, ENLIGHTENMENT AND SITTING STILL, AMERICAN STYLE
by Dinty W. Moore (Algonquin, 1997, paperback)

Can a guy with an off-beat sense of humor find enlightenment? It won't be easy. Moore can't help putting a funny spin on some fundamental Buddhist practices, such as giving up attachment to material things: ("Why do Tibetan Buddhists have such trouble with their vacuum cleaners? They lack attachments.") The basics of zazen, or sitting meditation, sound to him like advice you give an antsy kid: ("Eat your rice, wash your bowl and just sit.")

In the end, Moore confesses that he's a "fairly lousy Buddhist," but Buddhism has taught him to incorporate the principles of kindness, compassion and awareness into his life.

THE LAZLO LETTERS (Vols. I & II)
by Don Novello (Workman, 1992, paperback)

Don Novello (a.k.a. Father Guido Sarducci) has an alter ego, Lazlo Toth, who has written some very strange letters—a request for an autographed photo of the Shah of Iran, notes of encouragement to the beleaguered Richard Nixon and Dan Quayle and a suggestion for a new Moldavian national anthem to the tune of Neil Diamond's "I Am, I Said." Stranger still are the straightforward replies he gets back. You won't find anything like this brilliantly funny collection of Lazlo's letters and responses (complete with autographed photos).

AGE AND GUILE:
BEAT YOUTH, INNOCENCE AND A BAD HAIRCUT
by P.J. O'Rourke (Atlantic Monthly Press, 1996, paperback)

I'm a middle-class male with a job. Of course I'm a Republican," says America's funniest political humorist, P.J. O'Rourke. Ah, but time was when O'Rourke was long-haired kid, denouncing the establishment, materialism, sexual hang-ups and engagement rings. This hilarious collection brings together 25 years of O'Rourke's funniest writing, from send-ups of Richard Nixon trying to speak hippie slang, to Truman Capote's society gossip, to O'Rourke's personal recollections of the down-side of the Sixties: "communal toothbrushes... women who thought they might be witches... jail." With O'Rourke, the laughs always cross party lines.

ALL THE TROUBLE IN THE WORLD
by P.J. O'Rourke (Atlantic Monthly Press, 1995, paperback)

With his jaundiced view of humankind and razor-sharp put-downs, O'Rourke is a modern H.L. Mencken. Now the best-selling political humorist crisscrosses the planet to eyeball, first hand, the problems that make the headlines. From overpopulation to deforestation to multiculturalism on his old college campus (it reminds him of Bosnia), O'Rourke is never at a loss for an outrageously funny opinion.

....

HOW TO PLAY WITH YOUR FOOD
by Penn and Teller, photographs by Anthony Loew, design by Robert Bull (Villard Books, 1992, paperback)

I f you thought playing with your food meant flinging mashed potatoes at whoever is sitting across the table from you, think again. Master magicians Penn and Teller have assembled a collection of devilishly clever food tricks that will amaze your friends at home or in your favorite bistro. There is "Stabbing a Fork in Your Eye," the ever popular "How to Get Your Ethical Vegetarian Friends to Eat Veal" and, of course, the "Bleeding Heart Gelatin Dessert." Even if you never learn to do a single trick, *How to Play with Your Food* will have you laughing all the way to the refrigerator.

....

PLUNKITT OF TAMMANY HALL:
A SERIES OF VERY PLAIN TALKS ON VERY PRACTICAL POLITICS
by William L. Riordon (1905; Signet Classics, 1995, paperback)

F rom his rostrum at the New York County Courthouse shoeshine stand, George Washington Plunkitt, one of the great Tammany Hall operatives, held forth on his fundamental political philosophy: "I seen my opportunities," he told New York Evening Post reporter William L. Riordon, "and I took 'em." With Riordon writing down every word he said, Plunkitt holds forth on "Honest Graft and Dishonest Graft," the "Curse of Civil Service Reform" and personal 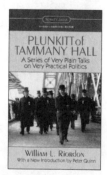 loyalty. "What," he muses, "is the Constitution between friends?" Shameless, pragmatic and born to win elections, Plunkitt is America's Machiavelli—only a lot funnier.

....

IN GOD WE TRUST, ALL OTHERS PAY CASH
by Jean Shepherd (Dolphin Books, 1991, paperback)

Few people remember growing up as well or as funny as Jean Shepherd. One of the most prominent humorists of the 1960s, Shepherd has an incredible memory for what it's like to be a kid. While In God We Trust is an authentic and hilarious portrait of small-town boyhood in the Depression years, it's humor transcends time. You'll find yourself laughing along with the misadventures of Ralph, his kid brother and his friends Flick, Schwartz and Kissel as if they were stories from your own youth.

Also by Jean Shepherd:

WANDA HICKEY'S NIGHT OF GOLDEN MEMORIES AND OTHER DISASTERS
(Dolphin Books, 1976, paperback)

The characters from In God We Trust return, a little older but— thankfully—no wiser in this hilarious follow up work.

BETTER THAN SEX
by Hunter S. Thompson (Ballantine, 1996, paperback)

The high priest of gonzo journalism is back and he's out of control as he spews his venom at Bill and Hillary Clinton, George Bush, James Carville and Ollie North. Plus, Thompson fires off one final barrage at his long-time nemesis, Richard Nixon. After tagging along with the 1992 Clinton campaign and eyeballing the Clinton presidency, Thompson concludes, "Bill Clinton would have played the Jew's harp stark naked on 60 Minutes if he thought it would help him get elected." Don't miss this literary wild man.

A THOMPSON CLASSIC: FEAR AND LOATHING ON THE CAMPAIGN TRAIL, '72
(Warner Books, 1985, paperback)

A hilarious collection of invective and wild, scurrilous attacks on the candidates of the 1972 presidential election campaign. (Nixon gets both barrels.)

THE THURBER CARNIVAL
by James Thurber (1945; Modern Library, 1994, hardcover)

This collection of classic essays, poems, stories, memoirs, fables and cartoons by the late New Yorker writer is all the proof needed that Thurber ranks with the truly great humorists of our age. Whether he's lampooning his youth in Columbus, Ohio, the battle of the sexes, Shakespeare, or the secret life of milquetoast Walter Mitty, he writes with a wit and wisdom that is timeless.

THE DOONESBURY CHRONICLES
by G.B. Trudeau (Holt, 1975, paperback)

Doonesbury first appeared in the *Yale Daily News* in 1968. In the 30 years since, Garry Trudeau, via his characters Mike Doonesbury, Mark Slackmeyer, Zonker Harris, Joannie Caucus, Roland Hedley, Boopsie, Phred the Viet Cong terrorist, Uncle Duke and others too numerable to mention, has satirized every newsworthy political and social anomaly to come down the pike—and made others newsworthy through his attention. This collection of strips from 1970 to 1975 (the year Doonesbury became the first comic strip to win a Pulitzer Prize for editorial cartooning) is guaranteed to give you the most enjoyable history lesson you've ever had.

LITTLE RED RIDING HOOD
retold and illustrated by William Wegman
(Hyperion, 1993, hardcover)

I magine a perplexed-looking weimaraner dog, dressed in a red hooded cape and "holding" a wicker basket of wildflowers. Wegman and his dogs, Bettina and Fay Ray, retell the story of the sweet, naive little puppy who forgets her mother's warnings about dawdling in the woods and talking to strangers. Absolutely hilarious.

Also by Wegman:

CINDERELLA
(Hyperion, 1993, hardcover).

The heroine wears a wig of cascading golden curls. The evil stepsisters, of course, are real dogs.

CARRY ON, JEEVES
by P.G. Wodehouse (1925; Penguin, 1975, paperback)

T o put it mildly, Wodehouse was a true comic genius, admired and imitated by some of the greatest writers of the 20th century. His novels and stories captured an era of Art Deco wackiness that is sadly gone for good. This classic collection contains ten misadventures of the intellectually challenged playboy, Bertram Wooster and his inimitable manservant, Jeeves and includes the episode where Jeeves first shimmers into Bertie's life to pull him out of the soup and a delightful diversion narrated by the brainy butler himself. ("In an employer," says Jeeves, "brains are not desirable.")

THE CODE OF THE WOOSTERS
by P.G. Wodehouse (1938; Vintage, 1975, paperback)

" M an and boy, Jeeves," says Bertie Wooster, "I have been in some tough spots in my time, but this takes the mottled oyster." In this classic country-house farce, Bertie comes to the aid of his Aunt Dahlia and his friends Gussie Fink-Nottle and Stiffy

Byng only to end up in imminent danger of matrimony, prison and being pounded to a pulp by the evil Sir Roderick Spode. Can Jeeves, that paragon of butlers, save the day? A work of diluted comic genius.

HOW RIGHT YOU ARE JEEVES
by P.G. *Wodehouse* (HarperCollins, 1990, paperback)

Foolishly, Bertie Wooster accepts an invitation to his Aunt Dahlia's country house while Jeeves is away on holiday. Of course, Bertie becomes ensnared in all sorts of trouble. Will Jeeves arrive back in time?

GODS & HEROES

THE SHADOW OF ULYSSES:
FIGURES OF A MYTH
by Piero Boitani, translated by Anita Weston
(Oxford University Press, 1994, hardcover)

Of all the epics of Western civilization, only the Odyssey has passed into our language as a term for a journey of discovery. Beginning with that curious fact, Boitani traces the hold Ulysses has had on the imaginations of some the West's greatest writers—including Dante, Tennyson, Borges and Joyce. This is an intriguing study of the connections between poetry, history and myth and why after 3000 years, we are still reading the story of Ulysses.

Brush up your classics:

THE ODYSSEY
translated by Robert Fagles (Penguin, 1997, paperback).

Man-eating cyclops, killer whirlpools, seductive nymphs, even a sidetrip to Hell. Come on! Give the classics a chance. By the way, Fagles' is widely considered the finest modern English translation of Homer's epic.

THE MARRIAGE OF CADMUS AND HARMONY
by Roberto Calasso (Random House, 1994, paperback)

The trouble with those thick collections of ancient myths is that they take stories of incredible power and boil them down to encyclopedia entries. In his retelling of tales from Greek mythology, Calasso unleashes the heroic—and erotic—power of the old stories. He brings to life the long-vanished age when gods and mortals ate and drank and made love with one another.

THE HERO WITH A THOUSAND FACES
by Joseph Campbell (1949; Princeton/Bollingen, 1973, paperback)

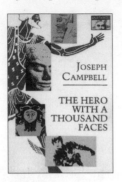

No one spoke more eloquently about the vital role mythology plays in our lives than Joseph Campbell. In this classic, Campbell argues that it does not matter who is the hero of the story—Apollo or Wotan, Moses or Jesus, Lao-tzu or the Old Men of Australia. Behind them all is a single hero, the archetype of all our legends.

THE ILLUSTRATED BULFINCH'S MYTHOLOGY
by Thomas Bulfinch, Illustrated by Giovanni Caselli
(1855; Macmillan, 1997, hardcover)

For some years now, this classic retelling of world mythology has only been available in cheaply printed one-volume editions. So, it's a real pleasure to find a beautifully designed, exquisitely illustrated, unabridged edition of *Bulfinch's Mythology*. This three-volume boxed set features The Age of Fable—the classic stories from the Greek and Roman pantheons, the myths of ancient Egypt, the legends of the Celts and the Norse; The Age of Chivalry—Arthurian legends, heroic tales of the Crusades, the story of Robin Hood; and Legends of Charlemagne, which includes a retelling of the Chanson de Roland.

GODS, GRAVES AND SCHOLARS
by C.W. Ceram (Vintage, 1986, paperback)

Ceram's classic celebrates the old-time, Indiana Jones-style archaeologists who combined genius with knowledge of arcane lore plus dumb luck to locate some of the great archaeological finds, including Troy, Pompeii and Babylon.

DATELINE: TROY

by *Paul Fleischman*, collages by *Gwen Frankfeldt & Glenn Morrow* (Candlewick Press, 1996, paperback)

To get kids interested in Homer's epic tale of the Trojan War, Fleishman, Frankfeldt and Morrow juxtapose an episode from the ancient legend with clippings of 20th-century newspaper articles that reflect the same theme. Paris' judgment of which goddess is most beautiful is set beside the results of the Miss Universe contest. Achilles sulking in his tent is compared to Darryl Strawberry's threat to walk out on the Mets. When the Trojan's drive the Greeks to the sea, the authors see a parallel with the Allies pinned down at Dunkirk. A fun, fresh way to convince kids of the relevance of classic stories.

HERCULES, MY SHIPMATE

by *Robert Graves* (Greenwood Press, 1979, hardcover)

The author who imagined the life of the Emperor Claudius now takes the myth of Jason and the Argonauts and tells it as if it were an actual historical event. (Jason, you remember, collected a crew of heroes to help him win the Golden Fleece and Hercules was among them). Robert Graves is completely convincing as he conjures up mythology's golden age, lending realistic details to the old legends and all the while telling a great adventure story.

More of Robert Graves:

HOMER'S DAUGHTER

(Academy of Chicago, 1987, paperback).

When Princess Nausicaa finds a handsome young seafarer washed up on the beach she is certain he is a gift from heaven, sent by Athene to help her drive out the 120 unwelcome, riotous and treacherous suitors who have descended on her palace. A great read, based on a number of episodes from Homer's *Odyssey*.

I, CLAUDIUS
by Robert Graves (1934; Vintage Books, 1989, paperback)

One of the best historical novels ever written! In old age, lame, stammering Claudius, once a major embarrassment to the Imperial family and now himself Emperor of Rome, writes an eyewitness account of the reign of the first four Caesars: the noble Augustus and his cunning wife Livia; the reptilian Tiberius; the monstrous Caligula; and finally old Claudius himself and his wife Messalina. Filled with poisonings, betrayals and shocking sexual excesses, *I, Claudius* is a real page-turner.

Also by Robert Graves:

CLAUDIUS THE GOD
(1934; Vintage Books, 1989, paperback).

The sequel features the epic adulteries of Messalina, King Herod Agrippa's treachery and the arrival on the scene of that slimy teenager, Nero.

....

HANNIBAL: THE NOVEL
by Ross Leckie (Regnery Press, 1996, hardcover)

Life is cruel. Mercy is weakness. And Rome is the enemy that must be destroyed. Those were the lessons the boy Hannibal learned from his father. So at 18, when he becomes king, Hannibal begins to hone the armies of Carthage into an unstoppable fighting machine whose only purpose is to crush Rome. Leckie takes us inside the psyche of a great military commander and carries us along on Hannibal's epic journey through North Africa, across the Alps and into Italy where he inflicts one humiliating defeat after another on the Romans. The novel is graphic and bloody—as befits the times—but it also brings a legendary character to life.

RED BRANCH
by Morgan Llywelyn (Ivy Books, 1990, paperback)

Llywelyn's big, swashbuckling novel retells the entire Cuchulain legend—his lifelong conflict with Morrigan the goddess of war, his epic battles for Ulster and the deadly enmity between the hero and Queen Maeve.

CAESAR
by Allan Massie

The narrator—once Julius Caesar's closest companion, now a captive of the barbarian Gauls—looks back on the final months of his commander's life and explains his motives for betraying Caesar and joining the assassins. By focusing on character (with a few digressions into the sexual decadence of ancient Rome), Massie gives new zest to a story we think we know. Worth searching for.

THE KING MUST DIE
by Mary Renault (1958; Random House, 1988, paperback)

You may never get around to reading Homer's *Iliad* and *Odyssey*, but there is a way to bone up on the old myths and at the same time discover what life was like in ancient Greece. Mary Renault writes what you might call mythological novels—her retelling of the legend of Theseus and the Minotaur is not only exciting but believable. And the young hero's perilous journey to the strange island kingdom of Crete is a great read.

Also by Mary Renault:

THE BULL FROM THE SEA
(1962; Vintage, 1975, paperback).

In this sequel, Phaedra, Theseus' wife, tries to seduce and then destroy her handsome stepson, Hippolytus.

THESEUS AND ATHENS
by Henry John Walker (Oxford University Press, 1995, hardcover)

The story of Theseus and the Minotaur has been popular for more than 2500 years. In ancient Athens, Theseus was such a favorite he was recast from an archaic hero-king to the founder of the city's democratic principles. Now, Henry John Walker sifts through the fragmentary evidence of the ancient world to see how Theseus' myth grew and how he was transformed from a monster-slayer into a enlightened Athenian gentleman. And he studies how the great Greek dramatists, Sophocles and Euripides, presented him in their plays. An interesting study of one of the most enduring heroes of Greek mythology.

WORLD MYTHOLOGY
Roy Willis, General Editor (Henry Holt, 1993, hardcover)

Every civilization has stories which give meaning to birth and death, sin and forgiveness, the seasons of life and the seasons of the year. Now, all the world's mythologies are assembled in a single volume. From Egypt comes the story of the Nine Gods of Heliopolis. From India, the tales of Krishna and Shiva. From Rome, the story of Romulus and Remus. From Japan, the story of Izanagi and Izanami, the primal couple. Every major culture is represented, from the Celts to the Mesoamerican civilizations, from the Polynesian Islanders to the Navajo to the Inuits. Lavishly illustrated with hundreds of stunning photographs, plus maps and genealogical charts, this volume is a superb book for browsers and researchers.

MEMOIRS OF HADRIAN
by Marguerite Yourcenar, translated by Grace Frick and Marguerite Yourcenar (Random House, 1995, hardcover)

Yourcenar wrote this extraordinary psychological novel as a memoir from the Roman Emperor Hadrian (76-138 A.D.) to his young successor, Marcus Aurelius. Imitating the forceful prose of the great Roman authors, Yourcenar follows Hadrian into battle with Emperor Trajan, portrays his love for the beautiful Antinous and tags along on Hadrian's own adventures to the frontiers of the Empire. A splendid reconstruction of actual events from ancient history.

GRAND PASSIONS

MADAME BOVARY
by Gustave Flaubert (1857; Doubleday, 1997, hardcover)

Flaubert's novel so shocked 19th-century French society that he was charged with "offenses against public morals and religion." In spite of official disapproval, the story of Emma Bovary, an entrancingly beautiful woman with the flighty disposition of a child, has always beguiled readers. Like Emma's lovers, we find her passionate, frivolous, enchanting, frustrating and ultimately unforgettable. She is one of the most perfectly created characters in modern fiction and the heroine of what many consider the first modern novel.

LOVE IN THE TIME OF CHOLERA
by Gabriel Garcia Marquez (Penguin 1989, paperback)

Set in Colombia at the turn of the century, this is the wildly romantic story of the beautiful Fermina Daza and the two men who loved her for 50 years. Florentino Ariza is the mysterious, intense young lover she rejected in her youth. Dr. Juvenal Urbino de la Calle is the illustrious gentleman she married. Through all those years, Ariza stayed close by, waiting. And when de la Calle dies, Ariza seizes his last chance for love.

THE VOLCANO LOVER
by Susan Sontag (Farrar, Straus and Giroux, 1992, hardcover)

Sir William Hamilton, British ambassador to Naples, is a renowned collector of beautiful things. The "object" this connoisseur loves best of all his wife, Emma. For her part, Emma has fallen in love with Horatio Nelson, whose victories over Napoleon have made him the British public's most beloved hero. With Mount Vesuvius and Naples (both by turns enchanting and horrible) as a backdrop, Sontag casts a pretty cold eye on collecting, celebrity and grand romantic passion. But the real pleasure of this novel is the humorous detachment with which she tells a familiar love story.

ANNA KARENINA
by Leo Tolstoy
(1876; Signet Classics, 1961, paperback)

"All happy families resemble one another, each unhappy family is unhappy in its own way." So begins what many readers believe to be the greatest novel ever written. Anna, beautiful and respectable, is lured away from her former life by the dashing Count Vronsky. Her gradual slide into decadence and despair is heartbreaking and you'll never forget the final scene. Only Tolstoy could have taken a story of seduction and elevated it to a masterpiece, filling his pages with some of the most psychologically complex characters in Western literature.

BRAZIL
by John Updike (Fawcett, 1994, paperback)

On a beach in Rio, Tristao, a 19-year-old black petty thief, spots the very voluptuous, very rich, very white Isabel. One forbidden kiss and they are in love—and also in deep trouble. Both Isabel's villainous father and Tristao's ferocious mother hate the idea of a mixed-race marriage. But nothing can keep these lovers apart and danger only fires their passion all the more.

Also by Updike:

COUPLES
(Fawcett, 1996, paperback).

A group of young couples in Tarbox, Massachusetts, go to work, raise their kids, throw dinner parties, but mostly commit adultery.

GREAT ADVENTURES

ORION AMONG THE STARS
by Ben Bova (Tor, 1995, paperback)

The Creators took Jack O'Ryan and made him Orion—somewhat more than human but a little less than a god—a champion to fight and die for them across the spectrum of time. Now a civil war has split the Creators, with Anya, Orion's lover, on one side and Aten, Orion's nemesis, on the other. Worse, Orion is centuries away, leading a regiment of humans in a vicious interstellar war. Can Orion live long enough to get back to Anya's side and crush Aten? A great sci-fi swashbuckler.

ORION IN THE DYING TIME
by Ben Bova (Tor, 1991, paperback)

The god-like Creators send Orion to the prehistoric age where the god Set, a living embodiment of pure evil, plots to destroy humankind and populate the Earth with a reptilian race made in his own image. If Orion fails to defeat Set and his horde of dragons, Orion himself will perish. And this time there will be no coming back.

VENGEANCE OF ORION
by Ben Bova (Tor, 1989, paperback)

The story opens with Orion as a galley slave on a Greek ship carrying fresh troops to Troy. The Creators have sent him back along the timeline to ancient Ilium where they want Orion to alter the course of the epic conflict and ensure a Trojan victory. An extremely clever fantasy novel by a six-time Hugo winner.

TARZAN AT THE EARTH'S CORE
by Edgar Rice Burroughs (1929; Ace, 1968, paperback)

This book marks one of the rare instances that Burroughs crossed over characters from his different adventure series. In the 13th novel of the Tarzan series, the Lord of the Jungle outfits an expedition to Pellucidar, the prehistoric land at the center of the earth. However, Tarzan is soon separated from his companions and must complete his mission to rescue the Emperor of Pellucidar from the depths of a Korsar dungeon alone, in a jungle far more savage than his own.

TARZAN OF THE APES
by Edgar Rice Burroughs (1914; Ballantine, 1984, paperback)

The story of the son of an English lord marooned on the coast of Africa and raised by a tribe of fierce apes has captured the imagination of readers of all ages for nearly a century. Tarzan's adventures in the jungle evidently speak to something savage within us all. The work has been translated into 32 languages and has sold millions of copies worldwide. Burroughs claimed he only wrote for those wanting entertainment and escape, but he penned a classic.

TARZAN: THE LOST ADVENTURE
by Edgar Rice Burroughs and Joe R. Lansdale.
(Dark Horse Comics, 1996, paperback)

If you're only familiar with the tame, domesticated Tarzan from the movies, brace yourself: the Tarzan of the Burroughs novels is a superhuman savage who tears his enemies apart with his bare hands and drinks their blood. (What would Jane have said?!?) Burroughs died before he could complete this adventure, so it has been finished by Joe R. Lansdale, a writer who recognizes man's darker impulses. To protect a band of archaeologists searching for the Lost City of Ur, Tarzan fights ferocious apes, bandits, the barbarous inhabitants of Ur and a monster from the earth's core. It's non-stop action.

AT THE EARTH'S CORE
by Edgar Rice Burroughs (Ballantine, 1998, paperback)

In nearly half a century of writing pulp fiction, Burroughs set his adventures in jungles, medieval castles and on planets well beyond the farthest star. But by far one of his most interesting settings was 500 miles below the surface of the earth. David Innes and his inventor friend Abner Perry take their new mechanical mole for a test drive only to end up in a primitive land of eternal daylight where Stone Age men and women struggle for their lives against prehistoric monsters.

* * *

CITY OF DIAMOND
by Jane Emerson (DAW Books, 1996, paperback)

Two rival city-ships, City of Diamond and City of Opal, are locked in an endless war for control of the galaxies. In a bold gamble, the Protector of Diamond reveals to young Adrian Mercati the hiding place of the Sawyer Crown, an talisman that will make Diamond invincible. Of course, Adrian's mission is plagued by all kinds of perils, not the least of which is a growing suspicion that the Sawyer Crown may bring about the downfall of both the Diamond and the Opal cities.

* * *

CAPTAIN HORATIO HORNBLOWER
by C.S. Forester (1937; Little, Brown, 1984, paperback)

A secret mission to the Pacific coast of Central America, a thrilling battle against Napoleon's navy and an encounter with a beautiful and headstrong Englishwoman named Lady Barbara. C.S. Forester certainly knew how to write stories of seafaring. The adventures come fast and furious in this novel, concluding with the Captain, his wounded first mate and his servant being captured by the French who intend to try them for piracy. Dive in.

Another Hornblower Novel:

LIEUTENANT HORNBLOWER
by C.S. Forester (1957; Little, Brown, 1984, paperback).

Forester imagines his hero as a green by eager and very perceptive young lieutenant. Among the finest scenes are a thrilling rescue of an English ship which had been captured by the Spanish and the beginnings of Hornblower's life-long friendship with Lieutenant William Bush.

....

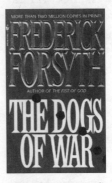

THE DOGS OF WAR
by Frederick Forsyth (Bantam, 1982, paperback)

The "dogs" of the title are a group of mercenaries hired by a ruthless British mining baron to overthrow an African dictator so he can get access to the country's platinum. Forsyth writes real spellbinders, peopled by flesh-and-blood characters. And his tough guys are really tough.

Another Forsyth adventure:

THE DAY OF THE JACKAL
(Bantam, 1982, paperback).

A book of incredible suspense about a plot to assassinate Charles de Gaulle. The French are tipped off, but they don't know who the assassin is and they don't know when he plans to strike.

NEGOTIATOR
(Bantam, 1990, paperback).

A gung-ho American conspirator is convinced the survival of the U.S. depends upon its control the oil-rich states along the Persian Gulf. He is willing to do anything to get America into a Mideast war. Real edge-of-your-seat reading.

....

THE POLISH OFFICER
by Alan Furst

As Warsaw is falling to the Nazis in 1939, Polish Captain Alexander de Milja undertakes a harrowing mission—to smuggle Poland's gold reserves out of the country by train. But that's just one of de Milja's escapades in this thrilling adventure novel. In occupied Paris, he collects valuable intelligence information and passes it on to the British. In the Ukrainian forests he's a saboteur, impeding the Nazis' invasion of Russia. If you like stories packed with plenty of action, lots of cliff-hangers and a protagonist who describes himself as "unafraid to die and lucky so far," this is your book. Worth searching for.

CELESTIAL MATTERS
by *Richard Garfinkle* (Tor Books, 1996, paperback)

In *Celestial Matters*, Richard Garfinkle has created a world in which the scientific beliefs of the ancient Greeks are literally true, the empire of Alexander the Great has lasted a thousand years and for all that time it has been at war with the Empire of the Orient. But the war may soon be won. Commander Aias plans to lead the first expedition to the sun to seize for the Greeks a weapon that will make them invincible: a burning fragment of the sun itself. An inventive combination of fantasy and hard science fiction.

THE BLACK MOON
by *Winston Graham*
(Doubleday, 1974, hardcover)

In the 1950s, Winston Graham began his enormously popular Poldark novels (later made into a Masterpiece Theatre series). At the heart of these novels is the antagonism between Ross Poldark and George Warleggen—a clash between new money and old gentry. In *The Black Moon*, looming over the private feud of Poldarks and Warleggens are larger issues: fear of the bloody Reign of Terror in France and anxiety that the Revolution will claim some of Poldark's friends and family. Worth searching for.

The Poldark saga continues:

THE TWISTED SWORD
(Carroll & Graf, 1991, hardcover).

It is 1815, the year Napoleon returned in triumph to Paris. Before the novel is over, Poldark's son, Jeremy will find himself on the field of Waterloo.

THE SECRETS OF THE HEART
by Kasey Michaels (Pocket, 1995, paperback)

Michaels' romantic romp in Regency England has a wonderful sense of humor. To his fellow aristocrats, Lord Christian St. Clair is a shallow, foppish fool. But under the persona of "The Peacock" he is the champion of the downtrodden. There's plenty here to keep you turning the pages—St. Clair's heroics, a lovely but penniless heroine and English high society's futile attempts to discover the true identity of "The Peacock."

THE HANDS OF LYR
by Andre Norton (Avon, 1995, paperback)

Once Ryft was the paradise garden of the goddess Lyr. Now it is a wasteland, devastated generations ago by evil powers. In this dark world two misfits come together: Alnosha, perhaps Lyr's last follower, blessed with the gift of divining by touch and Kryn, an angry outlawed highborn youth, pursued by the bloodthirsty disciples of the false god. Against his better judgment, Kryn becomes the swordsman and champion of Lyr and together he and Alnosha begin a perilous quest to restore Ryft. If they fail, the entire world will be plunged into eternal darkness.

THE FAR SIDE OF THE WORLD
by Patrick O'Brian (Norton, 1992, paperback)

Jack Aubrey is a gallant captain in the Royal Navy. Stephen Maturin is the ship's surgeon, polymath, spy, ladies' man and a bit of an eccentric. Together, they have weathered some of the most extraordinary adventures in contemporary fiction. This time out, the War of 1812 is raging and Aubrey's mission is to intercept a powerful American frigate before it wrecks Britain's whaling trade. But there are shipwrecks, typhoons, murder and many more disasters looming on the horizon. Start with *The Far Side of the*

World and immerse yourself in Aubry and Maturin's intelligent, witty, thrilling world.

More by O'Brian:

THE THIRTEEN GUN SALUTE
(Norton, 1992, paperback).

In the South China, Sea, Aubrey and Maturin are pitted against barbaric Malay princes and the cunning envoys of Napoleon.

CAPTAIN BLOOD
by Rafael Sabatini (1922; Buccaneer Books, 1990, paperback)

Why aren't novels set on the Spanish Main anymore? If you like swashbuckling adventures, you'll find the career of the dashing Peter Blood—sometime soldier, physician, slave, pirate and finally Royal Governor of Jamaica—irresistible.

BIRDS OF PREY
by Wilbur Smith (St. Martin's Press, 1997, hardcover)

After an intense apprenticeship at sea, young Hal Corteney is serving aboard his father, Sir Francis', privateer. When a Dutch treasure galleon comes in sight, Sir Francis sweeps down and seizes the ship. Bad luck, because Holland and England have just concluded a treaty. Accused of piracy, the Corteneys head for the high seas—and plenty of adventures. Young Hal's coming of age includes sea battles, dungeons, temptresses, buried treasure, plus an epic voyage up the coast of Africa to the Red Sea.

Another Wilbur Smith Adventure:

DIAMOND HUNTERS
(Crest, 1990, paperback).

On his death bed, the founder of Africa's Van Der Byle Diamond Co. urges his son to make his inheritance secure by destroying his best friend. A satisfying, old-fashioned story of greed, hatred, vengeance and murder.

KIDNAPPED
by Robert Louis Stevenson (1886; Harper, 1995, paperback)

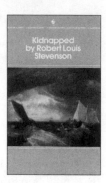

They don't write adventure stories like this anymore. In 18th-century Scotland, orphaned David Balfour is swindled out of his estate by his wicked uncle. That's just for starters—before the story is over, David is kidnapped (you knew that), shipwrecked, accused of murder and pursued through the Scottish Highlands. With nonstop action from page one, *Kidnapped* is one of Stevenson's best books.

TREASURE ISLAND
by Robert Louis Stevenson (1883; Putnam, 1997, hardcover)

Wily Jim Hawkins gets his hands on a treasure map and sets sail with his friends to collect the loot. There are pirates among the crew, led by Long John Silver, one of the most charming villains in English literature.

THE MASTER OF BALLANTRAE
by Robert Louis Stevenson
(1889; Everyman's Library, 1992, hardcover)

A subtle, complex novel of rivalry between two brothers for possession of their family's estate. For this one, Stevenson pulled out all the stops: Bonnie Prince Charlie's rebellion, duels by moonlight, even the return of the dead.

....

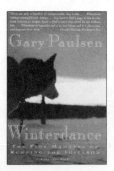

WINTERDANCE: THE FINE MADNESS OF RUNNING THE IDITAROD
by Gary Paulsen
(Harcourt Brace, 1994, hardcover)

The Iditarod is a 1150-mile winter sled-dog race between Anchorage and Nome. Gary Paulsen was a rank amateur who decided to take part in this grueling and extremely dangerous trek across Alaska. And while other contestants purchase special equipment and dogs specially bred for this marathon, Paulsen took an almost reckless approach to outfitting himself and picked up his dogs at the pound. Somehow, he made it, and when he was coming in after seventeen days in a breathtaking, unforgiving country, he didn't want the trek to end. You'll probably feel the same way.

FOREVER AMBER
by Kathleen Winsor (1944; Buccaneer Books, 1991, hardcover)

Winsor chose her 24th birthday—October 16, 1944—as the publication day for her romance-adventure novel that would become a national blockbuster. Amber St. Clair is a gorgeous, ambitious country girl determined to carve out a place for herself in the decadent court of Charles II. This is not your standard bodice-ripper romance. Winsor was meticulous in her research of 17th-century England and populated her novel with full-blooded characters. If you've never read a historical romance, start here:

GREAT GOSSIP

THE LAST OF THE DUCHESS
by Caroline Blackwood (Pantheon, 1995, hardcover)

In her final years, Wallis Warfield Simpson, Duchess of Windsor, the Baltimore belle who came this close to being Queen of England, lived in her grand but shuttered house in Paris, with her virago of a lawyer guarding the door. "She is as lovely and captivating as ever," lawyer Suzanne Blum told the world. "She's a wizened old crone, completely bald, her complexion turning black and on her way to being absolutely gaga," snorted the Duchess' closest friends. A naughty, nasty, often uproarious gossip-biography.

LEAVING A DOLL'S HOUSE: A Memoir
by Claire Bloom (Little, Brown, 1996, hardcover)

Claire Bloom maintains a remarkable calm in her memoir of her disastrous relationship and marriage with author Philip Roth. Nonetheless, there's great gossip here—the draft of a novel Roth gave Bloom that told the story of an English actress named Claire married to a writer named Philip who cheats on her incessantly with younger women; Roth's banishment of Bloom's 16-year-old daughter because she disrupted his routine; and the final indignity when Roth filed for divorce and accused Bloom of "cruel and inhuman treatment." How Bloom managed to write this book without being vindictive is as much a wonder as the fact that she stayed with the man for 18 years.

SHE MADE FRIENDS AND KEPT THEM:
AN ANECDOTAL MEMOIR
by Fleur Cowles, with an introduction by Carlos Fuentes
(HarperCollins, 1996, paperback)

Fleur Cowles is one of those people who knew Everybody Who Was Anybody—and at the conclusion of her book she provides a master list of more than 1000 notables and celebrities of the 20th century. Marilyn Monroe was a houseguest. Fleur and the Queen Mother continue to throw dinner parties for each other. But Fleur Cowles didn't simply know people, she also did interesting things. She was Clare Luce Booth's representative at the coronation of Elizabeth II. She witnessed the signing of the Korean Armistice. Reading this memoir is like catching up on a century of celebrity gossip.

MODEL:
THE UGLY BUSINESS OF BEAUTIFUL WOMEN
by Michael Gross (Warner Books, 1996, paperback)

In what must be the dishiest book to come along in years, Michael Gross tells all about the women whose faces and bodies launch a thousand fantasies and the agents, designers, photographers, stylists and fashion editors who create them. He gets the straight poop from stars like Cindy Crawford and dishes the dirt on mega-agents like Eileen Ford. A very naughty read.

BEHIND THE OSCAR: THE SECRET
HISTORY OF THE ACADEMY AWARDS
by Anthony Holden (Plume, 1994, paperback)

Is it all hype, self-promotion and Hollywood propaganda? Or does that golden figurine actually stand for quality? Going back to the birth of the Academy Awards in 1927, Holden offers a sweeping history of the Oscars with loads of gossip, pages of photos and plenty of lists of who won, who lost and who never even made the short list. Once you start, you won't be able to put this book down.

IN AND OUT OF VOGUE
by Grace Mirabella with Judith Warner
(Bantam Doubleday Dell, 1995, hardcover)

The fashion industry was stunned in 1971 when Grace Mirabella replaced Diana Vreeland as editor of Vogue. Seventeen years later, Mirabella herself was surprised when she was shown the door to make way for Anna Wintour. In this forthright memoir, she recalls the designers she championed— Geoffrey Beene, Giorgio Armani, Calvin Klein, Ralph Lauren, Halston—and she settles old scores. Photographer Richard Avedon is described as a "royal pain." Andy Warhol and his crew smelled "like unwashed underwear and pot." Anna Wintour is "a vision of skinniness in black sunglasses and Chanel suits." Worth searching for.

WILLS OF THE RICH AND FAMOUS
by Herbert E. Nass, Esq. (Warner Books, 1991, paperback)

Assuming that Elvis really is dead, do you know who he left his money to? Guess what part of his anatomy Einstein bequeathed to science? Did JFK have a will? This is an entertaining compendium of how 20th-century celebrities—from Marilyn Monroe to Andy Warhol—disposed of their estates.

LIFE OF THE PARTY:
THE BIOGRAPHY OF PAMELA DIGBY
CHURCHILL HAYWARD HARRIMAN
by Christopher Ogden
(Warner Books, 1995, paperback)

The crowning achievement of Pamela Harriman's long career was serving as U.S. Ambassador to France, the most glamorous position in the diplomatic corps. She had begun her rise by marrying Winston Churchill's son, Randolph. During World War II she had affairs with Edward R. Murrow and Averill Harriman.

Her postwar lovers included Aly Khan and Elie de Rothschild. She was friends with Kathleen Kennedy, knew JFK and claimed she met Hitler. It all must be true. Who would have the nerve to make it up?

....

IT WASN'T PRETTY, FOLKS, BUT DIDN'T WE HAVE FUN?
ESQUIRE IN THE SIXTIES
by *Carol Polsgrove* (Norton, 1995, hardcover)

Life at Esquire, once a staid men's fashion magazine, changed when iconoclast Harold Hayes took over as editor. He welcomed the "New Journalism" of Tom Wolfe and Gay Talese and published the short stories of Raymond Carver. Meanwhile, Esquire's art director George Lois gave the magazine a wild new look: he put Muhammed Ali on the cover as St. Sebastian and brought in Diane Arbus' unsettling photographs. Here's the story of an insanely inventive band of editors, journalists and designers, having a great time during the Sixties.

....

AMERICAN EMPRESS:
THE LIFE AND TIMES OF MARJORIE MERRIWEATHER POST
by *Nancy Rubin* (Random House, 1995, hardcover)

When her father committed suicide, Post inherited the Postum Cereal Co. and become one of America's wealthiest women. With E.F. Hutton, her second husband, she bought Clarence Birdseye's General Foods company. With her third husband, Joseph Davies, FDR's ambassador to Stalin's Soviet Union, she witnessed the horrors of a police state. Her fourth marriage ended in divorce when a blackmailer sent her photos of her husband's homosexual liaisons. Rubin laces her rollicking story of money, international intrigue and sexual scandals with plenty of juicy gossip. Worth searching for.

THEY CAN KILL YOU... BUT THEY CAN'T EAT YOU
by Dawn Steel (Pocket, 1994, paperback)

While Dawn Steel was in labor, the boys back at Paramount were working to dump her as president of production. Steel's rise and fall and rise in Hollywood is laced with glamour: *Fatal Attraction* and *Top Gun* are among her hits; Tom Cruise, Jodie Foster and Barbra Streisand are her friends; Richard Gere and Martin Scorsese were her lovers. Steel dishes up the dirt and reveals what it's like to be a powerful woman in Hollywood.

FORTUNE'S CHILDREN:
THE FALL OF THE HOUSE OF VANDERBILT
by Arthur T. Vanderbilt II (Quill Paperbacks, 1991, paperback)

A member of the Vanderbilt family offers an insider's account of how the descendants of that crusty old robber baron, Commodore Vanderbilt, frittered away one of the world's largest fortunes. Among the skeletons hauled out of the closet is the story of Alva Vanderbilt who shot her daughter's fiancée and then faked a heart attack. Scandalous doings, beautifully told.

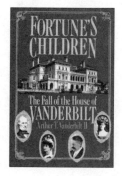

From Another Vanderbilt:

THE GLITTER AND THE GOLD
by Consuelo Vanderbilt Balsan

The daughter of one of America's wealthiest families recalls life at the height of the Gilded Age. Worth searching for.

GREAT NOVELLAS

ANGELS & INSECTS
by A.S. Byatt (Random House, 1994, paperback)

The novella is a wonderful genre. It has all the intensity of a short story, but enjoys the luxury of a little more length to develop plot and character. Novellas are rare these days, but perhaps these two enchanting creations will spark a renaissance. *Morpho Eugenia* draws parallels between the insect and the human world. William Crompton, a Darwinian scientist in the Victorian era, longs to possess two things: a lovely young woman named Eugenia and a rare  Amazon butterfly. *The Conjugal Angel* is a ghost story that reveals the source of Tennyson's inspiration for his poem, "In Memoriam." Together, these novellas are A.S. Byatt at her enchanting best.

A MONTH IN THE COUNTRY
by J.L. Carr

Two veterans, both scarred by what they endured in World War I, meet in a tiny Yorkshire village. One is an art restorer hoping to uncover a great medieval fresco in the village church. The other is an archaeologist searching for the tomb of a medieval lord who was denied burial in consecrated ground. A lovely evocation of another time and place. Worth searching for.

THE AWAKENING
by Kate Chopin (1899; Dover, 1993, paperback)

Just beneath the surface of this sad story is a feminist manifesto. At home in New Orleans, Edna Pontellier, a young wife and

mother, had been feeling vaguely discontented with her marriage to Léonce, a respectable, fortyish stockbroker. But summering among Creoles at a resort called Grand Isle, Edna encounters an intoxicating freedom—and a gallant young suitor named Robert Lebrun. Alas, Edna was looking for a rescuer, while Robert was looking only for a summer dalliance. After the season is over, Edna makes a fatal decision. The plot is a bit melodramatic, but Chopin's prose is lush and sensuous.

DAISY MILLER
by Henry James (1878; Penguin, 1984, paperback)

James did have a tendency to run on in his novels. But in *Daisy Miller*, he was wonderfully succinct. Aristocratic Frederick Winterbourne meets the terribly rich but dreadfully common Miller family in Switzerland. Mrs. Miller is a flighty nouveau riche. Her son Randolph is unspeakable. But her daughter Daisy has an audacious streak that Winterbourne finds attractive. They meet again in Rome, where Daisy scandalizes society and Winterbourne tries to reconcile his obvious sexual attraction to Daisy with his contempt for her lack of discretion. A little gem.

A TURN OF THE SCREW
by Henry James (Prometheus Books, 1996, paperback)

Henry James writes horror fiction? It's not as bizarre as it seems. For the master of the psychological novel, it was a short step to mastery of psychological terror. In a lonely English manor house, an inexperienced governess realizes that her young charges have fallen under the influence of two malevolent ghosts. Her battle for the children's souls is the most blood-curdling scene in English literature.

INDECENT DREAMS
by Arnost Lustig,
(Northwestern University Press, 1990, paperback).

Appearing here in an omnibus edition are three novellas set in Prague under Nazi occupation. In "Blue Day" a German prostitute hides a Nazi military judge on the day the city falls to the Allies. "The Girl with the Scar" is the story of an adolescent Czech girl in a Nazi orphanage who is fascinated by way her women teachers behave when Nazi men are around. The title story, "Indecent Dreams" tells of a cinema cashier trapped in Prague, 1945, as the doomed Nazis indulge an insane rage to kill. You'll admire Lustig's psychologically acute portrayal of his characters. And, you'll find that Lustig is an author whose conscience is as highly developed as his narrative gifts.

DEATH IN VENICE
by Thomas Mann (1912; Vintage, 1989, paperback)

On a trip to Venice, Gustav von Aschenbach, a successful author, sees Tadzio, a 14-year-old Apollo and falls hopelessly in love. Mann's story is at once an erotic classic and an eerie tale of a city on the verge of an epidemic. There has never been a novella to equal this exquisite little book.

THE COMFORT OF STRANGERS
by Ian McEwan (Vintage International, 1994, paperback)

It's late and Colin and Mary are lost in an eerie, unnamed city that from its description sounds an awful lot like Venice. Then from the shadows steps a man named Robert who offers his assistance. First in desperation, then out of good manners and finally compelled by some kind of strange attraction, Colin and Mary permit themselves to be drawn time and again into the peculiar orbit of Robert and his wife, Caroline. On the surface, it is all kindness and generosity, but soon the reader detects a sinister undercurrent beneath Robert and Caroline's hospitality. An absolutely mesmerizing modern gothic novella.

Another novella by McEwan:

BLACK DOGS
(Bantam, 1994, paperback).

Terrifying visions of black hounds draw a woman toward the dark forces of natures and alienate her from her husband's rational but soulless world.

BILLY BUDD
by Herman Melville
(1886; Oxford University Press, 1997, paperback)

Most readers agree that Billy Budd is the greatest short novel in English. Melville, however, did not write it until he had given up his literary career and the book wasn't published until long after Melville was dead. In this "parable of innocence," the handsome sailor and natural man Billy Budd is destroyed by two much more sophisticated men.

BLOODSHED AND THREE NOVELLAS
by Cynthia Ozick (Syracuse University Press, 1995, paperback)

A Polish Jew serves as a diplomat for an African nation, a naive scholar gives up her Fulbright to work as a servant in the home of a glamorous couple, a charlatan's tall tales come back to haunt him—literally and in a Hasidic community, a man meets a stranger who sees through all his defenses. Four great stories, by turn comical and mystical.

RAISE HIGH THE ROOFBEAM
Carpenters & Seymour, with an Introduction by J.D. Salinger
(Little, Brown, 1991, paperback)

These two novellas concern one Seymour Glass, an enigmatic, Buddha-like member of a family of whiz kids growing up in New York City before, during and after WWII. In telling Seymour's story, Salinger writes with an eye for the truth that will take your breath away. A real gem from the small but impressive body of work of the reclusive author of *The Catcher in the Rye*.

....

PUDD'NHEAD WILSON
by Mark Twain (1894; Bantam Books, 1987, paperback)

For this one, Twain combined the old switched-at-birth motif with the modern detective story. On the day a rich slaveholder has a son, his nearly white slave, Roxy, also gives birth to a boy. Roxy nurses both babies, but to save her child from ever being sold away by her master, she switches them in the cradle. Through a series of clever plot twists, the boys' story emerges in a celebrated trial in which an eccentric lawyer, Pudd'nhead Wilson, arrives at the truth of a murder and the truth of the boys' identity through the new science of fingerprints. One of Twain's overlooked gems.

More of the old switcheroo:

THE PRINCE AND THE PAUPER
by Mark Twain (1882; Random House, 1994, paperback).

Edward VI meets his double, a beggar boy named Tom. When they switch clothes for the day, the prince is tossed out of the palace and the pauper is mistaken for the prince. The prince has all the best adventures, running around the country with a courageous knight. And there's a splashy finish in Westminster Abbey on Coronation Day.

....

ETHAN FROME
by Edith Wharton (1911; Simon & Schuster, 1987, paperback)

In a departure from her usual stories about the upper classes, Wharton set this haunting, melancholy tale among working people in a small New England town. Ethan is married to Zeena, a bitter hypochondriac, but falls in love with Zeena's pretty young cousin, Mattie. Of course, Zeena becomes jealous and when she throws Mattie out it's more than Ethan can stand. On their way to the train station, he stops at their favorite sledding hill for what Ethan plans will be their one last ride. But it doesn't go quite the way he had hoped. A novella as cold, desolate and beautiful as a New England winter.

More of Edith Wharton:

THE HOUSE OF MIRTH
(1905; Penguin, 1993, paperback).

At 29, the lovely Lily Bart is dangerously close to spinsterhood. To make matters worse, she's not a very good judge of the male character. A tragedy of a young woman who followed conventional standards for a good match rather than her own good sense.

. . . .

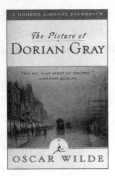

THE PICTURE OF DORIAN GRAY
by Oscar Wilde
(1890; Signet Classics, 1995, paperback)

"If it were I who were to be always young and the picture to grow old... I would give my soul for it," says the radiantly handsome Dorian Gray. So runs the premise of Wilde's famous, unsettling novella that scandalized Victorian England.

. . . .

THE BARRACKS THIEF
by Tobias Wolff (Ecco Press, 1993, paperback)

It was this exhilarating novella that won Tobias Wolff the PEN/Faulkner Award. On a sweltering afternoon, three young soldiers stand guard at an ammunition dump, hoping a forest fire will pass them by. Tobias complicates his coming-of-age story by throwing in a little recklessness, violence and betrayal.

. . . .

HARD-RIDING
WESTERNS

THE OX-BOW INCIDENT
by Walter Van Tilburg Clark
(1940; New American Library, 1996, paperback)

Two young riders fall in with a posse on the trail of rustlers who murdered their friend Kinkaid. When they come across some likely suspects, the posse decides to take the law into their own hands. Clark is a master of subtle shifts in characterization as he shows essentially decent men turning into a mob, their mood shifting from rage to doubt to stubborn resolve and finally to self-loathing. A tough, hard-hitting story that transcends time and place.

TALLGRASS
by Don Coldsmith (Bantam, 1997, paperback)

The year is 1541. Spaniards have arrived in the tallgrass country of the place we call Kansas. Although they will not remain long, their coming means that life will never be the same for the Osage, Pawnee, Comanche and Cheyenne who have lived here for thousands of years. The characters are the thing in Don Coldsmith's epic tale of the American prairie. Heron Woman, who is inexplicably drawn to a white man, Washington, a freed slave who chooses to begin his new life among the Comanches and Jed Sterling, a Princeton man who seeks his fortune out West.

NO MERCY
by Jack Curtis (Walker, 1995, hardcover)

Young Clint Durby lives free and easy, working for a wealthy rancher in Montana. His brother Lee, college-educated and ambitious, is visiting from Chicago. Soon the boys come up against a powerful syndicate that doesn't like the way Lee has been snooping around. When Lee is murdered, Clint and some friendly "sporting women" go after the killers. This is the best kind of Western—lots of action, lots of gunplay and lots of bodies crumpling in agony on the ground.

THE MASSACRE AT SAND CREEK:
NARRATIVE VOICES
by Bruce Cutler (University of Oklahoma Press, 1995, paperback)

This unusual historical novel imagines how eyewitnesses would have told the story of the Colorado militia's attack on a peaceful Cheyenne encampment on November 29, 1864. The narrative voices include Colonel John Chivington who led the assault; Captain Silas Soule, the only officer who refused to join in the massacre; John Smith, a mountain man who witnessed the murder of his half-Cheyenne son at Sand Creek; and Black Kettle, the chief who trusted the white officers' promises of protection and waved a white flag of surrender throughout the attack. Cutler has a strong poetic style that makes this terrible moment in American history especially haunting.

TERROR AT HELLHOLE
by L.D. Henry

Among the Quechan, Honas is the best man in the tribe—tall, powerful, an expert tracker. But, Honas thinks he understands which way the wind is blowing and tries to live with and like the white man. When escapees from Yuma's Hellhole Prison rape and murder his wife, Honas is stunned by the light sentences they receive. So he returns to the old ways and sets out to settle the score himself. Worth searching for.

SLAUGHTER
by *Elmer Kelton* (Bantam, 1994, paperback)

Jeff Layne, a young Confederate veteran on the lam from carpetbagger justice in Texas, heads for the Staked Plains to become a buffalo hunter. But Crow Feather, a fierce Comanche warrior, is waiting to turn back all whites who encroach on Comanche land and threaten the buffalo herds on which the tribe's life depends. You'll like Kelton's spare, sophisticated style and his gift for evoking the land and the people who love it.

The Sequel:

THE FAR CANYON
(Bantam, 1995, paperback).

Layne tries to return to Texas, hoping for a peaceful life, but is forced to take sides in a border war between dispossessed Mexican ranchers and his old nemesis, Crow Feather.

THE CHEROKEE TRAIL
by *Louis L'Amour* (Bantam, 1982, paperback)

Anything a man can do, Mary Breydon can do better. In 1860s Colorado, she's the only woman operating a way station on the Cherokee Trail. But with guts, brains, a steady aim and a little help from her neighbors, Mary is holding her own on the frontier. If you've never read a Western before, start with Louis L'Amour; he goes easy on romanticism and is dead-on accurate in his details.

KID RODELO
by *Louis L'Amour* (Bantam, 1971, paperback)

Harbin, Badger and Kid Rodelo busted out of prison together, but that doesn't make them friends. They've got 50 miles of desert between them and freedom and a savage band of Yaquis on their tail. Worse still, they've picked up a pretty woman named Nora along the way. Only Rodelo has the skills and the courage to bring them all safely across the desert, but can they trust this cold, aloof loner? A classic from the master storyteller of the Old West.

More by L'Amour:

UTAH BLAINE
(Bantam, 1995, paperback).

Blaine, an escapee from a Mexican prison, takes the first job he can find-as foreman for an old Texas rancher so unpopular his own cowboys tried to hang him.

BLOOD MERIDIAN, OR THE EVENING REDNESS IN THE WEST
by Cormac McCarthy (Vintage Books, 1992, paperback)

Cormac McCarthy based his story on historical incidents which took place in the American Southwest and northern Mexico in 1849 and 1850 when a ragtag band of American mercenaries was hired by the Mexican government to kill Indians and bring in their scalps. Working from the premise that black hair is black hair, the scalphunters augment their earnings by killing Mexicans as well as Indians. Soon, Anglos, Indians and Mexicans are locked in as vicious a cycle of violence as ever was depicted in fiction. A nasty journey into the dark side of human nature. Most readers find it impossible to put down.

DEAD MAN'S WALK
by Larry McMurtry (Pocket Books, 1996, paperback)

This is the beginning of the trail for Gus McCrae and Woodrow Call. They are not even 20 years old and have joined the Texas Rangers just in time for an ill-fated expedition to capture Santa Fe. Part of their adventure is a desperate trek across the Jornada del Muerte—the Dead Man's Walk—stalked the whole way by two implacable foes, an Apache named Gomez and a Comanche war chief named Buffalo Hump.

LONESOME DOVE
by Larry McMurtry (Pocket Books, 1998, paperback)

Many readers say this is the best western novel ever written. Two former Texas Rangers collect their compadres, pull up stakes and start moving their herd north to a new ranch in Montana. Along the trail, boys become men, friends become traitors and love and loyalty prove to be stronger than death.

ZEKE AND NED
by Larry McMurtry and Diana Ossana (Simon & Schuster, 1997, hardcover)

If Zeke Proctor didn't have a wandering eye and lousy aim, none of the trouble would have happened. But Zeke—a married man and the father of five-was chasing T. Spade Beck's wife, Polly. To pay him back, T. Spade put weevils in Zeke's ground corn. So Zeke went over to the Becks' place to settle the issue, took aim at T. Spade, but hit and killed Polly instead. From that point on, events begin to spin out of control, dragging in Zeke's best friend Ned and his beautiful wife Jewel. The body count (especially after the shoot-out in the courtroom) just gets too high to keep track of. Hands down, this is McMurtry's best book since Lonesome Dove.

THE WEST: AN ILLUSTRATED HISTORY
by Geoffrey Ward
(Little, Brown, 1996, hardcover)

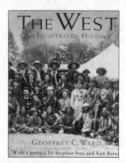

What Geoffrey Ward achieved with Ken Burns in The Civil War and Baseball, he's accomplished again in this magnificent companion volume to the acclaimed PBS series, *The West*. The illustrations are the heroes— breathtaking, rarely seen shots of the West, reproduced on oversized spreads. But don't just look at the pictures. The text is one of the most enlightening accounts of the frontier ever written. It studies the role of explorers, mountain, settlers, soldiers, miners, railroad builders, ranchers and takes a hard look at the collision of Indians, Mexicans, Anglos, ex-Confederates, European immigrants and Chinese. Ward has captured the grandeur of the West without getting sentimental about it. Do not let this book get away.

....

FOOLS CROW
by James Welch (Penguin, 1987, paperback)

It is 1870 and the Blackfeet of western Montana still follow their ancient ways—pursuing game across the plains, hunting blackhorn sheep in the mountains, raiding the camps of enemy tribes. But all that is certain to change now that white settlers are moving into Blackfeet land and bringing their cavalry along to protect them. More than a novel, Welch's book is an experience of total immersion in the culture, customs, religion, visions and tribal politics of the Blackfeet.

....

THE VIRGINIAN
by Owen Wister (1902; Penguin Classics, 1988, paperback)

This is the Western novel that started the whole genre. *The Virginian* is the quintessential American cowboy: brave, honest, cool, always in control, but quick to draw his six shooter if insulted. He's a handy man to have on a ranch and soon becomes foreman. He rescues and woos the schoolteacher from back East, Miss Molly Wood. Sure, he bides his time with his nemesis, Trampas, but you know that in the end there's going to be a dramatic showdown in some dusty street. A great all-American read. By the way, this is the book that gave us the expression, "When you call me that, smile."

HIGH CULTURE:
ART,
ARCHITECTURE,
MUSIC & DANCE

PIANO LESSONS:
MUSIC LOVE AND TRUE ADVENTURES
by Noah Adams (Delacorte Press, 1996, paperback)

At age 52, Noah Adams, the host of NPR's *All Things Considered*, fulfilled a life-long dream and began taking piano lessons. In 12 chapters that follow the calendar year, he recounts his progress as a student, culminating at Christmas when he appears in a tuxedo on a snowy night and by candlelight serenades his wife with a piece any third year student could pull off, but which proved sheer hell to a novice like Adams. A perfect real-life story about pursuing a dream.

More Divine Music:

PIANO PIECES
by Russell Sherman
(Farrar Straus & Giroux, 1996).

A classical pianist reflects on his art and on the marvel of a machine (that's what a piano is, after all) that can convey such a range of emotion.

THE SITWELLS AND THE ARTS OF THE 1920S AND 1930S
Edited by Sarah Bradford
(University of Texas Press, 1996, paperback)

Edith, Osbert and Sacheverell Sitwell were the Andy Warhols of the Jazz Age—bohemian, outrageous, adopting new affectations almost every day. This book looks at their often eccentric crusades to reinvent the arts in Great Britain, their friendships with Cecil Beaton and Evelyn Waugh and their feuds with Aldous Huxley and D.H. Lawrence (who committed the unpardonable offense of refusing to take the Sitwells seriously.)

THE CAVE PAINTINGS OF BAJA CALIFORNIA: DISCOVERING THE GREAT MURALS OF AN UNKNOWN PEOPLE
by Harry W. Crosby (Sunbelt Publications, 1997, hardcover)

Thirty years ago, while Harry W. Crosby was making maps of Baja California, he came upon two prehistoric paintings. Like a good tourist, he took a couple of photographs and continued on his way. What was he thinking? Later, he realized his blunder and returned to Baja to explore the region thoroughly. Guided by local ranchers, he found more than 200 previously unrecorded examples of prehistoric cave art. This magnificent volume chronicles Crosby's journey of discovery and reproduces his finds in full color. A revelation.

ATGET PARIS: THE PHOTOGRAPHS OF EUGÈNE ATGET
(Gingko Press, 1993, hardcover)

An arrondissement by arrondissement documentary of Paris, by the city's most beloved photographer. More than 800 photographs are reproduced in a brick-shaped book that is, literally, the size of a Parisian paving stone.

THE STORY OF PAINTING:
THE ESSENTIAL GUIDE TO THE HISTORY OF
WESTERN ART
by Sister Wendy Beckett (D.K. Publishing, 1997, hardcover)

Sister Wendy draws upon her considerable charm, wit and intelligence to trace the history of art from cave paintings to postmodernism. An enlightening book, packed with 450 color reproductions.

PAOLO UCCELLO
by Franco and Stefano Borsi (Abrams, 1994, hardcover)

"What a beautiful thing this perspective is!" Paolo Uccello used to exclaim. The Renaissance master would stay up all night, playing and experimenting with this newly discovered technique (Mrs. Uccello, waiting in bed, wasn't amused). In 170 dazzling color reproductions, you'll see for yourself the pleasure Uccello took in perspective—from the swift hunters and sleek greyhounds that vanish into the fairy tale forest of "The Hunt" to "St. George and the Dragon," painted in the soft, warm tones of the Tuscan countryside. Paolo Uccello is ideal for anyone who loves Renaissance painting and is ready to move beyond The Big Three (Leonardo, Michelangelo, Raphael).

HOW BUILDINGS LEARN:
WHAT HAPPENS AFTER THEY'RE BUILT
by Stewart Brand (Penguin, 1995, paperback)

The most beloved building on MIT's campus is an unpretentious World War II-era surplus structure called Building 20. For years, it has served a variety of creative uses. Meanwhile, the Media Lab, a "masterpiece" by architect I.M. Pei is an ominous, inhospitable structure that is already obsolete. Stewart Brand reveals why some buildings are adaptable and others are white elephants. This is one architecture book you're going to enjoy.

THE ROUGH GUIDE TO JAZZ: THE ESSENTIAL COMPANION TO ARTISTS AND ALBUMS
by Ian Carr, Digby Fairweather and Brian Priestly
(Viking, 1995, paperback)

Admit it. You don't know much about jazz. But now with *The Rough Guide to Jazz* you can get a comprehensive education in America's one true indigenous musical art form. More than 1,600 jazz artists and 3,000 recordings are surveyed here—Duke Ellington, Charlie Parker, Satchmo, Billie Holiday, Miles Davis, Ella and Count Basie; Joe Henderson, Shirley Horn and Wynton Marsalis. A great introduction for novices but packed with plenty of insights for connoisseurs, this book even brings to your attention the sidemen, accompanists and arrangers who too often are overlooked. Very cool.

NATIVE NATIONS: FIRST AMERICANS AS SEEN BY EDWARD S. CURTIS
Edited by Christopher Cardozo, Foreword by George P. Horse Capture
(Bulfinch Press, 1993, hardcover)

In 1898, photographer Edward Curtis began a 30-year-long endeavor to photograph Native American traditions before they disappeared. This splendid volume reproduces 125 of his most evocative photographs. You'll find magnificent portraits of Indians in traditional garb, photos of tribal rituals and shots of Indian villages and camps from the Canyon de Chelly to the Rocky Mountains. Accompanying these superb images is Curtis' own writings about the first Americans. Elegantly designed, beautifully produced, this will be one of the finest volumes in your personal library.

CIVILISATION
by *Kenneth Clark* (Harper, 1969, hardcover)

There has never been a better one-volume survey of Western art and culture than this superb book. In the conversational tone of a favorite dinner companion, Clark discusses the extraordinary achievements of men and women of genius who gave new meaning to our lives. From the last gasps of the Roman Empire to the glories of Renaissance Florence to the boundless energy of the United States, Clark explores the ideas that have made Western civilization great.

THE NUDE:
A STUDY IN IDEAL FORM
by *Kenneth Clark* (Princeton/ Bollingen, 1956, paperback)

Botticelli's Venus. Michelangelo's David. Pretty boys and girls chasing each other around a Greek urn. One of the most erudite (and readable) art historians of the 20th century, Kenneth Clark, explains the essential difference between "naked" and "nude" through 3000 years of Western art. In this richly illustrated book, Clark proves there's no separating life and art.

THE COLLECTION OF FRANCIS I:
ROYAL TREASURES
by *Janet Cox-Rearick* (Abrams, 1995, hardcover)

For his spectacular chateau Fontainebleu, France's Renaissance king, Francis I, collected masterworks from the greatest artists of his age. The king's agents acquired works by Michelangelo, Raphael, Titian and Cellini. Francis himself persuaded the elderly Leonardo da Vinci to come to France—and bring the Mona Lisa with him. More than 400 color plates of the king's treasures, each aptly described and explained by art historian Janet Cox-Rearick, illustrate Francis' desire to impress his visitors and enhance his reputation as a cultivated monarch.

THE CIVIL WAR IN POPULAR CULTURE: A REUSABLE PAST
by Jim Cullen (Smithsonian Institution Press, 1995, hardcover)

Did you know that Elvis took the music to "Love Me Tender" from a Civil War hit called "Aura Lee"? Or that Carl Sandburg's revered biography of Lincoln is little more than historical fiction? Throughout the 20th century, the Civil War has kept the molders of our popular culture (Cullen calls them "the myth-makers") very busy. Here then is a straightforward yet entertaining analysis of how we have portrayed the Civil War through such cultural icons as *Gone With the Wind*, Joan Baez's "The Night They Drove Old Dixie Down" and the Matthew Broderick-Denzel Washington film, *Glory*.

THE FOUR BOOKS ON ARCHITECTURE
by Andrea Palladio, translated by Robert Tavernor and Robert Schofield (1570; MIT Press, 1997, hardcover)

The circle, the square, the triangle. With these three essential shapes Andrea Palladio developed a theory of architecture that produced some of the most glorious structures of the Reanissance. More than 400 years later, it's safe to say that Palladio's book is the most influential work on architecture ever written. So why hasn't there been an English-language edition of this classic since 1738? Don't ask. Just be happy the book is back in a deluxe edition with reproductions of hundreds of large-format woodcuts which illustrate how Palladio's principles of judgment and proportion lead to works of great beauty.

GIOTTO, FRANCESCA FLORES D'ARCAIS
translated by Raymond Rosenthal (Abbeville, 1995, hardcover)

The best word for this book is "ravishing." More than 200 full-color reproductions chart the brilliant career of Giotto, the "Renaissance" painter who lived 200 years before the Renaissance began. Francesca d'Arcais, an art history professor in Verona, introduces you to the master's greatest works, including his fresco cycles in Assisi and Padua and his architectural commissions (he designed Pisa's Leaning Tower). And she teaches us that through his "avant-garde" colors, his gift for creating the illusion of space and his eye for the telling details of everyday life, Giotto was truly a revolutionary painter. The perfect gift to give yourself.

THE MYSTERIOUS FAYUM PORTRAITS: FACES FROM ANCIENT EGYPT
by Euphrosyne Doxiadis (Abrams, 1996, hardcover)

Perhaps you've seen them in museums, the hauntingly realistic portraits of Egyptian men, women and children painted in the first three centuries of our era. Doxiadis, an artist, traveled to art collections and galleries around the world to study these superb works of art. She explains the cosmopolitan culture of Fayum, a well-to-do community where Greeks, Romans, Hellenized Jews, Syrians and Nubians had adopted the Egyptian cult of the dead. She reveals the artists' techniques. And she places the Fayum paintings within the continuum of Greek painting, from the naturalism of the 4th century B.C. through the earliest centuries of Byzantine icons. A fascinating study, filled with magnificent color reproductions.

SKYSCRAPERS: THE HISTORY OF THE WORLD'S MOST FAMOUS AND IMPORTANT SKYSCRAPERS
by Judith Dupré
(Black Dog & Leventhal Publishers, 1996, hardcover)

From the ancient Pharos Lighthouse of Alexandria to the Leaning Tower of Pisa to the Chrysler Building to the Petronas Towers in Malaysia, here is a magnificent, imaginative history of humankind's tallest structures, illustrated with almost 200 black and white photographs. By the way, the book itself is 18" tall.

OPERA: WHAT'S ALL THE SCREAMING ABOUT?
by Roger Englander (Walker, 1994, paperback)

Many of us have never heard the fat lady sing. Roger Englander has written a friendly, accessible companion to the grand art of opera. You'll get the basics about the greatest composers, performers and productions; one-line summaries if the most famous operas (La Bohème: "Seamstress coughs to death as friends look on"); plus who qualifies as a "twenty-four-carat prima donna." There's even a CD of Carmen, featuring the legendary Maria Callas. You won't find a more entertaining guide to opera.

THE SQUARE HALO & OTHER MYSTERIES OF WESTERN ART:
IMAGES AND THE STORIES THAT INSPIRED THEM
by Sally Fisher (Abrams, 1995, hardcover)

Have you ever wondered why some medieval paintings of the Virgin Mary show her with a breast exposed? Why did Michelangelo give Moses horns? And what's the story of the saint who carries eyeballs in a dish? Sally Fisher, a staff member at the Metropolitan Museum of Art in New York for 17 years, explains that medieval, Renaissance and Baroque art tell stories and employ symbols that were once almost universally familiar to viewers, but today are known mostly to specialists. Through fascinating text and 150 illustrations—134 of them in full color— she casts new light on ancient symbols and tells marvelous stories, all to help you appreciate sublime works of Western art wherever you may find them.

OBJECTS OF DESIRE
by Thatcher Freund (Penguin, 1995, paperback)

When was the last time you read a book in which the three heroes were pieces of furniture? Freund writes so lovingly about three 18th-century American antiques, you'd think they had lives all their own. But the real story is about the collectors, dealers and auctioneers who would die for these pieces.

AMERICAN COLONIAL:
PURITAN SIMPLICITY TO GEORGIAN GRACE
by Wendell Garret, Edited and designed by David Larkin, photography by Paul Rocheleau (Monacelli Press, 1995, hardcover)

Wendell Garrett of Sotheby's leads you on a dazzling tour of architectural styles and decorative arts that are uniquely American. The itinerary includes the timber-framed Whipple House, built about 1639 in Ipswich, Massachusetts, the Huguenots' sturdy stone houses in New Paltz, New York and the majestic Tryon Palace of New Bern, North Carolina, completed in 1770. More than 200 color plates illustrate sites from New England parsonages to Williamsburg workshops. And the enlightening text explains how colonists adapted traditional English styles to their new life in the New World. A splendid history of the first flowering of American style.

NOA NOA
by Paul Gauguin, with an introduction by W. Somerset Maugham (Chronicle Books, hardcover)

Everyone knows that Paul Gauguin produced masterpiece after masterpiece on the paradise island of Tahiti. But Gauguin's racy Tahitian journal, accompanied by his own erotic woodblock illustrations, has been kept under wraps for decades. Now, for the first time since 1918, here is the complete journal of Gauguin's amorous adventures and his inspirations for future paintings, accompanied by the 10 woodblock illustrations he created for the book, plus the full-color sketches and doodles he drew in the margins. Worth searching for.

THE WAKING DREAM:
PHOTOGRAPHY'S FIRST CENTURY
by Maria Morris Hambourg, et al.
(Metropolitan Museum of Art, 1993, hardcover)

The Gilman Paper Company Collection is the world's most important private collection of photography. This volume brings together the collection's finest images from photography's first 100 years, 1839-1939. Some of the photographers will be familiar to you: Mathew Brady, Lewis Carroll, Man Ray, Alfred Steiglitz, Eugène Atget. Whether or not you know the name of the photograph, you'll find the photographs in this album exquisite. Vanished moments from Queen Victoria's Britain, Abraham Lincoln's America and Paris in the years before World War II are captured here in the eye of the camera.

ANDREW WYETH: AUTOBIOGRAPHY
introduction by Thomas Hoving (Bulfinch Press, 1995. hardcover)

Andrew Wyeth, one of America's most popular and most respected artists, looks back upon 60 years of his life and his paintings. He discusses his famous "Helga paintings," his classic work in Chadds Ford and Maine, as well as his more recent work. With 138 color illustrations-including works that are rarely seen—this is the most comprehensive retrospective of Wyeth's work to date.

HIDDEN TREASURES REVEALED
by Albert Kostenevich (Abrams, 1995, hardcover)

For 50 years, an attic room of the Hermitage Museum in Leningrad (now St. Petersburg) held a secret trove of 74 masterpieces by Renoir, Degas, Cezanne, Monet, Gauguin, Van Gogh and other Impressionist and post-Impressionist masters. Art historians in the West believed these paintings had been destroyed during World War II. In fact, they had been looted by Soviet troops from museums and private collections in Germany. This sumptuous book reproduces—for the first time ever—all of these superb paintings in full color.

THE BRANCACCI CHAPEL
by Andrew Ladis (George Braziller, 1993, hardcover)

Across the Arno, away from all the major sites on the standard tourist route of Florence, in a nondescript church is a little chapel where the walls are covered with some of the most glorious paintings of the early Renaissance. The frescoes have just been cleaned and to celebrate the restoration, Ladis offers this beautiful volume. The reproductions are excellent and the text is an education.

RISE OF THE NEW YORK SKYSCRAPER, 1865-1913
by Sarah Bradford Landau and Carl W. Condit
(Yale University Press, 1996, hardcover)

The invention of the elevator, a rapid increase in the number of office workers and the geographical limitations of downtown Manhattan combined to bring about the birth of the skyscraper. The authors begin with the Equitable Building of 1868, where for the first time elevators were used to lift people rather than freight and end at the Woolworth Building, a "Cathedral of Commerce" deemed so significant that President Woodrow Wilson came for its grand opening. A landmark history of the American skyscraper that blends interesting stories with intriguing technical details.

THE NATIONAL GALLERY COMPANION GUIDE
by Erika Langmuir (National Gallery Publications, 1994, hardcover)

Da Vinci. Piero della Francesca. Titian. Ingres. Renoir. London's National Gallery is one of the world's greatest collections of paintings. And this beautifully produced, easy-to-use softcover volume is the ideal companion when you're wandering through the galleries. The collection's major works are highlighted here, with excellent full-color reproductions and enlightening text that analyzes composition, technique and symbolism. From van Eyck's enigmatic "Arnolfini Marriage" to Seurat's groundbreaking "Bathers at Asnières," this is a handbook brimming with intriguing information about extraordinary works of art.

FLORENCE AND THE RENAISSANCE:
THE QUATROCENTO
by Alan J. LeMaître, translated by Jean-Marie Clarke, photographs by Erich Lessing
(Stewart Tabori & Chang/Editions Terrail, 1995, hardcover)

Florence and the Renaissance is the first in a series of well-written, beautifully illustrated, historically accurate and affordable art books. Alan LeMaître explains what made 15th-century Florence one of the most exciting places the world has ever known. He explores intriguing personalities such as Fra Angelico, Leonardo da Vinci, Lorenzo the Magnificent and Savonarola. And he offers detailed commentary on major works of art. This series could be the cornerstone of any art library.

Other titles in the series:

THE PHARAOHS MASTER BUILDERS
by Henri Stierlin.

THE FAUVES: THE REIGN OF COLOR
by Jean-Louis Ferrier.

AFRICAN OBJECTS:
EVERYDAY LIFE, RITUALS AND COURT ART
by Laure Meyer.

RODIN: A PASSION FOR MOVEMENT
by Dominique Jarrassé (Stewart Tabori & Chang/Editions Terrail, 1995, hardcover)

....

THE NPR GUIDE TO BUILDING A CLASSICAL CD COLLECTION
by Ted Libbey (Workman, 1993, paperback)

Newcomers to classical music and connoisseurs will profit from this excellent directory of the best classical music recordings.

JAZZ: PHOTOGRAPHS OF THE MASTERS
by Jacques Lowe with Cliff Preiss
(Artisan/Workman, 1995, hardcover)

Internationally acclaimed photographer Jacques Lowe is most famous for his photographs of President John Kennedy. Now he turns his attention to the best jazz performers. You'll find unforgettable portraits of Dave Brubeck, Ray Charles, Quincy Jones, Peggy Lee, Betty Carter, Shirley Horn, as well as Oscar Peterson, McCoy Tyner and Cecil Taylor. Jazz connoisseur Cliff Preiss offers a history of jazz and adds a personal dimension to the text by drawing on his own interviews over a period of 15 years with the top guns of the jazz world. A virtuoso collection of 200 jazz greats.

EDWARD HOPPER AND THE AMERICAN IMAGINATION
by Deborah Lyons and Adam Weinberg with Julie Grau, Editor
(Whitney Museum of American Art/Norton, 1995, hardcover)

What an extraordinary exhibition catalog this is. Published by New York's Whitney Museum, this remarkable volume brings together 65 full-color plates of Edward Hopper's most important paintings with original works of fiction by such writers as Ann Beattie, Norman Mailer, Walter Mosley, Paul Auster and Grace Paley. The book also featured an essay on Hopper and the enduring influence of his art by art historian, Dr. Gail Levin. Certainly this is one of the most innovative, accessible books on an American artist ever compiled.

THE VOICES OF SILENCE
by André Malraux (Princeton University Press, 1978, paperback)

The Voices of Silence is one of those big, sweeping books that are rarely written anymore. André Malraux is an artistic polymath, traveling from prehistoric caves to Sung China, from the tombs of Egypt to the Gothic cathedrals of France, from

Uccello to Cézanne, all in search of what a work of art meant in the day when it was created and what it means to us now. This is a grand tour that helps all of us who love the visual arts arrive at a greater appreciation of what we see. By the way, don't skip over the introductory essay on how the relatively modern invention of the art museum has changed our perception of art—it's an education in itself.

THE HOURS OF SIMON DE VARIE
with essays by James H. Marrow and François Avril
(J. Paul Getty Trust Publications, 1994, hardcover)

In 15th-century France, the painter Jean Fouquet had no rivals. In our own day, his tiny, sumptuous paintings have been especially prized. When Simon de Varie's "Book of Hours" emerged from a private collection in 1984, it was the first discovery of new paintings by Fouquet in 80 years. A jewel.

MARSALIS ON MUSIC
by Wynton Marsalis (Norton, 1995, hardcover)

A jazz musician, composer, classical trumpet virtuoso and teacher, Wynton Marsalis stands at the top of the musical world. In this book-and-CD set, he teaches you how to appreciate good music—both classical and jazz. To understand rhythm, he urges you to listen to your own pulse, a car horn honking in traffic and a ball bouncing on a basketball court. He helps you hear the musical connections that link Prokofiev, Ives, Gershwin and Ellington. He traces the evolution of American music from John Philip Sousa's wind band to Scott Joplin's ragtime to the birth of New Orleans jazz to the incredible achievements of Louis Armstrong. If you want to understand "serious" music, you can do no better than studying with Maestro Marsalis.

CHARTRES CATHEDRAL
by Malcolm Miller, photographs by Sonia Halliday and Laura Lushington (Riverside, 1998, paperback)

Malcolm Miller has devoted his life to this most perfect of all Gothic cathedrals. In fact, every day between Easter and November he guides small groups of visitors around the church, enlightening them on the principles of flying buttresses, the symbolism in the sculptures and the stories that unfold in the glorious stained glass. Now all of Miller's love and erudition are brought together in this wonderful book, with fine color photographs that complement his text.

More about the Gothic Age:

THE AGE OF THE CATHEDRALS
by Georges Duby (University of Chicago Press, 1983, paperback).

France's premier medievalist and one of the great narrative historians immerses us in the daily life of monasteries, cathedrals and palaces.

FONTEYN AND NUREYEV:
THE GREAT YEARS
by Keith Money.

Seeing Margot Fonteyn and Rudolph Nureyev dance together was one of the most thrilling experiences of our age. There, recording every moment—from rehearsals to final performances—was photographer Keith Money. Now, Money has released 300 stunning master prints—many of them never before published—of Fonteyn and Nureyev when they were at the zenith of their careers, with scenes from Giselle, Swan Lake, La Bayadére, Romeo and Juliet. Worth searching for.

ANCIENT IRELAND:
FROM PREHISTORY TO THE MIDDLE AGES
by Jacqueline O'Brien and Peter Harbison (Weidenfeld & Nicolson, 1996, hardcover)

It isn't often you find a book that is both beautiful and authoritative, yet that's what you get in this magnificent oversize architectural history of Ireland. The authors don't miss a single high point—Newgrange, Skellig Michael, Cashel, St. Patrick's Cathedral in Dublin. But the real joy of this book is discovering a host of significant, lovely and frequently overlooked sites, including the perfectly preserved Cahir Castle and the faintly pagan 7th-century sculptures on White Island. Scholars will appreciate the meticulous text and everyone will love the 300 full-color photographs.

WILLIAM MORRIS
Edited by Linda Parry (Abrams, 1996, hardcover)

In painting, typography, furniture, stained glass, tapestries—in any medium, William Morris (1834-1896) was a virtuoso. To mark the centenary of Morris' death, London's Victoria and Albert Museum mounted an eyefilling tribute to the master designer. This companion volume—more a full-scale biography than an exhibition catalog—is brimming with photographs of artwork and artifacts from the V&A exhibition, including examples of his famous textiles and the beautiful books Morris designed for Kelmscott Press. Here is a ground-breaking history of a brilliant designer whose influence is still felt today.

THEN & NOW
by Stefania & Dominic Perring (Macmillan, 1991, hardcover)

All your life, you dream of visiting the Palace at Knossos or the Roman Forum. Then one day you get there and see a pile of rocks and some shattered columns. The sad truth is lots of ancient sites are a disappointment. The Perrings have documented what the best sites—including the Acropolis of Athens, the Temple of Karnak and Rome's Colosseum—looked like in their prime. Just flip the full-color, transparent overlays over photos of the sites as they appear today and you get a technicolor vision of the past. Plus, they include lively, informed discussions of the historical and cultural significance of the sites. An inspired book.

JOHN SINGLETON COPLEY IN AMERICA
by Carrie Rebora and Paul Staiti, et al.
(Metropolitan Museum of Art, 1995, paperback)

I n colonial Boston, anybody who was anybody had their portrait painted by John Singelton Copley—from General Thomas Gage and his wife Margaret Kemble Gage, to John Hancock, Samuel Adams and that hard-riding silversmith, Paul Revere. Copley was a genius—a painter who could capture a likeness and convey a personality. The authors argue that Copley was an original who introduced a new aesthetic to portraiture while still managing to appeal to the conservative Anglo-American temperament. A wonderful exhibition catalog and a fascinating book that takes you back to the age of our Founding Fathers and Mothers.

John Singleton Copley
in America

....

PEGGY GUGGENHEIM:
A COLLECTOR'S ALBUM
by Laurence Rumney and Jack Altman
(Flammarion, 1996, hardcover)

P eggy Guggenheim was rich, outrageous and an insatiable collector of modern art. This biography tells her life story through more than 250 never-before-published photos selected from Guggenheim's own albums. The book chronicle's her bohemian phase in Paris' Montparnasse; her escape from France just one step ahead of the Nazis; her landmark exhibits of Jackson Pollack and Mark Rothko; and her retirement to a luxurious palazzo on Venice's Grand Canal. Among the photos are candids of Samuel Beckett, Max Ernst, Djuna Barnes, as well as artful shots by Guggenheim's friends, Berenice Abbott and Man Ray. No other book offers such a detailed look at the extravagance of Guggenheim's art collections and her life.

....

FLEMISH ILLUMINATED MANUSCRIPTS 1475-1500
by Maurits Smeyers and Jan Van der Stock
(Harry N. Abrams, 1996, hardcover)

Gutenberg's invention of the printing press threatened to put manuscript illuminators out of business. But, in the Low Countries, the artists weren't going down without a fight. For 25 years, these gifted miniaturists created the most exquisite paintings that had ever been seen between the covers of a book. In this handsome volume, two Belgian art historians chronicle the last—and perhaps most glorious—years of the art of manuscript illumination. The reproductions showcase the inventive, complex designs that filled the margins and pages. Even if you've never looked at a manuscript illumination before, you'll fall in love with this superb book.

THE SYMPHONY:
A LISTENER'S GUIDE
by Michael Steinberg (Oxford University Press, 1995, paperback)

You love classical music. But wouldn't it be nice if you understood what you were listening to? Michael Steinberg, the distinguished music critic and program annotator for the Boston Symphony, the New York Philharmonic and the San Francisco Symphony, has written a vastly informative and entertaining guide to 118 works by 36 composers. You get analyses of all the symphonies of Beethoven, Brahms, Mahler and Sibelius; the major symphonies of Haydn, Mozart, Dvorak and Tchaikovsky; plus modern works up to Harbison and Górecki. Whether you are a newcomer to classical music or a veteran concert-goer, there's a lot you can learn from Steinberg.

IMPRESSIONISTS SIDE BY SIDE:
THEIR FRIENDSHIPS, RIVALRIES AND ARTISTIC EXCHANGES
by Barbara Ehrlich White (Alfred Knopf, 1996, hardcover)

How did Renoir paint Monet's garden at Argenteuil? How did Mary Cassatt and Berthe Morisot portray a lady of fashion? How did Degas and Manet record a day at the races? In *Impressionists Side by Side*, Barbara Ehrlich White pairs up paintings of identical subjects by the great masters of Impressionism. White has filled her book with 284 illustrations, including scores of pictures never before published in color. This is a wonderfully fresh perspective that will help you recognize the varied approaches to Impressionism as never before.

VERMEER: THE COMPLETE WORKS
by Arthur Wheelock (Abrams, 1997, hardcover)

Art lovers rediscovered the 17th-century Dutch artist Jan Vermeer at the National Gallery's blockbuster 1995 exhibition of his paintings. Now Arthur Wheelock, curator of the Washington exhibit, has created a poster-sized volume filled with gorgeous full-color reproductions of every single one of the master's known works (many of them recently cleaned and all of them newly photographed). Wheelock provides an accessible commentary on each painting. For example, he shows us the "Woman in Blue Reading a Letter" "immersed in her private life...unaware of the presence of the viewer." A sublime volume that belongs in every art library.

A BESTIARY
compiled by Richard Wilbur, illustrated by Alexander Calder (Pantheon, 1993, hardcover)

What a beauty this books is. Large, handsome and illustrated with the playful line drawings of Alexander Calder, this book assembles a delightful assortment of poetry and prose to celebrate 33 creatures—both real and mythical. You get William Faulkner on the dog, Benjamin Disraeli on the Ape, Plato on the grasshopper, Machiavelli on the centaur.

BERENICE ABBOTT: CHANGING NEW YORK
by Bonnie Yochelson
(The New Press/Museum of the City of New York, 1997, hardcover)

Funded by the New Deal's WPA, sponsored by the Museum of the City of New York and inspired by the Paris street photography of Eugène Atget, Berenice Abbott spent the years between 1929 and 1939 photographing New York just at the point when the old 19th-century town was being overwhelmed by a modern urban metropolis. 307 photos record the landmarks that are still there-the Brooklyn Bridge and the Flatiron Building—but also the things that have vanished, such as the wooden pre-Civil War houses of "Irishtown" in Fort Greene, Brooklyn and the Triboro Barber School (haircuts 10 cents). A true American masterpiece.

IN HIS/HER/THEIR OWN WORDS

THE BOOK OF ABIGAIL AND JOHN:
SELECTED LETTERS OF THE ADAMS FAMILY
Edited by L.H. Butterfield, Marc Friedlander, Mary-Jo Kline
(Harvard University Press, 1977, paperback)

In their immensely entertaining correspondence, the Adams clan recorded the progress of the American Revolution, from the Boston Massacre to independence.

TWENTY YEARS AT HULL HOUSE
by Jane Addams
(1910; University of Illinois Press, 1990, paperback)

At the turn of the century, social reformers—men and women—were convinced that America had paid too high a price in human suffering to achieve its astonishing industrial growth and the time had come to put matters right. Jane Addams and her friend Ellen Starr (both ladies of excellent families) decided to put their beliefs into action. They bought a dilapidated mansion in a Chicago slum and began acting, as they put it, like good neighbors. Addams' memoir of her years at Hull House is as relevant today as it was almost a century ago—it is a clarion call for social justice, for America to help the urban poor find a way out of poverty.

SISTERS OF THE SPIRIT:
THREE BLACK WOMEN'S AUTOBIOGRAPHIES OF THE NINETEENTH CENTURY
Edited by William L. Andrews
(Indiana University Press, 1986, paperback)

Jarena Lee, Julia A. J. Foote and Zilpha Elaw recount their lives as itinerant preachers and reveal to us what life was like for free-born black women of the North in the decades before the Civil War.

WOULDN'T TAKE NOTHING FOR MY JOURNEY NOW
by Maya Angelou (Bantam, 1997, paperback)

Since Maya Angelou read her poem, "On the Pulse of the Morning" at Bill Clinton's first inauguration, her audience has grown and grown. Now she speaks with humor and eloquence about the wisdom she has acquired over a lifetime—what it means to be a woman, a single mother and an African-American.

Also by Maya Angelou:

I KNOW WHY THE CAGED BIRD SINGS
(Bantam, 1983, paperback).

Her first autobiographical novel follows her difficult childhood in Arkansas and St. Louis.

THE CIVIL WAR DIARY OF CLARA SOLOMON: GROWING UP IN NEW ORLEANS
1861-1862, Edited, with an Introduction, by Elliott Ashkenazi (Louisiana State University Press, 1995, paperback)

The best personal record we have of what it was like to live in New Orleans during the Civil War comes from a teenage Sephardic Jewish girl named Clara Solomon. Witty, perceptive, a staunch Confederate and hopelessly romantic, Clara records such momentous historical events as David G. Farragut's fleet bombarding New Orleans' defenses as well as such private sorrows as the deaths of dashing hometown officers. Like Mary Boykin Chesnut, Clara Solomon is one of the brightest, most engaging, most poignant eyewitness historians of the Civil War.

OUTWITTING THE GESTAPO
by Lucie Aubrac (University of Nebraska Press, 1993, paperback)

Vichy France, 1943. Lucie Aubrac is pregnant when her husband, a member of the Resistance, is arrested by the Gestapo. While Aubrac tries to bear up under torture in a Nazi prison, Lucie hatches a dangerous scheme to rescue him. One of the great real-life stories of heroism in World War II.

THE HONE & STRONG
DIARIES OF OLD MANHATTAN
Edited by Louis Auchincloss (Abbeville Press, 1998, hardcover)

Just about everybody kept a diary in 19th-century Manhattan, but nobody filled the pages with so much fascinating information about the old town as Philip Hone and George Templeton Strong. They witnessed the conflagrations and riots that nearly destroyed Manhattan, reported (unfavorably) on the great waves of Irish and German immigrants and evaluated the character of every famous person they met, including Abraham Lincoln, Daniel Webster and the Prince of Wales. Worth searching for.

WARRIORS DON'T CRY
by Melba Pattillo Beals (Pocket Books, 1998, paperback)

The author was one of the nine black students chosen to integrate Little Rock's Central High. For the first time, we learn what integrating the high school was like. Melba and her companions were kicked, pushed down stairs and received threatening phone calls. All her friends from her old school dropped her—they were afraid to be seen in public with her. But at Central High she found a teacher who wouldn't tolerate racist behavior, a soldier who became her guardian angel and a white boy who called her secretly every night to warn her what to expect the next day.

SISTER OF THE WIND:
VOICES OF EARLY WOMEN AVIATORS
Edited by Elizabeth S. Bell (Trilogy Books, 1995, paperback)

I n the 1920s and 1930s, an easy-going male aviator might regard women who flew airplanes as a bit unconventional. More often than not, however, the reaction to women aviators was much more hostile. In *Sister of the Wind*, Bell has brought together the autobiographies of the first generation of American and British women aviators. It records their courage, their troubles, their determination and their growing sense of purpose and self-worth. But perhaps most important, it reveals the remarkable record of the women who helped advance a revolutionary new field of technology.

WRITING HOME
by Alan Bennett (Random House, 1995, paperback)

M ention Alan Bennett's name to anyone from Britain and you are likely to hear effusive praise. The British seem to have unlimited respect and affection for this brilliant but self-effacing playwright, actor and screenwriter. Now, with this eccentric collection of humorous essays, conversations and reminiscences, Bennett is likely to become beloved on this side of the Atlantic, too. Two personal favorites: Bennett and Dudley Moore are tossed out of the Hotel Pierre lobby on suspicion of being petty thieves and Bennett invites an elderly homeless woman to set up house in a van in his garden.

MATISSE, PICASSO, MIRÓ, AS I KNEW THEM
by Rosamond Bernier (Knopf, 1991, hardcover)

B ernier was the first person Matisse told when he accepted the commission to decorate the Chapel of the Rosary at Vence. Picasso sent Bernier to his family in Barcelona, where she found a cache of his early paintings unknown to the world for 37 years. Miró took her on a week-long private tour of Catalan art and culture. One of America's most engaging art lecturers has written a highly personal book, illustrated with 205 color plates and dozens of photographs of the artists, that intertwines the life and art of three modernist masters.

· · · · · · · · · · · · ·

WE ARE WITNESSES:
THE DIARIES OF FIVE TEENAGERS WHO DIED
IN THE HOLOCAUST
Edited by Jacob Boas (Henry Holt, 1995, paperback)

A nne Frank was not the only victim of the Holocaust to keep a diary. Boas, who was born in the Westerbork concentration camp, has found other young writers who chronicled the disintegration of their world, from a small Polish village to the Vilna ghetto to Brussels to Hungary. The excerpts are sizable and are accompanied by expert commentary.

· · · · · · · · · · · · ·

DAVID BRINKLEY: MEMOIRS
by David Brinkley (Knopf, 1995, paperback)

I n his early twenties, David Brinkley was already covering FDR at the White House. In 1946, he heard Winston Churchill's "Iron Curtain" speech. He witnessed Harry Truman's miraculous election in 1948. And his career as a reporter only got better in the 1960s and 1970s. Robert Kennedy was a friend; LBJ confided to him an outrageous story of how he got votes from a graveyard; and he was #1 on Richard Nixon's enemies list. Wonderfully written and packed with terrific anecdotes about the great and the near-great.

· · · · · · · · · · · · ·

TESTAMENT OF YOUTH
by Vera Brittain (1933; Penguin, 1989, paperback)

V era Brittain's autobiography is one of the few—perhaps the only—first-person accounts of World War I written by a woman. Brittain was an intelligent but sheltered young woman who, on the eve of the war, fell in love with a man named Roland— a close friend of her beloved brother Edward. Both men, in fact virtually all the young men of Brittain's acquaintance, were killed in World War I. The shock of it all changed Brittain as much as it changed her society. She became a life-long pacifist, an advocate of women's rights and began a career as a journalist. *Testament of Youth* weaves together the private experiences of an exceptional young woman with larger events that shaped our century.

MARY CHESNUT'S CIVIL WAR
Edited by C. Vann (Yale University Press, 1981, paperback)

From one of the most articulate voices of the American South comes a remarkable journal that chronicles the antebellum period, the Civil War and Reconstruction. Chesnut was a member of the South's plantation aristocracy and the best friend of Lavinia Davis, the First Lady of the Confederacy. Her diaries are rich in intimate details, psychological insight and as works of literature, they are a real treasure.

ENOCH'S VOYAGE:
LIFE ON A WHALESHIP 1851-1854
Edited by Elizabeth McLean (Moyer Bell, 1994, hardcover)

In the summer of 1851, young Enoch Cloud shook the dust of Ohio from his feet and headed for New Bedford, Massachusetts and a life of adventure aboard a whaler. He kept a journal throughout the voyage, recording storms at sea and near mutinies; adventures in Japan, New Zealand and among Pacific islanders; and the dangers of hunting whales in small wooden boats with nothing but hand-held harpoons. Then, he went home to Ohio and put his journal away. Now, thanks to his great-great-granddaughter, we can experience Enoch's greatest adventure.

NARRATIVE OF THE LIFE OF FREDERICK DOUGLASS
Written by Himself, Edited by Henry Louis Gates
(Dell, 1997, paperback)

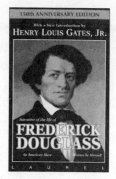

When he was 20 years old, Frederick Douglass "stole" himself from his owners in Maryland and escaped north. Seven years later he published this masterful autobiography. Douglass' account of the cruelty of slavery, of his own daring efforts to defy the law and teach himself to read and write and of his thrilling escape to freedom electrified readers and drew thousands to the abolitionist cause. A work of extraordinary power.

Also by Frederick Douglass:

MY BONDAGE AND MY FREEDOM AND LIFE AND TIMES OF FREDERICK DOUGLASS
Edited by William L. Andrews
(University of Illinois Press, 1988, paperback).

These two volumes include Douglass' meetings with John Brown, Harriet Beecher Stowe and Abraham Lincoln.

ZLATA'S DIARY:
A CHILD'S LIFE IN SARAJEVO
by Zlata Filipovic, translated, with notes, by Christina Pribichevich-Zoric (Penguin, 1995, paperback)

Not since Anne Frank's diary has a child's journal made such an impression on the world. Thirteen-year-old Zlata begins her story in a Sarajevo when children could still go out for pizza and play tennis in the park. But soon Zlata and her family are huddling in basement shelters, struggling to find food, water and fuel, watching hopelessly as friends and neighbors are killed in the daily shelling.

FAMILY
by Ian Frazier (HarperPerennial, 1995, paperback)

A hunter was slain by the Indians he was tracking. During the Revolution, an ancestress saved the family fortune by hiding the silver from marauding British troops. Drawing upon private papers and public documents, Frazier tells the history of his clan, stretching back 300 years. There are lots of great stories, but the best part of this book is the way Frazier summons up a vanished world, where young couples courted in orchards and, more likely than not, the kids you'd played with all day were going to stay to supper. This is Ian Frazier's masterpiece and the book all of us wish we could write about our family.

MUSCLE: CONFESSIONS OF AN UNLIKELY BODYBUILDER
by Samuel Wilson Fussell (Avon, 1992, paperback)

Here's an intriguing book about what motivates people to reinvent themselves. One day, a nice Oxford grad named Sam Fussell saw a man attacked on a New York subway platform. The incident scared Fussell so much that he joined a gym. But what began as a little strength training for self-defense purposes became an obsession. Fussell started spending eight hours a day pumping iron, hanging out with guys named Nimrod and Bam Bam. And, he was juiced up on enough steroids to be a contender for the title of Mr. San Gabriel Valley.

COLORED PEOPLE
by Henry Louis Gates, Jr. (Knopf, 1994, hardcover)

Today, Henry Louis Gates is a respected writer and teacher at Duke University. But in the 1950s and '60s, he was just another kid growing up in a paper-mill town called Piedmont, West Virginia. With warmth and humor, he recalls life in Piedmont's flourishing black community, his generally good relations with the town's white residents, his first encounters with racism and the path that led him from West Virginia to Yale and Harvard.

A MASS FOR THE DEAD
by William Gibson (A Common Reader Edition, 1996, hardcover)

Don't be put off by the title. Gibson's memoir of his family is anything but gloomy. In some of the most gorgeous prose you're likely to encounter, Gibson conjures up memories from his own childhood in turn-of-the-century New York, when there were lots of green open spaces in the Bronx and Harlem was a nice neighborhood for families. The reminiscences are wonderful, but at the heart of this book are the mystic chords that bind families together, from one generation to the next. There has probably never been a better book about growing up than *A Mass for the Dead*. It is a joy to have it back in print.

SHOT IN THE HEART
by Mikal Gilmore (Doubleday, 1995, paperback)

The name "Gilmore" probably rings a bell. Mikal is a writer for Rolling Stone. His brother, Gary, was the convicted killer executed by a firing squad in Utah in 1977 and later the subject of Norman Mailer's *The Executioner's Song*. This is Mikal's memoir of a violent, messed-up family. With all the alcoholism, bigamy, abuse and crime, it's no wonder that Gary went bad and a miracle that Mikal got away.

THE DELIGHTS OF GROWING OLD
by Maurice Goudeket, translated by Patrick O'Brian
(A Common Reader Edition, 1996, paperback)

Maurice Goudeket was in his mid-seventies when he wrote this memoir of a long and happy life. At age 30, he married Colette. When Colette died, he assumed his life was over. Then he fell in love again, with a young woman named Sanda, who soon became pregnant. When she woke him in the middle of the night to say it was time to go to the hospital, he asked her to wait a moment so he could shave: "The man who presents himself before his fate in an unshaved condition does so in an undeniable state of inferiority." A stylish, self-deprecating memoir you won't want to miss.

MEMOIRS

by Ulysses S. Grant (The Library of America, 1990, hardcover)

An eloquent autobiography of a man who was an absolute failure at everything—except waging war.

....

LAKOTA AND CHEYENNE: INDIAN VIEWS OF THE GREAT SIOUX WAR, 1876-1877

Compiled, edited and narrated by Jerome A. Greene
(University of Oklahoma Press, 1994, paperback)

History, as you know, is written by the winners. So Jerome Greene, a historian with the National Park Service, set out to collect accounts of the Great Sioux War as Lakota and Cheyenne veterans saw it. Here are eyewitness accounts of Custer's defeat at Little Big Horn, the famous clashes at Powder River and Cedar Creek and the death of Crazy Horse. The book's 34 illustrations include photographic portraits of Sitting Bull, Dull Knife and other warriors, as well as Indian pictographs of the battles. This an excellent way to balance our perceptions of the Indian Wars.

On the other hand...:

BATTLES AND SKIRMISHES OF THE GREAT SIOUX WAR, 1876-1877: THE MILITARY VIEW

Compiled, edited and narrated by Jerome A. Greene
(University of Oklahoma Press, 1993, paperback).

This companion volume offers eyewitness accounts by officers, enlisted men, surgeons and journalists.

....

A DRINKING LIFE

by Pete Hamill (Little, Brown, 1995, paperback)

Hamill's father was an alcoholic. Pete hated him for it, but that didn't stop his own drinking. In fact, booze seemed an essential component of friendship, manhood, even creativity (after all, Hemingway drank hard). But whatever Hamill thought alcohol was supplying, it was also taking away the things any writer values most: clarity of thought, a good memory, objectivity. So, he quit in 1972. A tough, honest memoir.

THE LAST GIFT OF TIME:
LIFE BEYOND SIXTY
by Carolyn Heilbrun (Bantam Diubleday Dell, 1997, hardcover)

For years, Carolyn Heilbrun had promised herself that she would commit suicide when reached 70. But when the day came, she found that aging was not the burden she had expected it to be. "My perspective is that of someone who has enjoyed many advantages," she writes. "I have had a privileged education, worked for over thirty years as a professor of English... and now enjoy a comfortable income. At the moment of recording this, I am in good health." At age 72, Heilbrun is delighted to find that there are so many new experiences to savor. And where once she feared aging, now she looks back and thinks youth isn't everything it's cracked up to be.

THE WAY OF A BOY: A MEMOIR OF JAVA
by Ernest Hillen (Penguin, 1995, paperback)

In 1942, 8-year-old Ernest Hillen, his older brother and his mother were interned in a Japanese camp on the island of Java. Hillen conjures up the harrowing experiences of life in the camp, the hunger, the brutal treatment of women and children and the aching fear of what had happened to their husbands and fathers. This chilling book concludes with an epilogue in which Hillen recounts the fate of many of the characters mentioned in his memoir.

SECOND SIGHT
by Robert V. Hine (University of California Press, 1993, paperback)

Robert Hine was barely 20 when the doctors told him that he was going blind. But before the darkness descended, Hine married, earned a doctorate, became a professor of history and published books on the American West. Then, after 15 years of total blindness, a 30-minute operation wrought a miracle. An overwhelming story.

. . . .

INCIDENTS IN THE LIFE OF A SLAVE GIRL, WRITTEN BY HERSELF
by Harriet Jacobs, Edited by Jean Fagan Yellin
(1861; Harvard University Press, 1987, paperback)

For more than 120 years, this autobiography was regarded as a work of fiction. It was Yellin who proved that Jacobs' book was an authentic autobiography that reveals what slavery was like for black women. It is a shocking story. Harriet Jacobs endured sexual abuse and the loss of the two children she bore by a white man. Once she escaped to New York, she feared white women would reject her book as indecent. "I do earnestly desire," she wrote, "to arouse the women of the North to a realizing sense of the condition of the two millions of women in the South, still in bondage, still suffering what I suffered and most of them far worse."

. . . .

THE REPUBLIC OF LETTERS:
THE CORRESPONDENCE BETWEEN THOMAS JEFFERSON AND JAMES MADISON 1776-1826
Edited by James Morton Smith (Norton, 1998, hardcover)

This is book is a landmark. For the first time, the 50-year-long correspondence of the two greatest philosopher-statesmen of the American Enlightenment is presented in its entirety, with superb essays by editor James Morton Smith to illuminate the personalities and private thoughts of these two brilliant men.

Jefferson on John Adams: *"His want of taste I had observed."*

Madison on Alexander Hamilton: *"We see every rhetorical artifice employed... to prop up his sinking reputation."*

Jefferson on the Louisiana Purchase: *"The less we say about constitutional difficulties respecting Louisiana the better."*

Since neither man kept a diary, these letters offer the most profound insights into the genius of Jefferson and Madison.

MY LIFE

by Earvin "Magic" Johnson with William Novak
(Fawcett, 1993, paperback)

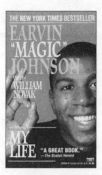

Magic confronts his personal tragedy of living with AIDS head on, yet fills his autobiography with his genuine upbeat spirit. Here's the story of his incredible seasons playing basketball for Michigan State and the L.A. Lakers; friendships with Pat Riley, Kareem Abdul-Jabbar and Michael Jordan; and the endless opportunities for sex on the road. It was from one of those encounters that Magic Johnson contracted the HIV virus.

THE LIAR'S CLUB: A MEMOIR

by Mary Karr
(Penguin, 1995, paperback)

The worst childhoods make for the best stories. Poet Mary Karr's tale of growing up in a swampy East Texas refinery town as part of a "terrific family of liars and drunks" is a dilly. Her saga, completely without self pity, of how an inheritance was squandered, liquor bottles were emptied, guns were drawn and of how life was casually and constantly thrown into turmoil, will have you turning pages late into the night. One of the best memoirs in recent memory.

LAND OF THE BURNT THIGH

by Edith Eudora Kohl
(1938; Minnesota Historical Society, 1986, paperback)

"We were young and demanded some fun and feminine enough to find life more interesting when the young men who were homesteading began gathering at the shack in little groups.... the romances which naturally developed made the winter less desolate."

Drought, prairie fires, snakes and claim jumpers didn't seem to trouble Edith Eudora Kohl. With her sister, she took easily to homesteading in turn-of-the-century South Dakota. And as the publisher of the local newspaper, she became the social and political heart of her little community. Kohl's autobiography is something out of the ordinary—it offers a comic, sometimes irreverent perspective on the perennial optimism of homesteaders.

UNDER MY SKIN: VOLUME ONE OF MY AUTOBIOGRAPHY TO 1949
by Doris Lessing (HarperPerennial, 1995, paperback)

Without flinching, Lessing recalls her early life when she abandoned her husband and two children for another man, joined the Communist Party and worked at becoming a writer. Lessing isn't proud of everything she's done, but she sees it all as part of her development and she apologizes for none of it. This is a no-holds-barred autobiography.

LONG WALK TO FREEDOM
by Nelson Mandela (Little, Brown, 1995, paperback)

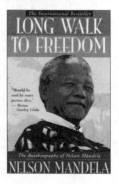

After everything he has suffered, how can Nelson Mandela's memoir be completely free from rancor? That is only one of the surprises you'll encounter in this compelling, heart-rending autobiography of the man who endured 27 years of harsh imprisonment, negotiated the peaceful end of apartheid, won the Nobel Peace Prize and was elected President of South Africa. For millions across the globe, Mandela is a legend, yet his true story is even more incredible.

DREAMS OF TRESPASS: TALES OF A HAREM GIRLHOOD
by Fatima Mernissi (Addison Wesley Longman, 1994, hardcover)

I was born in a harem in 1940 in Fez, a ninth-century Moroccan city," Mernessi tells us. In this near-mythical world, women were forbidden to step beyond the harem's sacred frontier, but nothing

could keep them from dreaming of freedom or urging one another to rebel: it was her own mother who told Mernessi that when her time came, she should "scream and protest." Now a sociologist and researcher at the University Mohammed V in Rabat, Mernessi looks back at her years of confinement with wit and candor.

• • • • • • • • • • • • • •

RED AZALEA:
LIFE AND LOVE IN CHINA
by Anchee Min (Berkley, 1995, paperback)

As a child during China's Cultural Revolution, Anchee Min was a dutiful member of Mao's Little Red Guards—she even betrayed one of her favorite teachers. To reward her for her devotion to the Party, Min at age 17 was given the "honor" of slaving as a peasant out in the countryside. But on the farm, Min was spotted by one of Madame Mao's talent scouts and whisked away to Beijing to sing in political operas. In stunningly beautiful prose, Min reveals the cruelty and hypocrisy of the Cultural Revolution. One of the best memoirs to emerge from modern China.

• • • • • • • • • • • • • •

HIS PROMISED LAND:
THE AUTOBIOGRAPHY OF JOHN P. PARKER,
FORMER SLAVE AND CONDUCTOR ON THE
UNDERGROUND RAILROAD
Edited by Stuart Seely Sprague (Norton, 1996, hardcover)

For decades, John Parker's oral history, written down by a journalist in the 1880s, sat in the archives of Duke University. This is the first published edition. In 1835, at age eight, Parker was sold from his home in Norfolk, Virginia and sent in chains to Mobile, Alabama. After ten years, he had earned enough in an iron foundry to buy his freedom and go north to Ohio. Between 1845 and 1865, Parker returned to the South repeatedly to smuggle other slaves to freedom. His life is a great adventure story, as well as a testament to the daring of men and women who would risk anything to be free.

TOMBEE:
PORTRAIT OF A COTTON PLANTATION
by Thomas Rosengarten (William Morrow & Co., 1986, hardcover)

In the 19th century, Thomas B. Chaplin of South Carolina owned five plantations and hundreds of slaves. Rosengarten reprints the complete journals-a bonanza of information about slave resistance, runaways and the complex relationship between master and slaves—and he includes a complete biography of Thomas B. Chaplin. Worth searching for.

LOST IN PLACE:
GROWING UP ABSURD IN SUBURBIA
by Mark Salzman (Vintage, 1995, paperback)

At age 13, Mark Salzman saw his first kung fu movie and announced to his parents that he was going to sell his possessions and live as a wandering Zen monk. They, of course, told him he wasn't going anywhere until he graduated high school. Until then, he could just practice his kung fu and meditate in the basement. And so, Salzman began pursuing Zen "with the kind of dedication that's possible only when you don't yet have to make a living, when you are too young to drive and you don't have a girlfriend." This is a lighthearted, self-deprecating memoir of adolescence.

IRON AND SILK
by Mark Salzman (Vintage, 1987, paperback)

Salzman went to China, to Hunan Province, in 1982 to teach English. There, he met Pan Qingfu, a renowned martial arts expert, who granted Salzman the rare privilege of being his only kung fu student. Salzman recounts the close master-student friendship that flowered between them and recalls the swordsmen, peasants, Communist Party bureaucrats, students and calligraphers he met during his stay. He brings warmth, humor and the gifts of a natural storyteller to this memoir of a journey in a strange land.

MEMOIRS OF GENERAL W.T. SHERMAN
by William Tecumseh Sherman
(The Library of America, 1990, hardcover)

All the people retire before us," Sherman wrote of his march to the sea, "and desolation is behind." A dazzling and aggressive commander of armies, Sherman also enjoyed an astonishing command of language. No Civil War memoir is more vivid than Sherman's.

REWRITES: A MEMOIR
by Neil Simon (Simon & Schuster, 1996, paperback)

Neil Simon is a funny guy who writes very funny plays. (Who can forget Oscar Madison and Felix Unger?) In this memoir, Simon talks about his career in a way that is refreshingly honest. He tells of the directors and actors who have helped him finish or polish his plays. He admits that given the size of the mutual egos involved, working with Bob Fosse on *Sweet Charity* wasn't easy. He has lots of humorous stories of the actors he's worked with, including George C. Scott's wildly unpredictable behavior during *The Gingerbread Lady*. Witty and wonderfully entertaining, this is going to be a theater classic.

WOMEN'S DIARIES OF THE WESTWARD JOURNEY
by Lillian Schlissel (Schocken Books, 1992, paperback)

Some of the most poignant, most eloquent, most hopeful writings of the American West are found in the diaries of the women who left their homes forever to start a new life on the frontier. Schlissel was one of the first scholars to bring these marvelous documents to light. Read them and you'll understand the sacrifice, the heartache, the courage of these pioneer women.

EIGHTY YEARS AND MORE:
REMINISCENCES 1815-1897
by Elizabeth Cady Stanton
(1898; Northeastern University Press, 1993, paperback)

It was in her father's law office that Elizabeth Cady Stanton learned how the legal code enforced women's subordination. For the rest of her life she would call for the overthrow of these laws, arguing that equality and liberty for women were logical extensions of the fundamental principles upon which the United States had been founded. Stanton's autobiography recalls her struggles against slavery, her 50-year political partnership with Susan B. Anthony and her successes—including securing passage of laws which guaranteed property rights to married women and ensured their right to retain custody of their children after divorce.

WE ARE YOUR SISTERS:
BLACK WOMEN IN THE 19TH CENTURY
Edited by Dorothy Sterling (Norton, 1984, paperback)

Using interviews collected by historians of the WPA Writers' Project of the 1930s, as well as original diaries, memoirs and letters, this book is an in-depth chronicle of the lives of black women—slave and free—who lived between 1800 and 1880. The women talk about childhood and family life, the mental anguish and physical abuse they suffered as slaves, their view of the Civil War and what they did after emancipation.

LETTERS OF A WOMAN HOMESTEADER
by Elinore Pruitt Stewart (Houghton Mifflin, 1982, paperback)

In 1909, Elinore Pruitt left Denver to become the housekeeper for a rancher in Wyoming. Six weeks later, they married. Her letters to friends and family back home read like short stories as she introduces new characters, goes on excursions into the Rockies and captures the details of a homesteader's life in the back country of Wyoming.

THE WAR THE WOMEN LIVED:
FEMALE VOICES FROM THE CONFEDERATE SOUTH
by Walter Sullivan (J.S. Sanders & Co., 1995, hardcover)

Mary Jones Mallard gave birth to her fourth child while Sherman's troops occupied her property. Nineteen-year-old Belle Boyd was arrested as a spy. Sarah Ida Fowler Morgan had brothers fighting on both sides of the conflict. Through the authentic accounts of 23 Southern women, Sullivan offers an informal history of the effects of the Civil War on domestic life in the Confederacy. Sullivan has edited out such extraneous matter as family affairs and political musings to keep the focus on the women and the war. As a result, these first-person accounts have an immediacy, precision and veracity no scholarly history can imitate.

WITH CUSTER ON THE LITTLE BIGHORN: A NEWLY DISCOVERED FIRST PERSON ACCOUNT
by William O. Taylor (Viking, 1996, hardcover)

Private William Taylor was a lucky man. He was among the 150 or so troopers under Major Marcus A. Reno to survive the massacre at Little Bighorn. With Custer on the Little Bighorn is Taylor's own graphic minute-by-minute account of the battle and its aftermath.

Full annotations and explanatory sidebars accompany the text and the book is illustrated with duotone photographs-many of which have never been seen before. This manuscript, found in 1995, gives us a fresh perspective on a tragic event in American frontier history.

GEORGE WASHINGTON:
COLLECTED WRITINGS
Edited by John D. Rhodehamel (The Library of America, 1996, hardcover)

Imagine reading George Washington's account of crossing the Delaware. Or his take on the British surrender at Yorktown.

Or tracing Washington's evolving attitudes about slavery. George Washington: Collected Writings is the most authoritative edition ever published of all of the great man's writings. You can follow through letters his difficult relationship with his mother, his lifelong love for Sally Fairfax and his interest in becoming a player in land speculation. A forceful, eloquent stylist, Washington's writings will delight anyone interested in history or politics.

THE JOURNAL OF JOHN WINTHROP: 1630-1649
Edited by Richard S. Dunn and Laetitia Yeandle
(Belknap Press, 1996, paperback)

On Easter Monday 1630, John Winthrop began his journal and kept on writing right up to his death in 1649. It's a wonderfully idiosyncratic history of the founding generation of New England Puritans. Winthrop faithfully recorded Anne Hutchinson's heresy trial and Roger Williams' exile from Massachusetts. But he also reported sexual naughtiness among the colonists and such newsworthy events as a woman who escaped drowning by grabbing her dog's tail. Anyone who loves diaries or early American history will welcome this new definitive edition.

BLACK BOY
by Richard Wright (1945; HarperCollins, 1993, paperback)

Wright tells the story of his life in the rural South up to age 19. It's a "portrait of the artist," rebelling against the authority of teachers, the piety of family and the racism of whites, while discovering a larger world in the books of H.L. Mencken, Theodore Drieser and Sinclair Lewis.

SOLDIER OF THE YEAR
by José Zuniga (Pocket Books, 1995, paperback)

Sergeant José Zuniga was a hard-core Republican. He served in the Persian Gulf War and was named the Sixth Army's Man of the Year for 1993. But gay men aren't welcome in the U.S.

Army, so he hid behind a sham marriage with a lesbian. When at last he made his coming out speech at a gay/lesbian rally in Washington, the Army stripped him of his rank. Expressing his disgust for Bill Clinton's "don't ask, don't tell" policy, arguing for gay rights, Zuniga is a powerful advocate who tells his story without becoming self-righteous or indulging in self-pity.

If you liked Soldier of the Year:

CONDUCT UNBECOMING:
GAYS & LESBIANS IN THE U.S. MILITARY
by Randy Shilts (Fawcett, 1994, paperback).

An incisive study of gay men and women who have served honorably in the U.S. Armed Forces since the Revolution.

HOLIDAY READING

JEWISH HOLIDAYS

JEWISH DAYS: A BOOK OF JEWISH LIFE AND CULTURE AROUND THE YEAR
by Francine Klagsbrun, Illustrated by Mark Podwal
(Farrar, Straus & Giroux, 1996, hardcover)

Passover and Hanukkah. Rosh Hashanah and Yom Kippur. All the major Jewish holidays are here, but so are less familiar observances and modern commemorations. For example, the eleventh day of Heshvan is observed as the day on which Rachel died; and the twenty-seventh day of Nissan is Yom ha-Shoah, a new holiday which remembers the victims of the Holocaust. Klagsbrun details the rituals associated with the festivals and draws upon such sources the Talmud and medieval texts to tell ancient stories about Abraham, Queen Esther and Rabbi Akiva. A wonderfully comprehensive book, enriched with beautiful illustrations.

FAST & FESTIVE MEALS FOR THE JEWISH HOLIDAYS: COMPLETE MENUS, RITUALS AND PARTY-PLANNING IDEAS FOR EVERY HOLIDAY OF THE YEAR
by Marlene Sorosky (Morrow, 1997, hardcover)

Marlene Sorosky blends respect for religious traditions while updating traditional holiday fare. Where else could you find a recipe for Salmon Gefilte Fish, Giant Potato-Carrot Pancake and Chocolate-Peanut Butter Hamantashen? Each chapter begins with a description of the significance of the holiday and includes the appropriate prayers—in English and transliterated Hebrew. Plus there are lots of activities for kids, from building a model sukkah out of breadsticks to planting seeds in cups for Tu B'-Shevat.

VALENTINE'S DAY

ROSES ARE PINK, YOUR FEET REALLY STINK
by Diane de Groat (Morrow, 1996, hardcover)

Gilbert gets back at two unpleasant classmates by sending them prank valentines. But never fear—the story comes to a happy resolution with apologies all around.

············

PASSOVER

THE MATZAH THAT PAPA BROUGHT HOME
by Fran Manushkin, illustrated by Ned Bittinger (Scholastic, 1995, hardcover)

*"This is the Passover Seder we shared
to eat the feast that Mama made
with the matzah that Papa brought home."*

Manushkin uses a "House That Jack Built" formula to tell the story of Passover and a big, happy family preparing for the Seder. Bittinger's illustrations are clear and colorful and will remind grown-ups of the luminous paintings of Marc Chagall.

············

THE NEVER-ENDING GREENNESS
by Neil Waldeman (Morrow Junior Books, 1997, paperback)

A young Jewish survivor of the Holocaust bonds with Israel, his new homeland, by planting seedlings on the barren hillsides.

············

HALLOWEEN

ADVENTURE IN THE WITCH'S HOUSE:
A BOOK TO READ BY FLASHLIGHT
by Lynn Gordon, illustrations by Susan Synarski

(Simon & Schuster/Little Simon, 1996, hardcover)

The story of creeping through a witch's scary house takes the back seat to a truly nifty gimmick. Every page contains an acetate; shine a flashlight through it and a huge spider web or a bunch of creepy bats, or some other spooky image is projected on the wall. Kids aged four through eight will love this book.

THANKSGIVING

STRANDED AT PLIMOTH PLANTATION 1626

by Gary Bowen (HarperCollins, 1994, paperback)

Thirteen-year-old Christopher Sears has no prospects in England, so he becomes the indentured servant of a ship's captain bound for a new settlement in Massachusetts. When winter sets in and Christopher is stranded, he starts to keep a diary of the Indians and English colonists he meets and his adventures in the New World. Packed with authentic details from the colony's history and illustrated with colored woodcuts, this engaging work of historical fiction is an exciting way for young readers to learn about life in early America.

OVER THE RIVER AND THROUGH THE WOODS: A MUSICAL PICTURE BOOK

by Lydia Maria Child, illustrations by Nadine Bernard Westcott (HarperCollins, 1995, hardcover)

"Over the River and Through the Woods" has always been fun for kids to sing. Now singing along is even easier with a computer chip playing the melody embedded in this wonderful book. Wescott's illustrations are perfect—wintry snowscapes, idyllic farmhouses and big happy families. The ideal accompaniment to celebrating Thanksgiving.

PILGRIM VOICES:
OUR FIRST YEAR IN THE NEW WORLD
Edited by Connie and Peter Roop, illustrated by Shelley Pritchett
(Walker, 1995, paperback)

Excerpts from the journals of the Pilgrims themselves tell the story of their journey to the New World, their friendship with Squanto and Samoset and their harvest festival that we call "Thanksgiving." Shelley Pritchett's paintings are stunning evocations of the New England landscape.

HANUKKAH

ONE YELLOW DAFFODIL:
A HANUKKAH STORY
by David A. Adler, Illustrated by Lloyd Bloom
(Gulliver Books/Harcourt Brace, 1995, paperback)

Morris Kaplan has a florist shop. He loves his flowers, he loves his customers. But Mr. Kaplan still feels hollow inside-he lost all his family and friends in Auschwitz. Then one day the Becker children, a brother and sister who buy flowers every Friday for their family's Sabbath table, invite Mr. Kaplan to come to their house for Hanukkah. The beauty of the holiday and the warmth of the Becker family finally heals Mr. Kaplan's broken heart. "I had no one," he tells the family. "Now you have us," says Mrs. Becker. A beautiful story, perfectly told.

HANUKKAH CHUBBY BOARD BOOK
AND DREIDELS
by Alan Benjamin, illustrated by Ellen Appleby
(Simon & Schuster/Little Simon, 1997, hardcover)

A very sweet story of a family playing dreidels. The book includes the rules of the game and includes two wooden dreidels.

WHILE THE CANDLES BURN:
EIGHT STORIES FOR HANUKKAH
by Barbara Golden, illustrated by Elaine Greenstein
(Viking, 1996, hardcover)

There's a story for each night of the Hanukkah holiday in this collection. For her stories, Barbara Golden draws upon Jewish folklore, the Talmud and the real-life accounts of Holocaust survivors and students of an Israeli school where Arabs and Jews study together.

A GREAT MIRACLE HAPPENED THERE
by Karla Kuskin, Illustrated by Robert Andrew Parker (HarperCollins, 1993, paperback)

Kuskin retells the story of the oil that burned in the Temple of Jerusalem for eight days and ties that ancient miracle to contemporary celebrations of the holiday.

THE STORY OF HANUKKAH:
A LIFT-THE-FLAP REBUS BOOK
by Lisa Rojany, illustrated by Holly Jones (Hyperion, 1993, hardcover)

Here's a charming way to teach children the story of the valiant Maccabees, wicked king Antiochus and the miracle of the oil lamp that burned in the Temple for eight days. The pop-ups are great and the lift-the-flap format is an ingenious way to teach children new words.

THE STORY OF HANUKKAH
by Norma Simon, illustrated by Leonid Gore
(HarperCollins, 1997, hardcover)

Leonid Gore's paintings for this book are wonderful—they have a soft, warm glow that make you believe you are viewing them in the light of Hanukkah candles. Author Norma Simon tells the historic origins of the holiday and the legends that have grown up around it. She goes on to explain how to play with a dreidel and even offers a recipe for latkes. A fresh, reverent and engaging approach to Hanukkah.

CHRISTMAS

A TAXI DOG CHRISTMAS
by *Debra Barracca and Sal Barracca, illustrated by Alan Ayers* (Dial, 1994, paperback)

While working the Christmas Eve shift in Manhattan, Jim the cabbie and Maxi the dog come to Santa's rescue and are rewarded by flying with the reindeer. A charmer that adults are going to love as much as the kids.

THE IT'S A WONDERFUL LIFE BOOK
by *Jeanine Basinger* (Knopf, 1990, hardcover)

Just about everything you might ever want to know about Frank Capra's classic Christmas film, *It's a Wonderful Life*, can be found in this comprehensive and exhaustively researched work. Basinger has assembled the finished screenplay (as well excerpts from earlier versions credited to writers such as Clifford Odets), the self-published short story on which it was based, contemporary reviews, interdepartmental RKO memos about the film, interviews with Jimmy Stewart, Capra and his cinematographer and plenty of movie stills and behind-the-scenes photographs. It's a fascinating look at how films were made at the end of Hollywood's Golden Age.

GOING HOME
by *Eve Bunting, illustrated by David Diaz* (HarperCollins, 1996, hardcover)

Every year, as Christmas approaches, Carlos and his family drive from their home in California to the town his family came from in Mexico. The journey gives Carlos a new appreciation for the beauty of his homeland and an better understanding of the sacrifices his parents make so that he and his sisters can have a better life. David Diaz, a Caldecott Medalist, has created brightly colored illustrations that convey the joy of Christmas in Mexico.

CHARLES DICKENS' A CHRISTMAS CAROL

by Charles Dickens, illustrations by Gustav Doré (1843; McE Publishing, 1996, hardcover)

Everybody loves Dickens' story of the cold-hearted old skinflint who is miraculously transformed on Christmas Eve by the visitation of three ghosts. Now this Christmas classic is available in a superb edition that features 45 engravings made by Gustav Doré for an 1861 edition of the story. Doré's images should go down as definitive: his ghosts are spookier and Scrooge nastier than in any other illustrated version of *A Christmas Carol*. This is the kind of book that becomes a family heirloom.

A DOZEN SILK DIAPERS

by Melissa Kajput, illustrated by Veselina Tomova

The mother spider and her little ones had never seen such a night. First a dazzling new star appears in the sky. Then a young couple takes refuge in the stable and the woman gives birth to a baby boy. Finally, one of the little spider brood falls into the manger and is rescued by the new mother. In gratitude, the mother spider spins 12 silk diapers for the new born Child. Worth searching for.

AMAHL AND THE NIGHT VISITORS

by Gian Carlo Menotti, illustrated by Michele Lemieux (Morrow Junior Books, 1986, hardcover)

As the Three Kings follow the star to Bethlehem, they stop at the house of a poor widow and her son, Amahl—a shepherd boy afflicted with a crippled leg. When the Kings explain where they are going and bring out the wondrous gifts they are bringing to the Christ Child, Amahl decides to send a gift, too. Then, something miraculous occurs. The story from Menotti's opera has become a Christmas classic and it is presented in an especially handsome version here, with the figures rendered in bright colors highlighted in gold.

O HOLY NIGHT!
MASTERWORKS OF CHRISTMAS POETRY
Selected, translated and Edited by Johann M. Moser
(Sophia Institute Press, 1995, hardcover)

It would be hard to surpass this collection of Christmas poetry. Johann Moser, himself a poet, has brought together in a single volume works by St. Augustine, Dante, Chaucer, Christina Rossetti, T.S. Eliot, Boris Pasternak, Gerard Manley Hopkins. Plus Milton's "On the Morning of Christ's Nativity" and Yeats' "The Mother of God." Moser even includes Virgil's *Fourth Eclogue*, the verses medieval Christians believed prophesied the coming of Christ. Truly, the perfect treasury of Christmas verse.

GOOD KING WENCESLAS
by John Mason Neale, illustrated by Christopher Manson
(Puffin, 1993, paperback)

Most readers are probably familiar with the first stanza of "Good King Wenceslas." But did you know the Christmas carol goes on through several more verses to tell a story of royal charity and the miracle that accompanied it? Manson has illustrated the carol, bringing it to life with superb, colorful, medieval-style paintings. And there are appendices that tell the story of the real Wenceslas and John Mason Neale who immortalized him in song.

THE ULTIMATE CHRISTMAS BOOK
by Jane Newdick (Houghton Mifflin, 1996, hardcover)

Make an Advent calendar with a little gift behind every door. Fashion beautiful silk balls for your Christmas tree. Deck your halls with wreaths and flowery garlands. Set a jewel-like candelabra at the center of your holiday table. Jane Newdick's all-in-one Christmas compendium has more than 100 festive ideas for original decorations, ornaments, gift wrap and cards. Plus she includes more than 50 traditional Christmas recipes from around the world. With lavish illustrations to inspire you and easy-to-follow directions for every project, *The Ultimate Christmas Book* can help you create the merriest Yuletide ever.

THE BATTLE FOR CHRISTMAS
by Stephen Nissenbaum (Knopf, 1996, hardcover)

Back in merry old England, Christmas was often an excuse for gluttony, gambling, power drinking, promiscuity and even gang violence (particularly among wassailing riffraff). No wonder the Puritans abolished it. Then in the 1820s, Washington Irving and some like-minded New York friends decided to make Christmas a respectable family holiday. From Clement Clark Moore's "'Twas the Night Before Christmas," to today's riot of consumerism, Nissenbaum's well-researched, beautifully illustrated book studies the sacred, the sordid, the sentimental and the even the silly customs of Christmas.

THE CHRISTMAS WITCH
written and illustrated by Ilse Plume
(Hyperion, 1993, paperback)

There's an old Italian legend that a witch, Befana, heard about the birth of Christ and set out with gifts for the newborn. When she couldn't find him, Befana began to leave her presents at every house where there were children.

KING ISLAND CHRISTMAS
by Jean Rogers, illustrated by Rie Munoz
(Greenwillow Books, 1985, paperback)

Astand out among holiday books is this story of the Inuit community of King Island who band together one Christmas to rescue their new priest who is stranded in the ice of the Bering Sea.

THE TWELVE DAYS OF CHRISTMAS: A POP-UP CELEBRATION
by Robert Sabuda (Simon & Schuster, 1996, hardcover)

Incredibly complicated pop-ups are the heroes in this enchanting book illustrating the popular Christmas song.

HOW THE GRINCH STOLE CHRISTMAS
by Dr. Seuss (Random House, 1957, hardcover)

*Every Who
Down in Who-ville
Liked Christmas a lot...*

The Grinch, on the other hand, was completely disgusted by the holiday and the unrelenting good cheer of the Whos. So on Christmas Eve, he dresses up as Santa Claus, makes his long-suffering dog Max play the part of a reindeer and creeps into Who-ville... well, you know how the story goes. Before you open your Christmas packages, boxes and bags, or carve your own roast beast, read *How the Grinch Stole Christmas* aloud. And don't be surprised if the entire household clasps hands and starts to sing.

THE TIME-LIFE OLD-FASHIONED CHRISTMAS COOKBOOK
(Time-Life Books, 1996, hardcover)

Roast Beef and Yorkshire Pudding. Roast Gingered Turkey Breast. Bûche de Noël. Chocolate Truffles. Bourbon Bread.

Here are hundreds of delicious recipes to help you spread holiday cheer.

. . . .

THE CHRISTMAS MIRACLE OF JONATHAN TOOMEY

by Susan Wojciechowski, Illustrated by P.J. Lynch
(Candlewick Press, 1995, hardcover)

Jonathan Toomey is a grumpy woodcarver. His wife and baby son died many years ago and Mr. Toomey hasn't been happy since. Then one December, a widow and her son come to the workshop and ask Mr. Toomey to carve a set of Nativity figures for them. Soon, the set is complete—except for the figures of the Mother and the Child. To finish these, Mr. Toomey brings out a sketch of his wife and son—they become the models for Mary and the Christ Child. A perfect Christmas story, illustrated with watercolors in the warm gold and brown tones of a wood-carver's workshop.

. . . .

THE CHRISTMAS BIRD

by Bernadette Watts (North-South, 1996, hardcover)

The only gift Katya has for the newborn Baby is her wooden bird whistle. But once she places it in the manger, it is miraculously changed into a living, singing bird. A heart-warming Christmas miracle, set in a wintry Alpine wonderland.

. . . .

WINDOWS OF CHRISTMAS:
A RENAISSANCE NATIVITY

(Simon & Schuster, 1997, hardcover)

There might be an unseemly scuffle under the Christmas tree as adults and kids all try to get their hands on this sublime book. Each page spread features a gorgeous reproduction of a Renaissance triptych—those hinged, three-panel paintings that served as altarpieces centuries ago. As with the originals, the flaps (or wings) of each painting open to reveal a scene from the story of the first Christmas. Among the masters represented are Gerard David, Robert Campin and Hieronymous Bosch. And the text is from the King James Bible. Absolute perfection.

HOMES & GARDENS

THE GARDEN TRELLIS:
DESIGNS TO BUILD AND VINES TO CULTIVATE
Written and illustrated by Ferris Cook
(Artisan/Workman, 1996, hardcover)

Very beautiful yet eminently practical, *The Garden Trellis* teaches you how to build simple, elegant trellises and then helps you choose the right vines—honeysuckle or morning glory, roses or moon flowers. Cook also includes a list of sources for ready-made trellises.

WRITERS' HOUSES
Prologue by Marguerite Duras, photographs by Erica Lennard, text by Francesca Premoli-Droulers (Vendome Press, 1995, hardcover)

The royalties from Mrs. Dalloway paid for a water closet in Virginia Woolf's simple house. Jean Cocteau surrounded himself with exotic curios. And Ernest Hemingway welcomed dozens of cats to his home in Key West. Through more than 200 illustrations, plus interviews with writers' children and companions, you'll see how authors as diverse as Mark Twain and Jane Austen, Beatrix Potter and Dylan Thomas designed their homes to reflect their personality and their vision of the world. A tantalizing glimpse of the private life of your favorite writers.

THE BOOK OF OUTDOOR GARDENING
by the Editors of Smith & Hawken with Sara Goodwin (Workman, 1996, paperback)

Among gardeners, Smith & Hawken is a firm legendary for its expertise on how to make beautiful things grow. But just

as important is Smith & Hawken's faith in gardening as a life-enhancing activity. Now, in this splendid book, you can learn to strengthen your ties to the earth through organic garden. It's packed with information, from making good compost to raising champion vegetables to getting your flowers to bloom early and often. And every method is environmentally sound. If you love to garden, you'll love this book.

BULBS:
FOUR SEASONS OF BEAUTIFUL BLOOMS
by Lewis and Nancy Hill
(Garden Way Publishing, 1994, paperback)

Practical advice on how to grow crocus, hyacinths, narcissus, tulips and other bulb flowers, in your garden, as well as forcing them indoors during the winter. Packed with useful information for novices and tips for seasoned gardeners, such as how to create your own hybrids.

GRANDMOTHER'S GARDEN:
THE OLD-FASHIONED AMERICAN GARDEN 1865-1915
by May Brawley Hill (Abrams, 1995, hardcover)

Harriet Beecher Stowe was an inveterate gardener. So were Emily Dickinson and Sarah Orne Jewett. In the mid- to late-19th century, gardening entered a golden age in America and women especially embraced it as a creative outlet. In Grandmother's Garden, May Brawley Hill, an art historian and herself a passionate gardener, explores the lush gardens of 100 years ago and their modern revival. An especially fine feature of this book are the 75 full-color plates of works by American Impressionists—including Childe Hassam—who saw in the gardens of America the same informal style they had admired at Monet's home in Giverny.

TAYLOR'S GUIDE TO CONTAINER GARDENING
Edited by Roger Holmes (Houghton Mifflin, 1995, paperback)

You love growing flowers, herbs and other plants, but you don't have a yard. The solution is growing plants in containers and no book is more helpful than this comprehensive guide from Taylor's, a respected name in gardening books. You'll discover which are the best annuals, perennials, bulbs, vines, even shrubs and trees to grow in containers. You'll learn to choose wisely among clay pots, wooden boxes, tin cans, plastic tubs and concrete whatnots. Plus you'll get details on how to grow 300 plants. And the 284 color illustrations take the guesswork out of selecting plants at the nursery.

HOUSE
by Tracy Kidder (Avon, 1986, paperback)

In a story about building a house, the carpenters are the heroes. The owners seem to think that every quoted price is up for negotiation. The architect gets touchy when the builders point out that his vision may not work in the real world. A completely absorbing story of what it takes to create a home from the ground up.

THE BACKYARD BIRD-LOVER'S GUIDE
by Jan Mahnken, color illustrations by Jeffrey Domm
(Storey Communications, 1996, paperback)

If you put out a bird feeder, they will come. But once the birds arrive, how do you identify them? *The Backyard Bird-Lover's Guide* has the color illustrations you need to identify birds, but features a whole lot more—such as information about the nesting and feeding habits of a variety of species to help you attract the kinds of birds you want to your backyard. Plus, you get instructions and diagrams for building birdhouses and birdbaths and tips on how to construct a birdfeeder that will be safe from those damn squirrels.

THE HERB GARDEN
by Susan McClure (Storey/Garden Way, 1996)

Fresh herbs are always welcome in the kitchen. But if you've always thought herb gardens were too much trouble, think again. In this comprehensive handbook, Susan McClure tells you everything you need to know to grow and dry your own herbs with a minimum of fuss. You'll learn how to lay out your garden, how to control pests, when to harvest and which herbs you can bring indoors for the winter. Plus, McClure includes a chapter of suggested herbal recipes and craft projects and a list of sources so you can shop for herb seeds by mail. There's never been a simpler, more practical guide for cultivating your own herb garden.

SHAKER BUILT: THE FORM AND FUNCTION OF SHAKER ARCHITECTURE
by Paul Rocheleau and June Sprigg, Edited and designed by David Larkin (Monacelli Press, 1994, hardcover)

An oversized volume brimming with powerful, luminous photographs that capture the secret details of Shaker architecture, *Shaker Built* is a work of love that draws the reader into the Shakers' world of ingenuity, hard work and perfect peace. Today, we look at Shaker buildings and fall in love with the generous space and handsome simplicity of the decor. But the Shakers had other things in mind when they built their communities—comfort, convenience and keeping the sexes segregated.

LIVING WITH WILDLIFE
FROM THE CALIFORNIA CENTER FOR WILDLIFE
With Diana Landau and Shelley Stump
(Sierra Club Books, 1994, hardcover)

These days, you don't have to live out in the country to encounter wildlife on a day-to-day basis. Deer have moved into the suburbs devouring prize flowers, expensive shrubs and whole vegetable gardens. Canadian geese spend the winter in town, fouling patios, decks and lawns. And basements and attics have become favorite raccoon habitats. Now you can learn how to handle wildlife problems humanely, with methods that respect wild animals but keep your home secure from intrusions.

* * *

JEFFERSON AND MONTICELLO:
THE BIOGRAPHY OF A BUILDER
by Jack McLaughlin (Owl, 1990, paperback)

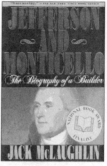

Thomas Jefferson spent virtually his entire life designing, building, improving and furnishing his home, Monticello. It was his greatest passion. But if Jefferson was the genius behind the finest 18th-century house in America, his slaves were the craftsmen.

* * *

COUNTRY LIVING SEASONS AT SEVEN GATES FARM
Mary Seehafer Sears and Keith Scott Morton, editors (Hearst Books, 1996, hardcover)

If you read *Country Living* magazine, you know that Seven Gates Farm in rural Maryland is the home and studio of designers James Cramer and Dean Johnson. Now they offer a season-by-season study of their farmstead through more than 300 glorious color photographs. Among their inspirations—embellish your spring and summer table settings with miniature topiaries; on cool autumn nights, throw dry rosemary on the fire and scent the air with the Herb's rich aroma; and as the holidays approach, Cramer and Johnson have wonderful suggestions for parties, gifts and festive decorations. *Country Living Seasons at Seven Gates Farm* is one of those rare design books that is both beautiful and useful.

* * *

THE GRAHAM STUART THOMAS ROSE BOOK

by Graham Stuart Thomas (Timber Press, 1994, hardcover)

Graham Stuart Thomas' trilogy, The Old Shrub Roses, Shrub Roses of Today and Climbing Roses Old and New, has been essential reading for gardeners for decades. Now these three classics have been updated and brought together in a single, magnificently illustrated volume. You'll rediscover all the ancient rose varieties that were the favorites of gardeners in the early 19th century, plus you get an excellent overview of climbing roses. For anyone who loves roses, this is the ultimate resource book.

LIFE IN THE ENGLISH COUNTRY COTTAGE

by Adrian Tinniswood (Orion Publishing Group, 1995, hardcover)

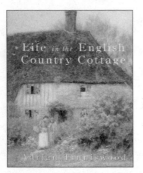

Real life in English cottages was not all cream cakes and hollyhocks, you know. According to Adrian Tinniswood, a consultant to Great Britain's National Trust, cottages were damp, gloomy, unsanitary warrens for the poor. In the Victorian Age— and then the Arts and Crafts period—well-to-do people gentrified old cottages, filled them with lovely antiques and fabrics and amused themselves waxing nostalgic about the simple life. Through engaging text and more than 300 illustrations, Tinniswood leads you on a private tour of the changing appearance and perception of cottage life.

BATTLEFIELD:
FARMING A CIVIL WAR BATTLEGROUND

by Peter Svenson
(Ballantine, 1994, paperback)

The author's life is transformed when he discovers that a Civil War battle was fought in the front yard of his Virginia farm.

BOB VILA'S WORKSHOP
by Bob Vila (Morrow, 1994, hardcover)

Bob Vila is the man you want to set up your home workshop. And in this detailed, profusely illustrated handbook, that's exactly what he does. Vila helps you find the best possible work space, tells you how to select essential tools and even teaches you how to build your own workbench. Indispensable advice from the star of Bob Vila's *Home Again* and *This Old House*.

In Style

AN AUTOBIOGRAPHY
by Richard Avedon (Random House, 1993, hardcover)

Only Avedon could do Avedon justice. Part life story, part retrospective, this smashing volume is filled with his stunning, provocative, seductive photographs. From cover shots for Vogue and Harper's Bazaar, to the quintessential candid of Eisenhower triumphant, to a series of nudes in Andy Warhol's Factory, to a uncanny portrait of Marilyn Monroe, no one captured the heart and soul of his subjects like Richard Avedon.

LOVE, LOSS AND WHAT I WORE
by Ilene Beckerman (Algonquin Books, 1995, paperback)

Ilene Beckerman writes about what all women know—that memories are often tied to favorite clothes. And so she uses her wardrobe to tell her life story. There's the dress her father bought her when her mother died, the maternity dress she wore through six pregnancies, the dress she was wearing when she caught her first husband cheating on her, her first mail order purchase (a brown wool pants suit from Spiegel's) and the interview suit she bought when she decided to re-enter the work force. Today, Beckerman's four-year-old granddaughter plays with these old outfits and Beckerman wonders if the little girl will remember them when she grows older.

MEN AND WOMEN: DRESSING THE PART
by Claudia Brush Kidwell and Valeria Steele (Smithsonian Institution Press, 1989, paperback)

C lothes do a lot more than keep us warm and cover up our naughty bits. What we wear and how we wear it communicates what we think of ourselves and how we want others to perceive us. Kidwell and Steele expand upon this idea, studying changes in fashion as a sign of changing ideas about masculinity and femininity. It's intriguing stuff as they examine shifting notions of ideal body types, appropriate hairstyles for men and women, the jeans revolution, even the history of lingerie (what's it for and who should wear it).

A THOUSAND DAYS OF MAGIC: DRESSING JACKIE KENNEDY FOR THE WHITE HOUSE
by Oleg Cassini (Rizzoli, 1995, hardcover)

D esigner Oleg Cassini knew Jackie Kennedy before she became First Lady. But the apex of their friendship was the thousand days when Cassini worked to make Jackie the most glamorous woman in America. This stunning book, packed with beautiful black-and-white and color photographs of Jackie in Cassini couture, is a loving tribute. And for readers who did not experience the Camelot years, this is a fascinating glimpse of the grace and style with which Jackie carried out her duties as First Lady.

COUTURE: THE GREAT DESIGNERS
by Caroline Rennolds Milbank (Stewart, Tabori & Chang, 1997, hardcover)

S aint Laurent. Dior. Chanel. Ralph Lauren. Valentino. Issey Miyake. This big, splashy book lets you explore the rarefied world of fashion designers and what the "look" says about us and our times. Lavishly illustrated with drawings from the designers' own sketch pads, spreads from fashion magazines and famous shots by such renowned photographers as Horst and Cecil Beaton, this is the ultimate look book.

....

SEX AND SUITS
by Anne Hollander (Kodansha Globe, 1995, paperback)

To Anne Hollander, fashion is not about vanity; it is an art with a history and formal laws just like painting or, better yet, architecture. Going back to the 16th century, she uses anthropology, sociology and psychology to reveal the changes in the way people dress. She finds the first example of sartorial nonchalance in the leather jerkins and loose breeches of 17th-century soldiers. And while for centuries a woman's pelvis and legs were always hidden, her bosom was subject to a "constantly changing theatrical presentation of some kind." Smart, witty, insightful, *Sex and Suits* is a marvelous introduction to the complexities of fashion.

....

QUILTS IN AMERICA
by Patsy and Myron Orlofsky
(Abbeville Press, 1992, hardcover)

Quilts are hot. Sotheby's and Christie's devote entire auctions to antique quilts and contemporary Amish quiltmakers can name their price for their creations. How did such a humble object (after all, it's just a blanket) come to be in such tremendous demand? Here is the definitive study on American quilts, from functional household items to masterpieces of design. And the Orlofskys have packed their book with a kaleidoscope of photographs that could transform you from an admirer to a collector.

More Quilts:

A GALLERY OF AMISH QUILTS
by Robert Bishop and Elizabeth Safanda
(Peter Smith Publisher, 1988, paperback).

One of the best books on the artistry of Amish quiltmakers.

Light Entertainment

WHY THINGS ARE: ANSWERS TO EVERY ESSENTIAL QUESTION IN LIFE
by Joel Achenbach (Ballantine, 1996, paperback)

Why are we here? Why don't Communist leaders ever get assassinated? And most importantly, why doesn't Lois Lane realize Clark Kent and Superman are the same person? Journalist and National Public Radio commentator Joel Achenbach isn't afraid to ask the tough questions. He also doesn't shy away from offering up some funny, insightful and downright plausible answers. *Why Things Are* is packed with just the type of fascinating yet useless ponderances your brain needs to stay in peak condition.

. . . .

NOW ALL WE NEED IS A TITLE: FAMOUS BOOK TITLES AND HOW THEY GOT THAT WAY
by André Bernard (Norton, 1995, hardcover)

"Trimalchio in West Egg." That's the title F. Scott Fitzgerald had in mind for the novel we know as *The Great Gatsby*. When it comes to titles, it seems even the great authors have a tin ear. In this funny, informative literary romp andré Bernard ferrets out the strange origins of some titles (Edward Albee found the line "Who's afraid of Virginia Woolf?" scrawled on the mirror in a men's room) and spills the beans about authorial suggestions that must have given editors nightmares. For instance, when he was told to dream up a Shakespearean title, Raymond Chandler suggested "Zounds, He Dies." Doesn't quite have the same ring as *Farewell, My Lovely*, does it?

. . . .

FIGHTING WORDS:
WRITERS LAMBASTE OTHER WRITERS—
FROM ARISTOTLE TO ANNE RICE
Edited by James Charlton, with illustrations by Tullio Pericoli
(Algonquin Books, 1994, hardcover)

"The effect upon women," Dorothy Parker wrote of Ernest Hemingway, "is such that they want to go right out and get him and bring him home stuffed." Ezra Pound said that if Ford Madox Ford were "placed naked and alone in a room without furniture, I would come back in an hour and find total confusion." A wicked collection of literary mudslinging.

THE LAST CUCKOO: THE VERY BEST
LETTERS TO THE TIMES SINCE 1900
Chosen and introduced by Kenneth Gregory
(A Common Reader Edition, 1996, paperback)

A gentleman laments "the disappearance of the chamber pot as an article of guest bedroom furniture." A lady marvels that French phrase books omit the question, "Madam, my son has been bitten by a mole. Has rabies reached this part of France?" Reading (and writing!) letters to *The Times of London* must be among Britain's more civilized pleasures. Kenneth Gregory's hilarious collection includes letters from perplexed vicars, flummoxed military men (ret.), indignant brides and such celebrity correspondents as Evelyn Waugh, T.S. Eliot, Vita Sackville-West and Benito Mussolini. Perfect for devoted Anglophiles.

More Loony Letters:

THE NEXT TO LAST CUCKOO AND THE
SECOND CUCKOO
Chosen and introduced by Kenneth Gregory
(A Common Reader Edition, 1997, paperback).

Pocket boroughs, turned-up trousers, memorable encounters between an actress and a bishop and "the earwig's better nature" are among the vital issues addressed in these sequels.

THE CARTOON HISTORY OF THE UNIVERSE
by Larry Gonick (Doubleday, 1994)

Of course you're buying this two-volume set for the kids. But you'll wind up reading it yourself. Larry Gonick is a guy who can goof on the Great Moments in History and still get all his facts straight. He starts with the Big Bang, concludes with the Fall of Rome and never leaves out the good parts (the orgies, the beheadings, the human sacrifices). You'll meet the first single-celled life forms, watch Bathsheba in her bathtub, witness Achilles' battlefield exploits, see the trouble Queen Hatshepsut caused when she declared herself King Hatshepsut and even get a two-page summary of the Mahabharata ("the very short version"). Funny and informative.

THE ART OF THE COMIC BOOK:
AN AESTHETIC HISTORY
by Robert C. Harvey
(University of Mississippi Press, 1996, paperback)

Harvey, a cartoonist himself, explains in a lively engaging way how comic books evolved in America. He introduces readers to the art of Will Eisner, creator of *The Spirit* and Art Spiegelman, who wrote *Maus* and *Maus II*. He explains why superheroes all wear costumes that resemble long underwear. And he reproduces the first Superman and Captain America strips. Plus he brings comics up to date with New Teen Titans and Zap. This book is so good, you'll not only look at the cartoons, you'll actually read the text.

ENDANGERED PLEASURES
by Barbara Holland
(HarperPaperbacks, 1996, paperback)

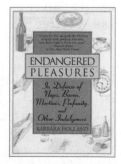

"Gloom we will always have with us," Barbara Holland writes. So she has taken it upon herself to defend the little indul-gences that make life livable. Like bacon. And martinis. And afternoon naps. And profanity. A witty, savvy book that laughs at the solemn warnings about things that aren't good for you.

....

ALL I REALLY NEEDED TO KNOW I LEARNED FROM WATCHING STAR TREK
by Dave Marinaccio (Crown, 1995, paperback)

Every episode of Star Trek taught an important lesson.

• Every alien life-form has a right to exist so long as it doesn't try to take over the universe.
• Correct your mistakes, even if it means that Joan Collins has to be run down by a speeding car to keep the Nazis from winning World War II.
• If everybody does his own job, the ship won't run into problems.

....

NOBLESSE OBLIGE
Edited by Nancy Mitford
(1955; A Common Reader Edition, 1997, hardcover)

Between the upper class and the middle class, Nancy Mitford observes, "there is a very definite border line, easily recognizable by hundreds of small but significant landmarks." And so Miss Mitford and her friends (including Evelyn Waugh and John Betjeman) help readers distinguish between upper class ("U") and the non-upper class ("non-U") behavior. The expression, "bye-bye" is very non-U ("It makes me blush for my country," says Miss Mitford). Mr. Waugh deplores fraudulent pedigrees some non-U parvenus have concocted for themselves. ("People," he writes, "have been caught filling their parish churches with bogus tombs.") It's all delightfully tongue-in-cheek and very, very English.

....

MILTON'S TEETH & OVID'S UMBRELLA: CURIOUS AND CURIOUSER ADVENTURES IN HISTORY
Michael Olmert (Touchstone Books, 1996, paperback)

Historians have found that if you want to know how ordinary people lived their ordinary lives, you've got to look in odd places. Michael Olmert does just that in this breezy collection of historical anecdotes. He recounts how a man named Crescens immortalized a night of hard drinking with his pals by scrawling the details on a wall in Pompeii. He ponders the mystery of how a West African monkey's bones found their way into an 18th-century rubbish heap in Williamsburg, Virginia. And he speculates whether the shiner the Archbishop of Rheims got during a English vs. French soccer match in 1439 prolonged the Hundred Years War. From 12th-century Irish to Aztec Mexico, this is fun, fascinating history.

THE COMPLETE LYRICS OF COLE PORTER
by Cole Porter, Edited by Robert Kimball
(Da Capo Press, 1992, paperback)

He's the tops. He's the Colisseum. He's the tops. He's the Louvre Museum. For anyone who loves Cole Porter's infectious, effervescent songs, here's a book that collects all the lyrics of every song Porter ever wrote (and he wrote 800!). "Begin the Beguine." "My Heart Belongs to Daddy." "Anything Goes." "Brush Up Your Shakespeare." "I Get a Kick Out of You." "You'd Be So Nice to Come Home To." "In the Still of the Night." "Always True to You in My Fashion." "Night and Day." They're all here and it's delightful, it's delicious, it's deductible, it's delirious, it's dilemma, it's delimit, it's deluxe, it's delovely.

ONE FROG CAN MAKE A DIFFERENCE
by Kermit the Frog as told to Robert P. Riger, illustrated by Tom Payne (Pocket Books, 1994, paperback)

The ultimate spokesfrog addresses the most important issues of our time:

• Finding the Tadpole Within.
• I'm Not an Amphibian American, I'm a Frog.
• French for Frogs [Je saute, donc je suis (I hop, therefore I am)].
• I'm Okay, You're a Pig.

THE COMPLETE HENRY ROOT LETTERS
by Henry Root (A Common Reader Edition, 1996, paperback)

On a lady columnist's threat to pull down Margaret Thatcher's knickers, Mr. Henry Root writes to the Director of Public Prosecutions: "Surely any unauthorized reference to Mrs. Thatcher's knickers is illegal and a threat to pull them down by a private citizen unacquainted with Mrs. Thatcher tantamount to civil disorder?" Since his retirement from the trade of wet fish merchant, Henry Root has been firing off eccentric, deliriously funny letters to a host of authorities: Her Majesty the Queen, the directors of the BBC, the ambassador of Greece. Almost as much fun to read as Root's originals are the perplexed replies he receives.

SHRINKLITS: SEVENTY OF THE WORLD'S TOWERING CLASSICS CUT DOWN TO SIZE
by Maurice Sagoff
(Workman, 1980, paperback)

"Monster Grendel's tastes are plainish.
Breakfast? Just a couple Danish."

Think of it! *Beowulf* cut down to 13 rhymed couplets. Darwin's *Origin of Species* condensed in 14 lines, *Moby Dick* in 8. This is the quick way to glean all the major ideas of 70 monumental classics—and they're uproariously funny.

OH THE PLACES YOU'LL GO
by Dr. Seuss (Random House, 1990, hardcover)

"You have brains in your head. You have feet in your shoes. You can steer yourself any direction you choose."

Theodore Geisel, better known to all as Dr. Seuss, penned over 40 children's books in his career. However, this inspirational guide to weathering the world's ups and downs was meant for boys and girls of all ages who are about to enter any of life's mazes.

The best of Dr. Seuss:

THE CAT IN THE HAT
(Random House, 1997, hardcover).

"The sun did not shine. It was too wet to play."

It looks like a dreary afternoon until the Cat in the Hat arrives and creates absolute chaos. A favorite with kids and parents for decades.

FIRST ENCOUNTERS:
A BOOK OF MEMORABLE MEETINGS
by Nancy Caldwell Sorel and Edward Sorel (Knopf, 1994, hardcover)

Dorothy Parker kissed Dashiell Hammett's hand. Sarah Bernhardt swooned into Thomas Edison's arms. Marilyn Monroe and Isak Dinesen danced wildly on a tabletop. First meetings have a peculiar effect on celebrities—as the Sorels know well. They've chronicled first encounters of The Great Ones for years in *The Atlantic Monthly*. Here are 65 of Nancy Caldwell Sorel's chatty, funny, completely factual accounts of what happened when giants met, accompanied by Edward Sorel's sardonic full-color drawings.

COMPLETE AND UTTER FAILURE
by Neil Steinberg (Doubleday, 1994, paperback)

Imagine pre-cooked bacon that you reheat by popping it into the toaster. Or root beer flavored milk. In this comic collection of human folly, Steinberg chronicles ideas, products and people who fell short of the mark. From the missteps of mountaineers to the guy who nearly invented the telephone, here is, as Samuel Johnson once put it, "Every failure of conduct joyfully published."

MADAME BLAVATSKY'S BABOON:
A HISTORY OF THE MYSTICS, MEDIUMS AND MISFITS WHO BROUGHT SPIRITUALISM TO AMERICA

by Peter Washington (Schocken Books, 1996, paperback)

Through sleight-of-hand "miracles" and brazen chicanery, Blavatsky and her cohorts played upon the gullibility of well-heeled clients as diverse as William Butler Yeats, Greta Garbo and Frank Lloyd Wright. Author Peter Washington revels in the details of the hoax Blavatsky played on a credulous public.

LITERARY LIVES

THE BRONTËS
by Juliet Barker (St. Martin's Press, 1995, paperback)

You can't discuss one of the Brontës without discussing them all. Their lives were just too tangled to separate the individual threads. So Juliet Barker has accepted the inevitable and written a biography of the entire family with fresh interpretations that at last sweep away the caricatures that have served as character analysis in previous biographies. For example, Barker dismisses the notion that Patrick Brontë was a loony pistol-packing parson. She concedes Charlotte could be opinionated and unpleasant. She suggests Branwell may have been unlucky. But Emily remains enigmatic. This is a tremendously impressive book, one that all Brontë fans will welcome.

OSCAR WILDE
by Richard Ellman
(Random House, 1988, paperback).

The flamboyant, extravagant, outrageous life of the most notorious literary man of the 19th century, by the master of modern literary biography.

CHARLOTTE BRONTË:
A PASSIONATE LIFE
by Lyndall Gordon (Norton, 1996, paperback)

How do you reconcile the meek, mousy personality of Charlotte Brontë with her passionate, sharp-tongued novels? It's always been a puzzle. So Lyndall Gordon takes a fresh look at the autobiographical roots of Brontë's fiction and casts new light on the turbulent emotions that lay just beneath the placid surface Brontë displayed to the world. Gordon even offers a solution to the vexing problem of why Brontë stopped writing.

HARRIET BEECHER STOWE
by Joan D. Hedrick (Oxford University Press, 1995, paperback)

As a member of the very outspoken Beecher clan, Harriet Beecher Stowe could never have settled into quiet domesticity. So she began to do a little writing in her spare moments at the kitchen table. With the publication of *Uncle Tom's Cabin*, Stowe began a career that eventually made her America's best-paid and most sought-after author. Hendrick's biography is the first full-scale life of Stowe in 50 years and offers an intimate portrait of this gifted, complex woman who threw herself into the great moral struggles of her time.

JAMES THURBER: HIS LIFE AND TIMES
by Harrison Kinney (Owl, 1997, paperback)

Hats off to Kinney for creating a book that is as lively and colorful as Thurber himself. For this biography, he's made extensive use of Thurber's essays, poems and one-liners and illustrated the book with the great man's hilarious cartoons. You'll learn that Thurber's mother was a madcap who embraced seances and numerology and kept the neighborhood entertained with her antics. Nonetheless, Thurber was not always a happy man and Kinney helps us understand how Thurber used his sly sense of humor to exorcise his personal demons.

The Best of Thurber:

MY WORLD AND WELCOME TO IT
by James Thurber (Harvest Books, 1969, paperback).

A hilarious collection of Thurber classics, including "The Macbeth Murder Mystery," "The Secret Life of Walter Mitty" and "Footnote on the Future."

GENIUS IN DISGUISE:
HAROLD ROSS OF THE NEW YORKER
by Thomas Kunkel (Random House, 1995, hardcover)

How do you build a great literary magazine? Well, if you're Harold Ross (1892-1951), you sign on E.B. White, Dorothy Parker, John Cheever and James Thurber, to name just a few stars of the literary galaxy he published in *The New Yorker*. Kunkel's biography is packed with great stories and juicy gossip, such as his battles with his eventual successor, William Shawn. A telling portrait of the man and the magazine he founded.

THE SAGEBRUSH BOHEMIAN:
MARK TWAIN IN CALIFORNIA
by Nigey Lennon (Marlowe & Company, 1994, hardcover)

Spanning 1861 to 1869, Lennon's off-beat and well-researched biography covers an important period in Twain's life—the years Twain spent honing his craft as a newspaperman and humorist in the wilds of California and Nevada. He chronicles the transformation of Sam Clemens, prospector, to Mark Twain, journalist, to the famous American author Mark Twain.

TOM: THE UNKNOWN TENNESSEE WILLIAMS
by Lyle Leverich (Crown, 1995, hardcover)

This first volume of a projected two-volume life of the great playwright Tennessee Williams takes us up to age 34. But by that time, Williams had experienced all the personal trauma he would need to create such fragile, neurotic char- 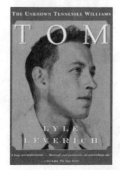 acters as Blanche DuBois. Williams early life isn't pretty. A self-sacrificing yet emotionally stifling mother. A whoring, brawling, bingeing father who ridiculed his son. Most tragic of all is Williams' older sister, Rose, who was subjected to a lobotomy. This isn't a fun book to read, but it reveals the real-life inspiration for Williams' emotionally charged plays.

NORA: THE REAL LIFE OF MOLLY BLOOM
by Brenda Maddox

For years, Nora Barnacle has been portrayed as a crude, semi-literate bimbo who was a lifelong embarrassment to James Joyce (even if he did eventually marry her). Brenda Maddox sweeps away those nasty slurs and proves that Nora was a witty, intelligent woman who was the most important person in Joyce's life and the model for all the women in his fiction. Worth searching for.

GERARD MANLEY HOPKINS:
A VERY PRIVATE LIFE
by Robert Bernard Martin (Putnam, 1991, hardcover)

Poet and priest he may have been, but Hopkins' irascible personality made him a real handful. Robert Bernard Martin's biography draws heavily on private papers of Hopkins which the Jesuits had not released previously.

WHAT FRESH HELL IS THIS?
A BIOGRAPHY OF DOROTHY PARKER
by Marion Meade (Penguin, 1989, paperback)

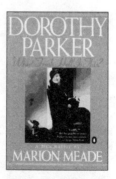

This is not a novel to be tossed aside lightly," Dorothy Parker once wrote in a book review. "It should be thrown with great force." Who doesn't love Dorothy Parker? Her perverse, penetrating one-liners are still repeated, 60 years after she first coined them at the legendary Algonquin Round Table. But a keen wit was only one facet of Parker's complex personality. Now Marion Meade has come forward with a new sympathetic portrait of the funny, glamorous and frequently self-destructive woman who was one of the great literary luminaries of New York in the 1920s and '30s.

SALEM IS MY DWELLING PLACE:
A LIFE OF NATHANIEL HAWTHORNE
by Edwin Haviland Miller
(University of Iowa Press, 1991, paperback)

Miller delves into the cryptic personality of Nathaniel Hawthorne, a shy, yet ambitious man who never escaped his fascination with ancient evils.

JANE AUSTEN: A LIFE
by David Nokes (Farrar, Straus & Giroux, 1997, hardcover)

In her letters, as in her novels, Jane Austen was a sharp observer of human folly. Biographer David Nokes leans heavily on Austen's letters for this enchanting life of everyone's favorite novelist. Austen, like so many of her heroines, had a tough time in the marriage market. She found that fame could be disconcerting (the Prince Regent hinted that she should dedicate a novel to him; Austen would have preferred not to since she disapproved of his morals, but she acquiesced). Nokes also reveals Austen's greatest fear-that she would end up an "old maid." Readers who want detailed analysis of Austen's novels will have to look elsewhere. But anyone who wants to become acquainted with Austen's prickly personality should pick up a copy of Nokes' book.

WALT WHITMAN'S AMERICA:
A CULTURAL BIOGRAPHY
by David S. Reynolds (Random House, 1996, paperback)

David S. Reynolds has accomplished what no other Whitman biographer ever has—a comprehensive reading of his poetry to find the ideas Whitman cherished. When the country threatened to split apart, Whitman pleaded for unity; when people argued over slavery, he wrote of human equality; and when the nation seemed lost, he found in Lincoln a redeemer-president.

EDGAR A. POE:
MOURNFUL AND NEVERENDING REMEMBRANCE
by Kenneth Silverman (HarperCollins, 1992, paperback)

Kenneth Silverman's book is a landmark biography that clarifies many of the enduring questions about Poe's character and literary influences and examines his emotional problems, alcoholism and hallucinations.

LITTLE-KNOWN
HISTORY

FOR THE PRESIDENT'S EYES ONLY
by Christopher Andrew (HarperPerennial, 1996, paperback)

George Washington relied on spies for information about foreign powers. But more than 100 years would pass before another U.S. President—Woodrow Wilson—would recognize the possibilities of espionage. Andrew takes the reader through all the presidents of the 20th century and their response to secret intelligence: FDR's haphazard approach, JFK's inexperience, Nixon's preference for personal diplomacy, Reagan's enthusiasm for covert action. And what president best understood the possibilities of secret intelligence? George Bush, himself a former head of the CIA.

VAMPIRES, BURIAL AND DEATH
by Paul Barber (Yale University Press, 1988, paperback)

In 17th-century Serbia, a man fell off a haywagon, broke his neck and died. But soon after he had been buried, he returned to his village, frightening his neighbors and even killing four of them. When his grave was opened, the villagers found tell-tale signs that the dead man was a vampire. That's just one of the strange tales Barber tells in this book that studies the history of vampires. To get at the heart of the legends, Barber sorts out fact and fantasy and 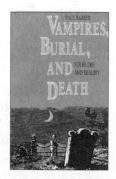 uncovers the points where mythology and biology converge. It's fascinating stuff.

For your vampire reference shelf:

THE VAMPIRE BOOK:
THE ENCYCLOPEDIA OF THE UNDEAD
by J. Gordon Melton (Visible Ink Press, 1994, paperback).

A compendium of vampires, from a blood-drinking demon of ancient Sumeria to the soap opera Dark Shadows. More than 400 entries, plus never-before-published illustrations gleaned from the files of the Vampire Studies Society(!).

HOW THE IRISH SAVED CIVILIZATION
by Thomas Cahill (Bantam, 1997, paperback)

Okay. So maybe the words "Irish" and "civilization" aren't often linked together. Nonetheless, Tom Cahill insists that if it hadn't been for the Irish scholars of the sixth to ninth centuries, the literary legacy of ancient Greece and Rome would have been lost forever. While the barbarians were raising hell on the Continent, in remote, peaceful Ireland monks were busily copying any ancient manuscript they could lay their hands on. And when things settled down on the mainland, the monks took their precious books and set out as missionaries, teachers and founders of schools and libraries all across Europe. It's a great story, and it's all true.

THE VANISHED LIBRARY:
A WONDER OF THE ANCIENT WORLD
by Luciano Canfora (University of California Press, 1990, paperback)

Thirteen hundred years after an Arab fanatic burned it to the ground, readers still wonder what was in the ancient Library of Alexandria. Canfora digs up everything he can find about the Egyptian and Greek scholars who built the library, the blend of Eastern and Western learning that thrived there and the insane competition between the Alexandrian librarians and their rivals at Pergamon to accumulate the best collection of rare books. (At one point, they were actually buying forgeries just in case these doubtful texts proved to be the real thing). A wonderful book that manages to be both anecdotal and erudite.

THE ILLUSTRATED HISTORY OF MAGIC
by Millbourne Christopher and Maurine Christopher, foreword by David Copperfield (Carroll & Graf, 1996, hardcover)

This mesmerizing history of magic was first published in 1973 but has been out of print for years. Now it's back in a new updated edition. The Christophers begin with the earliest known depiction of magic—a conjuring trick painted on the wall of an Egyptian tomb about 2500 B.C. Then it's on to 18th-century magician Jean Eugene Robert-Houdin, the astounding escapes of Harry Houdini and the feats of Doug Henning, David Copperfield and Las Vegas performer Melinda Saxe. A work of pure enchantment, illustrated with more than 300 pictures.

The Most Famous of All Magicians:

THE LIFE AND MANY DEATHS OF HARRY HOUDINI
by Ruth Brandon (Kodansha Globe, 1995, paperback).

A biography that explores Houdini's preoccupation and constant flirtation with death, his intense love for his mother and why he detested mediums.

SEEKING PLEASURE IN THE OLD WEST
by David Dary (Knopf, 1995, paperback)

It wasn't all bar room brawls and poker games out West. Troopers of the U.S. Army whiled away their free time playing baseball. Lots of cowboys preferred dominoes to cards. And wealthy cattle ranchers even took to collecting fine art. Of course, there was still plenty of gambling, drinking and prostitution going on. Nonetheless, Dary offers an expanded vision of how territory folks amused themselves around campfires, in saloons, on steamboats. And with 110 photographs and engravings, readers get an especially graphic image of just how diverse the diversions were out West.

CHRONICLES OF THE FRIGATE MACEDONIAN, 1809-1922
by James Tertius de Kay (Norton, 1995, hardcover)

The frigate Macedonian began life in 1809 as a British ship, but during the War of 1812 Stephen Decatur captured her (something of a miracle since the Macedonian carried more than 40 cannons and the fledgling US Navy was not exactly a power on the high seas). After the war, the ship chased Barbary pirates, joined a blockade to stop the African slave trade, ran a relief mission to Ireland during the Potato Famine and was there when Commodore Perry broke Japan's isolation. She ended her life in the Bronx as a hotel off City Island before burning down in 1922. In de Kay's hands, this history reads like a great historical novel.

ENTERTAINING SATAN: WITCHCRAFT AND THE CULTURE OF EARLY NEW ENGLAND
by John Putnam Demos (Oxford University Press, 1982, paperback)

John Putnam Demos is in a unique position to write about New England witchcraft: he is a direct descendant of the Putnams of Salem, the clan that surpassed all their neighbors in spurring on the notorious witch trials of 1692. In this fascinating study, Demos examines in detail some 100 accusations of witchery in early America: well-to-do women who fell on hard times; cantankerous, solitary men who may have been homosexual; willful children. A remarkable book that attempts to understand the kind of society that could have sparked a witch hunt.

SERVING WOMEN: HOUSEHOLD SERVICE IN 19TH-CENTURY AMERICA
by Faye E. Dudden (Wesleyan University Press, 1983, paperback)

Faye Dudden's social history strips away the romantic Upstairs Downstairs view of servant life. She begins with the distinction between "help" (women who came in for the day and went home to their own families in the evening) and "domestics" (women who lived on the premises). As the wages, hours and working conditions got worse, however, the native-born American help withdrew from service. Immigrant women didn't like the situation either, but they had fewer choices and so they became live-in domestics. Through family papers, letters, diaries and reminiscences, Dudden studies the biases and assumptions of both employers and employees about life in household service.

. . . .

WOMEN IN THE CLASSICAL WORLD: IMAGE AND TEXT
by Elaine Fantham et al. (Oxford University Press, 1993, hardcover)

Readable, reliable and sumptuously illustrated, this survey introduces you to slaves, prostitutes, housewives and empresses. You'll also find fascinating chapters on the reported wild behavior of Spartan women and traces of women's lives preserved at Pompeii.

. . . .

RED SCARE: MEMORIES OF THE AMERICAN INQUISITION-AN ORAL HISTORY
Edited by Griffin Fariello (Norton, 1995, hardcover)

Robert Meeropol, son of Julius and Ethel Rosenberg, remembers spending his childhood running from one haven to the next as neighbors found out who he and his brother Michael were. Irwin Silber and Bob Black recall the Peekskill Riot of 1949, when residents of the Hudson River town attacked Communists who were attending a fund-raising concert. And FBI agent M. Wesley Swearingen reveals that he maintained a list of Americans to be placed in concentration camps if a "declared national emergency" ever arose. Filled with the testimony of the accused, the informants and the FBI agents, this is an excellent eyewitness history of a troubled time.

. . . .

THE BUCHENWALD REPORT
Edited and translated by David A. Hackett
(Westview Press, 1997, paperback)

After the liberation of the Buchenwald concentration camp, U.S. intelligence officers arrived to interview survivors and collect material for the impending war-crimes trials. Jews, homosexuals, clergymen, Poles, Russians and political prisoners offered chilling testimony of what they endured and what they saw. For decades this invaluable document was thought to be lost, but the head of the intelligence team, Albert Rosenberg, kept his copy of the original German text. Here it is, translated for the first time into English.

PYRAMIDS OF TÚCUME:
THE QUEST FOR PERU'S FORGOTTEN CITY
by Thor Heyerdahl, Daniel H. Sandweiss and Alfredo Narvaez
(Thames & Hudson, 1995, hardcover)

You'll remember Thor Heyerdahl as the anthropologist/adventurer who sailed a balsa log raft named Kon-Tiki from Peru to the Tuamotu Islands of the South Pacific. Now Heyerdahl and his archaeologists colleagues Sandweiss and Narvaez, tell how their excavations of unexplored pyramids at Túcume, Peru, revealed carvings of birdmen, identical to the ones found on Easter Island. This is a great read, part exacting archaeology, part treasure hunt, with the surprise discovery of artifacts which could revolutionize our understanding of the settlement of the Pacific Islands.

500 NATIONS: AN ILLUSTRATED HISTORY OF NORTH AMERICAN INDIANS
by Alvin M. Josephy, Jr. (Knopf, 1994, hardcover)

Enrique, an Arawak Indian on the island of Hispaniola, led a successful revolt against the Spanish in the 16th century. Between 850 and 1150, the city of Cahokia on the Mississippi had 100 pyramids and earth mounds and more than 10,000 inhabitants within its walls. Using rare documents, oral history and private papers of Native Americans, Josephy offers a comprehensive overview of the 500 tribes of the Americas, reclaiming a part of America's history we rarely hear about. A triumph that balances good storytelling with judicious interpretation.

SAVAGES
by Joe Kane (Knopf, 1995, paperback)

There are only 1300 Huaorani in the Ecuadorian Amazon forests, yet they have always been such ferocious warriors that for thousands of years they have successfully defended their homeland—a territory about the size of Massachusetts—against all comers. But now the tribe is besieged by a host of new invaders—rapacious oil companies, cockeyed environmentalists, zealous American missionaries and corrupt government officials. Kane, who lived with the Huaorani, chronicles their ordeal and their decision to accept "development" and "progress" only on their own terms.

THE DEVIL IN THE SHAPE OF A WOMAN:
WITCHCRAFT IN COLONIAL NEW ENGLAND
by Carol F. Karlsen (Vintage books, 1989, paperback)

Connecticut hanged a servant, Mary Johnson, for witchcraft in 1648. Ann Hibbens, a wealthy Boston widow, was executed in 1656 for casting spells. This study broke new ground in understanding the witchcraft trials of 17th-century New England. Studying original documents, Karlsen discovers what types of women were most likely to be accused of witchcraft and suggests that witch hunts were manifestations of sexual, religious and economic tensions.

BEHIND THE SCENES,
OR THIRTY YEARS A SLAVE AND FOUR YEARS IN THE WHITE HOUSE
by Elizabeth Keckley (Oxford University Press, 1988, hardcover)

Elizabeth Keckley was Mary Todd Lincoln's dressmaker in the White House and her confidante after Abraham Lincoln"s assassination. Mary Lincoln had always been unpopular with the press and never more so than after the assassination. Keckley hoped that by offering an insider's glimpse of family life among the Lincolns-their profound grief at the death of their son, Willie, Mrs.

Lincoln's straitened circumstances after her husband's murder—the public would judge her friend "more kindly than she has been." A unique document that gives us a fresh perspective on the Lincoln family private life.

....

THE DEATH OF THE CHILD VALERIO MARCELLO
by Margaret L. King (University of Chicago Press, 1994, paperback)

When his eight-year-old son, Valerio, died on New Year's Day 1461, Venetian patrician Jacopo Antonino Marcello called upon men of great learning to help put his anguish into words. Margaret King examines this literary tribute from two perspectives: a man's efforts to cope with a personal tragedy as an ancient Roman would have and a father's desire to give full voice to his grief. Worth searching for.

....

DEATH BE NOT PROUD
by John Gunther (1949; Harper Perennial, 1989, paperback).

To fend off despair after the death of his 17-year-old son, Gunther, an author and journalist, wrote this now-classic memoir. A wise, powerful book that has never gone out of print.

....

ROANOKE: THE ABANDONED COLONY
by Karen Ordahl Kupperman (Rowman & Littlefield Publishers, 1984, paperback)

Drama, tragedy and mystery are all bound up in the story of Roanoke, the colony Sir Walter Raleigh established in 1587 in what is now North Carolina and which disappeared about 1590. Drawing upon a wealth of 16th-century English documents, as well as other materials discovered in this century in Spanish archives, Karen Ordahl Kupperman reconstructs the story of the first English colony in America and how the colonists were received by the Indians. And while Kupperman has no hard and fast answer to the fate of the colonists, she has found some tantalizing clues in the Spanish sources.

THE ARCHITECT OF DESIRE: BEAUTY AND DANGER IN THE STANFORD WHITE FAMILY
by *Suzannah Lessard* (Dial, 1996, paperback)

Suzannah Lessard's great-grandfather was Stanford White, the celebrated architect during America's Gilded Age, the friend of the rich and the famous, the lover of a beguiling showgirl named Evelyn Nesbit. In 1906, at Madison Square Garden, White was shot and killed by Nesbit's jealous husband. This murder lies at the heart of Lessard's multigenerational history of her family, in which she finds recurring strains of genius and sexual perversion. Here are tales of wealth and power and glamour, as well as a host of unpleasant secrets Lessard's family has tried to suppress. Candid, complex and completely absorbing, this is superb family history.

THE STORY THE SOLDIERS WOULDN'T TELL: SEX IN THE CIVIL WAR
by *Thomas P. Lowry* (Stackpole Books, 1994, paperback)

Did Robert E. Lee do the wild thing? What were Abe and Mary Todd up to after the lights went out in the White House? Was Walt Whitman the only gay man out and about during the Civil War? Here is the first and only book ever to study the extremely intimate details of the Civil War. From the antics of the boys in blue and gray to the proclivities of generals and presidents, this books uncovers a dimension of the Civil War we've never seen before.

EXTRAORDINARY POPULAR DELUSIONS & THE MADNESS OF CROWDS
by *Charles MacKay* (1841; Crown, 1995, hardcover)

Why did sensible people leap lemming-like into the junk bond market in the '80s? Why did they do it all over again with high-tech stocks in the '90s? The answers may lie in a work first published in 1841. Charles MacKay offers some very illuminating and vastly entertaining examples from history—the 17th-century craze that valued tulip bulbs higher than gold, the mania for the meaningless prophecies of Nostradamus. MacKay suggests reasons why smart people permit themselves to be scammed and reminds us that the power of greed is stronger than we like to think. A classic study of humankind's willingness to be bamboozled.

THE ULTIMATE SPY BOOK
by H. Keith Melton, Foreword by William Colby, Former Director of the CIA and Oleg Kalugin, Former Major-General of the KGB (DK Publishing, 1996, hardcover)

As an adviser to U.S. intelligence agencies, Melton is just the man to tell you how to begin a career in espionage and what kind of cool stuff you get to play with once you're on the job. There's the wire garrote—indispensable for strangling sentries; crossbows and dart guns—ideal for silent, long-distance kills; an inconspicuous mechanical pencil—that's really a pistol. Plus, Melton tells the stories of some the most famous spies—Mata Hari, Guy Burgess, Gary Francis Powers and the legendary "Ace of Spies" Sidney Reilly. Brimming with photographs, this is a would-be secret agent's dream.

ARGUING ABOUT SLAVERY: THE GREAT BATTLE IN THE UNITED STATES CONGRESS
by William Lee Miller (Knopf, 1996, hardcover)

Between 1833 and 1844, a gag rule was in effect in the U.S. Congress forbidding any discussion of slavery on the floor of the House of Representatives. Leading the fight to repeal the rule and to abolish slavery was John Quincy Adams, former President and the son of Founding Father John Adams. Miller does a superb job capturing the dramatic—often vitriolic—confrontations in the House, the eloquence of the speakers and the drive among slavery's supporters to have Adams formally censured. A beautifully rendered study of a dark and forgotten moment from American history.

THE RAPE OF EUROPA: THE FATE OF EUROPE'S ART TREASURES IN THE THIRD REICH AND THE SECOND WORLD WAR
by Lynn H. Nicholas (Vintage, 1995, paperback)

Overshadowed by the Nazis other crimes is their theft of untold thousands of works of art from across Europe. In France, Holland, Russia, even Florence, the Nazis looted museums, private collections and art dealers. Nicholas details what was lost, what was regained and was is still missing.

THE CREATURE IN THE MAP: A JOURNEY TO EL DORADO
by Charles Nicholl (Morrow, 1996, paperback)

In May 1595, Sir Walter Raleigh was forty, broke and out of favor with Queen Elizabeth I when he decided on a mad scheme to restore his fortunes. He would go to the New World and find the fabled golden city of El Dorado. He figured it was somewhere up the Orinoco River in South America. Nicholl has a genius for drawing us into the spirit of Raleigh's time, helping us comprehend just how strange, even weird, it must have been to leave behind the tidy familiar world of Elizabethan England and plunge into a vast, unknown wilderness where anything could happen (and frequently did).

THE RECKONING: THE MURDER OF CHRISTOPHER MARLOWE
by Charles Nicholl (University of Chicago Press, 1995, paperback)

Any graduate student will tell you that Christopher Marlowe was killed in a barroom brawl at age 29. But Charles Nicholl has a different view. This first full-blown investigation into the untimely death of the No. 2 playwright of Elizabethan England reveals an underworld of espionage and betrayal. Based on clues buried for centuries in a host of archives, Nicholl finds evidence that Marlowe's death was a setup.

THE EXPLORERS:
FROM THE ANCIENT WORLD TO THE PRESENT
by Paolo Novaresio (Stewart, Tabori and Chang, 1996, hardcover)

Paolo Novaresio lets the discoverers themselves tell their story through their own ship's logs, diaries and memoirs and he reproduces the maps they would have used, or drew themselves on their journeys. You'll voyage with the Phoenicians and the Vikings, explore the Indies with Vasco da Gama, join Balboa and Coronado in the Americas, cruise the South Pacific with Captain James Cook and explore Tibet with Sven Hedin. More than 400 color photographs and illustrations, plus 90 maps, help you trace great adventures that changed human history—from the migrations of homo erectus to Neil Armstrong's walk on the moon.

FATAL SUBTRACTION:
HOW HOLLYWOOD REALLY DOES BUSINESS
by Pierce O'Donnell and Dennis McDougal
(Doubleday, 1992, hardcover)

In 1988, humorist Art Buchwald sued Paramount Pictures for failing to give him original story credit for Eddie Murphy's smash hit Coming to America. Not a petty matter, for aside from the cash, Buchwald and his partner had been promised a share in the film's net profits, which although it grossed $350 million, the studio claimed were nil. (Apparently the most creative people at the studios are the accountants.) Co-authored by Buchwald's attorney, Pierce, it's a riveting, blow-by-blow account of a history-making trial that at least exposed, if not changed, the way Hollywood does business.

AT BECK AND CALL:
THE REPRESENTATION OF DOMESTIC SERVANTS IN NINETEENTH CENTURY AMERICAN PAINTING
by Elizabeth O'Leary
(Smithsonian Institution Press, 1996, hardcover)

Elizabeth O'Leary studies paintings for clues about the changing imagery of servants—from the fairly egalitarian view during the early years of the Republic to often derisive depictions in the late 19th century. In addition, she reveals what the paintings tells us about the place of immigrants, blacks and the working class in America.

BAD BLOOD
by Judith Reitman (Kensington Publishing, 1996, hardcover)

How could the American Red Cross have knowingly exposed millions of innocent people to a blood supply contaminated with HIV and other diseases? Why did officials at the Red Cross refuse to admit that AIDS was spread through transfusions? And when at last the organization agreed to blood testing, why did it choose the least accurate method? Reitman found people who were willing to answer her questions: doctors at the Center for Disease Control and former Red Cross employees. The most shocking, most appalling exposé to come along in decades.

LANDSCAPE AND MEMORY
by Simon Schama (Random House, 1996, paperback)

Anyone who has read Citizens, or *The Embarrassment of Riches*, or *Dead Certainties* knows that Simon Schama is one of the most gifted narrative historians our of time. Well, in *Landscape and Memory* he outdoes himself. Page after page, he sucks us in with completely absorbing tales of bison in Lithuania, Hasidic lumberjacks in the Baltics, the Nazi cult of the forest, Bernini's fountains in Rome and America's love affair with Mount Rushmore. But the real genius of this book is how Schama connects these disparate elements into a unified whole that tells us alot about how we see our forests and mountains and rivers.

Also by Schama:

DEAD CERTAINTIES
(Knopf, 1991, hardcover).

Two extraordinary stories: James Wolfe at the Battle of Quebec and how a Harvard chemistry professor became a murderer.

A FOREST OF KINGS:
THE UNTOLD STORY OF THE ANCIENT MAYA
by Linda Schele and David Friedel (Quill Paperbacks, 1992, paperback)

Schele and Friedel have been among the handful of scholars who cracked the ancient Mayan language and now can read the incredibly difficult Mayan glyphs. In these ancient texts, they found the story of the Maya, from the time of their first kings to the destruction of the civilization under the Spanish conquistadors 1000 years later.

Also by Schele:

THE BLOOD OF KINGS
(George Braziller, 1992, paperback).

The ground-breaking book on the bizarre, blood-soaked rituals of the Maya.

GOD'S CHINESE SON
by Jonathan Spence (Norton, 1996, hardcover)

It may surprise you to learn that Jesus Christ had a younger brother. His name was Hong Xiuquan and he was one of the most important players in the last decades of China's imperial age. In this superbly crafted narrative, Spence explores the life and times of this strange visionary who firmly believed that he had been chosen to complete the work of his Heavenly Elder Brother. With hundreds of thousands of well-armed followers, Hong established himself in Nanjing, keeping government forces at bay for ten years until the city and Hong's movement collapsed in the bloody Taiping Rebellion. Spence is in top form as he explores Hong's complex character and captures his turbulent times.

MORE CHINESE HISTORY:
THE SEARCH FOR MODERN CHINA
by Jonathan Spence (Norton, 1990, paperback).

The 400 years that made modern China, from the fall of the Ming Dynasty to Deng Xiaoping's death blow to the democracy movement. A definitive, monumental work presented in the engaging style that makes Spence such an effective guide through the unfamiliar terrain of China's history.

. . . .

THE MAN IN THE ICE
by Konrad Spindler (Crown, 1996, paperback)

In 1991, entirely by chance, two hikers in the Tyrolean Alps discovered a 5300-year-old body, frozen in a glacier. The discovery became an instant international sensation — for the first time, scientists had a perfectly preserved Stone Age man to study. Spindler, the archaeologist in charge of examining this astounding find, offers a detailed account of the Iceman's physical condition, his clothes and the equipment he was carrying. An extraordinary book, part scientific analysis, part thriller.

. . . .

THE SECRET OF THE INCAS: MYTH, ASTRONOMY AND THE WAR AGAINST TIME
by William Sullivan (Crown, 1996, hardcover)

In a single afternoon, Francisco Pizarro and 170 Spaniards defeated a warrior empire of six million souls. How did it happen? William Sullivan believes the answer lies in the stars. Before Pizarro arrived, the Inca astronomers saw Mars ascendant in the night sky and believed they were doomed. Then they faithfully recorded their observations in their arcane code and waited for the inevitable. Now, using a software program that recreates the night sky at any point in history, Sullivan has been able to see what the Inca stargazers saw, crack their secret code and discover the reason why the empire surrendered without a fight.

. . . .

ASSASSINATION AT ST. HELENA REVISITED: THE CLASSIC INVESTIGATION EXPANDED WITH NEW EVIDENCE
by Ben Weider and Sten Forshufvud
(John Wiley & Sons, 1995, hardcover)

More than 30 years have gone by since forensic scientists discovered abnormally high concentrations of arsenic in samples of Napoleon's hair. Yet the academic community has resisted the suspicion that the emperor was poisoned to death. The authors of this deeply researched, intriguing study are historian-sleuths collecting and finding that one of Napoleon's closest personal attendants, the man who served as his night nurse, had the motive, the method and the opportunity to kill his emperor.

THE PRINCES IN THE TOWER
by Alison Weir (Ballantine, 1995, paperback)

Who killed 12-year-old King Edward V and his 10-year-old brother Richard, Duke of York? This royal murder mystery has puzzled historians and common folk for 500 years. By reconstructing the chain of events that led to the death of the princes in the Tower of London, Weir reveals how, when and why the boys were killed and who was their killer.

KILLING CUSTER: THE LITTLE BIG HORN AND THE FATE OF THE NATIVE AMERICANS
by James Welch with Paul Stekler (Penguin, 1995, paperback)

Custer had it coming." You see that on bumper stickers all through the West. Here, then, is the first book to tell the story of the Battle of the Little Big Horn from the Indians' perspective. It is the first book to present eyewitness accounts of the Indians who fought Custer and the 7th Cavalry—testimony that most historians have ignored for more than 100 years.

A FOOL AND HIS MONEY
by Ann Wroe (Hill and Wang, 1995, hardcover)

In 1369, in the town of Rodez, the drain outside Peyre Marques' cloth shop had become clogged and began to stink. As workmen cleared the mess, they discovered a clay jug packed with gold coins. Whose gold was it? The scramble to claim the cache produced a small mountain of documents—all of them preserved in the Rodez archives. Now Ann Wroe, perhaps the first person to read these records in 600 years, has written a captivating account of this forgotten mystery, and a detailed portrait of life in Rodez during the Hundred Years War. But best of all is the verbatim testimony of the people of Rodez— it's the closest you'll ever come to hearing voices from 14th-century France.

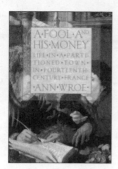

THE BLACK DEATH
by Philip Ziegler (HarperTorchbooks, 1971, paperback)

Ziegler's classic account of the pestilence that swept through Europe in 1347 makes for chilling reading. Before the Black Death had run its course, whole villages were emptied, farms were abandoned, monasteries and convents lost all their inhabitants and unmanned ships drifted aimlessly across the seas. A highlight is the beautiful period illustrations from medieval manuscripts at the time of the plague.

LIVING WITH BOOKS

A GENTLE MADNESS:
BIBLIOPHILES, BIBLIOMANES AND THE ETERNAL PASSION FOR BOOKS
by Nicholas A. Basbanes (Henry Holt, 1995, hardcover)

Basbanes has divided his book into two sections: first, the history of collections, beginning 2,200 years ago with the Library of Alexandria, which believed it had all of human knowledge shelved and catalogued under one roof; and second, lively stories of devoted, sometimes larcenous, often loony collectors who would do damn near anything to get the books they wanted. Haven O'More, for instance, talked a rich young man into giving him $17 million to buy the rarest books, while Stephen C. Blumberg just stole what he wanted from 300 libraries before he was caught. An irresistible tribute to the love of books and the passion for collecting them.

AMERICAN TREASURES IN THE LIBRARY OF CONGRESS
Introduction by Garry Wills, Foreword by James H. Billington, Librarian of Congress (Abrams, 1997, hardcover)

The curators of the Library of Congress have rooted around and brought to light some of the most significant, remarkable and delightful objects in their collections. Here's *The Bay Psalm Book*, printed in Massachusetts in 1640. From 1839 comes the earliest surviving photographic portrait in America. There's Lincoln's copy of the Gettysburg Address and the contents of his pockets on the night he was assassinated. You can study George Gershwin's score for *Porgy and Bess*, Maya Lin's drawing for the Vietnam War

Memorial, even the papers of Groucho Marx. With 97 illustrations, this book highlights 300 years of American life.

....

USED AND RARE:
TRAVELS IN THE BOOK WORLD
by Lawrence and Nancy Goldstone (St. Martin's, 1997, hardcover)

The year Lawrence and Nancy Goldstone moved to the Berkshires they agreed to buy each other inexpensive birthday presents. He gave her a bath brush. She gave him a $10 used hardcover copy of *War and Peace*. That's all it took. Soon, they were rummaging in antique shops and garage sales for nice, old books, cheaply priced. They eventually graduated to first editions, out-of-prints and leather-bounds. The Goldstones invite you to tag along and learn the fine points of collecting as they hunt rare books from Boston to Manhattan. Even if you never become a dealer or collector yourself, you'll enjoy the Goldstone's passion for rare books.

....

BOOKNOTES
by Brian Lamb (Times Books, 1997, paperback)

Book lovers have made Brian Lamb's "Booknotes," a weekly program on C-SPAN, an unexpected success. In this anthology, Lamb has picked his favorite bits from 150 interviews with authors as diverse as Simon Schama, Doris Kearns Goodwin, Richard Nixon and Shelby Foote (who, you'll be interested to know, writes with a dip pen). You get David McCullough's impression the first time he saw Harry Truman ("My God, he's in color!"). And Joseph Ellis' summary of what it's like to read the papers of John Adams ("Adams was just a hoot!"). Like the program itself, Booknotes deserves to be a runaway hit.

....

THE HISTORY OF READING
by Alberto Manguel (Viking, 1996, hardcover)

Anyone who loves books will agree with Alberto Manguel that "reading, almost as much as breathing, is our essential function." Now in this learned yet friendly book, Manguel weaves the story of reading over the last sixty centuries. Did you know that silent reading led to the development of punctuation? Manguel's book is brimming with such information. In addition to wonderful stories, you get a Reader's Timeline tracing great moments in reading from 4000 B.C., as well as over 100 illustrations of notable readers, writers and books. Ideal for anyone with a passion for a good read.

OLD BOOKS, RARE FRIENDS:
TWO LITERARY SLEUTHS AND THEIR SHARED PASSION
by Leona Rostenberg and Madeleine Stern
(Doubleday, 1997, hardcover)

For 50 years Stern and Rostenberg have been business partners and legends in the antiquarian book world. Their joint memoir conveys the thrill of the chase and the satisfaction of bagging a truly rare book.

A MASTERPIECE
YOU MIGHT HAVE
MISSED

NIGHT OF THE SILENT DRUMS
by John L. Anderson (Mapes Monde, 1992, paperback)

1733 was a bad year for the Danish West India Company on the Virgin Island of St. John. There had been a brutal drought, a deadly fever and everyday more slaves were escaping into the forest. On November 23, all hell broke lose. John L. Anderson became fascinated with the story of the western hemisphere's first slave rebellion while honeymooning on the sleepy Caribbean island in 1935 and began to research the event as a hobby. Forty years later he had learned to read nine languages, scoured archives from Berkeley, California, to Copenhagen, Denmark and penned this even-handed yet gripping novel about the bloody uprising.

ALL SOULS' RISING
by Madison Smartt Bell (Pantheon, 1995, paperback)

Only a novelist of Bell's gifts could weave all the complexities of revolution in late 18th-century Haiti into a seamless epic. The story covers 12 brutal years on the island and follows the fortunes of Toussaint L'Ouverture, the cunning leader of the revolt; a runaway slave who perhaps desires freedom more than any other character in the novel; the unhinged mistress of a sugar plantation; and a French doctor who has fallen in love

with a mulatto woman. Through all the twisting alliances and animosities of Haiti's factions, Bell keeps a firm hand on his story. And his beautiful epilogue is mercifully free of the triumphalism common in novels about revolution.

TALK BEFORE SLEEP
by Elizabeth Berg (Doubleday, 1997, paperback)

I have been on an airplane twice when it suddenly lost altitude. It felt just like this." That's how Ruth explains that she's been diagnosed with breast cancer to her friend, Ann. Suddenly shy, conventional Ann finds she has untapped reserves of strength to help the normally gregarious Ruth get through this ordeal. Berg takes the mundane details that fill up their days and blends them with unexpected revelations to show just how beautiful and absurd life is. This a wise, funny story of friendship and heartbreak.

WORLD'S END
by T. Coraghessan Boyle (Penguin, 1990, paperback)

In the Hudson River Valley, three families have been at odds for 300 years: the aristocratic Van Warts, the working-class Van Brunts and the Native American Mohonks. One of America's most inventive writers, Boyle draws on his considerable imagination to spin a story that moves easily between the 17th century and the late 1960s.

THE CHANEYSVILLE INCIDENT
by David Bradley (HarperPerennial, 1990, paperback)

At the heart of this novel lies a bit of forgotten history—the murder of 13 escaped slaves who believed they had found safety and freedom in Pennsylvania. John Washington, the protagonist, returns home to Chaneysville to be with a dying friend, Moses. In their conversations, Washington finds himself reviewing his life, the story of his ancestors and his connection with the 13 murdered slaves. His new interest in his family saga puts a strain on his relationship with his white lover, but Washington keeps at it and eventually understands his own place in history.

THE FIRST MAN
by Albert Camus (Random House, 1996, paperback)

A t the time of his death in 1960, Camus had outraged the intellectual left by refusing to support terrorism to free Algeria from France. To his widow and friends, publishing a Frenchman's love song to old colonial Algeria seemed tactless. So three decades later it comes to us—transcribed by his daughter and completely unedited. This is the book Camus left behind. It is an autobiographical novel of a 40-year-old man who returns to his childhood home in Algeria to see his aged mother. Recalling old friends, old feuds and his love for this exotic land, Camus fills the pages with a wealth of sensuous details. *The First Man* is Camus at his most poetic.

MY ANTONIA
by Willa Cather (1918; Vintage Classics, 1994, paperback)

W illa Cather grew up among pioneers in Nebraska and knew that the true hardships of the West were not long wagon train journeys and Indian raids but the day-to-day struggles to build a home and keep a family together. This story of a Bohemian immigrant girl, Antonia, who fights to preserve her integrity through all the calamities life can throw at her, may be Cather's finest work.

Another Cather classic:

O PIONEERS!
(1913; Signet Classics, 1989, paperback)

A Swedish immigrant woman, Alexandra Bergson, embodies all the heroic and creative energy of the passing frontier. Although her homestead flourishes, she remains dissatisfied because she has no one to share it with.

THE CONNOISSEUR
by Evan S. Connell (North Point Press, 1987, paperback)

A Manhattan executive named Muhlbach wanders into a curio shop in Taos, New Mexico and among the trinkets he finds a terra-cotta figurine of a Mayan nobleman. "It's a reproduction," the shop owner assures him. But the figurine exerts a strange power over Muhlbach, so he buys it. On a whim he takes it to the university where the experts tell him he has just bought a real Mayan antiquity. Muhlbach is hooked. Soon he is studying up on Mayan art, haunting galleries, making unwise purchases at auctions. An intelligent tale of how an obscure and beautiful object changes a man's life. Worth searching for.

....

SIGNALS OF DISTRESS
by Jim Crace (Farrar, Straus and Giroux, 1995, paperback)

N ear a hard-up fishing village in 1830s England, an American steamer has foundered and its captain, crew and a black slave named Otto have come ashore. At the same time, Aymer, scion of a manufacturing family, has come to town with bad news for the villagers. These two plots converge when Aymer takes it upon himself to free Otto and unleashes a flood of resentment in the village. Crace has a shrewd eye for delineating character and a tremendous gift for evoking the details of life in English sea towns in the early part of the 19th century.

More by Crace:

ARCADIA
(Ecco Press, 1997, hardcover).

A rich, solitary man plans to mark his 80th birthday by doing something extraordinary that will leave a lasting impression on his city.

....

A FEAST OF SNAKES
by Harry Crews (Scribners, 1998, paperback)

M ystic, Georgia, is a hardscrabble town of dirt farmers, bootleggers, lecherous sheriffs, ex-varsity football stars and high school beauty queens who have lost their looks. But once a year, Mystic comes alive when crowds of sportsmen, rednecks and wild-eyed fanatics come to town for the Rattlesnake Roundup. At the heart of the story is Joe Lon Mackey: a former football hero who is washed up at age 20. He's in an ugly mood and it's all going to come to a head at the roundup. Crews writes a hard-bitten prose that makes you want to laugh and leaves you feeling uneasy when you do.

More by Harry Crews:

THE KNOCKOUT ARTIST
(HarperPerennial, 1989, paperback).

A boxer, a natural athlete with astonishing power and agility, discovers he has a glass jaw so fragile he can even knock himself out. It's a skill that makes him famous. But when he comes up against a fresh young fighter, he decides to reclaim his self-respect.

CORELLI'S MANDOLIN
by Louis De Bernieres (Pantheon, 1995, paperback)

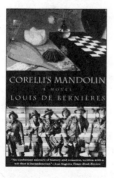

W ar seems especially cruel when a brutal Axis force occupies the paradise island of Cephallonia. Suddenly the islanders are caught up in a conflict they hoped would pass them by. But for some, it appears the war will make no real difference. For instance, the lovely Pelagia's biggest worry is how to choose between two suitors. But for others, the war changes everything. Mandras was once a fisherman; now he kills soldiers. By the way, the Corelli of the title is not the composer but the mandolin-playing Captain Corelli, a reluctant officer of the Italian garrison.

LIBRA
by Don DeLillo (Penguin, 1991, paperback)

Long before he took his place in a window of the Texas Book Depository, Lee Harvey Oswald imagined he was an agent of history. When two CIA agents approach him with a plan for an unsuccessful assassination attempt of the life of John F. Kennedy, Oswald knows his moment has come. This eerie novel is DeLillo's masterpiece. And by the way, the description of the teenage Oswald riding the New York subways is unforgettable.

RAGTIME
by E.L. Doctorow (Plume, 1996, paperback)

Doctorow's dazzling novel of New York in the early years of the 20th century is told through the stories of fictional characters— as well as historical figures such as Stanford White, Evelyn Nesbit, J.P. Morgan, Emma Goldman and Henry Ford. The plot comes to a head with a terrorist take-over of the Morgan Library.

STONES FOR IBARRA
by Harriet Doerr (Viking Press, 1988)

Sara and Richard Everton pack up and leave a comfortable life in California to live in a small village in Mexico. While Sara restores the ruined hacienda they call home, Richard revitalizes the village by opening a copper mine. If the Evertons have given something to the village, they have received even more in return as they participate in the daily joys and sorrows and traditions of the villagers of Ibarra. When Richard is diagnosed with leukemia, it is with the help of her neighbors that Sara finds the strength to go on.

More by Doerr:

CONSIDER THIS SEÑORA
(Harcourt Brace, 1993).

Three American women buy land on a hill near a poverty-stricken Mexican village. A memorable story of the search for something that will give life purpose.

PADDY CLARK, HA HA HA
by Roddy Doyle (Penguin, 1993, paperback)

Ten-year-olds, like the rich, are different than you and me. In this beautifully written novel, Roddy Doyle captures in wonderful first-person detail—and with humor and deep feeling—the specific and utter strangeness of boyhood (specifically boyhood in Dublin during the 1960s). Paddy's life bounces between wild fun and bleakness (his parents' marriage is floundering; he never knows when some neighborhood toughs may try to beat him up). Yet, Paddy and his friends have plenty of high times. Finally, an Irish novel that is about neither politics nor religion.

A Roddy Doyle Classic:

THE COMMITMENTS
(Vintage, 1989, paperback).

One of the great comic novels of all time features a rag-tag group of young men and women from a ratty neighborhood in Dublin who try to start a band.

THE ISLAND OF THE DAY BEFORE
by Umberto Eco, translated from the Italian by William Weaver (Penguin, 1996, paperback)

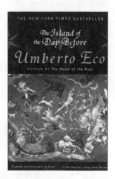

Since The Name of the Rose, readers have been waiting for Umberto Eco to write another spellbinding story. A young Italian is shipwrecked in the South Pacific, but he isn't washed up on an island; instead, he climbs aboard a deserted but extremely well-stocked ship. There are echoes of *Robinson Crusoe*, Jules Verne's *Mysterious Island* and even Dante, in this imaginative story of an intelligent, capable man who is nonetheless a prisoner of his circumstances.

THE PIANO MAN'S DAUGHTER
by Timothy Findley (HarperCollins, 1995, paperback)

In Canada, readers admire Timothy Findley for his baroque, almost sumptuous prose. But In the United States, Findley is barely known. A good way to introduce yourself to this award-winning author is to begin with this novel, the portrait of an Irish family in turn-of-the-century Toronto. Charlie Kilworth, a young piano-tuner, is haunted by two questions: Who was his father? And does he dare become a father himself, given the madness of his mother, Lily? There's an operatic grandeur (and maybe a touch of hysteria) to this story of Lily and Charlie that makes the novel hard to put down.

COLD MOUNTAIN
by Charles Frazier (Atlantic Monthly Press, 1997, paperback)

In the final weeks of the Civil War, Inman, a wounded Confederate veteran, decides to return home to his beloved, Ada, who is waiting for him at her farm deep in the Carolina mountains. Like Odysseus, Inman has his share of run-ins with hostile strangers. Meanwhile, Ada, like Penelope, is learning to handle loss and loneliness and is making an inner journey of her own. There's nothing grand and mythological about these journeys—no Cyclops, no lotus-eaters—but the story is definitely mystical as both Inman and Ada travel into regions where they would never have ventured before.

THE RECOGNITIONS
by William Gaddis (Penguin, 1993, paperback)

Wyatt Gwyon forges paintings of the Flemish Renaissance masters. Yet he instills such care and devotion into these "fakes" that they become as luminous and haunting as the originals. A monumental story of fraud in the art world and fraud in the larger outside world.

MICKELSSON'S GHOSTS
by John Gardner

Peter Mickelsson's life is a mess. He's driven away the woman he loves, ruined his finances and started a clandestine war with a gnomish colleague. To bring some order to his life, Mickelsson buys and begins to restore an old farmhouse haunted by the spirits of its former occupants. Finally Mickelsson's life has a purpose—to learn why his ghosts can't rest and to do something about it. Worth searching for.

Also by Gardner:

GRENDEL
(Random House, 1989, paperback).

The legend of Beowulf told from the monster's point of view. A real tour de force.

FREDDY'S BOOK

A distinguished author meets a giant man-child who has written an extraordinary novel. Worth searching for.

....

THE TENTH MAN,
by Graham Greene (Pocket Books, 1986, paperback)

In a Nazi prison, 30 French hostages draw lots to see who will be executed. The loser is Louis Chavel, a Paris lawyer. Desperate to live, Chavel makes his cellmates an offer—everything he owns to the man who dies in his place. Chavel will even draw up a will so his replacement can bequeath his new wealth to his family. Janvier, a poor young man, accepts. After the war is over, Chavel does what he never expected he would do: he goes home—to meet Janvier's family.

....

ULYSSES

by James Joyce (1922; Oxford University Press, 1997, paperback)

When the greatest novel of the 20th century was first published, the Irish were furious, the English were outraged and the Americans were scandalized—so they all banned it. But in time, readers began to see that, naughty words notwithstanding, the story of Leopold Bloom's interesting encounters in Dublin on June 16, 1904, was an absolute marvel, that Joyce had taken ordinary English and transformed it to pure gold. So if somebody asks you if you're going to read *Ulysses*, make like Molly Bloom and say, "yes I said yes I will Yes."

ULYSSES: THE MECHANICS OF MEANING

by David Hayman
(University of Wisconsin Press, 1982, paperback).

If you'd feel more comfortable with a key to the novel by your side, we recommend this admirably short and lucid study.

THE GREEK PASSION

by Nikos Kazantzakis

Kazantzakis' greatest novel is also his least known. As Holy Week approaches, the priest and elders of Lycovrissi choose the villagers who will re-create Christ's Passion. When refugees from a devastated village arrive and beg for asylum, the elders drive them out, by the new Passion players are moved to pity. Slowly, they find that the sacred roles they are to play will change their lives. A magnificent tale of ordinary people trying to live moral lives in a fallen world. Worth searching for.

Also by Kazantzakis:

THE LAST TEMPTATION OF CHRIST
(Touchstone Books, 1988, paperback).

As Jesus hangs on the cross, Satan offers him one final temptation—happiness in this world as an ordinary man.

．．．．．．．．．．．．．．

IRONWEED
by William Kennedy (Penguin, 1996, paperback)

Francis Phelan, once a professional baseball player, is now a 58-year-old bum. Years before, Francis dropped his infant son and the child died. Unable to cope with the guilt, he left his family in Albany and began wandering. But lately, Francis has been having hallucinations—or maybe they're visions—of his dead son. So, he comes home to Albany. Maybe he can put his child's spirit to rest. Maybe he can get off the booze. Maybe he can even effect a reconciliation with his family. A hope-filled and often funny novel set during the 1930s.

Another Albany story:

QUINN'S BOOK,
by William Kennedy (Penguin, 1989, paperback).

Daniel Quinn, a renowned Civil war correspondent, recalls his adolescence in Albany and his 15-year-old pursuit of Maud Fallon, an actress famous for her nude interpretations of characters from Keats and Shelley.

THE FLAMING CORSAGE
by William Kennedy (Viking, 1996, hardcover)

With his left hand he pulled the burning stick from her breast and hugged her to his chest to quench the flaming corsage." Bet you haven't read anything like that before. But it demonstrates how, as William Kennedy's *Albany Cycle* expands, his literary imagination does, too. At the heart of the story is the marriage of Edward, a brilliant writer from an Irish working-class family, to the aristocratic Katrina and how a dark past can overwhelm even the most promising future. Beautifully plotted and blessed with dialogue that's dead-on, *The Flaming Corsage* is the best of Kennedy's Albany books.

CHINA MEN
by Maxine Hong Kingston (Vintage, 1989, paperback)

It's hard to distinguish history from legend in Kingston's account of the men in her family who for three generations struggled to be recognized as Americans. Her great-grandfather was enslaved in the pineapple fields of Hawaii; grandfather hacked through the granite of the Sierras to build the railroad; uncle was a riverboat pirate. It's all true, but it reads like a fabulous novel.

Also by Kingston:

THE WOMAN WARRIOR
(Vintage, 1989, paperback).

A young Chinese woman in America longs to assimilate but doesn't want to abandon the ancestral heritage she loves.

THE PAINTED BIRD
by Jerzy Kosinski (Grove Atlantic, 1995, paperback)

During World War II, a little boy wanders through Poland, where his dark hair and dark eyes make him different from the blond peasants. In this ambitious, sometimes disturbing novel, Kosinski tries to filter a cruel, ignorant, superstitious world through the logic of a child.

Also by Kosinski:

BEING THERE
(Bantam, 1985, paperback).

Kosinski's immortal parable of Chance the Gardener who becomes a world figure by offering garden analogies for complex problems.

THE GOLDEN NOTEBOOK
by Doris Lessing (1962; HarperPerennial, 1994, paperback)

Since it was first published, this novel has been one of the defining works for two generations of women. The story follows Anna Wulf, a writer who declares herself "a free woman" and vows never to marry. As her story unfolds, we encounter Lessing's ideas about men and women, sex and politics, love and children.

HENRY AND CLARA
by Thomas Mallon (Picador USA, 1995, paperback)

At the last minute, General Ulysses S. Grant and his wife Julia canceled their plans to attend the theater with the Lincolns. So the President and his wife invited two young friends to join them, Major Henry Rathbone, a Civil War hero and Clara Harris, a favorite of Mrs. Lincoln. Henry and Clara were engaged to be married. They were also stepbrother and stepsister. What Henry and Clara witnessed in the Presidential box at Ford's Theater on April 14, 1865, changed them forever. Thomas Mallon has spun a gripping novel of two forgotten young lovers, trapped in a downward spiral of guilt, madness and murder.

THE DEATH AND LIFE OF MIGUEL DE CERVANTES
by Stephen Marlowe (Arcade, 1996, hardcover)

Many writers attempt historical novels based on the life of a famous person, but few succeed as brilliantly as Stephen Marlowe. Granted, Cervantes' real life story gave Marlowe plenty of material—he fought at Lepanto against the Turks, he was captured by pirates and he was sold as a slave to the Moors. He did all that before he even began writing *Don Quixote*. Marlowe adds his own interesting flourishes: Cervantes' friendship with a cross-dresser named Micaela; his career in espionage; his encounters with the playwrights Christopher Marlowe and Lope de Vega; and his quixotic battle against the Knight of the Moon. An ingenious work of storytelling you won't want to miss.

THE CROSSING
by *Cormac McCarthy* (Vintage, 1995, paperback)

In the 1930s, the 16-year-old son of small-time cattle ranchers sets out to kill a wolf, an animal of almost human cunning. The boy's dangerous quest leads him across the Rio Grande into Mexico, where it seems that every denizen of the desert means to do him harm. McCarthy tells his story in stark, even ferocious prose that will take your breath away.

TENDING TO VIRGINIA
by *Jill McCorkle* (Algonquin Books, 1987, paperback)

During a difficult pregnancy, Virginia Suzanne Ballard (Ginny Sue to her family) returns home to eastern North Carolina where her clan is eager to take care of her. To while away the time, her mother, aunt, great-aunts and grandmother tell her stories about their lives—some shocking, some sad, some hilarious. With each telling, Ginny Sue understands something new about her family and herself. Most importantly, she recognizes that she and her unborn child belong to the past—as well as the future.

RAJ
by *Gita Mehta* (Fawcett, 1991, paperback)

This glorious book immerses you in the exotic traditions of the maharajas and the tense relations between Indians and British under the Raj. Mehta tells her tale of colonial India through princess Jaya, who longs for independence from the men in her family just as India struggles for independence from the British Empire.

BLACK ROBE
by *Brian Moore* (HarperCollins, 1996, paperback)

A Jesuit missionary named Laforgue, his Huron escorts and one young French companion begin a mystical, dark-night-of-the-soul journey into the Canadian wilderness. Moore's thrilling tale of adventure is played against the frightening grandeur of a

Quebec winter. And what really sets this book apart is the intelligence and sympathy with which Moore writes about both French and Indian culture—you won't find a single Indian or priest cliché in this splendid novel.

. . . .

THE STATEMENT
by *Brian Moore* (Plume, 1997, paperback)

In 1944, when he was an officer in Vichy's pro-Fascist militia, Pierre Brossard murdered 14 French Jews. For 50 years, sympathetic elements in the French government and a host of conservative clergy have helped Brossard elude justice. But now, at age 70, assassins are gaining on Brossard. Worse, many of his monastic hosts—recognizing (a little late) that they've been duped by an unrepentant killer—are politely turning him away. This could have been a straight-forward thriller. Instead, Brian Moore has written a novel that explores the self-deceptions and conflicting impulses that torment the human heart. Hands down, *The Statement* is Moore's most interesting novel to date.

. . . .

LEMPRIÈRE'S DICTIONARY
by *Lawrence Norfolk* (Ballantine, 1993, paperback)

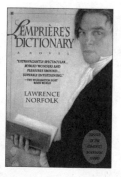

This beautifully written, exiting first novel set in the late 18th century is grounded in historical details, shows a good understanding of 18th-century culture, but breaks free of history to pull the reader into a fantastic series of mysterious events. The hero of the novel is the youthful John Lemprière, a historical person whose "Dictionary of Classical Mythology" was highly influential in the 19th century. Here, he is the reluctant participant in a series of strange adventures, including a political conspiracy of enormous proportions. Working with both fact and fantasy, Norfolk has created one of the most dazzling literary thrillers ever.

GOING AFTER CACCIATO
by Tim O'Brien (Dell, 1992, paperback)

One day, Cacciato gets up and decides he's tired of fighting in Vietnam's jungles. He's quitting; he's going to walk to Paris. Of course, his squad goes after him. You'll find that the chapters on individual members of Cacciato's unit are perfect—they could stand alone as short stories. And in fact, one of them won an O. Henry Award for short fiction.

THE LAST HURRAH
by Edwin O'Connor (1956; Little Brown, 1985, paperback)

Edwin O'Connor based his story of a crooked but lovable Boston politician on the real-life career of the city's long-time mayor, James Michael Curley. As the story opens, the glory days of the ward heelers are over. New, slick, packaged candidates are using television to garner votes. But the old pol has one more campaign in him and so he takes his nephew (and the reader) through the old neighborhoods of Boston where the old days and the old ways of doing business aren't forgotten. A very affectionate farewell to the old fashioned way of practicing politics.

THE DROWNING ROOM
Michael Pye (Viking, 1996, paperback)

Pye stumbled upon the bare facts of this story while researching a history of New York City. There really was a Gretje Reyniers who came to New Amsterdam from Holland in the 17th century with her husband, called the Turk. She was apparently a colorful character who once on the Manhattan waterfront used a broomstick to measure the genitalia of three sailors. In this novel, Gretje passes a long winter with a teenage boy who wrangles her life story out of her—her legal troubles, prostitution and flights from the plague and a marriage to the Turk. A captivating story of 17th-century life in Europe and the New World.

BANISHED CHILDREN OF EVE
by Peter Quinn (Penguin, 1995, paperback)

Hands down, this is one of the best historical novels ever written about New York. In the summer of 1863, the most popular play in New York is the melodrama, *Uncle Tom's Cabin*; the most beloved songwriter is the hopeless alcoholic, Stephen Foster; the two most hated minority groups are the blacks and the immigrant Irish. Keeping an eye on the underclass are New York's old aristocrats and the new robber barons. Pulling all of these threads together, Quinn tells a magnificent story of a conservative city about to erupt in an enormous riot. This a story you are going to love.

ALL QUIET ON THE WESTERN FRONT
by Erich Maria Remarque (1929; Fawcett, 1987, paperback)

You may be shocked when you first begin this novel: it is written from the German point of view. But what Remarque has to say about war and its effects on fighting men is universal. In the trenches, young Paul loses his friends, his innocence, his idealism, but never his humanity. truly one of the most shattering books on warfare ever written.

THE GOD OF SMALL THINGS
by Arundhati Roy (Random House, 1997, paperback)

A word-of-mouth publicity campaign among readers made Arundhati Roy's first novel a literary sensation. At a funeral, Rahel is reunited with her twin brother Estha, 25 years after they were separated and raised apart. Flashing back to 1969 when the children were seven years old, Roy reveals the events that forced sister and brother apart. There's a drowning, a betrayal, a banishment, a murder and a brief love affair between Rahel and Estha's mother and their best friend—a young untouchable carpenter. Roy's prose is gorgeous and her understanding of the human heart is profound.

WATERLAND
by Graham Swift (Vintage, 1992, paperback)

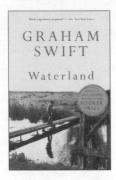

Blending family history and his own memories, Swift's narrator carries us from the disappointing present to two much more resplendent worlds: the Victorian era, when his mother's family prospered but also planted the seed of future disasters; and World War II, when the narrator was a boy learning about sex and death and family secrets. *Waterland* is a great novel that deserves a wider audience.

THE HUNDRED SECRET SENSES
by Amy Tan (Ivy, 1996, paperback)

Two sisters emigrate from China to San Francisco. Kwan, the elder, never loses touch with the old ways. In fact, she believes she has "yin eyes," the gift of seeing ghosts. Olivia has become Americanized and Kwan's constant conversations with invisible spirits drive her nuts. Nonetheless, there is one story Kwan has heard from her ghosts that fascinates Olivia, a tale of an American missionary in love with an evil general. Kwan tells it in installments and like Olivia you will savor the stories, too.

THE SECRET DIARY OF ADRIAN MOLE, AGED 13 ³/₄
by Sue Townsend (Methuen, 1996, paperback)

Townsend's hilarious memoir of a deadly-serious British teenage boy became a publishing sensation on both sides of the Atlantic when it first appeared in the early eighties. It spawned a hit musical, a popular television series, received critical raves and sold over five million copies—all with good reason. Townsend puts Adrian through the paces of modern puberty—love, pimples, rebellion, divorce-with warmth and affection, brilliantly balancing the sadness and absurdity of his situation. You'll laugh loud and long.

Worth Searching For:

THE GROWING PAINS OF ADRIAN MOLE
(Avon Books, 1982, paperback).

Adrian; Pandora, his love interest; Nigel, his best friend; and Bert the geriatric are back as Townsend scores again with more of Adrian's adventures.

....

THE CENTAUR
by John Updike (Fawcett, 1996, paperback)

Readers who are accustomed to Updike's suburban restraint will be bowled over by this visionary novel that places Greek mythology in contemporary America. On one level, it is the story of a high school teacher, George Caldwell and his son Peter. On another, it is a retelling of the myth of Chiron, wisest of the Centaurs, who surrendered his immortality to Prometheus. The line between modernity and myth shifts all the time in this novel, but Updike exercises perfect control over his material. A beautiful, intellectually stimulating work.

....

THE BOOK OF SECRETS
by M.G. Vassanji (McClelland & Stewart, 1995, paperback)

Through the eyes of a retired schoolmaster living in the shadow of Mount Kilimanjaro we read the diary of Alfred Corbin, an Englishman who had been posted to East Africa in the first days of the Great War. It's easy to become caught up in Corbin's life, especially when he writes of meeting a young Indian woman named Miriamu. But then Corbin becomes evasive and we—like the schoolmaster—are left wondering: Did Miriamu become Corbin's lover? Was he the father of her child? Vassanji lets the mysteries resonate through the century, capturing the life of Africa's Indian, Swahili and British communities.

....

BURR

by Gore Vidal (Ballantine, 1986, paperback)

Vidal's finest novel is the story of Aaron Burr, after Benedict Arnold the most infamous man in early American history. Aged 77 when the book opens, Burr is settling old scores with the Founding fathers:

George Washington: *"[His] judgment sometimes disallowed facts."*

Thomas Jefferson: *"Only slave-holding aristocrats like Jefferson can afford to believe in democracy."*

Alexander Hamilton: *"All his life he was attracted to women of the lowest class."*

MASTERS OF THE MACABRE

THE FAN
by Peter Abrahams (Warner Books, 1996, paperback)

Gil Renard, a Boston knife salesman, is passionate about baseball, particularly about the Red Sox and their new slugger Bobby Raymond. When Raymond hits a slump, Renard decides to help him out by murdering his closest rival. Little by little, Renard worms his way closer to his hero, even breaking into Raymond's home for a frightening confrontation. One of the scariest books ever written about obsession.

DRACULA UNBOUND,
by Brian Aldiss

Dracula sends vampire assassins to kill Bram Stoker before he can write his novel/exposé *Dracula*. So Joe Boderland hijacks a time-travel train to 1896 London and teams up with Stoker to defeat the legions of the undead. Worth searching for.

THE GREEN MAN
by Kingsley Amis (Academy Chicago Publishers, 1997, paperback)

Be warned! This macabre tale of terror could give you a month's worth of nightmares. Maurice Allington, a drunk, a lecher, a bon vivant and the owner of a posh hotel and restaurant housed in a medieval manor, begins to see apparitions of Dr. Thomas Underhill, a 17th-century clergyman who practiced the black arts. When Underhill promises Maurice that he can have whatever he desires most, Maurice is strongly tempted. Truly frightening. One of the great modern ghost stories.

THE REGULATORS
by Richard Bachman (Signet, 1996, paperback)

It's a perfect summer day in Wentworth, Ohio. Nothing is out of the ordinary on Poplar Street, except for the nondescript red van idling up the way. But then the van starts to roll and the carnage begins. Strangely spared from all the mayhem is 247 Poplar Street, the house where Audrey Wyler lives with her eight-year-old autistic nephew, Seth. At nightfall, the surviving residents of Poplar Street have a few questions. Why were Audrey and Seth left unscathed? Who are "the Regulators," said to be on their way? And can they be stopped? The answers will scare you to death. By the way, there is a plausible rumor that Bachman is the alter ego of Stephen King.

SOMETHING WICKED THIS WAY COMES
by Ray Bradbury (1962; Bantam, 1990, paperback)

To a nice, quiet, normal Midwestern town comes Cooger and Dark's Pandemonium Shadow Show. Lured by a flyer, two best friends, Jim and Will, both 13 years old, go to the show and get caught up in a carnival of unrelenting evil. Before the night is over, the boys will be at each throats on an out-of-control carousel. But worse still is the vision each will have of their own deaths and of the damnation of their entire town. A novel so shocking, thrilling and vivid it's been known to give readers nightmares.

Bradbury in Brief:

THE ILLUSTRATED MAN
(1951; Avon, 1997, paperback).

The classic collection of short stories united by a man covered with tattoos, each of which introduces a new tale.

GHOSTLIGHT
by Marion Zimmer Bradley (Tor, 1995, paperback)

A little Gothic romance, some contemporary occult "magick" and a classic haunted mansion make this ghost story out of the ordinary. The heroine is a forceful character named Truth Jourdemayne, the daughter of a celebrated occultist. Truth has decided to write a book about her father and she begins by visiting his estate in the Hudson Valley. There she finds a occult group her father founded, led by the attractive Julian Pilgrim. There are some supernatural flourishes in this novel, but the real story is Truth's own journey of self-discovery.

TREASURE BOX
by Orson Scott Card (HarperCollins, 1996, paperback)

Quentin Fears was ten years old when his sister was killed in a car crash. Since that day he has become a recluse who has nonetheless made millions as a creator of software. So it is a shock when Quentin meets Madeleine, a lovely woman who appears to be as socially naive as he is. Only after they are married does Quentin learn that Madeleine is not an innocent but the guardian of a malevolent force which she is preparing to loose upon the world. Quentin is terrified of what this evil thing will do, but he is just as frightened of going into the outside world to stop it.

WHERE ARE THE CHILDREN?
by Mary Higgins Clark (Pocket, 1996, paperback)

Even if you don't especially like children, this story will make your blood run cold. In the middle of a snow storm, Nancy Eldredge's son and daughter vanish from the front yard. Under hypnosis, Nancy reveals long-suppressed details of the disappearance of her first two children from her first marriage, with very scary parallels between what happened then and what's happening now. A suspenseful plot, great characterizations and killer descriptions of winter landscapes.

THE BLOOD COUNTESS
by Andrei Codrescu (Dell, 1996, paperback)

Elizabeth Bathory (1560-1613), the Blood Countess, was real. Beautiful, wealthy, educated as a Renaissance woman, she may have been the most infamous serial killer in history. It's said the countess murdered 650 virgin girls to bathe in their blood. And although the charges could not be proved in court, she was walled up in a room of her castle for five years anyway—just to be on the safe side. In this novel, Codrescu links the Countess' story with a tale of her 20th-century descendant, a Hungarian émigré in America, who can't escape the eternal fascination with his notorious ancestor.

THE TRICKSTER
by Muriel Gray (St. Martin's Press, 1997, paperback)

There's trouble in the idyllic Rocky Mountain valley town of Silver. A young cop has been murdered and his body mutilated. A trucker is found frozen to death in his cab amid drifts of snow—although all the doors and windows are shut. And a hotshot skier is slain on the slopes, where his murderer left no footprints in the deep snow. The only man in town with the guts to take on this demonic killer the Indians call the Trickster is Sam Hunt, the son and grandson of Indian shamans. Sam has felt something reawaken in him—and he has heard a call to meet his foe on the summit of Wolf Mountain. An original suspense thriller from a promising newcomer.

THE SILENCE OF THE LAMBS
by Thomas Harris (Simon & Schuster, 1992, paperback)

Perhaps the most chilling story of our time. To stop a brutal serial killer, FBI agent Clarise Starling enlists the aid of a brilliant but sociopathic psychiatrist—Hannibal "the Cannibal" Lecter. From his ultra-maximum-security prison cell, Lecter doles out his help in tantalizingly small portions. Each clue brings Clarise closer to the killer, But will she be able to piece the puzzle together in time to save his latest victim?

....

LORD OF THE DEAD,
by Tom Holland (Pocket, 1996, paperback)

Having come of age at last, Rebecca Carville receives the keys to the family crypt from her attorneys. Down among the tombs she hopes to find the sole manuscript of Lord Byron's memoirs. Instead, she finds Byron himself. He tells Rebecca how he became a vampire in Greece and about his efforts to resist becoming one of the undead. he reveals the true nature of his friendship with Shelley and his awful discovery that only the blood from a member of his family will maintain his youthful beauty. Effortlessly, Tom Holland combines period details and incidents from Byron's life to spin a very convincing horror novel. And the ending is a real shocker.

....

THE HAUNTING OF HILL HOUSE
by Shirley Jackson (1959; Viking, 1984, paperback)

Like Hawthorne's *House of the Seven Gables* (only more so), Hill House has a personality. And it isn't a nice one. Something terrible lurks in the stately old place, as an intrepid party of psychics confirm when they decide to investigate. Among them is Eleanor Vance, a woman in whom the house's evil presence has taken a special interest. Jackson is the master of ominous foreshadowing, a genius at building suspense. Waiting for the story's climax is almost unbearable. There's no gore or mayhem in this classic ghost story, just a eerie old house where someone is going to remain forever.

....

DESPERATION
by Stephen King (Viking Press, 1996, hardcover)

A nice young couple is driving along a nasty stretch of road in Nevada. Up ahead is a dead cat, nailed to the speed limit sign. Welcome to Stephen King Country. In a dried-up town called Desperation our couple meet a handful of other travelers who may never get to where they're going—a famous author; a clever 20-something woman; an 11-year-old boy who hears supernatural voices, not all of them of heavenly origin. And of course, there is something else in Desperation that will manifest itself in time. In the tradition of *The Stand*, this a tightly plotted, absolutely terrifying novel of ordinary people grappling with unfathomable evil.

CARRIE
by Stephen King (New American Library, 1994, paperback).

The novel that put King on the map. Carrie, a slightly off-balance teenager, takes revenge on her heartless classmates at the senior prom.

INSOMNIA
by Stephen King (Signet, 1995, paperback)

Ralph Roberts, a widower in a small Maine town, is sleeping less and less each night and seeing things that are stranger and stranger each day. Ralph thinks he's hallucinating until two messengers come to him and announce that his visions are signs that he has been chosen to fight in an earth-shaking conflict between good and evil. The story of Ralph's war against the Crimson King and his hellish legions is chilling.

ROSE MADDER
by Stephen King (Viking, 1995, hardcover)

Rosie Daniels has escaped her monstrously cruel husband, police detective Norman Daniels and started a new life hundreds of miles away. In her new home hangs an old oil painting of a Greek mythological scene that attracts Rosie's gaze and eventually draws Rosie herself into the picture. And when she emerges, she is no longer the frightened runaway housewife. Now she is a powerful creature named Rose Madder—she wants revenge.

Every Author's Nightmare:

MISERY
by Stephen King (Penguin, 1987, paperback).

Crippled in car accident, an author is trapped in the home of an unbalanced woman who claims she is his greatest fan. Spine-tingling.

THE STAND
by Stephen King (NAL Dutton, 1994, paperback)

An old Chevy rolls out of the night and crashes into a gas station in East Texas. Inside are a dead woman, a dead child, a dying man and a plague virus that will wipe out almost everyone on earth. As if the survivors don't have enough to contend with, a new horror comes along: the Dark Man is abroad, drawing the weak and the corrupt to himself. Can the handful of the good and the true defeat the powers of evil? This suspense-filled epic is King's first novel and it is still one of his best, packed with characters you care about and scenes you'll never forget.

A DRY SPELL
by Susie Maloney (Delacorte, 1997, paperback)

A killer drought and a spate of suspicious fires are destroying Goodlands, North Dakota. When a drifter and rainmaker named Tom Keatley wanders into town, Karen Grange, manager of the local bank, believes he may be Goodlands' last hope. What neither Tom nor Karen suspect is the disasters that afflict Goodlands are acts of vengeance by the ghost of a woman who was murdered a century ago—whose bones lie buried beneath Karen's house. A very spooky novel; savor it on a dark and stormy night.

LIE TO ME
by David Martin (Pocket, 1990, paperback)

One night, a madman breaks into the home of a wealthy Washington, D.C. couple. The husband and wife are afraid he will torture and rape them, but he does something worse—he reveals their secrets, the ones each of them was certain no one else knew. When the cops arrive the next morning, the husband is found to have committed suicide in a particularly gruesome manner—according to his wife.

LIVING WITH GHOSTS:
ELEVEN EXTRAORDINARY TALES
by Prince Michael of Greece, translated by Anthony Roberts, Photographs by Justin Creedy Smith (Norton, 1996, hardcover)

A slaughtered Renaissance princess. A foul Irish dragon. A baroness whose lover was killed by her husband in a duel. The castles of Europe are thick with ghosts. As a member of one of Europe's royal families with a special gift for ferreting out tormented spirits, Prince Michael of Greece has seen them all. In this eerie book, Michael doesn't just recount old ghost stories, he claims to have made contact with the dead so they can tell us what happened to them. Whether you are a firm believer in the supernatural or a skeptic, you'll enjoy these unusual tales of hauntings.

EDGAR ALLAN POE:
POETRY AND TALES
Edited by Patrick F. Quinn
(1984 The Library of America, 1984, hardcover)

You mean you've never read "The Tell-tale Heart"? "The Masque of the Red Death"? "The Cask of Amontillado"? Not even "The Pit and the Pendulum"? Poe is the macabre master of the American short story—if you haven't read Poe, you don't understand horror fiction. So start with the aforementioned four short stories. If they don't scare the bejesus out of you, nothing will. Then move on to "The Fall of the House of Usher." And don't skip "The Raven."

EXPIRATION DATE
by Tim Powers (Tor Books, 1996, paperback)

Young Koot Parganas has absconded from his parents' house with the ghost of Thomas Edison, which they kept locked in a glass vial. On the run, he loses himself in the underworld of Los Angeles, where strange creatures revitalize themselves by devouring the ghosts of the dead. And if they can find the ghosts of geniuses like Edison, these dark hordes could increase their powers a hundredfold. A chilling, wildly inventive work of fantasy told by one of the masters of the genre.

RELIC
by Douglas Preston & Lincoln Child (Tor, 1996, paperback)

Imagine Alien meets Jurassic Park. That's what Preston and Child have dreamed up in this eerie tale of a creature that is wreaking mayhem in Manhattan. A team of archaeologists is massacred in the Amazon Basin. Their artifacts and specimens are carted up, shipped to New York and stored in a museum basement. When mutilated corpses begin turning up in the museum corridors, Margo Green, a graduate student, starts assembling the evidence. And when she reaches her terrifying conclusion, she wonders if she has the courage to face the beast before it strikes again.

THE BRIDESMAID
by Ruth Rendell (Bantam, 1990, paperback)

Rendell is at her most thrilling in this tale of Philip Wardman, a civilized London man who meets a mysterious actress named Senta at his sister's wedding. To prove their love, Senta demands that they each murder someone—and then admits that she has killed one of Philip's enemies. A chilling novel that sets polite English society on its ear—and will keep you on the edge of your seat.

A GRACIOUS PLENTY
by Sheri Reynolds (Harmony Books, 1997, paperback)

A childhood accident badly disfigured Finch's face, so she has taken a job as caretaker of her hometown's cemetery. As she tends the graves and headstones, she hears the voices of the departed revealing the secrets of their lives. Little Marcus, an infant who died before he could speak, just wails. To bring peace to the child, Finch finds she will have to go back among the living whom she has avoided for so long.

INTERVIEW WITH THE VAMPIRE
by Anne Rice (Ballantine, 1986, paperback)

This is the novel that made Anne Rice an overnight sensation. Louis, a 200-year-old vampire, tells his story to a New Orleans reporter, revealing how he was made one of the undead by his friend Lestat, his love for the child vampire Claudia and the agony of meaningless immortality.

Also by Rice:

THE VAMPIRE LESTAT
(Ballantine, 1986, paperback).

Journeying back to 18th-century France, Rice tells how Lestat and Louis became vampires and eternal enemies.

SERVANT OF THE BONES
by Anne Rice (Knopf, 1996, paperback)

On a wintry night in upstate New York, an archeologist is dying alone. Suddenly, a beautiful young man appears, restores the scholar to health and asks him to write down his incredible story. The apparition is Azriel, originally a Jewish boy who was sacrificed to the god Marduk in 600 B.C. and transformed at the last excruciating moment into a spirit known as the Servant of the Bones. In human form, Azriel sought to save the Jews during the Black Death and now he is in the present battling the leader of a diabolical cult. *Servant of the Bones* is everything you hope for in an Anne Rice novel—scary, sexy and wildly imaginative.

More Chills from Anne Rice:

THE MUMMY
(Ballantine, 1989, paperback).

Pharaoh Ramses the Great drinks the elixir of life and is doomed to wander eternally in search of his beloved lost queen.

....

HAUNTED AMERICA
by Beth Scott and Michael Norman (Tor, 1995, paperback)

You've probably heard that Lincoln walks the corridors of the White House. But did you know that Custer still rides across the battlefield at Little Bighorn? Or that spectral mourners gather beside the grave of Edgar Allan Poe? Scott and Norman find eerie tales of hauntings for every state in the Union. A personal favorite—in Horicon, Wisconsin, a ghost rises out of the floor before the Tallman family and drives them from their house.

....

CITY OF DREADFUL NIGHT
by Lee Siegel (University of Chicago Press, 1995, hardcover)

Both a meditation on horror fiction and a succession of Gothic tales, this novel is skillfully constructed in three layers. The first is Siegel's own account of a trip to India to research tales of terror. The second is the life of Brahm Kathuwala, a professional storyteller, narrated by Brahm himself. The third comprises the horror stories of India, from ancient legends of vampires to the modern story of the "human bomb" who assassinated Rajiv Gandhi. A wonderfully inventive novel.

....

PERFUME:
THE STORY OF A MURDERER
by Patrick Süskind (Penguin, 1997, paperback)

This may be the only book ever written based on the sense of smell. Jean-Baptiste Grenouille is a sinister creature whose sense of smell is so uncanny that he can read hidden secrets about people or objects simply by breathing in their odor. When he turns his eerie gift to creating perfumes, his scents become the rage of 18th-century Europe. But Grenouille has a darker purpose in mind—to distill a secret fragrance just for himself from the most beautiful women in France.

JACK FAUST
by Michael Swanwick (Avon, 1997, paperback)

After a lifetime of study, Dr. Jack Faust is forced to admit that most of what his books tell him is outright nonsense. So he offers himself to whatever power will give him the knowledge he craves. The Devil, of course, takes him up on the offer. Soon, Faust is playing with electricity, manned flight and who knows what other advanced technologies. In the back of his mind, Faust may recall that all this hard science will end in his own damnation. What Faust doesn't realize is that Satan is using him as a tool to destroy humankind.

More by Swanwick:

THE IRON DRAGON'S DAUGHTER
(Avon Books, 1997, paperback).

A young slave escapes from the factory where she made "dragons"—huge flying machines piloted by humans—only to find herself in a world that is much worse.

THE WEATHERMAN
by Steve Thayer (Signet, 1996, paperback)

Every time the weather turns ugly, a serial killer strikes. Suspicion falls on Dixon Bell, a Minneapolis TV weatherman who has a genius for predicting violent storms, even ahead of the National Weather Bureau. But two men believe Bell is innocent— one of his fellow newscasters and a Vietnam vet who conceals his deformed features behind a blue mask. Whether in a courtroom or in the path of a killer tornado, Thayer builds the suspense beautifully. Sit down in a bookstore and read the first few pages. You'll be hooked.

NIGHT MAGIC
by Tom Tryon

Michael Hawke was a popular street performer in New York, amusing the crowds with his magic tricks. But then he meets an old man whose powers clearly go beyond sleight-of-hand. Seduced by his first encounter with real magic, Michael finds himself drawn deeper and deeper into the mystical arts, all the while trying to balance his love for his girlfriend, Emily, with the demands of his sorcerer-teacher who lures him with the incredible powers of Night Magic. Worth searching for.

MEN AT ARMS

D-DAY JUNE 6, 1944:
THE CLIMATIC BATTLE OF WORLD WAR II
by Stephen E. Ambrose (Touchstone, 1995, paperback)

The Allied troops who made it alive to Omaha and Utah beaches realized that nothing about the landing was as they had expected. So these citizen-soldiers took the initiative, struggling forward inch by inch under heavy German fire, until—by their individual acts of heroism—Hitler's Atlantic Wall was smashed. Drawing upon interviews with more than 1400 American, British, French, Canadian and German veterans and working with newly disclosed government documents, Ambrose tells the definitive story of the most important day of the 20th century.

SON OF THE MORNING STAR:
CUSTER AND THE LITTLE BIGHORN
by Evan S. Connell (HarperPerennial, 1991, paperback)

The Arikara Indians called Custer "Son of the Morning Star." His own men called him "Hard Ass," "Iron Butt" and "Ringlets." With a scholar's skill and a storyteller's gifts, Connell sorts through the tall tales and outright lies that have accumulated around Custer and finds something much more interesting: the truth about the man and what happened at the Battle of the Little Bighorn.

HITLER'S LAST GAMBLE
by Trevor N. Dupay, David L. Bongard and Richard C. Anderson, Jr.

On the morning of December 16, 1944, American forces were about to cross into Germany. But then they met a surprise in Belgium's Ardennes Forest. Incredibly, Hitler had amassed 410,000 men, 1400 tanks and thousands of artillery pieces and rocket-launchers for a final, daring counterattack against the Allies. Where did Hitler find these resources? And why did Allied intelligence miss the massive Nazi build-up? With unprecedented access to original documents and using a unique computer simulation system developed by the Army, the authors found the answers by recreating and analyzing every detail of the Battle of the Bulge. Worth searching for.

PATTON: A GENIUS FOR WAR
by Carlo D'Este (HarperCollins, 1995, hardcover)

Carlo D'Este has written the most incisive biography yet of one of America's most popular commanders. Working with new material from the George Patton family archives, D'Este shows us a man who believed God would intervene to give him victory and who compensated for his severe, life-long dyslexia by driving himself and his men to achieving one great objective after another. Unlike so many other biographies of Patton, D'Este's portrait looks at the whole man.

THAT DARK AND BLOODY RIVER:
CHRONICLES OF THE OHIO RIVER VALLEY
by Allan W. Eckert (Bantam, 1995, paperback)

Between 1768 and 1799, thousands of white settlers followed the Ohio River through Pennsylvania, Ohio and Indiana to Illinois, looking for new lands to farm. Allan Eckert tells the story as if it were an epic novel, introducing pioneer families like the Zanes, the Bradys and the Wetzels, following the heroic exploits of Daniel Boone, George Rogers Clark and Tecumseh and chronicling the bloody and tragic wars between the Indian tribes and the settlers. This is American history with a grand narrative sweep.

THE FIRST WORLD WAR: A COMPLETE HISTORY
by Martin Gilbert (Henry Holt, 1996, paperback)

Who will return us our children?" Rudyard Kipling cried when his son was killed in World War I. It was a lament echoed by millions of parents across the globe between 1914 and 1918. In this heroic history, Gilbert balances historical insights with human anecdotes. And he reveals some of the unexpected side effects of the war—such as the rise of both Arab separatism and Zionism. An incredible one-volume account of the cataclysm that shaped the 20th century.

GOOD-BYE TO ALL THAT
by Robert Graves (1929; Smith Publishing, 1992, paperback)

Graves, whom you know as the author of *I, Claudius* and *Claudius the God*, fought in the trenches of World War I and survived. This memoir of his experiences combines eyewitness testimony with black farce and outbursts of bitterness. The book was extremely controversial when it first appeared and still has the power to unsettle its readers.

THE FACE OF BATTLE
by John Keegan (Penguin, 1983, paperback)

It's no exaggeration to say that John Keegan is the most original military historian of the planet. Here he immerses readers in three landmark battles—Agincourt 1415, Waterloo 1815, the Somme 1916—as they were viewed by the men who fought them. A thrilling achievement.

Also by Keegan:

THE MASK OF COMMAND
(Penguin, 1988, paperback).

The front-line heroism of Alexander, the cool professionalism of Wellington, the "just folks" leadership of Grant, the false heroics of Hitler. A penetrating study of how commanders lead.

. . . .

CRUSADER CASTLES
by Hugh Kennedy (Cambridge University Press, 1994, hardcover)

To find the perfect castles, the ones with massive walls and soaring towers, the ones that could hold a garrison of thousands and withstand any siege, you have to travel to Syria, Jordan and Lebanon. There, between the 11th and the 13th centuries, the Crusaders built 60 grand bastions designed to keep the Holy Land in Christian hands. With spectacular photographs and a lively narrative, medieval historian Hugh Kennedy explores these citadels, tells the stories of the warlords who built them and studies the conflict between Christians and Muslims. The perfect book for anyone who has never gotten over a childhood fascination with castles.

The best book on how castles were built:

CASTLE
by David Macaulay (Houghton Mifflin, 1982, paperback).

From design through construction to a siege that tests the strength of the fortress, Macaulay shows step-by-step how a castle would have been built in 13th-century Wales. Packed with wonderful illustrations and lively details.

. . . .

CONQUERING THE VALLEY:
STONEWALL JACKSON AT PORT REPUBLIC
by Robert K. Krick (Morrow, 1996, hardcover)

The first months of 1862 were disastrous for the Confederacy. They lost Kentucky and west Tennessee, New Orleans,

Natchez and Memphis. But, Stonewall Jackson's triumphs over three Union armies in the Shenandoah Valley gave the South the psychological edge they needed to fight on and launched Jackson's reputation as a brilliant commander. Marked by exceptional research and a strong narrative style, Krick's study blends the general's grand strategic designs with details of how the fighting men actually experienced the battle. A splendid book that throws new light on one of the Confederacy's most jubilant moments.

THE RAILWAY MAN
by Eric Lomax (Norton, 1995, hardcover)

As a prisoner of the Japanese, Eric Lomax, a train buff, drew a detailed map of a new railway the Japanese were constructing. When the radio and the map were discovered, Lomax and his friends were subjected to days of torture and spent the rest of the war locked in filthy cages. For almost 50 years, Lomax nurtured his hatred for his torturers—especially his interrogator. One day, he learned that his interrogator was still alive. Hard as it may be to believe, Lomax went to meet him. Moved by the man's overwhelming sense of remorse for what he had done half a century ago, Lomax did what he thought he could never do—he forgave him.

PICKETT: LEADER OF THE CHARGE
by Edward G. Longacre (White Mane, 1996, hardcover)

George Pickett, of course, is the Confederate general who led the disastrous Pickett's Charge on the last day of the Battle of Gettysburg. Longacre's book is the first modern biography of Pickett and he dismisses the two most common misconceptions about Pickett–that he was a foppish cavalier or a military incompetent. Instead, Longacre shows Pickett to have been dependable man on the battlefield. Perhaps most interesting of all is his exploration of the tensions that sprang up between Robert E. Lee and Pickett after Gettysburg.

COLDER THAN HELL: A MARINE RIFLE COMPANY AT CHOSIN RESERVOIR
by Joseph R. Owen (Naval Institute Press, 1996, hardcover)

In December 1950, Joseph R. Owen was a Marine lieutenant of a rifle company fighting to stay alive as they battled North Koreans and temperatures of 25 degrees below zero. Owen brings the Korean War down to the level of individual soldiers who "functioned at a primal level: they ate, slept and fought and they tried to get warm." Owen's combat memoir is harsh, hard-boiled and authentic as he leads his readers into battle across blood-splotched snow in bone-chilling weather. It is a valuable, unforgettable account of the hardships American fighting men endured in an almost forgotten war.

MICHAEL COLLINS AND THE TROUBLES
by Ulick O'Connor (Norton, 1996, hardcover)

The opening chapters of this narrative history read like scenes from Doctor Zhivago, as Anglo-Irish aristocrats and visiting British officers pass their evenings at the dinners and balls of Dublin's glittering "season." It is something of a shock when galas give way to assassinations. Rebel leader Michael Collins knew that every Irish uprising had been betrayed by informers, so he began by ordering the assassination of anyone connected with Britain's Irish intelligence network. O'Connor writes history with just the right balance between interesting anecdotes and serious analysis, keeping his readers well entertained all the while they are being well informed.

CATAPULT:
HARRY AND I BUILD A SIEGE WEAPON
by Jim Paul (Avon, 1992, paperback)

In a moment of pure whimsy, the author and his pal Harry decide to build a medieval catapult and fling rocks into the Pacific. But before they toss a single stone, they learn the history of siege warfare, the physics of the humble rock and the strain one crazy impulse can put on a friendship. A very funny book and a great read.

NO MAN'S LAND
by John Toland

In the final year of World War I, millions of men were locked in a stalemate in the trenches, yet the German command was confident that one final assault would defeat the Allies. Toland summons all of his considerable narrative powers to describe the devastation of the war, its horrific cost in human life, as well as the events of that fateful year that gave victory to the Allies. Worth searching for.

THE CLASS OF 1846
by John C. Waugh

Review the roster for West Point's Class of 1846 and you'll find some of the greatest names of the Civil War listed.

No one thought that strange mountain boy from Virginia, Thomas "Stonewall" Jackson, would amount to much.

At Gettysburg, George Pickett led the immortal charge against a Union position held by his friend, John Gibbon.

At the Point, George McClellan and A.P. Hill were roommates, best friends and rivals in love. But, on the bloody field of Antietam, they were deadly enemies.

Fascinating reading about a fated class of military men. Worth searching for.

IN PHARAOH'S ARMY:
MEMORIES OF THE LOST WAR
by Tobias Wolff (Knopf, 1995, paperback)

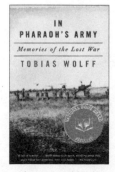

Like Hemingway, Tobias Wolff produces incredible vivid scenes and characters out of lean, spare prose. In this superb literary memoir, he recalls his tour of duty in Vietnam, where he was an advisor to a Vietnamese battalion in a small Mekong Delta town. He draws us in to the terror of the Tet Offensive, the close calls he survived—thanks only to dumb luck and the boredom of hanging around a backwater day after day. Best scene: Wolff is determined to celebrate Thanksgiving by watching *Bonanza* on his own color TV. A brutally honest war memoir and beautiful to read.

THE REASON WHY
by Cecil Woodham-Smith (Penguin, 1991, paperback)

Theirs not to reason why,
Theirs but to do and die:
Into the valley of Death
Rode the six hundred.

—Tennyson

The first and still the definitive modern study of the famous Charge of the Light Brigade reveals the petty rivalries among the officers that nudged the gallant cavalrymen to their doom. Woodham-Smith's description of the charge is one of the most moving accounts in military history.

MIND & BODY

A NATURAL HISTORY OF LOVE
by Diane Ackerman (Vintage, 1995, paperback)

For love of Eurydice, Orpheus went to Hell and back (literally). Abelard paid the ultimate price for his love for Héloïse. Aeneas ditched Dido for love of... Rome (what was he thinking?). Ackerman draws upon mythology, psychology, philosophy and literature to explore everybody's favorite emotion. She studies up on what Plato, Stendahl and Freud have to tell us about love. She wonders why girls love horses and men love cars. And she traces erotic history through fashion and hairstyles. A fun, sensuous tour of romantic conquests, infidelities, obsessions, even sexual ambiguities.

JANE BRODY'S COLD AND FLU FIGHTER: PREVENTING THEM, TREATING THEM, WHAT WORKS, WHAT DOESN'T
by Jane Brody (Norton, 1996, paperback)

Do you know the difference between viral and bacterial infections? Or which over-the-counter remedies work for which cold and flu symptoms? After years of catching colds, you ought to know this stuff. But never mind, Jane Brody, the Personal Health columnist for *The New York Times*, has collected the answers in this invaluable guide. You'll find preventive measures, what to do if you get sick anyway, how to nurse sick children, even how to make killer chicken soup. How did we ever get through the cold and flu season without Jane Brody?

THE HUMAN BODY:
AN ILLUSTRATED GUIDE TO ITS STRUCTURE, FUNCTION AND DISORDERS
editor-in-chief Charles Clayman, M.D.
(Dorling Kindersley, 1995, hardcover)

Without a doubt, this is one of the most beautiful, most accessible, most fascinating books on the human body to come along in years. More than 1000 full-color microphotographs and medical illustrations let you explore the intricate structure of human anatomy. The clear, concise text helps you grasp (at last!) such complex processes as how DNA conveys genetic information and how neurotransmitters send messages between cells. Plus you'll learn about the diagnosis and treatments of more than 150 diseases and disorders.

WHY IS SEX FUN?
by Jared Diamond (Basic Books, 1997, hardcover)

Birds do it. Bees do it. But humans want to do it all the time. Does that mean we're smarter than birds and bees? Or is a libido in overdrive part of nature's plan? Jared Diamond's good-humored, thought-provoking book is brimming with interesting information about sexuality and biology. For example, did you know that while the human male has the largest penis of all the primates, the orangutan's 1.5" member makes him more versatile (he can "perform in a variety of positions... while hanging from a tree.") *Why Sex Is Fun* is the smart, savvy, sassy book you wanted in high school sex-ed class.

THE MALE EGO
by Willard Gaylin, M.D.

Gaylin, a practicing psychoanalyst and psychiatrist, says that men set unrealistic goals for themselves and then feel frustrated when they don't achieve them. It's damaging to men, says Gaylin, bewildering to the women who love them and dangerous to society at large. But in this landmark work, the good doctor offers some excellent suggestions for bolstering the fragile male ego. Worth searching for.

....

PAIN REMEDIES:
FROM LITTLE OUCHES TO BIG ACHES
by Philip Goldberg and the Editors of Prevention Magazine Health Books
(Rodale Press, 1997, paperback)

In a perfect world, there would be no paper cuts. Or tennis elbow. Or wrenched backs. Or hangovers. But now, there is speedy relief. *Pain Remedies* gives you fast, effective treatments for more than 1000 aches and pains. You'll learn how a compress of fresh ginger can heal a sore knee. What to do to help a hangover. How to ease the pain of a lost filling until you can get to a dentist. And, what to do before you apply salve to a burn. These quick fixes to a host of common ailments will get you back on your feet—fast.

....

MEMORY: REMEMBERING AND FORGETTING
IN EVERYDAY LIFE
by Barry Gordon, M.D., Ph.D.
(Master Media Ltd., 1995, hardcover)

You can improve your memory by as much as 40%-that's what Dr. Barry Gordon, head of the Cognitive Neurology Division at Johns Hopkins University, argues in this intriguing book. In plain English, Gordon takes on the myths and anxieties associated with memory loss. He explores such interesting questions as whether a busy lifestyle can cause forgetfulness, or if a woman's memory works differently than a man's. He also helps you recognize if someone you love is suffering from Alzheimer's. Drawing upon the latest research into the functions of the brain, Gordon explains how you remember, why you forget and how you can improve your memory no matter how old you are.

....

ARISE FROM DARKNESS: WHAT TO DO WHEN LIFE DOESN'T MAKE SENSE
by Benedict J. Groeschel, C.F.R. (Ignatius Press, 1995, paperback)

As both a psychologist and a priest whose community works with the poor and desperate in the South Bronx, Benedict Groeschel has heard more than his share of stories of fear, grief and loss. In most cases, he admits that he has no answers why horrible things happen, but he does have suggestions for dealing with the pain and learning once again to live a life filled with hope. Drawing upon the insights of modern psychology as well as ancient spiritual wisdom from traditions around the globe, Father Groeschel has written a book of comfort for anyone who feels overwhelmed by sorrow.

WHO DO YOU THINK YOU ARE?
by Keith Harary, Ph.D. and Eileen Donahue, Ph.D.
(Harper San Francisco, 1994, paperback)

Does the real you emerge at a cocktail party, a private dinner with a lover, or when you're giving a business presentation? Do your neighbors think you are cold and aloof, while you consider yourself just a bit shy? Through the Berkeley Personality Profile, a ground-breaking method of self-discovery, two psychologists show you how to recognize the multidimensional you. Instead of being labeled a certain personality type, you'll discover the different ways you relate to diverse people and situations and learn how to work toward achieving your ideal personality.

THE PSYCHOLOGIST'S BOOK OF SELF-TESTS
by Louis Janda, Ph.D. (Berkley, 1996, paperback)

How comfortable are you in social situations? What do you believe controls your fate? How romantic are you? After years of research, psychologists have developed a collection of personality tests to profile the human character. Now you can use these tests yourself to gain valuable insights into your personality. And at the end of each test, an expert summary helps you read the results properly and points you in the right direction so you can change for the better. Whether you are wondering about your love life, your intelligence, or your career, these tests developed by professional psychologists can help you discover the real you.

....

THE HEALING HAND:
MAN AND WOUND IN THE ANCIENT WORLD
by Guido Majno, M.D. (Harvard University Press, 1991, paperback)

Life is fragile," Dr. Majno writes, " to be hurt is part of the game." Today, of course, we feel pretty confident that our doctors can patch us up, but what happened in ancient Egypt, Greece, Rome, India and China? Starting with some medical basics such as why cuts bleed and how they close and heal, Majno moves on to how physicians in ancient times treated wounds and whether it did the wounded any good. A completely absorbing read.

....

DOCTORS
by Sherwin B. Nuland (Vintage Books, 1995, paperback)

To tell the story of the evolution of medical science, Nuland begins with Hippocrates and then traces the development of modern medicine through the lives and achievements of such doctors as William Harvey, the discoverer of the circulation of the blood, Ignace Semmelweis, who formulated the theory of germs and Helen Taussig, who developed the "blue-baby operation" and other men and women who advanced our understanding of how the body works and how to heal it.

....

THE WISDOM OF THE BODY
by Sherwin B. Nuland (Knopf, 1997, paperback)

Even Dr. Nuland—who is not of a theological turn of mind—admits the way every part of the body works to keep itself alive is damn near miraculous. So in this fascinating book he not only delineates the principle of self-preservation as it is revealed in the chemistry of the cells, but he also addresses a question which physicians and philosophers have contemplated for centuries: Is biology destiny? Along the way, Nuland takes readers on a "voyage through the gut," explains why the blood is life and leads an in-depth tour of the nervous system, the brain and the heart. And each section is introduced with an actual life-or-death incident that could be an episode from E.R.

HOW WE DIE:
REFLECTIONS ON LIFE'S FINAL CHAPTER
by Sherwin B. Nuland (Knopf, 1994, hardcover)

Remarkably, this is not a depressing book. As a surgeon and teacher of medicine, Nuland knows that every death—like every life—is unique. In sensitive, uplifting prose, always mindful of the humanity of the patients, Nuland explains what happens to the body when someone is dying. This may be the moving book you ever read.

DOCTOR, WHAT SHOULD I EAT?
by Isadore Rosenfeld, M.D. (Warner Books, 1996, paperback)

The subtitle to this medically sound guide is "Nutrition Prescriptions for Ailments in Which Diet Can Really Make a Difference." Rosenfeld, who teaches at New York Hospital/Cornell Medical Center and is an attending physician at Memorial Sloan-Kettering Cancer Center, teaches you why a turkey sandwich and a glass of milk can reduce stress, how chili peppers can be an asthmatic's best friend and why zinc is for lovers. A warm, witty guide to more than 70 health problems you can handle right now with the right foods.

AN ANTHROPOLOGIST ON MARS:
SEVEN PARADOXICAL TALES
by Oliver Sacks (Vintage, 1996, paperback)

You know Dr. Oliver Sacks: Robin Williams played him in the film *Awakenings*. In seven case studies, Sacks introduces men and women whose physical or mental ailments have spilled over into moral dilemmas. A tumor changed a young man named Greg's personality beyond recognition—his father says he became like a changeling in the old stories. Virgil, who gained his sight after 45 years of blindness, could make no sense of the images he was now seeing for the first time. Dr. Sacks writes most eloquently of men and women trying to create a coherent picture of themselves and their world.

THE PDR FAMILY GUIDE TO NUTRITION AND HEALTH
(Medical Economics, 1995, hardcover)

From the publishers of the *Physicians' Desk Reference* comes this up-to-date compendium on eating healthy. You'll find lists of the best and worst diet books and cookbooks, a break-down by calories, fat and sodium of fast food, even which ethnic dishes are your healthiest choice. Chapters are devoted to the special health requirements of children, pregnant women and the elderly. Weight loss, eating disorders and the links between diet and hypertension, heart disease, cancer and diabetes are discussed in a scientific manner, without any of the usual myths that plague pop nutrition books. An authoritative reference on health and nutrition.

THE ORIGIN OF EVERYDAY MOODS: MANAGING ENERGY, TENSION AND STRESS
by Robert E. Thayer (Oxford University Press, 1996, paperback)

If you're feeling stressed, do you go to the gym, go to a bar, or go to bed? *The Origin of Everyday Moods* suggests that our moods aren't purely emotional reactions to what is going on around us, but are determined by our psychology and our physiology. Pioneering biopsychologist Robert Thayer explains why our troubles seem much worse late at night. And he shows that the best way to deal with tension or a bad mood is to exercise. More than an intriguing study of moods, this book offers sound advice on how to handle stress.

CHOLESTEROL CURES
by Richard Trubo and the Editors of Prevention Magazine
(Rodale Press, 1996, paperback)

From almonds and antioxidants to wine and yogurt, this A-to-Z compendium teaches you how to feel better by eating right. Plus, it comes with a 30-day eating program that can lower your cholesterol by 30 points and a handy "fat and cholesterol counter" for 500 foods.

TWELVE STEPS TO A BETTER MEMORY
by Carol Turkington (Macmillan, 1996, paperback)

If you have trouble remembering names, dates and day-to-day stuff like where you left your keys and whether you turned off the oven before you left the house, you need this book. *Twelve Steps to a Better Memory* teaches you fast, easy methods to learn facts, retain them and trot them out again the moment you need them. You'll get a proven method for remembering numbers, a sure-fire technique for memorizing a speech, tips to help you overcome "tip-of-the-tongue" phenomenon. From family birthdays to the name of that really attractive person you met at a cocktail party last month, this book can help you pump up your memory.

THE ART OF LIVING
by Dietrich and Alice von Hildebrand
(Sophia Institute Press, 1994, paperback)

A husband-and-wife team of distinguished teachers and philosophers recommend seven essential virtues to embrace if you hope to foster within yourself a more positive personality. The Hildebrands teach you how to make fundamental changes to your outlook on life by cultivating responsibility, veracity, hope, goodness, faithfulness and gratitude. They explore the ways these virtues can have a powerful impact on your actions, give you a more positive mental outlook and enrich your spiritual life. *The Art of Living* is a step-by-step course for anyone who hopes to make lasting improvements to their character.

THE DOUBLE HELIX
by James D. Watson (Norton, 1980, hardcover)

James Watson is not a self-aggrandizing man. Even in this personal account of how he and his colleague Francis Crick discovered the structure of DNA—our fundamental genetic material—he admits with absolute candor that there's often tension between a scientist's sense of fair play and his ambition to make a discovery before the next guy. Watson and Crick faced that dilemma; how they resolved it is every bit as interesting as the story of how they mapped the structure of DNA.

RACING TO THE BEGINNING OF THE ROAD:
THE SEARCH FOR THE ORIGIN OF CANCER
by Robert A. Weinberg (Harmony Books, 1996)

It was Dr. Weinberg who first identified and described the aberrant sequences in DNA which begin the cellular changes that result in cancer. Modest man that he is, he insists that his discovery could not have been possible without the discoveries his predecessors made in viral, chemical and genetic constructs. *Racing to the Beginning of the Road* offers a vivid record of the personalities, accomplishments and idiosyncrasies of these scientists. Weinberg is one of those rare scientists who can discuss his work with drama and clarity.

SEX FOR DUMMIES™
by Dr. Ruth K. Westheimer (IDG Books, 1995, paperback)

It had to happen eventually. Sooner or later Dr. Ruth was bound to hook up with the "_____ for Dummies" people and put out a book for the erotically challenged. So here it is, from tips for women on how to find a good partner to tips for men on how to give women orgasms. Plus you get Dr. Ruth's top ten lists, including: "10 Dumb Things People Believe About Sex" and "10 Mistakes Men and Women Make." From the absolute basics to the fine points of sensual massage, this is the ultimate user friendly guide for lovers and lover wannabes.

MYSTERIOUS DOINGS

BLIND JUSTICE
by Bruce Alexander (Berkley, 1995, paperback)

Admit it. London in the 18th century was a lot more fun than the stuffy Victorian town of Sherlock Holmes. There were rascals on every corner, whores in the Haymarket and the streets were crammed with bright orphan boys ready to seize an opportunity. Jeremy Proctor, for instance, is a street-smart kid who helps magistrate Sir John Fielding solve the murder of a dissipated nobleman. This is the first time out for Jeremy and Sir John, so its good to see that they chose a classic "murder-in-a-locked-room" caper for their debut. Keep on an eye on Bruce Alexander. *Blind Justice* looks to be the beginning of a very promising series.

THE FASHION IN SHROUDS
by Margery Allingham (1938; Carroll & Graf, 1995, paperback)

Allingham's undisputed masterpiece is set in a dress designer's studio—a hothouse of over-developed egos and over-the-top emotional outbursts. When some fashion designs are stolen, Albert Campion is summoned. Complicating his case is a little blackmail, a murder that's three years old and the theft of 69 cages of canaries. It's a beautiful thing to watch Campion in action and Allingham never loses control of the convoluted twists and turns of her plot. If Margery Allingham is new to you, you're in for a treat.

Campion's Second Best Caper:

DANCERS IN MOURNING
(1937; Carroll & Graf, 1996, paperback).

The cast of characters is especially good in this mystery, probably because they're almost all prodigies, performers, or narcissists. Campion is a bit slow sorting out the clues, but he's fallen in love in this novel so you'll excuse him if he appears distracted.

....

THUS WAS ADONIS MURDERED
by Sarah Caudwell (Dell, 1981, paperback)

Barrister Julia Larwood has run off to Venice to escape the British Inland Revenue Service. There she encounters the beauteous Ned and falls instantly in love. But Julia's beloved is himself a tax man for the Inland Revenue. Even more disconcerting is the arrival of the Venetian police who charge Julia with Ned's murder. (It appears Ned's corpse was found with Julia's copy of the Finance Act lying beside it). Julia's colleagues back in London know she could never kill anyone. But how will they ever convince the Venetians that Julia is too clumsy to stab a man to death? A laugh-out-loud funny, fiendishly plotted and very, very English murder mystery.

Another by Caudwell:

THE SHORTEST WAY TO HADES
(Dell, 1995, paperback).

A devilishly clever Oxford don, Hilary Tamar, comes to the aid of a group of bungling young barristers when one of their clients, a wealthy heiress, is murdered.

....

THE BODY IN THE LIBRARY
by Agatha Christie (HarperCollins, 1992, paperback)

In case you don't know, Miss Jane Marple is a quiet, reserved lady of a certain age who possesses an encyclopedic knowledge of human evil. This time out, Miss Marple uses her unique gifts to solve one murder, predict a second and prevent a third. A virtuoso performance from one of the greatest figures in detective fiction.

Also by Christie:

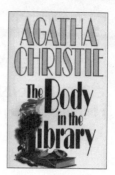

AT BERTRAM'S HOTEL
(HarperCollins, 1992, paperback).

A story rich in atmosphere that shows off Christie's talent for well-drawn characters.

A MURDER IS ANNOUNCED
(1950; Berkley, 1995, paperback).

Blackmail and murder in a rural village. Christie's 50th story is solid gold.

AND THEN THERE WERE NONE
[OR TEN LITTLE INDIANS]
(1939; Berkley, 1995, paperback)

Christie's undisputed masterpiece. ten people, each of whom has killed someone, is invited to an island for a party. On the island is an unseen avenger who eliminates the guests, one by one. Christie handles the rising tension beautifully. If you read only one Christie novel, make it the flawless *And Then There Were None.*

THE PALE HORSE
(HarperCollins, 1994, paperback).

Christie is fresh and full of surprises in this tale of murder and the black arts.

DEATH COMES AS THE END
(HarperCollins, 1995, paperback).

Absolutely unique in the Christie canon—a murder set in 2000 B.C. in Thebes on the Nile. based on actual ancient Egyptian documents.

THE HOLLOW
by Agatha Christie (Berkley, 1984, paperback)

Droll, elegant, Hercule Poirot is Agatha Christie's most charming character. In this tale of an amorous man and three ladies each of whom has reason to kill him, Christie is in absolute control as she increases the tension and builds motive. *The Hollow* is Agatha Christie at her personal best.

More from the Casebook of Hercule Poirot:

CARDS ON THE TABLE
(Berkley, 1987, paperback).

A psychological thriller that reveals which of four bridge players killed someone in the cardroom.

THE MYSTERIOUS AFFAIR AT STYLES
by Agatha Christie (1920; Berkley, 1995, paperback)

Agatha Christie's first Hercule Poirot mystery is a triumph. Mrs. Inglethorpe, a widow, holds an estate in trust for her two stepsons. But once she marries a young gigolo, the old lady is markedly less generous to the boys. When she turns up dead of strychnine poisoning, Hercule Poirot is called in to solve the case. "The Pride of Belgium" has a wonderful time wading through the knot of complicated clues, with more than a few red herrings thrown in.

One More Christie Classic:

MURDER ON THE ORIENT EXPRESS
(1934; HarperCollins, 1991, paperback).

This devilishly clever murder on the renowned luxury train was originally titled *Murder in the Calais Coach*. It is in every respect one of Christie's finest achievements.

THE IRON HAND OF MARS
by Lindsay Davis (Ballantine, 1994, paperback)

Marcus Didius Falco, ancient Rome's greatest private detective, has his problems. The emperor's son would like to see him dead. A Teutonic queen would like to see him roasted alive. And Falco's current lady friend just doesn't want to see him. Of course, the situation doesn't improve when Falco is sent on an imperial mission to the frontier, where lately the barbarians have been more barbarous than usual.

14 PECK SLIP
by Ed Dee (Warner Books, 1995, paperback)

One nasty winter night on the Lower Manhattan waterfront, two New York cops, Anthony Ryan and Joe Gregory, see a barrel being rolled into the East River. Recognizing a mob burial at sea when they see one, they call for the divers. The boys bring up the wrong barrel, but it is worth investigating just the same. Inside are the remains of Jinx Mulgrew, a crooked cop who disappeared 10 years earlier just before he was scheduled to testify before an ethics commission. Now the cops Mulgrew was about to finger are after Ryan and Gregory. And Mulgrew's old mob connections would like to "talk" to them, too. This is one tough, gritty detective novel.

THE WATERWORKS
by E.L. Doctorow (Plume, 1997, paperback)

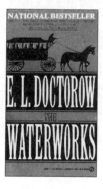

The soul of the city was always my subject," says the narrator of *The Waterworks*, but it could just as easily be the voice of Doctorow himself. In this dazzling novel, Doctorow conjures up New York in 1871. On Broadway, Martin Pemberton, a freelance journalist, sees a horse-drawn omnibus filled with old men dressed in black. Among them he recognizes his father, supposedly dead and buried. No sooner does Martin tell his strange tale to his editor than Martin himself disappears. The search for Martin and the quest to discover if his wicked old father is truly alive, reveals a part of New York no one has ever encountered before.

THE SHAMAN LAUGHS
by James D. Doss (St. Martin's Press, 1995, paperback)

On Ute tribal land in Colorado, somebody—or something—has been slaughtering prize bulls and cutting off their ears and testicles. Then, a businessman who suggested the tribe could make a lot of money storing nuclear waste in a sacred canyon is found slain and mutilated in the same way. And witnesses are reporting sightings of a large, hairy, horned creature with a single burning eye. Clearly, Ute reservation police sergeant Charlie Moon and Anglo police chief Scott Parris have their hands full as they try to make sense of a series of mystical clues. A flawlessly plotted mystery from a welcome newcomer to the genre.

Doss' debut mystery

THE SHAMAN SINGS
(St. Martin's Press, 1994, paperback).

A series of unpleasant omens alerts Ute shaman Daisy Perika that the Dark One is at work among her white neighbors. So Perika joins forces with police chief Scott Parris to find a killer before he finds another victim.

THE HOUND OF THE BASKERVILLES
by Sir Arthur Conan Doyle (1902; NAL Dutton, 1997, paperback)

Reports of a phantom hound bring Holmes and Watson to the ancestral hall of the noble Baskerville family. This full-length Sherlock Holmes novel reveals Doyle at the height of his powers, with plots and subplots flawlessly integrated and plenty of false clues sprinkled about to bedevil the reader.

Also by Doyle:

ADVENTURES OF SHERLOCK HOLMES
(Bantam, 1997, paperback).

A blockbuster collection of Holmes short stories, including the fiendishly clever "Redheaded League" and "Adventure of the Speckled Band."

A TIME FOR THE DEATH OF A KING
by Ann Dukthas (St. Martin's Press, 1995, 1995, paperback)

Did Mary, Queen of Scots, conspire to murder her husband? It's a question people have been asking since that February night in 1567 when the house where the handsome, dissolute Henry Darnley was staying inexplicably blew up. Why was Darnley's body found strangled in the garden rather than mangled in the ruins? What is the meaning of the chair, the rope and the dagger found beside his corpse? What are we to make of the widow remarrying within days of the murder? In this richly atmospheric tale, Dukthas attempts to solve a the mystery 429 years after the crime occurred.

THE BOOKMAN'S WAKE
by John Dunning (Pocket Books, 1996, paperback)

Cliff Janeway gave up being a cop and began a second career as a rare book dealer. But his law enforcement training will not go to waste as long as there are fetching felons like Eleanor Rigby—a young lady who has stolen a priceless copy of Poe's "The Raven." Janeway follows Rigby to Seattle, where he finds the usually civilized city is crawling with people who want Rigby's purloined copy of Poe and don't care what they have to do to get it. An entertaining detective story that also teaches you a lot about the rare book business.

The first Janeway case:

BOOKED TO DIE
by John Dunning (Avon Books, 1993, paperback).

The novel that introduced Cliff Janeway, the tough, homicide detective and bibliophile. To find the murderer of a down-and-out rare-book hunter, Janeway beats up a suspect. The off-duty interrogation costs Janeway his badge, but as far as he's concerned, he's still on the case.

COMEBACK
by *Dick Francis* (Fawcett Crest, 1994, paperback)

When several race horses die under suspicious circumstances, the veterinarian is suspected. But bit by bit, hero Peter Darwin uncovers the conspiracy that is truly behind the slayings. Hang on for the big finish.

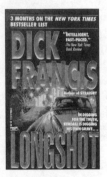

LONGSHOT
by *Dick Francis* (Fawcett Crest, 1992, paperback)

Dick Francis is the master of thoroughbred mysteries. In Longshot, a hungry writer between jobs takes an assignment to write the biography of a racehorse trainer and discovers that the perils of England's horse country are as deadly as the jungles and deserts he describes in his travel books.

TO THE HILT
by *Dick Francis* (Putnam, 1996, paperback)

Francis' latest mystery begins with four thugs breaking into the Highlands cottage of artist Alexander Kinloch, beating the hell out of him and screaming, "Where is it?" The "it" is the solid gold, jewel-encrusted sword hilt Bonnie Prince Charlie gave Kinloch's ancestor. And the beating is just the beginning of Kinloch's problems. His mother wants him to save the family brewery from total ruin. His spiteful stepsister plans to steal the family's thoroughbred steeplechaser. His relative, the earl, wants Al to hide the priceless sword hilt. And the thugs return with some ghastly methods of persuading Kinloch to reveal the location of the heirloom. With his usual skill, Francis, resolves all these plot lines. It is no wonder the Mystery Writers of America named him a Grand Master.

DEATH OF A GOD,
by S.T. Haymon (St.Martin's Press, hardcover)

A band named Second Coming arrives in town and within hours the band's charismatic lad singer is found crucified in the market square. As Detective Ben Jurnet investigates the murder, he finds that the rock star's gruesome death provokes an unusual response from the people who knew him: they are absolutely gleeful about it. Haymon deserves a larger following among readers of British murder mysteries. Worth searching for.

Also by Haymon:

STATELY HOMICIDE.

There's a body in the moat at historic Bullen Hall. But rivaling the corpse for attention is a packet of love letters from Anne Boleyn—to her brother George! A great caper of past crimes that that return to bedevil the present. Worth searching for.

....

THE TALENTED MR. RIPLEY
by Patricia Highsmith
(1955; Black Lizard/Vintage Books, 1992, paperback)

Like a figure out of a Henry James novel, Tom Ripley has been sent to Italy to bring a prodigal young American back home to his wealthy father. On the surface, Ripley is charming, sophisticated, a perfectly correct gentleman. In fact, the only time his emotions rise to the surface is when he is in the act of killing a carefully selected victim. Cool, detached and daring, Ripley leaves a trail of corpses from America to Europe—and he is never so calculating as when he is disposing of a corpse. A real shocker of a crime novel.

Another Highsmith Shocker:

EDITH'S DIARY
(Atlantic Monthly Press, 1989, paperback).

A woman's incremental descent into madness is chronicled through diary entries that become ever more cheerful. Subtle and horrifying.

A MONSTROUS REGIMENT OF WOMEN
by Laurie R. King (St. Martins Press, 1996, paperback)

Mary Russell made her debut as Sherlock Holmes' most promising student in *The Beekeeper's Apprentice*. Now, she dives into her second case, in which she meets a former classmate from Oxford who has become enmeshed in a bizarre secret society—part religious cult, part women's suffrage movement. Mary Russell observes that something peculiar appears to be going on behind the scenes, so she launches her own investigation, unaware of the danger that stalks her.

Sherlock's Successor:

THE BEEKEEPER'S APPRENTICE,
by Laurie R. King (St. Martins Press, 1994, paperback).

Now retired and enjoying a late-life career as a beekeeper, Sherlock Holmes becomes the mentor of a promising young sleuth named Mary Russell. Their adventures together become increasingly dangerous until Holmes' life is in peril and Mary must prove herself a worthy successor to the great detective.

THE DEBT TO PLEASURE
by John Lanchester (Henry Holt, 1996, hardcover)

"**T**his is not a conventional cookbook," says Tarquin Winot, gourmand, aesthete, savant and wit as he begins his story. In fact, as you'll discover once you are immersed in the novel (and you will find it hard to break away from it), the menus Winot describes are tied to mysterious disclosures about Winot's character. When he speaks learnedly about "the erotics of dislike" you can't help wondering if Winot is holding back something vital. And when he turns his attention to the binding properties of blood.... A tour de force that teases all the senses.

BLOOD RED ROSES
by Margaret Lawrence (Avon, 1997, paperback)

The year is 1786. Hannah Trevor, a young widowed midwife in the little settlement of Rufford, Maine, is trying to talk herself into entering a loveless marriage so she and her eight-year-old daughter will enjoy some security. But her marriage plans are put on hold when a man Hannah knew is found murdered in a rich man's rose garden—and she is suspected of the killing. Blending early American history with a complex murder plot, *Blood Red Roses* will keep you on the edge of your beach chair.

Another Hannah Trevor Mystery:

HEARTS AND BONES
by Margaret Lawrence (Avon Books, 1996, paperback).

Hannah unravels a series of brutal killings during an especially cruel Maine winter.

TIME'S WITNESS
by Michael Malone
(Washington Square Press/Pocket Books, 1994, paperback)

Cuddy Mangum, Chief of Police in a small North Carolina town, finds himself tangled in a web of intrigue when he tries to solve the murder of a black political activist who has just won a reprieve for his brother unjustly waiting on Death Row. From the Klan's secret meeting places to the highest offices of state government, Malone has written a funny, suspenseful mystery story that is also a gripping social commentary on the New South.

AFTER DARK
by Phillip Margolin (Bantam, 1996, paperback)

When an attractive law clerk is murdered and the judge she worked for is blown up in his car, suspicion falls on the judge's estranged wife, Abbie. She gets an attorney, Matthew Reynolds, who specializes, by his own admission, in "sociopaths, misfits [and] psychotics." Reynolds is certain Abbie is innocent, but his law clerk isn't so sure. A master at contriving new plot twists and devilishly clever clues, Phillip Margolin has written a mystery thriller that will keep you on the edge of your seat.

THE MARSHAL AT THE VILLA TORRINI
by Magdalen Nabb

While most police procedurals are set in America or Great Britain, Magdalen Nabb locates hers in Florence. Marshal Salvatore Guarnaccia commands the Pitti Palace Station on the far side of the Ponte Vecchio, across the Arno from the Uffizi. The case that is bedeviling him is the murder of an Englishwoman. Guarnaccia is sure the woman's husband is the culprit, even though he didn't leave a single clue. You'll like Nabb's genial style and it's refreshing to hang out with a detective who relies on intuition to solve his case. Worth searching for.

Another Florentine mystery:

THE MARSHAL'S OWN CASE
by Magdalen Nabb. (Scribner's, 1990, hardcover)

Guarnaccia is flustered and embarrassed when ordered to investigate the murder of Lulu, a transsexual prostitute. In Florence's underworld, the Marshal finds that Lulu had many enemies and a mysterious client named Nanny. Worth searching for.

THE MAN WHO CAST TWO SHADOWS
by Carol O'Connell (Putnam, 1995, paperback)

Kathleen Mallory was a wild kid with a penchant for petty theft. Now she's a police sergeant and a computer wizard, but she still lives by her own rules. A young writer has been murdered and the clues to her killer are scattered throughout her last manuscript. Combining intuition and a little computer burglary, with an assist from a genius private investigator friend, Mallory turns up three celebrity suspects. A great read, from a great newcomer to suspense fiction.

TRAITORS GATE
by Anne Perry (Fawcett, 1996, paperback)

Colonial Office Superintendent Thomas Pitt and his glamorous wife, Charlotte, are the best Victorian sleuthing team since Holmes and Watson. This time, they have to ferret out a nest of aristocratic traitors who are feeding secrets about British colonies in Africa to the envious Germans. Perry keeps the suspense going from page one and packs her book with plenty of accurate period details and lively, passionate characters as well. But be warned: read just one Anne Perry mystery and you'll be hooked.

More by Anne Perry:

BELGRAVE SQUARE
(Fawcett, 1993, paperback).

In the desk of a murdered moneylender, Thomas Pitt finds a list of distinguished names and a case of scandal that could damage aristocratic families throughout England.

FARRIER'S LANE
(Fawcett, 1994, paperback).

A Jewish actor is convicted of ritual murder. The judge who proposes to reopen the case is poisoned. There are no leads, until Charlotte Pitt's social connections provide a few clues, with some additional help from Oscar Wilde.

THE SUMMER OF THE DANES
by Ellis Peters (Mysterious Press, 1992, paperback)

On a diplomatic mission to his native Wales in Summer 1144, Brother Cadfael is caught up in a feud between two Welsh princes. When one of the antagonists lands an army of Danish mercenaries on the Welsh coast, Cadfael is taken prisoner. Sharing his confinement is a young woman who may or may not have been involved in a murder. With escape impossible, Cadfael has a lot on his mind. How can he prevent a full-scale war from breaking out? Will he ever see his abbey again? And how can he solve a murder if he can't examine the clues?

Another Brother Cadfael adventure:

THE HERMIT OF EYTON FOREST
by Ellis Peters (Mysterious Press, 1988, paperback).

First Cadfael's abbey gets in a row with a local noblewoman. Then, just as a hermit arrives in the neighborhood, a series of mishaps befalls the monks. Finally, a corpse turns up in the hermit's forest.

MURDER AT THE GOD'S GATE
by Lynda S. Robinson (Ballantine, 1996, paperback)

How do you tell a 14-year-old god that starting wars is for grown-ups? That's just one of the dilemmas in this beautifully plotted mystery set in the Egypt of Tutankhamen, the boy-king. While the young pharaoh dreams of conquest, Lord Meren, his adviser and Kysen, Meren's adopted son, try to solve the puzzling rash of murders at court.

MURDER IN THE PALACE OF ANUBIS
by Lynda S. Robinson (Ballantine, 1994, paperback)

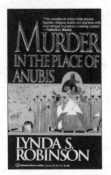

Lord Meren, the Eyes and Ears of the Pharaoh Tutankhamen, must find who has murdered the scribe Hormin and desecrated the sacred embalming chamber by depositing his slaughtered corpse there. Since everyone who knew Hormin hated him, there are plenty of suspects. Meren's investigation leads him to Thebes, where Hormin's sons and concubine plot revenge; through the court of Pharaoh, where intrigue is a daily past time; to the terrifying palace of the god Anubis, where the souls of the unquiet dead dwell. A fascinating mystery, in an intriguing setting.

THE DEVIL IN THE MUSIC
by *Kate Ross* (Viking, 1997, hardcover)

Julian Kestrel, English dandy and amateur sleuth, is enjoying the luxurious, sometimes scandalous, hospitality of the Marquesa Malvezzi's villa on Lake Como. But life is more than a little slap and tickle in the marquesa's box at La Scala. The marquesa's late husband died under mysterious circumstances and an English tenor who goes by the stage name of Orfeo appears to have been involved. Is Kestrel so besotted with his hostess that he will let the crime go unsolved and permit the murderer to get away? Don't bet on it.

CUT THE QUICK
by *Kate Ross* (Penguin, 1993, paperback).

At an opulent country house in 1820s England, sparring between the families of a bride and a groom ends in murder. This is Julian Kestrel's debut.

THE UNPLEASANTNESS AT THE BELLONA CLUB
by *Dorothy Sayers* (HarperPaperbacks, 1995, paperback)

The distribution of a legacy worth half a million pounds depends on discovering what time 90-year-old General Fendman died. But that's just one of the mysteries that are puzzling Lord Peter Wimsey about the general's passing. Why wasn't he wearing a red poppy in his lapel on Armistice Day? How did the Bellona Club's phone get repaired when no repairman came? And why does the general's knee swing freely when the rest of him is locked in rigor  mortis? It is a joy to see Wimsey solve and knit together these seemingly unconnected clues.

MEMENTO MORI
by Muriel Spark (Avon, 1990, paperback)

A group of elderly people are beginning to feel ill at ease. All of them have received an anonymous phone call with the voice on the other end saying, "Remember, you must die." And some of them do! It's all very unsettling and you won't feel any better when you discover who the caller is.

THE LOVER OF THE GRAVE
by Andrew Taylor (St. Martin's Press, 1997, hardcover)

A ndrew Taylor puts a new spin on the English country mystery. The folk of Lydmouth village are cunning rather than kind, cruel rather than quaint. And boy do they hate strangers—as the Italian P.O.W. who stayed on after the war to farm found out. So, when the village school teacher is found dangling from the Hanging Tree (with his pants down around his ankles), the vicar calls in Inspector Richard Thornhill. Morose and lecherous, Thornhill would have sent Agatha Christie running for the hills. But he's the perfect man for this dark mystery.

BRAT FARRAR
by Josephine Tey (1949; Collier Books, 1988, paperback)

E ight years have gone by since Patrick Ashby, the young heir to a considerable fortune, disappeared. He is presumed dead. Then Brat Farrar presents himself as the long lost Patrick. Farrar, who could pass as Patrick's twin, has been coached in every detail of the missing heir's personality and bearing. He gives a completely convincing performance. But just as it appears that the impersonation has been a success, the false Patrick develops a passion for Farrar's cousin. Then, some murderous old family secrets surface which threaten to undermine the whole imposture.

Also by Josephine Tey:

THE DAUGHTER OF TIME
(Simon & Schuster, 1995, paperback)

If the clues to a double murder are 500 years old, would you say they were a bit stale? That doesn't seem to deter Alan Grant of Scotland Yard, who decides to solve one of the great murder mysteries of English history: did Richard III kill the Little Princes in the Tower? Or was he framed by those upstart Tudors and their cronies?

THE LAWS OF OUR FATHERS
by *Scott Turow* (Farrar Straus & Giroux, 1996, paperback)

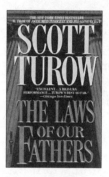

Sonia Klonsky, who appeared as a young prosecutor in *The Burden of Proof*, is now a Superior Court Judge presiding over a murder trial. The victim was June Eddgar, an old activist from the Sixties, who was shot and killed in a ghetto. Charged with ordering the hit is her son, Nile. As you'd expect from Scott Turow, there are lots of intriguing plot twists before the case comes to a close, plus flashbacks to the golden years of anti-war activism. The theme is interesting: how can children break away from strong, ideologically committed parents? And some readers say the defense attorney Hobie Tuttle reminds them of Johnnie Cochran.

NO NIGHT IS TOO LONG
by *Barbara Vine* (Harmony Books, 1995, hardcover)

Tim was on an Alaskan cruise with his lover Ivo when he fell in love with the mysterious Isabel. Leaving his boyfriend for a girlfriend proved messy, so Tim solved the problem by knocking Ivo on the head and leaving him for dead on an uninhabited island. Safe back in England, Tim believes he has executed the perfect murder—until he starts receiving anonymous letters about a castaway. A nerve-wracking thriller from suspense-writing persona of Ruth Rendell.

IMPERFECT STRANGERS
by Stuart Woods (HarperCollins, 1995, paperback)

Two strangers meet on a flight from London to New York. Both are successful businessmen. Both have troublesome wives. By the time the plane is ready to land, they have come to an understanding. "You and I are contemplating each committing a murder on a stranger. Do you think you can actually do that?" the one asks. "All I have to do is pretend she's my wife," the other answers. A stylish, chilling update of the famous Hitchcock film, *Strangers on a Train*.

PANAMA
by Eric Zencey (Berkley, 1997, paperback)

For seven years after his wife Clover killed herself, Henry Adams traveled the world, meditating on the riddles of human life. In this mystery novel, Zencey places Adams first in Panama, where he surveys the wreckage of France's canal and then on to Paris. In a capital of the Industrial Revolution, Adams meets a woman who wants to introduce him to the beauties of the Middle Ages. But when his new friend disappears, Adams adopts the role of detective. Zencey has succeeded in writing a very evocative historical novel and an intriguing mystery story.

NOTABLE
BIOGRAPHIES

EDISON: INVENTING THE CENTURY
by Neil Baldwin (Hyperion, 1996, paperback)

A survey of prominent Americans made during the Chicago Exposition of 1893 posed this question: "What American (now living) will be the most honored man in the 1990s?" The overwhelming choice was Thomas Edison. Baldwin's superb biography explores Edison's innumerable achievements (he held 1000 patents, including his invention of the light bulb, the phonograph and the motion picture). But Baldwin also reveals
Edison's eccentricities: he virtually exiled the children of his first marriage, had no use for the telephone and thought radio was a "craze." A balanced, intelligent biography of the great inventor.

LOUIS ARMSTRONG:
AN EXTRAVAGANT LIFE
by Laurence Bergreen (Broadway Books, 1997, hardcover)

This is the first biography I have written," Bergreen says, "in which my opinion of my subject kept improving as I worked." Bergreen's enthusiasm shows on every page of this lively life story of the jazz pioneer. Armstrong's own reminiscences—recorded on tape, in letters and in diaries—helped Bergreen create an especially vivid picture of life in New Orleans in the first years of this century. We see how Armstrong's genius enabled him to escape from crippling poverty, the extraordinary contributions he made to jazz and his unshakable optimism. This is certain to be the definitive life of an American musical legend.

FOUNDING FATHER:
REDISCOVERING GEORGE WASHINGTON
by Richard Brookhiser (The Free Press, 1996, hardcover)

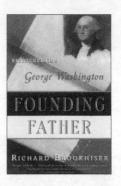

George Washington seems awfully dull when compared with the genius of Thomas Jefferson, or the quirky personality of Benjamin Franklin. So why did all the Founding Fathers consider him indispensable to the cause of American independence? To answer that question, Richard Brookhiser explores Washington's character, his accomplishments, even his physique—and finds a lot to admire. (For example, Jefferson talked about freeing his slaves; Washington actually freed his). If Washington has always seemed more an icon than a man, read *Founding Father*: it is a biographical tour de force.

THE INNER JEFFERSON:
PORTRAIT OF A GRIEVING OPTIMIST
by Andrew Burstein (University Press of Virginia, 1995, hardcover)

Throughout his public life, Thomas Jefferson strived to project a cool, rational image as the "Sage of Monticello." But privately, our most brilliant president was frequently tormented by strong emotions and less-than-generous impulses. Drawing upon Jefferson's voluminous correspondence, Burstein examines the great man's complex character. He offers fresh insights into Jefferson's friendship with Madison, Washington and Maria Cosway and explains why John Adams, Alexander Hamilton and Patrick Henry brought out the worst in Jefferson. A learned, subtle study of Jefferson's interior life.

THE KENNEDYS: AN AMERICAN DRAMA
by Peter Collier and David Horowitz (Warner Books, 1989, paperback)

Out of the mountain of books published about the Kennedys, this one stands out. Collier and Horowitz's solid scholarly approach enables them to offer a fair assessment of the clan, from Patrick and Bridget Murphy Kennedy, the founders of the dynasty in 1849, through the innumerable grandchildren of Joe and Rose Fitzgerald Kennedy.

LINCOLN
by David Herbert Donald (Simon & Schuster, 1996, paperback)

T his long-anticipated biography of America's greatest and most beloved president was worth waiting for. Pulitzer Prize winner David Herbert Donald demonstrates an uncanny ability to draw the facts out of a mountain of folklore while still conveying brilliantly Abraham Lincoln's remarkable character and intellect. He shows us a man of principle who was not adverse to being pragmatic, a man of ambition who wanted to be president, not a hero, yet grew to greatness when the future of the United States was at stake.

PASSIONATE SAGE: THE CHARACTER AND LEGACY OF JOHN ADAMS
by Joseph J. Ellis (Norton, 1994, paperback)

R arely does a biographer focus on the final years of his subject's life, yet Ellis has found that John Adams' last 25 years were worth a book all their own. Once he left public life, Adams was afraid his fellow Americans would forget everything he had done for them, from the stormy days before the Revolution through his years as President. So he reminded them, firing off angry letters to historians and newspaper editors who he thought had slighted his contributions. An engaging portrait of a cantankerous Founding Father.

DANIEL BOONE: THE LIFE AND LEGEND OF AN AMERICAN PIONEER
by John Mark Faragher (Henry Holt, 1993, paperback)

Absolutely the definitive biography of the famous 18th-century frontiersman. Among the surprises that Faragher unveils is Boone's sympathy for American Indians and their plight and the trouble he had during the Revolution convincing American officers that he was not a Tory.

WASHINGTON: THE INDISPENSABLE MAN
by James Thomas Flexner (Little, Brown, 1994, paperback)

Flexner's book is the best one-volume life of our first president. Here is the "kid" who escalated the French and Indian War by ambushing the French ambassador; the commander who took foolhardy risks in battle; the President who showed the kings of Europe that a republic could work; and the famous old man who wrote to his former sweetheart that "those happy moments, the happiest of my life," had been spent with her. A touching, insightful biography that makes Washington a living, breathing human being.

CROMWELL THE LORD PROTECTOR
by Antonia Fraser (Smithmark Publishers, 1996, hardcover)

A very detailed life of the Puritan who signed his king's death warrant and tried to eliminate monarchy in England forever.

BEARING THE CROSS: MARTIN LUTHER KING, JR. AND THE SOUTHERN CHRISTIAN LEADERSHIP CONFERENCE
by David J. Garrow (Vintage, 1988, paperback)

Late one night in 1956, Martin Luther King sat in his kitchen thinking about stepping back from the civil rights movement.

But then he heard a voice say, "Stand up for justice. Stand up for truth." From that moment, he was committed. Garrow has written a strong, personal, larger-than-life portrait of Dr. King, focusing on what gave him strength for his historic struggle.

RICHARD FEYNMAN: A LIFE IN SCIENCE
by John and Mary Gribbin (Dutton, 1997, hardcover)

Richard Feynman is remembered as one of the great minds of our century—and one of its greatest characters whose antics inspired his students and his fellow scientists. His gifts as a teacher became clear early: he taught his little sister math by letting her pull his hair every time she got a problem right. Later, Feynman went on to work at Los Alamos and won a Nobel Prize for his research in quantum electrodynamics. Feynman was a funny guy: you have to love a scientist who observes that while people are easily fooled, nature never is.

One by Feynman:

SIX EASY PIECES:
ESSENTIALS OF PHYSICS EXPLAINED BY ITS MOST BRILLIANT TEACHER
by Richard P. Feynman, Introduction by Paul Davies
(Addison Wesley Publishing, 1994, paperback).

Six of Feynman's most entertaining lectures explain the basics of physics—from the enormous significance of those tiny little atoms to Newton's law of gravitation and why it is wrong.

THE LAUREL AND THE IVY:
THE STORY OF CHARLES STEWART PARNELL AND IRISH NATIONALISM
by Robert Kee (Viking, 1998, paperback)

For a few short years in the 1880s, Ireland was tantalizingly close to home rule, thanks to an aristocratic Protestant landlord, Charles Stewart Parnell. But Parnell had a guilty secret— his affair with a married woman, Katharine O'Shea. When Mrs.

O'Shea's husband went public, the scandal destroyed Parnell's political power and divided the Irish people into two bitter camps. Kee tells the story well, recreating the tensions of the Parnell-O'Shea triangle and shrewdly analyzing Irish and British politics.

FIORELLO H. LA GUARDIA AND THE MAKING OF MODERN NEW YORK
by Thomas Kessner

La Guardia was not the man you think he was. His constituents may have called him "the Little Flower" but he was a Protestant. Sure he was the greatest supporter of the New Deal in New York, but he was still a Republican. He may have acted and talked like a quintessential New Yorker, but he grew up in Arizona. And yes, he was the city's first Italian mayor, but he was also half Jewish. As the director of The Fiorello H. La Guardia Archives at Columbia University, Kessner is the best man to tell the story of this dynamic and compassionate statesman. Worth searching for.

LINCOLN: AN ILLUSTRATED BIOGRAPHY
by Philip B. Kunhardt, Jr., Philip B. Kunhardt III and Peter W. Kunhardt (Knopf, 1992, paperback)

The homeliest face in the American pantheon belongs to Abraham Lincoln. This biography tells the great man's story through 900 photographs, many of them from private collections rarely made accessible to the public. Among these images are photos of the tumbledown log cabin where Lincoln was born, the small derringer Booth used to assassinate the President and an eerie photo of Lincoln's body lying in state.

W.E.B. DUBOIS 1868-1919
by David Levering Lewis (Henry Holt, 1998, hardcover)

In the first years of this century, when the Ku Klux Klan was widely admired and the film Birth of a Nation expressed the white mainstream view of American history, W.E.B. DuBois took the radical position that blacks should be allowed to compete equally with whites. Now Lewis tells the story of this brilliant activist who graduated from Harvard, founded the NAACP and presented a daring and militant agenda for black liberation.

A classic work by W.E.B. DuBois:

THE SOULS OF BLACK FOLK
(1903; Viking, 1996, paperback).

In 15 essays, DuBois reveals the lives of black sharecroppers, interprets the power of music in black church services and works out his own ambivalent feelings for Booker T. Washington.

MORNINGS ON HORSEBACK
by David McCullough (Simon & Schuster, 1981, hardcover)

From his stolid New York Dutch forebearers, Theodore Roosevelt got his sense of duty, of moral rectitude, of living a life active in the pursuit of good works. From his mother's family, those Georgia plantation aristocrats, the Bullochs, Teddy got his impulsive nature, his love for poetry, his romantic attachment to heroic exploits and gallant gestures. In this dazzling account of T.R.'s early years, David McCullough, our finest narrative historian, explores the influences that made Roosevelt one of the most remarkable men ever to sit in the White House.

TRUMAN
by David McCullough (Touchstone Books, 1993, paperback)

Many of us do not remember Harry Truman. Now, thanks to David McCullough, no one will ever forget him. Truman was the man who dropped the bomb on Hiroshima and Nagasaki. He was responsible for the Marshall Plan, NATO and the near-miraculous Berlin Airlift. He went toe-to-toe with Stalin, recognized Israel, desegregated the armed forces and sent the first ever civil rights message to Congress. (Not bad for a Missouri farm boy.) It took McCullough more than 10 years to write this highly documented, beautifully written life of Truman. Don't miss it.

ANCESTRAL PASSIONS:
THE LEAKEY FAMILY AND THE QUEST FOR HUMANKIND'S BEGINNINGS
by Virginia Morell.(Simon & Schuster, 1995, hardcover)

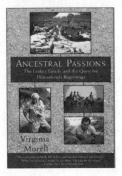

Between Louis and Mary Leakey's astonishing discoveries in Olduvai Gorge and their son Richard's discovery of the Turkana Boy, it is no exaggeration to call them the First Family of Paleoanthropology. In Morell's multi-generational biography, we get the first complete warts-and-all history of the Leakeys. Louis, the shameless self-promoter. Mary, a better scientist than her husband. And Richard—according to Morell—slandered by his arch-rival, Donald Johanson, the paleoanthropologist who discovered the "Lucy" fossils. Worth searching for.

ADMIRAL OF THE OCEAN SEA
by Samuel Eliot Morison (M.J.F. Books, 1997, hardcover)

It stands to reason that one of the greatest naval historians would produce a never-to-be-equaled biography of Columbus. Morison focuses his biography on three aspects of Columbus' life: "what he did, where he went and what sort of seaman he was."

GLENN GOULD:
THE ECSTASY AND TRAGEDY OF GENIUS
by Peter F. Ostwald (Norton, 1997, hardcover)

Peter F. Ostwald's book is more a reminiscence of his 20-year-long friendship with Glenn Gould than an analysis of the great pianist's life. Gould, in spite of his virtuosity, was a deeply troubled man who felt uncomfortable perfoming in public and generally shunned human contact. As Gould's friend, a psychiatrist and the founder of the Health Program for Performing Artists, Ostwald is in an enviable position to describe how eccentricity—even madness—and genius were inextricably intertwined in Gould.

In Gould's Own Words:

CONVERSATIONS WITH GLENN GOULD
by Jonathan Cott (A Common Reader Edition, 1997, hardcover)

Cott's conversations with Gould about Bach, Beethoven, the Beatles, Barbra Streisand, solitude, eccentricty and more (originally published in the 1970s in *Rolling Stone*) are collected here in a handsome volume which features many black and white photographs of Gould.

MOZART: A LIFE
by Maynard Solomon (HarperPerennial, 1996, paperback)

Maynard Solomon is the ideal man to tell Mozart's story: He is an award-winning biographer and a distinguished musicologist who can explain Mozart's sublime music in terms lay people understand. Here is Mozart the child prodigy, who played at virtually every royal court in Europe; the lover, who wrote his first sweetheart the infamous ca-ca letters; and the neurotic son, who craved his father's approval while he struggled fiercely to escape the old man's control. This is a vivid biography that reveals Mozart's work habits, captures the gaiety of 18th-century Vienna, but best of all, enchants us with the story of his music.

JOHANNES BRAHMS: A BIOGRAPHY
by Jan Swafford (Knopf, 1997, hardcover)

Johannes Brahms hated being hailed as the heir of Beethoven (he was afraid he could never live up to the title). He took rooms in cheap boarding houses even at the height of his wealth (he dreaded falling into poverty). He also tried to keep himself above ordinary human concerns so he could devote his energies to composition (which did not come easy to him). Convinced that "his life must not sully his music," Brahms destroyed as many private documents about himself as he could get his hands on. Nonetheless, biographer Jan Swafford has tracked down enough surviving material to give us a lively portrait of the artist.

PAUL GAUGUIN: A COMPLETE LIFE
by David Sweetman (Simon & Schuster, 1996, hardcover)

David Sweetman's new biography of Gauguin shatters a number of myths about the artist. Far from a conventional bourgeois businessman, Gauguin was the grandson of one of France's first feminists and had an unconventional childhood (including six years living in Peru). Furthermore, he did not desert his wife: he and Mette-Sophie—a mannish, cigar-smoking woman—had separated before he left for Tahiti. And finally, Sweetman's study of Gauguin's paintings has found not just Polynesian myths, but also motifs from pre-Columbian and Christian mythologies. A very well-written, scrupulously researched biography.

NOTORIOUS

AGRIPPINA: SEX, POWER AND POLITICS IN THE EARLY EMPIRE
by Anthony A. Barrett (Yale University Press, 1996, hardcover)

She was Caligula's sister and lover; the emperor Claudius' niece, wife and murderer; and Nero's mother and lover and victim. Tacitus portrayed her as one of the greatest villains in Roman history, a sluttish woman who left a trail of corpses behind her. And when she got to be too much to handle, Nero tried to kill by luring her onto a "trick" ship rigged to sink. Could all this be true? Could any of this be true? Historian Anthony Barrett searches the ancient sources and offers the most evenhanded biography ever of notorious Agrippina.

......

CALIGULA: THE CORRUPTION OF POWER
by Anthony A. Barrett (Yale University Press, 1990, hardcover)

Barrett is the first modern scholar in more than half a century to reassess the life of Rome's most notorious emperor. Was Caligula mad? Did he make his favorite horse a senator? Did he sleep with his sisters? Barrett studies the surviving evidence closely to determine the true character of the man. Worth searching for.

......

CAPONE: THE MAN AND HIS ERA
by Laurence Bergreen (Touchstone Books, 1996, paperback)

When in 1930 the students of Chicago's Medill School of Journalism named the top ten "outstanding personages of the world," their list included Gandhi, Albert Einstein, Henry Ford and Al Capone. Despite of his brutality, Capone was a celebrity. With energy and style, Bergreen captures the fast pace of the 1920s, explains how a mobster could become a hero and debunks the myth that Eliot Ness brought down Capone.

....

THE MAN IN THE MIRROR:
A LIFE OF BENEDICT ARNOLD
by Clare Brandt

E arly on in the American Revolution, Benedict Arnold established himself as a patriot, a hero and a skilled commander— so much so that Washington gave him the command of West Point. So why did he turn traitor? Brandt's biography is the best to date. She probes Arnold's character, his psyche and his relationship with his 19-year-old wife Peggy Shippen to discover the motives that led a great American to betray his country. Worth searching for.

....

ALL GOD'S CHILDREN:
THE BOSKET FAMILY AND THE AMERICAN
TRADITION OF VIOLENCE
by Fox Butterfield (Knopf, 1995, paperback)

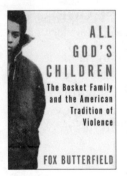

ALL
GOD'S
CHILDREN
The Bosket Family
and the American
Tradition of
Violence

FOX BUTTERFIELD

T he past is not dead," William Faulkner once wrote. "It is not even past." This statement seems especially true for the Boskets, a family of legendary bad men sprung from an especially violent corner of the South. Butterfield, a New York Times reporter, began covering the case of murderer Willie Bosket, but soon found himself reading documents from 18th-century Edgefield, South Carolina, the most murderous spot in colonial America and the ancestral home of the Boskets. Reading 250 years of criminal activity is at once ghoulish and fascinating. This book is bound to be a classic study of violence in America.

....

THE POLITICS OF RAGE:
GEORGE WALLACE AND THE TRANSFORMATION
OF AMERICAN POLITICS
by Dan T. Carter (Simon & Schuster, 1995, hardcover)

Carter calls George Wallace of Alabama "the most influential loser in twentieth-century American politics." He shows us a wily, ambitious, charismatic man who was willing to do anything—even exploit racial hatred—to hold on to political power. The chapters on Wallace's willing collaboration with the Klan's terrorism campaign in 1960s Alabama are especially unnerving. And Carter argues that Wallace laid the foundation for the suspicion of the federal government that flourishes today.

PLOTTING HITLER'S DEATH: THE GERMAN
RESISTANCE TO HITLER, 1933-1945
by Joachim Fest (Henry Holt, 1996, hardcover)

By 1944, it had become obvious that if the Nazi regime was to be stopped, Hitler had to die—and only insiders would be able to carry out the assassination. Joachim Fest, best known for his biography of Adolf Hitler, focuses on Claus von Stauffenberg, Carl Goerdeler, Julius Leber and their military and civilian fellow conspirators. They were rank amateurs and their non-stop bungling—confidential papers left on trains, incriminating conversations conducted over open phone lines—made it difficult even for the Gestapo to take them seriously. Fest tells their story as if it were a thriller.

THE KINGFISH AND HIS REALM:
THE LIFE AND TIMES OF HUEY LONG
by William Ivy Hair
(Louisiana State University Press, 1991, paperback)

The author takes a hard look at Huey Long, the flamboyant "dictator of Louisiana" in the 1930s and exposes the ruthless quest for power he concealed behind his charisma.

MY FIVE CAMBRIDGE FRIENDS:
BURGESS, MACLEAN, PHILBY, BLUNT AND CAIRNCROSS-BY THEIR KGB CONTROLLER
by Yuri Modin (Farrar Straus & Giroux, 1995, hardcover)

The amount of intelligence information Guy Burgess, Donald MacLean, Kim Philby, Anthony Blunt and John Cairncross passed to the Soviets was astounding. Between 1944 and 1947, it was Yuri Modin who translated, assessed and passed their material along to Moscow. Later, Modin was their KGB controller in London. Where others have caricatured these five notorious spies as drunks and lechers, Modin accentuates their engaging personalities and keen intelligence—the qualities which won the confidence of their colleagues and made them such successful operatives.

RASPUTIN: THE SAINT WHO SINNED
by Brian Moynahan (Random House, 1997, hardcover)

In long-suppressed Russian documents, including confidential police reports, Moynahan has found a Rasputin that is beyond the sordid myths. Moynahan details Rasputin's youthful religious and sexual excesses. He follows Rasputin to St. Petersburg where he became the pet holy man of the aristocracy. And he studies in detail how Rasputin's fateful encounter with the Romanovs brought about the downfall of tsarist Russia. The original documents give us what we have never had before—candid portraits of Rasputin and his circle.

ANATOMY OF THE NUREMBERG TRIALS
by Telford Taylor (Little, Brown, 1993, paperback)

As the Allies' chief prosecutor at Nuremberg, no one is better qualified to tell the inside story of the prosecution of Nazi war criminals than Telford Taylor. His gripping narrative reveals the conflicts among the Allies themselves as they try to define "war crimes," the occasional blunders of the prosecution, the behind-the-scenes comments of the judges and Taylor's own impressions of the Nazi defendants.

THE PRIVATE LIFE OF CHAIRMAN MAO
by Dr. Li Zhisui with Anne F. Thurston
(Random House, 1996, paperback)

For 22 years, Dr. Li had only one patient, a man who would not wash or brush his teeth, was hopelessly addicted to sleeping pills and cigarettes and believed fervently that frequent sexual intercourse with young women would prolong his life. Dr. Li's patient was Mao Tse-tung. In his memoir, Dr. Li reveals absorbing bits of history we never knew—from the virtuoso performance the deathly ill Mao staged for Richard Nixon to the royalties from all those little red books that made the Chairman a millionaire.

PAGE-TURNERS

THE SOUVENIR
by *Patricia Carlon* (Soho Press, 1996, paperback)

Four years before this story begins, two teenagers, Sandra and Peta, ran away from home together. But their hitchhiking adventure ended badly when a young man named Burton tried to settle an argument between the two girls: Burton wound up stabbed to death. The girls had unshakable alibis and the cops had no evidence to link them to the crime. Now Burton's sister, Marion, has hired Jefferson Shields, a private investigator, to try to settle the case. Carlton moves skillfully between the past and the present, assembling clues, revealing secrets, building a case. Best scene: Shields' face-to-face confrontation with Sandra and Peta. A tight, tense thriller that will keep you reading far into the night.

THE LOST WORLD
by *Michael Crichton* (Ballantine, 1997, paperback)

Remember *Jurassic Park*? Well the raptors and T-Rexes are back in this spine-tingling sequel. This time the hero is Ian Malcolm, the mathematician with attitude. It seems InGen, the genetics firm that engineered the Jurassic Park dinosaurs, had a second island as a breeding ground for the creatures that would be shown in the park. Malcolm, a beautiful scientist named Sarah, a technical whiz named Eddie and two smart stowaway kids head off for this new island and, of course, all hell breaks loose. Face it, once you start reading, it's going to be impossible to put this book down.

A SEASON IN PURGATORY
by Dominick Dunne (Bantam, 1994, paperback)

Constant Bradley, a handsome Congressman from a wealthy and powerful Irish Catholic family in New England, is on trial for a murder that occurred 20 years before. It seems that 15-year-old Winifred Utley, daughter of the Bradleys' neighbor, was beaten to death with a baseball bat after a country club dance. The man pointing the accusing finger is Constant's best friend from prep school, Harrison Burns. The Bradleys are a big family, but there are plenty of skeletons and peccadilloes to go around. And it turns out that Harrison Burns has one or two things to complicate his past as well.

THE TWO MRS. GRENVILLES
by Dominick Dunne (Bantam, 1994, paperback)

Money, scandal and venom are Dominick Dunne's specialty and he's at his best in *The Two Mrs. Grenvilles*. Wealthy socialite Alice Grenville is appalled when her only son marries a second-rate actress but accepts the gold digger into the family rather than lose her boy. When the actress kills her husband, Alice covers for her daughter-in-law to avoid a scandal. Now two women who loathe each other are bound together for life.

PLAYLAND
by John Gregory Dunne (Random House, 1994, paperback)

Blue Taylor, a child star of the 1940s, won an Oscar at age 10. She was the only survivor in the plane crash that killed Carole Lombard. And then she disappeared, emerging 45 years and 11 husbands later as a bag lady in Detroit. To unravel the mysteries that still cling to Blue, the screenwriter who narrates this novel tracks down a oddball bunch of the faded star's friends. A hit man. A mogul. An ex-Commie homosexual who named names to the House Un-American Activities Community. Dunne carries off the story with his usual wry wit, high style and wonderful ear for dialogue.

More by Dunne:

TRUE CONFESSIONS
(Signet, 1977, paperback).

Two Irish brothers, one an up-and-coming monsignor, the other a going-nowhere police detective, are linked by the S&M murder of a porn star. Worth searching for.

A DANGEROUS FORTUNE
by Ken Follett (Delacorte, 1993, paperback)

In 1866, at an exclusive boys school, one of the students drowns. Three of his friends were present at the time of the tragedy: the aggressive Hugh Pilaster; his already depraved older cousin Edward, heir to the family fortune; and Micky Miranda, the good-looking son of a tyrannical South American landowner. Over the course of three decades, the lies and betrayals the boys launched back on the day of the drowning spin out of control, pulling more and more people into their vortex. A mesmerizing plot and solid characterizations make this thriller a stand-out.

More by Follett:

NIGHT OVER WATER
(NAL-Dutton, 1992, paperback).

The cast's the thing in this novel set aboard a deluxe seaplane about the time of World War II. On board are a Nazi sympathizer and his family, a Jewish physicist, a Hollywood star, a jewel thief, a Russian princess and a bored housewife and her lover. What they all don't know is the pilot is going to sabotage the flight.

BEHIND THE LINES
by W.E.B. Griffin (Jove Publications, 1996, paperback)

Griffin writes about the U.S. Marine Corps during its glory days in World War II. This time out, a radio message is received from one Wendell Fertig, a self-proclaimed general who claims to be leading a guerrilla movement against the Japanese in the Philippine islands. Once the transmission is verified, a team of Marines is sent in to supply the insurgents, evacuate any wounded and evaluate Fertig's leadership capabilities. If you like interesting characters, tough-talking dialogue and lots of action, you'll love this and other Griffin's novels.

THE LONG WALK
by Slavomir Rawicz (1956; Lyons & Burford, 1989, paperback)

On Easter Sunday, 1941, 26-year-old Slavomir Rawicz and six companions—one an American-escaped from a Soviet prison camp in Siberia and fled south toward British India and freedom. For the next year, they walked: through Siberia, across the Gobi Desert, through the Himalayas. They had no regular supply of food and water. Their only tools were an ax-head and a homemade knife. They had no medicines, no map, not even a compass. It's an incredible story and Rawicz's simple, direct, vivid prose makes you feel like you are enduring it all with them. A true masterpiece.

THE SEVENTH SCROLL
by Wilbur Smith (St. Martin's Press, 1995, paperback)

An ancient papyrus bears the location of the lost tomb of a Pharaoh, its fabulous treasures still intact. Searching the highlands of Ethiopia for the tomb is a beautiful Egyptologist, Royan Al Simma and an English adventurer, Nicholas Quentin-Harper. It's bad enough that their way to the tomb is beset by ancient traps designed to eliminate grave robbers. But then Royan and Nicholas notice that someone is following them.

JURY DUTY
by Laura Van Wormer (Crown, 1996, paperback)

The author's own experiences as a sequestered juror in a Manhattan murder trial were the inspiration for this lively, witty page-turner. Hanging out in the jury room, Libby Winslow, a freshman juror, is first attracted to fellow juror Alex, a ruggedly handsome renovation contractor. But there's something about the man that gives Libby bad vibes. Then she finds herself drawn to William, a quiet investment banker. The development of Libby and William's relationship parallels the evolution of the trial. The story has an exciting finish during the jury's final deliberations.

WHAT MATTERS MOST
by Cynthia Victor (NAL Dutton, 1996, paperback)

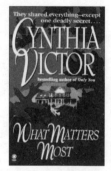

There are lots of romance authors out there, but when it comes to writing stories with carefully crafted plot lines, discriminating readers turn to Cynthia Victor. *What Matters Most* focuses on a woman with an exciting career as a New York designer. She's successful, self-sufficient, but she's alone. When her best friend and her friend's husband are mysteriously murdered, this independent career woman discovers that she has been named guardian of their children. Suddenly she's a "mom" with two young children to raise and a house in the suburbs to run. Just as challenging as these lifestyle changes is her determination to solve the murder.

JUBILEE
by Margaret Walker (Bantam, 1991, paperback)

Margaret Walker says she heard these stories from her great-grandmother. You might think of *Jubilee* as *Gone With the Wind* told from a slave woman's point of view. Like Margaret Mitchell's more famous epic, this novel stretches from Georgia's ante-bellum years through the Civil War and into Reconstruction. The heroine is Vyry, who grows up a slave on her white father's plantation. The story is a real page-turner: a great love story, an exciting escape attempt, Sherman's March to the Sea, Emancipation and the struggle to begin a new life without being lynched by the Klan. Enhancing this novel further is Walker's solid command of the history of the South and of slavery.

PERSONAL
FINANCE

BUFFETTOLOGY:
THE PREVIOUSLY UNEXPLAINED TECHNIQUES
THAT HAVE MADE WARREN BUFFETT
AMERICA'S MOST FAMOUS INVESTOR
by Mary Buffett and David Clark (Scribner's, 1997, paperback)

Mary Buffett was married to Warren Buffett's son. David Clark is a portfolio analyst and a friend of the Buffett family for more than 30 years. Using their insider's knowledge, they give you a peek inside one of this century's greatest investment minds. You'll get all of the billionaire investor's strategies (including how to recognize a company that has what Buffett calls a "consumer monopoly"). Plus, you get a never-before-published list of 54 companies that Buffett himself has invested in and the mathematical formulas he uses to determine if the price is right to buy a company or stock.

THE WARREN BUFFETT WAY:
INVESTMENT STRATEGIES OF THE WORLD'S
GREATEST INVESTOR
by Robert G. Hagstrom, Jr.
(John Wiley & Sons, 1995, paperback)

In case you didn't know, Warren Buffett is worth $10 billion. And he made it all by buying stocks in companies that meet three criteria:

• its profits are at least $10 million after taxes.
• it offers good returns on equity without using much debt.
• you can understand what the company makes

(if the product is too complicated for you to figure out, don't get involved with it).

Sound too simple? Bear in mind that nobody in America is a better stockpicker than Warren Buffett.

INVESTOR'S BUSINESS DAILY GUIDE TO THE MARKETS
(John Wiley & Sons, 1996, hardcover)

Investor's Business Daily is the fastest growing, most widely read investment newspaper in the country—so who better to explain to you the entire investment and financial marketplace? You'll learn how to pick winning stocks and avoid losers; how to pick the right mutual fund; where bonds fit in your portfolio; and how to understand—and profit from—the volatile futures market. Here at last is a comprehensive, authoritative, easy-to-understand, handbook you can use today to build a profitable portfolio.

MONEY TROUBLES:
LEGAL STRATEGIES TO COPE WITH YOUR DEBTS, 3RD EDITION
by Robin Leonard (Nolo Press/Berkley, 1995, paperback)

J ust about everybody you know is weighed down by debt. But if you are feeling especially burdened, the money and credit advisor on Good Morning America and CNN can help you. Attorney Robin Leonard will show you how to prioritize your debts, cut back on expenses, correct and rebuild your credit and learn your rights so you can negotiate with creditors from a position of strength. Whether you're struggling with endless credit card debt, behind on your student loans, or want to challenge wage attachments, *Money Troubles* can help you make a fresh financial start.

KIPLINGER'S INVEST YOUR WAY TO WEALTH

by Theodore J. Miller (Kiplinger Books, 1996, hardcover)

The editor of the widely respected *Kiplinger's Personal Finance Magazine* offers commonsense advice on how you can build your personal fortune. If you're picking stocks, look for companies that have had five years' worth of good earnings and reinvested at least 35% of their profits. If you're a skittish investor, Miller suggests money-market funds: they pay more than savings accounts and are virtually as safe. From investment basics to the ins and outs of pumping up your portfolio, this is an invaluable first step on the road to financial success.

THE WALL STREET JOURNAL LIFETIME GUIDE TO MONEY

by The Personal Finance Staff of The Wall Street Journal, Edited by C. Frederic Wiegold, Personal Finance Editor (Hyperion, 1997, hardcover)

For the first time ever, the editors of *The Wall Street Journal* have written a guide that gives you everything you need to know about managing your finances. This book highlights financial issues for three age groups: 20s-30s, 40s-50s, 60s and over. You'll get solid advice on how to build a portfolio, choose the right kinds of insurance, maximize your company's retirement benefits, manage your debts, buy a house, survive unemployment, even start your own business.

POETS & POETRY

ANTS ON THE MELON:
A COLLECTION OF POEMS
by Virginia Hamilton Adair (Random House, 1996, paperback)

Virginia Hamilton Adair has written poetry for most of this century (she's 85 years old). But she didn't publish anything until 1996. So *Ants on the Melon* isn't just another slender volume of verse; it's the distillation of a lifetime of work. "Surfers" reflects on the transience of youth. The book's title poem is an offbeat commentary on overpopulation. And "Peeling an Orange" recalls a private moment with a lover: "Your bare arm hard, furry and warm on my belly/Your fingers pry the skin of a navel orange/ Releasing tiny explosions of spicy oil." Little wonder Galway Kinnell has said Virginia Hamilton Adair has "arrived in our world like a comet."

JUST GIVE ME A COOL DRINK OF
WATER 'FORE I DIIIE
by Maya Angelou (Random House, 1997, hardcover)

Angelou's first collection of poems ranges from the personal and the tender to the strident and militant.

THE COMPLETE POEMS: 1927-1979
by Elizabeth Bishop (Farrar Straus Giroux, 1984, paperback)

I am in need of music that would flow
Over my fretful, feeling finger-tips,
Over my bitter-tainted, trembling lips,
With melody, deep, clear and liquid-slow.

here is remarkable intimacy in the poetry of Elizabeth Bishop. Her own gift for casting a fresh light on the ordinary encourages us to see the world as ever new. This book represents a lifetime of brilliant work from one of the greatest poets of the 20th century.

....

SO FORTH
by Joseph Brodsky (Farrar, Straus and Giroux, 1996, paperback)

As I lay dying
here, I'm eyeing
stars. Here's Venus;
no one between us.

So Forth is the final book of verse by Joseph Brodsky, the Russian exile who won the Nobel Prize for Literature and served as Poet Laureate of the United States. Fate is a common theme of Brodsky poems and he approaches the subject with humor, or resignation, or anxiety, as the mood strikes him. But Brodsky was also a great traveler and you'll find striking vignettes of his visits to Venice, Ischia, Lisbon, even the dump on Nantucket.

....

C.P. CAVAFY COLLECTED POEMS
Translated by Edmund Keely & Philip Sherrard, Edited by George Savidis (Aristide D. Caratzas Publisher, 1988, paperback)

May there be many summer mornings when,
with what pleasure, what joy,
you enter harbors you're seeing for the first time.-Ithaka

When Cavafy's "Ithaka" was read at Jacqueline Kennedy Onassis' funeral in 1994, it had a tremendous emotional impact on the American public. Here, then, is the first complete, bilingual edition of Cavafy's poetry, filled with his profound love for Greek culture, his sharp/funny cynical outlook and his frank eroticism.

....

THE COMPLETE POEMS OF EMILY DICKINSON
Edited by Thomas H. Johnson
(Little, Brown, 1960, paperback)

What is-"Paradise"-
Who live there-
Are they "Farmers"-
Do they "hoe"-
Do they know that this is "Amherst"-
And that I-am coming-too-

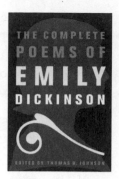

I s there any poetry lover who does not love Emily Dickinson? Witty, innovative, passionate, she is one of the geniuses of American literature. If you haven't read her in a while, it's time to make her acquaintance once again.

MORNINGS LIKE THIS: FOUND POEMS
by Annie Dillard (HarperCollins, 1995, paperback)

D illard has taken a unique approach in this book. She has crafted wonderful poems, brimming with remarkable images from 19th-century books on navigation, 20th-century science texts, even from the letters of Vincent Van Gogh. These poems are all "objets trouvés," she says, "the literary equivalents of Warhol's Campbell's soup cans and Duchamp's bicycle." This is certain to be one of the most interesting little volumes of verse you've ever seen.

COLLECTED POEMS: 1909-1962
by Thomas Stearns Eliot
(Harcourt Brace, 1963, paperback)

T .S. Eliot is foremost among the many great poets of the 20th century. Intellectual, witty, often mystical, Eliot developed a style that was markedly different from traditional Victorian and Romantic verse. This collection ranges from his challenging masterwork, *The Waste Land*, to *Old Possum's Book of Practical Cats*, the playful poems that inspired a Broadway musical. For many readers, his best poems are the *Four Quartets*-also included here. If you've never read Eliot, this collection is an excellent way to make his acquaintance.

THE WASTE LAND
by T.S. Eliot (1922; Harcourt Brace, 1997, paperback)

Edmund Wilson said Eliot's epic "enchanted and devastated a generation." That may be hyperbole, but certainly no serious reader (or writer) of modern literature has ever been able to ignore *The Waste Land*. Eliot weaves together images from Shakespeare, Dante, the Bible, the Grail legend and the Upanishads with snatches of overheard conversations as he portrays European society in the aftermath of World War I as a spiritual and cultural desert. Beneath all the dark imagery there is an undercurrent of hope and the promise of redemption.

SEEING THINGS
by Seamus Heaney (Noonday Books, 1993, paperback)

His hands were warm and small and knowledgeable.
When I saw them again last night, they were two ferrets,
Playing all by themselves in a moonlit field.

One of the best contemporary Irish poets, Heaney takes memorable moments and changes them into something otherworldly.

GERARD MANLEY HOPKINS
Edited by Catherine Phillips
(Oxford University Press, 1989, paperback)

The world is charged with the grandeur of God.
It will flame out like shining from shook foil.

One of the most innovative poets of the 19th century, Hopkins' verse is still a powerful influence on contemporary poets.

You'll enjoy his peculiar rhythms and striking imagery. In fact, Hopkins' poems are always filled with surprises. This Oxford Authors edition collects all his poetry, including his handful of verses in Latin.

JOHN KEATS
Edited by Elizabeth Cook
(Oxford University Press, 1990, hardcover)

Ay, in the very temple of Delight
Veil'd Melancholy has her sovran shrine,
though seen of none save him whose strenuous tongue
Can burst Joy's grape against his palate fine.

The greatest loss to English poetry was the death of Keats at age 26. Sensuous, sometimes humorous, always richly atmospheric, Keats' poems are the pride of the Romantic Age. This Oxford Authors edition collects all his poetry and prose.

THE WOMEN OF PLUMS,
by Dolores Kendrick
(Phillips Exeter Academy Press, 1990, paperback)

Look lively, child. We be sold,
but we ain't bought.

Kendrick has done extensive research to create a modern poetic interpretation of the lives of black women enslaved in America. Each poem addresses a different facet of slavery—enduring the "Middle Passage" from Africa, attempting to escape, secret efforts to learn to read (which the voice of the poem calls a "baptism of words"). The poem quoted above represents an auction in which a mother and daughter are relieved because they have been purchased together. You'll be amazed by Kendrick's mastery as she creates dozens of distinctive voices.

HERO AND LEANDER,
by Christopher Marlowe (1593; A M S Press, 1997, hardcover)

An erotic masterpiece. Every night, the handsome Leander swims the Hellespont to be with his beloved Hero. But problems arise when Neptune takes a shine to Leander. A beautiful, sensual narrative poem.

A SCATTERING OF SALTS
by James Merrill (Knopf, 1996, paperback)

Eyes shut in all but visionary
Consent, he lets the words reorganize
Everything he lives for, until it all fits
Or until he forgets them.

These poignant lines could be Merrill's epitaph: he died in 1994. In this final book of poems, he returns to two forms that made his career—the short lyric and the dramatic narrative poem. And as always, he keeps control over the intense emotion of his poems through intricate structure and rare rhyme schemes.

SELECTED POEMS
W.S. Merwin

Your absence has gone through me
Like thread through a needle.
Everything I do is stitched with its color.

Intense, vivid, a little existential from time to time, Merwin is one the best poets in America. This collection draws upon his finest work over a 30-year period. Worth searching for.

MOST ANCIENT OF ALL SPLENDORS
by Johann Moser (Sophia Institute Press, 1989, hardcover)

Aged rafters bend and sigh
Beneath the frosty hush of winter.

U nlike some modern poets who prefer to write obscure, self-referential verse, Moser writes in concrete images about icy blue New Hampshire lakes, Mozart and old-fashioned spiritual values. Give him a try.

SELECTED POEMS OF OGDEN NASH:
808 LIGHT-HEARTED VERSES
Introduction by Archibald MacLeish
(Black Dog & Leventhal, 1995, hardcover)

Behold the hippopotamus
we laugh at how he looks to us,
And yet in moments dank and grim
I wonder how we look to him.

H aving tried his hand at teaching, selling bonds and writing advertising copy, Ogden Nash took up poetry. In 1931 *The New Yorker* hired him and Nash was on his way to becoming the best-loved poet-humorist in America. These 808 poems are fun reading for adults, who will enjoy his off-beat rhymes and they are excellent way to introduce kids to poetry.

TOUCHSTONES:
AMERICAN POETS ON A FAVORITE POEM
Edited by Robert Pack and Jay Parini
(Middlebury College Press, 1996, paperback)

M axine Kumin tells of reciting A.E. Housman's "A Shropshire Lad" to herself while she endured an MRI scan. Richard Wilbur pulls out all the stops to analyze Tennyson's "Ulysses." Julia Alvarez writes a warm tribute to Elizabeth Bishop's mastery of the villanelle in "One Art." And Erica Jong admits that she can hear Shakespeare's private voice in his sonnets. In *Touchstones*, 59 American poets pick the poems that mean something special to them. It's an inspired idea and one which fulfills Matthew Arnold's exhortation "to have always in one's mind lines and expressions of the great masters... as a touchstone to other poetry."

THE MOON IS ALWAYS FEMALE
by Marge Piercy (Knopf, 1980, paperback)

"Why do you lie on the telephone, your voice fuzzy with the lint of guilt?" Marge Piercy is the queen of the memorable poetic one-liner. Read just one of her funny, beautiful, poignant poems and you'll be hooked.

THE FIGURED WHEEL:
NEW AND COLLECTED POEMS 1966-1996
by Robert Pinsky (Farrar, Starus and Giroux, 1996, paperback)

Under the ceiling of metal stamped like plaster
And below the ceiling fan, in the brown luster
Someone is reading, in the sleepy room
Alert, her damp cheek balanced on one palm.

Critics say that since the death of Robert Lowell, Robert Pinsky has been the most influential poet in America. His beautiful, intelligent poems have won him a devoted readership and the title Poet Laureate of the United States.

Pinsky's Dante:

THE INFERNO OF DANTE:
A NEW VERSE TRANSLATION
translated by Robert Pinsky
(c.1315; Farrar, Straus & Giroux, 1994, hardcover).

The 20th century's most powerful translation of the medieval masterpiece.

SELECTED POEMS OF ANNE SEXTON,

Edited with an Introduction by Diane Wood Middlebrook and Diana Hume George (Houghton Mifflin, 1988, paperback)

Wait Mister. Which way is home?
They turned the light out
and the dark is moving in the corner.
There are no sign posts in this room....

Before she committed suicide at age 45, Anne Sexton's poems were appearing in the most prestigious journals and she had won virtually every important prize awarded to American poets, including the Pulitzer. These 100 poems are her best work and serve as an excellent introduction to one of the most distinctive voices of American poetry.

SELECTED POEMS

by James Tate (Wesleyan University Press, 1991, paperback)

I am surrounded by the pieces of this huge
puzzle: here's a piece I call my wife and
here's an odd one I call convictions, here's
conventions, here's collisions, conflagrations . . .

Brainy, funny, humane and always delightful, James Tate is a poet other poets love to read. He makes you laugh even when he's writing about the absurdity of the human condition. This selection draws upon nine books of Tate's verse, representing 25 years of work and it won the Pulitzer Prize in 1992.

TUNES FOR BEARS TO DANCE TO

by Ronald Wallace

Funny title for a poetry collection. But then Ronald Wallace has a distinctively funny outlook that takes his poetry in all kinds of unexpected directions—the lunch line at McDonald's, a belly dancer in a nursing home. You'll like "Facts of Life," in which a six-year-old girl refuses to believe in penises and vaginas and is only content when her parents "try cabbages, storks... magic seeds, good fairies, god." Worth searching for.

NEW AND COLLECTED POEMS
by Richard Wilbur (Harvest Books, 1989, paperback)

Five soldiers fixed by Matthew Brady's eye
Stand in a land subdued beyond belief.
Belief might lend them life again. I try
Like orphaned Hamlet working up his grief
To see my spellbound fathers in these men.

Wilbur was named Poet Laureate of the United States in 1987. This collection spans four decades of his work, offering a superb sampling of the graceful, compassionate, humorous verses that make Wilbur such a joy to read.

PRIZE WINNERS

POSSESSION
by A.S. Byatt (Vintage, 1991, paperback)

England's Booker Prize went to *Possession*, a tour de force that transforms a scholarly paper chase into a completely absorbing mystery. In an abandoned wing of an old manor house Roland Mitchell, a starving graduate student and Dr. Maud Bailey, an aloof English professor, discover a treasury of manuscripts by Christabel LaMotte, a 19th-century poet. With careers and reputations hanging in the balance, the old adage "publish or perish" takes on a new meaning for Roland and Maud. By the way, the final scene in a graveyard in the middle of a hurricane is marvelous.

THE ADVENTURES OF AUGIE MARCH
by Saul Bellow (Penguin, 1985, paperback)

Bellow's first novel was extremely ambitious and extremely successful. His story of a young Jewish man who tries to create an exciting new life for himself on the streets of Chicago in the 1930s and '40s is a masterwork of strong characterizations.

BLACKWATER
by Kerstin Ekman, translated by Joan Tate
(Doubleday, 1996, paperback)

One night in midsummer, Annie Raft arrives in Blackwater, a remote Swedish village, where she expects to meet her boyfriend. He never shows. But the next morning, while out for a walk, Annie discovers the bodies of two murdered campers. The suspects include the village doctor who might have mistaken the campers for his wife and her lover. Or perhaps it is the odd Brandenberg clan who don't like strangers. 18 years will pass before the mystery is finally unraveled. In Sweden, Kerstin Ekman won several literary prizes for this wonderfully dark novel. It is her debut book in English.

A LESSON BEFORE DYING
by Ernest Gaines (Vintage Books, 1994, paperback)

In Louisiana's Cajun country in the late 1940s, a young black man has been sentenced to death for a murder he did not commit. To get him off, his attorney had argued that this client was more like a hog than a man and didn't know what he was doing. Now the condemned man's aunt goes to the local schoolteacher with a strange request: give her nephew an education before he dies. "I don't want them to kill no hog," she says. "I want a man to go that chair, on his own two feet." How Gaines managed to write such a poignant story without being cloying or manipulative is a marvel. It won him the National Book Critics Circle Award for fiction.

Gaines' Most Famous Novel (Before Oprah's Book Club):

THE AUTOBIOGRAPHY OF MISS JANE PITTMAN
(Bantam Books, 1989, paperback).

A grand saga of a black woman who lives through slavery, Jim Crow and segregation to take part in the Civil Rights movement.

JULY'S PEOPLE
by Nadine Gordimer (Penguin, 1982, paperback)

From the moment this book hit the bookstores, critics and readers alike acclaimed it as Nobel Prize-winning author, Nadine Gordimer's best. After a racial revolution in South Africa, a well-to-do white family is taken by their black servant, July, to his village in the bush for safety. You'll find that Gordimer is an intellectually honest author who can study the explosive issue of race relations in South Africa without ever settling for the easy, sentimental "black=good, white=bad" equation.

Also by Gordimer:

A GUEST OF HONOR
(Penguin, 1983, paperback).

A newly independent African nation tries to lift itself out of third-world status. A biting story of the tensions that often tear apart the postcolonial countries of Africa.

. . . .

SNOW FALLING ON CEDARS
by *David Guterson* (Vintage Contemporaries, 1995, paperback)

San Piedro Island off the coast of Washington is a little place of "five thousand damp souls." Many of the men on the island fought in World War II and some of those who did still carry physical and emotional scars. Even in 1954, the town isn't ready to let the war go. When a veteran is found mysteriously drowned, Kabuo Miyamoto, a first-generation Japanese American who fought for the U.S. against Japan, is charged with the murder. His trial becomes another round in the Anglos' quarrel with their Asian neighbors. A very impressive first novel that won the 1995 PEN/Faulkner Award.

. . . .

THE REMAINS OF THE DAY
by *Kazuo Ishiguro* (Vintage, 1990, paperback)

Anthony Hopkins and Emma Thompson notwithstanding, the movie version of this Booker Prize winner was...umm, shall we say...well, it was slow. The book, on the other hand, moves along at a brisk pace. On one level, this is a masterful comedy of manners about a cast-iron society and a poignant story of the seemingly perfect English butler. But Ishiguro's eye for the telling detail, the subtle undercurrent of sexual tension and his breathtaking gift for creating mood elevate The Remains of the Day to one of the finest novels of our time. Best scene: the tiger under the dining room table.

. . . .

TO KILL A MOCKINGBIRD
by Harper Lee (1960; Warner Books, 1988, paperback)

Lee won a Pulitzer prize for this poignant story of racial injustice viewed through the eyes of a six-year-old girl. In 1935, Jean Louise (Scout) Finch and her younger brother Jem are whiling away the summer in their sleepy Alabama town. But when their father, Atticus, agrees to defend a black man accused of raping a white woman, Scout and Jem learned some hard lessons about hatred. As powerful today as when it was first published.

. . . .

THE BEGINNING AND THE END
by Naguib Mahfouz (Doubleday, 1989, paperback)

Nobel Prize-winner Mahfouz is the premier writer of fiction in Egypt, perhaps in all the Middle Eastern and North African world. This novel is considered his finest work—a tale of a troubled Egyptian middle-class family trying to pretend that they are an ideal, cohesive family unit.

Also by Mahfouz:

WEDDING SONG
(Doubleday, 1989, paperback).

Actors in a play are stunned when a new script reveals that the playwright has murdered his wife.

. . . .

THE BUTCHER BOY
by Patrick McCabe (Doubleday, 1994, paperback)

When I was a lad twenty or thirty or forty years ago I lived in a small town where they were after me on account of what

I done on Mrs. Nugent." That's how Patrick McCabe begins his tale of a truly bad boy. The story of Francie Brady, a lovable little psychopath with a sharp tongue, a chip on his shoulder and mayhem on his mind, won Ireland's coveted Irish Times-Aer Lingus Prize.

ALL THE PRETTY HORSES
by Cormac McCarthy
(Vintage, 1993, paperback)

Two teenage boys ride down to Mexico for some adventure, but in the badlands across the Rio Grande, they find they must be men if they are to survive. McCarthy won the National Book Award for this harsh coming-of-age novel.

THE SAILOR WHO FELL FROM GRACE WITH THE SEA
by Yukio Mishima (1963; Vintage International, 1994, paperback)

A ship's officer falls in love with a woman and they begin a passionate affair. The woman has a son who belongs to a gang of degenerate boys who despise the sailor for what they believe to be unmanly weakness. So, the boys plan a suitable punishment. A chilling novel from the Nobel Prize winner.

More by Mishima:

PATRIOTISM
(1960; New Directions, 1995, paperback)

The sensuous tale of a beautiful young couple who make love for the last time and then commit suicide.

HOUSE MADE OF DAWN
by N. Scott Momaday (HarperPerennial, 1989, paperback)

With this book, Momaday became the first Native American novelist to win the Pulitzer Prize. Almost 30 years have passed since then, but this is still a powerful story. Abel, a part-Navajo World War II veteran, drifts through the Army, prison and menial jobs. Tired at last of the violence and humiliations of the white world, Abel goes home to cleanse himself in the purifying ritual of "the dawn race." There is real mythic power to this novel—don't miss it.

SONG OF SOLOMON
by Toni Morrison (Signet, 1993, paperback)

When Morrison won the Nobel Prize for Literature, this novel was cited. If you've never read Morrison before, begin with this lyrical novel of a prosperous black landlord who returns South to see if there is any truth to the near-legendary accounts of his family's origins. A novel that is part fantasy, part allegory and pure magic.

Also by Toni Morrison:

SULA
(Knopf, 1973, paperback).

A story of the ties that bind two women for 40 years and how they were severed.

BELOVED
(Knopf, 1987, paperback).

At the end of the Civil War, a runaway slave is haunted by the ghost of the daughter she killed to escape slave hunters. A miracle of the storyteller's art.

THE SEA, THE SEA
by Iris Murdoch (Penguin, 1980, paperback)

Murdoch won the 1978 Booker Prize for this novel about an English playwright who retreats to a house by the sea. He imagines a life of perfect peace and privacy, until a series of uncanny, perhaps supernatural, events overtake him.

More by Murdoch:

THE GREEN KNIGHT
(Penguin, 1993, paperback).

Medieval romances and the Arthurian legend inspired this unusual novel set in contemporary London where three lovely young sisters live happily in the enclosed world they've created in their mother's house. Disturbing their serenity are an angelically beautiful young man with a crippling wound that just won't heal; two stepbrothers divided by a fierce hatred; and a mysterious "murdered" man who refuses to remain dead.

THE ENGLISH PATIENT
by Michael Ondaatje (Vintage Books, 1993, paperback)

At the end of World War II, four survivors meet in an Italian villa: a Canadian nurse who has expended all her energy on nursing the damaged and the dying, a thief whose hands have been hopelessly maimed, an Indian sapper who searches compulsively for bombs and a mysterious, horribly burned English patient. Part romance, part mystery (the final revelation of the true identity of the patient is a shocker), part meditation on the horrors of war, *The English Patient* is a splendid achievement that won Ondaatje the Booker Prize.

Another Ondaatje Novel:

IN THE SKIN OF A LION
(Penguin, 1989, paperback).

Sitting in his car in the early hours of the morning, Patrick Lewis tells his girlfriend stories of actresses, millionaires, nuns and thieves—and how these characters have intersected with his own life.

DOCTOR ZHIVAGO
by Boris Pasternak
(1957; Pantheon, 1991, paperback)

This lush panoramic novel of Russia in the first three decades of our century is Pasternak's greatest achievement. Essentially, the novel is the love story of Yuri and Lara, but it also celebrates the joys of artistic expression and proclaims the integrity of the individual over the state. An absolute triumph that so offended the Soviet authorities, they forced Pasternak to decline the 1958 Nobel Prize for Literature.

THE SHIPPING NEWS
by E. Annie Proulx (Scribners, 1994, paperback)

When his adulteress wife meets an untimely but well-deserved end, Quoyle, a small-time newspaperman, withdraws with his two daughters and an aunt to the family home on the coast of Newfoundland. While writing the Shipping News column for the local paper, he runs up against a quirky cast of north country natives who help him exorcise his personal demons and see a future that holds the possibility of love without heartache. This comic and beautifully written tale of a life reclaimed won a 1994 Pulitzer Prize, the National Book Award for fiction and the Irish Times' International Fiction Prize!

JEAN-CHRISTOPHE
by Romain Rolland (Carroll & Graf, 1996, paperback)

Rolland won the Nobel Prize of 1915 for this epic novel. In the years before the first World War, Jean-Christophe leaves his home in the Rhineland and travels to Paris. In those years, the city is at its most exciting and there Jean-Christophe is swept up in a round of new friendships, new sexual experiences and new ideas—about art, politics, music, you name it. Rolland captures perfectly the fervor of a young man desperate to find something great to which he can dedicate his life. In many respects, this is a young person's book, but you may be surprised when the energy of the story suddenly grabs you and carries you along in its fast-moving current.

THE KILLER ANGELS
by Michael Shaara (Ballantine, 1993, paperback)

Shaara won the Pulitzer Prize for this griping recreation of the Battle of Gettysburg. Here is the one book that lets you experience the sheer terror and exhilaration of Pickett's Charge, makes you privy to the late-night councils of Lee and Longstreet and sets you down beside the men of North and South who fought like avenging angels to decide the fate of a nation.

THE STONE DIARIES
by Carol Shields (Viking, 1994, paperback)

Shields won the National Book Critics Circle Award for this unconventional chronicle of the 20th century. All the upheavals of an age are seen through the prism of a seemingly unexceptional woman—Daisy Goodwill Flett, who was born in 1905 and survives into the 1990s. While history must cling to the cold, bare facts, Shields goes deep into the interior life of her characters to gauge the impact of modern events on ordinary people. A rare and wonderful novel you won't want to miss.

ENEMIES: A LOVE STORY
by Isaac Bashevis Singer (1972; Farrar Straus Giroux, 1997, paperback)

Let's get the plot straight: a Jewish refugee from Poland believes his wife is dead and marries the Catholic peasant girl who saved him from the Nazis. They emigrate to New York, where he takes a mistress and when she becomes pregnant, he marries her too. Then his first wife (the one who's supposed to be dead) shows up." When I was a little boy," Nobel Prize-winner Isaac Bashevis Singer once said, "they called me a liar. But now that I am grown up, they call me a writer."

Also by Singer:

GIMPEL THE FOOL
(1957; Noonday Press, 1988, paperback).

A collection of tales set in the ghettos of Eastern Europe and populated by bizarre characters.

············

A THOUSAND ACRES
by Jane Smiley (Ivy, 1997, paperback)

Smiley won the Pulitzer Prize for this update of the King Lear legend. Larry Cook decides to turn over his prosperous, 1000-acre, debt-free farm to his three daughters. When the youngest tries to dissuade him, he cuts her off. When the remaining two sisters and their husbands begin a series of "improvements," the debts start to pile up. Then, Larry begins to act peculiar.

············

THE FIRST CIRCLE
by Aleksandr Solzhenitsyn (Northwestern University Press, 1997, paperback)

This is Solzhenitsyn's greatest novel. In Stalin's Soviet Union, if one had to be in prison, a sharashka was the best place to be. Here scientists and intellectuals continued to work in their particular fields, but solely for the regime. Nerzhin, a 31-year-old mathematician and a veteran of World War II, has been imprisoned for years and has virtually no hope of release. Rubin, a devout Communist, tries to stay loyal to the Party despite the injustices it has committed against him. Best scene: the prisoners put the medieval Russian hero Prince Igor on trial for crimes against the state.

Also by Solzhenitsyn:

ONE DAY IN THE LIFE OF IVAN DENISOVICH
(Noonday Books, 1984, paperback).

Drawing on his own experiences in a Soviet prison, Solzhenitsyn follows an innocent man's struggle for survival in a labor camp, from reveille to lights out.

THE GRAPES OF WRATH
by John Steinbeck (1939; Penguin, 1996, paperback)

When their farm is consumed by the Dust Bowl, the Joad family heads west to California, hoping to start a new life. Adversity, bigotry and exploitation dog them every step of the way. A novel that is by turns heartbreaking and uplifting, *The Grapes of Wrath* won Steinbeck the Pulitzer.

THE DIAMOND AGE
by Neal Stephenson (Bantam Books, 1996, paperback)

Neal Stephenson won the Hugo Award for Best Novel for this futuristic tale of a brilliant nanotechnologist who breaks a cardinal law of his tribe. By making an illicit copy of *A Young Lady's Illustrated Primer*, a work which encourages adolescent girls to think for themselves, John Hackworth has defied the Neo-Victorians, as the ruling class is known. It's a classic story of one man taking on an oppressive regime. Stephenson makes the science of nanotechnology comprehensible. But even if you aren't much interested in the techno-details, you'll enjoy the exciting, intricate plot and the interesting characters.

Another by Stephenson:

SNOW CRASH
(Bantam, 1992, paperback).

Hiro Protagonist is a pizza delivery boy in the real world. But in the computer-generated Metaverse he's a warrior prince. His mission: find and destroy a dark, enigmatic virtual villain before he launches the Infocalypse.

THE AGE OF INNOCENCE
by Edith Wharton (1920; The Library of America, 1985, hardcover)

Wharton's biting yet nostalgic tale of old New York pits conventional, upright Newland Archer and the bohemian Countess Olenska against the taboos of Manhattan society. This is Wharton's finest novel—a rare study of a long-vanished world—that won her the Pulitzer Prize.

REAL-LIFE DISASTERS

LET US NOW PRAISE FAMOUS MEN

by *James Agee, photographs by Walker Evans*
(1941; Houghton Mifflin, 1989, paperback)

Haunting photos—some of the finest ever taken—and impassioned text record the pain, humanity and terrible beauty of three sharecropper families in Alabama during the Depression.

RISING TIDE: THE GREAT MISSISSIPPI FLOOD OF 1927 AND HOW IT CHANGED AMERICA.

by *John M. Barry* (Simon & Schuster, 1997, hardcover)

Three million cubic feet of water per second surged down the Mississippi during the great flood of 1927. It took thousands of lives and left one million people (in a nation of 120 million) homeless. And its effects were felt throughout the country. The wretched treatment of black victims in refugee camps accelerated the great migration north. Disgust with Calvin Coolidge's inaction swept Herbert Hoover into the White House, Huey Long into the Louisiana governor's mansion and laid the groundwork for federal involvement in state affairs. *Rising Tide* is superb narrative history of a natural disaster that changed American politics and society.

THE GREAT CRASH OF 1929
by John Kenneth Galbraith (Houghton Mifflin, 1997, paperback)

The wild, desperate panic on the floor of the Stock Exchange was so awful that the visitors' gallery was closed so outsiders would not witness the fearful scenes below. How did it happen? How did America go from boom to bust overnight? America's most respected economist takes the U.S.'s biggest economic disaster and turns it into a great story.

TITANIC
by Colonel Archibald Gracie
(1913; Academy Chicago Publishers, 1996, paperback)

No novel or film can compare with a first-hand account of the Titanic disaster. Although he survived the tragedy, Colonel Gracie's freezing night in an open boat damaged his health permanently. He barely got this story down on paper before he died, just a year after the ship sank.

Another perspective:

EVERY MAN FOR HIMSELF
by Beryl Bainbridge (Carroll & Graf, 1996, hardcover).

The sinking of the Titanic fascinates us in a way few other disasters ever have. Beryl Bainbridge, who distinguished herself by recounting Robert's Scott's tragic Antarctica expedition in *The Birthday Boys*, is the right novelist to tell the story. With a few penetrating details offered in a casual, almost off-handed way, Bainbridge makes her readers understand instantly the animosities between steerage and first class passengers and between first class passengers and the crew. And when the ship starts to go down, Bainbridge's pacing is perfect, as arrogance and Edwardian chivalry give way to animal panic.

HIROSHIMA
by John Hersey
(Random House, 1989, paperback)

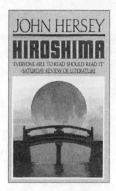

A clerk. A widowed seamstress. A physician. A Methodist minister. A German Jesuit. A young surgeon. Hersey begins with what these six ordinary people were doing at 8:15 a.m. August 6, 1945, when the atomic bomb was dropped on Hiroshima and then follows them hour-by-hour through their ordeal. Simply heartbreaking.

THE PERFECT STORM:
A TRUE STORY OF MEN AGAINST THE SEA
by Sebastian Junger (Norton, 1997, paperback)

When meteorologist say a storm is "perfect," they mean it couldn't be any worse. Such was the case in the last days of October, 1991, when an impossibly violent gale caught the swordfishing boat *Andrea Gail*, off the coast of Nova Scotia. In hundred-foot waves and eighty-mile-an-hour winds, the six crew members didn't have a chance. Sebastian Junger takes us into the heart of this terrifying storm, imagines the final moments of the *Andrea Gail* and recounts the heroism of the National Air Guard jumpers who attempted daring rescues by leaping from helicopters into the storm-tossed sea. Be prepared: *The Perfect Storm* will keep you reading far into the night.

INTO THIN AIR,
by Jon Krakauer (Villard Books, 1997, paperback)

If you believe the outfitters, anybody can get to the summit of Mount Everest. So in 1996, *Outside* magazine asked Jon Krakauer—himself a life-long mountain-climber—to sign up with a company that escorted amateurs to the summit of Everest. It turned out to be the most disastrous ascent ever made, taking the lives of 12 climbers, Sherpa guides and outfitters. Krakauer is a master storyteller who conveys the mind-numbing terror of the climbers caught in a killer storm on the mountain. Dramatic, horrific and completely absorbing, most readers get through this book in a day. You just can't tear yourself away from it.

INTO THE WILD
by Jon Krakauer (Villard, 1996, paperback)

In April 1992, Chris McCandless, a 24-year-old from the suburbs of Washington, D.C., walked into the Alaskan wilderness in search of "pure experience" with nothing but a small caliber rifle and a 10-pound bag of rice. Four months later a moose hunter found McCandless' emaciated corpse. Krakauer discloses the mystery of what happened in between and the events that led up to McCandless's fatal adventure.

LEFT TO DIE:
THE TRAGEDY OF THE USS JUNEAU
by Dan Kurzman (Pocket, 1994, paperback)

On November 13, 1942, as a convoy traveled along the coast of Guadalcanal, a Japanese torpedo hit the light cruiser USS Juneau and split the ship in two. The convoy commander was certain that no crew members could have survived the hit and ordered the convoy to move on. But 140 men did survive. Kurzman, a respected naval historian, makes excellent use of the Navy's archives as well as interviews with survivors to tell this moving story of tragedy and courage.

ENDURANCE
by Alfred Lansing (Carroll & Graf, 1986, paperback)

A master of suspense, Alfred Lansing was born to tell this story. In 1914, Sir Ernest Shackleton and his team sailed to Antarctica where they would disembark and cross the White Continent overland. But before they even reached their base camp arctic ice destroyed their ship. Marooned on drifting ice floes, somehow they survived a 1000-mile voyage and then an overland trek through the most unforgiving climate on the planet.

......

YOUNG MEN AND FIRE
by Norman Maclean
(University of Chicago Press, 1992, hardcover)

In 1949 a forest fire in Mann Gulch, Montana, claimed the lives of 12 young firefighters. For 40 years, Norman Maclean studied the tragedy, visited the site and finally got the only two survivors to agree to an interview. A compassionate, genuinely poetic book of an all-but-forgotten disaster.

......

HIROSHIMA NOTES
by Kensaburo Oe, Edited by David L. Swain, translated by Toshi Yonezawa (Grove Atlantic, 1996, paperback)

These grim essays were written between 1963 and 1965 when Kensaburo Oe made frequent visits to Hiroshima to interview survivors of the atomic blast that flattened the city in 1945. Some of the stories, like the Japanese medical community's denial that people exposed to radiation could contract leukemia, are not pretty. But there are also tales of heroism, of doctors and nurses who worked tirelessly with the victims in spite of their own injuries, the courage and dignity of the survivors and the movement in Japan to ban nuclear weapons.

......

AT DAWN WE SLEPT:
THE UNTOLD STORY OF PEARL HARBOR
by Gordon W. Prange (Penguin, 1982, paperback)

Prange's account of what happened at Pearl Harbor the morning of December 7, 1941, is the most complete, the most authoritative (he interviewed participants on both sides) and in many ways the most surprising study of "the day that will live in infamy."

THE HOT ZONE
by *Richard Preston* (Anchor Books, 1995, paperback)

As the African rain forest disappears, a new Ebola virus is discovered, one that turns vital organs to liquefied mush. Then one day, the virus shows up among monkeys in a lab in Virginia. What happens next is as frightening as anything Stephen King has ever dreamed up. Worse yet, it's a true story.

DISASTER ON THE MISSISSIPPI
by *Gene Salecker* (Naval Institute Press, 1996, hardcover)

On April 27, 1865, the boilers of the Mississippi steamboat Sultana exploded, killing more than 1700 of its 2200 passengers—many of them Union soldiers who had survived the Confederate prisons at Cahaba and Andersonville. It was a horrific disaster, yet in the grief over the assassination of Abraham Lincoln and the euphoria at the end of the Civil War, the Sultana tragedy was forgotten. Until now. After 15 years of research, Gene Eric Salecker has written the most comprehensive chronicle of the disaster. Filled with contemporary accounts and testimony of survivors, this is a graphic, gripping story of a forgotten moment in American history.

SMOLDERING CITY: CHICAGOANS AND THE GREAT FIRE, 1871-1874
by *Karen Sawislak* (University of Chicago Press, 1996, hardcover)

Around 10 o'clock one night, a spark in a Chicago family's barn started a fire that grew to be one of the most destructive conflagrations in American history. To tell the story, Karen Sawislak blends careful historical research with plenty of vivid personal anecdotes from survivors of the inferno, plus dozens of period illustrations. Then she goes on to chronicle the aftermath of the disaster, when city officials debated what to do about the homeless, how to feed almost the entire population of Chicago and how to organize rebuilding programs that were working at cross purposes. And she settles once and for all the story of the O'Leary's cow.

AND THE BAND PLAYED ON
by Randy Shilts (Penguin, 1993, paperback)

Randy Shilts was the first journalist to begin covering the AIDS crisis full-time. His account of the origins of AIDS in the United States is tragic, haunting, sometimes even infuriating as he exposes the criminal indifference of the Reagan Administration and members of the medical community, as well as the near-hysterical denials from some quarters within the gay community.

PERILS OF A RESTLESS PLANET:
SCIENTIFIC PERSPECTIVES ON
NATURAL DISASTERS
by Ernest Zebrowski, Jr.
(Cambridge University Press, 1997, hardcover)

The eruption of Vesuvius. The Black Death. The Johnstown Flood. The San Francisco Earthquake. Ernest Zebrowski relishes describing natural disasters. But he takes even greater pleasure in discussing how scientists have tried to forecast them. While Zebrowski's scientific slant is fascinating, the stories are the most fun. Two favorites: the eyewitness account of five English monks who saw an asteroid hit the moon in 1178 and the tsunami that lifted a U.S. man-of-war from its anchorage on the coast of Peru and deposited it 2 miles inland in the Atacama Desert.

REDISCOVERED CLASSICS

A LONG FATAL LOVE CHASE
by Louisa May Alcott (1866; Random House, 1995, paperback)

More than 100 years ago, Alcott sent this manuscript around to the publishers, but every one of them rejected it as being too sensational. In 1993, this long-forgotten manuscript was rediscovered in its entirety. This time, it had no trouble finding a publisher. The story of a young woman who discovers her husband is a bigamist, flees and then is stalked by him all across Europe makes an afternoon with the March girls seem pretty tame.

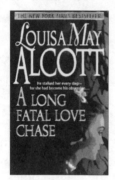

A MODERN MEPHISTOPHELES
by Louisa May Alcott (1877; Bantam, 1987, paperback)

I am tired of providing moral pap for the young," Louisa May Alcott once said. So she spun this Faustian fable of Felix Canaris, a destitute and desperate poet who, in return for money and fame, sells his soul to the wealthy and devilish Jasper Helwyze. Helwyze takes Canaris under his wing and even provides him with a lovely young wife. Here Alcott displays her powers as a novelist, drawing psychologically complex characters, introducing a dark undercurrent of sexuality, even violating taboos by introducing drug abuse to her readers. Sex, drugs and satanic compacts—it's a far cry from *Little Women*.

NIGHTWOOD
by Djuna Barnes (1936; Dalkey Archive Press, 1995, paperback)

T.S. Eliot, who edited *Nightwood* for his friend Djuna Barnes, once said that this novel reminded him of an Elizabethan tragedy. James Joyce was a great admirer of this story of five eccentrics in Berlin and Paris: in fact, readers often comment on the similarities between *Nightwood* and *Finnegans Wake*, except that *Nightwood* is more readable. Now this often overlooked classic of 20th-century literature is available in an excellent new edition that comes as close to Barnes' original intention as possible. If you've never read Djuna Barnes before, here is your chance to discover an author whose prose is so gorgeous it is almost poetry.

THE DIARY OF A COUNTRY PRIEST
by Georges Bernanos (1936; Carroll & Graf, 1984, paperback)

Georges Bernanos' story of a sensitive young French priest assigned to a remote rural parish explores the inexplicable workings of divine grace in the world. From all outward appearances, the Curé seems to be bumbling his way through life. Yet as the priest comes into conflict with one parishioner after another, Bernanos reveals, almost imperceptibly, the tremendous reserves of spiritual strength this young man possesses and his profound insight into human nature. For the first 50 pages you may think this novel is going nowhere, but hang on—you'll be surprised by how deeply moving it is once you reach the end.

THE BRIDGE OVER THE RIVER KWAI
by Pierre Boulle, Translated by Xan Fielding
(1952; Bantam, 1990, paperback)

Colonel Nicholson was a brilliant British officer and an exemplary prisoner of war who believed so strongly in a code of military honor that when his Japanese captors ordered him to build a railroad bridge for them, he not only built it, but built the best bridge possible in record time. But even as his men labored in the hot tropical sun, "Force 316" of British Intelligence was plotting to blow the bridge up before the enemy could put it to use. Boulle drew on his own experiences in Southeast Asia to write this suspenseful, ironic thriller that will keep you on the edge of your seat.

SHADOWS ON THE ROCK
by *Willa Cather* (1931; Viking/Library of America, 1990, hardcover)

Seventeenth-century Canada is an unusual setting for Cather, an author we generally associate with the western United States. Yet expanding her horizons appears to have expanded Cather's gifts as a writer—*Shadows* is one of her more mature works. Euclide Auclair, an apothecary and his daughter Cecile, newcomers to Quebec, are swept up in the excitement of life on the edge of an endless wilderness. But the main conflict here is a love story—will Cecile choose Jacques the sailor, or Charron the coureur de bois? A fine novel that deserves a wider audience.

THE WAPSHOT CHRONICLES
by *John Cheever* (Random House, 1992, paperback)

John Cheever won a national reputation thanks to this lively, ironic, event-filled novel. In a grungy seaport that's declining into staid respectability live the Wapshot clan. Old Captain Leander Wapshot lives only for his ferryboat. His sons, Coverley and Moses, have gone out into the world to sire heirs so they can inherit a fortune from loony Aunt Honora. Readers new to Cheever will be delighted by the poignant, sexy, funny story he spins.

Also by Cheever:

THE WAPSHOT SCANDAL
(Random House, 1992, paperback).

It seems that Aunt Honora has never paid her income taxes, but that's just the start of the family's intriguing troubles.

LORD JIM
by Joseph Conrad (1900; Everyman's Library, 1992, paperback)

A t age 24, Jim is chief mate on a steamer carrying 800 pilgrims to Mecca. In the middle of the night, the ship strikes something and the panicked crew takes to the lifeboats, leaving the pilgrims behind. At the last moment, Jim abandons his ship, too. To atone for his cowardice, Jim accepts a position as an agent on a remote Asian island. He becomes popular—the chief calls him Lord Jim. When a band of cut-throats arrives on the island, Jim believes he can handle the situation without bloodshed. Of course, he's wrong.

Conrad's Most Famous Novel:

HEART OF DARKNESS
(1899; Everyman's Library, 1995, paperback).

A European trading company sends a man named Marlow up a great African river to bring home their agent, Kurtz. Through the whole awful journey, Marlow looks forward to meeting this living saint renowned for his intelligence, refinement and compassion. Instead he finds a degraded, depraved man who has set himself up as a god.

THE CITADEL
by A.J. Cronin (1937; Little, Brown, 1983, paperback)

A ndrew Manson, a sincere, conscientious young physician, begins his practice with his wife Christina in a gritty Welsh mining town. But soon a desire for a fine practice in London tempts him to compromise his honor and even jeopardize his marriage. Cronin tells a moving story, especially the scenes in which Manson realizes his ambition may cost him Christina's love.

Another Cronin classic:

THE KEYS OF THE KINGDOM
(1941; Little, Brown, 1984, paperback).

C onin follows the long, active career of Father Francis Chisholm, a Scottish priest who spends most of his life as a missionary in China. A touching story of a man's struggle against intolerance, smug clergymen and his own pride. The characterizations of the women in the novel are especially strong.

THE GHOST AND MRS. MUIR
by R.A. Dick (1945; Lightyear Press, 1996, paperback)

Part of the reason Gull Cottage rented so cheaply was that it was haunted. But after years of living under the thumb of her oppressive husband and his strong-minded sisters the prospect of living with the ghost of a salty old sea captain seemed like a vacation to Lucy Muir. Still, she hadn't bargained for the blustery, opinionated spirit of Captain Daniel Gregg. This haunting (no pun intended) love story inspired both a classic 1947 romantic comedy starring Rex Harrison and Gene Tierney and a popular 1960s sitcom.

THE OLD CURIOSITY SHOP
by Charles Dickens (1841; Penguin, 1972, paperback)

Only a master like Dickens could manage a novel that is at once biting social satire, laugh-out-loud comedy and a three-handkerchief tearjerker. Nell Trent lives with her dotty old grandfather in his shop of curiosities. Unbeknownst to little Nell, Grandfather is a compulsive gambler who has gotten into debt with the odious moneylender, Daniel Quilp. To escape the villain they runaway to the countryside where they meet an endless string of kind people who help them. But Quilp is hot on their trail. This is Dickens at top form: lovable heroes and heroines, irredeemably wicked villains, a large cast of eccentric bit-players and lots of suspense.

More by Charles Dickens:

DOMBEY AND SON
(1848; Penguin, 1970, paperback).

A businessman is so single-minded in his desire for a son that he cannot respond to the love of his only child, a daughter. Critics say this novel makes the beginning of Dickens' mature style—less wild improvisation and more careful plotting.

MANHATTAN TRANSFER
by John Dos Passos
(1925; Houghton Mifflin, 1991, paperback)

Suicides, drunkards, aesthetes, bootleggers, corrupt politicians, much-married actresses. Dos Passos' Manhattan is a decadent but definitely lively city. These days, most authors shy away from such panoramic stories, but Dos Passos handled them with aplomb.

AN AMERICAN TRAGEDY
by Theodore Dreiser (1925; Signet, 1964, paperback)

Clyde Griffiths, the son of street-corner evangelists, yearns for wealth and social position-so he runs away. He begins an affair with a working girl named Roberta, but Clyde has his eye on a debutante named Sondra. When Roberta becomes pregnant and demands that Clyde marry her, he hatches a scheme to rid himself of his lower class encumbrances forever. Not a pretty story, but hard to put down nonetheless.

THE THREE MUSKETEERS
by Alexandre Dumas (1844; Penguin, 1982, paperback)

A young, gallant Gascon named D'Artagnan arrives in Paris in 1625 and manages to get involved in three duels on the same day. Nonetheless, his opponents—Athos, Porthos and Aramis—become his closest friends and together they embark on a series of adventures as they attempt to save the lovely Queen Anne from the machinations of the wicked Cardinal Richelieu and the even more wicked Milady.

Filled with swordplay, daring escapes and lush romance, this is a triumph of adventure fiction.

More of Dumas:

QUEEN MARGOT
(1845; Hyperion, 1994, paperback).

The recent visually stunning French film version of Dumas' novel has brought this overlooked classic a host of new readers. Set in 1575 at the time of the St. Bartholomew Massacre, this is the story of the ravishing Margot, her vacillating husband Henry of Navarre, her valiant Protestant lover, Le Mole and her ruthless mother, Catherine de Medici. A great story of intrigue, betrayal, lust, poisoning, religious hatreds and murderous squabbling among France's Royal Family.

FRENCHMAN'S CREEK
by Daphne Du Maurier
(1942; Robert Benchley Publishing, 1971, hardcover)

Lady St. Columb is bored by London society and sick to death of her boorish husband. So one night she climbs into her coach and drives away to the family's disused estate on the wild coast of Cornwall. There she meets a French pirate who uses a creek on the estate as a hideout for his ship and his crew. The lady and the pirate begin a passionate affair and Lady St. Columb embarks on the adventure of her life.

REBECCA
by Daphne Du Maurier. (1938; Avon, 1998, paperback)

Only eight months after the death of his wife, Maxim de Winter brings a new bride home to his magnificent house, Manderley. A novel rich in atmosphere, part mystery, part ghost story, part Gothic romance.

UNPUNISHED

by Charlotte Perkins Gilman (1929; Feminist Press, 1997, paperback)

Charlotte Perkins Gilman, the renowned author of *The Yellow Wallpaper*, wrote this murder mystery in 1929, yet it was never published. Until now. New York attorney Wade Vaughn is found in his office with a bullet hole in his temple, a wound on his scalp, a knife in his back, a cord around his throat and a glass of poison on the desk in front of him. Husband and wife detectives, Jim and Bessie Hunt, start investigating and learn that lots of people hated Vaughn's guts: his family, his servants, his neighbors, his clients, his colleagues, his doctor. It's a classic mystery, into which Gilman cleverly weaves a subtle commentary on the class and gender posturings of the early 20th century.

KON-TIKI

by Thor Heyerdahl
(Simon & Schuster, 1990, paperback)

To prove cultural links between the ancient Peruvians and Polynesians, Heyerdahl and five companions built a balsa log raft and sailed it 4300 miles from Callao, Peru to Tuamotu Island. A tremendous modern adventure story that made Heyerdahl's name a household word.

GOOD-BYE, MR. CHIPS

by James Hilton (1934; Bantam Books, 1983, paperback)

James Hilton's story follows Mr. Chipping, a teacher at an English school for boys, over the course of a career that stretches from 1870 to the years immediately following World War I. Chipping is shy, uncertain and rather dull. But on a tour of the Lake District he meets a young woman named Katherine. She is pretty, vivacious, confident—everything Chipping is not—and she has fallen in love with him. Katherine renames him "Chips" and takes his career in hand until he becomes the favorite master at the school. From that time on, through all the tragedies of life, through all the calamities of the times, the affection of his boys sustains Mr. Chips. A very sweet story. After you've read it, rent the movie starring Robert Donat and Greer Garson.

LOST HORIZON
by *James Hilton* (1933; Amereon Ltd., 1983, paperback)

Four explorers from the West discover a lost kingdom in the mountains of Asia whose people seem free from anxiety and where an aged lama keeps a profound secret.

BEYOND THE AEGEAN
by *Elia Kazan* (Knopf, 1994, hardcover)

Twenty years have passed since Stavros—the boyish hero of *America, America*—fled his home in Anatolia to escape Turkish brutality. Now World War I is over and Stavros has decided to return to his village, find a submissive wife and live like a rich man. But nothing happens as Stavros intends. He falls in love with headstrong Thomna. In spite of his dreams of peace and security, he finds himself drawn into the Greco-Turkish War that will drive Greek Christians from Anatolia forever.

Worth searching for:

AMERICA, AMERICA
by *Elia Kazan.* (Stein and Day, 1962, hardcover)

The beginning of the Stavros story is out of print, but scour the used bookstores and visit your public library to find this wonderfully moving immigrant's tale.

A SEPARATE PEACE
by *John Knowles* (1959; Bantam, 1985, paperback)

Gene and Phineas are roommates and best friends at an expensive New Hampshire boarding school. But, beneath their deep friendship is an uneasy rivalry and a secret they can't admit even to themselves. Though set in the 1940s, this is a timeless story—and so poignant it hurts.

ELMER GANTRY
by Sinclair Lewis (1927; Signet, 1967, paperback)

A brash ex-football player forges a new career for himself as a revivalist preacher. Almost overnight Gantry, with his good looks, gift for self-promotion and sermons plagiarized from legitimate evangelists, becomes an enormous success. When it was first published, Lewis' story of a sensational hypocrite rang so true, it offended believers and unbelievers alike,

Also by Lewis:

BABBITT
(1922; Penguin, 1986, paperback).

From this stinging satire came the word "babbitt," a synonym for mindless conformity. George Babbitt is a regular guy, successful, dependable, unimaginative, certain that all America's ills can be solved by "a sound business administration in Washington." As relevant today as it was in 1922.

WEST WITH THE NIGHT
by Beryl Markham (1942; North Point Press, 1982, paperback)

After Ernest Hemingway read Beryl Markham's book, he wrote to his editor and friend, Maxwell Perkins, "she has written so well and marvelously, that I was completely ashamed of myself as a writer." Markham's autobiography is certainly interesting: an English girl grows up in East Africa; native Africans teach her to hunt with a spear in the jungles; British colonials teach her to ride thoroughbreds at the club; in time, she takes up the adventurous career of bush pilot. But what elevates this book from a good read to a masterpiece is the incredible beauty of Markham's prose. Make a point of getting a hold of this book—you won't be disappointed.

Markham's Fiction:

SPLENDID OUTCAST
(Spoken Arts, 1987, paperback).

All Markham's short stories are set in her beloved Africa. While there are tales of adventure and romance, many of the stories are based on events in her life, such as flying a plane through a violent thunderstorm, or witnessing a lion's attack.

THE RAZOR'S EDGE
by W. Somerset Maugham (1945; Penguin, 1978, paperback)

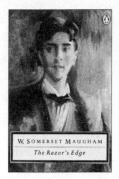

While F. Scott Fitzgerald was dressing Jay Gatsby in gold shirts and silver ties, Somerset Maugham decided to tell the story of Larry Darrell, a dashing World War I aviator who gives up everything to find the answers to the great spiritual questions: Does God exist? Why is there evil in the world? Do I have an immortal soul? Larry's quest for the truth carries him from America to bohemian Paris to remote monasteries in India. It's a great read, with plenty of satiric jabs at the pretensions of the British, French and American upper classes. *The Razor's Edge* is Maugham at his best.

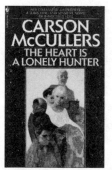

THE HEART IS A LONELY HUNTER
by Carson McCullers
(1940; Bantam, 1983, paperback)

John Singer is an intelligent, sensitive deaf-mute living in a small Georgia town. The only person with whom he can communicate is another deaf-mute, Spiros Antonapoulos. Then Spiros is sent to an institution. The other townspeople "adopt" John, visiting him, confiding to him their deepest feelings and enjoying a tremendous sense of peace after each visit. But John himself lives only for visits to his friend Spiros. A very poignant novel that deserves a wider audience.

More Carson McCullers:

MEMBER OF THE WEDDING
(1946; New Directions, 1963, paperback).

Twelve-year-old Frankie Adams is thrilled when her brother and his fiancée ask her to be a member of their wedding party—she thinks it means they will all live happily in a new home together! Best scene: Frankie the bridesmaid refuses to get out of the honeymoon car.

CRAZY WEATHER
by Charles L. McNichols
(1944; University of Nebraska Press, 1994, paperback)

Under the scorching Arizona sun, two boys, one half white and half Native American, the other a full-blooded Mohave, begin a journey of adventure and self-discovery. All the big themes that make a great novel are here: the pain of growing up, the intensity of real friendship and the confusion of two adolescents trying to make their own way in the world.

A DEVIL IN PARADISE
by Henry Miller (New Directions, 1993, paperback)

One day Conrad Moricand, a French astrologer, decided to leave his homeland and move in with an acquaintance in Big Sur-Henry Miller. As a houseguest, Moricand was belligerent, disagreeable and demanding. Yet Miller put up with him for a reason-Moricand gave him plenty to write about. If you think Miller is only bitter, caustic and obscene, *A Devil in Paradise* is certain to surprise you—it's a very funny book, free of the usual Miller-esque qualities that put off some readers.

BURMESE DAYS
by George Orwell (1934; Harvest Books, 1974, paperback)

O rwell was born in India and served there as a young man with the Imperial Police in Burma. He drew on this experience to create this fast-paced story about a group of whiskey-swilling Englishmen in a remote Burmese outpost at loggerheads over whether to admit an "Oriental" into their European club. Only a social critic as talented as Orwell could weave such an absorbing masterpiece of waning colonial rule. This novel will come as a pleasant surprise to readers who know Orwell only through 1984.

NORTHWEST PASSAGE
by Kenneth Roberts (1937; Fawcett, 1983, paperback)

O ne of the best historical novels by an American author also turned out to be an exciting event in historical research. While digging through archives for fresh material on his subject, Roberts unearthed long-forgotten documents on the French and Indian War. Set in 1759, this thrilling adventure yarn follows Major Robert Rogers and his men on a mission to destroy a hostile Indian town and discover the overland route to the Northwest Passage.

OLIVER WISWELL
by Kenneth Roberts (Doubleday, 1940, hardcover)

T he title character of Kenneth Roberts' clever novel is a young American who views the Revolution from a different perspective. You see, Oliver Wiswell and his family have remained loyal to England. From his vantage place in Boston, Wiswell comments on the character of such revered Founding Fathers as John Hancock (a smuggler), Patrick Henry (a fire-breathing rabble rouser), Sam Adams (a man with a pronounced weakness for the bottle). But the British don't fare much better as Wiswell observes and laments the tactical stupidities which will eventually cost the Crown their most valuable colonies. This historical novel was enormously popular in the 1940s and should be easy to find in your local library or used book store.

ALL PASSION SPENT
by Vita Sackville-West (1931; Carroll & Graf, 1991, paperback)

N ow in her eighties, Lady Slane, widow of a prime minister, gives up her large elegant home and moves to a charming cottage in Hampstead. Four of her six children are appalled; the other two are deeply confused. Lady Slane is restored by her new surroundings and the friends she makes in the village are delightful. There is a wonderful surprise awaiting her—a suitor from 60 years previous comes calling again. A very fine novel about the thrill of breaking out of the mold and the joy of finding freedom at last.

More of Vita Sackville-West:

THE EDWARDIANS
(1930; Amereon Ltd, 1989, paperback).

A meticulous portrait of the English aristocracy on the eve of George VI's coronation, told through the lives of Sebastian, the young heir to a dukedom and his mother, a famous hostess.

....

FRANNY AND ZOOEY
by J.D. Salinger (Bantam, 1991, paperback)

B efore Salinger headed off for a reclusive life in the hills of New Hampshire, he left behind a small but impressive body of work. Much of this work was part of a long-term project of short stories about the Glass family, a large and somewhat opinionated clan of New Yorkers who inhabited that city before, during and after WWII. Franny and Zooey concerns the two youngest of the seven Glass children. With the help of her brother Zooey, Franny is trying to find some meaning in her life. Salinger is one of the most widely read authors in the English language. These stories are two of the reasons why.

....

THE PRIME OF MISS JEAN BRODIE,
by Muriel Spark (1961; Harper Perennial Library, 1994, paperback)

Before Muriel Spark became famous for devilish mysteries, she wrote this modern classic. In 1930s Edinburgh, an unorthodox teacher gathers a group of schoolgirls about her and promises to transform them into the "crème de la crème." It's one thing for a teacher to treat her students like adults, but is Miss Brodie going too far when she starts telling her girls the details of her current love affair? Even after more than 30 years, there is a contemporary ring to Spark's story of an intimate friendship between a teacher and her students.

THE MOON IS DOWN
by John Steinbeck (1941; Penguin, 1995, paperback)

Set in an unnamed country, *The Moon is Down* chronicles the fascist occupation of small town and its citizens' resistance. Written in 1941, Steinbeck's novel was immediately translated into nearly a dozen languages and hundreds of thousands of copies were smuggled throughout Europe. Just owning a copy of this novel in Fascist Italy carried a death sentence.

Also by Steinbeck:

THE WINTER OF OUR DISCONTENT
(1961; Penguin, 1996, paperback)

The proud descendant of the Pilgrim Fathers, Ethan Hawley now toils as a lowly clerk in the village grocery. His wife is restless and his teenage children are anxious for the tantalizing material things that the world offers and their father cannot provide. Let's just say Ethan is not where he expected to be in life. Steinbeck sets his rigidly scrupulous hero on a collision course with moral crisis and doesn't let up until the last page.

THE MAGNIFICENT AMBERSONS
by Booth Tarkington
(1918; Indiana University Press, 1989, paperback)

There's a romantic, even elegiac tone of Tarkington's account of the decline of the Ambersons, a powerful, well-to-do, socially prominent family in a modest Indiana town. George Amberson Minafer, the heir to the family fortune, is arrogant to the point of insufferability. His pride and fixation on the things of the past is so strong he would rather see his mother lonely and unhappy than bless her marriage to a wealthy automobile inventor. (George considers the man common). A fascinating story set at the moment in American history when industrial tycoons and land developers were displacing the stuffy, old, aristocratic families.

INNOCENTS ABROAD
by Mark Twain (1869; New American Library, 1982, paperback)

Twain based this travelogue-with-attitude on his extended 1867 tour of Europe, Egypt and the Holy Land. The scenes of shrewd Yankees tormenting their guides (the American tourists insist they've never heard of Christopher Columbus), comparing Lake Como with Lake Tahoe (Tahoe wins, hands down) and going up against con men in the Old World are plenty of fun. Twain has a wonderful time asserting that the peculiar national traits of the democratic American surpass all the sophistication of Europe. Innocents Abroad is a great leap forward in Twain's writing style and the beginning of one of his most productive periods.

20,000 LEAGUES UNDER THE SEA:
THE DEFINITIVE UNABRIDGED EDITION
by Jules Verne, Edited by Walter J. Miller & Fredrick P. Walter
(1870; Naval Institute Press, 1993, hardcover)

Like so many of his novels, Verne's story of a submarine was prophetic. Captain Nemo, an Indian prince with a fierce hatred of the British Raj, travels the world in his opulently appointed submarine, destroying warships and their crews in the name of universal peace. When a hapless band of seafarers are imprisoned on the sub, they struggle with the dilemma of admiring Nemo's obvious genius yet deploring his megalomania. A classic adventure story, now in an excellent edition.

The sequel:

MYSTERIOUS ISLAND
by Jules Verne (1874; Signet Classics, 1986, paperback).

Union soldiers who escaped from a Confederate prisoner-of-war camp in a hot-air balloon crash land on a deserted island. Soon they are joined by two shipwrecked English ladies. Together they battle humungous beasts, pirates and eventually Captain Nemo himself.

ALL THE KING'S MEN
by Robert Penn Warren (1946; , paperback)

Robert Penn Warren based this story on the career of Huey Long, the backwoods demagogue who was essentially "King" of Louisiana in the 1930s. The story follows Willy Stark, unscrupulous and power-hungry and his unlikely crony, Jack Burden, a journalist with a conscience but not much of a backbone. Their uneasy partnership reaches a crisis when Willy sends Jack on a mission to blackmail Judge Irwin, an honorable man who acted as Jack's second father. Warren spins out a wonderful plot, filled with sudden twists and surprises and writes some of the most gorgeous prose in American literature.

THE DAY OF THE LOCUST
by Nathanael West (1939; Signet Classics, 1983, paperback)

When West died at age 36 in a car crash in 1940, he had published four novels. His best was *The Day of the Locust*, an unflinching study of the dark side of Hollywood. Turning his back on the glitz, West focused on the town's misfits and failures like Tod Hackett, the would-be-screenwriter and Faye Greener, the beautiful extra who yearns for stardom and turns tricks until her big break arrives. At its publication, Dorothy Parker called this novel, "brilliant, savage and arresting."

More by Nathanael West:

MISS LONELYHEARTS
(1933; New Directions, 1962, paperback).

A newspaperman takes on the job of writing an advice-to-the-lovelorn column and finds himself being drawn into the sad lives of the desperate souls who write to him.

THE GLIMPSES OF THE MOON
by Edith Wharton (1922; Macmillan, 1994, paperback)

You might call this Edith Wharton's "lost" novel. Two years after she won the Pulitzer Prize for *The Age of Innocence*, her compelling period piece of repressed sexuality, she published this sexy contemporary tale set in the Jazz Age. Nick Lansing and Suzy Branch have the right pedigree, but not much cash. So, they devise a simple plan. They'll marry and "honeymoon" at the estates of wealthy acquaintances. If either of them meets someone suitable (read, "stinking rich"), they'll divorce and marry the new candidate. Filled with Wharton's biting irony, this forgotten classic is sure to become one of your favorite Wharton novels.

THE GOSHAWK
by T.H. White (Lyons & Buford, 1996, paperback)

You remember T.H. White as the author of the Arthurian novel, *The Once and Future King*. This little book is White's diary from 1936 when he bought a German goshawk and set about trying to learn the medieval art of falconry. The story of White's successes and failures with the bird are interesting, but what truly sets this book apart is the effort of a 20th-century man to teach himself an ancient skill and the intense interaction between man and bird.

THE REFERENCE SHELF

THE NEW FOWLER'S MODERN ENGLISH USAGE, THIRD EDITION
Edited by R. W. Burchfield (Clarendon Press, 1996, hardcover)

For the first time in 70 years, this landmark guide to English grammar, syntax, style and vocabulary has been revised and updated. The project was spearheaded by *The Oxford English Dictionary's* Robert Burchfield to bring issues of usage up to date. For example, there is a thorough exploration of the "his/her" dilemma after indefinite pronouns. Burchfield has even augmented the book's famous illustrative sentences with examples from the novels of Martin Amis, Saul Bellow, Ruth Rendell and John Updike. With the new *Fowler's* you'll learn something from every entry, sometimes even from every sentence.

THE WOLF ALMANAC:
A CELEBRATION OF WOLVES AND THEIR WORLD
by Robert H. Busch (Lyons & Buford, 1995, hardcover)

Wolves are making a comeback—in the United States, Canada and Mexico, in Europe, even in Israel. Yet, wolves are still objects of irrational fears, old myths and chronic misunderstanding. In this beautifully illustrated almanac, nature writer Robert Busch offers a comprehensive, authoritative reference to wolves: their behavior, biology, their place in current conservation politics and their influence on cultures and religions from American Indian tribes to the ancient Romans. This is the definitive sourcebook on one of our most endangered wild creatures.

PAST IMPERFECT:
HISTORY ACCORDING TO THE MOVIES
Edited by Mark C. Carnes (Henry Holt, 1995, hardcover)

This book is inspired. Sixty-one world-class historians review famous movies for their historical accuracy. You get Antonia Fraser on *Anne of the Thousand Days*, James M. McPherson on *Glory*, Dee Brown on *Fort Apache*, Stephen Jay Gould on *Jurassic Park*, Gerda Lerner on *Joan of Arc*. Plus, you'll find out if George C. Scott was right on the money when he played Patton, if Errol Flynn went a little over the top when he played Custer and if Faye Dunaway did justice to Bonnie Parker. *Past Imperfect* is a terrific idea and it's fun to read.

THE MATHEMATICAL UNIVERSE
by William Dunham (John Wiley & Sons, 1997, paperback)

For every letter of the alphabet Dunham finds a great mathematician or a great mathematical idea. "B" is for the battling Bernoulli brothers (Jakob taught math to Johann and then Johann showed him up). "D" is for differential calculus (Isaac Newton and Gottfried Liebnitz exchanged nasty letters over which of them had discovered it). High school algebra should have been this much fun.

THE ELVIS ATLAS: A JOURNEY THROUGH ELVIS PRESLEY'S AMERICA
by Michael Gray and Roger Osborne (Henry Holt, 1996, hardcover)

Gray and Osborne have managed to write a book about Elvis that is as informative as it is fun. Their *Elvis Atlas* explores the King's musical roots in country, blues, gospel and jazz and includes spreads on his early influences—Jimmie Rodgers, Hank Williams, Hoyt Axton, Mario Lanza (Mario Lanza?!). Best of all are 150 unique full-color maps especially created for this volume, from the route of Elvis' tour through the South in 1955 to the look of Las Vegas in the 1970s. There's never been a more lavish, more entertaining Elvis encyclopedia.

∙∙∙∙∙∙∙∙∙∙∙∙∙

THE NPR CLASSICAL MUSIC COMPANION:
TERMS AND CONCEPTS FROM A TO Z,
by Miles Hoffmann (Houghton Mifflin, 1997, paperback)

In more than 100 witty and informative entries, NPR's popular commentator Miles Hoffman demystifies the terms and concepts of classical music—from "a cappella" to "zarzuela." Hoffman's irreverence makes classical music less threatening and his colloquial style makes these odd words and phrases accessible even to new listeners. And by defining the terms in the context of famous composers and famous works, Hoffman makes his readers feel smart.

∙∙∙∙∙∙∙∙∙∙∙∙∙

FOR KEEPS: THIRTY YEARS AT THE MOVIES
by Pauline Kael (Plume, 1996, paperback)

From her 10 previous collections of movie reviews written for *The New Yorker*, Kael offers this monumental anthology—her personal selection of her personal best. You'll find reviews of *Dances With Wolves*, *Platoon*, *Fellini Satyricon* and *West Side Story* (hated them) as well as *Prizzi's Honor*, *Tootsie*, *My Beautiful Launderette* and *Z* (loved them). Kael is unpredictable, merciless, insightful and infuriating. Movie lovers are going to love and cherish this book.

∙∙∙∙∙∙∙∙∙∙∙∙∙

THE FILM ENCYCLOPEDIA
by Ephraim Katz
(HarperCollins, 1994, paperback)

Just what does a "gaffer" do? How many films did Hitchcock make? What film won Best Picture in 1934? This comprehensive, one-volume reference work can answer just about any question you could have about films and the film industry. From Abbott and Costello to Edward Zwick it has over 7,000 entries on actors, directors, producers, screenwriters, cinematographers, studios, styles, genres, unions and technical terms. It's an indispensable addition to any film-lovers library.

WHAT EVERY AMERICAN SHOULD KNOW ABOUT WOMEN'S HISTORY
by *Christine Lunardini, Ph.D.* (Bob Adams, 1994, paperback)

Lunardini's fascinating book is packed with significant events concerning women in America. Anne Hutchinson defies Puritan authority in the 17th century. Phyllis Wheatley publishes her poetry in the 18th century. Dorothea Dix exposes the cruel treatment of the mentally ill, 1843. Victoria Woodhull runs for the Presidency, 1872. The Food and Drug Administration approves "the Pill", 1960. Iris Rivera refuses to make coffee for her boss, 1977. Sally Ride becomes the first American woman in space, 1983. Here is a collection of 200 events that shaped the destiny of all Americans-not just American women.

TOTAL TELEVISION
by *Alex McNeil* (Penguin, 1996, paperback)

Want to know what the Skipper's real name was on *Gilligan's Island*? When the Sid Caesar show ran? Who starred in *77 Sunset Strip*? Then turn to *Total Television*. This well-researched tome follows the rise and fall of nearly 5,000 TV series-network, syndicated, prime time, daytime and cable. There's even an easy-to-read chart of prime time shows from 1948 to 1991. This is an indispensable companion for any TV fan, be they couch potato or connoisseur.

THE GUYS' GUIDE TO GUYS' VIDEOS
by *Scott Meyer* (Avon, 1997, paperback)

It is Saturday night and you want to rent a video. As a regular guy, your requirements are simple: the movie should have gorgeous women, lots of explosions and a reasonably high body count. This indispensable handbook will help you zero in on the videos that fit the bill. Scott Meyer rates each film for violence, profanity, babes, cool cars and hero worship. He includes meaty plot summaries, spotlights scenes you're gonna love and even includes arguments you can use to convince the woman in your life that Bruce Willis is just as sensitive and caring as Brad Pitt.

NATIONAL GEOGRAPHIC ATLAS OF THE WORLD: REVISED SIXTH EDITION
by The Editors of the National Geographic Society (National Geographic Society, 1993, hardcover)

For exploring the secrets of the ocean floor or the quasars of outer space—and everything in between—*The National Geographic Atlas of the World* is a work of unsurpassed beauty and accuracy. An index of more than 150,000 place names helps you locate even the most obscure villages and islands. Thematic maps detail populations, land use, resources and more. Spectacular satellite images bring the universe into focus while city, country and continent maps (measuring 18 1/4" x 24") present information in astonishing detail.

THE OXFORD DICTIONARY AND THESAURUS: AMERICAN EDITION
(Oxford University Press, 1997, hardcover)

The *Oxford Dictionary and Thesaurus* is the reference writers have been waiting for: a book which provides both synonyms and definitions in the same entry. Among the more than 200,000 entries are hundreds of new words including "shareware," "grunge" and "downsize." Plus there are terms for animal groups (a clowder of cats, a skulk of foxes), English terms from around the globe (billabong, brassed off, high tea) and much, much more. Truly, this is the most reliable, up-to-date and wide-ranging resource on words available.

THE OXFORD DICTIONARY OF FOREIGN WORDS AND PHRASES

Edited by Jennifer Speak (Oxford University Press, 1997, hardcover)

So what exactly is nouvelle cuisine? How do you know if you are in an authentic bistro? Is falsetto a bad thing? This reference defines more than 8000 foreign words and phrases that have passed into common usage in contemporary English. Entries cover the arts, science, medicine, food, literature, making it a joy for browsers. But the dictionary is also authoritative. You'll find the date of the term's introduction into English, its origin, its definition, any alternative spellings and other interesting facts. A fun and useful guide to English's ever-growing lexicon.

THE MILLENNIUM WHOLE EARTH CATALOG

Edited by Howard Rheingold
(Harper San Francisco, 1994, hardcover)

For 25 years, *The Whole Earth Catalogs* have been in the cultural vanguard, promoting recycling, holistic health care and personal computers when such things were virtually unheard of. The "Millennium" edition is a complete revision of this endlessly fascinating reference. Attractive, easy to use and packed with surprises, you'll find valuable information on how to make your home more energy efficient, where to get the best videos at the best price, even how to navigate the Internet. A fun, fact-filled resource for the 21st century.

THE NEW ROLLING STONE ENCYCLOPEDIA OF ROCK 'N' ROLL, COMPLETELY REVISED AND UPDATED

Edited by Patricia Romanowski, Holly George-Warren and Jon Pareles
(Fireside, 1995, paperback)

Was Ray Charles born blind? (No) Where did Rap come from? (Black Discos of New York City in the 1970s) Who won the Grammy for best new group in 1964? (The Beatles) Is singer Pat

Boone descended from pioneer Daniel Boone? (That's what he says) If these kinds of questions keep you up at night, then keep this book by your bedside. Chosen by the Rock & Roll Hall of Fame as their official source of information, this exhaustively researched volume contains nearly 2000 entries on the music and the infamous music makers of Rock.

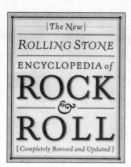

VIDEOHOUND'S GOLDEN MOVIE RETRIEVER™
(Visible Ink Press, 1997, paperback)

The mother of all video guides is *Video Hound's Golden Movie Retriever*™. This new edition adds hundreds of new reviews to the more than 22,000 critiques that have already been assembled by *VideoHound's* editors. Feature-length movies, documentaries, made-for-TV movies and animated films are rated from "Four Bones" (a must-see) to a "Woof" (better you should spend the evening cleaning the oven). With this comprehensive, authoritative and opinionated guide, you'll never rent a turkey again.

ROYAL LIVES

ELIZABETH:
A BIOGRAPHY OF BRITAIN'S QUEEN
by Sarah Bradford (Farrar Straus & Giroux, 1996, hardcover)

As an insider at the British court, Sarah Bradford, Viscountess of Bangor, is in an enviable position to draw a complex, life-like portrait of Elizabeth II and her family. Bradford shows us a woman worthy of our admiration: Elizabeth has overseen the dismantling of the British Empire and witnessed the collapse of her children's marriages, yet she has proven to be an outstanding constitutional monarch. Bradford does not shy away from the scandals (Prince Philip's adulteries, the rumor of Prince Edward's homosexuality, the "guttersnipe life" of Princess Margaret), but she doesn't let them overwhelm her book.

TO THE SCAFFOLD:
THE LIFE OF MARIE ANTOINETTE
by Carolly Erickson

To the French court, she seemed sweet-natured and almost childlike. But on the streets of Paris the mob called her "the Austrian bitch." Prize-winning historian and biographer Carolly Erickson offers the most psychologically acute study of Marie Antoinette to date. A heartbreaking story of the naive, extravagant queen who acquired good sense only when it was too late. Worth searching for.

Also by Erickson:

BLOODY MARY:
THE REMARKABLE LIFE OF MARY TUDOR
(St. Martin's Press, 1998, paperback).

Erickson's in-depth biography of Henry VIII's eldest daughter attempts to see Mary afresh, without the prejudices and myths that have accumulated around her over the last 400 years.

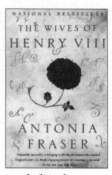

THE WIVES OF HENRY VIII
by Antonia Fraser (Vintage, 1993, paperback)

England's most marrying monarch went through six wives in 40 years. Now one of England's foremost biographers reviews the lives of the six ill-fated women who took on the perilous task of marrying Henry VIII. Fraser unearths the sexual tension of Anne Boleyn's reign, the tragedy of Jane Seymour's early death and the disastrous philandering of Catherine Howard.

Also by Antonia Fraser:

MARY, QUEEN OF SCOTS
(Delta, 1993, paperback).

The definitive biography of Scotland's most romantic, most tragic queen.

THE UNRULY QUEEN:
THE LIFE OF QUEEN
Caroline, by Flora Fraser (Knopf, 1996, hardcover)

If you think the Charles and Diana split was bad, wait until you read about the George IV and Caroline. They separated less than a year after they were married, but that was nothing compared to Caroline's trial for adultery. It was the greatest scandal ever to hit the British monarchy—and the English people sided with Caroline. Although the couple did not divorce, on Coronation Day, Caroline was barred entrance to Westminster Abbey—she would have the title and dignity of Queen, but she would never be crowned. Flora Fraser's biography is frank about Caroline's many indiscretions, but is essentially a sympathetic account of a woman who was outrageously misused.

CONSTANTINE THE GREAT
by Michael Grant (Scribner, 1994, hardcover)

Who'd have thought the grandson of a goat herder would ever become Emperor of Rome, much less the first Christian emperor. Although early in his career Constantine pledged himself to the Christian God, he waited until his deathbed to be baptized and he never let piety stop him from disposing of anyone who got in his way (including his wife and his eldest son). Utilizing new research in fields as diverse as archaeology and art history, Grant draws a detailed portrait of a complex man, arguably the most important emperor since Augustus.

ALEXANDER OF MACEDON, 356-323 B.C.
by Peter Green (University of California Press, 1991, paperback)

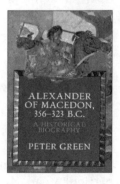

One of the most distinguished scholars of the ancient world presents an exciting, in-depth biography of Alexander the Great. Green studies the people who had the strongest influence on the young conqueror: Philip, his warlike father; his ambitious mother, Olympias; and his brilliant tutor, Aristotle. Then Green takes the reader on campaign with Alexander, a supremely confident commander who would do anything to win.

CLEOPATRA:
HISTORIES, DREAMS AND DISTORTIONS
by Lucy Hughes-Hallett (publisher?)

For more than 2000 years, Cleopatra has been the epitome of the sultry temptress. Now Hughes-Hallett has written the first biography that examines Cleopatra's life and the impact her legend has had on the Western imagination. This is a book packed with surprises: for instance, Cleopatra was Greek; she was rather homely; and she was no spring chicken when she met Mark Antony. Worth searching for.

YOUNG BESS, ELIZABETH, CAPTIVE PRINCESS, ELIZABETH AND THE PRINCE OF SPAIN
by Margaret Irwin (Ulverscroft Large Print Books, 1974, hardcover)

These long-lost biographies of Elizabeth I's youth first appeared in the 1940s. In Young Bess, 12-year-old Elizabeth carefully threads her way through the menacing Tudor court. Elizabeth, Captive Princess finds Elizabeth suspected of treason by her insecure half-sister, Queen Mary. And Elizabeth and the Prince of Spain imagines a dangerous love triangle of Mary, Elizabeth and Philip of Spain.

RICHARD THE THIRD
by Paul Murray Kendall (Norton, 1956, paperback)

This book is still the best biography of Richard, the last of the Plantagenets and England's last medieval king. Kendall sorts out the myths from the facts, studies Richard's character and weighs the evidence of the murder of the Little Princes with particular care.

PETER THE GREAT: HIS LIFE AND WORLD
by Robert K. Massie
(Ballantine, 1986, paperback)

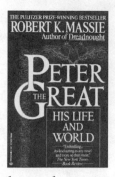

Nobody tells the story of the Russian tsars better than Robert Massie and this biography of Peter the Great is his masterpiece. Massie draws us into Peter's world and reveals the essence of this giant who dragged his semi-barbarous country kicking and screaming into the modern age. Truly one of the best biographies ever written.

THE ROMANOVS: THE FINAL CHAPTER
by Robert K. Massie (Random House, 1995, paperback)

Massie, the Pulitzer Prize-winning historian, biographer and author of Nicholas and Alexandra, unravels the final mysteries that surrounded the death of the Romanovs. Here is the story of the six amateur archaeologists who found the mass grave in 1979 and kept it secret until 1991; the exhumation of the remains; the DNA evidence (which finally puts to rest the story that Anastasia survived the massacre); and the ongoing squabbles among forensic experts, Romanov descendants and the Russian Orthodox Church over the proper disposal of the bones. A book that is by turns fascinating, chilling and sad.

CAESAR: A BIOGRAPHY
by Christian Meier (Basic Books, 1996, paperback)

The Romans had a lot of trouble dealing with Gaius Julius Caesar. He was, after all, a marked individualist in a society that discouraged individualism and his conquests were not for the greater glory or security of the Republic, but to satisfy his own craving for power. In ancient Rome, hubris like that could get you assassinated. Classical historian Christian Meier has written a provocative biography that casts a critical eye on a world conqueror and would-be emperor. Nonetheless, Meier can't help relishing the incredible drama of Caesar's life. You will, too.

DIANA: HER TRUE STORY
by Andrew Morton (Pocket Books, 1992, paperback)

This is the biography that shocked the world. Morton reveals that virtually from day one, Princess Diana had second thoughts about marrying Prince Charles and that she described her wedding day as the "most emotionally confusing day" of her life. Here are all the revelations of Diana's bulimia, her suicide attempts and Charles' callous indifference to his wife and the mother of his sons.

AN UNCOMMON WOMAN:
THE EMPRESS FREDERICK
by Hannah Pakula (Simon & Schuster, 1995, hardcover)

Her real name was Victoria and she was the first child of Queen Victoria and Prince Albert. Raised by her father to believe in the principles of constitutional monarchy and parliamentary government, the princess was married to Frederick of Prussia as a kind of political missionary to bring liberal principles to an autocratic kingdom. Drawing upon vast archives on both sides of the English Channel, Pakula tells the Empress' event-filled story, including rejection of her progressive views by her son, Kaiser Wilhelm II and his adherence to a form of monarchy that was passing away. A fascinating story of a great lady.

FAMILY FEUD: DREADNOUGHT:
BRITAIN, GERMANY AND THE COMING OF
THE GREAT WAR
by Robert K. Massie (Ballantine, 1992, paperback).

A monumental history of Great Britain's slow realization that Kaiser Wilhelm II was determined to be a world power. Especially interesting is the ambivalent relationship between the Kaiser and his uncle, Edward VII of England.

THE LAST TSAR:
THE LIFE AND DEATH OF NICHOLAS II
by Edvard Radzhinsky

The bodies were put in a hole... and generally doused with sulfuric acid," wrote Yakov Yurovsky, the man who supervised the execution of the tsar and his family. But for decades the Soviets denied the existence of the document that became known as "The Yurovsky Note." Then Radzhinsky found it. And so began his poignant, heartbreaking quest to solve the riddles that still surround the murder of the Romanovs. Worth searching for.

ISABELLA OF CASTILLE:
THE FIRST RENAISSANCE QUEEN,
by Nancy Rakin

Most likely, the only thing you remember about Queen Isabella is that she pawned her jewels so Columbus could discover America. Now Rakin has come forward with the first modern scholarly biography of this shrewd, pious, cultivated woman. Rakin's portrait of this complex woman reveals how Isabella achieved power in a world of men, why she backed Columbus and why she expelled the Jews and brought the Inquisition to Spain. Worth searching for.

RICHARD II
by Nigel Saul (Yale University Press, 1997, hardcover)

Some of us were taught that Richard II had been deposed because his affectation of blowing his nose in a handkerchief offended the virile nobility of England. Happily, in Nigel Saul's book, we get a more nuanced portrait of the king. England in the 1380s was in straitened circumstances, its peasants were in open rebellion and its nobles were edgy. The whole situation made Richard, who came to the throne at age 10, insecure. Throw in a few royal tantrums and you begin to understand how Henry Bolingbroke (soon to be Henry IV) could have seized the throne. The handkerchief theory may be easier to remember, but Saul's Richard is much more human.

NAPOLEON BONAPARTE
by Alan Schom (HarperCollins, 1997, hardcover)

Alan Schom takes a fresh approach to Napoleon, telling the story of the emperor's career in light of his character. At every stage of his life, whether he was playing politics during the risky days of the French Revolution or taking on the might of Russia and England, Napoleon's lust for ever greater challenges led him to one brilliant success after another. Ultimately he reached too far and was crushed by his own ambition. But it's a long road to Napoleon's defeat and the trip is thrilling as we witness his peak performances as a general, his passion and then contempt for Josephine and finally his exile and murder.

THE FALL OF THE ROMANOVS
by Mark D. Steinberg and Vladimir M. Khrustalev, Russian documents translated by Elizabeth Tucker
(Yale University Press, 1995, hardcover)

An American historian at Yale University and an archivist-historian at the State Archive of the Russian Federation in Moscow discovered this treasure trove of original materials from eye-witness reports of the imprisonment of the Imperial Family, to the final letters and diary entries of the victims, plus many photographs. It is almost all new material and much of it is heartbreaking.

SUETONIUS: THE TWELVE CAESARS
translated by Robert Graves (Penguin, 1979, paperback)

Suetonius was director of the imperial libraries and the collection of the Caesars' correspondence, a post he held from A.D. 117 to 138. Out of those documents, he created this excellent history of Rome's first emperors—from Julius to Domitian. Today, historians are still impressed by Suetonius' scholarly objectivity and his gift for telling a good story.

ARISTOCRATS:
CAROLINE, EMILY, LOUISA AND SARAH LENNOX, 1740-1832
by Stella Tillyard
(Farrar, Straus & Giroux, 1994, paperback)

The four Lennox sisters were well-connected. Charles II was their great-grandfather. Bonnie Prince Charlie was their cousin. Their husbands were peers of the realm and leading men in Parliament. But what really mattered to the sisters was their private world and this they shared with one another through hundreds of newsy letters. Stella Tillyard has woven a fascinating narrative around the Lennox sisters' correspondence that lets us explore the family scandals (elopements, huge gambling debts, marrying an Irishman!) But more interesting still is what these privileged women tell us about British society.

VICTORIA: AN INTIMATE BIOGRAPHY
by Stanley Weintraub (Dutton/Truman Talley, 1988, paperback)

Today it is hard to imagine a constitutional monarch having the influence Victoria once asserted over England, the Empire and even much of Europe and the United States. Weintraub's life of the queen and empress discovers the origins of her strong will and utter self-confidence and reveals Victoria and Albert's plan to create a new Europe by marrying their children into every royal house on the Continent. Perhaps most interesting of all is how this woman bent her large family and the British government to her will.

THE HABSBURGS: EMBODYING EMPIRE
by Andrew Wheatcroft (Viking, 1995, hardcover)

The Habsburgs pursued power as few royal families ever have. Maximilian I wanted to be both Holy Roman Emperor and Pope. Ferdinand II dreamed of turning back the tide of the Protestant Reformation. But as Holy Roman Emperor, King of Spain and sovereign over all the Spanish colonies in the New World, Charles V came closest to his family's ideal. Wheatcroft chronicles the lives of such Habsburgs as Marie Antoinette, Crown Prince Rudolf who committed suicide with his mistress and the last Habsburg emperor Karl, whose case for canonization is under review in Rome. Packed with great history and juicy family gossip, this is a wonderful account of Europe's longest-reigning dynasty.

················

KING EDWARD VIII
by Philip Ziegler (Knopf, 1991, hardcover)

Good gossip and a definitive biography in the same volume! In the United States, the story of Edward VIII giving up the British throne for the woman he loves seems awfully romantic. But Ziegler, working with unrestricted access to the Royal Archives, consulting documents never before accessible to the public, even interviewing the Queen, finds an entirely different character. Edward was a shallow, selfish, idle playboy and Wallis Simpson a shrill virago who never forgave the Royal Family for refusing to give her the title-and the cash settlement—she wanted. Worth searching for.

················

SACRED HISTORY

JERUSALEM: ONE CITY, THREE FAITHS
by Karen Armstrong (Knopf, 1996, hardcover)

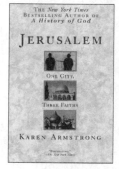

"The ancient city had been built as an enclave of safety against the demonic realm of the desert, where no life was possible," says Armstrong as she recounts the history of Jerusalem. She chronicles the first cults that worshipped on Mount Zion; David's transformation of Jerusalem into a Jewish city; the Roman, Muslim and Crusader conquests and the bloodshed that accompanied their arrival. And Armstrong brings her story up to our own time—the Jewish repossession of the Western Wall in 1967 and the ongoing conflict between Israelis and Palestinians. A balanced, insightful account of a city that arouses love in the hearts of millions.

THE TRIAL OF THE TEMPLARS
by Malcolm Barber (Cambridge University Press, 1993, paperback)

On October 13, 1307, every Knight Templar in France was arrested by order of the king, Philip IV. Once the guardians of Jerusalem, the pride and joy of popes and princes throughout Christian Europe, one of the wealthiest orders in the Church, the Templars were now accused of the vilest crimes, including satanic worship. Under torture, almost all the Templars confessed, including the Grand Master of the order, Jacques de Molay. Were they guilty? Or were they victims of the French king's avarice? In this richly detailed narrative history, Barber re-examines the charges, studies the character of the participants and essentially tries the Templars all over again. A gripping story, from Cambridge University Press' excellent *Canto* series.

PLAIN AND SIMPLE:
A WOMAN'S JOURNEY TO THE AMISH
by Sue Bender (Riverside, 1991, paperback)

One day, Sue Bender walked into a men's clothing store and was captivated by the Amish quilts hanging on the walls. So began a 25-year odyssey among the "plain people" that culminated with a privilege rarely offered to outsiders: Bender became the live-in guest of two Amish families. In prose as spare, clean and uncluttered as an Amish home, Bender draws back the veil that separates us from the Amish and teaches us how to incorporate the best of their world into our own harried lives.

ARROW OF THE BLUE-SKINNED GOD:
RETRACING THE RAMAYANA THROUGH INDIA
by Jonah Blank (Doubleday, 1993, paperback)

Part spiritual quest, part travelogue, part epic adventure. Jonah Blank's first book chronicles his own attempts to retrace the Hindu god Rama's route across India as described in the 3000-year-old sacred poem Ramayana.

THE BODY AND SOCIETY:
MEN, WOMEN AND SEXUAL RENUNCIATION
IN EARLY CHRISTIANITY
by Peter Brown (Columbia University Press, 1990, paperback)

Where did Western society get the idea that nudity is bad, virginity is good and sex is only for married people? Not from the rabbis of Judea, sassy Peter Brown, scholar of the ancient world, but from the pagan Stoics of Greece and Rome. A fascinating study of how the West came to believe that what you do in your bedroom is everybody's business.

IN THE YEAR 1096: PERSECUTION,
RESISTANCE, REVERBERATIONS
by Robert Chazan (Jewish Publications, 1996, hardcover)

Nine hundred years have passed since some crusader bands attacked the Jews of the Rhineland, but it is still an explosive issue. Now Robert Chazan has written an eye-opening study of what happened. Drawing upon original Jewish and Christian sources, he studies the actions and hesitations of a complex cast of characters—the crusaders, the Christians of the Rhineland and the Jews themselves. Best of all, in the place of good-guy/bad-guy stick figures, Chazan shows us living men and women forced by circumstances to make cruel choices.

A CHRONICLE OF THE LAST PAGANS
by Pierre Chauvin

How the religious, intellectual and political life of pagans in the Roman Empire became complicated under Christian emperors. Worth searching for.

THE STRIPPING OF THE ALTARS: TRADITIONAL RELIGION IN ENGLAND, 1400-1580
by Eamon Duffy (Yale University Press, 1994, paperback)

A groundbreaking book that uses original documents to explore what it meant to ordinary Englishmen and Englishwomen when Henry VIII's Reformation swept away the Church they loved.

WHO WROTE THE DEAD SEA SCROLLS: THE SEARCH FOR THE SECRET QUMRAN
by Norman Golb
(Touchstone Books, 1996, paperback)

Since their discovery in 1947, the Dead Sea Scrolls have attracted world-class scholars and world-class loonies. Now Dr. Norman Golb, a respected Scrolls scholar for decades, offers a fresh interpretation of these ancient treasures.

He attributes their authorship to several religious groups—not just the Essenes—and reveals fresh links between the communities and the early Christian Church, both of whom who shared a number of ideas and practices, including baptism, a sacred meal and the belief in a dying messiah who is the son of God.

THE BIBLE AND THE ANCIENT NEAR EAST, FOURTH EDITION
by Cyrus H. Gordon & Gary A. Rendsburg
(1953; Norton, 1997, hardcover)

Since it was first published more than 40 years ago, this invaluable reference has helped readers of the Hebrew Bible (what Christians call the Old Testament) make sense of enigmatic references to the world of the ancient Near Eastern. For example, what was "Ur of the Chaldees" out of which the Lord led Abraham? Did the Israelites interpret dreams differently than their neighbors? There are also fascinating sections on Israel as a league of tribes and the role David and his dynasty played in uniting the Israelites. This excellent resource supplies accurate, succinct answers so you can make sense of the biblical narratives.

CROWNING GLORY:
SILVER TORAH ORNAMENTS OF THE JEWISH MUSEUM, NEW YORK
by Rafi Grafman, Edited by Vivian B. Mann
(David R. Godine/The Jewish Museum, 1996, hardcover)

The collection of Torah ornaments in New York's Jewish Museum stands among the top three in the world, as this sumptuously illustrated volume demonstrates. More than 1000 sacred objects are displayed here—silver Torah crowns, shields, cases, finials and pointers. Some date back to the Middle Ages, many come from the destroyed Jewish community of Danzig: on the eve of World War II, they sent their treasures to New York for safe keeping. Rafi Grafman, formerly of the Israel Museum, describes each object in loving detail, explains its significance and discusses the variations in style from one country and century to the next. A magnificent chronicle of religious devotion.

CELTIC GODDESSES:
WARRIORS, VIRGINS AND MOTHERS
by Miranda Green (British Museum Press, 1995, hardcover)

Morrigan was a goddess who didn't take no for an answer. When the Irish hero Cuchulain refused to put off battle to go to bed with her, she herself attacked him on the battlefield. In this scholarly but completely accessible study of Celtic goddesses, Green looks to archaeological evidence and Celtic myths to discover the character of the goddesses who presided over healing, childbirth and warfare, assured good harvests, protected animals and, when Christianity arrived, passed on their best attributes to female Celtic saints.

STATIONS OF THE SUN:
A HISTORY OF THE RITUAL YEAR IN BRITAIN
by Ronald Hutton (Oxford University Press, 1996, hardcover)

Beltane and Samhain. Whitsun Ales and Corpus Christi plays. May Day and Harvest Home. In medieval Britain, the year was an endless cycle of festivals and feast days. Now folklorist Ronald Hutton helps readers experience vicariously the rituals of these forgotten holidays. Best of all, he cites literary works that throw light on the old customs: Chaucer on Valentine's Day, Milton on harvest queens, Sir Gawain and the Green Knight on New Year's celebrations and Thomas Hardy on Guy Fawkes Day. A wonderful compendium of the merriest days of the old English year.

BLASPHEMY:
VERBAL OFFENSES AGAINST THE SACRED, FROM MOSES TO SALMAN RUSHDIE
by Leonard W. Levy
(University of North Carolina Press, 1995, paperback)

Who better than a legal historian to take on the task of explaining the ancient sin of blasphemy. Levy looks at the famous people who have been charged with blaspheming—Socrates, Jesus, Thomas Paine, Martin Scorsese—and reveals cases in which the charge has been used to abridge intellectual or religious liberty.

THE EXCELLENT EMPIRE: THE FALL OF ROME AND THE TRIUMPH OF THE CHURCH
by Jaroslav Pelikan

When Rome fell to the barbarians in 410, the pagan Romans blamed the Christians for corrupting their ancient imperial city. Yale professor Jaroslav Pelikan, the most respected writer on early Christian history, finds that modern pagans and Christians are still debating what the Fall of Rome means. Worth searching for.

JESUS THROUGH THE CENTURIES
by Jaroslav Pelikan (HarperCollins, 1987, paperback)

For 2000 years, men and woman have taken Jesus Christ to their hearts and adapted him for their own particular time. Jaroslav Pelikan, the most respected historian of Christianity, traces how the image of Jesus has changed through the ages—in theology, in popular devotion and in art. A wonderfully enlightening book.

MARY THROUGH THE CENTURIES: HER PLACE IN THE HISTORY OF CULTURE
by Jaroslav Pelikan (Yale University Press, 1996, hardcover)

From America's foremost scholar of the history of religion comes the finest study of the Virgin Mary ever written. Pelikan examines why some churches accord her honors second only to God and others want nothing to do with her. In fact, Pelikan's approach is so comprehensive he includes an absolutely fascinating chapter on Mary in Islam (a lengthy sura is dedicated to her in the Koran). And he becomes positively lyrical when discussing the art, music and poetry Mary has inspired over the last 2000 years. Written in a conversational style and filled with wonderful illustrations, there is nothing on the market nearly as good as Mary Through the Centuries.

RETURN TO SODOM AND GOMORRAH
by *Charles Pellegrino* (Random House, 1994, paperback)

The archaeological sites of the Near East may be one of the few spots on earth where science and biblical scholarship are not strange bedfellows. The fascinating stories here include finding evidence of the ruins of Sodom, the Israelites' path through the wilderness and the plagues that afflicted Egypt.

A HISTORY OF HEAVEN:
THE SINGING SILENCE
by *Jeffrey Burton Russell*(Princeton University Press, 1997, paperback)

Russell hasn't just read up on Heaven, he's been contemplating it. Like a mystic, he defines Heaven as "where God is, in the rose of fire that keeps opening dynamically in one eternal moment." Here you'll find information about the Heaven the Jews expected and the afterlife the Greeks believed in. Plus there are very interesting accounts of a 12th-century Irish knight's journey to Heaven and the near-death experience of an 8th-century Anglo-Saxon layman. But the best chapters are on Dante, who pushed language, metaphor, theology and even physics beyond their limits to describe the light, the splendor, the incomparable beauty of eternity in union with God. A book that is at once informative and inspiring.

JERUSALEM:
AN ARCHAEOLOGICAL BIOGRAPHY
by *Hershel Shanks* (Random House, 1995, paperback)

Few people are better qualified to tell the story of Jerusalem's archaeological treasures than Hershel Shanks. As editor of

Biblical Archaeology Review magazine, he is one of the leading authorities on what lies beneath the surface of contemporary Jerusalem. In this spectacularly illustrated volume, Shanks takes readers on an enthralling tour of the city's past, from King Solomon's Temple to the gate through which Jesus entered the city on Palm Sunday to the city of the Crusaders. Plus, he shows us archaeological finds that match perfectly with biblical texts.

WHAT THE BUDDHA NEVER TAUGHT
by Tim Ward (Celestial Arts Publishing, 1995, paperback)

In 1985, Ward, a Canadian journalist, entered Pah Nanachat Monastery deep in the jungles of Thailand. He knew the monks would expect him follow all 227 precepts of the Buddha, including rising at 3 a.m. to meditate and begging rice daily from local villagers. What he didn't expect to find at the monastery was s corpions, cobras and a large contingent of Westerners seeking enlightenment. Ward offers a frank, often humorous account of a world most of us will probably never experience.

ENCOUNTERING MARY
by Sandra Zimdars-Swartz (Avon, 1991, paperback)

From suburban backyards in New Jersey to oak groves in Spain to mountainsides in Croatia, people keep insisting that they're meeting the Virgin Mary. Sandra Zimdars-Swartz's fascinating study is the first objective attempt to understand the visions-of-the-Virgin phenomenon. She examines Lourdes, Fatima, Medjugorje, among other apparition sites over the last 150 years, to find what they have in common and why some sites are the goal of millions of pilgrims while others are lost in obscurity. This is an engrossing, non-judgmental exploration of Marian sightings and what they tell us about our civilization.

SAINTS & SINNERS (& SOME OTHER FOLKS IN BETWEEN)

VISIONS OF GOD:
FOUR MEDIEVAL MYSTICS AND THEIR WRITINGS
by Karen Armstrong (Bantam Doubleday Dell, 1994, hardcover)

Karen Armstrong says the mystics of the 12th and 13th century "blazed a new trail to God and to the depths of the self." Focusing on four English mystics—Richard Rolle, Walter Hilton, Dame Julian of Norwich and the anonymous author of *The Cloud of Unknowing*—Armstrong introduces readers and seekers to some of the greatest mystical writing of all time. Their passionate desire for God, the intensity of their experiences once they had some inkling of the Divine, is beautiful, startling and impossible to forget.

HERE I STAND: A LIFE OF MARTIN LUTHER
by Roland H. Bainton (NAL Dutton, 1989, paperback)

This is the definitive, most readable biography of the man who started the Protestant Reformation. Bainton offers fascinating insights into the character of the German monk who began by asking a few innocent questions about indulgences and ended up defying the Pope, battling with the Holy Roman Emperor and shattering 1500 years of tradition.

HIS HOLINESS: JOHN PAUL II AND THE HIDDEN HISTORY OF OUR TIME
by Carl Bernstein and Marco Politi (Doubleday, 1996, paperback)

There have been other biographies of Pope John Paul II, but none has focused so intensely on John Paul as a player in world politics. Nor have any other biographers enjoyed such unparalleled access to rare sources of information in Rome, Washington, Warsaw and Moscow. Bernstein and Politi discuss the factors which led to John Paul's election to the Papacy, the extent to which he participated in the collapse of Communism in Eastern Europe. This is a monumental biography, but the authors are such first-rate storytellers they will hold your interest from page one.

THE BAD POPES
by E.R. Chamberlin (Dial Press, 1969, hardback)

John XII, just 18 when he became pope in a rigged election in 955, spent his pontificate chasing women through the streets of Rome. Late 14th-century Europe endured Urban VI, a wildman who tortured his own cardinals. And in 1492, Alexander had his children serve as artists' models for frescoes of his favorite saints. Racy reading from Rome's bad old days. Worth searching for.

THOMAS MORE
by R.W. Chambers (Jonathan Cape, 1949, hardback)

Thomas More, saint and martyr, was profoundly human. he was happily married (twice!), fathered many children, became a wealthy lawyer and was a mover and shaker in the court of Henry VIII. Why did he give it all up? The answers may surprise you. Of all the books on More, Chambers' is still the best. Worth searching for.

AUGUSTINE
by Mary T. Clark (Georgetown University Press, 1994, hardcover)

He lived in sin with a woman for 13 years, had a son out of wedlock and enjoyed the blood sport of dueling gladiators in the arena. No one who knew him at that stage of his life would have expected Augustine to become Christianity's most influential philosopher. In this concise, accessible study, Mary T. Clark traces the intellectual and spiritual development of Augustine from a young libertine to one of the most formidable minds ever to join the Church.

AUGUSTINE'S IDEAS:
AUGUSTINE OF HIPPO: SELECTED WRITINGS
Edited and translated by Mary T. Clark (Paulist Press, 1984, paperback)

An anthology of Augustine's major works in a new translation that captures his vigorous, lively style. From Paulist Press' excellent *Classics of Western Spirituality* series.

ST. PATRICK'S WORLD
by Liam de Paor (Four Courts Press, 1997, hardcover)

This is a book in two parts. The first is a learned yet completely accessible discussion of Christian Europe in the 5th century and where Ireland fits into the picture. The second part is de Paor's own translations of ancient texts about early Irish Christianity. The selection is the best ever. It includes the two authentic works by St. Patrick, the earliest life of St. Brigid and a wonderful letter from St. Columbanus to Pope Boniface IV lamenting that the Pope, intimidated by the Emperor, has fallen into heresy. But Columbanus assures the Holy Father that in Ireland everyone is perfectly orthodox!

CONSCIENCE AND COURAGE:
RESCUERS OF JEWS DURING THE HOLOCAUST
by Eva Fogelman (Doubleday, 1995, paperback)

Fogelman began this book as a tribute to the Polish baker who saved her father's life in 1942. As she tells the stories of Gentile housewives and telephone operators, farmers and nurses who risked their lives to save Jews, Fogelman asks: What made these people different from those who stood by and did nothing?

HELOISE AND ABELARD
by *Etienne Gilson* (Ann Arbor Paperbacks, 1992, paperback)

Gilson was a professor at the Sorbonne when he wrote this classic history of the Middle Ages' most famous love story. More than sixty years later, it is still the best account available of Abelard's tragic passion for Heloise, her family's terrible revenge and of the lover's mutual retirement into the religious life. Gilson brings the old story to life while also introducing modern readers to the genius of two of medieval Europe's finest minds.

SAINT PETER: A BIOGRAPHY
by *Michael Grant* (Simon & Schuster, 1995, hardcover)

When the gospels list the apostles, Peter's name always comes first. Michael Grant, a distinguished scholar of the ancient world, studies the information the New Testament supplies about Peter's complex, often impulsive personality, then he sorts out the legends that have accumulated around the man, analyzing them for any shreds of historical accuracy. Finally, Grant reviews the evidence to see if Rome's Basilica of St. Peter is truly built over the apostle's grave and if archaeologists did find the actual tomb of St. Peter in this century. A fascinating history of one of the most intriguing and likable personalities of the early Christian era.

MARY MAGDALEN:
MYTH AND METAPHOR
by *Susan Haskins* (Berkley, 1997, paperback)

You probably think Mary Magdalen was a repentant prostitute. That is not, however, the case. The Gospels never identify Mary's profession and there isn't even a hint that she was promiscuous. So who was she really? In one of the best books ever devoted to the study of a single saint, Susan Haskins examines the historical Magdalen and the many ways each age has reinvented her: a Christian Venus in the Renaissance, a sacred joke in the decadent courts of 17th-century Europe, a patron of fallen women to the Victorians, an image of fully realized womanhood to modern feminists. A beautifully written study, filled with surprises.

MONTAILLOU:
THE PROMISED LAND OF ERROR
by LeRoy Ladurie (Random House, 1979, paperback)

Around the meticulous records of Bishop Jacques Fournier (the future Pope Benedict XII), Ladurie reconstructs the strife between Albigensians and Catholics in Montaillou, a remote mountain village in southern France. Fournier was a consummate examiner, able to elicit the intriguing information from the peasants and shepherds who came before his tribunal. This book is a rare glimpse into a long-vanished world.

IGNATIUS OF LOYOLA:
THE PSYCHOLOGY OF A SAINT
by W.W. Meissner, S.J., M.D.
(Yale University Press, 1992, hardcover)

St. Ignatius began life as a professional soldier, ladies' man and bon vivant. So why did this intense yet essentially frivolous young man suddenly convert and found the Jesuit order? Meissner, a psychologist and a Jesuit, studies the personality of the man who became one of the most accomplished figures in Western Christianity. From Ignatius' own voluminous writings, Meissner uncovers the interplay between human needs and spiritual motivations.

WISDOM OF THE CELTIC SAINTS
by Edward C. Sellner, illustrations by Susan McLean-Keeney
(Ave Maria Press, 1993, paperback)

Most people see the world "Celtic" and think "Irish." But Sellner uses the term in the wider sense of the Celtic world, including Britain, Wales, Cornwall and Scotland, as well as Ireland. Moving easily between authentic biographies, venerable legends and ancient poems and hymns, Sellner examines the personality of the holy men and women of the Celts—their love of study, their passion for solitude, the joy they felt in the beauty of the natural world, their intimate friendship with God. Enhancing the stories are Susan McLean-Keeney's illustrations—handsome, modern interpretations of the manuscript illuminations of the old Celtic scribes.

ST. EDMUND CAMPION
by Evelyn Waugh (1935; Sophia Institute Press, 1996, paperback)

Evelyn Waugh wrote his life of the Elizabethan Jesuit, Edmund Campion (1540-81) to understand the character of a man who gave up a stellar career at Oxford and preferment at the court of Elizabeth I for a faith in which he had not been raised. Yet the book is also an adventure story. Jesuits were outlaws in Elizabethan England and Campion had his share of narrow escapes. When at last he was captured, he was racked in the Tower of London before being hanged, drawn and quartered. As you'd expect, Waugh writes an elegant biography without ever becoming saccharine or strident. It's a pleasure to have this book in print again.

SAGES AND DREAMERS:
BIBLICAL, TALMUDIC AND HASIDIC PORTRAITS AND LEGENDS
by Elie Wiesel (Touchstone Books, 1993, paperback)

Elie Wiesel never tires of probing the boundaries of Jewish history and memory. In this collection of 25 stories from the Bible, the Talmud and the tales of Hasidim, he brings new insight to such puzzling questions as how Jephthah could have sacrificed his own daughter and why Rabbi Hanina ben Dossa never spoke about the destruction of Jerusalem.

SHAKESPEARE— IN A CLASS BY HIMSELF

RICHARD III
by William Shakespeare (1595; Bantam Books, 1995, paperback)

Even if you think the real-life Richard was framed for the murder the little princes in the Tower, you can still love the sly, cunning, duplicitous devil Shakespeare created. This is an early play and the speeches are filled with the energy of a young writer ambitious to become a great poet. Among the scenes to savor: the great opening speech, poor pathetic Gloucester's dream, the grief of the three queens and of course, Richard's seduction of the Lady Anne—in the middle of a funeral no less!

HAMLET
by William Shakespeare
(c.1601; Norton Critical Editions, 1991, paperback)

Few things in life are as difficult as choosing just one play by Shakespeare and declaring it "the best." So pardon, gentles all, if your favorite is *King Lear*, or *Othello*, or *A Midsummer Night's Dream*. We chose *Hamlet* because it stands at the heart of Shakespeare's career, the point where he appears to have achieved mastery of his art; because the figure of Hamlet intrigues readers, audiences, actors and scholars like no other character in Shakespeare; and because in *Hamlet* Shakespeare explores the link between theater and daily life—in other words, the compulsion we all feel to play a part.

HENRY IV, PART 1
by William Shakespeare (1597; Norton, 1969, paperback)

Swilling ale. Roguish escapades. Great speeches. A little treason. And a battle to the death. Shakespeare knew how to write a great history play and this is probably his overall best of this kind. The story, you'll remember, is this: Prince Hal has fallen under the influence of a comical, rotund, disreputable knight named Falstaff. Meanwhile, Hotspur, Hal's contemporary and the pride of the Percy clan, is covering himself with glory in battle for King Henry IV. But then, Hotspur's hot temper gets the best of him and he switches loyalties from Henry to the Welsh rebel Glendower. Prince Hal's not so much of a party boy that he's going to take treachery lying down. He and Hotspur fight it out in one of Shakespeare's most stirring climaxes.

KING LEAR
by William Shakespeare (1605; Bantam, 1988, paperback)

It starts out as a fairy-tale plot: an arrogant old king rejects his plain-speaking daughter in favor of her two flattering sisters and then is destroyed by them. As all comfort is stripped away from Lear, Shakespeare widens the significance of this simple story until it broods over questions of human heartlessness and the mystery of evil. Especially memorable is the scene in the hovel: as a storm rages outside, Lear raves, Edgar chatters away as "Poor Tom" and the Fool chimes in with crack-pated, riddling comments. This is Shakespeare's darkest and most stirring play, a work almost without precedent in Western literature.

MACBETH
by William Shakespeare
(1606; Routledge, Chapman & Hall, 1985, paperback)

Chances are, this is the one Shakespeare play you liked in high school—probably because it was the only one you could understand. So imagine how much more you'll get out of it now. The poetry is thrilling, the murders and hauntings keep you on the edge of your seat and is there anyone in literature who can compare with Lady Macbeth?

THE TEMPEST
by William Shakespeare (1611; Cambridge University Press, 1995, paperback)

You can hardly call yourself a book lover if you ignore the greatest writer in the English language. So read *The Tempest*, Shakespeare's most enchanting lay (and also one of his shortest). There's a wizard, a shipwrecked prince, an island maiden who has never seen a man, a few spirits, a monster, drop-dead gorgeous poetry and a happy ending.

THE TEMPEST
by William Shakespeare, retold by Ann Keay Beneduce, illustrated by Gennady Spirin. (Philomel, 1996, paperback)

While most retellings of Shakespeare are pale, lifeless things, Anne Keay Beneduce has managed to convey in prose the beauty of Shakespeare's most magical play. But best of all are Gennady Spirin's sumptuous illustrations, painted in the style of the Renaissance masters. If this book doesn't get kids interested in Shakespeare, nothing will.

NORTHROP FRYE ON SHAKESPEARE
by Northrop Frye (Yale University Press, 1988, hardcover)

If you need a little friendly assistance, the dean of modern Shakespeare criticism explains it all for you in clear, understandable language that will enhance your enjoyment of ten plays, including *Romeo and Juliet*, *Hamlet* and *The Tempest*.

SCI-FI CLASSICS

THE GODS THEMSELVES
by Isaac Asimov (Bantam, 1990, paperback)

Asimov said that among all his books, this story of Earth scientists who receive messages from their counterparts in a parallel universe was his favorite. Asimov juggles these two worlds easily and fills readers with a chilling sense of dread every time the beings from the other universe communicate with people on Earth. Winner of science fiction's prestigious Hugo Award.

Also by Asimov:

I, ROBOT
(Warner Books, 1994, paperback).

Nine short stories about robots that made Asimov an international sensation among readers of science fiction.

FAHRENHEIT 451
by Ray Bradbury (1953; Ballantine, 1987, paperback)

Fahrenheit 451 is the temperature at which paper burns. In some dark future time, all information comes through television. "Firemen" are state functionaries who burn books and anyone who owns them. It's just a job. But then one Fireman discovers that books convey information, too. More to the point, they convey ideas. So he starts to read them in secret, until he is betrayed. Most readers consider this Bradbury's greatest novel and one of the finest works of science fiction ever written.

More of Ray Bradbury:

THE VINTAGE BRADBURY
(Random House, 1990, paperback).

All of his greatest short stories: "The Illustrated Man", "Dandelion Wine", "The Veldt", "The Fog Horn" and "The Wonderful Ice Cream Suit".

THE MARTIAN CHRONICLES
by Ray Bradbury (1950; Bantam, 1984, paperback)

One of the most significant books in the science fiction canon is Bradley's novel of humankind's repeated efforts to colonize Mars and their unsettling encounters with shapeshifting Martians. The book is really a series of independent stories, but Bradbury binds them together through common themes and haunting recurring images. One of the real masterpieces of science fiction.

FIREDANCE
by Steven Barnes Tor, 1993, paperback)

Aubry Knight, trained as a street fighter, has turned his back on the Ortega crime organization and joined the resistance in the ruins of central Los Angeles. But nobody gets away that easily. Knight's enemies have made accelerated clones of him, trained them as assassins and sent them after the original Aubry. An original and thrilling work of science fiction.

THE GODS OF MARS
by Edgar Rice Burroughs (1913; Ballantine, 1991, paperback)

Burroughs conceived his Martian Tales while he was the regional manager of a group of pencil sharpener salesmen, an occupation which gave him plenty of time to ruminate on the world's problems. His second Martian novel focuses on organized religion. To find his incomparable Dejah Thoris, John Carter travels down "the river of life" at the end of which Martians expect to find their eternal reward, only to discover that "heaven" is not quite what the priests promised.

DAWN

by Octavia E. Butler (Warner Books, 1997, paperback)

Octavia Butler puts a new spin on an apocalyptic tale. After a nuclear holocaust, aliens rescue as many human survivors as they can. The humans are put in a state of suspended animation while the aliens rehabilitate devastated planet Earth. The first human to be awakened is Lilith Iyapo. She finds the aliens absolutely terrifying and the prospect of resettling the wilderness Earth has become is anything but comforting. Worse yet, as Lilith resists the aliens' ongoing interference in human affairs, the human survivors begin to turn against her. A very inventive story by one of science fiction's top authors.

ENDER'S GAME

by Orson Scott Card (Tor, 1992, paperback)

At the age of six, Ender Wiggin, a military prodigy, is taken from his family and sent to battle School in outer space. For years, Ender and his team of child warriors learn war games that one day may save Earth from an alien invasion. But are these contests really just games?

The Sequels:

SPEAKER FOR THE DEAD
(Tor, 1986, paperback).

Ender tries to prevent a war of annihilation with an alien planet.

XENOCIDE
(St. Martin's Press, 1992, paperback).

Humans and aliens share a planet, but a virus essential to the aliens is proving lethal to humans.

THE ANDROMEDA STRAIN

by Michael Crichton (Ballantine, 1997, paperback)

A unmanned research satellite returns to Earth and brings with it a mysterious, lethal disease. The first victims are the inhabitants of a little town in Arizona where everyone—except an infant and an elderly derelict—have died of the plague. In a secret laboratory five stories beneath the Nevada desert, four American scientists try to find an antidote to the killer microbe and the reason why the infant and the old man survived. But then the virus breaks out of its hypersterile environment and suddenly the scientists are facing a global disaster.

LORD FOUL'S BANE, THE ILLEARTH WAR, THE POWER THAT PRESERVES

by Stephen R. Donaldson (Del Rey Books, 1997, paperback)

A mong readers of science fiction and science fantasy, the tales of Thomas Covenant and his epic battles against Lord Foul have always been wildly popular. These books are works of high fantasy and are very addictive. If you've never read science fiction, this entertaining trilogy is a good place to start.

THE ESSENTIAL ELLISON

by Harlan Ellison, Edited by Terry Dowling with Richard Delap and Gil Lamont (Nemo Press, 1987, paperback)

I f you're already a Harlan Ellison fan you need this in your library. If you're new to the outspoken Science Fiction author, this 35-year retrospective is a good jumping off point. Sandwiched between his first story, published in 1945 at the age of 15 and a piece published in Los Angeles magazine in 1983, you'll find classic tales such as "I Have No Mouth and I Must Scream" and "A Boy and His Dog," as well as reviews and essays. Particularly good is Ellison's account of his 1960 arrest in New York City.

An Ellison Graphic Novel:

HARLAN ELLISON'S DREAM CORRIDOR
(Dark Horse Comics, 1995, paperback).

The graphic novel format is especially well-suited to Ellison's explicit and thoroughly unpleasant dreams that feature a brutal dictator who hides out in a prehistoric age, a stoolie who has a really close encounter with a nasty sharp-toothed creature and more.

PERMUTATION CITY
by Greg Egan (HarperPrism, 1995, paperback)

Egan imagines a world in which you can copy your memories and personality, upload them into a computer generated universe, live there and return at will. The good news is that this is a type of immortality. The bad news is something or someone has blocked the Return option. Then you discover who has locked you out—yourself. Or rather, it is the other you—the one who wants to keep you locked in the cyberworld forever.

BECOMING HUMAN
by Valerie J. Freireich (NAL Dutton, 1995, paperback)

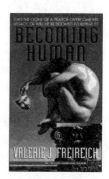

Alexander and August are Toolmen, genetically altered creations superior to humans but loyal and obedient servants nonetheless. The Electors, the ruling elite of their interstellar society, have chosen Alexander and August for a special function—spying. They watch every human facial expression and body gesture, vigilant for any sign of hostility to the Electors. But Alexander and August are growing unhappy with their role and are beginning to wonder if the Electors are worth serving. Freireich brings a thrilling intensity to her first science fiction novel.

FOREVER PEACE
by Joe Haldeman (Ace Books, 1997, paperback)

It's the year 2043 and the war between the American-led Alliance and the third world confederation Ngumi is in its eighth year. Most of the fighting is done by soldierboys: robot killers run by remote control. Physicist Julian Class is one of the mechanics who operate the remotes. Meanwhile, his lover, Ameilia Harding, discovers that a project to explore Jupiter has the potential to vaporize the entire universe. Haldeman creates some of the most complex characters in science fiction and he writes intelligently about humankind's violent tendencies. This novel shows all the signs of becoming a classic.

THE LATHE OF HEAVEN
by Ursula K. LeGuin (Avon, 1976, paperback)

LeGuin is one of the top authors of science fantasy. This profound book takes on the tension between nations, between races, even between doctors and patients. George Orr goes into therapy when his dreams start coming true in disastrous ways. But the dreams (and their effects) get worse as George's therapist uses them to advance his medical career.

REMNANT POPULATION
by Elizabeth Moon (Baen/Pocket Books, 1996, paperback)

Ofelia was an old woman when her failed colony was evacuated. But rather than leave the planet, she stays behind to enjoy the freedom of living alone and the privilege of dying in peace. Then, to Ofelia's sorrow, a new band of human settlers arrives. At about the same time, aliens appear on the scene. In this ticklish situation, Ofelia finds herself thrust into the role of ambassador. A very clever first contact novel.

Another Moon:

HUNTING PARTY
(Baen/Pocket Books, 1994, paperback).

Heris was forced to resign her commission in Space Service. Now she is the unwilling captain of an interstellar luxury yacht, taking her wealthy employers around the galaxies. A little excitement arrives at last in the guise of "sportsmen" who hunt humans.

RED MARS
by Kim Stanley Robinson (Bantam Books, 1993, paperback)

Kim Stanley Robinson won the Nebula Award for Best Book for this novel of the first human settlement on Mars. The pioneers have a found lifeless planet: some want to alter the ecosystem and make it habitable for humans, others believe the planet should be preserved in all its stark beauty. But no one—not the naive idealists nor the would-be exploiters—can say for certain if "terraforming" will work on Mars, or what the repercussions might be if they attempt it.

HOLY FIRE
by Bruce Sterling (Bantam Books, 1996, paperback)

Earth in the late 21st century has become a paradise. Crime and sickness have all but disappeared. And advances in cybernetics and nano- and virtual technology have put immortality within everyone's grasp. But the technology isn't flawless, as Mia Ziemann, a 94-year-old medical economist, is about to learn. After an experimental rejuvenation procedure, Mia looks like she's 20, but she's acting like a psychotic. On the streets she encounters an underclass of young artists and anarchists. At first, they strike Mia as colorful bohemians. But their sense of frustration has made them radicals and they want Mia to help them put an end to the earthly paradise.

SHORT TAKES

SHIP FEVER AND OTHER STORIES
by Andrea Barrett (Norton, 1996, paperback)

By imagining moments from the lives of great scientists and exploring the limits of the scientific method, Barrett has created an uncommon collection of short stories. "Ship Fever" finds a Canadian physician in a quarantine hospital, trying to reconcile his obligation to heal the sick with his contempt for the Irish refugees who are his patients. "The English Pupil" is an intimate story of the great Swedish botanist, Carolus Linneaus, coping with the double frustrations of memory loss and physical paralysis. A truly exceptional book that contrasts the cold certainty of science with the more chaotic movements of the human heart.

SWIMMING IN THE CONGO
by Grace Berggren (Milkweed, 1995, paperback)

This collection of luminous short stories chronicles the adventures of Margaret Meyers, the daughter of missionaries stationed on the banks of the Congo River. While the missionaries attempt to maintain Western standards, young Margaret is entranced by the lush magnificence of the Congo, finds freedom swimming in the river and is charmed by a community of free-thinking European expatriates. Berggren spent much of her own childhood in the Congo—now known as Zaire—and her experience of the place and its people raises these stories from a handful of exotic tales to an intelligent portrayal of the troubles that still beset Africa.

THE DEVIL'S MODE
by Anthony Burgess (Random House, 1989, paperback)

Here is a collection of witty, allusive short stories that shows Burgess at the top of his game. "1889 and the Devil's Mode" draws together characters from the literary and artistic culture of France, England and Ireland in 1889—the intellectual milieu from which early modernism emerged. "Meeting in Valladolid" imagines a conversation between Shakespeare and Cervantes on the rival claims of comedy and tragedy as visions of life. Especially memorable is "Hun," an exciting novella of Attila the Hun, a barbarian genius who feels seduced and repelled by Christian Rome—Christian Romans feel the same way about him.

THE MATISSE STORIES
by A.S. Byatt (Vintage, 1996, paperback)

The paintings of Matisse are the starting pint for three stories of women who experience unsettling surprises. From the author of Possession.

THE PALACE THIEF
by Ethan Canin
(Picador USA, 1995, paperback)

Halfway between the short story and the novella are these four luminous tales by Ethan Canin. By playing two sides against the middle with his genres, Canin has given his characters and story lines more room to develop, but kept the length down so you can still digest these wonderful pieces in a single sitting. An accountant confesses the strange revenge he took on a more successful friend. A boy unravels the many mysteries of older brother's genius; a son teaches his father about the joys of falling in love; a prep school history teacher spars with a sly student underachiever. Don't miss these profoundly beautiful stories.

EXILES: THREE SHORT NOVELS
by Philip Caputo (Knopf, 1997, hardcover)

Philip Caputo takes his readers on three journeys into Vietnam, Micronesia and Connecticut. But they are all really journeys into the heart of darkness. "In the Forest of the Laughing Elephant" five American soldiers crash through a Vietnamese jungle, chasing a huge man-eating tiger that has carried off one of their friends. "Paradise" finds an American expatriate on an island in the South Pacific where he is determined to "improve" the islanders by having them work in his fish processing plant. (The islanders appear to have other ideas). In "Standing In" a wealthy Connecticut couple take in a young drifter who bears a striking resemblance to their dead son. If you've never read Philip Caputo, these stories are a good place to start.

TROUBLE IS MY BUSINESS
by Raymond Chandler (Vintage, 1988, paperback)

On nights like that every booze party ends in a fight. Meek little wives feel the edge of a carving knife and study their husbands' neck. Anything can happen." Raymond Chandler was a journalist, soldier and oil company executive before he turned his hand to fiction at the age of 45. The seven novels and handful of short stories he published in his career practically defined the hard-boiled detective genre and gave us one of its most enduring private eyes, Philip Marlowe. This collection of 12 early mysteries, including the classic "Red Wind," is Chandler at his best.

A LONG DESIRE
by Evan S. Connell (North Point Press, 1988, paperback)

An English explorer returns to London with 1300 tons of precious metal, only to learn it is fool's gold. Thousands of German and French children form an army to liberate Jerusalem from the infidels. An Incan king is smeared with sticky balsam and his entire body is sprinkled with gold dust, making him the living idol of his tribe. Reading this collection is like listening to a master storyteller spin fantastic tales on a long winter night.

THE LITERARY GHOST:
GREAT CONTEMPORARY GHOST STORIES
Edited by Larry Dark
(The Atlantic Monthly Press, 1991, paperback)

Everybody loves a good ghost story, so it's good to know that the genre is alive and flourishing among our best contemporary authors. But some of these stories are ghostly tales with a twist. The ghost is the narrator in stories by Anne Sexton, Muriel Spark and Nadine Gordimer. The ghosts never quite materialize in Tim O'Brien's "The Ghost Soldiers." But Penelope Lively and V.S. Pritchett tell more conventional stories of haunted houses and Jack Matthews has his ghosts cruising around in automobiles. A feast for lovers of a good scare.

ECLOGUES: EIGHT STORIES
by Guy Davenport (North Point Press, 1981, paperback)

At the sophisticated end of the short story spectrum you'll find Guy Davenport. His writing is allusive, sometimes enigmatic, always beautifully crafted. "Idyll" begins as a vividly imagined pastoral scene in ancient Greece which dissolves into a Civil War field hospital where Walt Whitman is tending the wounded. "On Some Lines of Virgil" is a beautiful homoerotic novella set in Bordeaux. "The Trees of Lystra" is based on an episode from the New Testament in which Paul and Barnabas try to preach Christianity and are run out of town—the narrator, a Greek boy, gives us the pagans' side of the story. Short stories as refined as these are very rare. Give Davenport a try.

LOVE MEDICINE
by Louise Erdrich (Henry Holt, 1993, paperback)

Erdrich's collection of interrelated short stories follow the misadventures of several Chippewa families in North Dakota. These aren't cheerful pieces: they address poverty, violence, crime and alcoholism, the burden of history and memory, the pressure to assimilate. Still, you can't help but enjoy the dark comedy of the title story in which a reputed healer tries to cast a spell that will keep his grandfather faithful to his grandmother, but winds up killing the old man instead. Erdrich's skillful blend of elements of Native American oral tradition and her own gifts as a poet bring moments of transcendent beauty to these tales.

Two More by Erdrich:

BEET QUEEN
by Louise Erdrich (Bantam Doubleday Dell, 1989, paperback).

A family saga that begins when two orphaned children arrive in a small North Dakota town to live with their aunt, uncle and cousin. Erdrich explores the tensions and tenacity of family ties.

TRACKS
by Louise Erdrich (HarperCollins, 1989, paperback).

Two narrators—an astute Chippewa tribal elder and an embittered young woman of mixed blood—grapple with the collapse of traditional Indian life.

THE SHORT STORIES OF F. SCOTT FITZGERALD
Edited by Matthew J. Bruccoli Free Press, 1990, hardcover)

Fitzgerald's short stories are among the most intense and vivid in American literature. These 43 stories span his all-too-brief career and display his seemingly effortless craftsmanship. Writing tales of love, beauty and ambition, Fitzgerald always addressed himself "to the youth of his own generation," yet these powerful, romantic stories speak eloquently to readers of every time and place.

OCTOPUSSY: THE LAST GREAT ADVENTURES OF JAMES BOND
by Ian Fleming (New American Library, 1965, paperback)

Here's a quick way to discover whether you're a Bond fan or not. Published as a posthumous collection in 1965, these three short stories, which originally appeared in Playboy and

Argosy magazines, contain some of Fleming's best work. Particularly good are the quite clever title story in which Bond plays somewhat of a minor, yet important, role and "The Living Daylights," which gets inside of Bond's mind as waits in a Berlin tenement to assassinate a rival assassin.

WOMEN WITH MEN: THREE STORIES
by Richard Ford (Knopf, 1997, hardcover)

In Richard Ford's follow-up to his award-winning Independence Day, three men muddle through their relationships with women. "The Womanizer" is a comic story of a man who tries to start an affair with a French divorcée buts ends up destroying his marriage and ruining his relationship with yet another lover. "Occidentals" finds an American novelist in Paris, trying hard to find a translator for his book and trying even harder to avoid his lover's cretinous friends. "Jealous" is the jewel of the collection. A teenage boy goes on a road trip with his attractive aunt; bad weather forces them to take refuge in a bar where the story comes to an unforgettable climax.

EGGS FOR YOUNG AMERICA
by Katherine L. Hester
(University Press of New England, 1997, paperback)

This oddly titled collection of short stories marks the debut of an expert storyteller. "Labor" is a beautifully crafted story of the life—and anatomy—of working man named Monroe. "The Hat" relates, from the woman's point of view, a disappointing act of adultery. And "Deadman's Float" is set in a summer camp where three girls have just about had it with their sexually precocious tent mate. Hester is a genius at spotlighting the little comedies, tragedies and farces of everyday life.

THE COLLECTED STORIES OF CHESTER HIMES
(Thunder's Mouth Press, 1991, paperback)

All 61 of Himes short stories are collected here, including some which were never published during his lifetime. With unsparing accuracy he depicts the American character and the prejudices among both whites and blacks.

·············

IRVING: HISTORY, TALES AND SKETCHES
Edited by James W. Tuttleton
(Viking/The Library of America, 1983, hardcover)

Sure, you know the stories of Rip van Winkle and the Headless Horseman, but have you actually read them? Irving was America's first best-selling author and the first of our guys to get respect from the highbrow European literary community. The academics will point out that he addresses real American themes like the frontier, constant mobility, individualism and democracy. But he also tells great stories. Start with "The Legend of Sleepy Hollow" and "Rip Van Winkle," move on to "The Spectre Bridegroom" and browse his richly satirical *A History of New York...* by Diedrich Knickerbocker. Available in the excellent Library of America edition.

Irving for kids:

THE LEGEND OF SLEEPY HOLLOW
retold and illustrated by Will Moses (Philomel, 1995, paperback).

The story of Ichabod Crane and the Headless Horseman, simplified for young readers and illustrated with brightly colored paintings by Grandma Moses' great-grandson.

·············

THE LOTTERY AND OTHER STORIES
by Shirley Jackson (Noonday Press, 1992, paperback)

"The Lottery" is believed to be the most anthologized short story in American literature. Read it again and you'll understand why. And then move on to some of Jackson's other work.

THE MAMMOTH BOOK OF DRACULA:
VAMPIRE TALES FOR THE NEW MILLENNIUM
Edited by Stephen Jones (Carroll & Graf, 1997, hardcover)

Imagine Dracula on the Côte d'Azur. Or on the Oregon frontier. Or in Communist Eastern Europe. Or how about Dracula in Raymond Chandler's Los Angeles (sort of throws a whole new spin on the expression, "Farewell, my lovely"). It seems we never lose our fascination with vampires. This collection of ghoulish tales comes with a foreword by Bram Stoker's great-nephew and the never-before-published prologue to Stoker's theatrical version of Dracula.

A FISHERMAN OF THE INLAND SEA
by Ursula K. LeGuin (Prentice Hall, 1995, paperback)

This latest collection of short stories from the most acclaimed author of science fiction is a catalog of wonders. Starships that sail on waves of song. Orbiting arks designed to save humankind. Devices for faster-than-light communications. LeGuin explores the enigmas of time and space and finds their solutions lie in the mysteries of the human heart. No one writing science fiction writes as beautifully as Ursula K. LeGuin.

THE FIVE THOUSAND AND ONE NIGHTS
by Penelope Lively (Fjord Press, 1997, paperback)

A sparring husband and wife are reunited by their mutual dislike of their marriage counselor. A teenage delinquent ties up the lady of the house and commits the unpradonable crime of devouring her boeuf en daube. The "sultan" of the title story dislikes his wife's habit of reading aloud to him from Jane Austen and Virginia Woolf. "I never know what's coming next," he complains. "And [the stories are] so long." This collection of lighthearted stories may be Penelope Lively's most amusing work yet. They're wry, witty and shamelessly entertaining—perfect for a lazy Sunday afternoon.

A LONG NIGHT AT ABU SIMBEL
by Penelope Lively (Penguin, 1995, paperback)

The three perfectly balanced and satisfying short stories in this compact little volume serve as an excellent introduction for American readers to one of Britain's finest contemporaries authors. The title story is a comic jewel-a tour guide harried by an especially difficult group of British tourists deserts them at the grubby airport of Abu Simbel. In "The Emasculation of Ted Roper," the ladies of an English village take matters into their own hands to curb the depredations of a randy tom cat and his cocky bachelor owner. And in "Pack of Cards," a down-at-heels young man makes a surprising discovering about a grand dame's celebrated library.

More by Lively:

MOON TIGER
(HarperCollins, 1989, paperback).

Lively won the Booker Prize for this novel of a dying historical novelist who reviews her personal history, focusing particularly on an idyllic and tragic romance in Cairo during World War II.

BERNARD MALAMUD:
THE COMPLETE STORIES
Edited and introduced by Robert Giroux (Farrar Straus & Giroux, 1997, hardcover)

In 1958, Flannery O'Connor wrote to a friend: "I have discovered a short story writer who is better than any of them, including myself." That writer was Bernard Malamud. Now, more than a decade after Malamud's death, Richard Giroux, the writer's friend and editor, has collected all of Malamud's stories in a single volume. Included are such classics as "The Silver Crown" and Malamud's famous "fictive biographies" of Virginia Woolf and Alma Mahler. A landmark book, perfect for anyone who loves good stories.

THE COLLECTED STORIES
by John McGahern (Vintage Books, 1994, paperback)

Most of John McGahern's tales are set in Ireland, a place he describes as exceptionally beautiful and unbearably mean. There's "Swallows," a poignant story of a rural police sergeant who used to play the fiddle. "Wheels" and "The Gold Watch" explore the tensions between fathers and sons. And "Along the Edges" is the story of lovers who recognize that their passion is both terrifying and a source for tremendous happiness. If you like stories with a definite edge to them, you'll enjoy John McGahern.

OPEN SECRETS
by Alice Munro (Vintage, 1995, paperback)

A wife suddenly realizes there is a link between her sexually aggressive husband and a missing schoolgirl. A middle-aged women is surprised by happiness when she marries a man she hardly knows. A young woman tries to shield her brother from the charge of murdering her brutal husband. You'll return to Munro's stories again and again for their quick-paced plots and sublime prose.

SELECTED STORIES
by Alice Munro (Knopf, 1996, paperback)

These 28 tales demonstrate that Alice Munro is a master of the short story form. Almost all the stories take place in Munro's trademark setting-the small towns and farms of western Canada. In "Walker Brothers Cowboy," a young girl accompanying her father on a sales trip meets his old girlfriend and is able to compare her mother's disappointment in marrying her father and the girlfriend's disappointment at losing him. "Material" is a wonderful story of a wife who reads her husband's latest short story and is surprised to see that he really does have talent. Then surprise gives way to envy as she thinks of the writing career she abandoned years before.

COLLECTED WORKS OF FLANNERY O'CONNOR
Edited by Sally Fitzgerald
(The Library of America, 1988, hardcover)

One-legged Hulga Hopewell winds up in the hayloft with a Bible salesman. A prim grandmother learns that good manners don't mean much to a murderer named The Misfit. In the short stories of Flannery O'Connor, just about every situation is hilariously funny and also a little grotesque. Start with "A Good Man Is Hard to Find." Then move on to "A Temple of the Holy Ghost" and "The River." Like Mark Twain, O'Connor is one of the distinctive voices of American fiction.

BASEBALL'S BEST SHORT STORIES
Edited by Paul D. Stadohar
(Chicago Review Press, 1995, paperback)

Romance, nostalgia, sex, greed, honor and that beautiful sound when the bat makes contact with the ball. Everything we associate with baseball is spotlighted in this excellent anthology that covers a century of good writing about America's game. There are classics like Thurber's "You Could Look It Up," P.G. Wodehouse's "The Pitcher and the Plutocrat" and Ring Lardner's "My Roomy." Plus you get new works by Garrison Keillor, Michael Chabon and T. Coraghessan Boyle. And of course, the one work without which no baseball anthology of any size is complete, Ernest L. Thayer's deathless, "Casey at the Bat."

THE HAT OF MY MOTHER: STORIES
by Max Steele
(Thunder Bay Press, 1994, paperback)

The title story is a gem. A woman's good manners compel her to attend the funeral of a person she never met, while back home her family is certain she's been kidnapped. "The Cat and the Coffee Drinkers" details the offbeat education a Southern maiden lady gives her kindergarten students. And don't miss "Color the Daydream Yellow"-Steele won the O. Henry Prize for this vivid reverie of a young husband in Santa Monica who imagines himself single and living in Paris with a Swedish lover.

THE AFTERLIFE AND OTHER STORIES
by *John Updike* (Fawcett, 1996, paperback)

The focus of this collection is the special wonders of middle age, when spouses quarrel, lovers part, children become adults and death draws a little closer.

WELCOME TO THE MONKEY HOUSE
by *Kurt Vonnegut, Jr.* (Bantam Books, 1991, paperback)

Twenty-five short stories about good, evil, men, women, sex, time, technology and outer space from the former public relations man from General Electric who went on to become a literary hero. Especially good are: "Epicac" a story about a computer who longs to be made of protoplasm so it can experience love; "Who Am I This Time?" about a couple who can only have a storybook romance; and a love story originally titled "Hell to Live With," that ran in the Ladies' Home Journal as the "Long Walk to Forever." It's a wonderful grab bag of Vonnegut's unique talents.

WHY I LIVE AT THE P.O. AND OTHER STORIES
by *Eudora Welty* (Penguin, 1995, paperback)

Read just one Welty story and you'll be hooked. Her delightfully eccentric characterizations and her flawless ear for Southern colloquial speech make every tale a thing of beauty. The title story draws you into a bizarre family dispute that ends with one of the daughters leaving home to live at the post office. Other stories in this compact volume include "Death of a Traveling Salesman," "Shower of Gold" and "Where Is the Voice Coming From"—three tales that make you privy to the nasty/funny intimacies of life in small Southern towns.

More by Welty:

DELTA WEDDING
(Harvest Books, 1979, paperback).

A youngster's astute, comic observations as the immense Fairchild clan prepares for a wedding.

SKINNED ALIVE
by Edmund White (Random House, 1996, paperback)

Over the past 15 years, Edmund White has built a reputation for sharp, funny, perceptive tales of gay life that are often based upon his own experiences. The eight tales in this collection are among White's best: "Pyrography" explores the tensions among three teenage boys of various sexual orientations on a camping trip; a grief-stricken American traveler finds new reasons to live in "The Oracle"; and a man suffering from AIDS goes back to his Texas hometown in "Running on Empty." These stories address the great universal themes: the power of beauty, the pain of loss, the yearning for love.

More by Edmund White:

THE BEAUTIFUL ROOM IS EMPTY
(Ballantine, 1989, paperback).

A young gay man's coming of age story and how the Stonewall Riot of 1969 became his personal turning point.

THE NIGHT IN QUESTION
by Tobias Wolff (Knopf, 1996, hardcover)

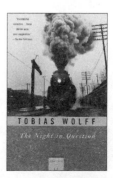

Tobias Wolff is one of the finest craftsmen of contemporary short stories. His prose is understated, yet intense emotions lie beneath the simple style. "Flyboys" examines an uneasy friendship among three young men. One violent act leads to another and then to another in "Chain," the story of a father's vendetta after his daughter is attacked by a dog. And in "Firelight," a son and his elegant yet penniless mother learn a new lesson about home and family as they look at an apartment they cannot afford. *The Night in Question* is Wolff's first collection of short stories in more than a decade and it's been worth the wait.

SPIRITUAL CLASSICS

A TESTAMENT TO FREEDOM:
THE ESSENTIAL WRITINGS OF DIETRICH BONHOEFFER
Edited by Geoffrey B. Kelly & F. Burton Nelson (Harper San Francisco, 1990, paperback)

In 1945, at age 39, Dietrich Bonhoeffer was executed in the Sachsenhausen concentration camp. This German Lutheran pastor and theologian had been an outspoken opponent of the Nazis from the beginning and a fearless defender of all the victims of Nazi terror. Bonhoeffer's most significant work is collected in this large volume: he calculates the cost of being Christian in a hellish world; and he explains the beliefs that gave him the courage and strength to pursue what was right. Bonhoeffer's sermons are unlike any you've ever heard before and his letters from prison are inspiring and beautiful.

THE LEGEND OF THE BAAL-SHEM
by Martin Buber, translated by Maurice Friedman (Schocken Books, 1969, paperback)

Israel ben Eliezar, known as the Baal-Shem (Master of God's Name), lived in Eastern Europe in the first half of the 18th century. He taught his followers an intense, ecstatic spirituality that has survived among Hasidic communities down to our own day. Martin Buber, whose philosophy echoes the teachings of the Baal-Shem, recounts 20 episodes from the life of the celebrated rabbi that reveal facets of his personality and illustrate his message of embracing a life of service, humility and religious exultation.

CARMINA GADELICA:
HYMNS AND INCANTATIONS
by Alexander Carmichael (1900; Lindisfarne Press, 1992, paperback)

Don't be put off by the Latin title—Alexander Carmichael was just trying to look scholarly. Actually, he was a tax collector in the Highlands and islands of Scotland under Queen Victoria. But in his wanderings, he became interested in folklore, especially the ancient traditions, prayers, hymns, charms and incantations of the people who lived in the remotest regions of Great Britain. He wrote down what he heard and included lengthy annotations about his sources who included shepherds, wise women, weavers, fishermen and farmers. And he explained the origins, the rituals and the significance of these incantations, some of which go back to pre-Christian times.

JOHN CLIMACUS:
THE LADDER OF DIVINE ASCENT
Edited and translated by Colm Luibheid and Norman Russell
(c.640; Paulist Press, 1982, paperback)

Among Eastern Christians, the most popular spiritual guide for 1300 years has been The Ladder of St. John Climacus (c.579-649). John takes his readers on a tour of desert monasteries and hermitages where the monks afflicted themselves with peculiar penances not uncommon at the time. Then, rejecting them, he offers instead a common-sense, step-by-step ascent from worldly temptations to union with God. A beautiful new translation, from the excellent Classics of Western Spirituality series.

DOROTHY DAY: SELECTED WRITINGS
Edited by Daniel Ellsberg (Orbis Books, 1982, paperback)

Dorothy Day (1897-1980) worked in the Communist/ Anarchist movements, entered into a common law marriage, had an abortion. Then, the birth of a daughter changed her life. In a relatively brief time, she received instruction in the Catholic faith, was baptized and founded The Catholic Worker movement to help the unemployed and the desperately poor. Yet she never gave up her radical political agenda—non-violence, social justice and freedom of conscience. Day's style is simple, but her ideas will challenge and inspire you.

FRANCIS AND CLARE: THE COMPLETE WORKS

translated and edited by Regis J. Armstrong OFM, Cap. and Ignatius C. Brady, OFM (Paulist Press, 1982, paperback)

I t's taken 700 years, but at last the writings of the two great saints of Assisi, Francis and Clare, have been collected in a single volume. Here are the letters of gentle encouragement and sound advice they wrote to their brothers and sisters; the Rule they created to define their commitment to radical poverty; plus their own sublime prayers—including Francis' magnificent Canticle of Brother Sun.

THE LITTLE FLOWERS OF ST. FRANCIS
(Daughters of St. Paul, 1976, paperback)

H is love for all humanity and the joy he took in all creation has made Francis of Assisi the most popular saint on the calendar. This book is a modern translation of one of the earliest medieval collections of stories from Francis' life and includes his taming of the savage wolf of Gubbio, his sermon to the turtledoves and the miracle of the stigmata.

KOL NIDREI-ITS ORIGIN DEVELOPMENT AND SIGNIFICANCE
by Rabbi Stuart Weinberg Gershon
(Jason Aronson, 1994, hardcover)

T he haunting prayer that inaugurates Yom Kippur asks for release from all vows made to God during the past year but not kept. With great warmth and enthusiasm for his subject, Rabbi Gershon explores the mystical and the historical elements of this prayer-including variants on the text and alternative musical arrangements. A thorough and completely accessible study of the Kol Nidrei.

THE ART OF PRAYING
by Romano Guardini
(1957; Sophia Institute Press, 1995, paperback)

If you pray, you know the problem. It often seems hard or fruitless. Your day has too many distractions. And then there are those times when you want to pray well, but nothing comes to mind. For more than 50 years, as a teacher and a pastor, Monseigneur Romano Guardini taught his students and his people how to pray. In clear, simple, direct language, he teaches the essential principles of prayer to you. He suggests when to use prayer books, how long your prayers should last, how to keep your prayers from being monotonous and so much more. Gentle, wise and accessible to anyone, this is an indispensable handbook for discovering the principles and methods of prayer.

THE LIVING GOD
by Romano Guardini
(1930; Sophia Institute Press, 1997, paperback)

As the pastor of a parish, Romano Guardini had the gift of making sacred mysteries accessible to people who had never set foot in a theology class. *The Living God* is one of his finest books. In brief but illuminating chapters he explains how God reveals himself to us, how God speaks to the human heart and how to recognize the hand of God in any event. Guardini writes beautifully about God's patience and compassion and becomes absolutely lyrical when he describes how God comforts us as a mother comforts her child. *The Living God* is a book that can transform your relationship with the Almighty.

THE LORD'S PRAYER
by Romano Guardini
(1932; Sophia Institute Press, 1996, paperback)

Everyday, hundreds of millions of Christians recite a prayer that Christ taught to his disciples almost 2000 years ago. But what do these ancient words mean? Romano Guardini unlocks the secrets of the Lord's Prayer. He explains why "Thy will be done"

is the heart of the prayer and what that means for us. He reveals that the "daily bread" the prayer asks for isn't necessarily what most people think it is. And he takes on the tough question of why sometimes God does not "deliver us from evil." A learned, profound book that will make the ancient Lord's Prayer seem new.

SHOWINGS

by *Julian of Norwich* (c.1393; Paulist Press, 1978, paperback)

On May 13, 1373, a nun named Julian had the first of her remarkable visions. *Showings* is the record of her mystical experiences, written in Julian's own rich, poetic style. There's a surprise here—a profoundly beautiful portrayal of God as Father and Mother. Since Julian's spiritual wisdom is direct and down to earth, you won't need a Ph.D. in theology to understand her.

THE IMITATION OF CHRIST

by *Thomas à Kempis, translated by William C. Creasy* (1425; Ave Maria Press, 1989, paperback)

This is one of those books virtually everyone has heard of, but almost no one has read. William Creasy's excellent modern translation should take care of that situation, because he has made Thomas à Kempis' (1379-1471) inspirational classic fresh and accessible. Kempis' main point: you develop a relationship with God the way you develop a friendship, by making time for private conversation.

MY SPIRIT REJOICES: THE DIARY OF A CHRISTIAN SOUL IN AN AGE OF UNBELIEF

by *Elisabeth Leseur* (1921; Sophia Institute Press, 1996, paperback)

Elisabeth Leseur (1866-1914) was a conventional, middle class French Catholic—until her atheist husband attacked her faith. To defend herself, Madame Leseur began reading the great mystics and she began this journal to reflect upon what she was learning. But the reader will see what perhaps Leseur herself did not—the lady's tremendous spiritual growth. When Leseur's husband found this journal after her death, he was so moved that he reconciled with the Church and in time became a priest. Elisabeth Leseur's journal was last printed in 1921, yet her little way of living a faith-filled life in a materialistic world is still valid today.

**C. S. LEWIS
A GRIEF
OBSERVED**

No one ever told me that grief felt so like fear. I am not afraid, but the sensation is like being afraid. The same fluttering in the stomach, the same restlessness, the yawning. I keep on swallowing...

A GRIEF OBSERVED
by C.S. Lewis (1962; Bantam, 1994, paperback)

C.S. Lewis is renowned as one of the 20th century's most eloquent advocates of traditional religious faith. Yet when his wife Joy died, Lewis found his faith badly shaken. "You never know how much you really believe anything until its truth or falsehood becomes a matter of life and death to you," he writes. As with all of his books, Lewis confronts the hard parts of Christianity head on to see if there is still reason to hope in the midst of pain.

THE SEVEN STOREY MOUNTAIN
by Thomas Merton (Harvest Books, 1990, paperback)

In 1941, Merton was a brilliant young professor at Columbia University. Yet his career, even his love life, left him restless and dissatisfied. To the horror of his colleagues and friends, Merton gave it all up and entered the silent, contemplative world of Gethsemani Abbey. In this profoundly eloquent book, he explains why he did it.

Also by Merton:

NO MAN IS AN ISLAND
(Harvest Books, 1978, paperback).

An especially rich work. Merton tests the limits of love—of self, of others, of God.

SIGN OF JONAS
(Harvest Books, 1979, paperback).

Outside the monastery walls, Merton celebrates the cycle of change and rebirth he find in the surrounding woods, ponds and meadows.

ASCENT TO TRUTH
(Harvest Books, 1981, paperback).

In a defense of the monastic life, Merton argues that contemplation is vital even in the Atomic Age.

CONJECTURES OF A GUILTY BYSTANDER
by Thomas Merton (Image Books/Doubleday, 1989, paperback)

What could a cloistered monk have to say about the more provocative issues of our time? If the monk is Thomas Merton, quite alot. In this collection of meditations, he takes on the controversial ideas of the last half of the 20th century: Communism, racial conflicts, "the death of God." He engages the ideas of such leading thinkers as Camus, Gandhi and Dietrich Bonhoeffer. Merton's tone may sound a bit detached, but his passion for intellectual inquiry is apparent. Conjectures of a Guilty Bystander is a thought-provoking book on how a believer might respond to the modern world.

More Merton:

LIFE AND HOLINESS
(Image Books/Doubleday, 1990, paperback).

Merton offers a handbook of simple steps one can take to practice holiness in the face of daily pressures, anxieties, distractions and obligations.

SOUL MATES
by Thomas Moore (HarperCollins, 1996, paperback)

Thomas Moore, a former monk, has taught millions how to incorporate the sacred into their daily lives. Now, he has written what he describes as a "handbook for ensouling our most ordinary and our most treasured relationships." Moore analyzes the risks involved in opening oneself to love, describes friendship as a "vessel of soul-making" and draws upon the wisdom of Emily Dickinson, Black Elk and ancient mythologies to help us understand the mysteries of love and relationships.

More by Moore:

CARE OF THE SOUL
(Walker, 1993, paperback).

The run-away best-seller that illuminates the complexities of the soul.

WRESTLING WITH ANGELS
by Naomi H. Rosenblatt and Joshua Horwitz (Delacorte Press, 1995, paperback)

With students like William Safire, Ted Koppel, Marvin Kalb and Senator Howard Metzenbaum, you could call Naomi Rosenblatt "Torah teacher to the stars." For 23 years, this psychotherapist and scholar of the Hebrew Bible has led Bible study classes, including weekly sessions for the U.S. Congress. Now, with her student Joshua Horwitz, she breathes new life into the stories from Genesis, finding lessons and illuminations in the sacred text that we can apply to our own lives as we wrestle with lust, greed, jealousy and fraternal rivalry and strive to live our lives with faith, social responsibility and compassion.

CREED OR CHAOS?
by Dorothy L. Sayers (Sophia Institute Press, 1995, hardcover)

C.S. Lewis' spiritual writings have never gone out of print and enjoy an enormous readership. But for inexplicable reasons, Dorothy Sayers' eloquent defense of traditional Christianity has been virtually forgotten. Now, it's back. In direct, concise, down-to-earth, conversational prose, Sayers (of Lord Peter Wimsey fame) ponders the great mysteries of faith—who God is, what Christ accomplished and what impact that has on our everyday lives. This is a little book (only 116 pages) but it is packed with great ideas. Believers, seekers and skeptics will find Sayers straightforward arguments and devastating humor refreshing.

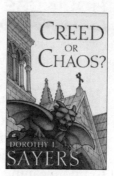

WHAT JESUS SAW FROM THE CROSS
by A.G. Sertillanges (1930; Sophia Institute Press, 1996, hardcover)

Originally published in Paris before World War II, this reflection on the last hours of Christ's life has been out of print for many years. Drawing upon studies of the daily life among the Israelites, Greeks and Romans and archaeological excavations in the Holy Land, Sertillanges offers authentic details of ancient life to help readers understand what it must have been like to witness the sufferings and death of Jesus. But then he takes these events which happened 2000 years in the past and reveals how they resonate for eternity.

THE DIALOGUE
by St. Catherine of Siena, translated by Suzanne Noffke, O.P. (1378; Paulist Press, 1980, paperback)

Of all the mystical works to emerge from 14th-century Italy, The Dialogue is arguably the most beautiful and the most profound. Catherine wrote it as a conversation between herself and God the Father, who at one point gives Catherine a vision of Christ as a bridge: "I made a bridge of my Son.... And though that living bridge has been taken away from your sight, there remains the bridgeway of His teachings." Savor this book by reading it in small portions.

HOLINESS FOR HOUSEWIVES AND OTHER WORKING WOMEN
by Dom Hubert van Zeller
(1957; Sophia Institute Press, 1997, paperback)

Women who run a house, or hold down a job, or do both, may find they have no time for prayer. So Dom Hubert van Zeller, a Benedictine monk who was a popular spiritual director for laypeople, developed this practical, encouraging handbook to help busy women grow in holiness day by day. Van Zeller shows you how to find meaning in even the most boring work, suggests ways to overcome weariness of spirit and inspires you to bear the stress of long days filled with responsibilities. A remarkable little book that reveals how you can place yourself in the presence of God no matter what you are doing.

CONFIDENCE IN GOD
by Dietrich von Hildebrand
(1948; Sophia Institute Press, 1997, paperback)

Dietrich von Hildebrand was fleeing from the Nazis when he wrote this pocket-sized guide on how to trust God and find peace even in the most desperate situations.

FOUR HASIDIC MASTERS AND THEIR STRUGGLE AGAINST MELANCHOLY
by Elie Wiesel (University of Notre Dame Press, 1978, paperback)

Elie Wiesel delivered these four essays as lectures to a packed house at the University of Notre Dame. In the stories of Rebbe Pinchas of Koretz, Rebbe Baruch of Medzebozh, Rebbe Yaacov Yitzchak Horowitz, the Holy Seer of Lublin and Rebbe Naphtali of Ropshitz, Wiesel offers examples of how to develop a deep friendship with God.

STAR QUALITY

WHO THE DEVIL MADE IT
by *Peter Bogdanovich* (Knopf, 1997, hardcover)

Here's a fascinating history of Hollywood straight from the lips of the men who made it (some of them even helped found it). Director, screenwriter, actor and critic, Peter Bogdanovich interviews sixteen of the greatest film directors of all time, including Sidney Lumet, Howard Hawks, Allan Dwan, Bugs Bunny creator, Chuck Jones, Fritz Lang (who envisioned his masterpiece, Metropolis, while awaiting entrance to the U.S. on a refugee ship docked on the West Side of Manhattan) and Alfred Hitchcock. ("Walt Disney, of course, has the best casting, if he doesn't like an actor, he just tears him up.")

ORSON WELLES: THE ROAD TO XANADU
by *Simon Callow* (Penguin, 1997, paperback)

Orson Welles was a brilliant raconteur, always ready to spin out some new version of his life for an interview. Callow, a talented, subtle writer and an English actor with an insider's knowledge of how plays and movies are produced, has researched his subject very carefully and offers the most reliable biography of Welles to date. He discusses Welles' exciting Federal and Mercury Theatre productions and his innovations for radio (including the famous "War of the Worlds" broadcast). But he also argues that even in his private life Welles was often more show than substance, just as his acting could sometimes be little more than a succession of clever effects. An excellent first volume of a two-book project which takes Welles' career up to age 26 and *Citizen Kane*.

THE LATE SHIFT: LETTERMAN, LENO AND THE NETWORK BATTLE FOR THE NIGHT
by Bill Carter (Hyperion, 1996, paperback)

When Johnny Carson retired, civil war erupted at NBC-with New York executives fighting for David letterman to get the Tonight show while the boys in L.A. championed Jay Leno. Bill Carter is television reporter for *The New York Times* and he brings a treasury of scoops, fresh details and inside stories to this chronicle about the ultimate network Battle of the Late-Night Stars.

MOMMIE DEAREST
by Christina Crawford

After a gruesome childhood, Joan Crawford's daughter gets her own back by revealing the hell her mother put her through as a child. This book is a revenge memoir par excellence.

STREISAND
by Anne Edwards (Little, Brown & Co., 1997, hardcover)

There is just not going to be another Barbra Streisand, now or ever," Alan Jay Lerner once said. "What she is, happens once." Anne Edwards, the biographer of Judy Garland and Katharine Hepburn, found plenty of admirers who were willing to talk to her about Barbra Streisand and lots of critics who refused to speak on record because they are so afraid of payback. Edwards follows the star's career from the singer in Greenwich Village who invented a new vocal style to the Hollywood perfectionist who is said to be impossible to work with. And of course there are details of her relationships with Elliot Gould and Jon Peters and her affairs with Omar Sharif and Pierre Trudeau. In Edwards' biography, Streisand's chutzpah and vulnerability come through on every page.

TARZAN OF THE MOVIES:
A PICTORIAL HISTORY OF MORE THAN FIFTY
YEARS OF EDGAR RICE BURROUGHS'
LEGENDARY HERO
by Gabe Essoe (Citadel Press, 1968, paperback)

Wrestling alligators, swinging from vines, righting wrongs, hanging around with Jane! Every red-blooded American boy wants to be a movie Tarzan, but only a few get the chance. This comprehensive, photo-filled volume is packed with trivia and behind-the-vines stories about the directors, producers and actors (Johnny Weismueller, of course, but also Lex Barker, Gordon Scott and Herman Brix) who gave us half a century of Ape Man cinema.

THE KID STAYS IN THE PICTURE
Robert Evans (Dove, 1995, paperback)

Now this is a Hollywood memoir. Rosemary's Baby, Love Story, The Godfather, Chinatown, no one had a hotter string of hits—or a more ignominious fall—than movie mogul and power player Robert Evans. He saved Paramount Studios from certain disaster, worked with the biggest names, took the biggest risks and paid the highest prices. Evans claims there are three sides to every story: yours, mine and the truth. Evans' version of his odyssey from the top of the Paramount mountain to his self-committal and escape from a mental institution and his journey back is nothing short of fascinating.

PIECES OF TIME:
THE LIFE OF JAMES STEWART
by Gary Fishgall (Scribner, 1997, paperback)

Actor Jimmy Stewart's sincerity and wholesomeness were the real thing. He got his faith in family, community and God from his upbringing in a small Pennsylvania town and he never lost them. Fishgall's comprehensive biography of one of America's most beloved actors includes highlights from Stewart's acting career (he made 79 films, 12 television programs and 10 stage plays), his service as bomber pilot during World War II and his stable marriage to Gloria Hatrick McLean. An affectionate, exhaustively researched life of an All-American star.

A DREAM IS A WISH YOUR HEART MAKES: MY STORY
by Annette Funicello with Patricia Romanowski
(Hyperion, 1995, paperback)

If you were a boy growing up in the 1950s and 1960s, you probably had a crush on Annette Funicello, She was wholesomely sexy on The Mickey Mouse Club, had a sweet singing voice when she was hitting the Top 40 and filled a bathing suit nicely in all those beach party movies. Now Annette reveals a few things we never knew: for instance, her first sweetheart, Paul Anka, wrote "Put Your Head On My Shoulder" for her. And she explains her reasons for giving up her film and recording career for her family. More poignantly, Annette also reveals her current battle with multiple sclerosis. This is a nostalgic, touching memoir from one of our favorite performers.

ADVENTURES IN THE SCREEN TRADE
by William Goldman (Warner, 1989, hardcover)

Oscar-winning screenwriter William Goldman offers a humorous and in-depth look at the complex and unpredictable machine that is Hollywood. From the sets of Marathon Man and Butch Cassidy and the Sundance Kid to the offices of high-paid executives, *Adventures* is filled with revealing anecdotes about stars like Olivier, Newman and Redford. If you've ever wondered how movies really get made, this is the book for you.

MY NAME ESCAPES ME:
THE DIARY OF RETIRING ACTOR
by Alec Guinness (Viking, 1997, hardcover)

In his movies, Alec Guinness appears so smart, funny and down-to-earth pleasant. It turns out that's really how he is. His memoir shows him happily installed with his wife Merula in their country house in Hampshire where they read Anthony Trollope, play with their dog and bicker over Puccini. They receive visits from long-time friends Alan Bennett, Tom Courtenay, Lauren Bacall. He praises his colleagues in the theater, Maggie Smith, John Gielgud, Nigel Hawthorne, Peggy Ashcroft. And he's humble. When a newspaper article asserts that Guinness has second sight, he comments: "News to me." A refreshing change from the mattress-hopping confessions of other stars.

LAST TRAIN TO MEMPHIS:
THE RISE OF ELVIS PRESLEY
by Peter Guralnick (Little, Brown, 1995, paperback)

Ed Sullivan assured his audience that for all the pelvic grinding, Elvis was "a real decent, fine boy." And so he was, says Guralnick in this meticulous new biography of The King. (Although, there was that time Elvis brought a stripper to his hotel room and said, "I'm as horny as billy a goat in a pepper patch. I'll race you to the bed.") Here, at last, is a serious study of the kid who crawled out of a shotgun shack to become a musical sensation.

MGM: WHEN THE LION ROARS
by Peter Hay (Turner Publishing, 1991, hardcover)

For nearly three decades Metro Goldwyn Mayer was the most glamorous, prestigious and prolific studio in Hollywood. It gave us *The Wizard of Oz*, *Gone with the Wind*, two versions of *Ben Hur*, *Andy Hardy*, *Tarzan*, "Tom and Jerry" cartoons, the

"Our Gang" comedies and nearly 2,000 other memorable films. Illustrated with hundreds of full-color and black-and-white photographs, *When the Lion Roars* chronicles the epic rise and fall of the studio and the moguls who ran it. Film historian Peter Hay has done a remarkable job in capturing the glamour, the intrigue and the behind-the-scenes drama that went into running Hollywood's most famous dream factory.

ME: STORIES OF MY LIFE
by Katharine Hepburn (Ballantine, 1996, paperback)

You won't be able to resist this stylish, clever, entertaining collection of anecdotes and reminiscences from one of the world's most beloved actresses. Hepburn writes the way she speaks—in that now-legendary style of short, clipped sentences and abrupt phrases. From cover to cover, pure Hepburn magic.

JAMES DEAN, LITTLE BOY LOST: AN INTIMATE BIOGRAPHY
by Joe Hyams with Jay Hyams

For an actor who only made three movies, James Dean had an astonishing impact on American films and American culture. Joe Hyams, a Hollywood insider, offers a candid, compassionate portrait of Dean, from the origins of his problems in his midwest Depression-era childhood to an honest assessment of his sexual promiscuity with women and men. The intimate story of a young man who lived fast and died young. Worth searching for.

MY MOTHER'S KEEPER
by B.D. Hyman

Bette Davis' estranged daughter revealed all her mother's nasty secrets while Davis was still alive. The histrionics, the drinking, the emotional blackmail, all the manipulative tricks Davis used on her only child. Worth searching for.

HIS WAY: THE UNAUTHORIZED BIOGRAPHY OF FRANK SINATRA
by Kitty Kelley (Bantam, 1987, paperback)

Nobody dishes up the dirt in such generous portions as Kitty Kelley—maybe that's why Sinatra tried to halt publication of this book with a $2 million lawsuit. Taking advantage of the Freedom of Information Act, Kelley brings forward new information about Sinatra's connections with the Mafia, plus she provides the inside scoop on the women, the music, the brawls.

THE BOX: AN ORAL HISTORY OF TELEVISION, 1920-1961
by Jeff Kisseloff (Viking, 1995, hardcover)

Kisseloff starts out with the farm kid named Philo T. Farnsworth who beat the scientists at RCA by inventing the television first, in 1921. Then he's off to quiz show scandals, the triumphs of Playhouse 90, how Red Channels derailed careers of stars like Kim Hunter and the nasty offscreen relationship between David Garroway and his chimpanzee sidekick, J. Fred Muggs.

SWIFTY: MY LIFE AND GOOD TIMES
by Irving Lazar, written in collaboration with Annette Tapert (Simon & Schuster, 1995, hardcover)

One of the most successful agents Hollywood and New York have ever seen was Swifty Lazar. His clients included Cole Porter, Moss Hart, Ira Gershwin, Truman Capote, Neil Simon. His pals were Bogart, Sinatra, Brando, Groucho and Sam Goldwyn. Lazar packed his memoir with anecdotes of over-inflated egos and the joy of stealing clients from his competitors and other golden moments from Hollywood's golden age. Read just one page of this rollicking, wisecracking memoir and you'll be hooked.

TRAMP: THE LIFE OF CHARLIE CHAPLIN
by Joyce Milton (HarperCollins, 1996, hardcover)

There have been many biographies of Charlie Chaplin, the world-renowned star of silent pictures. But Joyce Milton's is the first ever to examine Chaplin's radical politics and his connections with the Communist Party—a foible that in time drove him out of the United States. Milton argues that Chaplin was in many was naive and even inconsistent in his politics. Yet she also follows his left-wing sympathies back to their source. A perceptive study of Chaplin that gives us new information about a facet of his personality that has troubled his fans for decades.

AFTER ALL
by Mary Tyler Moore (Putnam, 1995, hardcover)

If you want to learn about the art of comedy, read Mary Tyler Moore's autobiography. As Laura Petrie on *The Dick Van Dyke Show* and Mary Richards on *The Mary Tyler Moore Show*, she showed us how she could blend the timing of Lucille Ball (without the clownish antics), the wit of Katharine Hepburn (without the highbrow accent) and create something new and hilarious. That wonderful sense of humor and respect for her audience is present in Moore's autobiography. She doesn't trash her family. She doesn't catalogue her lovers. She doesn't try the shock the hell out of us. Instead, she discusses her life with wit and candor.

AUDREY HEPBURN
by Barry Paris (Putnam, 1996, hardcover)

Audrey Hepburn has everything we hope for in a celebrity biography: lots of gossip, a little psychological insight and plenty of photographs. We get the details of her relationships—personal and professional—with Gregory Peck, William Holden, Cary Grant, Fred Astaire; and of the commotion when Hepburn rather than the Julie Andrews was cast as Eliza Doolittle in the film version of *My Fair Lady*. On the more serious side, Paris suggests that it was Hepburn's childhood in Nazi-occupied Netherlands that gave her a modest demeanor that made her appear approachable despite her tremendous glamour. A very satisfying biography of a great star.

MARLENE DIETRICH
by Maria Riva
(Random House, 1995, paperback)

Exotic, sexy, dangerous—both Germany and America claimed Marlene Dietrich as their own. Now Dietrich's daughter reveals the truth about the private and professional lives of her glamorous mother. A startling, compelling biography that makes all others obsolete.

MUSICAL STAGES: AN AUTOBIOGRAPHY
by Richard Rodgers with a new introduction by Mary Rodgers
(Da Capo Press, 1995, paperback)

The composer of some of Broadway's most beloved musicals— *Oklahoma!*, *Carousel*, *South Pacific*, *The King and I*, *The Sound of Music*—tells the inside story of his success and his collaborations with Lorenz Hart and Oscar Hammerstein. Especially interesting are anecdotes of working with Mary Martin, Agnes de Mille and Yul Brynner and the evolution of such songs as "If I Loved You," "Younger Than Springtime," "Some Enchanted Evening" and "Surrey with the Fringe on Top." The perfect book for anyone who loves American musical theater.

THINKING IN PICTURES:
THE MAKING OF THE MOVIE MATEWAN
by John Sayles (Houghton, Mifflin, 1987, paperback)

A film script, says writer/director, John Sayles, is "a potential for action, a story waiting to get told." Using his film, Matewan, a period piece about a West Virginia coal miners strike, as a model, America's best known independent filmmaker takes us behind the camera to offer a rational and complete look at the thought processes and physical labor that go into actually transforming a script into a film. Includes the complete shooting script as well as chapters on writing, fund raising, location scouting, editing and, as they say, much, much more.

BRANDO: A LIFE IN OUR TIME
by Richard Schickel (St. Martin's Press, 1993, paperback

Time magazine's film critic offers an in-depth, objective and ultimately admiring portrait of Marlon Brando, one of Hollywood's greatest if most erratic stars. Schickel casts new light on Brando's sometimes bizarre political stands, his messy private life and his family tragedies. Plus, he unlocks the secret to Brando's checkered career-why 14 flops stood between the triumphs of *Streetcar, On the Waterfront* and *The Godfather*.

MARILYN MONROE: THE BIOGRAPHY
by Donald Spoto (HarperPaperbacks, 1994, paperback)

Donald Spoto was the first biographer ever granted access to the sealed files containing Marilyn Monroe's letters, diaries, appointment books, medical history, her psychiatrist's papers and recently declassified government files. The result is a full-scale, definitive life of Hollywood's most glamorous star. Many Marilyn "biographers" have been little more than lurid gossipmongers, but Spoto tries to be scrupulous in everything he writes. And there are plenty of surprising revelations about her marriages, her affairs, her career, plus the real story of how Marilyn died.

NOTORIOUS: THE LIFE OF INGRID BERGMAN
by Donald Spoto (HarperCollins, 1997, paperback)

Ingrid Bergman is one of those rare actresses who actually lives up to her legend. She was stunningly beautiful and astonishingly talented. Spoto plays particular attention to the films Bergman made with Alfred Hitchcock, but he does not omit her affairs with Gary Cooper and director Victor Fleming. And

Spoto shows his readers how, after her adulterous affair with Roberto Rossellini, Bergman rebuilt her career and won public acclaim once again. While there are no new revelations about Bergman's life in Donald Spoto's biography, he does offer a sympathetic, well-rounded, well-told account of Ingrid Bergman's life.

A HELL OF A LIFE: AN AUTOBIOGRAPHY
by Maureen Stapleton and Jane Scovell
(Simon & Schuster, 1995, hardcover)

Some 50 years ago, when Maureen Stapleton was a kid at the Actors Studio in New York, she and two girlfriends gave themselves "a crash course in offensive language." It must have been a very successful class, because some of the most outrageously funny bits in this autobiography—like Stapleton's eulogy at Colleen Dewhurst's funeral—are unprintable. So take us at our word that this one of the most entertaining celebrity books to come along in years. Stapleton was pals with everybody—from Marlon Brando to Marilyn Monroe, Elizabeth Taylor to Tennessee Williams—and her stories of half a century of life in the theater are a laugh riot.

PERPETUAL MOTION: THE PUBLIC AND PRIVATE LIVES OF RUDOLF NUREYEV
by Otis Stuart (NAL Dutton, 1996, paperback)

Nureyev's insatiable appetites for dance, money and sex are revealed by dance critic and insider Otis Stuart.

FIVE SCREENPLAYS
by Preston Sturges (University of California Press, 1985, paperback)

Preston Sturges's films were so smoothly written that the actors seemed to be making up the dialogue as they went along. Nothing could be farther from the truth. Critics have called Sturges "Hollywood's greatest writer-director, with the emphasis on the former" and hailed him as "by far the wittiest scriptwriter the English-speaking cinema has known." This collection includes in-depth introductory essays as well as the complete screenplays for *Sullivan's Travels, The Great McGinty, The Lady Eve, Christmas in July* and *Hail the Conquering Hero*. Reading them is nearly as delightful as seeing the wonderful screwball films they inspired.

JOHN WAYNE'S AMERICA: THE POLITICS OF CELEBRITY
by Garry Wills (Simon & Schuster, 1997, paperback)

Fourteen years or so after his death, John Wayne is still ranked #1 in a Harris poll of favorite movie stars. That's the reason Garry Wills is studying John Wayne. Wills argues that Wayne defined essential masculinity where other stars were "naked gods" (Charlton Heston), "conflicted men" (Montgomery Clift), or "troubled adolescents" (James Dean). And Wills spends plenty of time discussing Wayne's movies—*Stagecoach, The Searchers, She Wore A Yellow Ribbon*. By the end, you can't help admiring John Wayne's gifts as an actor. Whether you're a fan or a skeptic, after this book, you'll never look at John Wayne the same way again.

SPLIT IMAGE: THE LIFE OF ANTHONY PERKINS
by Charles Winecoff (Dutton, 1996, hardcover)

Playing a knife-wielding transvestite in Alfred Hitchcock's shocker, *Psycho*, did not make Anthony Perkins a superstar. And marriage to a socialite did not make him any less a gay man. To chart the life of Anthony Perkins, Charles Winecoff appears to have interviewed everyone the star ever met-including his alleged lover, Tab Hunter. Packed with fascinating stories about Alfred Hitchcock, Sophia Loren, James Dean, Jane Fonda (at one point, Perkins and Jane shared the same boyfriend) and a host of other stars, Split Image unravels Perkins' life. This is one of the best researched, best written celebrity biographies to appear in years.

Also of interest:

ALFRED HITCHCOCK AND THE MAKING OF PSYCHO
by Stephen Rebello (HarperCollins, 1991, paperback).

A behind-the-scenes history of how Hitchcock created his shocker, based on Hitchcock's own private files, plus interviews with writers, crew, Janet Leigh and Anthony Perkins.

BRING ON THE GIRLS!
by P.G. Wodehouse and Guy Bolton (1953; A Common Reader Edition, 1997, paperback)

What's the one thing that pushed a hundred musical comedies "over the thin line that divides the floperoo from the socko?" Chorus girls! P.G. Wodehouse and Guy Bolton learned that lesson during the early years of this century when they were writing musicals on Broadway. This rollicking memoir includes unforgettable encounters with W.C. Fields ("the comedian was very sensitive about [his nose which] he considered the only flaw in an otherwise classic countenance"), Marion Davies ("Girls get mink the same way the minks do"), plus Ethel Merman, George M. Cohan, George Gershwin, Charlie Chaplin and chorus girls named Pickles St. Clair and Dawn O'Day.

SULTRY ROMANCES

PRISONER OF DESIRE
by Jennifer Blake (Fawcett, 1991, paperback)

Jennifer Blake is famous for her steamy tales of the Old South and the seductive charms of her iron-willed characters. In Louisiana before the start of the Civil War, a young woman has imprisoned her family's most implacable enemy, but slowly she finds herself falling in love with her prisoner. A lush, sweeping romance.

Also by Jennifer Blake:

LOUISIANA DAWN
(Fawcett, 1993, paperback).

A sexy adventure of a rogue who seduces the innocent young woman who saved his life.

SPANISH SERENADE
(Fawcett, 1994, paperback).

A headstrong heiress is kidnapped by an outlaw noble in this romantic adventure set in Spain.

SILVER-TONGUED DEVIL
by Jennifer Blake (Fawcett, 1996, paperback)

Angelica Carew awakens from a riverboat accident to find that she is married to the man who saved her life. But her new husband, Renold Harden, is not your ordinary spouse: his family lost their plantation at the gaming tables to Angelica's father and Renold has sworn revenge. How long will it take before Renold's righteous anger is replaced by passion for the lovely Angelica?

THE INVITATION
by Jude Deveraux (Pocket Books, 1994, paperback)

Jackie O'Neill was a daredevil pilot. But after the death of her husband, she returns home to Colorado to begin a new, more sedate life. There, she meets William Montgomery—formerly little Billy who used to follow her everywhere when she was a teenager. Now, he is definitely a man and he is still in love with her.

REMEMBRANCE
by Jude Deveraux (Pocket Books, 1995, paperback)

Hayden Lane, a successful romance writer, has an idea for a new novel about lovers whose present lives are complicated by their past lives. To help her understand reincarnation, Hayden consults a psychic and learns that in a previous life she was an Edwardian aristocrat named Lady de Grey. It's said that Lady de Grey poisoned her husband before mysteriously disappearing herself and that her ghost haunts her husband's home. Curious to learn more, Hayden asks a hypnotist to help her go back in time, where she encounters the most desirable man she has ever seen and embarks on the greatest adventure of her life.

FIRE DANCER
by Colleen Faulkner (Zebra Books, 1997, paperback)

It is 1759 in Pennsylvania and Mackenzie Daniels has come to Fort Belvedere to paint the French, Indian and British participants of peace talks. There she falls passionately in love with a Shawnee warrior named Fire Dancer. When the fort is attacked, Fire Dancer spirits Mackenzie away to his village for safety. Mackenzie is still intensely in love with Fire Dancer, but Shawnee life is hard for her. She is not certain she wants to give up her family and friends forever. Always lurking in the background is a Shawnee named Okonsa who hates Mackenzie. By drawing complex characters, Colleen Faulkner takes the popular historical romance genre and pushes it up a notch.

More by Colleen Faulkner:

TO LOVE A DARK STRANGER
(Kensington, 1997, paperback).

M eg Randall has killed the scoundrel she was forced to marry. Fleeing from the law, she meets Captain Scarlett, a dashing highway man. They begin a passionate affair, of course, but they are also caught up in the royal intrigues of Restoration England.

....

ALINOR
by *Roberta Gellis* (Leisure Books, 1994, paperback)

I f you're accustomed to "formula" romances, get ready for a surprise. Sure, Alinor has a gorgeous, strong-willed heroine, a hunky hero, lots of intrigue and plenty of steamy love scenes. But unlike so many romance authors, Gellis doesn't stop there. Her characterizations are strong, her historical details are accurate and her style is more in the tradition of Gone with the Wind. This classic, first published in 1978, sets the troubled love of the beautiful Lady Alinor Lemagne and the buff Ian de Vipont during the unpleasant reign of King John in early 13th-century England.

The prequel:

ROSELYNDE
by *Roberta Gellis* (Dorchester, 1994, paperback).

As Richard the Lionheart's Crusade heads for Jerusalem, the lovely young Alinor of Roselynde meets the man of her dreams.

....

THE BLACK OPAL
by *Victoria Holt* (Fawcett, 1993, paperback)

A s a child, Carmel was suddenly bundled up and sent from her home in England to Australia. Now, as a lovely young woman, she has come back and soon learns that she witnessed a murder all those years before. As long-repressed memories begin to return, Carmel becomes convinced that the wrong man has been imprisoned for the crime. She also questions the secretive behavior of her friend Lucian, and she wonders why black opals have always surfaced at critical moments in her life.

THE CAPTIVE
by *Victoria Holt* (Fawcett, 1990, paperback)

Holt is one of the most prolific authors of historical romances, weaving spellbinding tales of adventure with careful attention to period details. In this sensuous thriller, Rosetta Canleigh, just 18, is shipwrecked with a mysterious sailor, John Player. Pirates find the pair and sell them into slavery in Constantinople, where Rosetta is purchased for the pasha's harem. Can she survive the intrigues of the seraglio? Will Rosetta and John ever escape?

SON OF THE MORNING
by *Linda Howard* (Pocket Books, 1997, paperback)

Linda Howard blends time-travel, romance and adventure in this stunning tale of scholar Grace St. John who discovers the story of an embittered Scottish knight, Black Niall, in 14th-century documents and suddenly is transported back to the Middle Ages. The hunt for a lost Celtic treasure draws Grace and Black Niall together. Soon their mutual attraction leads to erotic fireworks, (Niall, after all, is the ultimate fantasy man). Fans agree that is one of Linda Howard's best novels ever.

A Linda Howard Classic:

ALMOST FOREVER
(Mira Books, 1994, paperback).

Claire Westbrook has the information Max Conroy needs to lead a corporate takeover, so he plans an elaborate seduction. But soon the callous seducer finds himself falling hard for his intended victim.

FLOWERS FROM THE STORM
by *Laura Kinsale* (Avon, 1992, paperback)

Laura Kinsale dares to do what most romance authors would never consider: she gives her heroes and heroines character flaws. And her readers appear to love Kinsale for it—she has one of the most loyal followings in romance fiction. Flowers from the Storm is a hot Regency romance that throws together the hunky Duke Christian Langland and a luscious Quaker woman named Archimedia Timms. Of course they fall in love, but when Christian becomes an invalid Archimedia must make a painful decision: to nurse her lover with little hope of recovery, or find love elsewhere. Readers agree it is one of the most emotionally powerful books Kinsale's ever written.

More by Laura Kinsale:

FOR MY LADY'S HEART
(Berkley, 1993, paperback).

A medieval romance with a difference: the self-assured Princess Melanthe takes up the role of aggressor, pursuing the dashing knight Ruadrik.

SAY YOU LOVE ME
by Johanna Lindsey (Morrow, 1996, paperback)

The roguishly handsome Lord Derek Malory spent a fortune to buy Kelsey Langton at a whorehouse auction. But once he gets her home, he finds himself falling in love with the woman he bought only for pleasure. And when Kelsey is kidnapped by the sadistic Lord Ashford, Malory sets out on a heroic rescue mission, determined to have the woman he loves—social conventions be damned. *Say You Love Me* is vintage Johanna Lindsey.

SURRENDER MY LOVE
by Johanna Lindsey (Avon, 1994, paperback)

When Selig the Viking is discovered outside the castle of the Anglo-Saxon noblewoman Lady Erika, he is seized, accused of spying and thrown into the dungeon. Tortured and starved, he clings to life, waiting for the day he will take his revenge. When at last Selig's family and friends win his release, he turns the tables on his captor and Lady Erika becomes Selig's prisoner. Now the Viking must choose between taking Erika's life and winning her love. Setting her story in the 10th century, when Saxons, Celts and Vikings were at each other's throats, Lindsey writes a classic romance, filled with adventure, treachery and passion.

···············

TENDER REBEL
by Johanna Lindsey (Avon, 1988, paperback)

Johanna Lindsey writes breathtaking historical romances filled with nonstop action and intrigue. In Tender Rebel, a Scottish heiress seeks refuge from her wicked cousin in the arms of a devilishly handsome English outlaw.

Also by Lindsey:

MAN OF MY DREAMS
(Avon, 1992, paperback).

A woman's plan to marry a great duke goes awry when she meets a virile commoner.

···············

THE FAIREST OF THEM ALL
by Teresa Medeiros (Bantam Books, 1995, paperback)

Holly de Chastel, a renowned beauty, has rejected scores of suitors. To force her to marry, she is made the prize in a tournament. But the headstrong young woman has a plan to thwart even this contrivance. She makes herself appear as homely as possible, certain that she will drive off all the contestants. But a dark, handsome Welsh knight named Austyn claims Holly nonetheless and carries her home to his castle. As Holly falls under Austyn's spell, she wonders how she can reveal herself—and what Austyn will do when he learns that he has been deceived.

More Medeiros:

BREATH OF MAGIC
(Bantam Books, 1996, paperback).

An enchantress from the 17th century travels forward in time 300 years where she encounters a dashing billionaire who has offered $1 million to anyone who proves to him that magic exists.

SECRET NIGHTS
by Anita Mills (NAL Dutton, 1994, paperback)

During the glory days of Regency England, Elise Rand finds herself confronted by a terrible dilemma. Her father has sought a marriage for her with the dashing Patrick Hamilton, London's most promising and ambitious trial lawyer. But Elise is stung when she finds that Hamilton wants her as his mistress, not his wife. Later, when Elise's father is falsely charged with murder, she knows only Patrick Hamilton can save him. And, she knows what price Hamilton will demand.

More Mills:

AUTUMN RAIN (NAL Dutton, 1993, paperback).

Elinor Ashton has been forced into a loveless marriage with the elderly but immensely rich Lord Kingsley. When she meets the bold, scandalous Lucien de Clare, Elinor is ripe for seduction. But soon Elinor and Lucien's love is caught up in a whirlwind of intrigue, danger and revenge.

MYSTIQUE
by Amanda Quick (Bantam Books, 1996, paperback)

Hugh the Relentless storms Lingwood Manor to capture a priceless green crystal—but the crystal is missing. So Alice, the lady of the manor, makes Hugh an offer: if he will deliver her from her reptilian guardian, she will help him find the jewel. Hugh agrees, but adds his own condition: Alice must become his betrothed. Together, Hugh and Alice set out on a quest that is both a romantic adventure and a grand detective story.

More Amanda Quick:

DECEPTION
(Bantam Books, 1994, paperback).

Olympia, a student of ancient legends and lost treasures, joins forces with Jared, a pirate masquerading as a tutor, to recover a fabulous golden horde.

WICKED: AN ANGELS TOUCH ROMANCE
by Evelyn Rogers (Leisure Books, 1996, paperback)

Amy Lattimer, fresh from convent school, has come out West to find her missing father. And she's willing to do anything to speed her search-even pose as a prostitute. But she finds an unlikely ally in Cad Rankin, an outlaw who can't bear to see her sell her body. As they ride together to find her father, Amy begins to ponder what secrets Cad is keeping and what she will have to do to earn his confidence and his love.

THE RANCH
by Danielle Steel (Delacorte, 1997, paperback)

Mary, Tanya and Zoe were inseparable in college. Twenty years later, they reunite for several weeks on a ranch in the foothills of Wyoming's Grand Tetons. They have a lot to talk about—failed marriages, old lovers who are turning up again, suicide, AIDS, the price of success. The conversations among the friends are perhaps the strongest part of this book., but Steel keeps the plot percolating by revealing plenty of secrets and having a couple of romances blossom.

THE RING
by Danielle Steel (Dell, 1983, paperback)

If you've never read any books by the wildly popular Danielle Steel, start with *The Ring*. Steel traces the fortunes of three generations of the von Gotthard clan, from their glory years before World War II, through the horrors of the Third Reich and finally to the clan's new life in America. A work of pure escapism, from page one.

Also by Danielle Steel:

FULL CIRCLE
Dell, 1985, paperback).

Steel is in top form in this tale of a young woman who grows from a chronic victim to a self-assured attorney and lover.

DADDY
(Dell, 1990, paperback).

A real departure for Steel. Modern women and the new sexual codes prove to be unexpected challenges for a single father.

• • • • • • • • • • • • •

RELATIVE SINS
by Cynthia Victor (Onyx, 1993, paperback)

Cynthia Victor is one of the very best writers of romance fiction. Every page is packed with real excitement and authentic passions. *Relative Sins* tells the story of a mother and a daughter and the man who betrays them both.

Also by Victor:

CONSEQUENCES
(Pocket, 1989, paperback).

Victor's debut novel of two sisters who grow up strangers, but find as adults that they share a passion for power, money and romance.

• • • • • • • • • • • • •

ONLY YOU
by Cynthia Victor (Onyx, 1995, paperback)

After years of childhood squabbling, Ben Dameroff and Carlin Squire find that as young adults their old antagonism has been replaced by deeper feelings. But tragedy separates the lovers and years pass before they are reunited—this time as joint suspects in a murder investigation. They begin their affair again, yet each harbors a secret suspicion about the other. as always, Cynthia Victor writes a stylish, carefully plotted tale of desire and betrayal.

ASHES IN THE WIND
by Kathleen E. Woodiwiss (Avon, 1990, paperback)

As Yankees rampage across her Virginia plantation, Alaina MacGaren disguises herself as a boy and flees. But she doesn't get far before she's nabbed by a band of Union soldiers, intent on roughing up this young Rebel. Fortunately, a handsome Yankee surgeon, Cole Latimer, happens by and he rescues Alaina. Once Latimer discovers that "the kid" is really a beautiful woman, he falls hard. How can he love a Rebel woman and remain faithful to the Union cause? What will take priority—his sense of loyalty and honor, or his passion?

THE FLAME AND THE FLOWER
by Kathleen E. Woodiwiss (Avon, 1977, paperback)

Among romance writers, Woodiwiss is a phenomenon whose readers look forward to each new novel of desire and suspense. Here, a beautiful young Englishwoman and the dashing aristocrat from the American South she has been forced to marry try to resist their secret passion for one another.

Also by Woodiwiss:

A ROSE IN WINTER
Avon, 1983, paperback).

Set in Scotland during the time of Bonnie Prince Charlie, a young woman longs for the American sea captain her family would not let her marry.

THRILLERS

THE TRIAL OF ELIZABETH CREE:
A NOVEL OF THE LIMEHOUSE MURDERS
by Peter Ackroyd (Doubleday, 1995, paperback)

A murderer is walking the gaslit streets of Victorian London's Limehouse district. His grisly butchering of two prostitutes, a venerable Jewish scholar and an entire family shocks the city. But soon, Londoners are distracted by the sensational trial of Elizabeth Cree, accused of murdering her husband. What no one suspects is that the shocking truth of the Limehouse murders lies hidden in Elizabeth Cree's story.

More by Peter Ackroyd:

HAWKSMOOR
(Harper Collins, 1985, hardcover)

The violence of 18th-century London reaches across 250 years, connecting 17th-century architect Nicholas Dyer with Nicholas Hawksmoor, a 20th-century detective investigating murders that have taken place in churches Dyer built. Worth searching for.

ACTS OF REVISION
by Martyn Bedford (Doubleday, 1996, paperback)

After the death of his mother, Gregory Lynn, 35 years old, finds his school report cards in the attic. Lynn reads, "Must work....Little progress....Disappointing," and suddenly all the little humiliations of childhood come rushing back to him. Where others might burn the report cards and forget the past, Lynn decides to correct his, to revise it and begins to plan how he will settle the score with seven former teachers. A very sinister story that will appeal to anyone who ever suffered an unkind word from a teacher.

THE INTRUDER
by *Peter Blauner* (Simon & Schuster, 1996, paperback)

The Schiff family—Jake, Dana and 16-year-old Alex—has everything. Money, successful careers, good looks, a great townhouse on Manhattan's perennially trendy Upper West Side. Then one of Dana's psychiatric patients, a homeless man named John Gates, starts stalking her and disturbing her family. Gates becomes more menacing; but the police write off his harassment of the Schiffs as a petty violation. So to protect his family, Jake makes a fatal decision. *The Intruder* is an urban nightmare, filled with unsettling surprises that will keep you reading all through the night.

THRILL
by *Robert Byrnes* (Carroll & Graf, 1995, paperback)

Nothing gets the adrenaline pumping like a ride on a California roller coaster named Thrill. It was designed by a master, so everyone is a bit surprised when a young woman is thrown from the ride and dies. Engineer Jack McKenzie is hired to oversee the redesign. Although there are inklings that someone is out to sabotage the project, Jack can't find the flaw in the rebuilt Thrill and even plans to take the inaugural ride himself. A different suspense story, with lots of information about the history of roller coasters and roller coaster groupies who will travel across country to get a new rush.

THE ALIENIST
by *Caleb Carr* (Bantam, 1995, paperback)

In 1896 Manhattan, the mutilated body of a boy prostitute is found atop the unfinished Williamsburg Bridge. Joining forces against the killer is a *New York Times* crime reporter, a psychologist (or "alienist," as they were called then), the New York police department's first aspiring woman detective and the city's gregarious police commissioner, Theodore Roosevelt. Carr's best-seller is a suspense-filled thriller that explores the dark side of the Age of Innocence.

THE ANGEL OF DARKNESS
by Caleb Carr (Random House, 1997, paperback)

Caleb Carr's smart, thrilling historical novel, *The Alienist*, was one of the most popular novels of the 90's. *The Angel of Darkness* is it's long-awaited sequel. The infant daughter of a Spanish diplomat was kidnapped by Libby Hatch, a fiendish woman who has murdered nearly a dozen children. The excitement mounts as Dr. Laszlo Kreizler, John Schuyler Moore, Sara Howard and Stevie Taggert try to find the child before it's too late. A new character is introduced in an unforgettable courtroom scene—the legendary lawyer, Clarence Darrow.

EXECUTIVE ORDERS
by Tom Clancy (Putnam & Sons, 1996, hardcover)

As all devoted Clancy readers remember, *Debt of Honor* ended with a suicide attack on the U.S. Capitol that killed the President, both Houses of Congress and all nine Supreme Court Justices. Only Jack Ryan, the newly sworn in Vice President, survived the massacre. In *Executive Orders*, Ryan isn't just the President, he's the whole federal government. And he's got plenty to worry about as enemies in Beijing, Tehran and other world capitals plot to take advantage of the chaos in America. This could be Clancy's best thriller ever.

More by Tom Clancy:

RED STORM RISING
(Berkley, 1993, paperback).

Russia starts a war in Europe to divert world attention from their real goal-the oil fields of the Middle East.

SUM OF ALL FEARS
(Berkley, 1996, paperback).

Terrorists explode an atomic bomb in Houston and Jack Ryan is called in to try to defuse a tense situation between the United States and the Soviet Union.

....

A STRANGER IS WATCHING
by Mary Higgins Clark (Pocket, 1991, paperback)

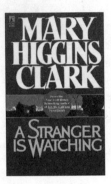

In two days, Ronald Thompson will be executed for the murder of Nina Peterson—a murder he knows he did not commit. But Thompson's imminent death is no comfort to the dead woman's husband, nor is it any consolation to her 6-year-old son who saw his mother die. While everyone waits for the execution, a stranger is watching outside the Peterson family's house where he has some unfinished business.

More of Mary Higgins Clark:

LOVES MUSIC, LOVES TO DANCE
(Pocket, 1992, paperback).

A killer lures his victims through personal ads in New York's upscale magazines.

....

CAUSE OF DEATH
by Patricia Cornwell (Putnam, 1996, hardcover)

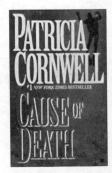

Ted Eddings, an investigative reporter who was a personal friend of Kate Scarpetta, has died while scuba diving in an ice-covered river. Was Eddings indulging some bizarre whim? Or was he after a story? After all, his body was found near a decommissioned Navy yard. Complicating the case is a neo-fascist cult that vows to "kill and maim, frighten, brainwash and torture" anyone who opposes their bid for world domination—that includes Scarpetta. Fortunately Kate has her niece Lucy, an F.B.I. agent and techno-genius, to help her out. A tightly plotted thriller with an opening scene that grabs you and won't let go.

Another Scarpetta Caper:

FROM POTTER'S FIELD
by Patricia Cornwell (Berkley, 1996, paperback).

Temple Gault, a psychopath Scarpetta has encountered before, returns with vengeance on his mind. The scenes played out in the subway tunnels beneath New York City will scare the wits out of you.

PLUM ISLAND
by Nelson DeMille (Warner Books, 1997, paperback)

It was one of those enchanted evenings, as they say," writes Nelson DeMille, "one of those magic nights that are often a prelude to something not so good." The first not so good thing that happens is NYPD detective John Corey finds two of his closest friends murdered. Then he learns they may have been selling genetically altered viruses. But who was the buyer? While Corey tries to sort this out, more of his friends and acquaintances fall victim to an unknown assassin. With lots of mayhem, a couple of love interests and an outrageous boat chase, *Plum Island* is vintage DeMille.

DARK SPECTER
by Michael Dibdin (Pantheon, 1996, paperback)

Connoisseurs have always appreciated Michael Dibdin's neatly crafted, literary thrillers. In Dark Specter, however, he took even his fans by surprise. Instead of a tidy mystery worked out in an enclosed setting, this novel highlights random mayhem all across the American landscape (this is his first novel set in the U.S.). The plot links together a man whose orderly life is violently torn apart, cops in several cities investigating multiple murders and a malevolent cult leader named Los. Backed up by a twisted interpretation of a prophetic poem of William Blake, Los sends his followers out in to the world to murder at will. Be warned: the violence is graphic.

WHITE JAZZ
by James Ellroy (Fawcett, 1993, paperback)

I t's 1958 (that's pre-Miranda Rights). Lieutenant Dave Klein's life is pretty complicated: he's accidentally killed one of the Feds' witnesses against the mob; he's fallen for a starlet he was supposed to mess up at the behest of Howard Hughes; and his partner is indulging in freelance shakedowns to make a few extras bucks on the side. Then Klein gets assigned to a bizarre breaking and entering at the home of a family of drug dealers who also dabble in incest. From page one of *White Jazz*, the plot sings, the dialogue is tremendous and the dark deeds are blacker than anything you've ever encountered in a lifetime of reading crime fiction.

More of James Ellroy:

AMERICAN TABLOID
(Knopf, 1996, paperback).

Meet three of the nastiest characters in contemporary crime fiction. Urbane Kemper Boyd, JFK's pimp and undercover agent for the CIA, the FBI, the Mob and Robert Kennedy. Pete Bondurant, Jimmy Hoffa's favorite hit man. Ward Little, an FBI wiretapper who's changed careers and become a mob lawyer. They all come together at JFK's assassination.

VERTICAL RUN
by Joseph R. Garber (Bantam, 1995, paperback)

First thing in the morning David Elliot's boss tried to kill him and his day has just gone downhill from there. Armed with only his wits and some office supplies, which in the right hands can be surprisingly deadly, the former Green Beret must outwit a squad of trained killers to escape his Park Avenue office building and find out why everyone wants him dead.

THE ART OF BREAKING GLASS
by Matthew Hall (Little, Brown, 1997, paperback)

A senator is vaporized by a bomb planted in his home computer. An especially well-connected doctor gets a 50,000-volt shock when he turns on his electric razor. A $53 million Van Gogh disappears from a gallery. Who is attacking New York's power brokers? Psychiatric nurse Sharon Blautner thinks she knows: after all, she's in love him. Sharon met Bill Kaiser at a Manhattan mental ward. He was handsome, intelligent, sensitive—not the kind of patient she expects to meet in her line of work. But once Bill escaped from the hospital, all hell broke lose in New York. And now it's up to Sharon to decide if her lover's reign of terror will come to an end.

MIAMI PURITY
by Vicki Hendricks (Vintage Books, 1996, paperback)

Sherri Parlay is a stripper who killed her boyfriend. But she got the court to believe it was in self-defense. With the murder safely behind her, Sherri decides to go straight. She lands a job at the Miami-Purity Dry Cleaners and almost immediately begins a steamy affair with the owner's son, Payne. But there are these strange burn marks on Payne's body—and, he and his mother seem awfully close-in a weird sort of way. Sherri finds lipstick on Payne's underwear and all her murderous impulses surface again.

THE PRESIDENT'S DAUGHTER
by Jack Higgins (Putnam, 1997, hardcover)

Twenty years earlier, in Vietnam, a heroic young man saved the life of a Frenchwoman and then had a brief affair with her. Now the hero is president of the United States. On a state visit to Paris, he meets his love again and is introduced to a stunning young woman: she is his daughter. Terrorists seize the young woman and threaten to kill her if the president does not order America's security agencies to submit to their demands. In desperation, the president turns to Sean Dillon, a former IRA enforcer who has become a security specialist. There's no break in the action as Dillon tries to save the president's daughter.

....

THE FUNHOUSE
Dean Koontz (Berkeley, 1989, paperback)

Years ago, Ellen ran away from home, joined the carnival, married a man she hated and had a kid she didn't love. Then she ran away again, began a new life, got a new husband, started a new family. Ellen is very happy. But now, the carnival is coming to her town and Ellen knows the people from her past will want revenge.

....

TICKTOCK
Dean Koontz (Random House, 1997, paperback)

Tommy Phan, a 30-year-old, Vietnamese-American detective, novelist and ardent pursuer of the American Dream, is being pursued across the Southern California landscape by a nasty little supernatural (and very resourceful) rag doll who, for reasons Tommy cannot fathom, wants him dead. Koontz gives readers a respite from his usual intense thrillers in this entertaining novel that strikes a masterful balance between terror and humor.

....

REQUIEM FOR A GLASS HEART
by David Lindsey (Doubleday, 1996, paperback)

David Lindsey is a spellbinder, one of the best writers of dark, intelligent, suspense fiction around today. In this novel he brings together two women from different worlds. Irina Ismaylova, an assassin "owned" by a brutal Russian mafiya czar and Cate Cuevas, the American undercover agent dedicated to catching him. From the moment they meet (at an international summit of crime bosses) the ladies play an erotically charged high-stakes game of truth or deception. Crafty, complex and very, very sexy.

Lindsey's Break-out Book:

MERCY
(Bantam, 1991, paperback).

David Lindsey became a household name with this best-seller. Carmen Palmer, a Houston homicide detective, teams up with an FBI expert on criminal personality profiling to track down a serial killer. Lindsey's gruesome scenes may shock some readers.

....

OMEGA
by Patrick Lynch (Dutton, 1997, paperback)

Something strange is happening at a hospital in South Central Los Angeles. Patients who come in with routine problems—minor stab wounds, food poisoning—are dying from a grisly secondary infection that resists every known antibiotic. Trauma surgeon Marcus Ford is especially worried about this new bacteria—his own daughter has become infected. There's a rumor of a powerful new antibiotic under development, so Dr. Ford begins a desperate search to find the cure before his daughter—and countless others—die. The twists and turns of this medical thriller are riveting. Hang on to your beach blanket!

....

LOST MAN'S RIVER
by Peter Matthiessen (Random House, 1997, paperback)

The hunters, farmers and moonshiners who were Edgar Watson's neighbors in the Florida Everglades feared him: he had a reputation as a killer. Then in 1910, Watson was gunned down by a posse. Now, forty years later, Watson's son Lucius, a college professor, receives a cache of documents about his father that draws him back to the Everglades to try to learn who his father really was and why he was killed. The theme may be commonplace, but Matthiessen elevates it to an elegy for a vanishing wilderness and study of the origins of violence in American life. His portrait of the long-dead Edgar Watson is nothing short of brilliant.

LIES OF SILENCE
by Brian Moore (Avon, 1991, paperback)

Michael Dillon has decided to leave his wife and move to London with his lover. But before he can leave, terrorists take over his home and demand that he participate in a terrorist attack, or they will kill his wife. A tense moral thriller that grabs you by the throat and won't let go.

GOOD INTENTIONS
by Patricia O'Brien (Simon & Schuster, 1997, paperback)

Rachel Snow, a popular Chicago radio talk show host, is being stalked by a shadowy killer who calls himself the Truthseeker. Unfortunately for Rachel, there are plenty of likely suspects. It might be Rachel's bitter ex-husband. Or the reformed alcoholic newspaperman who is dying to crack a big story. Or it could be her daughter's boyfriend—a scumbag hacker who posts pornography about Rachel's daughter on the Web. Or maybe it's Rachel's newest love interest. Settle back in your favorite chair for a great read.

SILENT TREATMENT
by *Michael Palmer* (Bantam Books, 1996, paperback)

Dr. Harry Corbett heads over to the hospital to visit his wife Evie the evening before she is scheduled for surgery. When he arrives at her room, Evie is dead. The cops suspect homicide— and they suspect Harry. Then the killer strikes again, murdering one of Harry's favorite patients. From his methods, Harry realizes the killer is trained in medicine and someone who knows his way around hospitals. As Harry pursues his own investigation, he uncovers a pattern that endangers the life of every patient in every hospital in the city. A harrowing medical thriller from a master of the genre.

KISS THE GIRLS
by *James Patterson* (Warner, 1995, paperback)

Bicoastal serial killers at are work in Los Angeles and in the North Carolina university towns of Chapel Hill and Durham. And as time goes by it appears that these two psychopaths are copying, perhaps even collaborating and most certainly competing with each other. For investigator Alex Cross, this is his most baffling case ever. Hint: watch for medically related clues.

ROAD RAGE
by *Ruth Rendell* (Crown, 1997, paperback)

Reginald Wexford, private citizen, is disgusted. A new super highway is about to barrel its way through the forest that surrounds his beloved Sussex village. So, it comes as no surprise that he has great sympathy for the band of conservationists who've camped out in the woods to protest the new highway. But then a militant fringe group called Sacred Globe comes to the village, kidnaps five innocent residents—including Wexford's wife—and threatens to kill them all unless the highway project is canceled. Suddenly Chief Inspector Wexford is on the job. Rendell captures Wexford's rage and writes eloquently about the issues that spawn eco-terrorism.

SIMISOLA
by Ruth Rendell (Random House, 1995, paperback)

A Nigerian doctor and his wife try to downplay their anxiety when they ask Chief Inspector Wexford to help them find their missing daughter. "It's probably nothing," Dr. Akande says. But soon Wexford finds the corpse of a young African woman and it appears that the case is solved, until the Akandes arrive to identify the body and tell the inspector that the only thing the dead woman has in common with their missing child is the color of her skin. Few authors understand the tangled motives of human nature better than Ruth Rendell. She is in top form in this disturbing thriller that explores the awful anonymity of urban life and the hurtful assumptions even fair-minded people make.

More by Ruth Rendell:

LIVE FLESH
(Ballantine, 1987, paperback).

After 14 years in prison for violent crimes, Victor Jenner tries to put his life back together. But he's chosen a peculiar way of doing it—he's contacting people he knew before his conviction. Of course, his ill-fated attempts to befriend them have grisly results.

....

THE HELLFIRE CLUB
by Peter Straub (Ballantine, 1997, paperback)

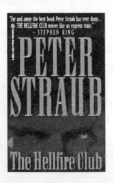

Peter Straub has all but given up writing novels of supernatural terror; apparently there's enough nastiness in real-life America these days to inspire him. In posh Connecticut, five women have vanished from their homes. Then at the police station, a lady named Nora Chancel is taken hostage by Dick Dart, a local man the cops have brought in for questioning. Dart is a formidable villain—and conspicuously hard to kill. He meets his match in Nora, a smart, tough woman who endures the worst Dart can do and still fights back.

Another Peter Straub thriller:

THE THROAT
(Signet, 1993, paperback).

A woman is murdered in an especially ghastly fashion that was the signature of a killer believed to be dead. Could the killer really be alive? Or is this the work of a copycat?

THE KILLER INSIDE ME
by Jim Thompson (Black Lizard/Vintage Books, 1990, paperback)

Everybody in the small Texas town where Lou Ford is deputy sheriff thinks he's a gentle, good-natured soul. But Ford's sweet exterior conceals a psychopathic personality. Bit by bit, author Jim Thompson draws his readers into the twisted mind of a born killer. The plot twists are devious; the murders are nasty, brutish and frequent; and the revelations are enough to scare the bejesus out of you. Connoisseurs of crime fiction agree that *The Killer Inside Me* is Thompson's masterpiece. For maximum effect, save it for a long, dark night when you're home alone.

AFTER DARK, MY SWEET
by Jim Thompson (Black Lizard/Vinatge Books, 1990, paperback)

William Collins, a former boxer, is very handsome, very polite, very friendly. He's also just busted out of his fourth mental institution. A con man and his alluring wife spot Collins, take him into their home and include him in on a little kidnapping and extortion job they're planning. But things have a way of going very wrong when Bill Collins is around.

TOUGH GUYS

THE POSTMAN ALWAYS RINGS TWICE
by James M. Cain (Random House, 1992, paperback)

A young drifter with no conscience. A beautiful woman who finds her husband to be a major inconvenience. A complicated problem that has one simple solution. When Cain's exquisite noir novel was published in 1934, it was banned in Boston for being too violent and too erotic. You decide.

THE BIG SLEEP
by Raymond Chandler (Random House, 1992, paperback)

I n the school of hard-boiled detective fic- tion, Chandler stands at the head of the class. Through Philip Marlowe, the all-American tough guy, Chandler explores the seamy side of life in 1930s California. In *The Big Sleep*, Marlowe takes on a paralyzed millionaire, his two psychopathic daughters and a little problem of blackmail complicated by murder.

Also by Chandler:

FAREWELL, MY LOVELY
(Random House, 1992, paperback).

Marlowe returns to take a case involving gambling, three very dan- gerous ladies and of course, murder.

THE LADY IN THE LAKE
(Random House, 1992, paperback).

Marlowe is hired by a husband whose wife has vanished just as she was about to leave him for another man. This is vintage Chandler, with a perfect ending.

DEBT OF HONOR
by Tom Clancy (Berkley, 1997, paperback)

Jack Ryan, Clancy's most enduring character, has taken the job of the President's National Security Adviser, just as a new world war seems to be brewing. A Japanese financier, whose parents were killed during WWII, has marshaled his immense wealth and power to avenge himself on the United States. Ryan and a team of his old colleagues join forces to frustrate the plot, neutralize hostile undercover agents and find and defuse hidden nuclear weapons. As usual, Clancy spins an exciting, complicated plot and brings it all together in a breathtaking climax.

Another Jack Ryan adventure:

PATRIOT GAMES
by Tom Clancy (Berkley, 1988, paperback).

In London, Ryan leaps in and foils an IRA plot to kidnap members of the British Royal Family. So the terrorists follow him back to the United States and make Ryan and his family their target.

RED STORM RISING
by Tom Clancy (Berkley, 1987, paperback)

Nobody does techno-thrillers like Clancy. He's a master storyteller with an absolute command of high-tech weaponry. This time out, the Soviets fake an attack on Western Europe to seize the oil fields of the Middle East. best scene: a fleet of Soviet subs attacks an American naval convoy. Buy a stack of Clancy's books, because one isn't going to be enough.

Also by Clancy:

THE HUNT FOR RED OCTOBER
(Berkley, 1992, paperback).

The first and arguably the greatest of Clancy's Jack Ryan stories. The captain of a Soviet submarine wants to defect—and bring his sub with him.

THE CARDINAL OF THE KREMLIN
(Berkley, 1989, paperback).

America's highest contact in the Kremlin is about to be betrayed to the KGB.

POSEIDON'S GOLD
by Lindsey Davis (Crown, 1994, hardcover)

Unique among the legion of private detectives is Marcus Didius Falco who operates in Rome during the 1st century A.D. This time out, Falco is accused of murdering a legionnaire who came to collect money Falco's feckless late brother owed him. Then, just as Falco is about to begin hunting for a rare sculpture of Poseidon his brother supposedly purchased with the soldier's money, Falco's roguish father (who deserted the family years before) shows up and decides to tag along. It's all good, rollicking, dangerous fun in the streets of ancient Rome.

Falco's debut:

SILVER PIGS
(Ballantine, 1991, paperback).

Two thugs are chasing a lovely young woman in the Forum, so the ever-chivalrous Falco intervenes. When Falco learns the young lady is the niece of a senator, he thinks he'll get rich. And when she tells him she knows about a cache of silver earmarked to finance a coup against the Emperor, Falco imagines himself a hero of the empire. Of course, you know Falco is in way over his head.

DEAD LAGOON
by Michael Dibdin (Pantheon, 1995, paperback)

If you've read any of Michael Dibdin's Aurelio Zen books, you know the inspector works out of Rome's Criminapol squad. But Zen is really a Venetian and this mystery takes him home to the eerie streets and desolate palaces of Venice. The story is the search for a kidnapped American, but it seems secondary to the pleasure Dibdin gets from describing the singular atmosphere of Venice where. Buy a copy before you go and savor it in a cafe overlooking the Grand Canal.

FROM RUSSIA WITH LOVE
by Ian Fleming (M.J.F. Books, paperback, 1994)

Fleming based the adventures of his suave, Cold War superspy on his own experience as a member of British Intelligence, giving his books a dark side that the Bond films never even attempted to re-create. In this particular page-turner, the Soviet anti-espionage agency SMERSH draws in 007 with a beautiful woman, then sends its number one assassin to take him out for good.

Also by Fleming:

THE MAN WITH THE GOLDEN GUN
(Signet, 1997, paperback).

Bond is brainwashed and sent out to do the KGB's bidding.

GOLDFINGER
(M.J.F. Books, paperback, 1994).

One of Fleming's most impressive Bond novels pits 007 against Auric Goldfinger, a villain determined to possess the world's gold supply.

....

THE DECEIVER
Frederick Forsyth (Bantam, 1992, paperback)

Sam McCready, chief of covert operations for Britain's Secret Intelligence Service, is a dinosaur in the new world order. He's being pushed out of his job and into early retirement, so McCready exercises his last option: a hearing to review his career. The confrontation becomes the frame for one exciting story after another, from the mission to subvert an alliance between Qaddafi and the IRA, to the time McCready revealed to the CIA their prize defector was actually a double agent.

D IS FOR DEADBEAT
by Sue Grafton (Bantam, 1988, paperback)

Private investigator Kinsey Millhone has got a problem. A deadbeat client has turned up dead and she's discovered a whole bunch of people who are happy to see him that way. Not only is she out 400 bucks, but her curiosity is compelling her to track down the killer and the investigation is taking some highly unsettling turns.

E IS FOR EVIDENCE
by Sue Grafton (Bantam, 1989, paperback)

In this case "E" also stands for exceptional, exciting and entertaining. When sarcastic, streetwise private eye Kinsey Millhone investigates a suspicious industrial fire it nearly costs her license, her reputation and her life. Once again, Grafton's offbeat sense of humor merges magically with her mastery of the detective genre.

I IS FOR INNOCENT
by Sue Grafton (Fawcett, 1992, paperback)

Grafton's celebrated "Alphabet Mysteries" continues with an artist who has been shot and killed. Her husband was acquitted of the murder, but now the victim's ex-husband is suing on behalf of the estate, claiming a miscarriage of justice. It's one of Kinsey Millhone's most complicated cases ever as she tries to sort out who's guilty, who's innocent and who's lying.

K IS FOR KILLER
by Sue Grafton (Fawcett, 1994, paperback).

Ten months after her daughter was murdered, a grieving mother comes to Kinsey for help in finding the killer. After almost a year, Kinsey would expect the trial to be cold. But once she discovers that the victim was involved in prostitution and pornography, the number of possible suspects multiplies.

M IS FOR MALICE
by Sue Grafton (Holt, 1996, paperback)

When this story opens, California private investigator Kinsey

Millhone is feeling a little depressed. But, a new case comes along to lift her spirits. Years ago, Guy Malek, heir to the Malek Construction company (worth $40 million) disappeared. Now the father has died and the family needs Guy back so the will can be enacted. Guy's brothers hire Kinsey to track down the prodigal son and she finds him without too much trouble. Of course, as soon as Guy is back all the real trouble begins. Once again, Sue Grafton delivers a completely satisfying mystery.

More from Millhone:

L IS FOR LAWLESS
by Sue Grafton (Holt, 1995, paperback).

Kinsey leaves southern California for Texas and Kentucky where a million dollars is missing and somebody's been murdered.

....

BLOOD AND HONOR
by W.E.B. Griffin (Putnam, 1997, paperback)

In spring 1943, Marine flyer Clete Frade is sent on an undercover mission to neutral Argentina. Ostensibly, he's bringing his father's body home for burial. In fact, he's instructed to prevent Nazi ships from re-arming and refueling in Argentina's coastal waters. Once in Buenos Aires, Clete hears of a plan to establish Nazis in South America after the war and of a racket that offers to ransom Jews from death camps. The trick for Clete is foiling all of these nefarious plots without causing an international incident. As usual, Griffin—a master of the military thriller—spins a complex, believable plot with lots of tension and plenty of action.

....

A THIEF OF TIME
by Tony Hillerman
(HarperCollins, 1990, paperback)

Hillerman's Navajo mysteries are clever, mystical and brimming with suspense. In what may be the best of his Officer Jim Chee and Lieutenant Joe Leaphorn series, an Anasazi archaeological site is plundered, an anthropologist disappears and a mystifying collection of murders has Chee and Leaphorn stumped.

Also by Hillerman:

COYOTE WAITS
(HarperCollins, 1992, paperback).

Jim Chee finds a friend shot and a Navajo shaman holding the murder weapon.

THE BLESSING WAY
by Tony Hillerman (HarperCollins, 1990, paperback)

Award-winning mystery author Tony Hillerman lives in Albuquerque and likes to set his literary cliffhangers among the picturesque buttes of his southwestern home. In this particular thriller, Lt. Joe Leaphorn of the Navajo Tribal Police encounters a murder scene without any tracks or clues—only a corpse with a mouthful of sand. Should he follow police procedure or turn to Navajo ritual to find what may be a supernatural killer?

Another Hillerman mystery:

PEOPLE OF DARKNESS
(HarperCollins, 1991, paperback).

When a wealthy white woman asks Navajo Tribal Police Detective Jim Chee to find a stolen box of trinkets, the trail leads to a mysterious Navajo cult known as the People of Darkness.

COTTON COMES TO HARLEM
by Chester Himes (Vintage Books, 1988, paperback)

A scam artist named Deke O'Hara has extorted $87,000 out of the residents of Harlem by posing as the leader of a "back-to-Africa" movement. The money has been stashed in a huge bale of cotton-but the bale has disappeared. Trying to track down the cotton, the money and the crooked O'Hara are two black detectives, Coffin Ed Johnson and Grave Digger Jones. This is classic detective fiction, with hard-boiled dialogue, a femme fatale and skillful use of light/dark imagery. But Himes (who started his writing career while he was in prison for jewel theft) also tackles the larger issues of racism and the problems faced by the residents of Harlem.

ORIGINAL SIN
by P.D. James (Warner, 1996, paperback)

P.D. James is a master of psychological suspense, with a special gift for creating atmosphere so intense it is almost a major character in its own right. Her latest Dalgliesh novel is set in an elite London publishing house. Life has been unsettling at Peverell Press, what with the series of nasty pranks, an editor's suicide and then the ghastly murder of the brilliant but thoroughly unpleasant new managing director, Gerald Etienne. When Commander Adam Dalgliesh and Detective Inspector Kate Miskin take on the case, they find Etienne was so unpopular, virtually the entire staff of Peverell Press is suspect.

More of P.D. James:

THE CHILDREN OF MEN
(Warner, 1994, paperback).

This is a departure for James. She sets her story in the year 2021 when males are sterile and the human race is dying. As society becomes increasingly cruel, Theodore Faron, an Oxford historian, is drawn to a band of revolutionaries.

THE BOURNE IDENTITY
by Robert Ludlum (Bantam, 1987, paperback)

Robert Ludlum specializes in old-fashioned, globe-trotting, non-stop action. Jason Bourne knows that he was left to die, but he doesn't know by whom. He doesn't even know if his name is really Jason Bourne. But he does know that assassins—from several governments—are after him. And he knows that a terrorist named Carlos may hold the key to his real identity. A classic of fast-paced espionage.

Also by Ludlum:

THE BOURNE SUPREMACY
(Bantam, 1987, paperback).

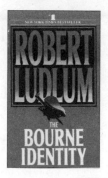

Jason Bourne takes on two assignments at once: rescue his wife from kidnappers and stop a Bourne impersonator before he plunges the Far East into a catastrophic war.

....

DARKER THAN AMBER
by John D. MacDonald
(Fawcett, 1997, paperback)

Travis McGee, a tough guy with a heart of gold, is always up to his neck in sex violence. This time out, the color amber refers to the eyes of the young woman McGee rescues from hoods in this classic that lets our hero show off both his guts and his brains.

....

BLACK BETTY
by Walter Mosley (Pocket, 1995, paperback)

It's a long, hot summer in L.A., 1961, when Easy Rawlins, a black private investigator, accepts a job to track down "Black Betty," a stunningly beautiful woman. But the path to Betty is strewn with corpses and Rawlins has all he can do to make sure he doesn't become one of them.

More by Mosley:

DEVIL IN A BLUE DRESS
(St. Martin's Press, 1993, paperback).

Mosley's debut novel finds Rawlins in 1940s L.A., taking a job from a mobster. he's supposed to locate a blond femme fatale who frequents black jazz joints, promises men love, but often delivers violent death.

A RED DEATH
(Pocket, 1992, paperback).

During the Red Scare of the 1950s, Rawlins is blackmailed by an IRS agent into infiltrating a black church and spying on a former Polish resistance fighter.

......

BROTHER CADFAEL'S PENANCE
by Ellis Peters (Mysterious Press, 1996, paperback)

If you've seen Derek Jacobi play Brother Cadfael, the clever Benedictine sleuth, on PBS, then you already know that Ellis Peters writes devilishly complex tales of medieval intrigue. Good as the Jacobi series is, the books are even better. In this one, Cadfael must leave the safety of his monastery and face the perils of 12th-century England's civil war. Olivier de Bretagne, Cadfael's own son (from the days when Cadfael was still a knight), has been taken prisoner and Cadfael will need all his cunning to save the young man.

Also by Peters:

THE HOLY THIEF
(Mysterious Press, 1994, paperback).

Floodwaters threaten the shrine of St. Winifred at Cadfael's abbey. He knows that if the relics are moved, a long-buried secret will be discovered. But even Cadfael is shocked with the saint's bones are stolen and the sin of sacrilege is compounded by murder.

......

CALAMITY TOWN
by Ellery Queen

Queen leaves his familiar Manhattan and ventures out to a small town where he falls in love and becomes entangled in murder. This story has the great courtroom scenes that are an EQ trademark, but the small-town atmosphere—the gossip, the rivalries, the cliques—give the story extra oomph. An excellent introduction to the master of laid-back detective fiction. Worth searching for.

Also by Queen:

AND ON THE EIGHTH DAY.

EQ stumbles upon a utopian community in the desert. In this strange environment he's called upon to solve a crime. Worth searching for.

·············

HIDE & SEEK
by Ian Rankin (St. Martin's Press, 1997, paperback)

Y ou are going to like Inspector John Rebus. He's an Edinburgh man, proud of his city. As a committed Calvinist, he disapproves of most of what goes on beneath the handsome, civilized surface of the old town. But as a shrewd cop, none of it surprises him. In this multi-layered tale of a gruesomely murdered male prostitute, everyone in Edinburgh seems to be a Jekyll-and-Hyde character. In fact, the prime suspect is a sanctimonious old villain named Dr. Jekyll. Complex, thrilling and completely satisfying, *Hide & Seek* is a classic police procedural.

More by Ian Rankin:

STRIP JACK.

First Gregor Jack, a popular young Member of Parliament, is caught in a police sweep of a notorious Edinburgh brothel. Then he disappears. Then his pals obstruct Rebus' investigation. Does the boy have more to hide than a single night's indiscretion? Worth searching for.

·············

THE WAY OF THE TRAITOR
by Laura Jon Rowland (Villard Books, 1997, paperback)

A new sleuth on the scene is Sano Ichiro. He's a samurai and Nagasaki's Most Honorable Investigator of Events, Situations and People. When the story opens in 17th-century Japan, Sano has two problems: he believes a highly placed enemy is setting him up for a fall and the director of the local Dutch trading company has been murdered. Tracking a murderer while trying to save his own neck keeps Sano pretty busy. But then the Dutch up the ante by training their cannons on the town and insisting that the murderer be found—pronto.

....

MURDER MUST ADVERTISE
by Dorothy L. Sayers (HarperCollins, 1995, paperback)

Mr. Bredon has just joined a Londona advertising agency, replacing a copywriter who took a nasty—and fatal—spill down an iron staircase. But strange and gruesome deaths continue to plague the agency. And now the office staff notice that Bredon is a bit peculiar, snooping around private offices, befriending his late predecessor's sister and spending his lunch hours on the roof with a catapult. It's all very puzzling and only Lord Peter Wimsey could make sense of this ingenious plot. A work of art from one the greatest mystery writers of the 20th century.

Also by Sayers:

THE NINE TAILORS
(Harvest Books, 1966, paperback).

On New Year's Eve, Wimsey's car goes off the road in a snowstorm but the rector of a rural village offers him refuge. During his enforced stay, Wimsey makes a dreadful discovery—a mutilated corpse in another man's grave.

....

TRAVELER'S TALES

THE MOST BEAUTIFUL VILLAGES OF THE DORDOGNE

by James Bentley, photographs by Hugh Palmer
(Thames & Hudson, 1996, hardcover)

You may know the Dordogne by another name—Périgord. It is famous for its superb examples of prehistoric art, dramatic scenery and exquisite cuisine (this is the home of the famous black truffles!). Now, accompanied by James Bentley and photographer Hugh Palmer, you'll explore the secret places of this enchanting corner of rural France. Some highlights include the majestic old houses of Brantôme on the river Dronne and the fortified medieval villages of Montfort and Monpazier. To help you plan your itinerary, the book offers a listing of hotels and restaurants, a calendar of market and festival days and a map.

Farther South:

THE MOST BEAUTIFUL VILLAGES OF PROVENCE

by Michael Jacobs, photographs by Hugh Palmer (Thames & Hudson, 1994, hardcover).

Explore the rustic villages and exquisite countryside that inspired Cezanne and van Gogh.

DAYS AND NIGHTS IN CALCUTTA

by Clark Blaise and Bharati Mukherjee
(Hungry Mind Press, 1995, paperback)

This husband-and-wife team have written the ideal travel book about Calcutta in particular and India in general. After many

years in America, Mukherjee returns to her home city, not altogether happily. Her half of the book immerses us in such everyday
occurrences as shopping for saris with her relatives, packing
medicines for a leper clinic and attending the premier of a film
(India's movie-making industry is the world's largest). Blaise's
half focuses on conversations he has with the Indians he meets—
in the shops and on the streets, at dinner parties and in the
"permanent theater" of his wife's family. Together, these two points
of view offer a rich, in-depth look at Indian life.

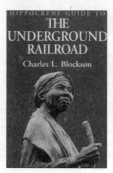

HIPPOCRENE GUIDE TO THE UNDERGROUND RAILROAD
by Charles L. Blockson
(Hippocrene Books, 1994, hardcover)

This is the essential companion for anyone
who wishes to retrace the routes of the
runaway slaves. Blockson includes stories of
narrow escapes and desperate acts of heroism.

YAK BUTTER AND BLACK TEA, A JOURNEY INTO FORBIDDEN CHINA
by Wade Brackenbury (Algonquin Books, 1996, paperback)

They say that in a mountain valley somewhere between Burma
and Tibet live a people called the Drung. No Westerner had
been in the valley or spoken with a Drung in more than a century.
And officials of the People's Republic of China are suspicious of any
outsiders interested in such a remote place. So of course Wade
Brackenbury, a footloose mountaineer from Utah and Pascal Szupu,
a photojournalist from France, were determined to go there. It is a
tremendous adventure as the two guys and their translator, Sophi,
slip pass border guards, cross cable bridges high above raging
torrents, survive brutal weather and scramble through mountains,
deserts and rainforests to reach a place that may not even exist.

VIEWS OF ROME
Photographs by Steven Brooke (Rizzoli, 1995, hardcover)

I f you've found that travel snapshots are unsatisfying and post cards are just a bit cheesy, you'll love Steven Brooke's wonderfully evocative black-and-white photographs of the Eternal City. The man's a genius who not only captures how the buildings look, but what it feels like to actually be in their presence. So if you're planning a trip to Italy, don't buy a dozen rolls of film. Buy this book instead.

THE LOST CONTINENT:
TRAVELS IN SMALL-TOWN AMERICA
by Bill Bryson (HarperCollins, 1990, paperback)

G ripped with nostalgia for the land of his youth, expatriate American Bill Bryson leaves London to undertake "what blurb writers like to call a journey of discovery." Piloting an aging Chevette, he transverses the beautiful if somewhat bizarre American countryside, visiting Elvis' Birthplace, Colonial Williamsburg and strange little places where it's possible to purchase an ice-cream cone the size of a baby's head. Bryson's account of his 14,000-mile odyssey into the heartland and psyche of America is not to be missed.

CELTIC SACRED LANDSCAPES
by Nigel Campbell Pennick (Thames and Hudson, 1996, hardcover)

I f we look at the landscape through contemporary eyes," Nigel Pennick writes, "our view can be only partial; people in other times, or with other beliefs, have seen things quite differently." Traveling throughout the British Isles and Brittany, Pennick locates the holy mountains, holy wells, mystical caves, fairy trees and sacred rocks the Celts venerated since pre-Christian times (he even supplies a gazetteer so you can find them yourself). But more importantly, he transports us back to a time when the whole landscape was crowded with loci of supernatural power.

IN THEIR FOOTSTEPS:
THE AMERICAN VISIONS GUIDE TO AFRICAN-AMERICAN HERITAGE SITES
by Henry Chase

Beale Street in Memphis, where the blues were born. The red-brick Dexter Avenue Baptist Church, where the world first heard the ringing oratory of Dr. Martin Luther King, Jr. The superb ante-bellum plantation house, now the President's House of Tuskegee University. In almost 600 pages, Chase urges you to discover fascinating sites of African-American history. Regional maps pinpoint the locations and famous authors enliven the guide with evocative essays, such as Gloria Naylor on her home in Mississippi and Amiri Baraka on Newarks' "tenderloin" district. Worth searching for.

CALIFORNIA FAULT:
SEARCHING FOR THE SPIRIT OF STATE ALONG THE SAN ANDREAS
by Thurston Clarke (Ballantine, 1996, paperback)

Living on top of California's San Andreas Fault is a bit like living on the summit of Mount Vesuvius: some day, the Big One is gonna hit and the people there will have no place to go. Travel writer Thurston Clarke follows the length of the Fault and finds that most of the folks there try to forget that they live on a lethal stretch of real estate. Sure, from time to time he runs into the stray loony (this is California, after all), but the big surprise is how many cheerful optimists he meets.

THE MOJAVE:
A PORTRAIT OF THE DEFINITIVE AMERICAN DESERT
by David Darlington (Henry Holt, 1996, hardcover)

The Mojave Desert is all arid mountains, salt flats and dried up lakes. It's the place where you find Death Valley and Joshua Tree. David Darlington explores these vast, hot and hostile badlands through stories: the belief in some quarters that extraterrestrials are especially fond of the Mojave; the way across the desert—from wagon train trails, to the road followed by the Joads in *The Grapes of Wrath* , to old Route 66. There are discussions of ranchers in the Mojave, gold miners in the Mojave and the military in the Mojave, and a look at people as disparate as motorcyclists and real estate developers who just can't seem to leave the desert alone.

ON THE NARROW ROAD:
JOURNEY INTO A LOST JAPAN
by Lesley Downer (Summit Books, 1989, paperback)

In 1649, just before he died, the haiku poet Matsuo Basho journeyed through Japan to see its beauties one last time. In the 1980s, Lesley Downer followed Basho's trail, hoping to find unspoiled corners of rural Japan. But her secret desire—like Basho's—was to visit the yamabushi, a particularly ascetic and secretive order of monks hidden deep in the mountains of northern Japan. Downer's journey and the discoveries she makes along the way, are both surprising and inspiring. This book is out of print, but try your local library and search used books until you find a copy.

THE PERFECT LONDON WALK
by Roger Ebert & Daniel Curley, photographs by Jack Lane (Andrews & McMeel, 1986, paperback)

Follow in the footsteps of Dick Whittington, Karl Marx, John Keats and Queen Boadicea (who is believed to be buried beneath Track 5 in Paddington Station).

A WELSH CHILDHOOD
by Alice Thomas Ellis (A Common Reader Edition, 1996, hardcover)

Alice Thomas Ellis' reflections on her childhood in Wales are funny, thought-provoking, uplifting. The black-and-white photographs by Patrick Sutherland that accompany the text are nothing less than stunning.

CHASING THE MONSOON:
A MODERN PILGRIMAGE THROUGH INDIA
by Alexander Frater (Owl, 1992, paperback)

Frater is one of those rare authors who can make you fall in love with a place you've never seen. His goal is Trivandrum on India's Malabar Coast, where the life-giving monsoon sweeps into the subcontinent every year at the end of May. On this rainy pilgrimage, Frater discovers all kinds of monsoon lore and introduces his readers to colorful characters who love nothing better than a good soaking downpour.

GREAT PLAINS
by Ian Frazier (Penguin, 1990, paperback)

Frazier covers 25,000 miles driving back and forth across the Plains states, visiting some of the most stirring and haunting spots in America: Sitting Bull's home on the Grand River in South Dakota; the Clutter family farmhouse, of *In Cold Blood* fame, in Holcomb, Kansas; plus sites associated with Bonnie and Clyde, Woody Guthrie, Doc Holliday and Crazy Horse.

FROM BEIRUT TO JERUSALEM
by Thomas L. Friedman (Farrar, Straus & Giroux, 1991, hardcover)

From *The New York Times*' correspondent in Lebanon and Israel comes these eyewitness accounts of carnage in Beirut during Lebanon's civil war, the Palestinian intifada and other examples of religious and ethnic hatreds in the Middle East.

SWIMMING TO CAMBODIA
by Spalding Gray
(Theatre Communications Group, 1985, paperback)

Multimedia mogul Spalding Gray played a very small role in the movie *The Killing Fields*. In *Swimming to Cambodia*, he turns his experiences filming that role into a fascinating, late-20th-century odyssey. In this witty account, he ruminates on Bangkok prostitutes, nuclear weapons, the entertainment industry and his own search for the elusive "perfect moment"—weaving them all into a mesmerizing tale.

••••••••••••

THE SIZE OF THE WORLD
by Jeff Greenwald (Globe Pequot Press, 1995, paperback)

On his 40th birthday, Greenwald challenged himself to prove "that the sidewalk in front of [his] house is connected, physically, with every other place on Earth." To demonstrate his theory, he would travel from Oakland, California, to Oakland, California, without ever leaving the ground. "I want... to ambulate [the world's] circumference," he writes, "and let the very fact of the planet's spheroid shape carry me back to where I started from." We won't spoil the story by telling you how he manages to get across the oceans. But we will say that Greenwald learns the world is full of very nice people and truly lousy roads.

For Goal-Oriented Travelers:

SHOPPING FOR BUDDHAS
by Jeff Greenwald (Lonely Planet, 1996, paperback).

During a journey in Asia, Greenwald began an obsessive search for the perfect statue of Buddha—an exercise that just begs for a spiritual message. In the back streets of Katmandu, Greenwald finds a statue, enlightenment and a whole lot more.

••••••••••••

MOTORING WITH MOHAMMED
by Eric Hansen (Vintage, 1992, paperback)

In 1978, Eric Hansen was shipwrecked on a deserted island off the coast of North Yemen. When rescue arrived, in the form of a leaky boat of goatherds, he buried his diaries which chronicled seven years of travel, expecting to return for them with a more reliable means of transportation. Motoring with Mohammed is the story of his search for those diaries—10 years later.

••••••••••••

Also by Eric Hansen:

STRANGER IN THE FOREST

A rmed only with a pair of trusty tennis shoes and a sack full of trinkets, the author sets out on foot across the Borneo rain forest.

LOST LHASA:
HEINRICH HARRER'S TIBET
by Heinrich Harrer (Abrams, 1997, paperback)

I n 1943, Heinrich Harrer, an Austrian, escaped from a British POW camp in India and fled into the Himalayas to Tibet, a land not especially fond of foreigners. Instead of being imprisoned or deported, he became adviser to the Dalai Lama and remained in Tibet until 1950, when he got out just ahead of the invading Chinese army. Illustrated with 200 of Harrer's photographs, *Lost Lhasa* is a gem of a book that captures the mysterious mountain kingdom in its final years.

MY OLD MAN AND THE SEA: A FATHER AND SON SAIL AROUND CAPE HORN
by David Hays and Daniel Hays (Algonquin Books, 1995, paperback)

T wo accomplished sailors, David (the father) and Daniel (his 24-year-old son) decide to tackle what has for them always been the ultimate seafaring challenge: rounding Cape Horn in a small boat. So they outfit a 25-foot cutter-rigged English sloop and set out on a 17,000-mile voyage. In alternate chapters, these two courageous mariners and gifted writers record their life together in cramped quarters and the climax of their adventure-coming upon the Horn in gale-force winds. A great read—don't miss it.

On a similar subject:

KAYAKING THE VERMILION SEA
by Jonathan Waterman (Simon & Schuster, 1995, paperback).

A fter the first stress-filled year of marriage, the author and his wife decide to test their endurance and their marriage on an extended kayak voyage along the harsh but spectacularly beautiful coast of Baja California.

....

ROME: THE BIOGRAPHY OF A CITY
by Christopher Hibbert (Penguin, 1988, paperback)

Hibbert brings Rome to life in a way no guidebook ever could. You can almost see the gladiators fighting before wild throngs in the Colosseum, the first Christians burying their martyrs in the gloomy catacombs, the Renaissance popes sinking to new levels of worldliness and even decadence while Michelangelo and Bernini lift St. Peter's Basilica to new heights of splendor. Whoever thought the history of a city could be such a great story?

....

POETS IN A LANDSCAPE
by Gilbert Highet (A Common Reader Edition, 1996, hardcover)

Gilbert Highet finds fresh insights into the work of ancient Latin poets by exploring the places in Italy where they lived. The result is a grand literary tour of "the Italy which was molded by Rome and educated by Greece." We study Catullus in Verona, Horace at Tivoli and Vergil in the bucolic countryside near Lake Garda. Plus there are excursions into the home territory of Ovid, Juvenal, Tibullus and Propertius. Then we conclude in Rome, for an in-depth tour of the city's ancient sites and their significance to the great poets. *Poets in a Landscape* is an ideal book for anyone who loves Italy, loves the classics, or loves poetry.

....

OFF THE ROAD:
A MODERN DAY WALK DOWN THE PILGRIM'S ROUTE INTO SPAIN
by Jack Hitt (Simon & Schuster, 1994, paperback)

One of the advantages of driving (instead of walking) the 500-mile Pilgrim Route from France to Spain's shrine of St. James in Compostella is that you won't smell bad when you finally arrive. But that did not deter Jack Hitt, who wanted his pilgrimage to be authentic. He hiked the entire trail and arrived at the church quite... fragrant. Along the way, he dodges lightning, fends off wild dogs and resists vendors of glow-in-the-dark rosaries. A lively, often hilarious account of a modern New Yorker trying to imitate medieval pilgrims.

AN ISLAND OUT OF TIME
by *Tom Horton* (Norton, 1996, paperback)

Nine miles out in Chesapeake Bay is Smith Island, one of the best places to harvest Maryland blue crabs. For generations the islanders have made their living from the Bay. But now environmentalists want to limit the crab harvest—and the islanders aren't about to take it lying down. "I respect science and education," one islander told Tom Horton, "but those people got to respect some things we know, too." Based on his two years living on Smith Island, Horton has written an in-depth portrait of this tight, traditional community, their concept of personal freedom and why one person's harvest is another's environmental exploitation.

BARCELONA
by *Robert Hughes* (Vintage, 1993, paperback)

Ask any Catalan and he'll tell you that Barcelona was a sophisticated city, a center of trade and culture, when Madrid was a dusty, hopeless backwater. Hughes hasn't written a travel book about a great city, he's composed a love song to the spectacular Gothic heart of the old town, to the Art Nouveau palaces and bizarre fantasies of Antonio Gaudí, to the poets and musicians and merchants and crusaders who made Barcelona one of the most vibrant cities in Europe.

TO TIMBUKTU:
A JOURNEY DOWN THE NIGER
by *Mark Jensen* (Morrow, 1997, hardcover)

Sure, you can pay outfitters to haul you to the top of Mount Everest, but how does anyone get to Timbuktu? Mark Jensen thought he'd get to the fabled city by kayaking down the Niger

River with three friends. Hundreds of miles before they even got near Timbuktu, the group broke up and Jensen continued on alone overland. His adventures with crocodiles, soldiers, waterfalls, swarms of killer bees and deserts will keep you turning the pages. His lyrical descriptions of the people he meets and the places he sees will make you want to follow Jensen's trail to Timbuktu.

PHANTOM ISLANDS OF THE ATLANTIC:
THE LEGENDS OF SEVEN ISLANDS THAT NEVER WERE
by Donald S. Johnson (Walker, 1996, hardcover)

Surely you've heard of Buss Island? How about the seven cities of Antillia? Any takers for St. Brendan Island? In the 16th century, these islands were on all the maps. Mariners swore they had seen them and even described them in detail. Now Donald S. Johnson, an intrepid sailor who has crossed the Atlantic in his 27-foot schooner more times than Columbus, explains how rumor, wishful thinking and mistaken identity kept these fantasy islands alive for centuries. Best part of the book: reproductions of blissfully misguided maps.

BALKAN GHOSTS:
A JOURNEY THROUGH HISTORY
by Robert D. Kaplan (Vintage, 1994, paperback)

Why have the Serbs, the Bosnians and the Croats always been at each other's throats? What could bring the Greeks, the Bulgarians and Romanians into the bloody strife? Kaplan draws us into "a time-capsule world, a dim stage upon which people raged, spilled blood, experienced visions and ecstasies." Finally, someone explains the ancient hatreds that flourish in the Balkans.

AN ARCHAEOLOGICAL GUIDE TO NORTHERN CENTRAL AMERICA: BELIZE, GUATEMALA, HONDURAS AND EL SALVADOR
by Joyce Kelly (University of Oklahoma Press, 1996, paperback)

If you like going off the beaten path, you need this book. Joyce Kelly has written an in-depth tour of 38 Mayan sites and 25 museums-more than any other guide book-in Belize, Guatemala, Honduras and El Salvador. Kelly has visited every site personally. And she has included many places which do not appear in any other guide book. Best of all for adventurous travelers, Kelly includes clear maps and precise directions so you can get to even the most remote sites. No other guide to the Mayan sites of Central America can compare with this compact, comprehensive, easy-to-use handbook.

With Kelly in the Yucatan:

AN ARCHAEOLOGICAL GUIDE TO MEXICO'S YUCATAN PENINSULA
by Joyce Kelly (University of Oklahoma Press, 1993, paperback).

Using the same format as her guide to Belize, Guatemala, Honduras and El Salvador, Kelly helps you get to 91 Mayan sites (and 8 archaeological museums) in Mexico.

THE KNOPF GUIDE TO LONDON
(Knopf, 1993, paperback)

More a pocket encyclopedia of London than a guidebook, this sturdy, magnificently illustrated volume is packed with information about every corner of the city and includes hotel, restaurant and shopping information, plus tips on how to navigate the Tube (London's subway).

CHARLES KURALT'S AMERICA
by Charles Kuralt (Doubleday, 1996, paperback)

You probably remember Charles Kuralt's ongoing "On the Road" series on the CBS News. After his retirement, Kuralt had some time to think about all the places he visited and in this beautiful book he goes gone back to "revisit my favorite American places at just the right time of year." He still finds the Alaska Panhandle breathtaking, revels in the peace of the Minnesota lakes and enjoys the "elaborately tolerant" inhabitants of Key West. With his simple, direct, almost folksy style and the wonderful color photos that accompany the text, this is a handsome book that makes you feel good about America and the people who live here.

PRAIRYERTH (A DEEP MAP)
by *William Least Heat-Moon* (Houghton Mifflin, 1991, paperback)

In *Blue Highways*, William Least Heat-Moon chronicled his 13,000-mile journey down the back roads of America. In PrairyErth he stops his car and sets out on foot across Chase County, a sparsely populated tract of tallgrass prairie in central Kansas. As an "inspector of the ordinary," he takes the reader on a journey through the time, landscape and history of the county, exquisitely describing the land and its plants, animals and people until he has created what he calls a "deep map." It's a beautiful map that will stay in your heart and mind for quite some time.

On the road with William Least Heat-Moon:

BLUE HIGHWAYS
(Houghton Mifflin, 1991, paperback).

On old maps, the two-lane back roads were printed in blue. So the author gassed up his Ford van and followed the blue lines on a 13,000-mile journey to the little-visited towns and regions of America.

FLORENCE: A PORTRAIT
by *Michael Levey* (Harvard University Press, 1996, hardcover)

Michael Levey's book is definitely unconventional. To prove that genius did not begin and end with the Renaissance, he introduces his readers to the best Florentine art over 700 years. And to dispel the myth of Florence as a serene "Athens-on-the-Arno," he tells stories of bloody feuds, riots in the streets and assassinations in the Duomo. But Levey is at his most entertaining when critiquing every work of art in the old town (he says Michelangelo's Medici Chapel "possesses the stark chill of a frigidarium").

ADVENTURES ON THE WINE ROUTE:
A WINE BUYER'S TOUR OF FRANCE
by Kermit Lynch (Noonday Books, 1990, paperback)

If wine buyers were merchant princes, Kermit Lynch would be a Medici. He is a man of strong opinions and a discerning palate. He knows what he likes and he's willing to scour every backroad in France to find it. This thoroughly enjoyable book takes you along on his French wine buying tours. In vineyards, caves and tasting rooms, he discusses what he looks for in a fine wine—a distinctive personality, some nuance, balance among the flavors, maybe a surprise. For anyone who loves wine, this is a delightful companion.

UNDER THE TUSCAN SUN:
AT HOME IN ITALY
by Frances Mayes (Chronicle Books, 1996, paperback)

I am about to buy a house in a foreign country," begins Frances Mayes in *Under the Tuscan Sun*. "It is tall, square and apricot-colored with faded green shutters, ancient tile roof and an iron balcony on the second level." In 1990, Mayes and her husband restored an abandoned villa in Tuscany. They found frescoes beneath the whitewash in the dining room and a vineyard under brambles in the garden. They also discovered the joys of regional cooking, such as Red Peppers Melted With Balsamic Vinegar and Pizza with Onion Confit and Sausage (recipes included). This is the best thing since *A Year in Provence*.

A YEAR IN PROVENCE
by Peter Mayle (Vintage, 1991, paperback)

Once you start reading, it's impossible to put this book down. On the surface, it's about Mayle and his wife moving to a

200-year-old stone farmhouse in Provence and trying to restore it. Actually, the book is about great food, heavenly wines eccentric neighbors, philosophical plumbers and a devilishly clever plan to have the house finished by Christmas.

THE STONES OF FLORENCE
by Mary McCarthy (Harvest Books, 1987, paperback)

In Florence, Mary McCarthy knows where all the best paintings are buried. Follow her through the cool shadows of empty churches and you'll encounter dazzling works of art the tourists haven't discovered yet.

GOD HAS NINETY-NINE NAMES:
REPORTING FROM A MILITANT MIDDLE EAST
by Judith Miller (Simon & Schuster, 1996, paperback)

To report on the militant Middle East, Judith Miller, former bureau chief for *The New York Times* in Cairo, distinguishes between Islam, the faith of hundreds of millions of peaceable believers and Islamism, a radical, extremist faction. She travels through eight Arab countries, plus Iran and Israel and observes that Arab states with close ties to the West tend to be led by incompetent governments, suffer from corruption or repression, or are simply too weak to resist a movement that promises justice, prosperity and the blessings of divine favor. An unsettling book that says what the leaders of the Western democracies need to hear.

SPELL OF THE TIGER:
THE MAN-EATERS OF SUNDARBANS
by Sy Montgomery (Houghton Mifflin, 1996, paperback)

Cyclones, venomous snakes, crocodiles and sharks all infest the mangrove swamp that stretches between India and Bangladesh on the Bay of Bengal. The most frightening creatures are the tigers. They swim in the bay and grab fishermen from their boats. They lie in wait and pounce on unwary woodcutters and honey-gathers in the forest. The tigers kill 300 people every year.

Studying the man-eaters of Sundarbans and the people they prey upon, Montgomery is surprised to find the local people don't hate the beasts-they fear and worship the tigers as manifestations of the tiger god Daksin Ray. A compelling read about a natural phenomenon and the myths humans tell one another to help make sense of it.

MAIDEN VOYAGES:
WRITINGS OF WOMEN TRAVELERS
Edited by Mary Morris in collaboration with Larry O'Connor
(David McKay, 1993, paperback)

T he exploring of foreign lands," Mabel Sharman Crawford wrote in 1863, "is more improving, as well as more amusing, than crochet work." No doubt the 51 women travelers in this collection would agree. Here is Edith Wharton marveling in a Marrakech palace garden; Mildred Cable hearing phantom voices in the Gobi Desert; Joan Didion meditating on power and violence in modern Bogotá; and Frances Trollope casting a pretty cold eye on domestic manners in early 19th-century America. From Willa Cather in Provence to Mary Wollstonecraft in Norway, this a literary banquet for armchair travelers.

SHAKER HERITAGE GUIDEBOOK:
EXPLORING THE HISTORIC SITES, MUSEUMS AND COLLECTIONS
by Stuart Murray (Golden Hill Press, 1994, paperback)

T urray begins his meticulous guide book with a history of the Shakers. Then he walks you through 26 Shaker communities— including the sole active community at Sabbathday Lake, Maine (established 1794). Each entry includes maps and a full description of the site. You can visit Hancock, Massachusetts, famous for the round stone barn; Pleasant Hill, Kentucky, renowned for its superb spiral staircase; and Gorham, Maine, home of the composer of "Simple Gifts." There's also a list, state by state, of museums with notable Shaker collections. Finally, the book is illustrated with period photographs, portraits, paintings and engravings of Shaker life.

Off the Map:

THE CURIOUS HISTORIES OF PLACE NAMES
by Derek Nelson (Kodansha America, 1997, hardcover)

There's a lot of wish fulfillment going on in maps. Syria never shows Israel on any of its maps. Rand McNally refused to recognize Idi Amin's decree to rename a lake in his honor. The Soviet city of Naberezhnyye Chelny, renamed Brezhnev, reverted only four years later. And Medieval and Renaissance mapmakers kept showing the paradise islands of St. Brendan in the Atlantic in the hope that someday someone would actually find them. Nelson's chatty chapters are filled with interesting factoids and amusing anecdotes. And of course, there are lots of reproductions of wonderful old maps.

DAKOTA: A SPIRITUAL GEOGRAPHY
by Kathleen Norris (Houghton Mifflin, 1994, paperback)

In Lemmon, South Dakota, Norris lives in the house her grandfather built. She's 40 miles from the next town, surrounded by open country where the antelope out number the automobiles. Through her eyes, we come to love this place, to admire the perseverance of the farmers and ranchers and to rejoice when at last Norris rediscovers her Christian faith. A beautiful book suffused with the splendor of the vast spaces and profound silences of the northern plains.

THE EXPLORERS: FROM THE ANCIENT WORLD TO THE PRESENT
by Paolo Novaresio (Stewart, Tabori & Chang, 1996, hardcover)

From the Phoenicians to Vasco da Gama to Captain James Cook to astronaut Neil Armstrong, the explorers tell their own stories through ship's logs, diaries, memoirs and the maps they themselves drew of their journeys.

THE HUDSON RIVER:
FROM TEAR OF THE CLOUDS TO MANHATTAN
photographs by Jake Rajs, writings edited by Arthur G. Adams
(Monacelli Press, 1995, paperback)

Forget the muddy, murky Mississippi. The grandest, most beautiful river in America is the Hudson. Jake Rajs proves it in 250 spectacular photographs that follow the river from its source in Lake Tear of the Clouds and meanders 315 miles downstream to the tip of Manhattan. Enhancing the magnificent photos are an anthology of writings from people who loved the Hudson, from Hudson River School artist Thomas Cole to Europhile Henry James.

LONDON
by John Russell (Abrams, 1996, paperback)

A London resident for some 50 years, Russell squires his readers along the grand streets and tiny alleys, through the interiors of stately homes and bustling coffeehouses. You'll even go boating on the Thames. Plus, Russell summons up great moments in London's history, from Christopher Wren rebuilding the city after the Great Fire of 1666 to Winston Churchill's funeral procession traveling by boat under Tower Bridge. Read this book before you head to the great city.

PARIS
by John Russell

New York, London and Rome are cities. Paris is drama, maybe even opera. In any case, everything is more intense in Paris. John Russell strolls down the grand boulevards, wanders along the banks of the Seine and explores the alleys of the Latin Quarter and Montparnasse to find the very essence of the world's most thrilling city.

ISLANDS OF STORM
by James Charles Roy (Dufour Editions, 1994, paperback)

You've probably never heard of this book, which is a tremendous shame. Nobody loves Ireland and the Irish like Roy and no author living can describe the place and its people—whether it's the contemporary Irish, medieval Celtic monks, or the vanished life of the Inishmurray islanders—as vividly or as eloquently as he does. A great book that combines a traveler's tale with Irish history and Celtic folklore.

Also by Roy:

THE ROAD WET, THE WIND CLOSE
(Dufour Editions, 1986, paperback).

Dozens of evocative black-and-white photographs capture the soul of old Celtic Ireland.

MILES FROM NOWHERE
by Barbara Savage (Mountaineers Books, 1985, paperback)

The idea of bicycling around the world started out as a joke. But in May of 1978 Barbara Savage and her husband actually set out on an unforgettable 20,000-mile journey of a lifetime. For two years they propelled themselves along the back roads, highways and dusty trails of 25 nations, seeing wonderful things that would have been only a blur through a car window. Savage's account of their trek is so vivid and full of life she makes you wish you had been along every pedal of the way.

SUSAN B. ANTHONY SLEPT HERE:
A GUIDE TO AMERICAN WOMEN'S LANDMARKS
by Lynn Sherr & Jurate Kazickas (Times Books, 1994, paperback)

More than 1500 sites are listed—including Georgia O'Keeffe's ranch in Abiquiu, New Mexico; the farmhouse of Rebecca Nurse, a victim of the Salem witch trials, in Danvers, Massachusetts; Harriet Tubman's birthplace in Cambridge, Maryland; and the house where Susan B. Anthony really did sleep in Rochester, New York.

WITHIN TUSCANY:
REFLECTIONS ON A TIME AND PLACE
by Matthew Spender (Viking, 1992, hardcover)

Feel free to hate Matthew Spender. For 20 years, he lived a dream life in Tuscany. In this memoir you'll meet Spender's neighbors—stonecutters, cabinetmakers, butchers, wild boar hunters, parish priests. You'll witness the Palio, Siena's no-holds-barred horse race. You'll follow the career of Savonarola, the Dominican friar who almost single-handedly derailed the Renaissance in Florence. You'll visit Michelangelo's favorite marble quarry. You'll also learn how to make really good olive oil (the secret: use traditional stone mills, not modern metal grinders).

DINNER WITH PERSEPHONE
by Patricia Storace (Pantheon, 1996, paperback)

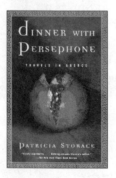

Patricia Storace, an award-winning poet who spent a year living in Athens, immerses you in the day-to-day life of the city where mythology and history are omnipresent and where politics and neighborhood life are almost operatic in their intensity. Sure, you scramble up to the Parthenon, but you also observe people on the bus, go to Greek movies (Storace provides plot summaries), attend religious and national celebrations and indulge in shopping expeditions. By the end of the book, you aren't a tourist in Athens anymore, you're a resident.

ALONGSHORE
by John Stilgoe (Yale University Press, 1996, paperback)

Stilgoe's subject is a twilight world, "the edge of the sea, the edge of the land, the frontier where ocean and land mingle, the coastal realm." He focuses on the strip of Massachusetts coast that runs between Boston and Plymouth, drawing us in with stories of pirates and smugglers, of little-known shelling from German and Japanese subs during World War II. And all the while Stilgoe weaves in the fragile ecology of the shore and the complex sociology of seafarers and land people, all illustrated with photographs ancient and modern. Reading Alongshore is as much fun as a barefoot stroll along the beach.

....

TRANSLATING L.A.:
A TOUR OF THE RAINBOW CITY
by *Peter Theroux* (Norton, 1995, paperback)

What are outsiders to make of L.A.? Is it all plastic surgeons, celebrity murders and endless summer? Theroux, whose permanent home is in the Middle East (of all places), seems to be endowed with a instinctual understanding of L.A.; he can even navigate the freeways. In this freewheeling tour of the city he takes in Hollywood, Santa Monica, Long Beach and Venice; talks to anybody who has a pulse; and is surprised when he finds himself seduced by L.A.

....

TIMPSON'S ENGLISH COUNTRY INNS
by *John Timpson* (Headline Books, 1995, hardcover)

One of the pleasures of traveling through the English countryside is coming upon a cozy rural pub or village inn where there's an endless supply of history, atmosphere and pints of high-octane stout. John Timpson's handsomely illustrated guide takes you to such venerable roadside attractions as The Eel's Foot, The Cat & Custard Pot, The Three Chimneys (there are only two) and The Case Is Altered, where you can meet the locals, knock back a few and hear strange stories from centuries past of hauntings and midnight riders.

....

TRAVELS WITH ALICE
by *Calvin Trillin* (Avon, 1990, paperback)

Calvin Trillin is the kind of traveler who tries to elicit better service from the Italian hotel staff by constantly referring to his wife Alice as "la principessa." He admits his French is a little incomplete "I know a number of nouns... it's verbs I don't do." And he considers a pinball game he played in Florence one of "Great Moments in Sports." Clearly, Trillin is a man who knows how to have a good time and his family's journeys to Sicily, Barbados, Spain and the South of France are a laugh riot.

ST. PETERSBURG: A CULTURAL HISTORY
by Solomon Volkov (Free Press, 1995, paperback)

Solomon Volkov has taken a truly unique approach to chronicling the city's cultural history, devoting each of his six chapters to a different set of influential artists. There's Gogol and Dostoyevski's anti-St. Petersburg writings; the passionate music Tchaikovsky, Rimsky-Korsakov, Mussorgsky and Borodin wrote for Petersburg audiences; Anna Akhmatova's St. Petersburg, nostalgic for the days of the tsars; the St. Petersburg-in-exile created by Balanchine, Stravinsky and Nabokov; Shostakovich's Leningrad, scarred by Stalin's purges and hanging on through Hitler's siege; and finally Joseph Brodsky's harried, insecure postwar town. A completely fresh perspective on a great city.

METROPOLITAN: A PORTRAIT OF PARIS
by Matthew Weinreb and Fiona Biddulph
(Chronicle Books, 1994, hardcover)

For most travelers to Paris, the city drifts by as a dream and we return home with a few soft-focus memories of one of the world's most beautiful capitals. In this magnificent book, Weinreb and Biddulph have decided to put Paris in really sharp focus. Their eye-filling photographs spotlight the superb architectural details that are scattered generously across the city, but that most of us miss as we wander from Notre Dame to the Louvre.

ALL THE TIME IN THE WORLD
by Hugo Williams (A Common Reader Edition, 1997, paperback)

For two years in the early Sixties, British poet and essayist Hugo Williams, traveled around the globe. Most of us wouldn't consider it a very pleasant journey-Williams was forever being robbed, bamboozled, even mistaken for a spy. Nonetheless, he never lost his sense of adventure or his sense of wonder, both of which he conveys in luminous prose: "You sit in the bus, waiting for it to go, knowing that where it stops will be infinitely far away and mysterious and that you are free to stay or leave there, too... a free agent in an anchored world."

IRELAND, A BICYCLE AND A TIN WHISTLE
by David A. Wilson
(McGill-Queen's University Press, 1995, paperback)

David A. Wilson was a man with a mission—to find the Irish pub with the best traditional music. Every day he peddled through the glorious Irish countryside. Every night he sought out a pub where he could restore himself with a few pints of Guinness and listen to the fiddlers. It was a grand tour, in spite of bicycle accidents in Dublin and a few rough mornings of biking with a hangover. With his fresh point of view, a fine sense of humor and beautiful pacing, Wilson has written the best kind of travel book.

DOWNCANYON: A NATURALIST EXPLORES THE COLORADO RIVER THROUGH GRAND CANYON
by Ann Haymon Zwinger
(University of Arizona Press, 1995, paperback)

Part of a volunteer team of naturalists and scientists, Ann Zwinger made a comprehensive study of America's most magnificent canyon. She investigates the impact a huge dam has on the river ecology, she counts bald eagles and she offers gorgeous descriptions of experiencing the shimmering heat of the canyon in high summer: "Rock made of seething, molten magma still pulses heat out... when its flat faces tilt to the sun like solar collectors." This is the best kind of outdoor writing that blends natural history with scientific observations and captures the joy of knowing a sublime landscape intimately.

TRUE CRIME

EROS, MAGIC & THE MURDER OF PROFESSOR CULIANU
by Ted Anton (Northwestern University Press, 1996, paperback)

Joan Culianu was a Romanian émigré who taught religion and magic at the University of Chicago and dabbled in the occult. On May 21, 1991, he was murdered. His murderer has never been found. In his search for a solution to the crime, Ted Anton makes some surprising discoveries: cells of Romania's fascist Iron Guard in the American Midwest, plots by the ultra-right wing Romanian Securitate forces to assassinate Culianu and a Chicago suburbanite whose dreams seem to offer clues to the identity of the murderer. With its unique blend of the occult and Eastern European vendettas, this true-crime book stands out from all the others.

IN MY FATHER'S NAME:
A FAMILY, A TOWN, A MURDER
by Mark Arax (Pocket, 1997, paperback)

In 1972, when Mark Arax was 15, his father was gunned down at the Fresno nightclub he operated. The murder was never solved. Arax went on to become a reporter for the Los Angeles Times and he used his investigative skills to learn why his father was killed and who did it. Arax found that when his father discovered drug dealers were making sales at his club, he told the cops. Unfortunately some of the police officers he talked to were on the dealers' payroll. For Mark Arax, this book must have been a catharsis. For readers, it is a shocking study of corruption.

MIDNIGHT IN THE GARDEN OF GOOD AND EVIL: A SAVANNAH STORY
by *John Berendt* (Random House, 1993, hardcover)

This is a masterfully written murder story set in a beguiling old Southern city and filled with remarkable characters and remarkable scandal made all the more remarkable by the fact that is a work of nonfiction. John Berendt, former editor of New York Magazine, weaves together a delightful account of his life in Savannah, Georgia, with the enthralling twists and turns of a murder case that shocked the city's well-bred society. Late one night, a gay antique dealer shot and killed Savannah's premier boy toy. Was it murder or self defense? Don't start reading late in the evening or you may be up all night.

HELTER SKELTER: THE TRUE STORY OF THE MANSON MURDERS
by *Vincent Bugliosi* (Bantam, 1996, paperback)

The #1 best selling true crime book of all time was written by the District Attorney who successfully prosecuted the Manson "Family." Bugliosi explores the question that baffled Amereicans in 1969: why did young men and women from decent middle class families commit such atrocities? It's hard to tear yourself away from his account of life among the "Family," their conspiracy, the details of their crime and the record of their trial. And there's a hefty insert filled with photographs of the victims, the killers and the evidence. For this 25th anniversary edition of *Helter Skelter*, Bugliosi as written a new Afterword telling where the killers are today.

IN COLD BOLD
by *Truman Capote* (1966; Vintage International, 1994, paperback)

I thought he was a very nice gentleman," Perry Smith said. "I thought so right up to the moment I cut his throat." In 1959, Smith and his partner, Richard Hickock, were in a black Chevy cruising to Holcomb, Kansas. There they entered the Clutter home and murdered the entire family. In preparation for this book,

Truman Capote spent thousands of hours with the Clutters' friends and neighbors, as well as with the two boys who killed them. This chilling tale of cold-blooded murder is Capote's masterpiece and probably the best true-crime book ever written.

MINDHUNTER: INSIDE THE FBI'S ELITE SERIAL CRIME UNIT
by John Douglas and Mark Olshaker (Publishers)

John Douglas is a behavioral psychologist working for the FBI. He travels to prisons interviewing serial killers and rapists. His goal is to create profiles of violent criminals, their techniques and their personality traits that would make it easier for the law to track down the perpetrator once a crime has been committed. So be warned—some of the scenes described in this book are pretty grisly. By the way, Douglas was the inspiration for the character of Special Agent John Crawford in Thomas Harris' *Silence of the Lambs*. Worth searching for.

THE COQUETTE
by Hannah W. Foster, with an introduction by Cathy N. Davidson (1897; Oxford University Press, 1986, hardcover)

Like Truman Capote's *In Cold Blood*, Foster's novel is based on an actual event: after being seduced and abandoned by her lover, a woman named Elizabeth Whitman gave birth to a stillborn child in a Massachusetts tavern and died alone. The story created a sensation in late Victorian New England; Foster, who was distantly related to Whitman, was in an excellent position to tell the woman's story. While Coquette may sound like a classic seduction novel, Foster elevates the genre to explore the motivations of a woman who tries to balance the conflicting demands of pleasing her family and conforming to society's standards, while striking out on her own in the world.

POISON MIND
by Jeffrey Good and Susan Goreck (Morrow, 1995, hardcover)

This real-life thriller begins with the death of a middle-aged waitress in Florida and the discovery that a Coke she had drunk had been laced with poison thallium. Police suspected a neighbor, George Trepal, but had little to go on. Until special agent Susan Goreck and St. Petersburg Times reporter, Jeffrey Good went undercover, met Trepal at a weekend sponsored by the high I.Q. group MENSA and insinuated themselves into Trepal's life. Especially interesting is Goreck's growing sympathy for the eccentric Trepal. A very unusual true crime story that reads like a John Grisham novel.

STORIES OF SCOTTSBORO:
THE RAPE CASE THAT SHOCKED 1930S AMERICA AND REVIVED THE STRUGGLE FOR EQUAL RIGHTS
by James Goodman (Random House, 1995, hardcover)

In 1931, outside Scottsboro, Alabama, two white women accused nine black youths of rape. Immediately, the case became a cause celebre and in time produced two Supreme Court decisions. Goodman tells the story from the perspectives of several participants. A penetrating work of history and a real page-turner.

THIS BLOODY DEED:
THE MAGRUDER INCIDENT
by Ladd Hamilton
(Washington State University Press, 1994, paperback)

In August 1863, Lloyd Magruder and several companions were gunned down on a lonely trail in Idaho's Bitterroot Mountains. After a prophetic dream, Magruder's friend Hill Beachey tracked the killers all the way to San Francisco and brought them back to Idaho for trial. Hamilton's book will remind you of *In Cold Blood* for its detailed portrayal of all the brutish nastiness of life in the Old West and the complex character of the people who lived on the frontier.

TREASURE HUNT:
A NEW YORK TIMES REPORTER TRACKS THE QUEDLINBURG HOARD
by William H. Honan (Fromm International, 1997, hardcover)

More than 1000 years ago, German kings bestowed upon the Cathedral of Quedlinburg remarkable treasures: sacred vessels of crystal and gold, sumptuous manuscripts bound between jeweled covers. Then, in 1945, an American soldier named Joe Tom Meador stole them and carried them home to Whitewright, Texas. After 40 years, one of the priceless lost treasures—the Samuhel Gospels, a 9th-century book written entirely in gold-reappeared when Meador's heirs tried to sell it. Once word got out, the chase to reclaim the looted treasures was on. Honan balances the excitement of the hunt for the horde, with titillating details about Meador himself, who used the treasures to entice sexual partners.

....

DR. MUDD AND THE LINCOLN ASSASSINATION: THE CASE REOPENED
Edited by John Paul Jones (The Free Press, 1996, hardcover)

In 1865, Dr. Samuel A. Mudd was convicted of conspiring with John Wilkes Booth to assassinate Abraham Lincoln and was sentenced to life imprisonment. But in 1869, President Andrew Johnson pardoned Mudd—not on the merits of the case, but for the heroic services he rendered in prison during an epidemic. Leap ahead to 1993 when the University of Richmond School of Law decided to reexamine the evidence and give Mudd a new "trail." Arguing for the defense were F. Lee Bailey and Candida Ewing Staempfli Steel, the great-great-granddaughter of Mudd's original defense attorney. Here are the complete proceedings of the retrial and you'll find that all the old passions and controversies come to life in this search for justice for Dr. Mudd.

....

CAT AND MOUSE:
MIND GAMES WITH A SERIAL KILLER
by Brian Alan Lane (Dove, 1997, paperback)

Even though his crimes were, if not more horrific, at least more numerous, America was so swept up in the O.J. Simpson circus that few people followed the trial of another California resident. Bill Suff, a.k.a. the Riverside Prostitute Killer, who in seven years murdered more than a dozen women, then posed their bodies in gruesome human sculptures for the police to find. In this true crime story, Brian Lane does not attempt to recount the facts of the trial for those of us who missed it. Instead, through extensive interviews and analysis of Suff's writings, (the killer is also a budding author) Lane gets inside the killer's mind to try and answer the most haunting question about mass murderers—why?

BIG TROUBLE:
A MURDER IN A SMALL WESTERN TOWN SETS OFF A STRUGGLE FOR THE SOUL OF AMERICA
by J. Anthony Lukas (Simon & Schuster, 1997, hardcover)

On a snowy night in 1905, a bomb killed Frank Steunenberg as he pushed open his front gate. Since Steunenberg was a former governor of Idaho, the local powerbrokers suspected the murder was politically motivated. The manhunt ended in the arrest of radical labor leader "Big Bill" Haywood and his trial rapidly became a showdown between the dynamic prosecutor, William Borah and a smart young defense attorney named Clarence Darrow. With cameo appearances by Theodore Roosevelt, Henry James and Ethel Barrymore, Pultizer Prize-winner J. Anthony Lukas tells a big, brawling story of America on the brink of class warfare.

SERPICO
by Peter Maas (Viking, 1973, paperback)

The only oath I ever took was to enforce the law—and it didn't say against everybody except other cops." An admirable philosophy which nearly cost Frank Serpico his life. In the late

Sixties, the enigmatic New York City cop launched a one-man fight against the graft and corruption he saw around him everyday on the force. In this gripping biography, Peter Maas chronicles Serpico's career, how he stood up for what he believed in, how his life was in danger from the crooked cops he worked with every day and how he ultimately triggered the most comprehensive investigation of police practices the U.S. has ever seen.

THE EXECUTIONER'S SONG
by *Norman Mailer* (Warner, 1986, paperback)

More than 20 years after it first appeared, Mailer's "true life" novel of Gary Gilmore is still controversial. is Mailer trying to glamorize a killer?

OSWALD'S TALE: AN AMERICAN MYSTERY
by *Norman Mailer* (Random House, 1995, paperback)

Most Americans have already written off Lee Harvey Oswald as a villain. Or a stooge. Or a brilliant conspirator. Or a madman. Only Norman Mailer would try to find the humanity in this century's most notorious assassin. During a six-month stint in Russia, Mailer interviewed Oswald's old colleagues and girlfriends and even was permitted to read transcripts of KGB surveillance of Oswald and Marina (the KGB had bugged their apartment). This docu-novel of the lonely, loveless man who shot JFK may be Mailer's finest work.

BLIND FAITH
by *Joe McGinnis* (Signet, 1990, paperback)

A wealthy husband, a beautiful wife, three strapping sons. The Marshalls are the picture-perfect American family-until Maria Marshall is murdered. But when investigators learn that Maria's husband is in the midst of a flamboyant affair, deeply in debt and has taken out a $1.5 million life insurance policy on his wife just weeks before her murder, Rob Marshall becomes the prime suspect. As the case goes to trial, only the three Marshall boys still have faith in their father. But how long will it last? A marvelous twisting plot with so many villainous characters and surprise revelations, you may forget it's a true story.

．．．．．．．．．．．．

FAMOUS TRIALS:
CASES THAT MADE HISTORY
by Frank McLynn (Readers Digest, 1995, hardcover)

Browsing through this book gives you a front-row seat at history's most famous trails. Start in ancient Athens with Meletus v. Socrates. Move on to Tudor England for the Crown v. Thomas More. Cross the sea to Massachusetts for the Community [of Salem] v. Alleged Witches. From Oscar Wilde v. the Marquis of Queensbury, to the Allied Nations v. Nazi Leaders, to the State of Mississippi v. Byron de la Beckwith, this is an entertaining and enlightening look at momentous court cases. Get a copy for yourself and for anyone you know who couldn't get enough of the O.J. and Menendez Brothers trials.

．．．．．．．．．．．．

CASE CLOSED: LEE HARVEY OSWALD AND
THE ASSASSINATION OF JFK
by Gerald Posner (Anchor Books, 1994, paperback)

Some 2000 books have been published about the assassination of John F. Kennedy, but this one is different: it is convincing. Posner settles each conspiracy theory, one by one and then argues only three points:

• *Three shots rang out in Dealey Plaza;*
• *All three came from Oswald's rifle;*
• *No way were Oswald and Jack Ruby conspirators.*

．．．．．．．．．．．．

A. LINCOLN: HIS LAST 24 HOURS
by W. Emerson Reck
(University of South Carolina Press, 1994, paperback)

A completely absorbing, hour-by-hour account of what happened on the last day of Lincoln's life. Reck strips away the myths that have accumulated around the assassination to reveal the bare, harsh, shocking truth.

....

DEAD BY SUNSET:
PERFECT HUSBAND, PERFECT KILLER?
by Ann Rule (Pocket, 1996, paperback)

To look at Brad Cunningham, you wouldn't think he was a killer. He was good-looking, smart, athletic. But his violent temper was a problem that destroyed his first three marriages. The marriage to Cheryl Keeton was different. In 1986, not long after Cheryl filed for divorce from Brad and sought custody of their three children, she was found bludgeoned to death in her car. Yet Brad was not charged with the crime until 1993. Ann Rule handles this unhappy story well and draws an incisive portrait of a charismatic con man.

....

LOW LIFE: LURES AND SNARES OF OLD NEW YORK
by Luc Sante (Vintage, 1992, paperback)

Return to the days when Bowery street gangs used cannons against their rivals; when a successful downtown abortionist outbid the Archbishop of New York for a fine uptown mansion; and when the toughest saloon in the city was McGurk's Suicide Hall. Luc Sante's book is like a walking tour of the wild side-teeming streets, rough neighborhoods and palaces of sin.

....

DEVIANT: THE SHOCKING ORIGINAL STORY
OF THE ORIGINAL "PSYCHO,"
by Harold Schechter (Pocket Books, 1991, paperback)

The killers in *Psycho, The Silence of the Lambs* and *Texas Chainsaw Massacre* were all based on a real person named Ed Gein. In the 1950s, his neighbors in the small Wisconsin town where he lived thought him a gentle if occasionally eccentric man.

They never knew what he was doing inside his "death house," as it came to be known later. Author Harold Schechter is a tireless researcher who has documented every gruesome detail and bizarre plot twist in the Ed Gein case. But the real strength of this book is the realization that as bad as Norman Bates and Hannibal Lechter were, Ed Gein was worse.

THE MYSTERIOUS DEATH OF MARY ROGERS
by Amy Gilman Srebnick (Oxford University Press, 1995, hardcover)

In the summer of 1841, a cigar store clerk named Mary Rogers disappeared. Three days later her body was found floating in the Hudson River. The murder was never solved and became a sensation—Edgar Allan Poe based his detective story, "The Case of Marie Roget" on the crime. While other authors have studied the mystery, Amy Gilman Srebnick is the first historian to study Mary herself. She was a member of that prominent New England clan, the Mathers and a participant in the great rural-to-urban migration of the mid-19th century. As a working woman she was a source of mystery, romance and forbidden sexuality. An intriguing look at the myths and realities of urban culture in ante-bellum New York.

SINS OF THE SON
by Carlton Stowers (Hyperion, 1995, hardcover)

Carlton Stowers writes true-crime books and has a reputation for grasping the intricacies of criminal behavior. None of his research among the criminal element has helped him deal with the sociopathic behavior of his own son. Anson Stowers was always an angry, rebellious boy. He ran away at age 15 and launched a criminal career that began with stealing cars and ended ten years later with the murder of his wife. Now Anson is in prison, serving a 60-year sentence. Carlton Stowers tries in this book to understand what happened to his boy. "I could not for the life of me see the kinship," he writes, "between my son and those criminal strangers I had encountered and written about."

UNDERSTANDING OUR WORLD

THE ORIGINS OF THE UNIVERSE
by John D. Barrow (Basic Books, 1997, paperback)

It would be so much easier if time, space and matter had simply been created in six days. Alas, it's more complicated than that. Still, John Barrow, a renowned astronomer, finds a way to explain how the universe began in terms that readers will understand. He can even make concepts such as the expansion of the universe, wormholes in the galaxy and COBE satellite findings instantly comprehensible. This is the best introduction around to one of life's most basic mysteries.

....

SNOW CRYSTALS
by W.A. Bentley & W.J. Humphreys (Dover, 1931, hardcover)

This is one of those unique books you will never part with. Wilson Alwyn Bentley was fascinated, maybe even obsessed, by snowflakes. Beginning in 1885 in Jericho, Vermont, he took thousands of photographs of snow crystals through a microscope. Some 2500 of Bentley's photos are displayed here, revealing the six-sided shape of all snowflakes, their delicate beauty and reassuringly, no two are exactly the same. A perfect book for browsing.

....

ARE WE ALONE?
by Paul Davies (Orion Productions, 1995, paperback)

The discovery a single extraterrestrial microbe," Paul Davies says, "could be the greatest scientific discovery of all time." But is there anything out there to discover? Davies discusses how the assumption that extraterrestrial life exists must alter our understanding of the laws of physics, evolution and the nature of life and intelligence. He reveals the impact such a discovery would have on the world's philosophical and religious systems. He asks, if evolution is random, the product of myriad accidents, could these random events happen twice? A concise analysis of one of the most compelling mysteries of our time.

THE LAST THREE MINUTES
by Paul Davies (Basic Books, 1997, paperback)

If you've ever wondered whether the world will go out with a bang or a whimper, this is the book for you. Paul Davies, a professor of natural philosophy, explains all the leading opinions and speculations about how the world will end. He suggests an immense comet could strike the earth and destroy it. he imagines what the last day of sunlight would be like. And he reviews the possibility that the world may never end at all. Indulging that secret desire of yours to stare into the abyss has never been so satisfying, or so interesting.

AN INORDINATE FONDNESS FOR BEETLES
by Arthur V. Evans and Charles L. Bellamy, photography by Lisa Charles Watson (Henry Holt, 1996, hardcover)

If all the beetles on earth disappeared, our ecosystem would soon die. This volume reveals the absolutely essential role beetles play on Earth, while also studying their anatomy, evolutionary history and their variety (there may be as many as 8 million species of beetles!). Plus the authors look at humankind's ongoing fondness for beetles in art and literature (think of Egyptian scarabs and Kafka's "Metamorphosis"). Illustrated with 140 beautiful color photographs plus dozens of black-and-white drawings, this is a beautiful reference to an amazing insect and its absolutely vital role in Earth's ecology.

THE WHOLE SHEBANG:
A STATE-OF-THE UNIVERSE(S) REPORT
by Timothy Ferris (Simon & Schuster, 1997, hardcover)

Timothy Ferris may be our greatest living science writer. His descriptions of the universe are personal, even poetic. In The Whole Shebang, Ferris explains what we currently know about the geometry of the cosmos ("literally the biggest problem in science"). He discusses black holes (where Einstein's theory of relativity breaks down), quantum physics (and why scientists call it "quantum weirdness"), worm holes, even the possibility that there are an infinite number of universes out there. *The Whole Shebang* is a voyage into the strangest corners of the cosmos.

More of Ferris:

COMING OF AGE IN THE MILKY WAY
(Anchor Books, 1989, paperback).

Ferris explores our conception of the universe, from earliest recorded history through Copernicus, Newton, Einstein and the repercussions each new theory has had on society.

THE QUARK AND THE JAGUAR:
ADVENTURES IN THE SIMPLE AND THE COMPLEX
by Murray Gell-Mann (W. H. Freeman & Co, 1994, hardcover)

Murray Gell-Mann won the Nobel Prize in physics for the discovery of the quark. He is renowned in the scientific community as one of the founders of the new science of complexity. In this intriguing book, he cuts across the spectrum of human knowledge to reveal to ordinary readers (like us) the connections between the basic laws of complexity and the diversity we have all observed in the natural world. To illustrate his points, he cites the behavior of chimpanzees, the mechanics of an avalanche and the operettas of Gilbert and Sullivan.

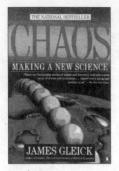

CHAOS: MAKING A NEW SCIENCE
by James Gleick (Penguin, 1988, paperback)

Anarchy makes humans uneasy. So imagine how frightening it must have been for scientists—the guys who spend their lives figuring out how the cosmos works—when they found themselves face to face with chaos. In this eerie yet fascinating book, James Gleick reveals the revolutionary aspects of the science of chaos and what it tells us about how clouds form, how smoke rises, what determines the shape of snowflakes.

BULLY FOR BRONTOSAURUS
by Stephen Jay Gould (Harmony Books, 1996, paperback)

Gould helps ordinary mortals grasp the mysteries of the natural world. Among his topics in this book: why men have nipples, the miracle of Joe DiMaggio's 56-game hitting streak, some surprises about kiwis and why there is an endless mania for dinosaurs.

DINOSAUR IN A HAYSTACK: REFLECTIONS IN NATURAL HISTORY
by Stephen Jay Gould (Harmony Books, 1996, paperback)

As an evolutionary biologist and paleontologist, Stephen Jay Gould is a natural to explain why Jurassic Park (the book) was interesting while Jurassic Park (the movie) was "gutless and incoherent." In this collection of off-beat yet informative essays he follows up the rumor that Edgar Allen Poe wrote a book on snails and tells how the discovery of a whale fossil in Pakistan exposes our "spin-doctored" view of evolution (it isn't a tidy, gradual process at all, but moves in fast and slow growth spurts). You'll like Gould's elegant, entertaining style.

HOW SCIENCE WORKS
by Judith Hann (Reader's Digest, 1991, hardcover)

A godsend to parents pestered by children who want to know why some balloons go up, what makes it rain and where electricity comes from. By the way, grown-ups can learn plenty from this simple, straightforward answer book, too—how magnetism works, for instance and why a little computer can hold all that information. This is going to be one of the most popular books in your house.

DIGGING DINOSAURS
by John Horner and James Gorman (HarperPerennial, 1990, paperback)

Fascinating discoveries in the Badlands of Montana reveal the social behavior of dinosaurs. Dr. Horner, by the way, was the model for Alan Grant, the hero in *Jurassic Park*.

THE GRAND TOUR: A TRAVELER'S GUIDE TO THE SOLAR SYSTEM
by Ron Miller and William K. Hartmann (Workman, 1993, paperback)

This spectacular book is the best way to understand our solar system. using dozens of gorgeous full-color paintings and NASA photographs and drawing upon the latest discoveries made by Voyager 2, Magellan and other space probes, Miller and Hartmann take you on a mind-boggling tour through our planetary neighborhood.

THE PHYSICS OF STAR TREK
by Lawrence Krauss, Introduction by Stephen Hawking (Basic Books, 1995, paperback)

But I canna change the laws of physics, Captain!" Ah, how many times did Scotty try to teach Captain Kirk that even warp drives and transporter beams have their limitations. Now

physicist Lawrence Krauss boldly goes where Star Trek's screenwriters have gone before. For example, he reveals how Einstein's theory of relativity implies that time travel is possible (as Captain Kirk and Captain Picard have learned over the years). From the difference between a hologram and a holodeck, to what warps at warp speed, to Star Trek's top 10 physics bloopers, this is a smart, enlightening, often funny volume that could even make a Vulcan smile.

THE ORIGIN OF HUMANKIND
by Richard Leakey (HarperCollins, 1990, paperback)

Nobody is better qualified to tell the story of human origins than Richard Leakey. His parents, Louis and Mary Leakey, made the astonishing discoveries of early humanoid fossils in Olduvai Gorge and Richard Leakey is keeping the family tradition alive. This concise book explains human evolution in a way ordinary people who are "dumb in science" can understand. For instance, he says that once our apelike ancestors began to walk upright, modern humans were inevitable. Plus, he clears up the misconception that we are descended from monkeys.

IMPACT JUPITER:
THE CRASH OF COMET SHOEMAKER-LEVY 9
by David H. Levy (Plenum, 1995, paperback)

There are probably only a handful of people in the world who can name a professional comet watcher. Yet in summer 1994, three previously unsung astronomers were virtually household names. David Levy and his colleagues, Eugene and Carolyn Shoemaker, first spotted their comet in 1993. In time, it became apparent that the comet that bore their name was heading for a particularly spectacular end—a collision with the planet Jupiter.

Levy writes a lively story about the thrill of discovery and the scramble among scientists around the world to record the fiery cataclysm.

WHY THE EARTH QUAKES
by Matthys Levy & Mario Salvadori (Norton, 1995, paperback)

What caused the 40-foot tidal wave that all but obliterated Lisbon in 1755? Why did Frank Lloyd Wright's Imperial Hotel survive a 1923 earthquake when everything around it crumbled? And how do seismologists know that "the Big One" will hit California in the next 30 years? Levy and Salvadori unravel the mystery of tectonic plates, discuss the latest architectural innovations that may foil the forces of nature and recount history's worst natural disasters, from Pompeii to China to San Francisco to Alaska and the scientific lessons to be learned from such tragedies. And the authors even offer some ominous predictions of their own.

More by Levy and Salvadori:

WHY BUILDINGS STAND UP AND WHY BUILDINGS FALL DOWN
(Norton, 1994, paperback).

These two books serve up a lively blend of science, engineering and historical anecdotes from two acclaimed architectural engineers.

WALKING WITH THE GREAT APES: JANE GOODALL, DIAN FOSSEY, BIRUTE GALDIKAS
by Sy Montgomery (Houghton Mifflin, 1992, paperback)

Louis Leakey, the renowned anthropologist, used to say that "women are better observers than men." In their groundbreaking studies of chimps, mountain gorillas and orangutans, Goodall, Fossey and Galdikas proved that their mentor was right. This book portrays the unique styles and distinctive personalities of each of these women and makes accessible the importance of their work among great apes.

THE PEOPLING OF AFRICA:
A GEOGRAPHIC INTERPRETATION
by James L. Newman (Yale University Press, 1995, hardcover)

An important book that offers fresh insights into Africa's past, from the emergence of the first hominids 2.5 million years ago to the civilizations of the Nile Valley, northern Africa and the Sahara, Highland Ethiopia, the Sahel and the Sudan. An excellent starting point for readers who are unfamiliar with African civilization.

THE CHEMICAL THEATRE
by Charles Nicholl (A Common Reader Edition, 1997, hardcover)

Most of us believe alchemists were hucksters who conned the gullible with promises of making gold. But Charles Nicholl, whose exhaustive research always turns up remarkable nuggets of history, has found that alchemists were more practitioners of a kind of sacred science designed to purify the self rather than transform base metals. Shakespeare knew this. In King Lear, he used the vocabulary of alchemy to say something new about the self, the unconscious, madness and sanity. Nicholl sees a connection between alchemists and dramatists because both "were penetrating into the unknown." It's a joy to have this illuminating book back in print.

MUSEUM OF SCIENCE AND INDUSTRY, CHICAGO
by Jay Pridmore (Abrams, 1997, hardcover)

Find me a Chicagoan who doesn't love the Museum of Science and Industry. It has a coal mine shaft, an actual captured World War II German submarine, the Apollo 8 spacecraft that circled the Moon in 1968 and a skeleton of Tyrannosaurus Rex dominating the magnificent great hall. Jay Pridmore's salute to the oldest, most comprehensive museum of technology in the United States uses spectacular photographs to capture the excitement of the place. From "Yesterday's Main Street," complete with some of the first automobiles, to "The War Within", a larger-than-life AIDS exhibit, this book puts you inside the museum.

AMERICAN MUSEUM OF NATURAL HISTORY-125 YEARS OF EXPEDITION AND DISCOVERY

by Lyle Rexer and Rachel Klein, Foreword by Edward O. Wilson (Abrams, 1995, hardcover)

To fill the Museum's galleries, a larger-than-life cast of scientist/adventurers battled bandits in Mongolia, fought leopards barehanded in Africa and lived off the land in the Arctic. The pages of this big anniversary volume read like an Indiana Jones adventure. The Museum is still questing—to unravel the mysteries of evolution, to protect Earth's biodiversity and to learn about life tens of millions of years ago through DNA. The most entertaining, eye-filling natural history book ever.

THE GLORIOUS CONSTELLATIONS

by Giuseppe Maria Sesti (out of print)

Why did our distant ancestors play "connect the dots" with the stars? Why did they populate the night sky with figures of Orion and Andromeda? Sesti asks the same questions and in this big, gorgeous volume, he digs deeply into history, mythology, astronomy and art to find the answers. The illustrations, by the way, are breathtaking. Worth searching for.

THE PLANET MARS: A HISTORY OF OBSERVATIONS AND DISCOVERIES

by William Sheehan (University of Arizona Press, 1996, paperback)

Human explorers will probably land on Mars by the middle of the 21st century. Until then, the best account we have of "the Red Planet" is William Sheehan's timely and beautifully illustrated book. He takes us back to the ancient Greek and Islamic scientists who came to important conclusions about the solar system based on what they could see with the naked eye. Then he traces the revolution in astronomy brought about by Copernicus, Galileo and Tycho Brahe and explains the confusion about "canals" on Mars. In the wake of NASA's 1996 "life on Mars" announcement, this is an excellent guide to what Mars has meant throughout history and what questions about it may be resolved in the near future.

FROM SO SIMPLE A BEGINNING:
THE BOOK OF EVOLUTION
by Philip Whitfield (Macmillan, 1995, paperback)

Face it: you're probably never going to sit down and read Darwin's Origin of Species. That's why Whitfield has written this brilliant, crystal-clear narrative of how life first developed to the present day with mind-boggling breakthroughs in genetic engineering. Read this and you'll feel smarter than you've felt in years.

NATURALIST
by Edmund O. Wilson (Island Press, 1994, paperback)

At Harvard, Edmund Wilson is an entomologist (he studies bugs). In fact, his observations of hundreds of species of ants led to his revolutionary work in sociobiology, the study of chemical communications among insects. In this erudite memoir, Wilson takes the reader on a field trip to some of the most astonishing natural realms: Caribbean islands, Alabama swamps, South Pacific cloud forests. Everywhere he brings to life such scientific theories as evolution and the mysteries of DNA and points our marvels that generally escape our notice.

A WAY WITH WORDS

THE JOY OF WRITING SEX:
A GUIDE FOR FICTION WRITERS
by Elizabeth Benedict (Story Press, 1996, paperback)

The only thing trickier than having sex is writing about it. On paper, you're more likely to embarrass yourself. And your audience is likely to be less forgiving. So author Elizabeth Benedict explains how to write sex scenes that are both erotic and true. A good sex scene, she says, "doesn't have to be explicit, but it must always be specific." With advice from John Updike, Carol Shields, Dorothy Allison and with examples culled from classic and contemporary works, you'll learn how to write sex scenes that will steam up the page but not make your readers burst out laughing.

....

ON GRIEF AND REASON
by Joseph Brodsky (Farrar, Straus and Giroux, 1995, hardcover)

In these essays, Brodsky, who won the Nobel Prize for Literature and served as Poet Laureate of the United States, reconsiders the case of double agent Kim Philby, appraises the work of Robert Frost and Thomas Hardy and writes an open letter to Czech President Vaclav Havel.

....

THE MOTHER TONGUE:
ENGLISH AND HOW IT GOT THAT WAY
by Bill Bryson (Avon, 1991, paperback)

Did you know that drumstick was coined in the 19th century because polite society could not bring itself to utter the word leg? Or that Shakespeare gave us no less than 1700 new words

including barefaced, frugal, dwindle and summit? Bryson, an American transplanted to England, traces the history of English on both sides of the Atlantic. He explains the evolutionary accident that altered the human larynx and enabled us to speak. He traces the origins of English's naughtiest words, and offers a paean to that extraordinarily versatile American contribution to the language: O.K. A smart, funny, irreverent overview of English.

TALKING HORSE:
BERNARD MALAMUD ON LIFE AND WORK
Edited by Alan Cheuse & Nicholas Delbanco (Columbia University Press, 1996, hardcover)

Bernard Malamud won two National Book Awards and a Pulitzer Prize. This collection of Malamud's essays, interviews and unpublished material on the nature of fiction is a rare glimpse of the life, art and philosophy of a great writer. He discusses the work of Flannery O'Connor, Saul Bellow and Ernest Hemingway. He talks about what he was thinking as he wrote *The Natural, The Fixer* and *The Magic Barrel*. He suggests ways a writer can find a subject and find a voice. And he reflects on the Jewish experience in American fiction. A book filled with revelations from an intensely private man.

NEW ENGLAND WRITERS AND WRITING
by Malcolm Cowley, Edited by Donald W. Faulkner (University of New England Press, 1996, paperback)

Malcolm Cowley was one of this century's most articulate critics of American literature. In these 26 essays, he reflects on the ways New England as effected writers such as Emerson, Melville, Henry James and Thornton Wilder. Cowley's essay on Hawthorne's *The Scarlet Letter* is masterful and his dissenting opinion on the poetry of Robert Frost is sure to get Frost's fans up in arms. More soothing are reflections on the character of the people of the Connecticut Valley and the wisdom of growing melons. Persuasive, perceptive and witty, Cowley's essays are perfect reading for anyone who loves American literature.

GREAT BOOKS:
MY ADVENTURES WITH HOMER, ROUSSEAU, WOOLF AND OTHER INDESTRUCTIBLE WRITERS OF THE WESTERN WORLD
by David Denby (Simon & Schuster, 1996, paperback)

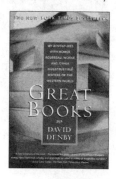

Thirty years after he entered Columbia University, New York film critic David Denby returned to his alma mater to study the Great Books. The outcome is this love song to the masterworks of Western literature and it's a joy to meet a reader who is carried away by the chaos of a Homeric battlefield and pulls no punches about his personal dislikes such as Goethe's *Faust* ("Noisy, redundant, crass, overbearing, dislikable"). You probably won't agree with everything Denby says about Plato, Dante and Austen, but he's certain to get you interested in reading these great books again.

THE ALPHABET ABECEDARIUM:
SOME NOTES ON LETTERS
by Richard A. Firmage (Godine, 1993, paperback)

Guaranteed, you've never seen a book like this one. An award-winning book designer and editor, Firmage offers a tour of the 26 letters of the modern alphabet, how the shape of each letter evolved, its history and the strange attributes each letter acquired. (For instance, "T" was thought to be the mark of Cain). And there are dozens of splendid illustrations by artists and typographers through the centuries. A real beauty.

ASPECTS OF THE NOVEL
by E.M. Forster (Harvest Books, 1956, paperback)

With the popularity of the recent films based on his novels, many modern readers are discovering the pleasures of E.M. Forster. In this captivating series of university lectures delivered in 1927, the author of *Howard's End* and *Room with a View* lets us in on some tricks of the trade. He examines aspects that all English-language novels, from Ivanhoe onward, have in common. Forster's casual wit and acute intelligence transform what could be a dull discussion of technique into a fascinating exploration of literary art.

MONSTER IN A BOX
by Spaulding Gray (Vintage, 1993, paperback)

Spaulding Gray's agent sold a major publisher on the idea that Spalding had a "novel in him" and suddenly it was up to Spalding to spit one up. However, when he sat down to write Impossible Vacation, a novel about his mother's suicide, he discovered just how hard writing fiction can be. He soon found himself wrestling with a severe case of writer's block and an unwieldy "monster" of a novel demanding an ending. Monster in a Box is his hilarious account of the lengths he went to avoid finishing the book. It is truly one of the funniest books ever written about not writing a book.

CHASING THE SUN:
DICTIONARY-MAKERS AND THE DICTIONARIES THEY MADE
by Jonathan Green (Henry Holt, 1996, hardcover)

The first dictionary was compiled in ancient Sumer to help conquerors understand the people they had just conquered. It's been a lexical free-for-all ever since. In *Chasing the Sun*, England's leading lexicographer undertakes the first history of people who produce dictionaries. There's Samuel Johnson, who assiduously ignored his creditors as he worked away at his magnum opus and Noah Webster, an industrious crank who created America's first dictionary. From the philosophy of pure language, to "indecent" dictionaries in Texas, this is an entertaining history of dictionaries and the quirks, passions and prejudices of the people who created them.

WRITING WAS EVERYTHING
by *Alfred Kazin* (Harvard University Press, 1995, hardcover)

This absorbing little memoir is filled with gems about writers, writing and reading. Kazin celebrates his favorite literature teachers such as Mark Van Doren and Lionel Trilling ("he mesmerized many of his Columbia students for life"). He tells great anecdotes about Hart Crane, Simone Weil, Flannery O'Connor, Robert Lowell, George Orwell and John Cheever. And he pours scorn on the dreary academic literary theorists who sap all the joy from literature. Finally, he assures us that writers are people who see "our life with the eyes of faith and so make the world shine again."

SEARCHING FOR A WRITER'S AMERICA:
LANDSCAPE IN LITERATURE
by *Alfred Kazin* (Knopf, 1988).

Jefferson on primeval America. Melville on the sea. Willa Cather on the prairies. Edith Wharton on New York City. F. Scott Fitzgerald on Hollywood. Saul Bellow on Chicago. Kazin offers a panoramic vision of America through the eyes of our greatest authors. Who let this book go out of print?

BIRD BY BIRD
by *Anne Lamott* (Pantheon, 1994, paperback)

Most "how to" writing books are not much fun to read. This one, however, is. One of the funniest authors working today, Anne Lamott possesses a wit and insight that cuts to the truth like a surgeon's scalpel. In Bird by Bird she uses her talents to offer some practical pointers on writing (a task about as "easy and pleasurable as bathing a cat"). She covers all the essentials: "Getting Started,"

"Character," "Plot," "Index Cards," "Looking Around," "Jealousy" and "How Do You Know When You're Done." If you've ever wanted to write, or ever wondered what your favorite authors face every day, *Bird by Bird* is the book for you.

AN EXALTATION OF HOME AND FAMILY
by James Lipton (Penguin, 1993, paperback)

James Lipton combines a wicked sense of humor with a flawless ear for language to create witty new collective terms for things domestic. If we can have a gaggle of geese and a pride of lions, why not a bicker of sisters, or a distraction of fathers, or a strain of in-laws, or a piddle of puppies, or a demolition of movers? Illustrated with elegant drawings in the style of 19th-century prints, this one-of-a-kind book is big fun.

Also by Lipton:

AN EXALTATION OF LARKS
(Penguin, 1993, paperback).

The classic that gave us "a charm of finches" and "a murder of crows."

DOWN AND OUT IN PARIS AND LONDON
by George Orwell (1933; Harvest Books, 1972, paperback)

George Orwell completely immersed himself in his work, as you'll see in this semi-autobiographical account of an impoverished British writer squeaking by in two European capitals. In Paris he ekes out an existence at the bottom of the culinary food chain as a dishwasher in chic French bistros. In London he spends his days with tramps and street artists while waiting for a job to materialize. Amazingly he never lets his desperate situation contaminate his keen observers eye. This is a riveting travel log through the world of poverty that still rings true today.

IN LOVE WITH NORMA LOQUENDI
by William Safire

For years, William Safire has had an all-consuming passion for Norma Loquendi—and Mrs. Safire doesn't mind. Norma Loquendi, of course, is Latin for "the everyday voice of the native speaker." In other words, plain English. Now America's language maven takes on the clichés, clumsy constructions and daily abuse English suffers at the hands of politicians and journalists. Safire duels with Senator Daniel Patrick Moynihan and comedian George Carlin over correct usage and he insists that plain English is always better than fancy, pretentious syntax. Worth searching for.

IF YOU CAN TALK, YOU CAN WRITE
by Joel Saltzman (Warner, 1993, paperback)

Any writer will tell you: there's nothing scarier than a blank sheet of paper. So if you would love to write but lack the courage to try, Joel Saltzman's handbook is just what you need. He loosens you up, encouraging you to "talk" on paper without worrying about grammar and style. He has useful exercises—like gagging your inner critic and "playing loose with the truth" to get your stories moving. With tips from authors like William Faulkner and Nora Ephron, he teaches you how to edit and rewrite your own work. Working with *If You Can Talk, You Can Write*, is like brainstorming story ideas with a pro.

RUINED BY READING: A LIFE IN BOOKS
by Lynne Sharon Schwartz (Beacon Press, 1996, paperback)

Schwartz was a child prodigy who could read when she was only three years old. According to her, she has been mesmerized by the written word ever since. Her book is a defense of the fine art of reading, how it develops the mind, shapes the soul, teaches us to be receptive and gives birth to ideas. She describes it as a private, addictive craving. Schwartz speaks for all readers when she says: "In daylight I would pay what I owed the world. Reading was the reward, a solitary, obscure, nocturnal reward. It was what I got everything else... out of the way to do."

JOURNAL OF A NOVEL:
THE EAST OF EDEN LETTERS
by John Steinbeck (Penguin, 1990, paperback)

Through letters to his editor at The Viking Press, Steinbeck reveals the day-to-day details of the creative process, from what he thinks about when he sharpens his pencils, to his petulant dismissal of the "silly business" of writing, tot he moments of thrilling exhilaration when he is completely caught up in forging his story. Reading these letters is like sitting beside Steinbeck as he works.

THE ELEMENTS OF STYLE
by William Strunk, Jr. and E.B. White
(Prentice Hall, 1979, paperback)

The one and only handbook you'll ever need to write clear English. Learn the proper use of the comma, how to avoid fancy words, even how to tighten up your sentence structure. Brimming with enlightening examples, this timeless work will teach you how to polish your prose.

THE WRITER'S JOURNEY:
MYTHIC STRUCTURE FOR STORYTELLERS
AND SCREENWRITERS
by Christopher Vogler
(Michael Weise Productions, 1992, paperback)

Why are some films quickly forgotten while others capture our imaginations and become part of the larger culture? Drawing on Joseph Campbell's *Hero with a Thousand Faces*, this book—which began its life as a seven-page memo the author wrote while a script reviewer for the Walt Disney company—attempts to answer that question. By applying Cambell's concept of the hero's journey to films such as *The Wizard of Oz* and *Star Wars*, Vogler reveals how the time-tested patterns of mythology are at work today in the movies.

A ROOM OF ONE'S OWN
by Virginia Woolf (1929; Harcourt Brace, 1989, paperback)

A woman must have money and a room of her own," Woolf says, "if she is to write fiction." As she develops her theme, Woolf pays tribute to great literary Englishwomen—Jane Austen, the Brontës, Aphra Behn—and laments all the women writers whose talents were thwarted by unjust laws and oppressive social customs. The part of this essay that everyone remembers is Woolf's fantasy that Shakespeare had a gifted sister named Judith who killed herself when she could find no audience or publisher for her work. *A Room of One's Own* has become a classic manifesto written especially for women, but also for anyone who is denied freedom of expression.

WISEGUYS

THE GOLD COAST
by Nelson DeMille (Warner, 1991, paperback)

On Long Island's north shore is an enclave of old families who have lots of old money. John and Susan Sutter count Astors, Vanderbilts and Roosevelts among their friends and enjoy a Gatsbyesque life that is just a little dull. Until Frank Bellarosa, the godfather of New York's most notorious crime family, muscles his way in and becomes the Sutters' neighbor. Many readers consider this clever story of two worlds colliding DeMille's best book.

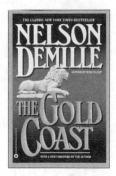

Also by DeMille:

SPENCERVILLE
(Warner, 1995, paperback).

A retired CIA man returns to his family farm outside Spencerville, Ohio and rekindles a love affair with the woman he lost 20 years early. We'd have a happy ending here if it weren't for the woman's psychotic husband, who's also the town's chief of police.

BLESS ME FATHER
by Mark Kriegel (Berkley, 1996, paperback)

Frank Battaglia was careless. When he killed his boss to move up in the mob's ranks, he left an eyewitness alive—a woman the tabloids have named "the mystery blonde." Now that a clever New York detective has picked up the case, things are getting pretty hot for Frank. Plus, he's having trouble with his sons—both of them want out of the world of wiseguys. For his debut as a novelist, New York Daily News columnist Kriegel has woven a tight plot with plenty of gritty atmosphere.

CHINA WHITE
by Peter Maas (Pinnacle Books, 1995, paperback)

Maas built his reputation as a writer whose cool narrative voice gives a nice edge to his investigative reporting. Now he brings that same acerbic quality to his first novel, a scary story of heroin and a mysterious Hong Kong businessman named Deng who plans to take over the drug trade in New York. Going up against Deng is a lawyer named McLean and his FBI-agent girlfriend, O'Shea. This is a tightly written, terrific book. Best scene: Deng and a Mafia kingpin lament the decline of traditional values in their crime families.

THE GODFATHER
by Mario Puzo (Signet, 1995, paperback)

The epic of Sicilian immigrant, Vito Corleone and how he built his extended "family" in America. If you liked the movie, you'll love the book.

THE LAST DON
by Mario Puzo (Random House, 1996)

On the day his grandson and his grandnephew are christened, Don Domenico Clericuzio tells his associates that once gambling is legalized in the United States, the boys "will never have to commit our sins and take our risks." Of course, it doesn't entirely work out that way. Grandson Dante grows up to be a sadistic enforcer. Grandnephew Crucifixio moves from Las Vegas casinos to new opportunities in Hollywood. The clash between the two cousins is inevitable. But along the way are dozens of colorful characters and incidents of mob vengeance that make the horse-head-in-the-bed seem pretty restrained.

WOMEN OF
SUBSTANCE

FIRST LADIES:
THE SAGA OF THE PRESIDENTS' WIVES AND
THEIR POWER, 1798-1961
by Carl Sferrazza Anthony (Quill Paperbacks, 1992, paperback)

R eporters trailed Martha Washington, waiting for the moment
when she would slip up and reveal herself to be a Tory. For
reasons she never understood, Mary Todd Lincoln ordered new
mourning clothes four weeks before her husband was assassinated.
FDR may have stopped sleeping with Eleanor, but he always
listened to her advice. Intriguing reading about the private lives
and public personae of the First Ladies.

MARY TODD LINCOLN: A BIOGRAPHY
by Jean H. Baker (Norton, 1989, paperback)

F inally, a serious biography that digs beneath
the myths, distortions and gossip to tell
the true story of Mary Todd Lincoln. Baker finds
an independent woman who refused to restrict
herself to a narrow Victorian code of behavior;
a mother who could not be stoic at the deaths
of all but one of her children; and a wife who
never recovered from the assassination of her
husband.

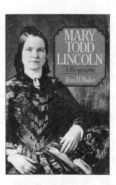

DAISY BATES IN THE DESERT
by *Julia Blackburn* (Vintage, 1995, paperback)

In civilized society, Daisy Bates was difficult on the best of days—strong willed, rebellious, almost a pathological liar. But then she found peace in the most unlikely setting—in the desert of Australia among the aborigines. From 1913 to 1934, this self-taught anthropologist thrived in circumstances most other Edwardian ladies would find horrific. Now Julia Blackburn has brought Daisy Bates' prickly personality and exceptional accomplishments back to an unsuspecting world.

MISTRESS OF RIVERSDALE:
THE PLANTATION LETTERS OF ROSALIE STIER CALVERT, 1795-1821
Edited and translated by Margaret Law Calcott

As someone who had barely escaped the French Revolution, Rosalie Stier had very little patience for democratic movements. Nonetheless, she stayed in America, married a relative of George Washington and waited for the United States to come to its senses and establish a monarchy. Her letters are a treasure trove of inside information about the first decades of the American republic. Worth searching for.

MARGARET FULLER: AN AMERICAN ROMANTIC LIFE-THE PRIVATE YEARS
by *Charles Capper* (Oxford University Press, 1994, paperback)

Louisa May Alcott and Ralph Waldo Emerson numbered Margaret Fuller among their closest friends. Nathaniel Hawthorne and James Russell Lowell modeled characters in their novels after her. Writer, activist, one of the leaders of the Transcendentalist movement and the author of the first mature study of women's place in 19th-century American society, Fuller possessed one of the finest minds of her age-and she wasn't shy about pointing this fact out to her friends. The first volume of

Charles Capper's two-volume life of Fuller reveals the beginnings of her intellectual life.

．．．．．．．．．．．．．．．

WOMAN OF VALOR:
MARGARET SANGER AND THE BIRTH CONTROL MOVEMENT IN AMERICA
by *Ellen Chesler* (Anchor Books, 1993, paperback)

At the turn of the century, Margaret Sanger came to the conclusion that women could not be truly free unless they had control over their reproductive system. In this landmark biography, Chesler follows the life of the woman who braved prosecution and personal attacks to provide women with safe, reliable forms of birth control.

．．．．．．．．．．．．．．．

WOMEN ON THE MARGINS:
THREE SEVENTEENTH-CENTURY LIVES
by *Natalie Zemon Davis* (Harvard University Press, 1996, paperback)

The 17th century was a time of tremendous economic, religious and intellectual ferment and these three women played a part in it. Glikl Bas Judah Leib founded a successful business in Hamburg. After the death of her husband, Marie Guyart entered the Ursuline order and went to Canada to establish a school for Indian women. And Maria Sibylla Merian, a Dutch painter and naturalist, traveled to Surinam to record the life cycles of butterflies. An intriguing triple biography of women who are all but forgotten, yet were very much a part of excitement of their age.

．．．．．．．．．．．．．．．

HYPATIA OF ALEXANDRIA
by *Maria Dzielska* (Harvard University Press, 1995, paperback)

A 60-year-old woman, an intellectual of liberal opinions, is attacked in the street and brutally murdered. It sounds like the type of crime that occurs every day in our cities, but in this case it happened in Alexandria in the year 415. In this fresh look at the life and death of one of the last great philosophy teachers of the pagan world, Maria Dzielska banishes the old myths and prejudices that have reduced Hypatia to a victim of patriarchy and religious fanaticism.

PRINCESS ALICE: THE LIFE AND TIMES OF ALICE ROOSEVELT LONGWORTH
by Carol Felsenthal
(St. Martin's Press, 1989, paperback)

Alice Roosevelt Longworth once described her cousin Franklin Delano Roosevelt as "two-thirds mush and one-third Eleanor." Here is the definitive biography of Teddy Roosevelt's flamboyant, sharp-tongued and often mean-spirited daughter who made herself the first lady of Washington society for 70 years.

APPETITE FOR LIFE: THE BIOGRAPHY OF JULIA CHILD
by Noel Riley Fitch (Doubleday, 1997, hardcover)

During the Second World War, Julia Child was working for the OSS in Ceylon and China when she began sampling regional cuisine as a way to escape the miserable fare served at the canteen. But her real culinary epiphany came a few years later at a bistro in Rouen. Child enrolled in the Cordon Bleu at Paris and in 1961, at age 49, published the heavy-weight of cookbooks (it tips the scales at three pounds), *Mastering the Art of French Cooking*. Soon she was on television and the rest is history. In this winning biography, Fitch has managed to convey Child's exuberance for food and and for life.

MARGARET BOURKE-WHITE
by Vicki Goldberg

This rich, in-depth biography tells the story of one of America's foremost photographers. Margaret Bourke-White did the cover shot for the premier issue of *Life* magazine and was the first photographer the editors of Fortune magazine ever hired. The evolution of Bourke-White's career makes fascinating reading—from her early "unfeminine" architectural shots to her photos of squalor among the poorest Americans. Worth searching for.

SISTER OF FORTUNE
by Nancy Coffey Heffernan and Ann Page Stecker
(University Press of New England, 1995, hardcover)

The three Wilson girls were ages 16, 18 and 24 when their widowed father ran off for the California gold fields in 1850. That left them with the responsibility for running the family farm in Keene, New Hampshire and raising their younger brother. In this amazing collection of letters that these young women sent to their wayward dad over the course of 12 years, the story of their hardscrabble but determined existence emerges. The letters themselves are a treasure, but Heffernan and Stecker have expanded on the original manuscripts to provide an in-depth look at rural life in New England in the mid-19th century.

THE EDUCATION OF MRS. HENRY ADAMS
by Eugenia Kaledin
(University of Massachusetts Press, 1994, paperback)

Marian Hooper Adams—known to her friends as "Clover"—was a gifted photographer, a witty free spirit, blessed with a sharp mind and a sharp tongue. When she married Henry Adams, great-grandson of the Founding father John Adams, everyone thought it was a splendid match. Why, then, did this vivacious independent woman swallow a lethal dose of potassium cyanide at age 42? And why is there no mention of Clover in her husband's autobiography, *The Education of Henry Adams*?

THE KENNEDY WOMEN:
THE SAGA OF AN AMERICAN FAMILY
by Laurence Leamer

No matter how much is written about them, the Kennedys remain a endlessly fascinating topic. Their good looks, successes, tragedies and scandals draw all eyes to them. But until now, no book has been devoted to the Kennedy women. Leamer goes back to 1849, to Bridget Murphy Kennedy, a poor widow, founder of the Boston clan and original well-spring of the Kennedy women's legendary courage. From the tough, pious Rose; to Pat and Eunice, both of whom dated Senator Joe McCarthy; to Jackie, the exemplary mother.

ABIGAIL ADAMS: A BIOGRAPHY
by Phyllis Lee Levin

Here is a grand, monumental biography of the most accomplished woman in 18th-century America. Abigail Adams did it all—gave herself an excellent education, raised four children ran the family farm single-handed while her husband was away at Congress, worked unceasingly for the success of the American Revolution, became the first First Lady to live in the White House and kept up a lively correspondence with virtually every great man and woman in America. Worth searching for.

PORTRAIT OF AN ARTIST:
A BIOGRAPHY OF GEORGIA O'KEEFFE
by Laurie Lisle (Pocket, 1997, paperback)

Two things Georgia O'Keeffe could not stand: erotic interpretations of her flower paintings and hearing herself described as "a woman artist" rather than simply as an artist. This definitive biography traces O'Keeffe's artistic development and her marriage to the photographer Alfred Stieglitz and reveals how the magnificent landscape and vibrant culture of New Mexico came to play such an important role in her work.

REBEL HEART:
THE SCANDALOUS LIFE OF JANE DIGBY
by Mary S. Lovell (Norton, 1995, hardcover)

Jane Digby (1807-81) shocked British society when she abandoned her husband and son for her lover, an Austrian diplomat. Her sensational divorce case in Parliament made the front page of the Times and forced her to retire to the Continent, where she took up with an endless series of men (including King Ludwig I of Bavaria). She married twice more and had five more children, but Jane was still unsatisfied. Then, at age 50, she met a man she could love—an Arab bandit named Medjuel. Jane adopted Islamic customs, lived among nomads for part of the year and entertained Western tourists at her home in Damascus. Lovell tells Jane's story vividly and fills this account with the details of Bedouin life that gave her such happiness.

THE SOUND OF WINGS:
THE LIFE OF AMELIA EARHART
by Mary S. Lovell (St. Martin's, 1989, paperback)

Recently declassified Navy documents and Earhart's own logbooks tell the story of her career as an aviator. Lovell also explores Earhart's complex relationship with G.P. Putnam, her husband, who very likely pressured Earhart to make her final flight.

SISTERS IN ARMS:
CATHOLIC NUNS THROUGH TWO MILLENNIA
by Jo Ann Kay McNamara (Harvard University Press, 1996, hardcover)

Sisters in Arms begins in Bethany with the sisters, Mary and Martha, the paradigms of the contemplative life and the active life. Then she moves on to the stories of women such as Thecla, the legendary companion of Paul, who baptized herself in preparation for facing the lions in the Roman arena. She tells how nuns resisted the "liberation" offered by the Protestant Reformers and acted heroically during the French Revolution. She brings the story up to the present when religious life is once again in upheaval. Jo Ann Kay McNamara has done what no one else ever has-written a comprehensive history of Catholic nuns while neither romanticizing nor minimizing these extraordinary women.

············

MARY BOYKIN CHESNUT: A BIOGRAPHY
by Elisabeth Muhlenfeld
(Louisiana State University Press, 1980, paperback)

From a life spent on plantations the aristocratic Mary Chesnut came to abhor slavery and to reserve a special contempt for masters who slept with their female slaves. Through her intimate friendship with Lavinia Davis, Jefferson Davis' wife, she knew all the troubles of the Confederacy. During the Reconstruction, Chesnut took over her impoverished family's finances and started small businesses that kept them afloat.

············

THE INSANITY FILE:
THE CASE OF MARY TODD LINCOLN
by Mark Neely et al.
(Southern Illinois University Press, 1993, hardcover)

Was Mrs. Lincoln mad? Here is a fresh examination of the notorious case that sent Abraham Lincoln's widow to an insane asylum. The letters, documents and other official records of the case were given to the authors in 1981 by the grandson of Robert Todd Lincoln who was responsible for having his mother committed.

············

A WOMAN OF VALOR:
CLARA BARTON AND THE CIVIL WAR
by Stephen B. Oates (The Free Press, 1995, paperback)

Clara Barton was 39 and unmarried (by choice) when the Civil War broke out. Zealous to do something constructive, she went to the front lines to nurse the wounded. She went on to serve at Second Bull Run, Antietam, Fredericksburg and The Wilderness. Later Barton founded the American Red Cross and through her truly heroic efforts, nursing became recognized as a trained, paid, respectable profession for women. This new biography of Clara Barton is definitive.

POCAHONTAS:
THE EVOLUTION OF AN AMERICAN NARRATIVE
by Robert S. Tilton (Cambridge University Press, 1995, paperback)

Thanks to Disney, if anyone in America didn't know the story of Pocahontas' rescue of Captain John Smith they know it now. But Tilton shows that the near-mythical Indian "princess" has always been popular, from the earliest days of the colonies. He shows the pride Southern aristocrats took in their descent from Pocahontas, how both 19th-century abolitionists and secessionists claimed her and he studies the endless series of images of the "Rescue" American artists turned out over the centuries. There is really nothing like this book.

FIRST LADIES
by Margaret Truman (Fawcett, 1996, paperback)

Former First Daughter Margaret Truman has known or met every First Lady since Frances Cleveland. Now she has written a comprehensive history of the Presidents' wives—women who have always drawn a lot of attention, even if their role has never been clearly defined. From Martha Washington to Hillary Rodham Clinton, Truman explores how these women saw themselves, how they were treated (and mistreated) by the press, what they accomplished and the impact their life in the public eye had on their marriages and their families.

A MIDWIFE'S TALE:
THE LIFE OF MARTHA BALLARD, BASED ON
HER DIARY, 1785-1812
by Laurel Thatcher Ulrich (Vintage, 1991, paperback)

Early America could not have survived without midwives. Among these skilled practitioners, perhaps the most gifted was Martha Ballard—in 27 years she delivered 816 babies, losing only 14 infants and 5 mothers. Among American historical documents, Ballard's diaries are a singular glimpse into life in the Maine wilderness.

Also by Thatcher:

GOOD WIVES:
IMAGE AND REALITY IN THE LIVES OF WOMEN
IN NORTHERN NEW ENGLAND, 1650-1750
(Vintage, 1991, paperback).

A landmark work of women's history that reveals the often extraordinary lives of ordinary New England women.

....

DIVIDED LIVES
by Elsa Walsh (Simon & Schuster, 1995, hardcover)

As she gave birth to her first child, a journalist is offered a job as a reporter on 60 Minutes. A classical music conductor marries the governor of West Virginia and finds herself recast as a First Lady. And the chief of breast surgery at Columbia Presbyterian Hospital discovers that she has to go toe-to-toe with the old boys' network. Washington Post reporter Elsa Walsh's profile of three accomplished women is a tremendous read. The women are outspoken and honest as they discuss sex, careers, marriage, children and the difficulty of balancing a public career while still enjoying a private life.

WORDS TO LIVE BY

THE STRAIGHT DOPE
by Cecil Adams (Chicago Review Press, 1984, paperback)

What's the most expensive thing in the world? Can a man live on bread alone? If so, how long? From the weight of whale poop to the depth of the dust on the moon, Cecil Adams, a legendary recluse and quite possibly the world's most knowledgeable human life form, has offered answers to the questions that torment us all in his outspoken and entertaining weekly syndicated newspaper column, "The Straight Dope." It's a simple formula: readers send in questions, Adams answers them (and he's almost always right). This collection of columns covers topics ranging from sex to the phone company and everything in between—and beyond.

THE PRACTICAL GUIDE TO PRACTICALLY EVERYTHING
by Peter Bernstein and Christopher Ma
(Random House, 1997, paperback)

Two top editors at *U.S. News & World Report* direct you to the best sources on almost everything you can imagine. Warren Buffett teaches you his secrets to picking winning stocks. Robert Parker tells you the best wines to drink now. Auto-racing champion Jackie Stewart gives you the inside scoop on becoming a world-class driver. Olympic champion Florence Griffith-Joyson offers on advice on developing good exercise habits in children. From keeping your computer virus-free, to paying less for your kids' college, to finding the perfect Caribbean beach, here is a reliable compendium of information you can really use.

THE PINBALL EFFECT
by James Burke (Little, Brown, 1997, paperback)

Did you know that the "Great Disappearing African Elephant Scare" of the 19th century led to the invention of pocket cameras (celluloid was developed as an ivory substitute)? Science writer James Burkehas one of those rare minds that not only study how inventions work, but also uncover the completely unexpected relationships between strange things—the permanent wave hairstyle and luxury liners, for example. Think how much more you would have learned in science class if your teacher could show how zoos, locomotives, air conditioning and "smart bombs" are related.

A MAN'S LIFE: THE COMPLETE INSTRUCTIONS
by Denis Boyle with a lot of help from Greg Stebben and A Whole Bunch of Other Guys (Rodale, 1996, paperback)

What do you say if your wife asks you if she looks fat? In an emergency, could you land a 747? Wouldn't you love to have some no-fail sex/basketball/investment tricks? In A Man's Life, lots of guys have pooled their knowledge to help you live a happier, more fulfilling life. You'll learn how to land a babe even if you don't look like Brad Pitt. And how to tell in 90 seconds or less if a TV show is worth watching (stay tuned if you see skin... a wide receiver in mid-air... a white Bronco driving slow down a California freeway). From how to change a diaper one-handed to how to carve a turkey, A Man's Life offers solid advice for all occasions.

HOW TO SELL YOUR HOME IN 5 DAYS
by William Effros (Workman, 1993, paperback)

In five days, you can get a fair-market price for your house and you don't need a real estate broker to do it. Effros shows you how to write the perfect classified ad, tells you what to fix and what not to fix, reveals the magic numbers that buyers find irresistible and talks straight about when you need a lawyer and when you don't. Here is a practical guide that takes the trauma out of selling your home.

THE COMPLETE SINGLE MOTHER: REASSURING ANSWERS TO YOUR MOST CHALLENGING CONCERNS
by Andrea Engber and Leah Klungness, Ph.D.
(Adams Publishing, 1995, paperback)

Two single moms offer a comprehensive, practical guide to raising good kids all by yourself. You'll learn how to get your financial house in order once you are on your own; what to do when the kids have made you furious; the mistakes to avoid when talking about Daddy; how to deal with family (including your ex's family); some tips about dating again; and knowledgeable advice on balancing home and career. Best of all, Engber and Klungness help you create what every single mom wants: a healthy environment for yourself and your kids.

1,101 BUSINESSES YOU CAN START FROM HOME, REVISED AND EXPANDED EDITION
by Daryl Allen Hall (John Wiley & Sons, 1995, paperback)

If you're independent by nature, or tired of 3% salary increases, then you should probably consider a home business. Whether you want to start a pet photography studio, make wooden lawn ornaments in your garage, or become a stocks and bonds advisor, you'll learn everything you need to know before you make the leap—from start up costs to how to build a client base. The perfect book for anyone thinking of becoming their own boss.

THE FRIENDLY GUIDE TO THE UNIVERSE
by Nancy Hathaway (Penguin, 1994, paperback)

If you fell into a black hole, what would happen? Why is the sky dark at night? What's the big deal about Stephen Hawking? And what the heck is a quark? In this fun, friendly reference, Hathaway answers tough questions so you can finally understand how the universe works.

More on what's out there:

THE STARS,
by H.A. Rey (Houghton Mifflin, 1973, hardcover).

A little course in astronomy that teaches you to identify the constellations and the planets.

....

ONE'S COMPANY:
REFLECTIONS ON LIVING ALONE
by Barbara Holland (A Common Reader Edition, 1996, paperback)

At last! Someone has written a manifesto for single people. In *One's Company*, Barbara Holland urges her solitary readers not to be shy but to take center stage in their own private dramas. Yet for all her bravado, Holland admits it isn't easy living on your own. "Preheating an oven," she writes, "and making it work for an hour just for our own personal dinner seems, well, disproportionate." Note that Holland uses the first person plural—our, we, us. It's a nice touch that binds her readers into a hearty band of solitaires. *One's Company* is a funny, assertive book that makes no apologies for being single.

....

DISCOVERING ANTIQUES:
GUIDE TO THE WORLD OF ANTIQUES AND COLLECTIBLES
by Eric Knowles (Stewart, Tabori & Chang, 1996, hardcover)

The best way to find out if an antique is genuine or a fake is to take an expert shopping with you. The next best way is to study *Discovering Antiques*, by Eric Knowles, director of Bonhams auction house in London. Knowles has filled his book with annotated full-color photographs of typical pieces that teach you how to date a piece accurately, spot a fake, detect damage or repairs and recognize makers, factories and their marks. With chapters devoted to furniture, pottery and porcelain, silver, toys and collectibles, *Discovering Antiques* is a comprehensive guide that could make you an antiques expert.

OPERATING INSTRUCTIONS
by Anne Lamott (Fawcett, 1996, paperback)

Y ou may find this book filed under "Baby Care," but don't let that fool you. Novelist and single mother Anne Lamott has created a hilarious, touching, sometimes heartrending journal of her first year with her son. Lamott holds her tiny family together with a little courage, some help from her friends, a new found faith in God and a wit that makes this book a delight to read. Give it to a new mom, or read it and understand what your own mother went through.

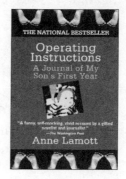

MISS MANNERS RESCUES CIVILIZATION
by Judith Martin, illustrated by Daniel Mark Duffy
(Crown, 1996, hardcover)

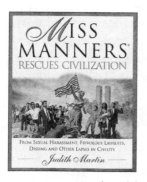

T he guardian of courtesy deplores applauding in church, wearing baseball caps indoors and corporate "retreats" in which employees are encouraged to divulge personal information in a misguided effort to establish a bizarre working place camaraderie. She also addresses such unpleasantness as the most effective yet polite way to banish houseguests who have overstayed their welcome; and how a vegetarian should respond when he or she receives from an employer the gift a turkey during the holiday season. From parrying the most annoying of current social questions, "How does that make you feel?" to recognizing those occasions when it is proper to be shocked, Miss Manners suggests a satisfactory solution to life's most vexing questions.

EVERYDAY SCIENCE EXPLAINED
by The Editors of National Geographic
(National Geographic Society, 1996, hardcover)

Why is water wet? Do we need 80,000 genes? Why are sunsets red and the sky blue? Ever wonder why stainless steel is stainless? Or why curve balls curve? Or why glass is transparent? Now you can find the answers to these and hundreds of other perplexing questions about matter, motion, chemistry, biology and the natural world. Cut-away diagrams and specially commissioned artwork give you an intimate look at the wonders of science. Plus the volume is illustrated with more than 400 spectacular photographs. Here at last is a perfect resource for perpetually curious adults-that will also answer those annoying questions small children tend to ask.

MOVING SUCCESSFULLY
by Tom Philbin and the Editors of Consumer Reports Books
(DIANE Publishing, 1998, paperback)

Only Consumer Reports could take the agony, hassles and expense out of moving. This handbook is loaded with clear-headed advice on how to move yourself, or get the best deal from a professional moving company. Plus you get checklists, inventory sheets and a "Countdown to Moving Day" schedule.

A GOOD PLACE TO LIVE
by Terry Pindell (Henry Holt, 1995, paperback)

Terry Pindell traveled coast to coast to find cities, towns, even suburbs that struck him as perfect places to live. He had a list of criteria: The Cheers Factor (everybody in town knows your name and you don't mind); The Foot Factor (you can get places you want to be without a car); The Cake Factor (you can have natural beauty and cultural amenities, too). Then he boils it down to 16 places, including Napa Valley (you expected that), Minneapolis and Corvallis, Washington, where bikers walk their Harleys past the local arts theater so as not to disturb the performance. (Yeah, we don't believe it either).

PAISLEY GOES WITH NOTHING:
A MAN'S GUIDE TO STYLE
by Hal Rubenstein with Jim Mullen
(Main Street Books, 1997, paperback)

The most important thing Rubenstein, editor-at-large of *In Style* magazine, teaches guys who want to be sophisticated urban males is that style and fashion are not the same thing. Then he explains how to take care of your skin and your hair, how to choose fragrances and eyeglasses, how to give dinner parties and how to act as a guest at one. From what to wear (never wear sneakers or designer jeans) to how to shop (alone), this is a chatty, opinionated, always entertaining guide for guys who want to make a great impression.

BUYING YOUR VACATION HOME FOR FUN & PROFIT
by Ruth Rejnis and Claire Walter (Dearborn Trade, 1996, paperback)

If you've ever dreamed of a getaway in the country, the mountains, or at the beach, this is the book you need. You'll learn which vacation home is the best buy, how to negotiate the purchase and get financing, even how to rent your vacation home for profit. A series of useful quizzes help you identify whether you should buy a traditional home, a resort condominium, a time share, or go for a house swap. There's even a list of "Try-Before-You-Buy" resources that let you sample vacation properties in the Caribbean, Mexico and Europe. From how to close up at the end of the season to important information about taxes and insurance, this is the book you need to read before you buy.

HOW COULD YOU DO THAT?!
THE ABDICATION OF CHARACTER, COURAGE AND CONSCIENCE
by Laura Schlessinger (HarperCollins, 1996, hardcover)

Dr. Laura Schlessinger has no patience for unprincipled weenies who do something dreadful and then offer the lame excuse, "I'm only human." Schlessinger urges her readers to show integrity, have some guts and take responsibility for their actions. She reminds us that there's a big difference between love and lust, that the pursuit of happiness doesn't mean you are free to bulldoze your way over other people, that parents have a special responsibility to be careful about what they do and say to their children and if you do something rotten, you have nobody to blame but yourself. *How Could You Do That?!* is tough medicine for a sick society.

THE LEGAL GUIDE FOR STARTING AND RUNNING A SMALL BUSINESS, SECOND EDITION
by Fred S. Steingold (Nolo Press, 1995, paperback)

An attorney explains to entrepreneurs and freelancers the ins and outs of whether you should incorporate or not, how to get licenses and permits, how to understand the tax requirements and more.

HOW TO INSURE YOUR LIFE: A STEP-BY-STEP GUIDE TO BUYING THE COVERAGE YOU NEED AT PRICES YOU CAN AFFORD
by Reg Wilson and the Merritt Editors
(Merritt Publishing, 1996, paperback)

How much life insurance do you need, really? Do you know the difference between whole and term life insurance? This comprehensive handbook tells the consumer, in plain English, everything you need to know before you buy a policy. You'll learn about the mechanics and pricing structures of various kinds of life insurance, the financial strength of major life insurance companies and how to avoid being misled by commission-hungry insurance agents.

WORKING STIFFS

WOMEN'S WORK: THE FIRST 20,000 YEARS
by Elizabeth Wayland Barber (Norton, 1995, paperback)

Mythology, literature and new archaeological finds from the caves of Lascaux to the tombs of Egypt supply the raw data for Barber's enlightening study of the importance of weaving in ancient societies. For example, she finds that 4000 years ago Mesopotamian women set up export companies to sell their cloth abroad. Especially intriguing is Barber's argument that if the Venus di Milo had arms, they would show her to be in the act of spinning.

DREAM REAPER
by Craig Canine (Knopf, 1995, hardcover)

Believe it or not, there is still such a thing as the solitary inventor working away on some gizmo that will actually change people's lives. Mark Underwood, a Kansas farmer and mechanical genius, is such a man. He built a machine called the Bi-Rotor Reaper that will revolutionize the way grain is harvested—if he can find a manufacturer for it. Here is the story of a modern-day McCormack and his attempts to get the farm machinery firms interested in his invention.

RIVETHEAD:
TALES FROM THE ASSEMBLY LINE
by Ben Hamper (Warner, 1992, paperback)

Ben Hamper pulls no punches in this darkly humorous, insider's portrait of the American automotive assembly line and the emotional toll exacted by the "lurching snake" on the men and women who work on it. He chronicles his career as a fourth-generation General Motors shop rat in Flint, Michigan— the drinking, the drugs, the hassles with the union and management and the desperate struggle to hang on to sanity while performing the same task all day, everyday, forever. It's a book you won't soon forget.

BOOK OF PLOUGH:
ESSAYS ON THE VIRTUE OF FARM, FAMILY AND THE RURAL LIFE
by Justin Isherwood (Lost River Press, 1996, paperback)

Isherwood is a farmer in central Wisconsin who writes the occasional essay for The Wall Street Journal. This book is a collection of funny, thought-provoking reflections farm life. He examines the farmer as a compulsive builder of sheds; explains why all farmers believe God invented the pick-up truck; becomes absolutely lyrical as he describes boiling field corn in a hub cap over a midnight fire; and offers two sure-fire cures for drought: leave your valuables outside over night and mow more hay than you can bale in a day. *Book of Plough* makes you wish your ancestors had never left the land.

HELLROARING:
THE LIFE AND TIMES OF A FIRE BUM
by Peter M. Leschak
(North Star Press of Saint Cloud, 1994, paperback)

As if battling an inferno weren't frightening enough, imagine running into an angry grizzly bear in the middle of it, or returning to your base only to find the camp has been taken over by refugee rattlesnakes. Peter Leschak and his companions fight forest fires out west. They string fire hoses over miles of terrain, lug chain saws up steep hillsides and battle the flames inch by inch, ember by ember. It is tough, dangerous, exhilarating work and Leschak loves it.

HOW TO TELL WHEN YOU'RE TIRED:
A BRIEF EXAMINATION OF WORK
by *Reg Theriault* (Norton, 1995, paperback)

Theriault began his working life as a "fruit tramp" in California and the Southwest. For the past 30 years he's been a longshoreman. In a freewheeling, articulate discussion, he looks at unions, management, accidents on the job and what makes work fulfilling. A fresh look at manual labor from an expert's point of view.

WORLDS OF WONDER

WATERSHIP DOWN
by Richard Adams (Macmillan, 1972, paperback)

Fiver had always been a little different from the other rabbits—thoughtful, mysterious. So when he has a vision about the bloody destruction of their beloved warren, he and his brother Hazel, accompanied by a band of loyal rabbits, defy authority and set out on an epic quest to find a new home and a better society.

THE ALTERATION
by Kingsley Amis (Carroll & Graf, 1988, paperback)

What if the Reformation, the Enlightenment and the Industrial Revolution had never happened? Amis fashions a world more medieval than modern around Hubert Anvil, a choirboy with a flawless, once-in-a-century soprano voice. To preserve this priceless gift, the authorities would like to make Hubert a castrato. But Hubert isn't sure he wants to cooperate.

A PRINCESS OF MARS
by Edgar Rice Burroughs (1912; Del Rey Books, 1985, paperback)

For 40 years Edgar Rice Burroughs reigned as king of pulp fiction. Although he is best known as the creator of Tarzan, it was *A Princess of Mars* that kicked off his literary career. Virginia gentleman John Carter is teleported to the red planet, where he battles with saber and laser across its barren plains to win the heart of the incomparable Dejah Thoris. A classic adventure that helped define the budding genre of science fiction.

THE MISTS OF AVALON
by Marion Zimmer Bradley (Del Rey Books, 1987, paperback)

The first version of the Arthurian legend told from the women's point of view. Morgaine, a priestess of the Celtic Mother Goddess, sacrifices her virginity to the Horned God and then learns that he was her younger brother, Arthur. But Arthur abandons the old religion and converts to Christianity in order to win the golden princess, Guinevere. The price of his betrayal is the doomed Arthur-Guinevere-Lancelot triangle and the end of the enchanted world of Avalon.

GLENRAVEN
by Marion Zimmer Bradley and Holly Lisle
(Baen Books, 1996, paperback)

Somewhere on the border between France and Italy is Glenraven, a Brigadoonish place ruled for the last 1000 years by an evil Watchmistress named Adris Akalan. Into this strange realm stumble a couple of ordinary American women, Jay Jay Bennington and Sophie Cortis, two mortals so out of touch with magic it is a long while before they even begin to notice where they are. Nonetheless, fate has selected one of the women (we won't say which one) to be the new Watchmistress of Glenraven. But how can two people with low self-esteem and zero magical skills defeat a wicked, all-powerful sorceress?

FIRST KING OF SHANNARA
by Terry Brooks (Del Rey, 1996, paperback)

The Druids cast Bremen out of their brotherhood, but he still feels loyalty and affection for the order. So when he learns that in the Northlands an immense Troll army is on the march with the fearsome Skull Bearers as their spies, Bremen takes on a seemingly impossible task. He will persuade the people of the Four Lands to unite. But Bremen's sense of urgency borders on panic as he learns that the dreaded Warlock Lord has come back to life and that all but a tiny handful of the Druids of Paranor have been massacred. An action-packed adventure from the hugely popular Shannara Cycle.

Another Chapter in the Shannara Cycle:

THE DRUID OF SHANNARA
by Terry Brooks (Ballantine, 1991, paperback).

Quickening, the daughter of the King of the Silver River and Walker Boh set out on a quest to find the Elfstone. But their adversary, the Stone King, has loosed his horde of monsters to stop them.

KINDRED
by Octavia Butler (Beacon Press, 1988, paperback)

Time travel novels are always popular (remember Mark Twain's *A Connecticut Yankee in King Arthur's Court?*). But Octavia Butler's story is time travel with a difference. Dana, a black woman of the late 20th century, keeps being called back to 19th-century Maryland to save the life of her ancestor, Rufus. If he dies, Dana will never be born. But there's a peculiar plot twist that makes Kindred singular: Rufus is a cruel, white slaveholder. With each successive journey back in time, Dana comes to a deeper understanding of the day-to-day horrors of slavery and wonders if Rufus' life is worth saving.

ALVIN JOURNEYMAN
by Orson Scott Card (Tor, 1995, paperback)

Orson Scott Card has dreamed up a parallel universe to colonial America, a world where the folk magic of the European settlers meets the enchantments of the Indians. This fourth volume in the series finds Alvin Miller—the seventh son of a seventh son, now a journeyman enchanter, or Maker—a very powerful man indeed. Alvin can conjure a fantastic future for this frontier land, but opposing him is the wicked Unmaker, who now invokes very human weapons—lies, false accusations and innuendo—to ruin Alvin. A brilliant blend of fantasy and colonial history.

SEVENTH SON, RED PROPHET, PRENTICE ALVIN
by Orson Scott Card (Tor, 1993, paperback).

Alvin's childhood, his early encounters with Native American magic and the maturation of his powers.

RUSALKA
by C.J. Cherryh (Ballantine, 1989, paperback)

In pre-Christian Russia, the most fearsome spirit was the Rusalka, the ghost of a murdered young woman who spent eternity trying to come back to life by draining the life force from any living thing she encountered. Pyotr, a young rake in the village, is hiding out in a wizard's cabin in the forest when he encounters the Rusalka. Worse yet, he falls in love with her— and she with him. But for a ghost, love is no substitute for life. An eerie evocation of a far away place and time.

More by Cherryh:

FOREIGNER
(Daw Books, 1994, paperback).

On a distant star, a small colony of humans lives in isolation from the planet's native inhabitants, the atevi, who tolerate the interlopers because of their technological expertise. The uneasy peace lasts 200 years, but when an assassin tries to kill the human's ambassador to the atevi, war seems inevitable. Can these two dangerous, violent, species get past their mutual distrust and build a permanent peace?

WARPATH
by Tony Daniel (Tor, 1993, paperback)

When space explorers travel to the stars, they discover that the Indians got there ahead of them. Long before the arrival of Columbus, a Mississippi tribe stumbled upon a mystical something they called "the Effect" which enabled them to paddle their canoes to a distant world. Now the technologically advanced white men are challenging these interstellar tribesmen (who are armed only with spears and guided missiles). It looks like history is about to repeat itself when Will Jones, an earth reporter with ties to both cultures, is put in the awkward position of trying to make peace.

TIME AND AGAIN
by Jack Finney (Scribners, 1995, paperback)

One day, Simon Morley steps outside his room in the Dakota Apartments on Central Park West and finds himself in 1882 New York. He had been selected by a top-secret government agency to travel back in time, but he never really believed it would work. Once he gets with the program, Morley immerses himself in his new surroundings, recording them with his camera and sketchbook—he even falls in love. But then, the agency asks him to alter history. Finney's superb re-creation of 1880s New York City life and mores is filled with unforgettable details and incidents. Arguably the most historically accurate about 19th-century New York ever written.

The Sequel:

FROM TIME TO TIME
(Scribners, 1996, paperback).

Simon Morley is asked to go to 1912 and alter events to keep America out of World War I. To complete his mission, he must sail from Europe back to America—aboard the Titanic.

HERLAND:
A LOST FEMINIST UTOPIAN NOVEL
by Charlotte Perkins Gilman (1915; Pantheon, 1979, paperback)

Three men—a sociologist, a doctor and a philanderer—discover a lush country inhabited solely by women. The place is called "Herland" and the women there explain that all the men were killed in a volcanic eruption 2000 years ago. The women who survived the disaster evolved to reproduce through parthenogenesis. But the contemporary Herlanders would like to be bisexual as their ancestors once were (provided some men were to come along). Naturally, the three adventurers fall in love and their conversations about gender are very interesting. Part Jules Verne, part Tarzan, part feminist track, this forgotten utopian novel is truly remarkable.

Also by Gilman:

THE YELLOW WALLPAPER AND OTHER WRITINGS
(1892; Bantam Books, 1994, paperback).

The lead story in this collection is Gilman's most famous work, the fearful tale of a woman suffering from a breakdown whose physician husband prescribes complete rest—no books, no writing materials, no visitors, no outside stimulation of any kind.

THE PRINCESS BRIDE
by William Goldman
(Ballantine, 1996, paperback)

This novel contains everything essential to a true adventure: sword fights, torture, dungeons, a dwarf, a giant, a beautiful princess, cowards, heroes, pirates, a zoo of death, chases, escapes, rats of unusual size, treachery, passion, great kisses and true love. Goldman combines his mastery of the cliff-hanger with an irrepressible wit to make Westley the farm boy's quest to save the beautiful Buttercup from the evil prince Humperdinck a rare gem of a read and an honest-to-goodness fairy tale that adults can sink their teeth into.

FIREHAND
by Andre Norton and P.M. Griffin (Tor, 1995, paperback)

The Baldies, predatory time-traveling aliens, have reduced the Dominion of Virgin to an ash heap. So Ross Murdoch and Gordon Ashe travel back to Dominion's feudal age to help the inhabitants win a war that will enable them to defeat the Baldies 400 years later. It seems like a simple assignment, but there's a catch: if Ross or Gordon reveal to anyone on Dominion that they are offworld humans, Earth will be annihilated.

Another Norton-Griffin Collaboration:

REDLINE THE STARS
(Tor, 1994, paperback).

A mysterious new crew member joins the Solar Queen and asks for passage to the port of Canuche. Then a plague of rats and a crisis on the planetary star docks threatens to the destroy the Solar Queen and Canuche's inhabitants.

....

ASSASSIN'S APPRENTICE
by Robin Hobb (Bantam, 1996, paperback)

As a bastard child of the royal house, Young Fitz can't expect to get ahead in life. Still, he does possess the Skill: the mystical powers that are the blood inheritance of all royalty. So the crafty (and aptly named) King Shrewd has Fitz trained as an assassin. As Fitz learns the dark arts, an especially vile nation of barbarians raid the kingdom's coastal towns, transforming the villagers into zombies. Once the apprentice assassin has honed his skills, the King has a mission for him that could save the kingdom.

The Sequel:

ROYAL ASSASSIN
by Robin Hobb (Bantam, 1997, paperback).

The King is dying, a host of usurpers have their eyes on the throne and Fitz's only ally at court is off on some silly quest. Once again, the fate of the kingdom is in the young assassin's hands.

....

TALIESIN:
BOOK ONE OF THE PENDRAGON CYCLE
by Stephen R. Lawhead (Avon, 1990, paperback)

In one of the most imaginative retellings of the Arthurian legend to come along in years, Stephen Lawhead combines the story of Celtic Britain's greatest king with the myth of Atlantis. Three battered shiploads of survivors from the Lost Continent, led by King Avallach and his daughter Charis, land at the Isle of Glass at a time when the Celtic chieftains are trying to fend off barbarian invaders. The Celts' one hope is young Prince Taliesin—as courageous, handsome and honest a hero as anyone could wish for. With Charis' help, Taliesin may save his people from being overwhelmed.

The sequel:

MERLIN
by Stephen Lawhead (Avon, 1990, paperback).

Merlin, a druid's son born with the gift of prophecy and a warrior's valor, seeks his destiny at the dawn of a new golden age for Celtic Britain.

MORDRED'S CURSE
by Ian McDowell (Avon, 1996, paperback)

For his first novel, Ian McDowell has taken his inspiration from the Arthurian legend. He focuses on Mordred, the boy born from the unholy union between Arthur and his half—sister, the enchantress Morgan le Fay. But McDowell's Age of Arthur is not all chivalry and romance. He captures the brutality of life in 6th-century Britain and portrays the youthful Mordred as a cunning, murderous little villain. This is Camelot from a fresh, twisted perspective.

FAIR PERIL
by Nancy Springer (Avon, 1996, paperback)

One day, while walking along a pond, Buffy Murphy, an overweight, fortyish, divorced mother, encounters a talking frog. One thousand years earlier he was handsome prince who refused to become the lover of a wicked sorceress, so she "transfrogrified" him. Naturally he wants to be kissed so he can return to human form. But Buffy sees that he's worth a small fortune as is. She takes him home, where her rebellious 16-year-old daughter delivers the magical kiss and a hunky prince appears. They run off to the land of Fair Peril. Now Buffy, of all people, has to travel into the faery realm to bring back her daughter. A very smart, often outrageously funny, modern spin on traditional fairy tales.

SIR GAWAIN AND THE GREEN KNIGHT
translated by J.R.R. Tolkien (Ballantine, 1980, paperback)

Tolkien, the immortal author of The Hobbit and The Lord of the Rings trilogy was also an internationally respected medievalist. His translation of the 14th-century tale of Sir Gawain is the best around, capturing all the beauty and mystery and enchantment of the greatest of all Arthurian legends.

THE HOBBIT
by J.R.R. Tolkien (Ballantine, 1990, paperback)

Bilbo Baggins is a hairy-toed hobbit who would much rather stay home by the fire and eat cakes than go off on any nasty old quest. But Bilbo has a role to play in the history of Middle Earth and it's up to Gandalf the wizard, assisted by a band of treasure-hunting dwarves, to see that he plays it. The prelude to Tolkien's epic, *The Lord of the Rings*, this tale of dragons and elves, trolls and kings is truly one of the most enchanting adventure stories if all time.

Tolkein's Trilogy:
THE LORD OF THE RINGS
(Houghton Mifflin, 1974, hardcover).

A saga that pits Bilbo's nephew, Frodo, and his companions against all the powers of darkness.

MISPLACED LEGION
by Harry Turtledove (Ballantine, 1991, paperback)

Asorceror casts a spell on 1000 Roman legionnaires and a Celtic chief which transports them all to the world of Videssos. In this new world, the Romans are welcome—the Emperor's throne is endangered by civil war and barbarian invasions; he could use a few well-trained mercenaries. Harry Turtledove, a gifted writer and storyteller, spins a tale of high adventure with plenty of court intrigue and exciting battle scenes. (You're going to love the brawny Haloga Guards who sing while they lop off heads and limbs on the battlefield).

The sequel:

AN EMPEROR FOR THE LEGION
by Harry Turtledove (Ballantine, 1988, paperback).

All the tension, energy and fun of the first book is carried over in this sequel. The Emperor is murdered and a free-for-all for the crown breaks out. Meanwhile, barbarian nomads are taking advantage of the chaos and pushing their way into the empire.

THE ICE-SHIRT
by William T. Vollmann (Penguin, 1993, paperback)

One thousand years ago, Norse settlers from Greenland begin a voyage to Vinland. But their way is beset by uncanny events—glaciers that are transformed into monsters, men and wolves who change shapes. Even after the adventurous colonists arrive, the strange events continue. Freydis, the bastard daughter of Eirik the Red, has made a pact with a demon in exchange for absolute power in the new land. Gudrid, a Christian, struggles to separate herself from her pagan Norse past and its shape-shifting shamans. Vollmann has fashioned an eerie, imaginative—sometimes surreal—novel of a world where nothing is as it appears.

UNCHARTED TERRITORY
by *Connie Willis* (Bantam, 1994, paperback)

Imagine a voyage of discovery in which the explorers could be charged with such a politically incorrect offense as "verbal abuse of indigenous fauna," or the eco-crime of "disruption of land surface." That's what two earthlings, Carson and Findriddy, are faced with when they try to survey the planet Boohte. To make matters worse, Carson and Findriddy can't tell which of their Boohtean hosts are male and which are female. Then, a sex specialist from Earth arrives, but she turns out to be a he.... *Uncharted Territory* is an entertaining, non-stop romp through the galaxy.

More by Connie Willis:

LINCOLN'S DREAMS
(Bantam, 1992, paperback).

A young woman dreams terrifying dreams and her psychiatrists are stumped. But, a Civil War historian recognizes parallels with the dark, prophetic dreams that tormented Abraham Lincoln.

....

SOLDIER OF THE MIST,
by *Gene Wolfe* (Tor, 1987, paperback)

Wolfe blends fantasy, mythology and history in this multilayered story. Latro, a Roman soldier, can see and speak with the gods, but cannot remember who he is himself from one day to the next. With a sorcerer, a slave and a poet, Latro wanders 5th-century Greece seeking a cure for his strange affliction

....

INDEX BY AUTHOR

INDEX BY TITLE

B

H

N

U